PAINTINGS OF IONA

CADELL
AND
PEPLOE

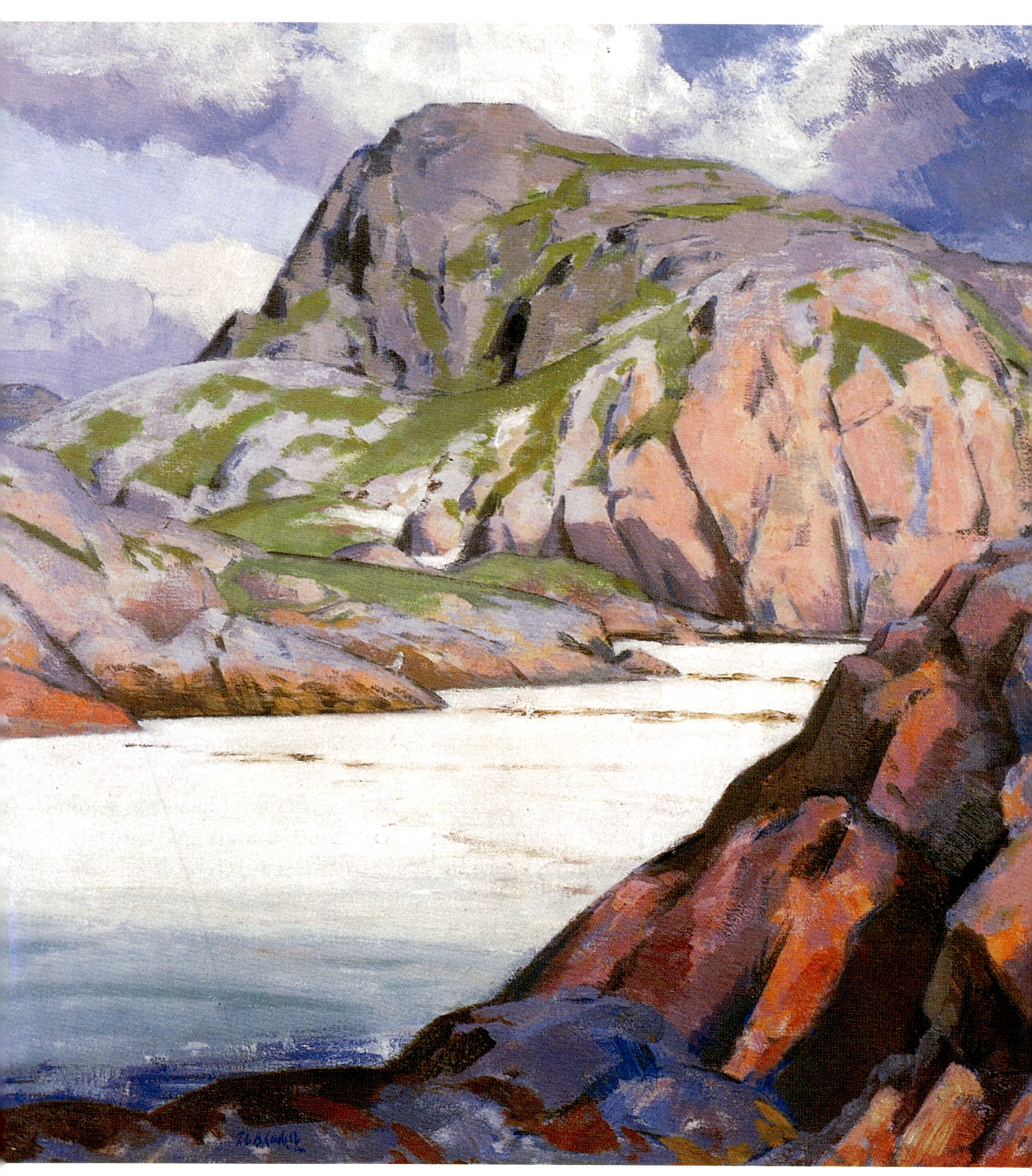

PAINTINGS OF IONA BY

F. C. B. CADELL

1883-1937

AND

S. J. PEPLOE

1871-1935

PHILIP MACLEOD COUPE

with foreword by
GUY PEPLOE

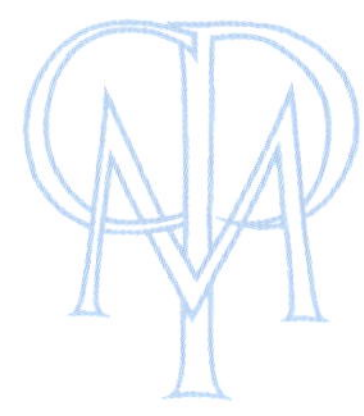

First published in 2014 by the heirs of Philip MacLeod Coupe

Heather Coupe
Holland Cottage
Broads Bank
Malvern
Worcestershire WR14 2HP

ISBN 978-0-9928597-0-1

Design by the author and Donna Holbrook, and typeset by her at
Ferguson Print Keswick Limited
Bakers Yard, St John Street
Keswick, Cumbria CA12 5AS

Printed on 150g silk paper by
Kent Valley Colour Printers Limited
Units 5/6, Chancel Place, Shap Road Industrial Estate
Kendal, Cumbria LA9 6NZ

This edition is limited to 500 copies of which this is
Number 311

Front cover: *Iona, a Cloudy Sky* by S. J. Peploe [134]
Back cover: *White Sands, Iona* by F. C. B. Cadell [78]
Frontispiece: *Dun Bhuirg from Port Bhan* by F. C. B. Cadell [188]

CONTENTS

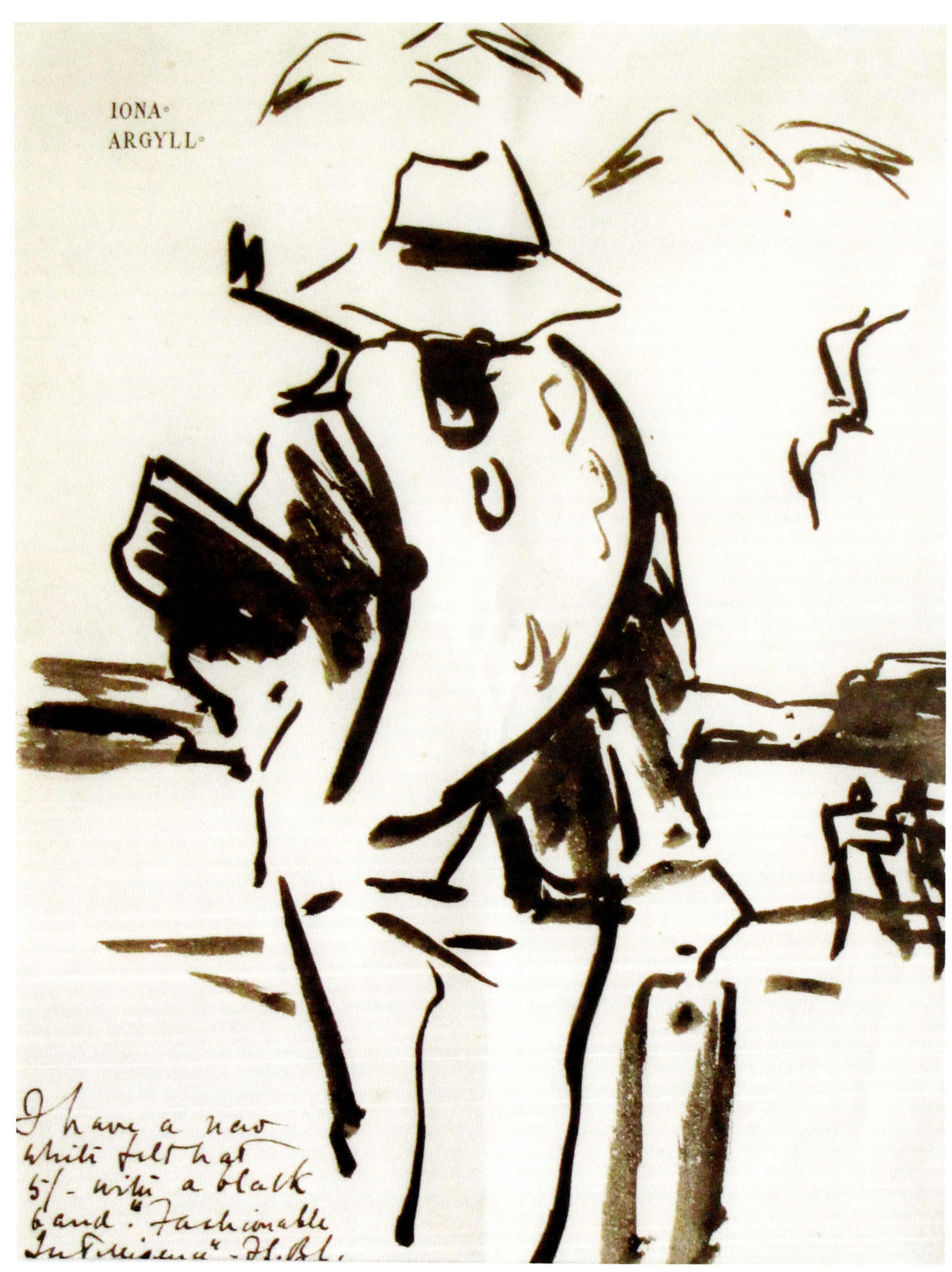
IONA
ARGYLL
I have a new
white felt hat
5/- with a black
band. "Fashionable
Intelligence" - F.C.B.

FOREWORD

I would like to congratulate Philip MacLeod Coupe on his book. It is a well researched, beautifully illustrated and produced work which will charm and inform in equal measure; it adds significantly to the Iona literature as well as that for the painters he follows.

Iona is a place of astonishing beauty, pristine in an ancient sense, essentially unchanged since its complex geology settled in the Torridonian Era. Sedimentary rocks give the character to the North End and the east shore and ancient Lewisian gneiss is exposed on the Atlantic side. Pink granites and green marble, commercially quarried in the nineteenth century, form a palette understood by the geologists and artists who have picked over the rocks. Bays, coves, perfect white strands and rocky headlands make up the curve of its coastline, as perfect as any Crusoesque idea of the desert island. But deserted it has not been for thousands of years. In the Iron Age our primitive ancestors eked out a subsistence, but by the time Columba fled there from Ireland in 563 and established his Christian mission the island could sustain a community and a centre of learning: a scriptorium saw the beginning of *The Book of Kells*, masons carved exemplary high crosses and missionaries went out to the Kingdoms of the mainland. The depredations of Viking invasion eventually led to the abandonment of the first monastery, but from the early thirteenth century a Benedictine Nunnery and Augustinian Monastery flourished, under the protection of the Scottish King, until the Reformation. The most recent renaissance of the spiritual came through the will of George MacLeod of Fuinary who founded the Iona Community in 1938 and adopted and restored the Abbey for ecumenical worship. Today the National Trust for Scotland owns the island and Historic Scotland preserves the ancient sites.

The island's character lies in its archaeological traces, pagan and holy, and in its remoteness: America is the first landfall due west and Mull is near but detached across the dangerous water of the Sound of Iona. Nature is relentlessly cyclical and the island changes with the seasons. The piece of Iona's history we are concerned with in this book is recent and the season is summer. As the sun climbs higher to its yearly zenith the machair becomes carpeted with wild flowers and the shallow seas around the North End become shades of blue and green. Generations of the same families have come to the island for their summer holidays, sustaining, enriching and invigorating the community. Amongst these visitors have been many painters and two in particular have shaped our understanding of the island and Scotland's landscape. Iona is so small that any visitor arrives and then looks outward; the view starts from where you have planted your feet but goes out to Mull, to Staffa and the Treshnish Isles, past Tiree and Coll to Rhum, south to Islay and Jura, or west to the vastness of the ocean. In this way Iona expands horizons and becomes a place of beginning and renewal. It is this marriage between the particular character of place and its location as a platform from which to see out and beyond which must have captivated Cadell and Peploe. Painting in the studio for both these men was a creative process born of rigour: the intellectual held sway; concerns with colour harmony, tonal contrast and proportion are paramount. On Iona the merest shift of viewpoint of a few degrees offered each a vista of new and perfect charms. Add the adventure of changing weather and the subject became limitless: an emotional and even spiritual response prevailed over the intellectual travails of winter in an Edinburgh studio, a tardy model or a wilting still life.

Cadell is supposed to have been the first to have visited the island and there are many works that date from before the First War. Peploe wrote to him from Edinburgh when Cadell was at the Western Front, giving him the gossip and looking forward to the end of war and a trip to the islands, to Iona, to somehow rediscover their innocence. Their visits would not always coincide but each made an annual pilgrimage to Iona for the rest of their lives, experiences valuable to them as artists and as friends. As this wonderful book amply illustrates, Cadell ventured all over the island to find his subjects while Peploe restricted himself to the North End and a few pictures of the Village. In the twenties Peploe would be accompanied by his family, wife Margaret, who came originally from Loch Boisdale in South Uist, elder son Willy, born in 1910, and second son Denis who was born in 1914. Cadell would often be accompanied by his manservant Charles, who would cook, model and act as sales agent at the rented cottage; selling work to the visitors was a vital part of Cadell's livelihood. They were not the only artists attracted to Iona. Peploe wrote to Margaret on his first visit, when he discovered the promise of the rocky North End, of how John Duncan was stalking the island looking for subjects, frustrated like Peploe by the poor weather. Cadell made caricatures of James Shearer (painstakingly "putting the finishing touches to a watercolour started in 1885") and of the celebrated resident silversmith Alec Ritchie, looking rather unsteady, "home from the fishing" *(right)*. And of himself, palette strapped to his back, pipe fuming, sporting a new panama hat with a black ribbon titled "fashionable intelligence" *(page 6)*. Cadell, in his Campbell tartan (he was a distant kinsman of the Duke at Inveraray), a loud check jacket and perhaps his lemon yellow waistcoat, certainly cut a dash. "Who's that man?" a young resident asked his father. "That's not a man, that's Mr Cadell" was the reply. Cadell found great entertainment in the comings and goings of locals and visitors like Sir Harold Boulton, the businessman and collector of Folk songs, who wrote the lyric of *The Skye Boat Song*, and his Canadian second wife. Margery and Patuffa Kennedy Fraser, both considerable performing artists of traditional music, were his friends as well as summer visitors like David Russell of Markinch and Ronald Service of Cove. The latter's family eventually numbered 10 and his collection of Cadells 100. Peploe would also have been a distinctive figure, tall and spare, immaculate in a three-piece summer suit, striding over the machair towards the north, sometimes accompanied by Denis helping to carry the painter's paraphernalia.

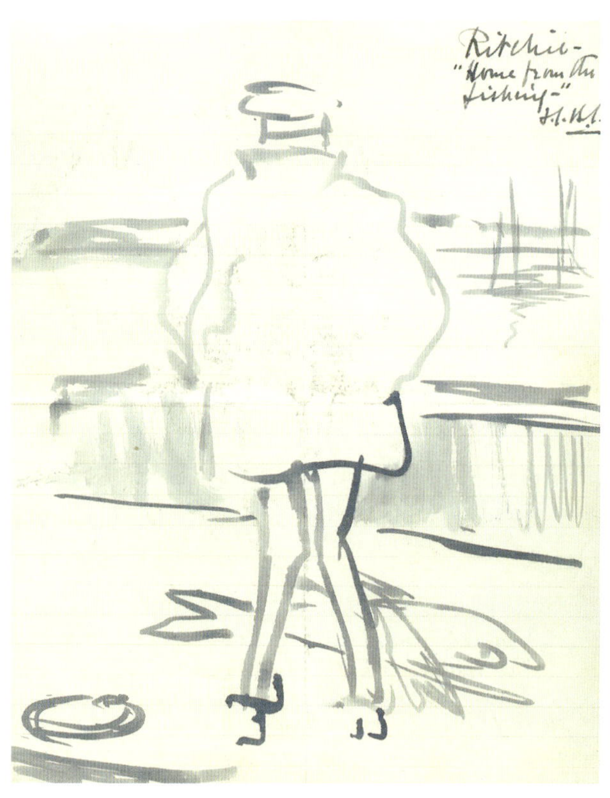

There are a few precious letters preserved by my family from Cadell, including one dated July 7th 1932, which gives us examples of his wit and a sense of the rich social life of the summer months as well as the travails and rivalries of the resident painter *(reproduced on pages 9 & 10)*.

Today both painters might remark how great a pity seems the encroachment of the grass of the machair, so well documented by the author, but I am sure they would find the visitors and residents just as interesting. If each had had another twenty-five years of visits I am also sure they would have continued to find new vistas. Peploe's shift of concern from rock to weather might have turned circle again. Cadell's unerring eye for form and brilliant palette would have found new charms looking towards Ben More on other days. What is certain from the pages of this book is that the manifest beauty of Iona required no feats of the imagination or artistic license for these two brother painters to be inspired and to leave a legacy in paint and a way of seeing now ingrained in how we feel about the Scottish landscape.

GUY PEPLOE Edinburgh, May 2013

July 7. '32 *Iona*

Dear Peploe,

How are you? It must have been rather awful in a way in Edinburgh all June if the weather there was as fine as it was here. But you didn't really lose much from the painting point of view. Little colour, not much wind and a cloudless sky for the most part. Though lying about doing nothing but benefitting the health was very pleasant. I have painted a few watercolours – 4 or 5 oil panels & a 24" square of the Nunnery, this not yet finished, as I have only done about ¾ of the stones! The panels consist of 2 of Calbha, one of Clachanach, one of the road running between the hotel & the cabin looking south from opposite the Reilig Odhrain & a portrait of myself done in a diseased mirror and not yet completed. Anything to escape the horrors of Ben More, Loch na Kiel & Bourg! The Orrs are here at the hotel & the other day – a wet one – Mrs O told me what an extraordinary man "Stewart" was – that she had offered to sit for her portrait, but that he apparently preferred to wander about the hill at the back of the hotel! She, I suppose, is his Ben More! Shearer has also arrived – Sir H & Lady Boulton were here for a bit. Patuffa K.F. goes tomorrow after being here for the burial at which MacNally wound up to the horror & astonishment of all present (except Ritchie who had given him permission) by playing reflections on the dulcimer – "Road to the Isles" etc. It really sounded <u>*awful*</u> *& quite knocked the stuffing out of Warr's concluding prayer. Quite the most outrageous thing I have ever heard. As for the stone – it is like a large size box of Bryant & May matches decorated with lettering & a* ball of wool that has been played with by a kitten. Tombstones have invariably (at least the recumbent ones) suggested the shape of an average human being, but this one calls up a corpse 3ft x 3 x 3 – As the body was cremated & in a square casket the stone should either have been of the usual proportions or the shape and size approximately of the thing it covers. Anyway it is perfectly bloody & compares very unfavourably with the work of the average monumental mason. Charlie Kirkpatrick's (though curious) is preferable with its china flowers and exotic shells – It only requires a boiled lobster to complete it. The inside of the shells is a delicate pink while the china flowers are the colour of the brow of a defunct virgin.

The Miss Storys are here having taken Cnoc More & Principal & Mrs Rait came to stay with them this weekend. Miss Reid has been here too but leaves today. Highland Cottage is no more & in its stead one of the usual protruding to the line of the Ritchies' porch. Seton Gordon here too – camping at Greenbank. Mrs Macdonald will be very sorry I think they took old M to Glasgow as he might as well have remained here as nothing was done to him there. Flora was here for a bit looking very well. Houston (George) appeared for one week in June & went off with 9 finished canvasses – 5 – 36 x 28 & 4 – 24 x 18, not to speak of a number of drawings. The "Loch Fyne" is now painted black instead of grey and looks better I think. I can think of no more local news to give you, except that this cottage has been re-thatched thank God & that sand is now piled quite high up in the "corridor" & the "cliffs" have in consequence lost their false majesty beloved by the designer of the "B & M" tombstone.

I hope you are all well & that no more accidents have happened to Dennis's masterpieces in clay.

Yours F. C. B. Cadell

P.S. Houston starts his pictures at the bottom & finishes them at the top.

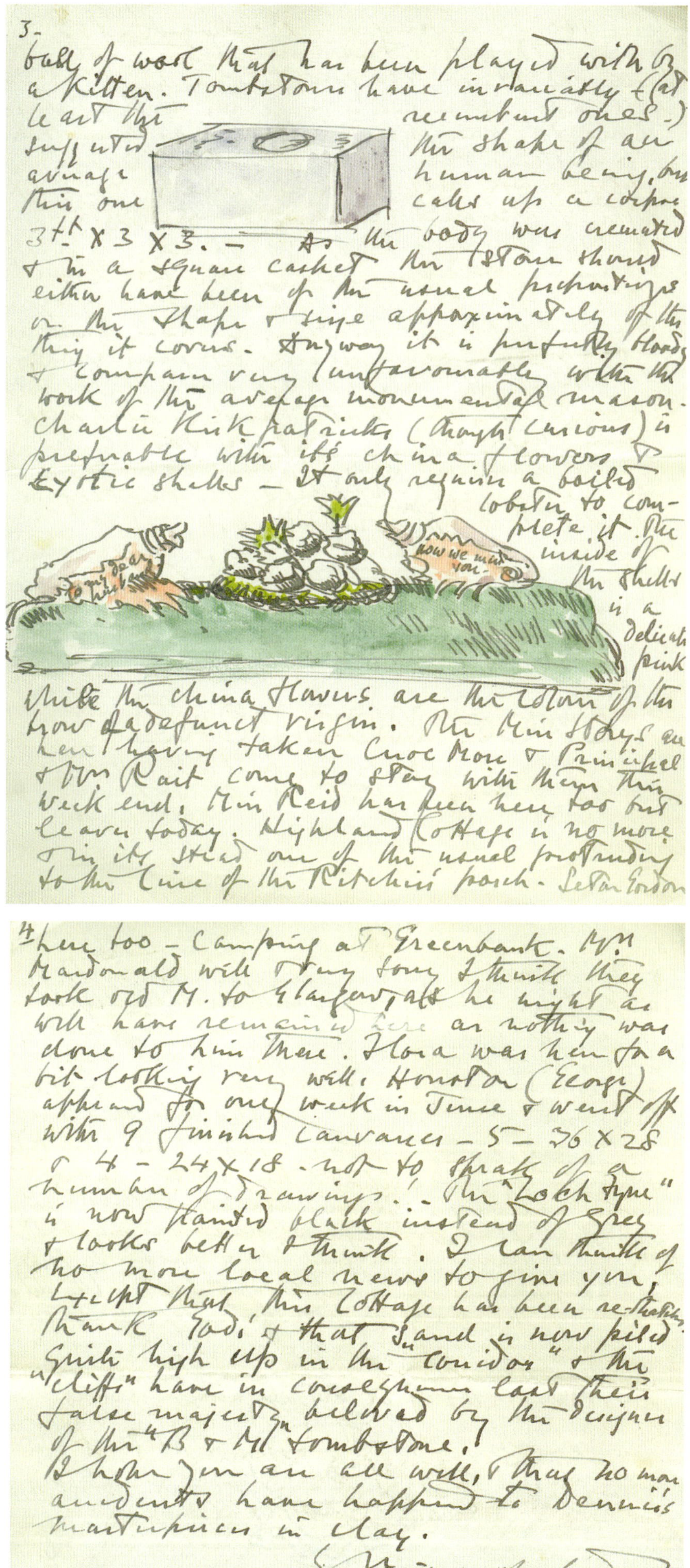

Acknowledgements

I would like to thank Guy Peploe for kindly writing the Foreword. His comments provide a fascinating glimpse into the social, personal, and historical background of the artists and their work on Iona. As grandson of Samuel John Peploe and a leading authority on the Scottish Colourists, he has provided a perfect opening for the book. Also I am grateful to him for his advice at various stages of writing.

A very great number of people have helped me through the long process of writing this study, but I feel special gratitude to Ewan and Carol Mundy (Ewan Mundy Fine Art) for their kindness and support. They read the draft of the book and made many helpful comments and also provided many of the images for the illustrations.

Similarly my thanks go to Alice Strang, Senior Curator of the Scottish National Gallery of Modern Art, without whose help the work would have taken considerably longer.

A quick flick through the pages will reveal that this is primarily a picture book, which could not have been put together without the generosity of all the galleries, public and private, auction houses, and private collectors who provided the images of the paintings. My sincere thanks go to:

• Aberdeen Art Gallery, Griffin Coe • Art Gallery and Museum, Kelvingrove, Glasgow • City Art Centre, Edinburgh, David Patterson and Ian O' Riordan • Dundee Art Galleries and Museums, Anna Robertson • Fleming-Wyfold Art Foundation, London, Sophie Midgley • The Hunterian, University of Glasgow, Anne Dulau • Fife Cultural Trust (Kirkcaldy Galleries), Jane Freel • Scottish National Gallery of Modern Art, Edinburgh, Alice Strang and Rachel Smith • Picture Library, National Galleries of Scotland, Shona Corner • The Roger Billcliffe Gallery, Glasgow, Roger Billcliffe • Bourne Fine Art, Edinburgh, Caledonia Armstrong • The Fine Art Society, London, Patrick Bourne • The Richard Green Gallery, London, Richard Green and Rachel Boyd • David Messum Fine Art, London, Andrea Gates • Duncan R. Miller Fine Arts, London, Duncan R. Miller and Sue Palmer • Ewan Mundy Fine Art, Glasgow, Ewan and Carol Mundy • The Portland Gallery, London, Tom Hewlett and Archie Wardlaw • The Scottish Gallery, Edinburgh , Guy Peploe and Elizabeth Wemyss • The Anthony Woodd Gallery, Edinburgh, Anthony Woodd • Bonhams, Dr. Chris Brickley, Edinburgh • Christie's • Lyon and Turnbull, Nick Curnow, Edinburgh and Gavin Strang, Glasgow • Sotheby's, Anthony Weld Forester, Edinburgh and Simon Toll, London • Giclee UK Limited, Edinburgh, Chris Pearson • And the private collectors who wish to remain anonymous.

The present day photographs in the book were taken by myself; however I am indebted to a number of sources for the historical photographs, and credits for these are listed together with the Picture Credits. My thanks to: Mrs Joan Faithfull • Tom Hewlett, Portland Gallery • Mairi E. MacArthur • Guy Peploe, The Scottish Gallery • National Library of Scotland, Edinburgh • R. Martin Tomlinson.

The maps are a vital component of the book; that on page 17 is reproduced by permission of Ordnance Survey. All the remaining maps are extracts from the map published by the Iona Community. This is the only map of the island of a sufficiently large scale to identify the painting locations, and I am very grateful to the Iona Community for their kind permission to use it, and to Susie Hay, Wild Goose Publications, the publishing house of the Iona Community, Glasgow.

I have relied heavily on local knowledge and am grateful to the following residents of Iona who kindly gave their time to provide me with the necessary information: Rev. Joanna Anderson (Director of the Iona Community), • Fiona Barker (The Iona Community Shop) • Jill Black • Iain Dougall • Michael and Kate Gordon (The Iona Craft Shop) • Gordon and Helen Grant • Mary Hay (Iona Heritage Centre) • Angus and Alison Johnston • David and Carol Kirkpatrick • Colin and Kate MacDonald • Margaret MacDonald • Jane MacFadyen • John and Annabel Macinnes • John MacLean • Jane Martin (Historic Scotland) • Ken and Janetta Tindal. Finally my thanks to Gordon and Fiona Menzies (The Iona Gallery and Pottery), who assisted in many ways including the search for illustrations. Also I am grateful to Fiona Menzies (nee Fraser, see Bibliography) for her expertise concerning the geology of Iona.

The book would have remained a mass of research notes and a pile of photographs without the work of the production team. I thank John and Linda Sinclair of Ferguson Print, Keswick, Cumbria for all their help, and use of their office and workshop, where I have spent so much time over the last few years that some visitors thought I worked there! My thanks to Donna Holbrook of Ferguson Print for typesetting the book, the layout of which was worked out between us. Her very considerable skills in this respect I find quite astonishing. Given also that the printworks are only five minutes' walk from my home, this has been an ideal association in every way.

The book was printed by Kent Valley Colour Printers of Kendal, Cumbria, with whom I have had a long association through the Lake Artists Society. My thanks to Tim Sarginson and Howard Duff, for their skills and attention to detail and for making the book a reality.

Although I come lastly to thanking my friends the painter John Rogers and his wife Judith, it was they who first encouraged me to go painting on Iona. John visited Iona as a boy of 13 in 1948, and came across postcards of paintings of the island by Cadell and Peploe. Inspired by these he later painted on the west coast of Scotland himself. He donated his copy of the 1985 Peploe Exhibition catalogue to me, and this was the beginning of my own collection of literature about Cadell and Peploe. Having worked in lithographic printing all his life, John gave expert advice on this aspect, and combined with Judith's facility with a computer their help was invaluable. I give them my grateful thanks.

Keswick, 2013

When Philip died suddenly in November 2013, this book was almost finished. It grew naturally out of his own life as an artist, reflecting his intimate knowledge of the Iona landscape and his respect for the remarkable artists who had preceded him there.

Our thanks to Guy Peploe, Alice Strang, and Fiona Menzies for their helpful advice. Thanks also to Katherine Marshall of Sotheby's for her kindness in supplying images, and to Andrew Currie of Bonhams and Charlotte Riordan of Lyon and Turnbull for allowing us to reproduce images. Finally, we are grateful to the staff at Ferguson Print and Kent Valley Colour Printers for giving the book its final form.

Robert and Rosemary Coupe
Vancouver, 2014

INTRODUCTION

THE Isle of Iona lies close to the southwest corner of the much larger Isle of Mull on the west coast of Scotland. It was an early outpost of Christianity and remains an important religious centre to this day. Historically, Iona was a crofting community, but tourism now plays a major part in the island's economy, and artists have been among the many visitors. The early painters recorded mainly the antiquities and ruins on the island. Later, especially after the Impressionist movement, the landscape itself became much more the focus of attention. During the twentieth century many artists came to Iona to paint the rocky shores, white sandy beaches and emerald seas. The two most celebrated were Samuel John Peploe (1871–1935) and Francis Campbell Boileau Cadell (1883–1937).

Their lives have been described in detail in a number of biographies, so it is not necessary to say more here. This is primarily a picture and reference book for those who love Iona, and admire the work of these two painters. For those interested in following in their footsteps, it identifies the location of each picture and gives directions on how to get there. In seeking out the viewpoints one is helped greatly by the excellent drawing skills of both artists, which result in a faithful rendering of the subject. In this respect the paintings are not only enjoyable as works of art, but also comprise an interesting historical record.

Contemporaries and close friends, Cadell and Peploe were the only members of the group known as the Scottish Colourists to paint on Iona. Cadell first visited in 1912 and returned most summers throughout his life. He encouraged Peploe to join him, which he did in 1920, after which he, like Cadell, returned most years. In a letter to his wife Margaret, Peploe refers, during his first visit, to having explored most of the island and finding the best subjects at the North End. This preference is certainly borne out in his paintings, which are almost entirely of that area. Cadell on the other hand painted subjects in many parts of the island.

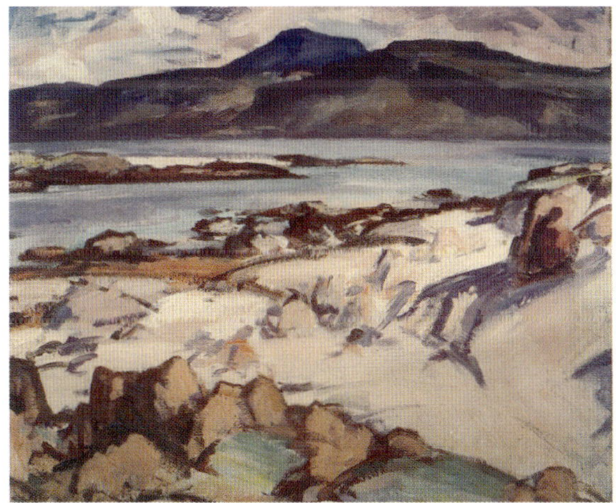

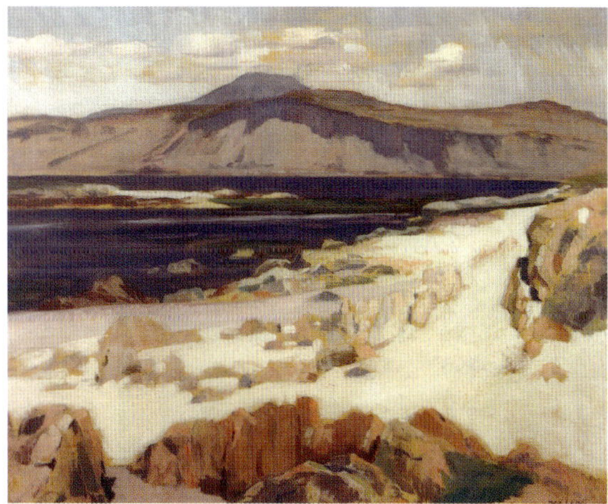

[FIGURE 1] Ben More painted by Peploe (left) and Cadell (right)

Among the Iona paintings there are examples of the two artists having painted exactly the same motif, (Figure 1), but it cannot be assumed from this that they were working at the same time side by side. However they would have seen each other's pictures and discussed them, and given that they both had the decisive and spontaneous handling required for outdoor painting, it is not surprising there are similarities in the work of the two artists. There are differences also; that of choice of subject has been mentioned already. In addition it will be noticed Cadell frequently included figures, or animals, or other signs of human activity, such as a yacht sailing by, whereas Peploe appears never to have done so. This may be a reflection of their respective personalities, Cadell an extrovert and Peploe a more private person.

Both artists repeated favourite motifs, but this is particularly true of Peploe, who worked almost in series or variations on a number of themes, such as his paintings of the White Strand, of which Plates 41 to 50 are a selection from a larger number of pictures of this subject. Cadell and Peploe followed similar working routines, painting landscapes en plein air in the summer and returning to their studios in the winter, Peploe to concentrate particularly on still life, the largest part of his total output, and Cadell to work on still life, portraiture, and his stylish interiors.

Peploe was nearly fifty when he first painted on Iona; he arrived with a fully developed mature style and worked fairly consistently within this. Cadell on the other hand was in only his late twenties and his work shows some changes in style. Typically in his early oil paintings he used long slashing brushstrokes of quite fluid paint, whereas the later works have a more broken touch of drier paint, and are topographically more specific. This change is seen on his return to Iona after the years away during the First World War, and maybe this is a factor, but it also coincides with Peploe's arrival and it is likely that his influence played a part in Cadell's work.

Regarding mediums, on Iona, Peploe worked only in oil paint. Cadell worked in both oil and watercolour. For oil painting both artists, but especially Cadell, often used 15" x 18" panels. Some of these had canvas laid down onto the board, and others were prepared with a gesso ground. Gesso is a mixture of chalk dust, zinc white, and hot glue size. Grounds of this sort are absorbent and many of Cadell's paintings have the instruction on the back, "never varnish". The larger oil paintings are on canvas on stretchers, 20" x 24" and 25" x 30" being frequently used sizes. It will be noticed that all the above sizes have a height to width ratio of 5:6 and this was the most frequently used shape by both artists. Some larger works have ratios of 5:7 and 2:3 (20" x 28" and 20" x 30"). Most of Cadell's watercolours are on 1/8th imperial sheets (approximately 7" x 10", or a little smaller when mounted). Nearly all Peploe's paintings and the majority of Cadell's are coastal subjects, and for these both artists used a high horizon for most of their pictures. More occasionally the composition comprised a large sky and low horizon.

Little has been written about the working methods of the artists, but the paintings themselves show that both had a brisk and confident style in oil, which would have allowed completion of the standard 15" x 18" panels in a single sitting, and possibly the larger works also. However, some of these reveal signs of a second working in their final brushstrokes dragged over previously dried paint (Figure 2). Both artists were skilled draughtsmen and underlying the loosely painted finish is secure and structured drawing. Cadell was extremely proficient in watercolour and his small paintings in this medium may well have been the product of less than an hour's work.

There is a photograph of the painter W. C. Crawford, a contemporary of Cadell, painting on Iona, sitting on a low stool and working with an open box on his knee (Figure 3). Such boxes are referred to as pochades, "pochade" being French for sketch. The painting is secured in the lid. The lower part of the box, which contains the materials, has a sliding top which also serves as the palette for mixing the colours. This design, which goes back many centuries, provides a very efficient means of working on small oil paintings out of doors, and the box may be closed quickly in the event of rain. Pochade boxes are frequently as small as 6" x 8". However the box that Crawford is using appears large enough to hold the 15" x 18" panels so frequently used, although it is possible that some form of easel may have been employed for this size. This would have allowed stepping back to view the progress of the painting, and a greater freedom of movement for the painting arm. The larger works would certainly have required an easel (Figure 4).

[FIGURE 2] *Opposite top:* Detail of *Ben More* by S. J. Peploe (Plate 155)
This detail, reproduced actual size, gives a vivid impression of the energy with which these works were painted. Stanley Cursiter in his biography *Peploe: An Intimate Memoir of an Artist and His Work* writes "The fast moving brush has the joy of the dancer, the dash of the figure skater, and the cut and thrust of the swordsman".

[FIGURE 3] *Opposite left:* W.C. Crawford, painting on Iona using a pochade box
[FIGURE 4] *Opposite right:* F.C.B. Cadell, painting on Iona, standing at an easel

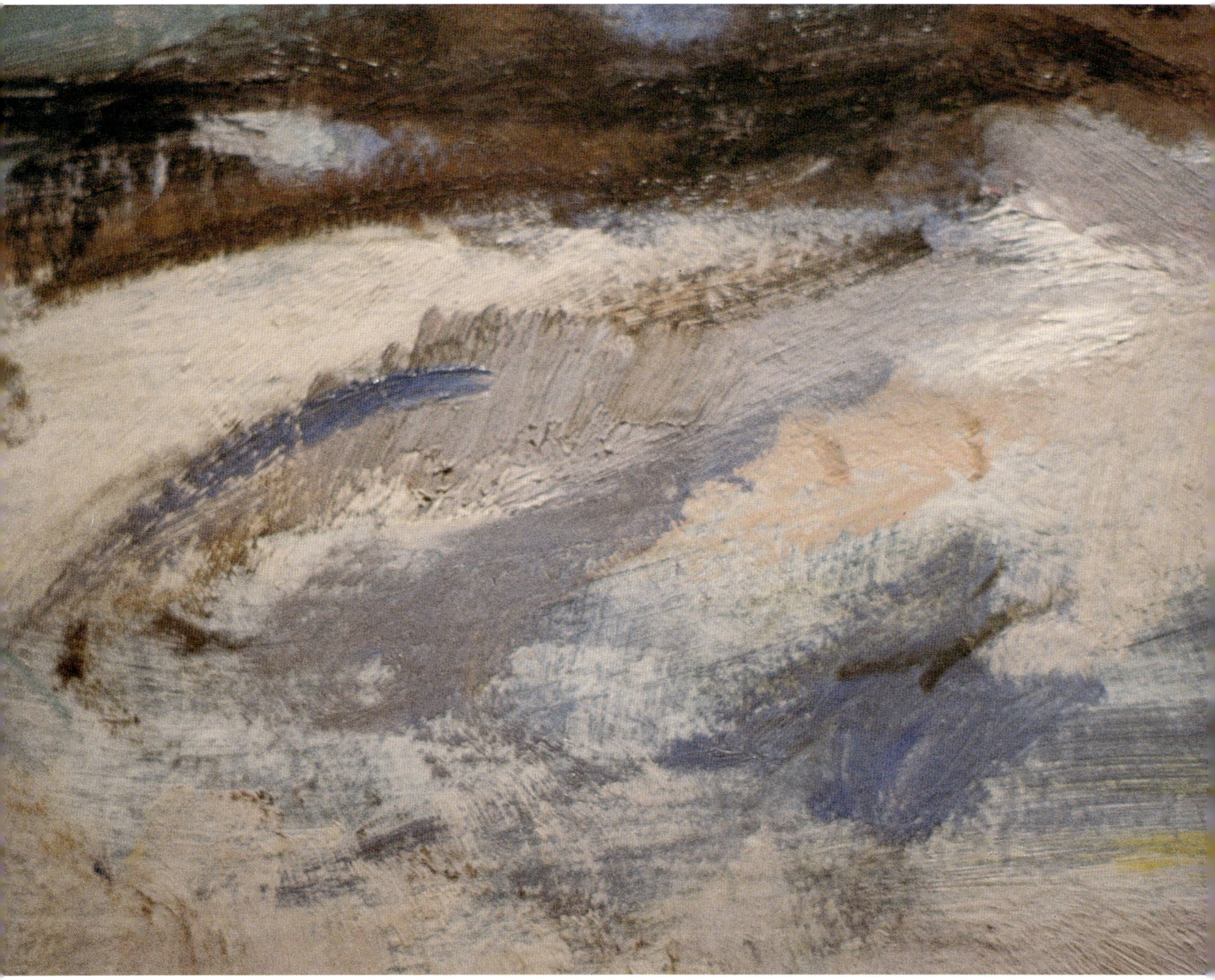

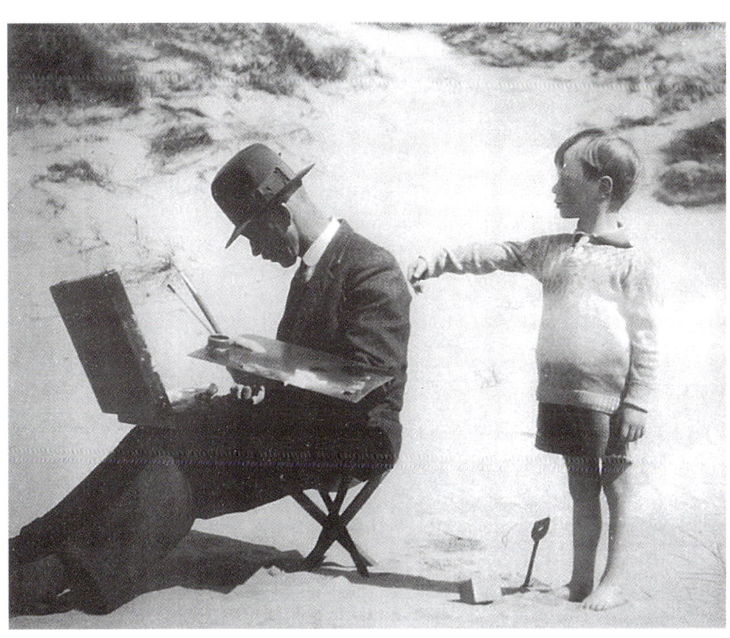

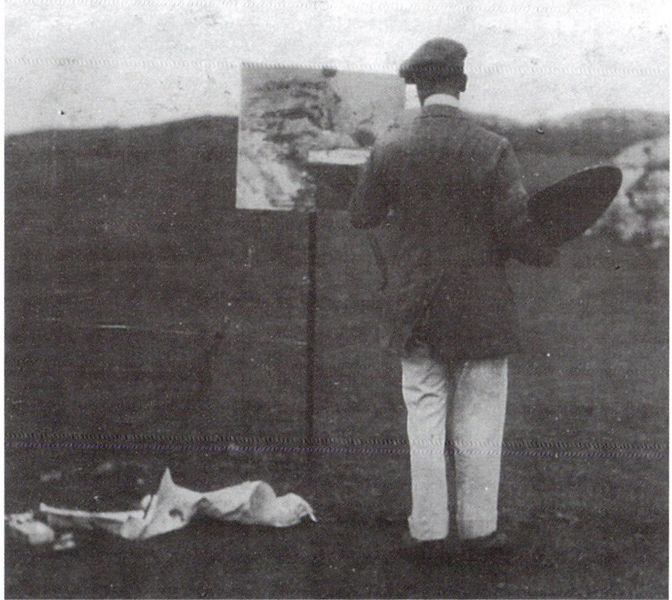

The paintings illustrated in the following chapters are not described in chronology, which in any case is not known precisely, but are grouped by location, and in a sequence that allows the reader to visit the site of each painting in turn during two circular walks on the island. Half a day should be enough for each walk. In most cases the illustrations of the paintings are accompanied by a present-day photograph of the same location. As may be seen from this comparison, many new buildings have been constructed and older ones altered and enlarged since the time that Peploe and Cadell painted here, including of course the extensive rebuilding of the Abbey. Visitors may perhaps assume that the landscape itself has remained unchanged. Indeed the rock profiles can hardly have altered since the last Ice Age, and this allows positive identification of the locations. However, the coastal subjects change in appearance with the shifting of sand with wind and tide. The sand levels appear to be lower now than in some of the paintings, a topic I shall return to in the relevant chapters. Naturally the tide affects the appearance of the subject; in many cases important features of a composition are submerged entirely at high tide. In order to see the coastal locations clearly, it is necessary to visit the beaches within the four-hour period from two hours before low tide to two hours after. A small number of paintings show relatively high tide levels (eg Plates 129 and 158).

As already noted nearly all Peploe's Iona paintings are of the northern beaches, and, although Cadell worked in a greater variety of locations, the majority of his paintings are also of the northern shores. Hence the first walk, from the Village round the north of the island, described in Chapters 1 to 5, takes in most of the paintings. The second walk, described in Chapter 6, round the west and south of the island via Port Bhan, The Machair, Marble Quarry and returning to the Village by Traigh Mhor, passes the sites of the remaining pictures (Figure 5). The second walk is rather longer but could be shortened by missing out the Marble Quarry and returning direct to Four Roads from The Machair. Larger scale maps are included in each chapter to pinpoint the painting locations.

Editorial procedure

Imperial units of measurement were in use at the time that these works were painted, and canvas stretchers were usually made in one-inch or two-inch increments (2.54cm or 5.08cm). The metric sizes given in the sources I have worked from show slight variations for the standard 15" x 18" panels. This may represent actual differences or just result from measurements having been taken to the sight lines of the paintings in frames with different widths of rebate. For simplicity I have given the nominal value of 15" x 18" for all these panels, and have also used inches for the other canvas sizes. Height precedes width.

Similarly I give the approximate size of 7" x 10" for watercolours on 1/8th imperial sheets.

For readers more familiar with centimetres than inches, the metric equivalents are listed below for the frequently occurring sizes of paintings:

7" x 10" – 17.8 x 25.4 centimetres
15" x 18" – 38.1 x 45.7 centimetres
20" x 24" – 50.8 x 61.0 centimetres
25" x 30" – 63.5 x 76.2 centimetres

Over the years some paintings have been known by different titles, and some have been incorrectly identified; a confusion between Lunga and the Dutchman's Cap occurs for example. Many paintings have been known simply as "Iona", a title which would have sufficed for a single work in a mixed exhibition.

However, in this book, since all the paintings are of Iona, I have given a concise topographical title to each work and omitted the word "Iona". Long-established descriptive titles such as *"Summer Day, Iona"* (Plate 87) are given in brackets. Longer explanatory notes and diagrams accompany some paintings.

For works in public Art Galleries and Museums the titles used by the gallery are shown in CAPITALS, followed, in some cases, by my own subtitle in *italics* where additional description is helpful. The book contains as many works as possible from public collections, so that the reader may have the opportunity of seeing the originals, but unless otherwise stated the paintings are in private collections.

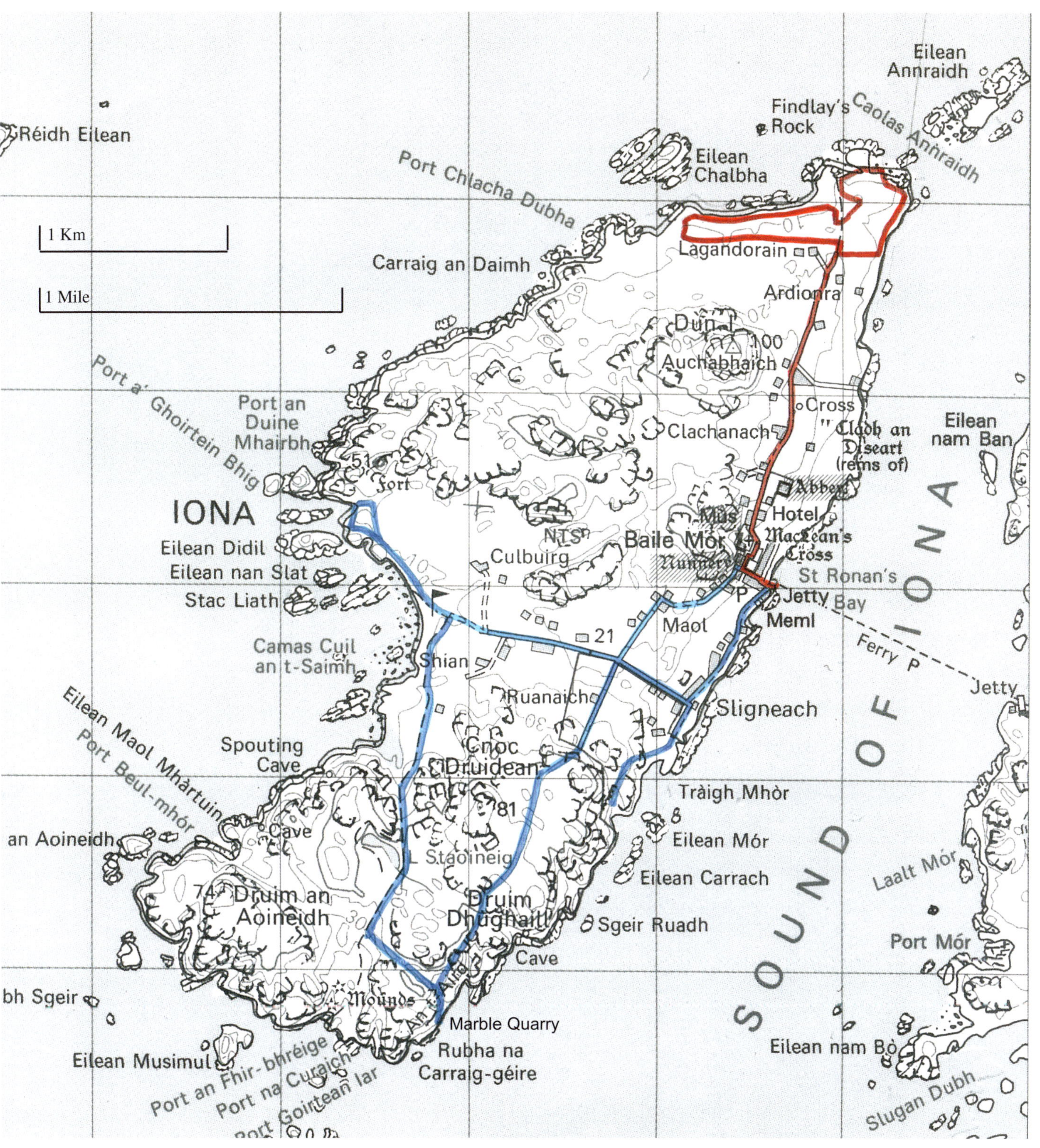

[FIGURE 5] MAP OF IONA showing the walks around the painting locations

The walk shown in red is described in chapters 1 to 5, and that in blue in chapter 6.
The larger scale (1:10,000) map published by the Iona Community is recommended as a guide to walking on the island, as it shows considerably more detail than that above.

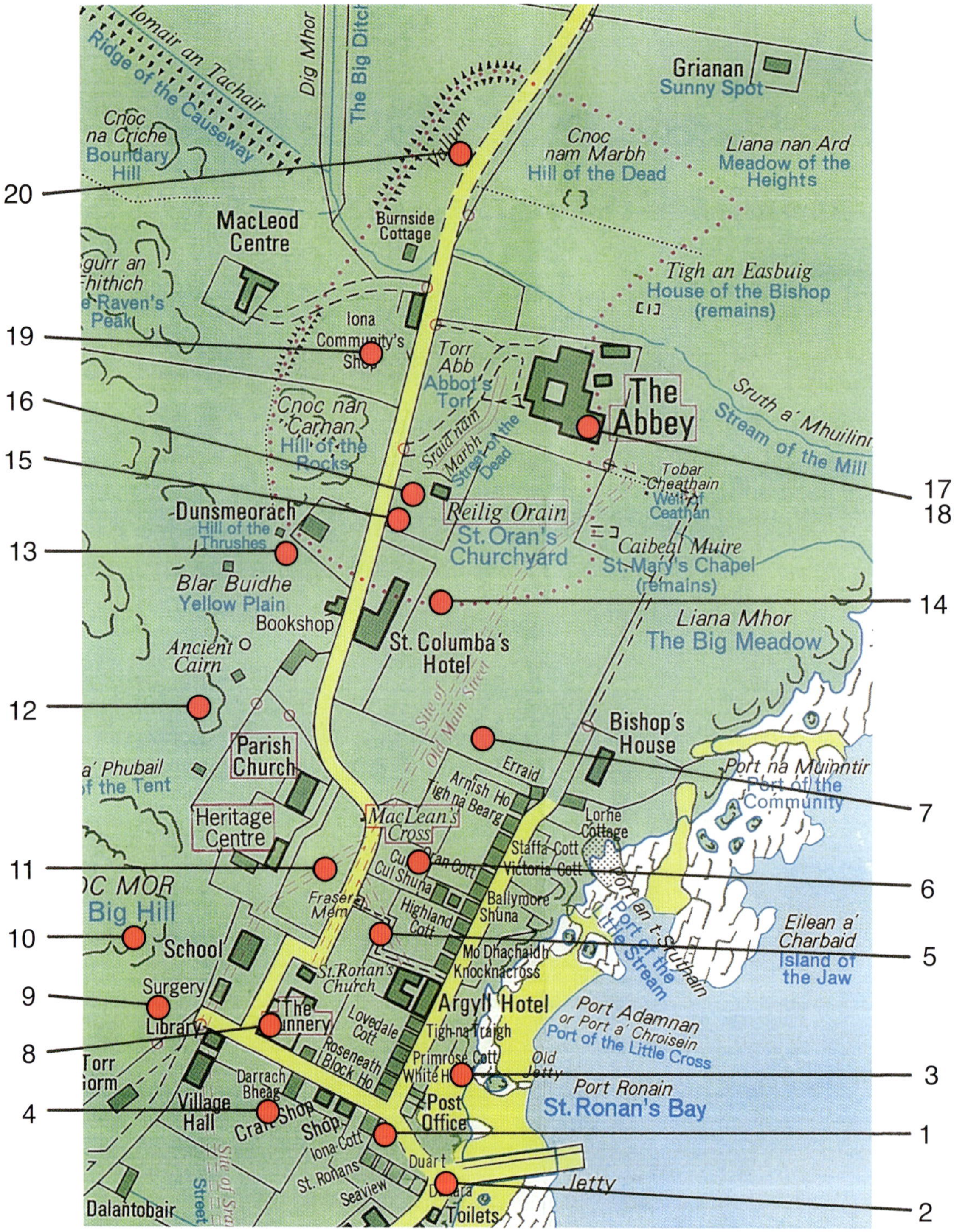

Iomair an Tachair
Ridge of the Causeway
Dig Mhor
The Big Ditch
Grianan
Sunny Spot
Cnoc na Criche
Boundary Hill
Vallum
Cnoc nam Marbh
Hill of the Dead
Liana nan Ard
Meadow of the Heights
20
MacLeod Centre
Burnside Cottage
Tigh an Easbuig
House of the Bishop (remains)
19
Iona Community's Shop
Torr Abb
Abbot's Torr
The Abbey
Sruth a' Mhuilinn
Stream of the Mill
16
Cnoc nan Carnan
Hill of the Rocks
Sraid nam Marbh
Street of the Dead
15
Tobar Cheathain
Well of Ceathan
17
18
Dunsmeorach
Hill of the Thrushes
Reilig Orain
St. Oran's Churchyard
13
Caibeal Muire
St. Mary's Chapel (remains)
Blar Buidhe
Yellow Plain
14
Liana Mhor
The Big Meadow
Bookshop
St. Columba's Hotel
Ancient Cairn
Site of Old Main Street
12
Bishop's House
Parish Church
Erraid
Arnish Ho
Tigh na Bearg
Port na Muinntir
Port of the Community
7
Heritage Centre
MacLean's Cross
Lorne Cottage
Staffa Cott
Victoria Cott
Cul Shuna
11
6
Fraser Mem
Ballymore
Shuna
Port an t-Sruthain
Port of the Little Stream
Big Hill
Eilean a' Charbaid
Island of the Jaw
10
School
Highland Cott
Mo Dhachaidh
Knocknacross
5
St. Ronan's Church
Argyll Hotel
9
Surgery
Library
The Nunnery
Lovedale Cott
Tigh-na-Traigh
Port Adamnan or Port a' Chroisein
Port of the Little Cross
8
Roseneath
Block Ho
Primrose Cott
White H
Old Jetty
3
Port Ronain
St. Ronan's Bay
4
Darrach Bheag
Village Hall
Craft Shop
Shop
Post Office
1
Iona Cott
Duart
St. Ronans
Seaview
Dalantobair
Jetty
Toilets
2

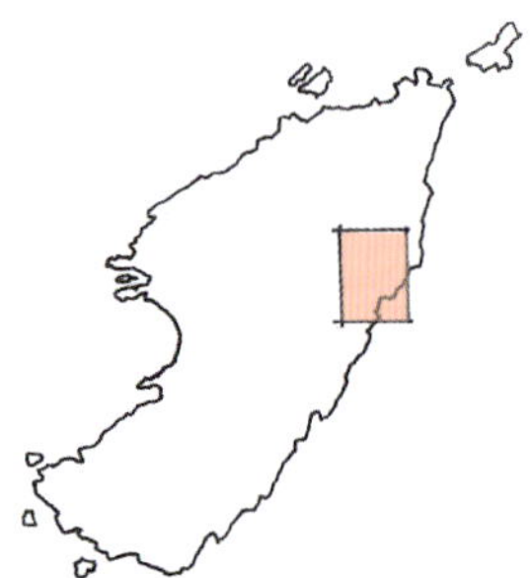

1/4 Mile (400 metres)

[FIGURE 6]
Locations of paintings illustrated in Chapter 1

1 · THE VILLAGE AND THE ABBEY

AS the jetty is the point of arrival, this seems a logical place to begin a walking tour of the painting locations, and given the importance of transport by boat to an island community, the picture by Cadell of the steamship Dunara Castle is an appropriate painting with which to start (Plate 1). The Dunara Castle made her maiden voyage in 1875 and was in service for nearly 73 years, sailing from Glasgow. She was a cargo vessel, but also carried a small number of passengers.

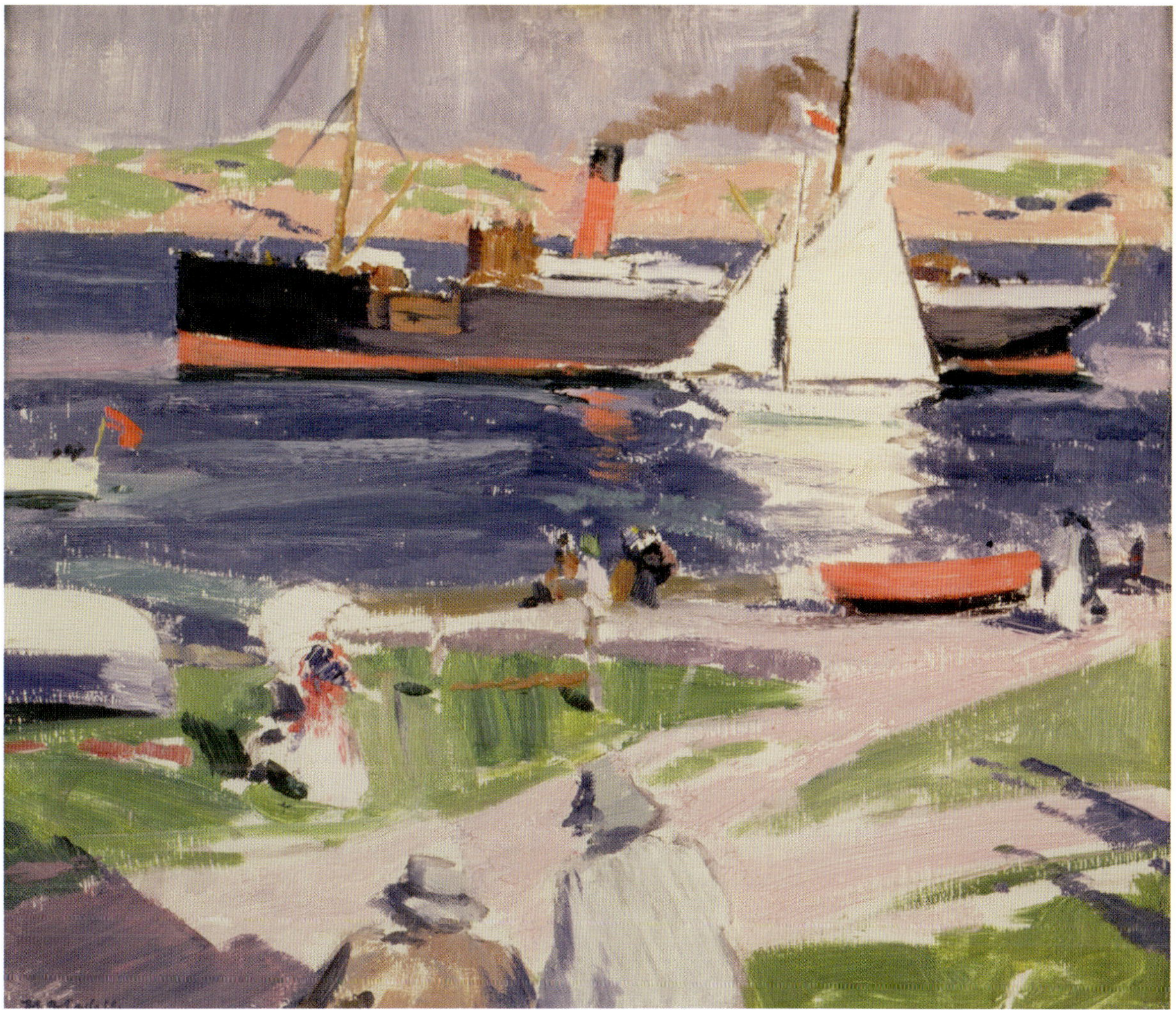

[PLATE 1]
F. C. B. Cadell

THE DUNARA CASTLE AT IONA
Oil 15 x 18

The Fleming-Wyfold Art Foundation

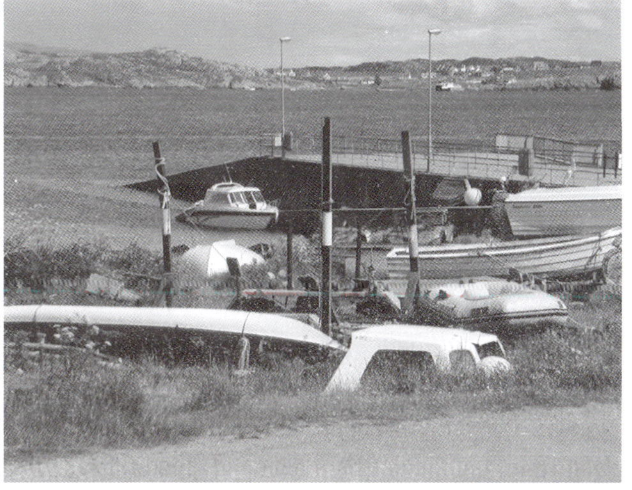

The lower jetty in the photograph, built in 1956, is in the same position as the old stone jetty in Cadell's painting. The higher jetty was built to accommodate the roll-on roll-off ferry which came into service in 1979.

Photograph 2010

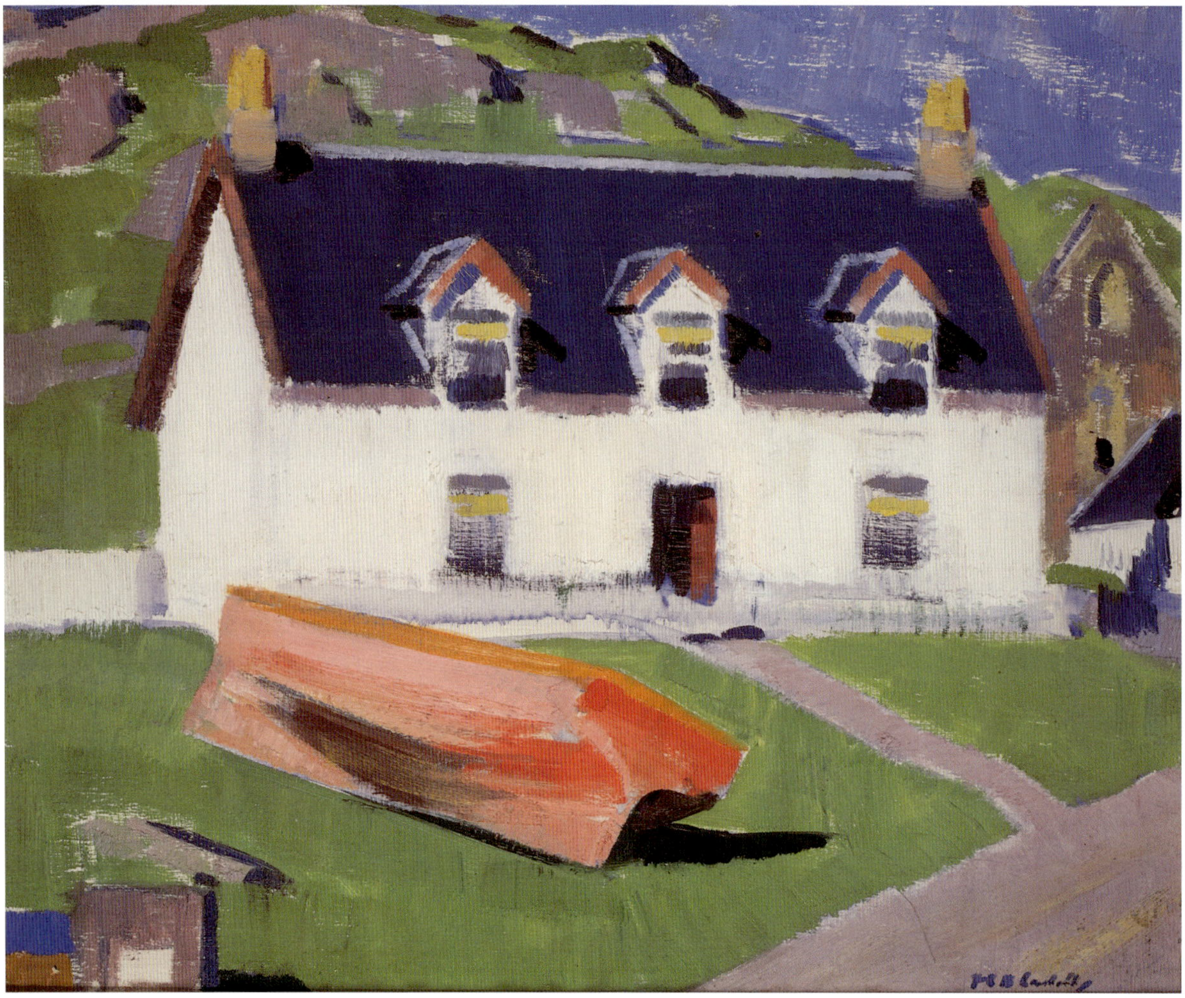

[PLATE 2]
F. C. B. Cadell
Iona Cottage
Oil 15 x 18

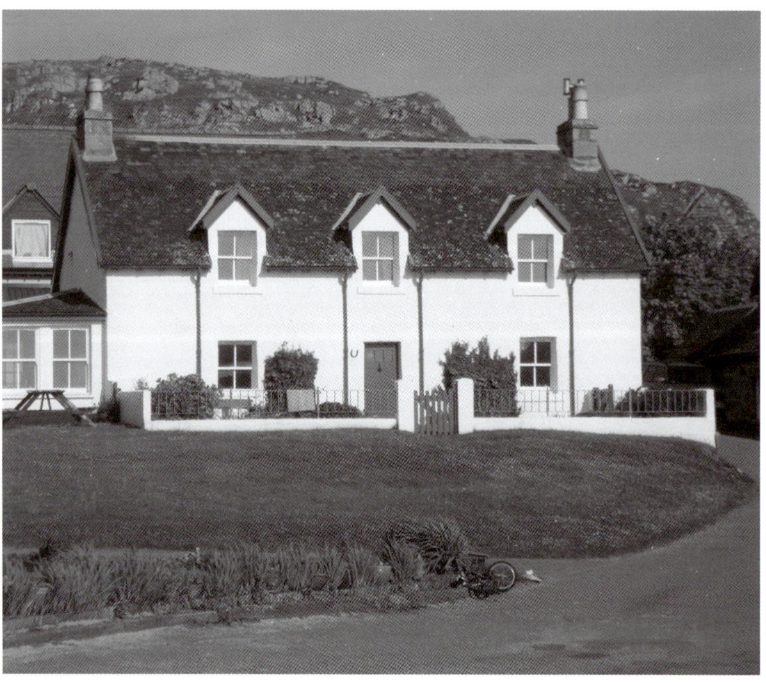

Photograph 2012

This was painted from close to the jetty. Cnoc Mor, the Big Hill, which rises behind the Village, is in the background, and a gable wall of the Nunnery can be seen at the right-hand side.

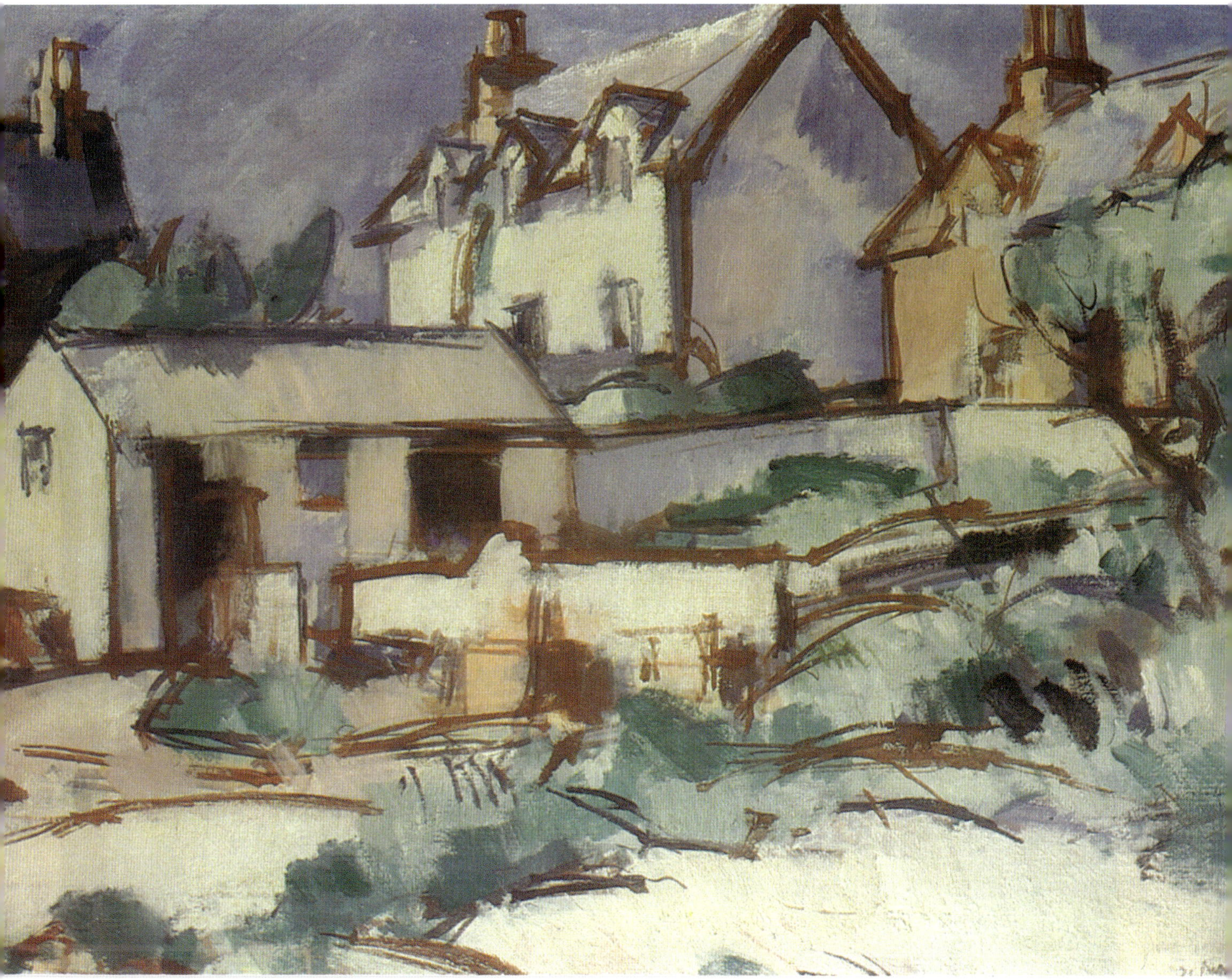

[PLATE 3]
S. J. Peploe
Iona Cottage
Oil 20 1/2 x 27

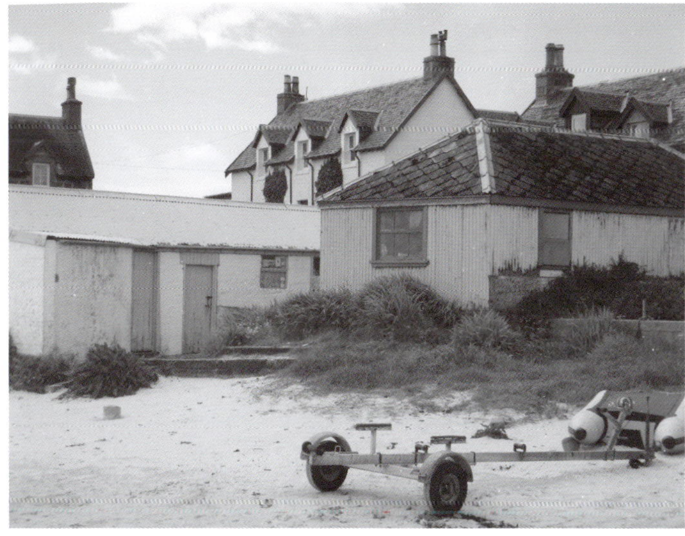

Photograph 2009

The houses in the background are St. Ronan's on the left, Iona Cottage in the centre, and Block House on the right. The small building in the left foreground was Mrs MacLeod's shop – a general store at the time, but now the Post Office. There is a painting by Cadell of the Post Office he would have used, which stood on the left of the road which leads up to the Nunnery (Plate 4).

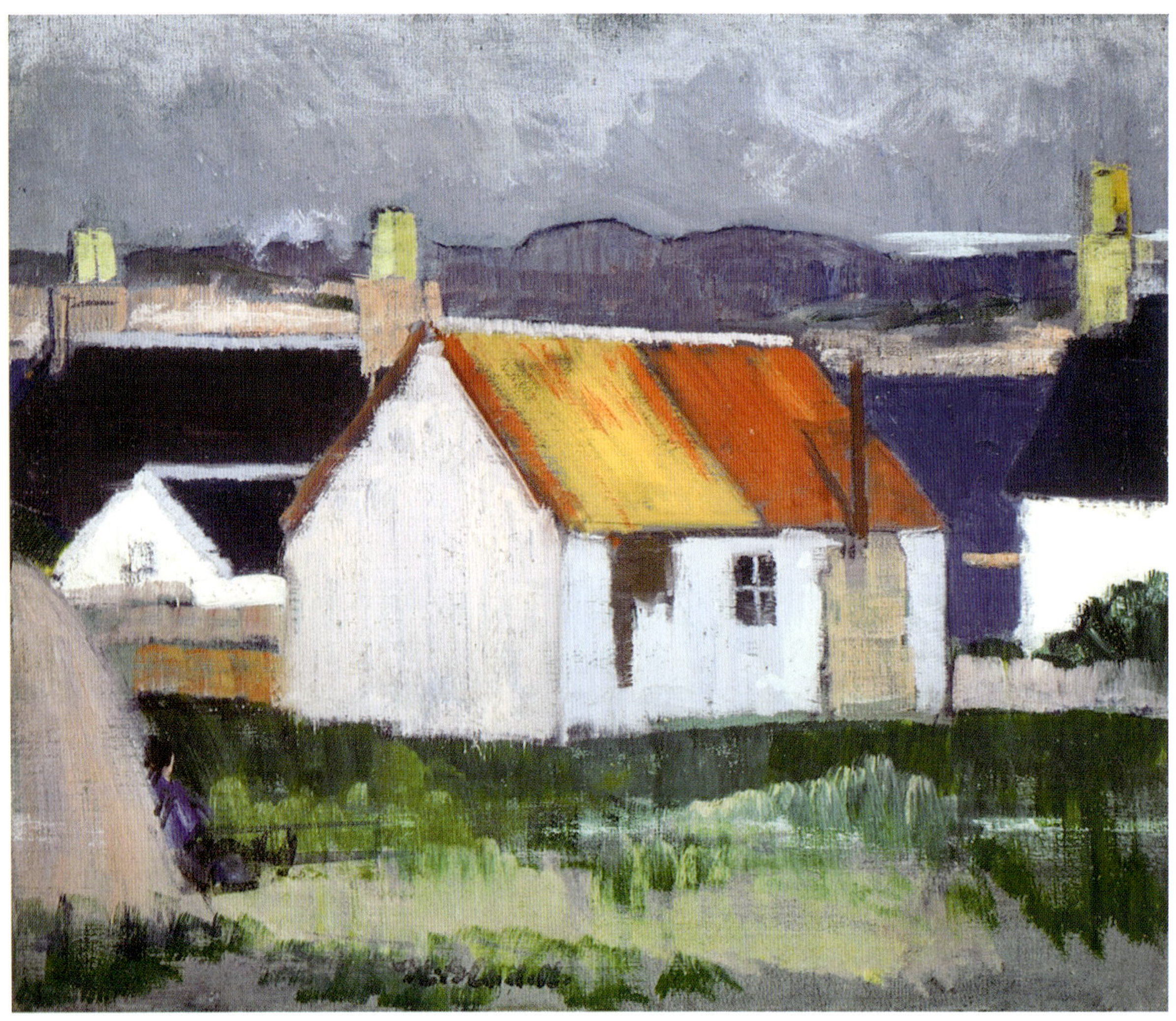

The Post Office is in the centre. To the left is Block House and to the right Iona Cottage, with a glimpse through the gap to the Sound of Iona. The Ross of Mull, which appears in many paintings across the narrow part of the Sound, is in the background.

Built in 1896, this served as the Post Office from that date through to 1988, when it was demolished and replaced by the Spar Shop.

[PLATE 4]
F. C. B. Cadell

IONA

The Post Office
Oil 15 x 18
Scottish National Gallery of Modern Art

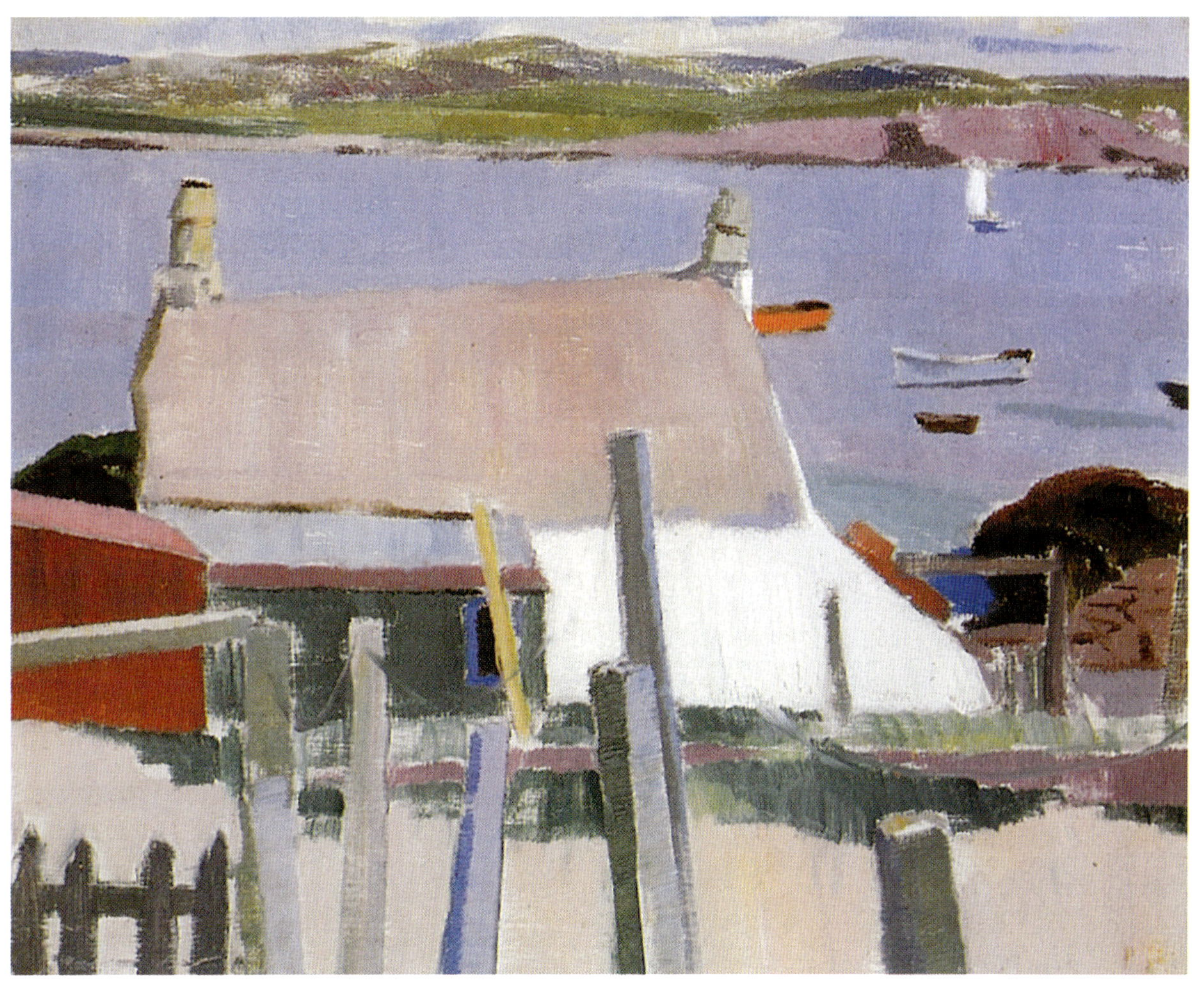

This cottage possibly stood on the site of the present house called Knocknacross. The view is from the back garden. The boats moored in the Sound were used to ferry passengers ashore from vessels such as the paddlesteamer Grenadier, as may be seen in another painting by Cadell (Plate 204).

The Ross of Mull is in the distance. Composed of Caledonian Granite formed over 400 million years ago, the rock is pink in colour, and when lit by the setting sun, glows in an unforgettable way. Quite different rocks are to be seen in other paintings of Iona, and on different parts of Mull which appear in other pictures. These will be described in the relevant sections in later chapters.

[PLATE 5]
F. C. B. Cadell
A Cottage on the Village Street
Oil 15 x 18

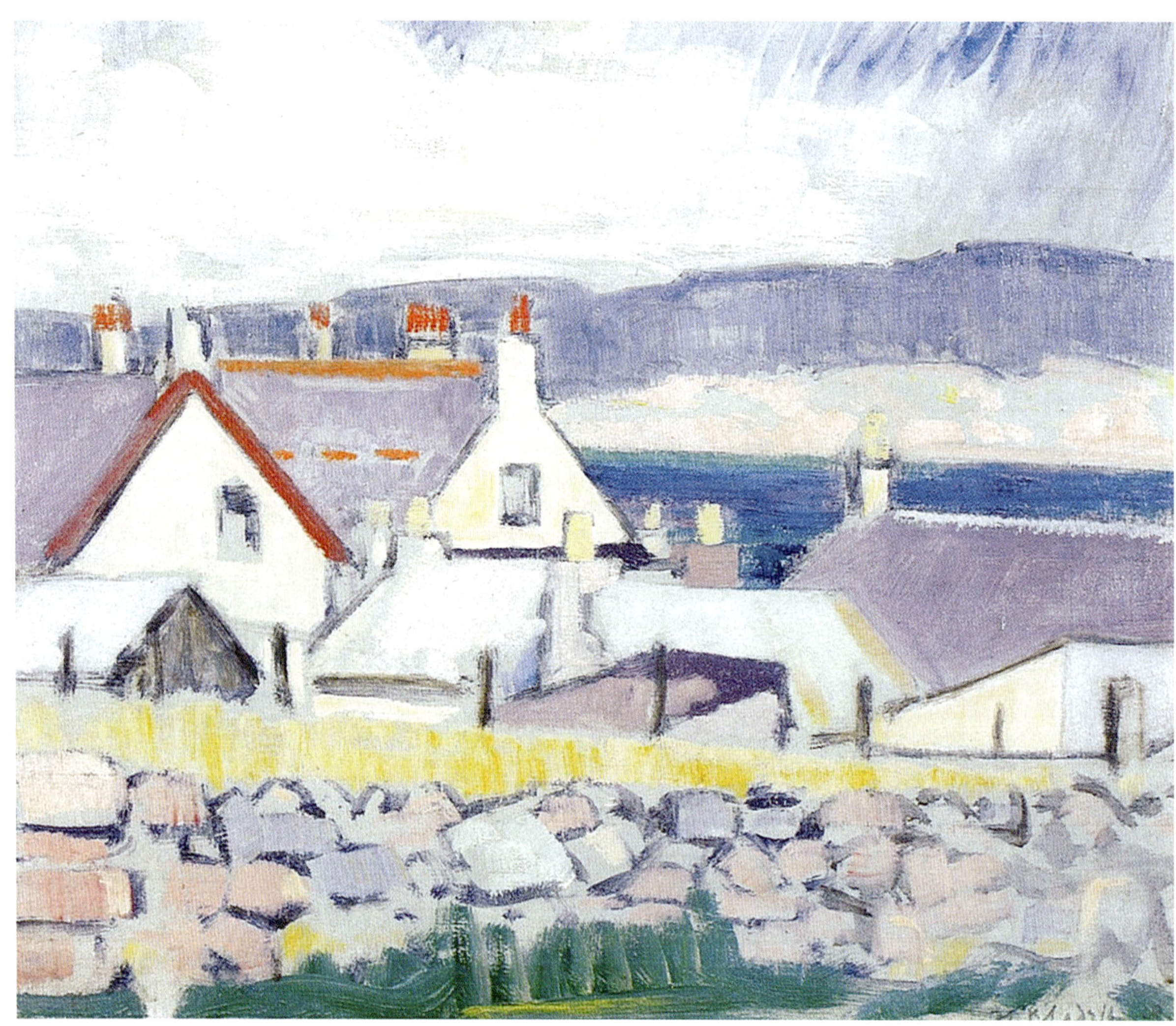

This group of buildings, which is also included in the middle distance of Plate 9, is at the north end of the Village Street. The gable wall just left of centre is that of Bishop's House, and the gable on the left is Arnish House. The picture was painted looking over the rear gardens; the backs of the houses Tigh na Bearg and Staffa Cottage are seen left of centre and on the right respectively.

The Sound of Iona, Ross of Mull, and the Burg are in the background. The location is easy to identify, but can no longer be seen from this position owing to the substantial growth of trees in the rear gardens.

[PLATE 6]
F. C. B. Cadell
Bishop's House
Oil 15 x 18

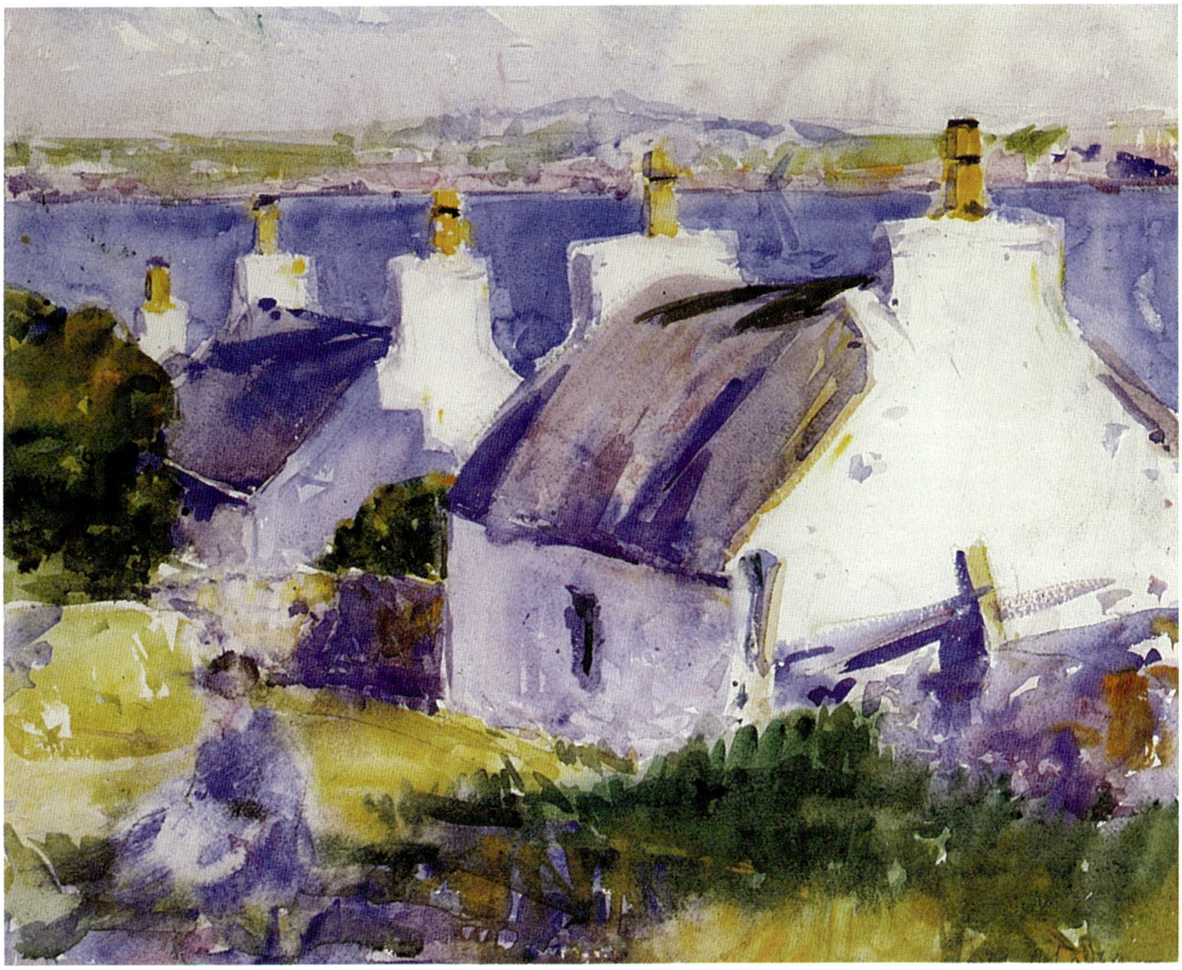

[PLATE 7]
F. C. B. Cadell
Rose Cottage
Watercolour 15 x 18

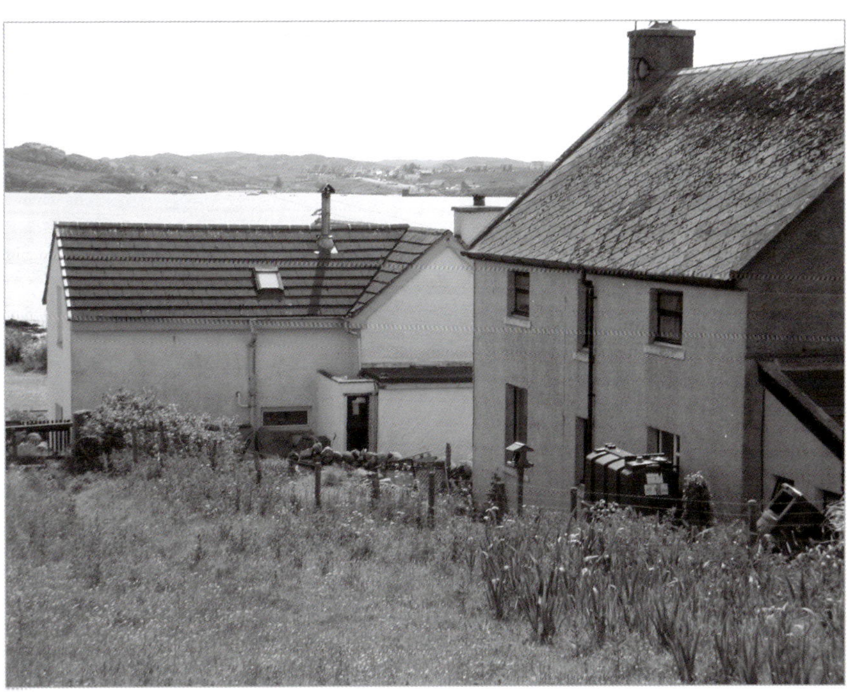

Photograph 2009

Rose Cottage is on the right, and Lorne Cottage beyond it on the left. A two-storey house, Erraid, now stands on the site of Rose Cottage. The Sound of Iona and the Ross of Mull are in the background.

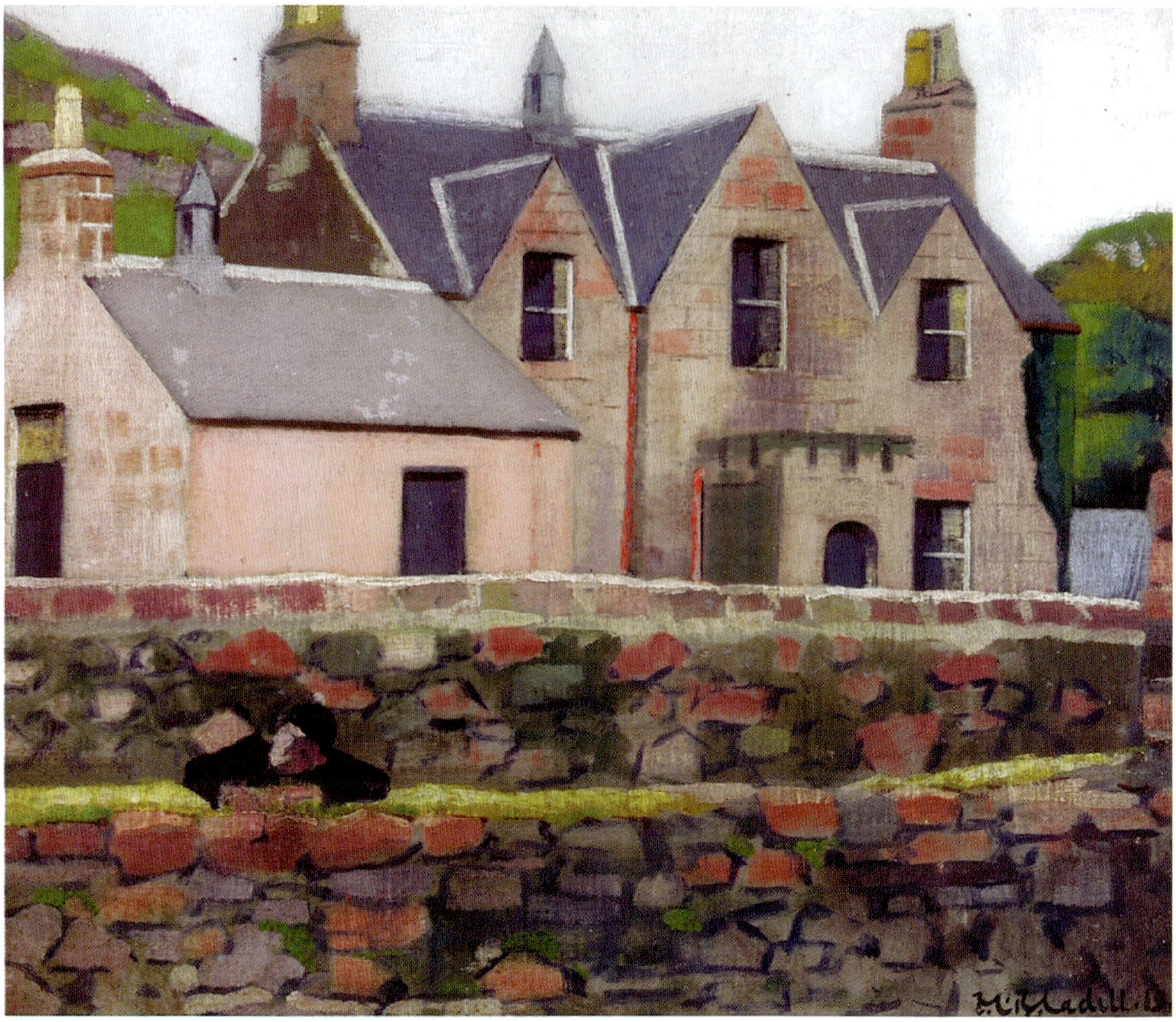

[PLATE 8]
F. C. B. Cadell
The Schoolhouse
Oil 15 x 18

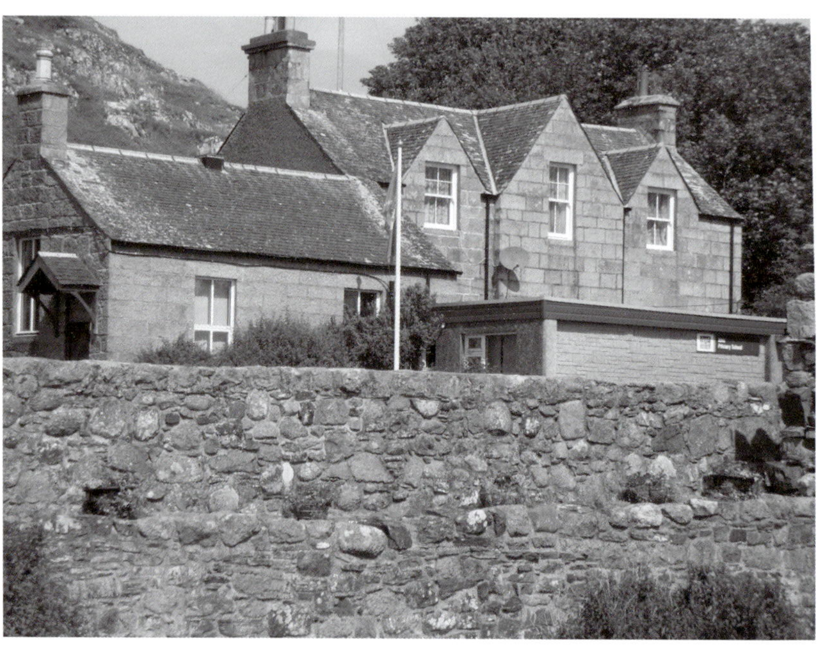

Photograph 2009

Here Cadell has painted the Schoolhouse from inside the Nunnery, and the wall of the Cloister occupies the lower forty percent of the painting. As in a number of pictures he has allowed the frame to cut the view at an unexpected point. Here the higher section of the wall on the right is just included (see also Plates 19, 40, 108, 183 and 195).

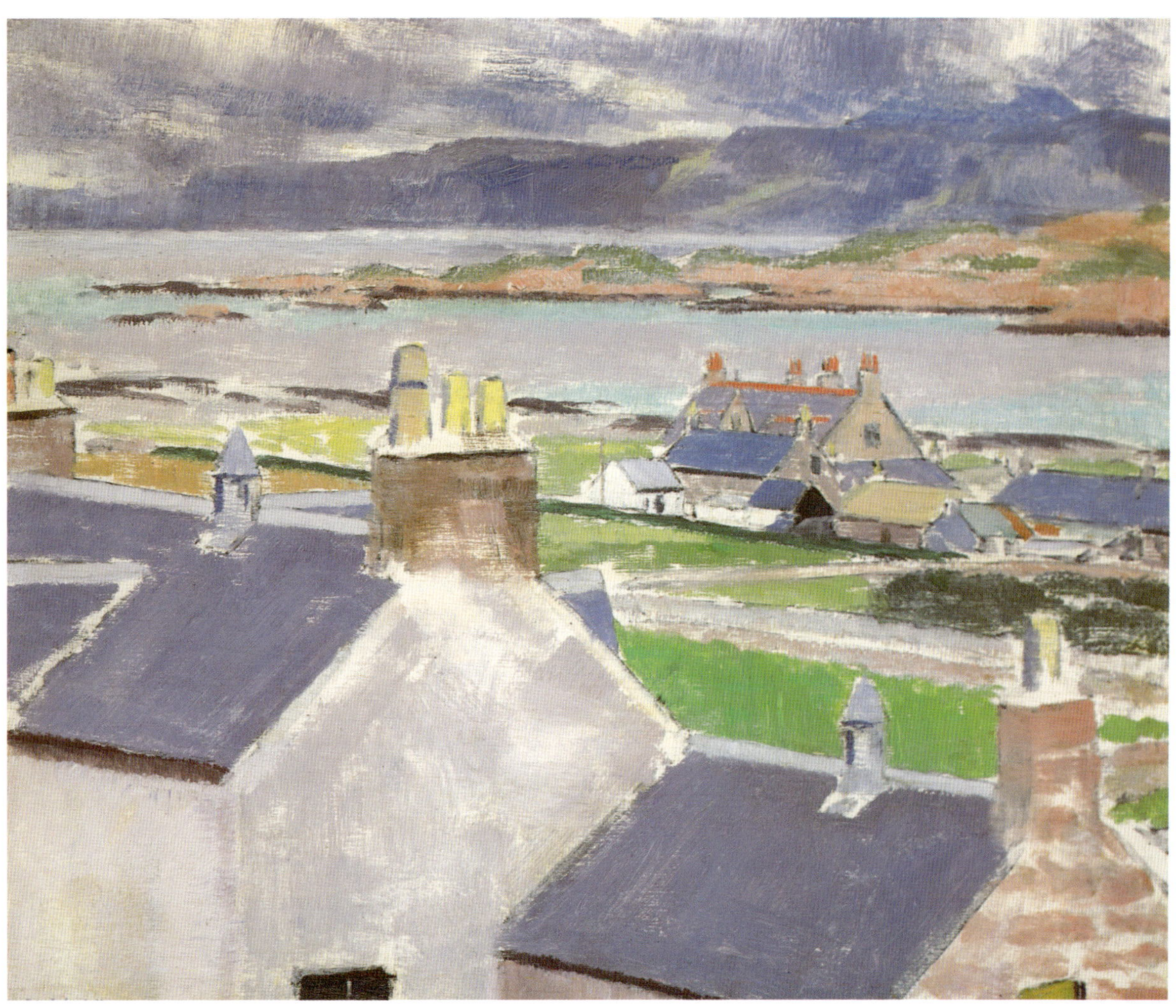

Painted from a short way up Cnoc Mor, this view is now partly hidden by trees. The roof of the Schoolhouse is in the foreground, and Bishop's House and the cottages at the north end of the Village Street can be seen in the middle distance. This group of buildings is the subject of Plate 6. The Ross of Mull is on the far side of the Sound, and Ben More can be seen in the top right corner partly obscured by cloud.

[PLATE 9]
F. C. B. Cadell
The Schoolhouse (Village Roofs)
Oil 15 x 18

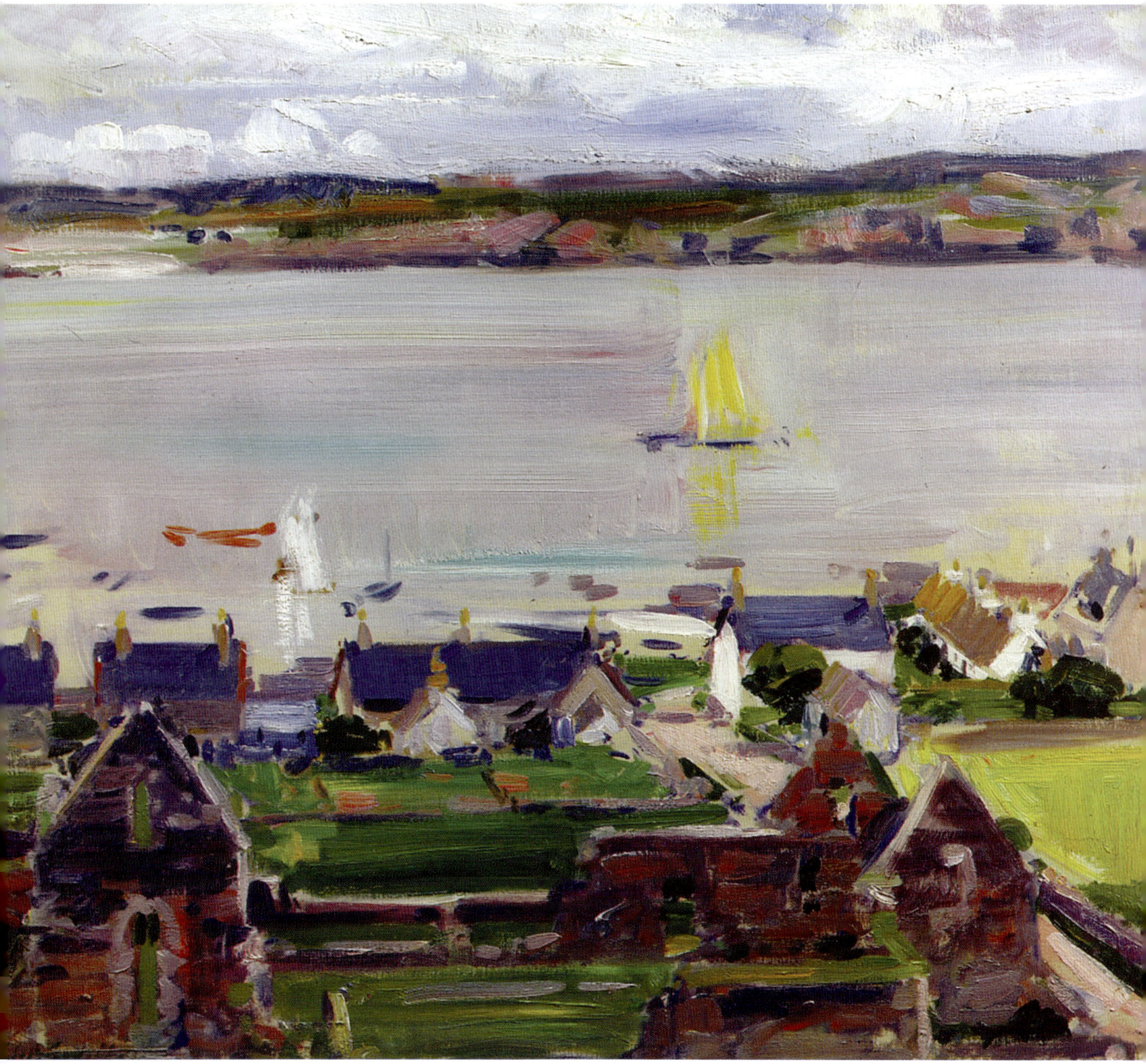

[PLATE 10]
F. C. B. Cadell
The Nunnery from Cnoc Mor
Oil 25 x 30

Cnoc Mor rises steeply behind the village. There is a broad grassy ledge part way up from where Cadell painted this view of the Nunnery, with the Village and Sound of Iona beyond. The new jetty and the Spar Shop, Craft Shop and Darrach Bheag on the right are obvious additions, but otherwise the view remains much as Cadell saw it.

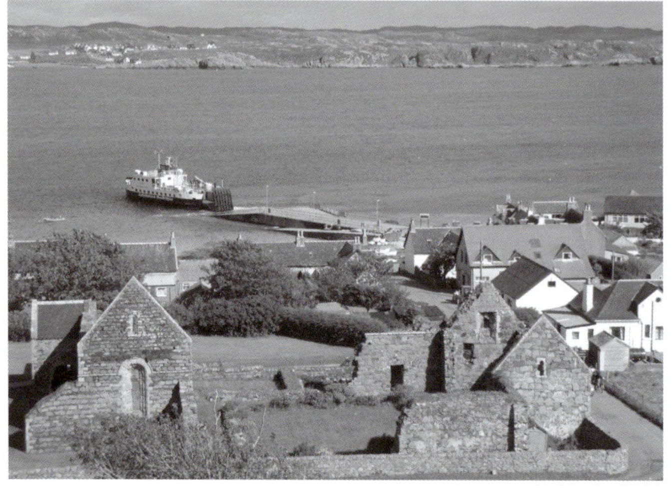

Photograph 2009

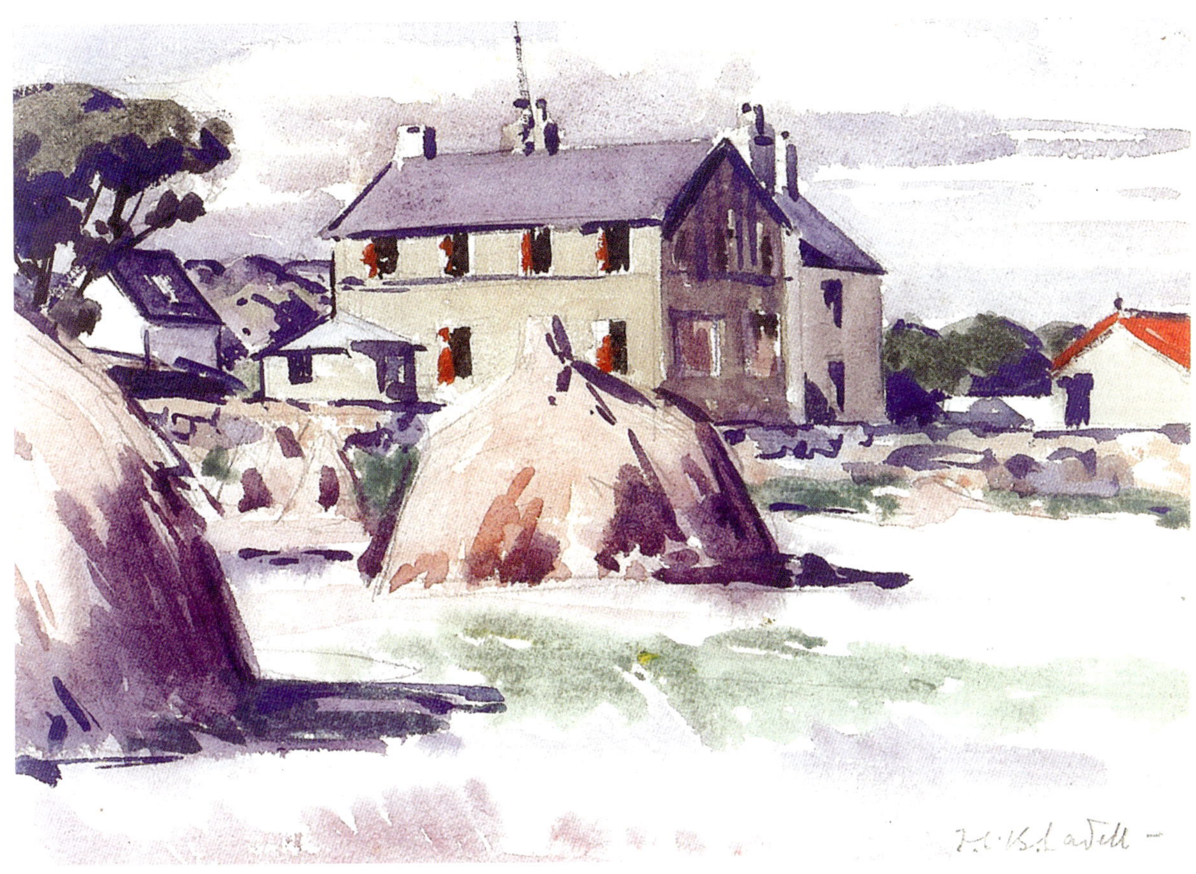

[PLATE 11]
F. C. B. Cadell
The St. Columba Hotel
Watercolour 7 x 10

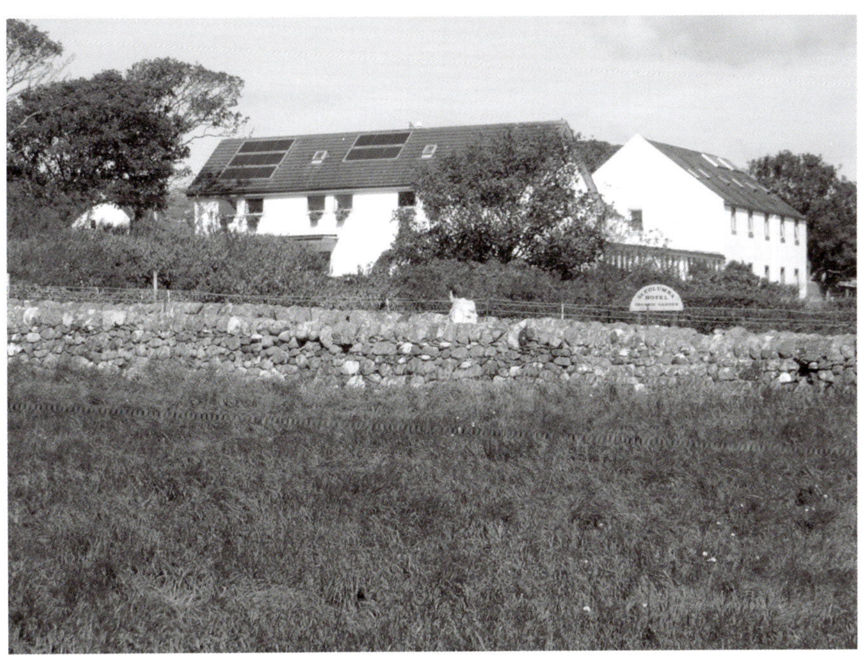

Photograph 2010

The hotel is in the centre, and the Bookshop can be seen at the left-hand side. The field in the foreground with the haystacks is in front of the Iona Heritage Centre and Tea Room, formerly the Manse.

The part of the hotel seen in the painting was built in 1926, and was clad in corrugated iron. It was demolished in 1966 and replaced in 1967 by the present building seen in the photograph. The building on the right is the northern extension of the hotel, which also appears in the photograph accompanying Plate 12.

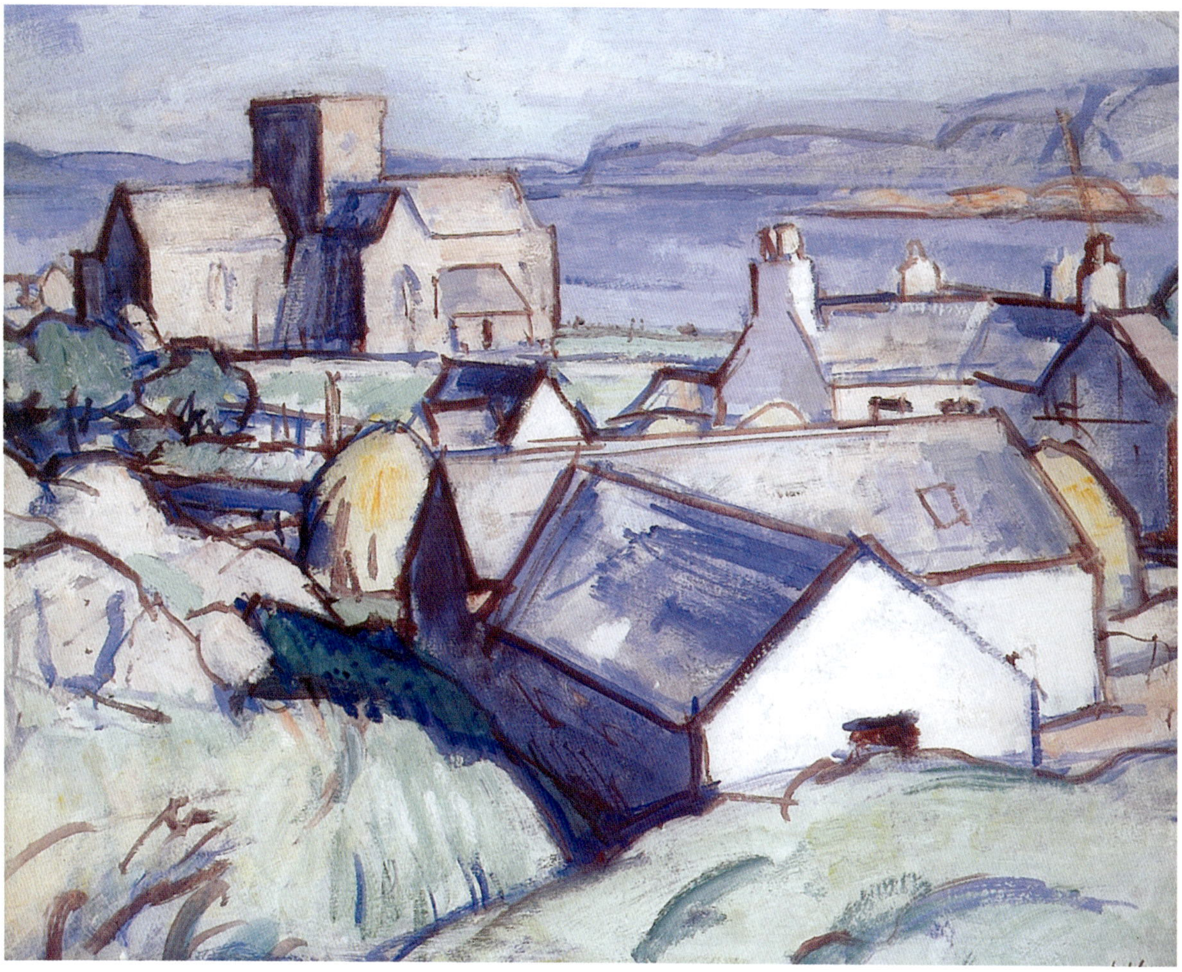

[PLATE 12]
S.J. Peploe
The Abbey and Hotel
Oil 25 x 30

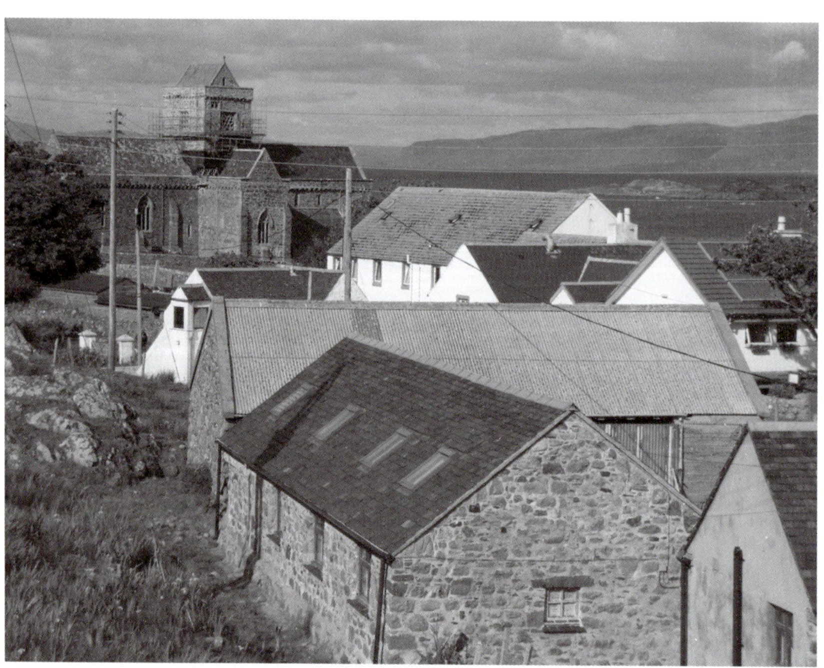

Photograph 2009

Peploe painted this large canvas from the top of a rocky outcrop above the former steadings, now an Arts Centre, which appears in the foreground. The Abbey is on the left and the St. Columba Hotel on the right. The view of the Sound of Iona through the centre of the painting is now closed off by the northern extension of the hotel.

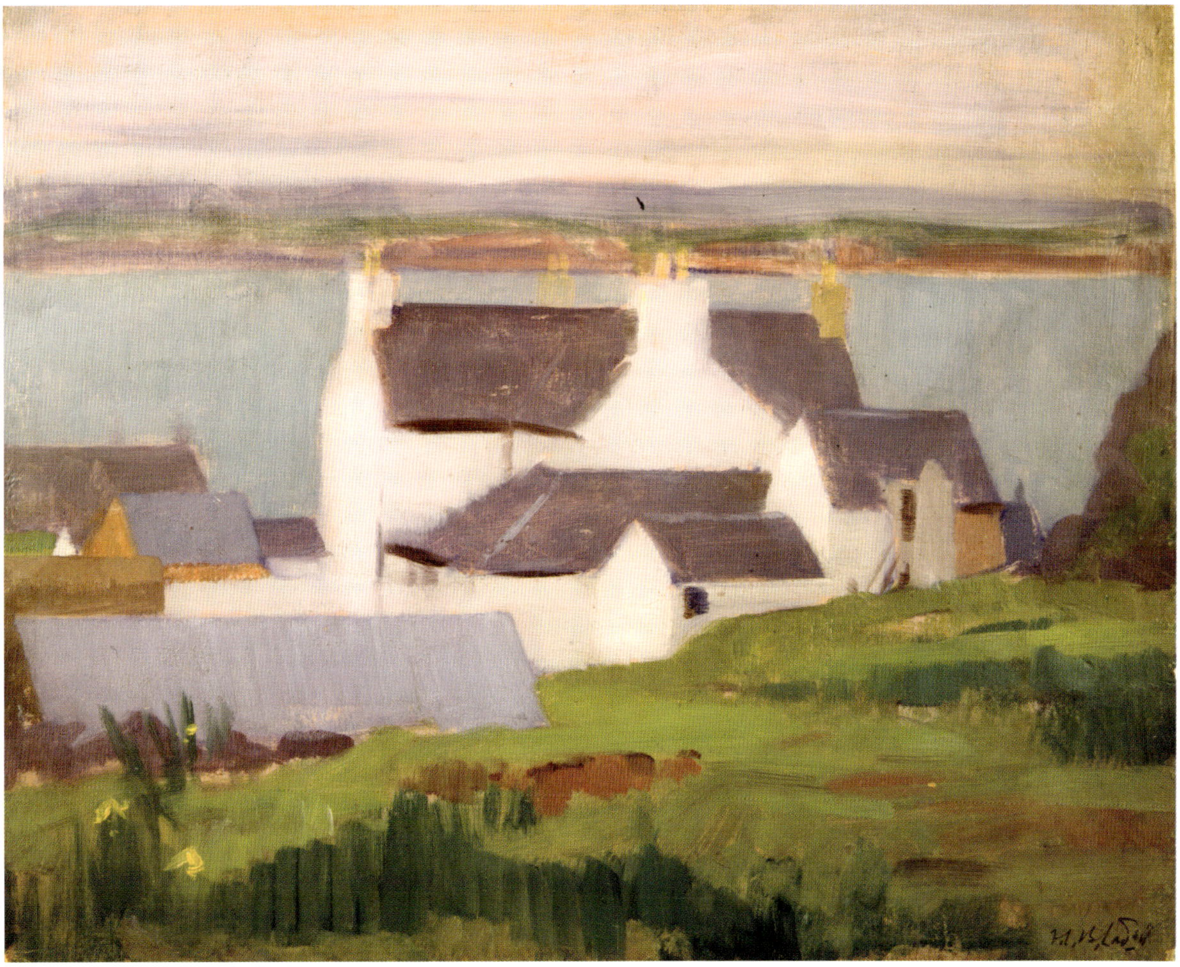

[PLATE 13]
F. C. B. Cadell
The St. Columba Hotel
Oil 15 x 18

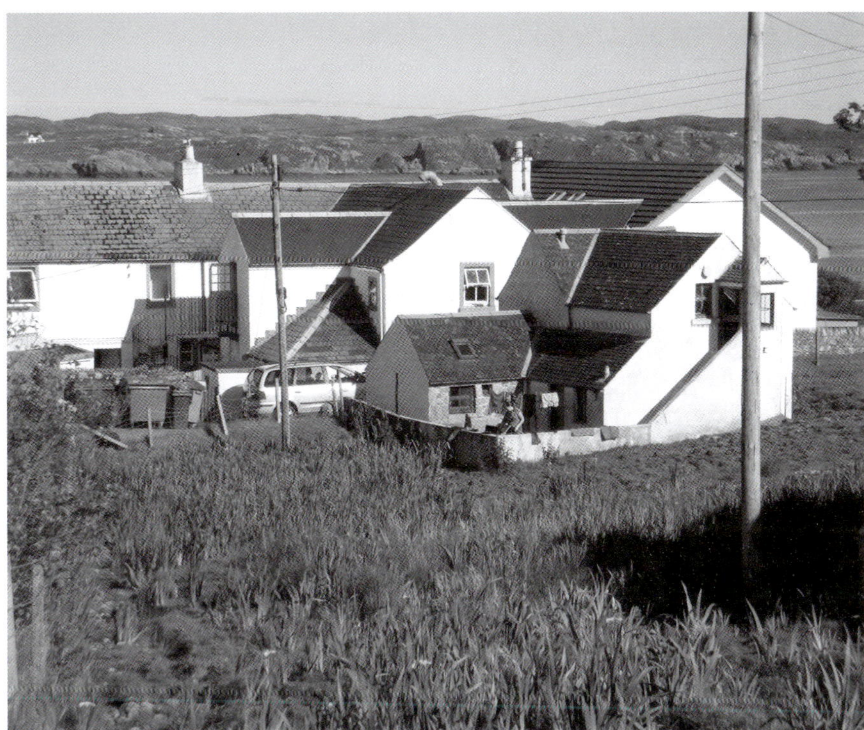

Photograph 2009

Cadell painted at least two versions of this subject, which shows the back of the Hotel. The building on the right with the external stair is the Bookshop; Cadell used the top floor on occasions, and referred to it as his “studio”.

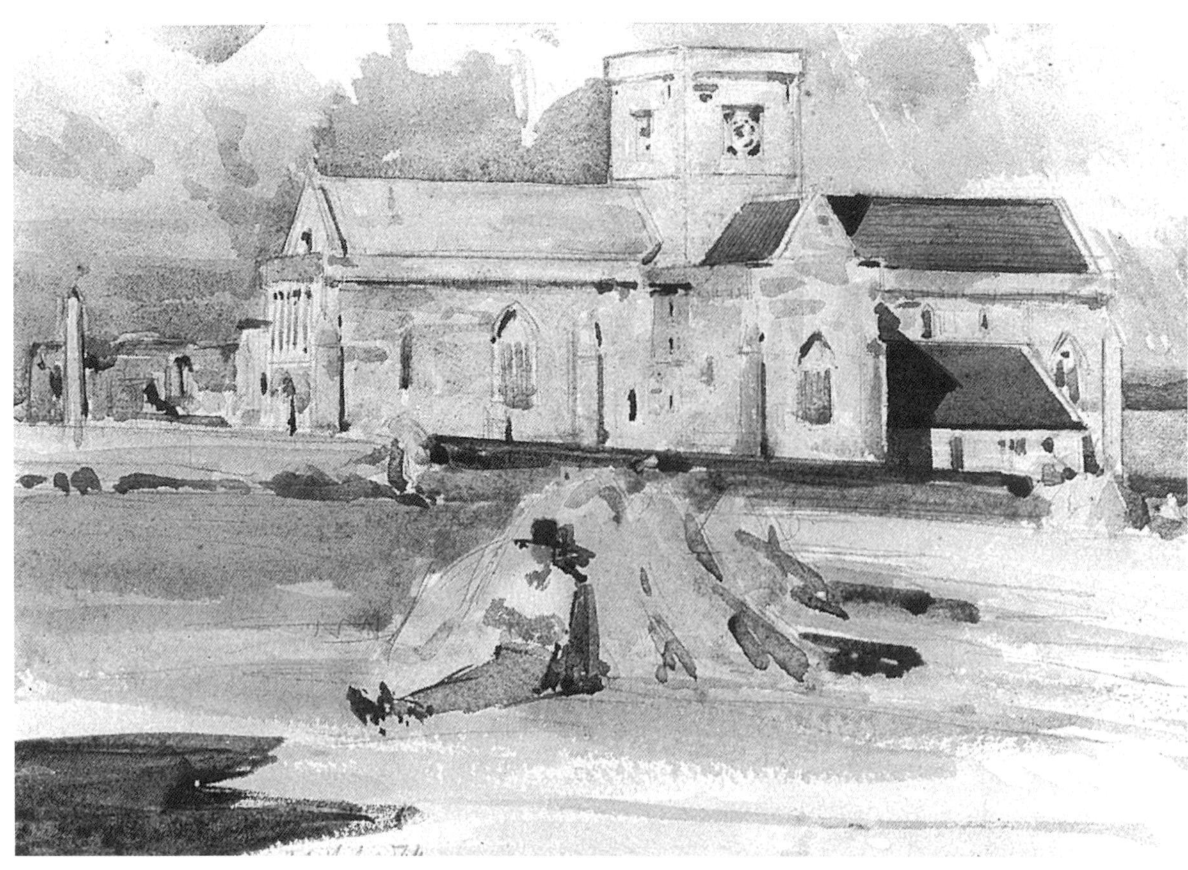

[PLATE 14]
F. C. B. Cadell
The Abbey from the south
Watercolour 7 x 10

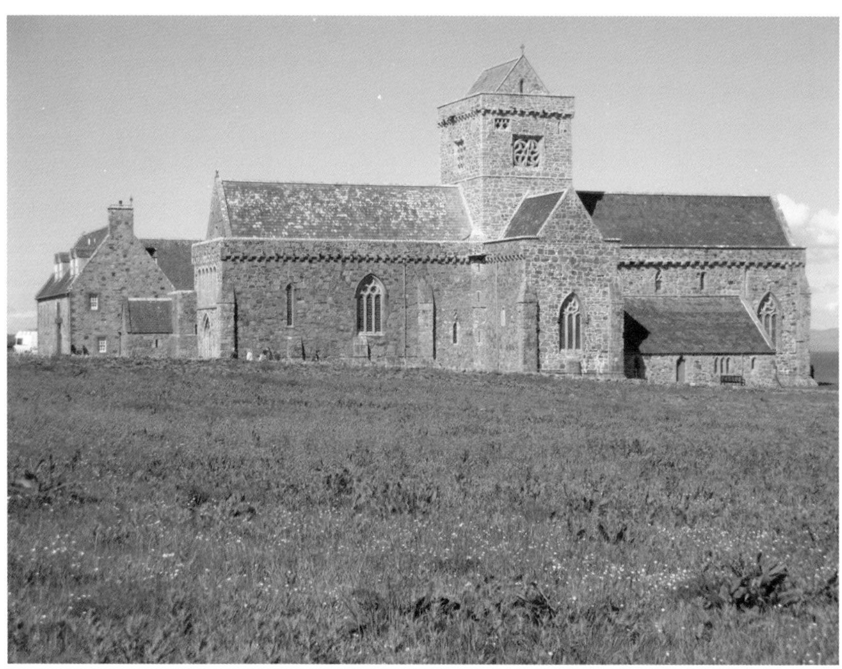

Photograph 2012

The gabled roof on the tower was added in 1996. Otherwise this side of the Abbey remains as Cadell painted it, and the picture is a good example of his sure draughtsmanship.

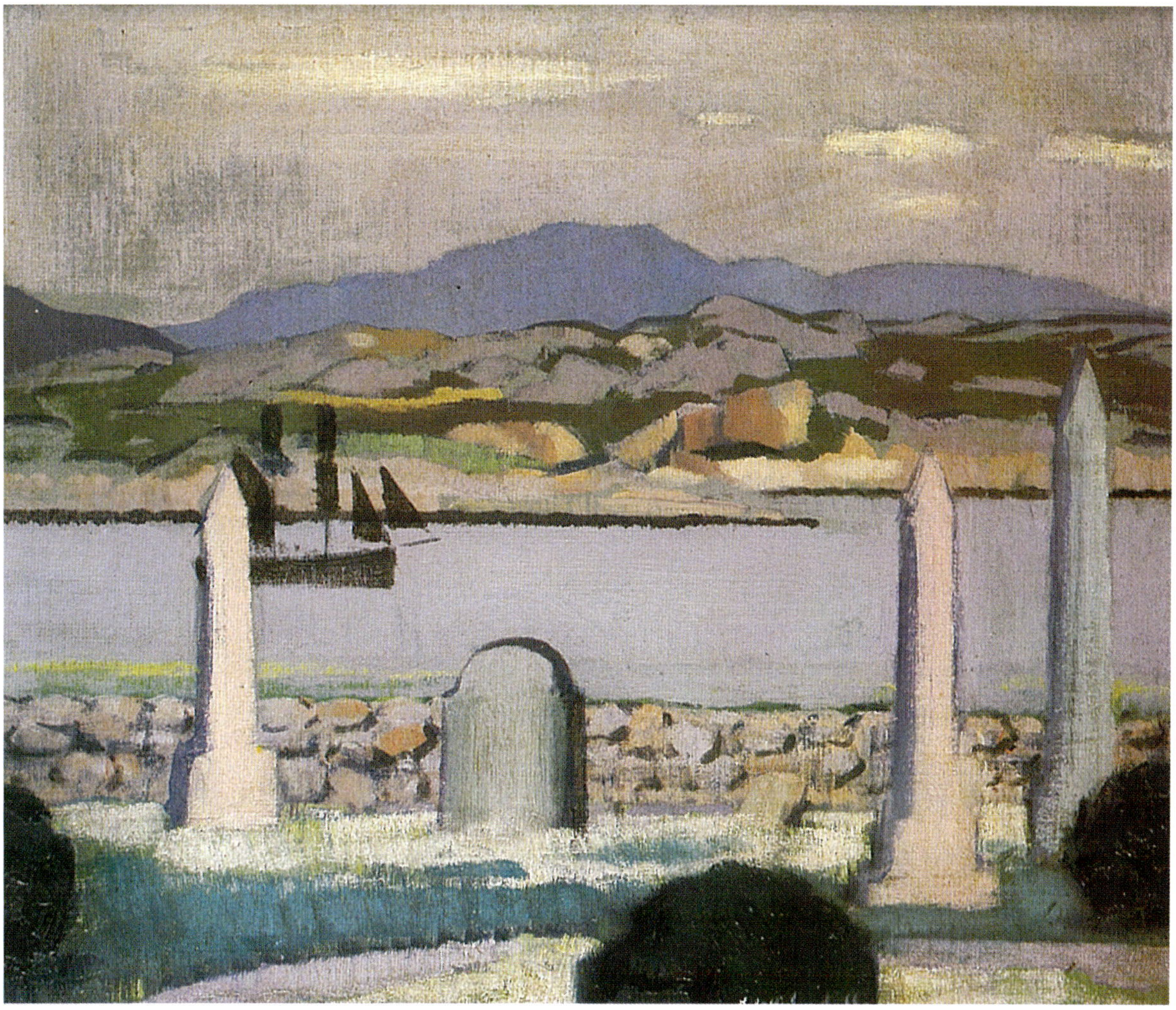

[PLATE 15]

F. C. B. Cadell

The St. Oran's Churchyard
(The Tiree coal gabbart)
Oil 15 x 18

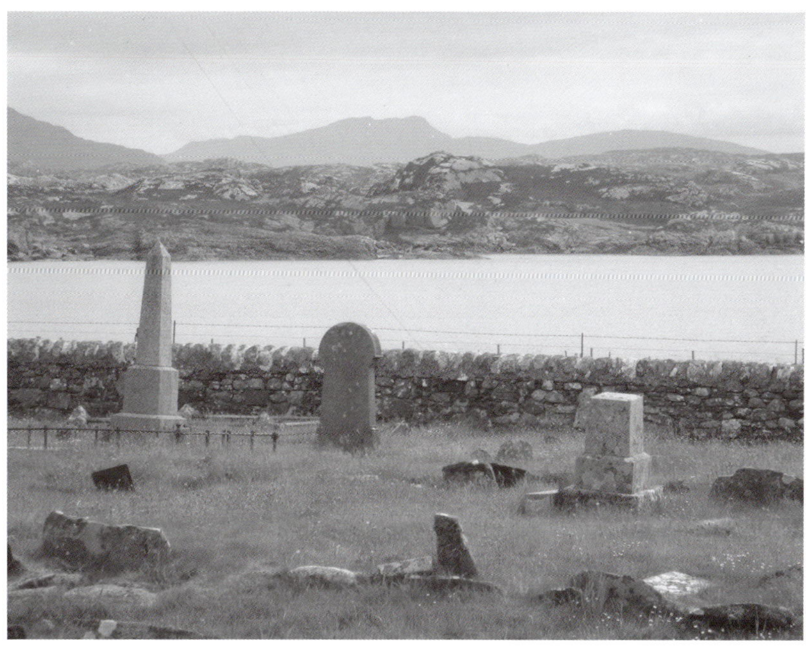

Photograph 2012

The shorter of the two obelisks on the right has fallen; the taller still stands in memory of the seamen and passengers who died on the American sailing ship Guy Mannering, which was wrecked on Iona in 1865. The actual position of this monument is some way further to the right out of the picture; perhaps Cadell included it to offset the duality caused by the symmetrical placing of the two smaller obelisks. The Ross of Mull is seen beyond the Sound, and Ben Buie is in the far distance.

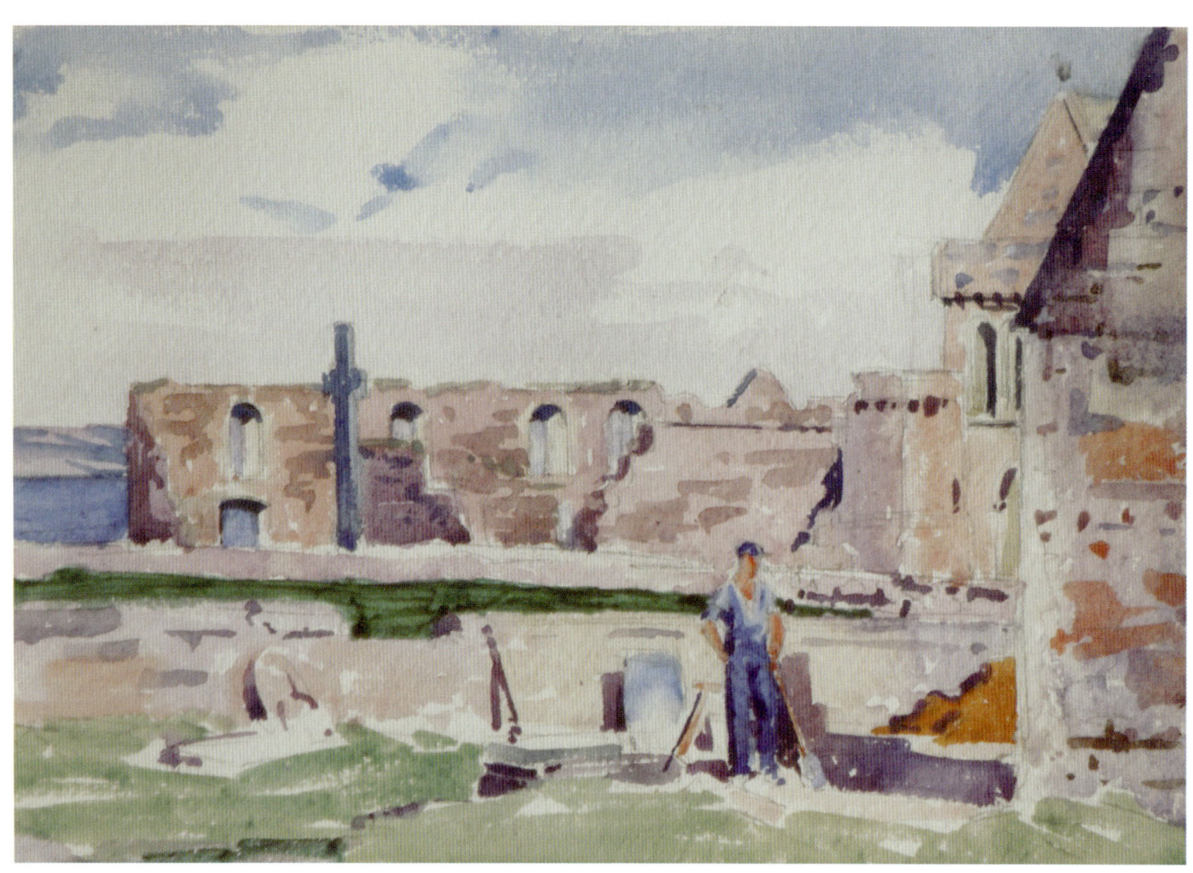

[PLATE 16]
F. C. B. Cadell
St. Oran's Churchyard
Watercolour 7 x 10

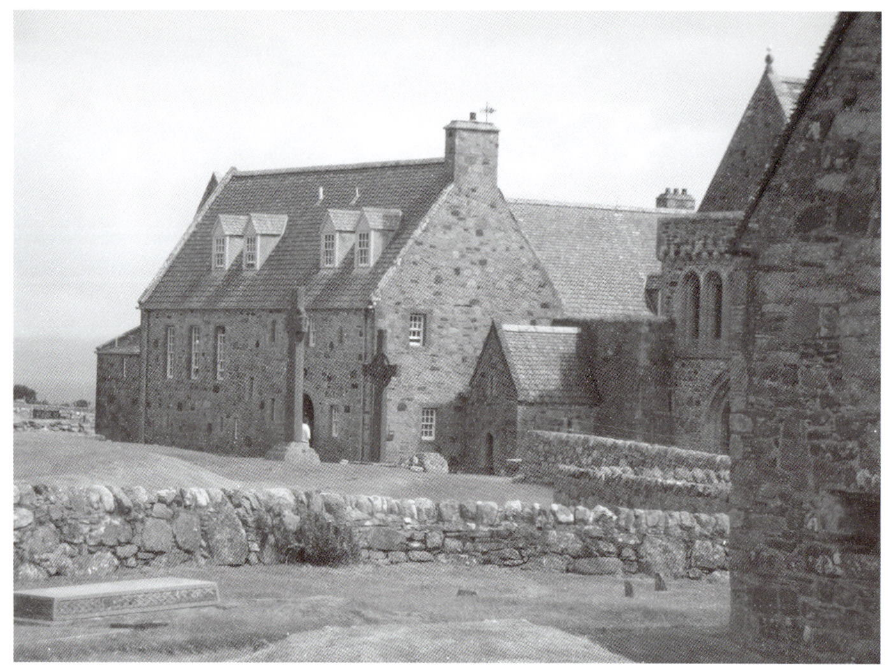

Photograph 2010

A gravedigger is working in the churchyard. The gable wall of St. Oran's Chapel, which had no roof at the time Cadell was there, is at the right-hand edge of the picture. Partly hidden by the Chapel is the west front of the Abbey, which was complete by this time, but the buildings on the north side of the Abbey were still in ruins.

[PLATE 17]

F. C. B. Cadell

Interior of the Abbey – The South Aisle

Oil 30 x 25

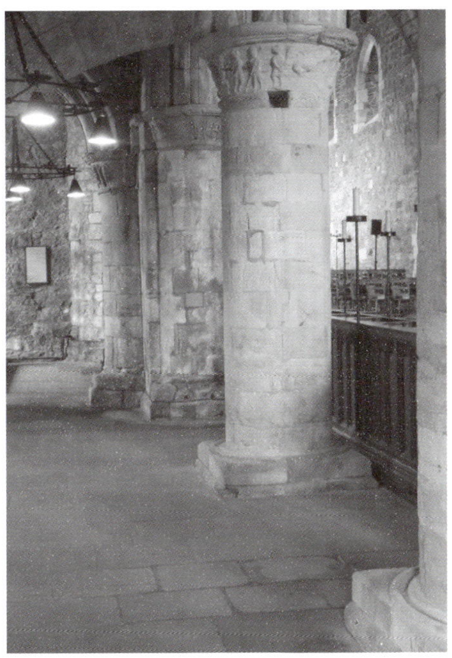

Photograph 2010

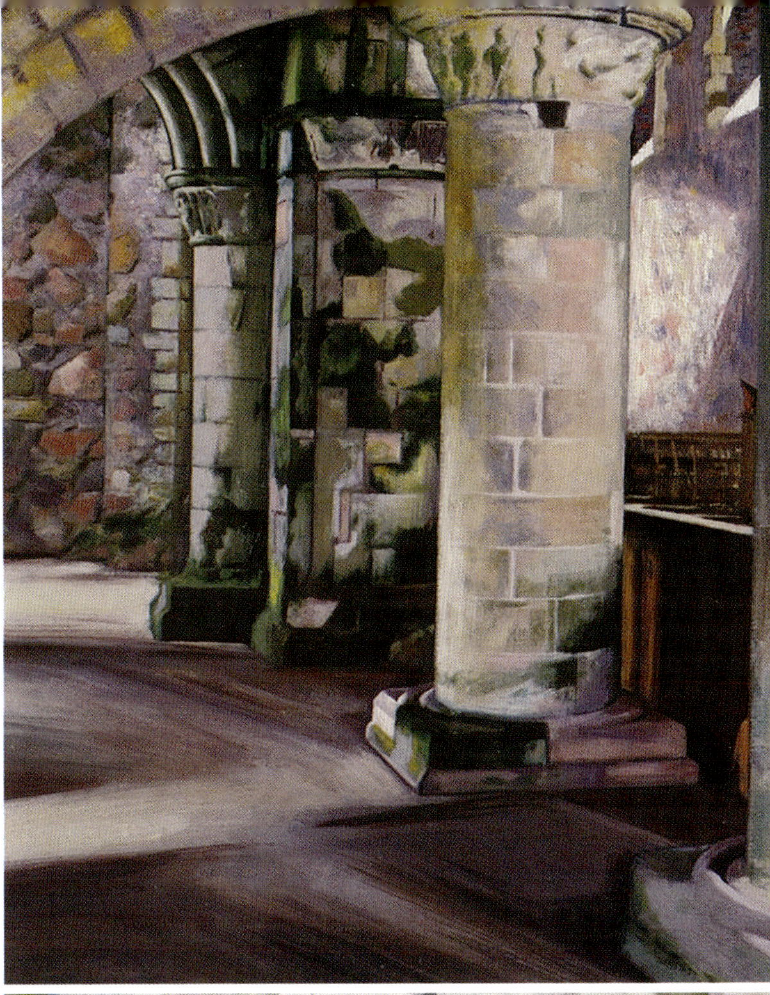

[PLATE 18]

F. C. B. Cadell

Interior of the Abbey – The Sacristy Door

Oil 28 x 20

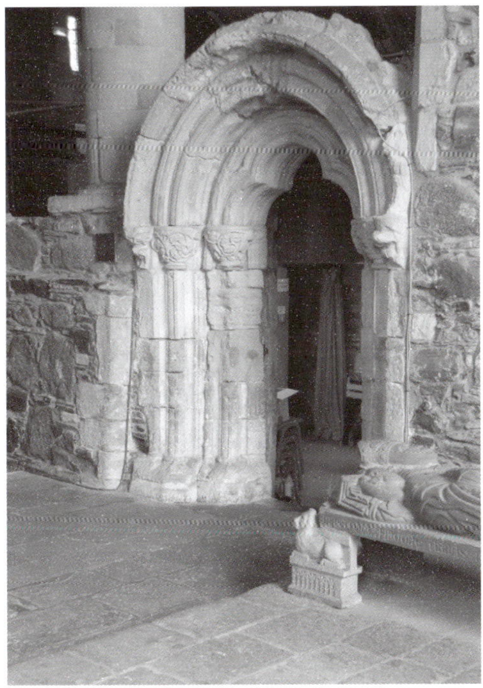

Photograph 2010

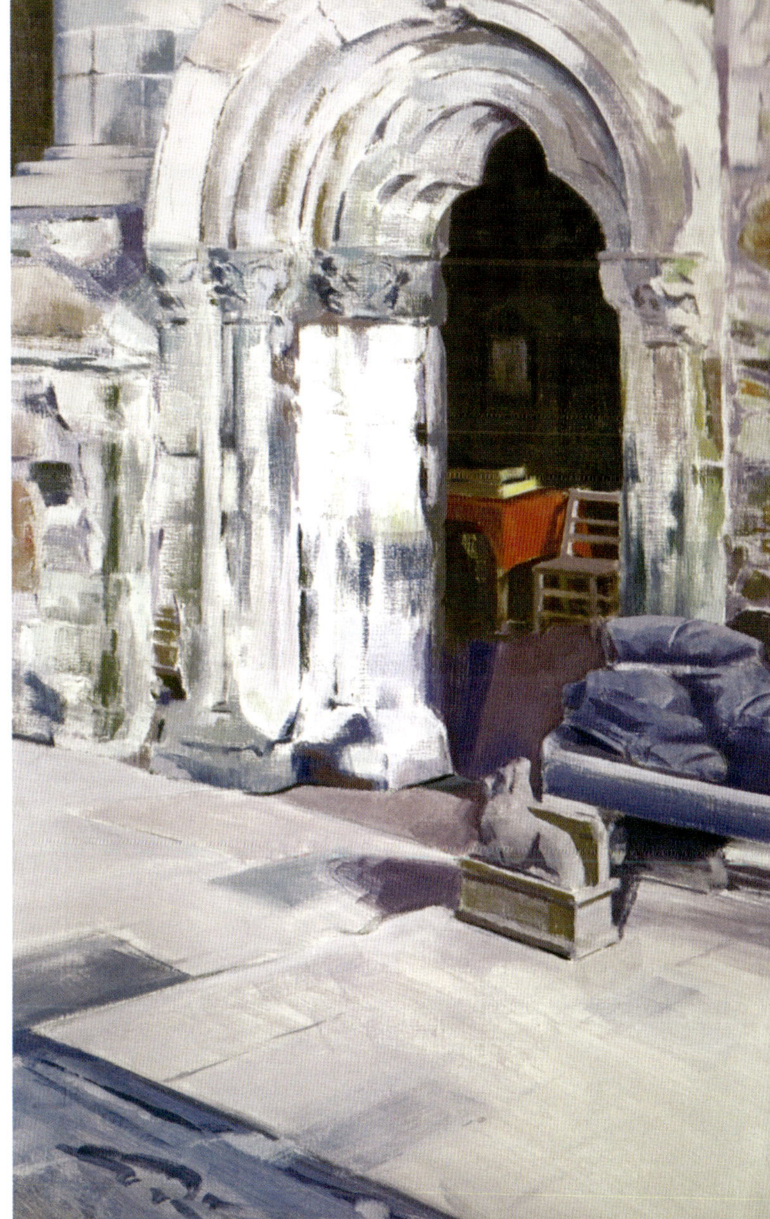

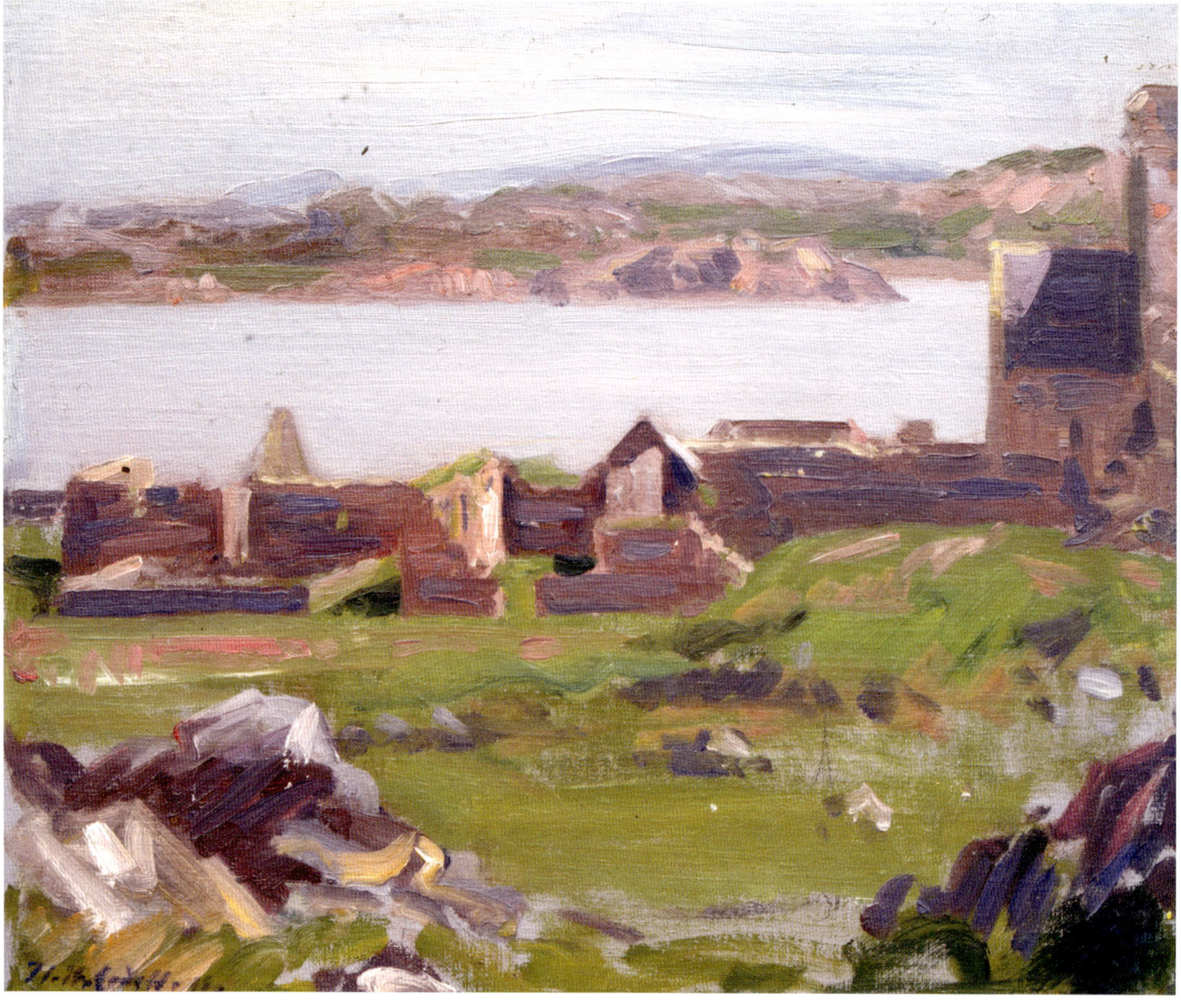

[PLATE 19]

F. C. B. Cadell

The Abbey

Oil 15 x 18

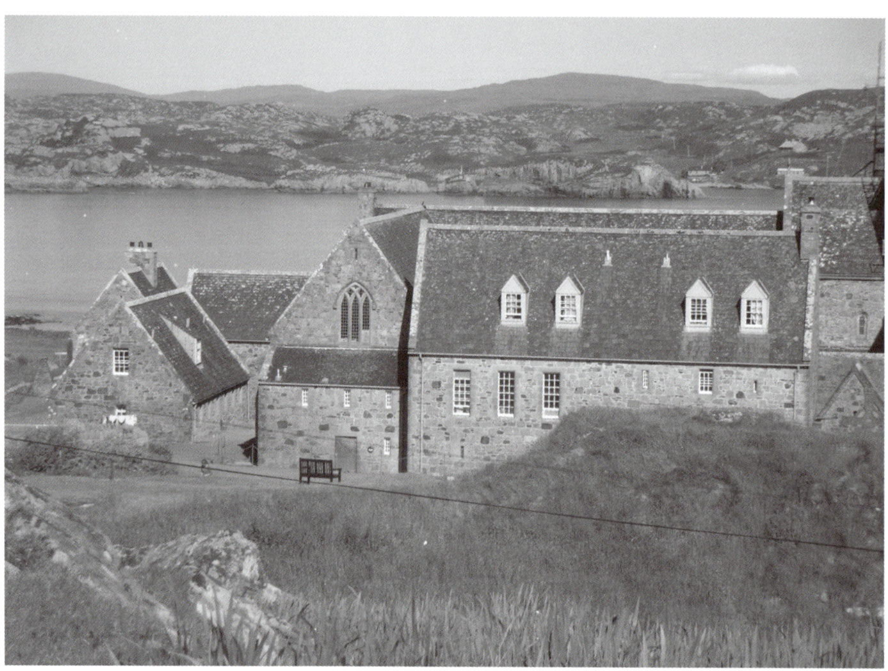

Photograph 2009

Painted from the rocky outcrop above the road, the picture shows the ruins on the north side of the Abbey prior to reconstruction. The north transept of the Abbey is on the right and the tower is at the extreme edge of the picture. The Sound of Iona and the Ross of Mull are in the background.

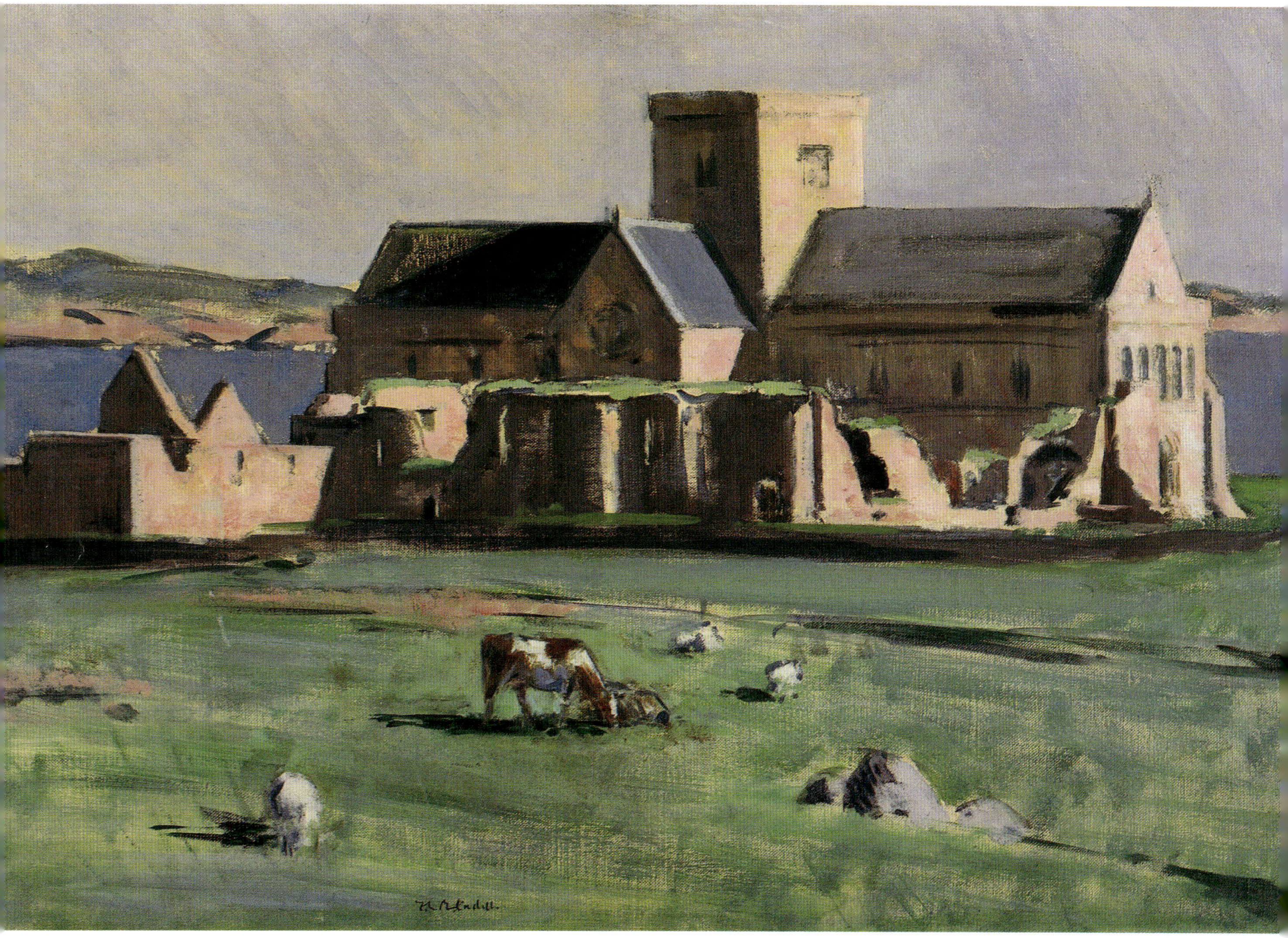

[PLATE 20]

F. C. B. Cadell

The Abbey from the northwest

Oil 20 x 30

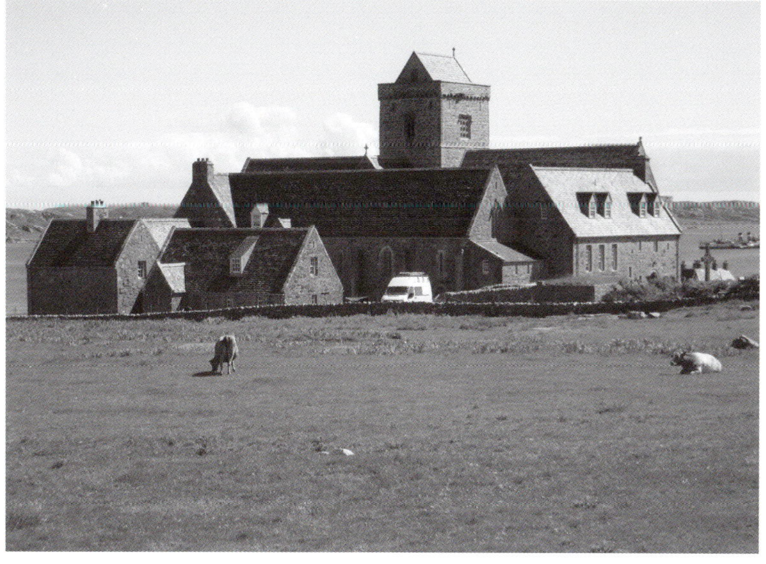

Photograph 2012

When Cadell painted this view of the Abbey, reconstruction of the ruined buildings around the Cloister had not been started, and the north elevation of the church could be seen almost in its entirety. Now, however, as may be seen in the photograph, only the tower and the top of the roof remain visible above the rebuilt West Range and Refectory.

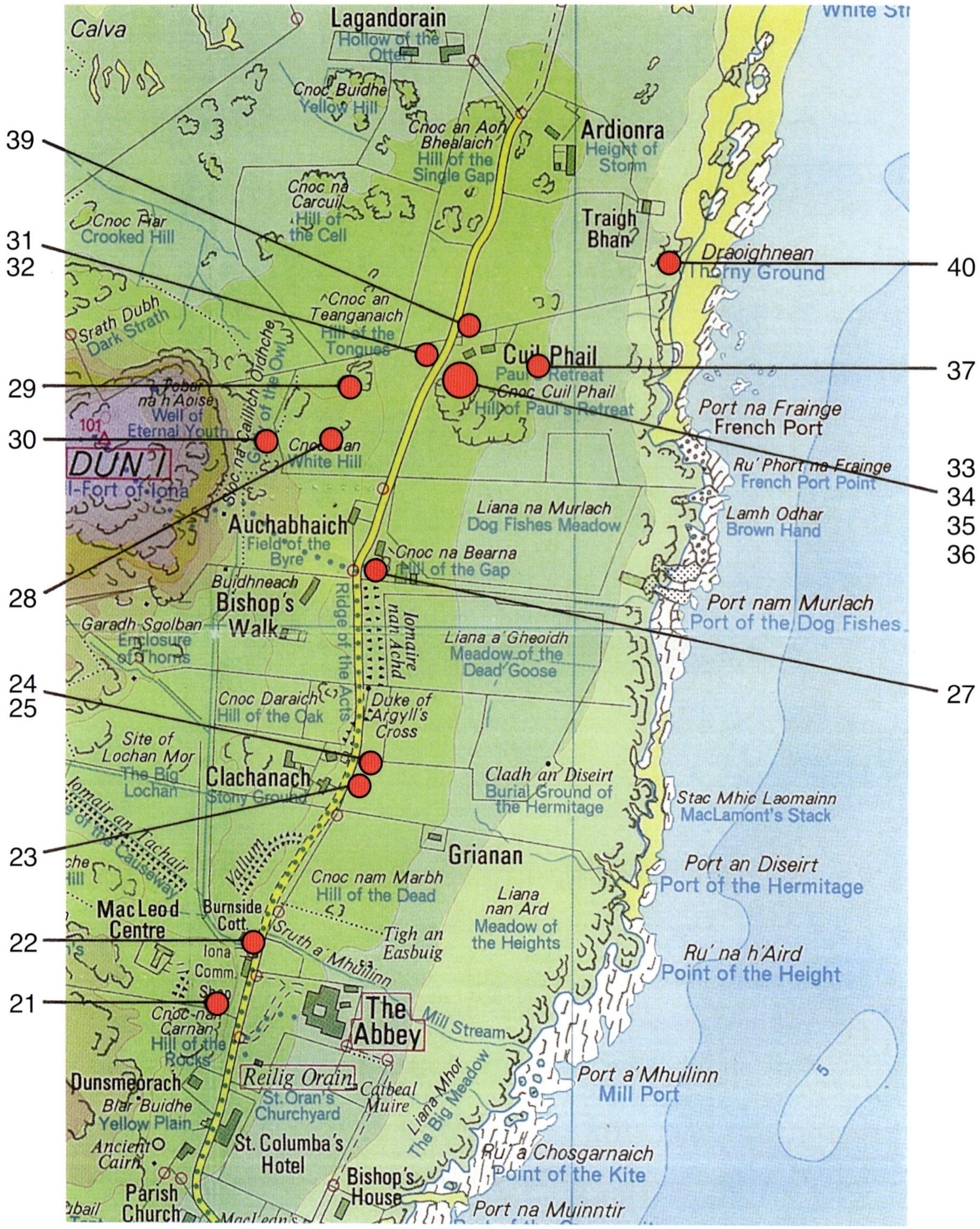

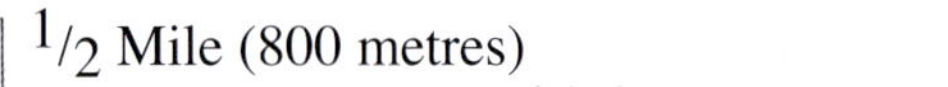

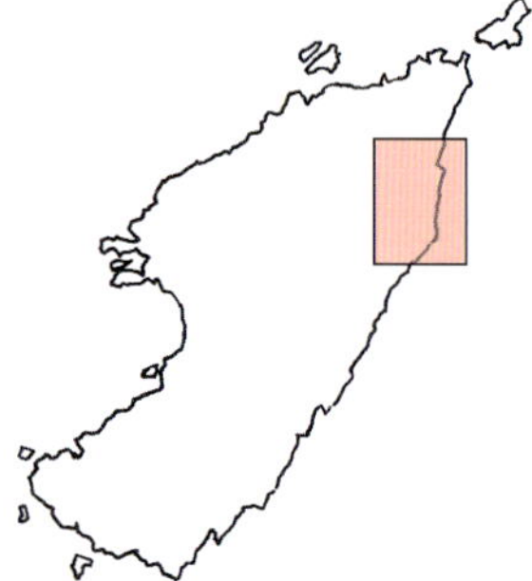

[FIGURE 7]
Locations of paintings illustrated in Chapter 2

2 · THE CROFTS NORTH OF THE VILLAGE

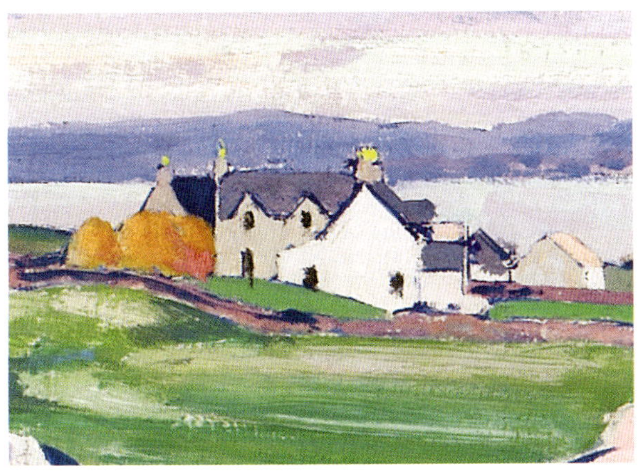
Clachanach

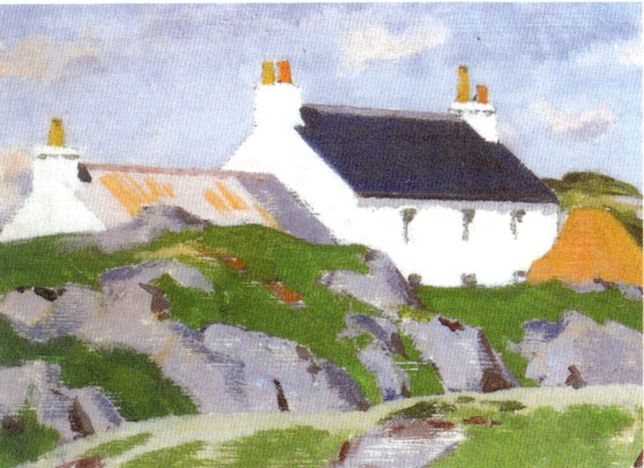
Auchabhaich

I AM unaware of any paintings of the crofts by Peploe, and therefore this chapter is devoted entirely to paintings by Cadell. The paintings illustrated show Clachanach, Auchabhaich, Cuil Phail (identified thus on the map, Figure 7, but often referred to as "Cnoc Cuil Phail") and Ardionra.

There are two other crofts north of the Village, both of which are only a few minutes' walk from Cuil Phail. Firstly, Lagandorain, which is also the most northerly croft, is at the end of the road on the left. This is a fine group of buildings beautifully sited, but over the period of my research I did not find any paintings of it by either artist.

The other is Bishop's Walk (originally known as Buidhneach, sometimes spelt Boineach, which means "The house at the foot of the hill"). This stands between Clachanach and Auchabhaich (Figure 8).

There are many paintings of Cuil Phail, which is hardly surprising, since this is where Cadell stayed during most of his visits to Iona. When he was there the tenant moved out and lived in the blue lean-to shed which appears in the paintings attached to the east gable. This way of letting houses to visitors was not uncommon and provided supplementary income.

Many of Cadell's paintings of the crofts show the bright red-painted iron roofs (or maybe just rusting) which were common at the time. Sadly, from a painter's point of view, these have now disappeared. Such regrets however are not new; there is a comment in the *Glasgow Evening Citizen* in 1887 which reads, "No doubt the artist grumbles. He laments the introduction of new villas, which are not to his taste, and the disappearance of the old thatched cottages. But the artist cannot always have what he wants."

Cuil Phail

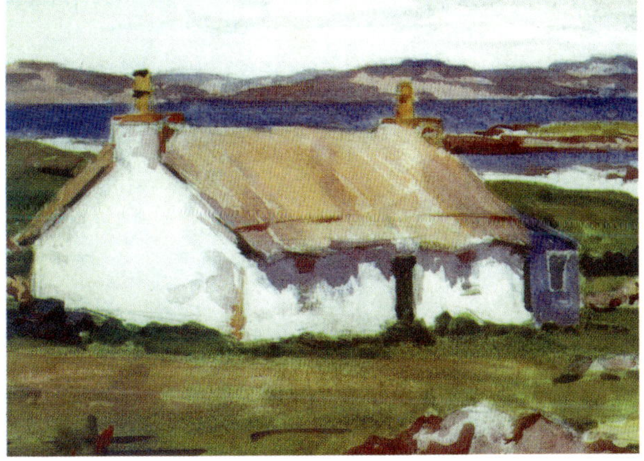

Ardionra

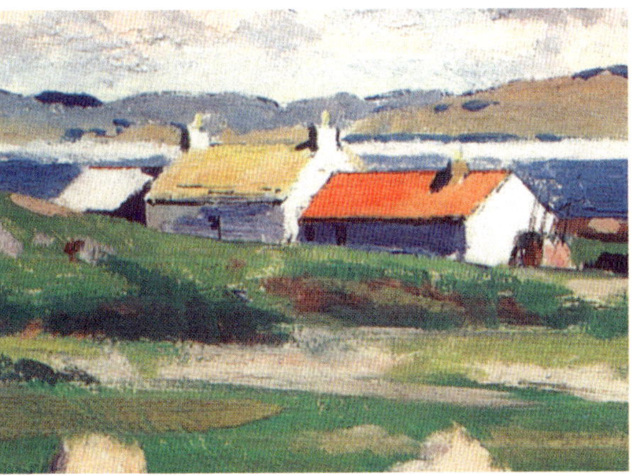

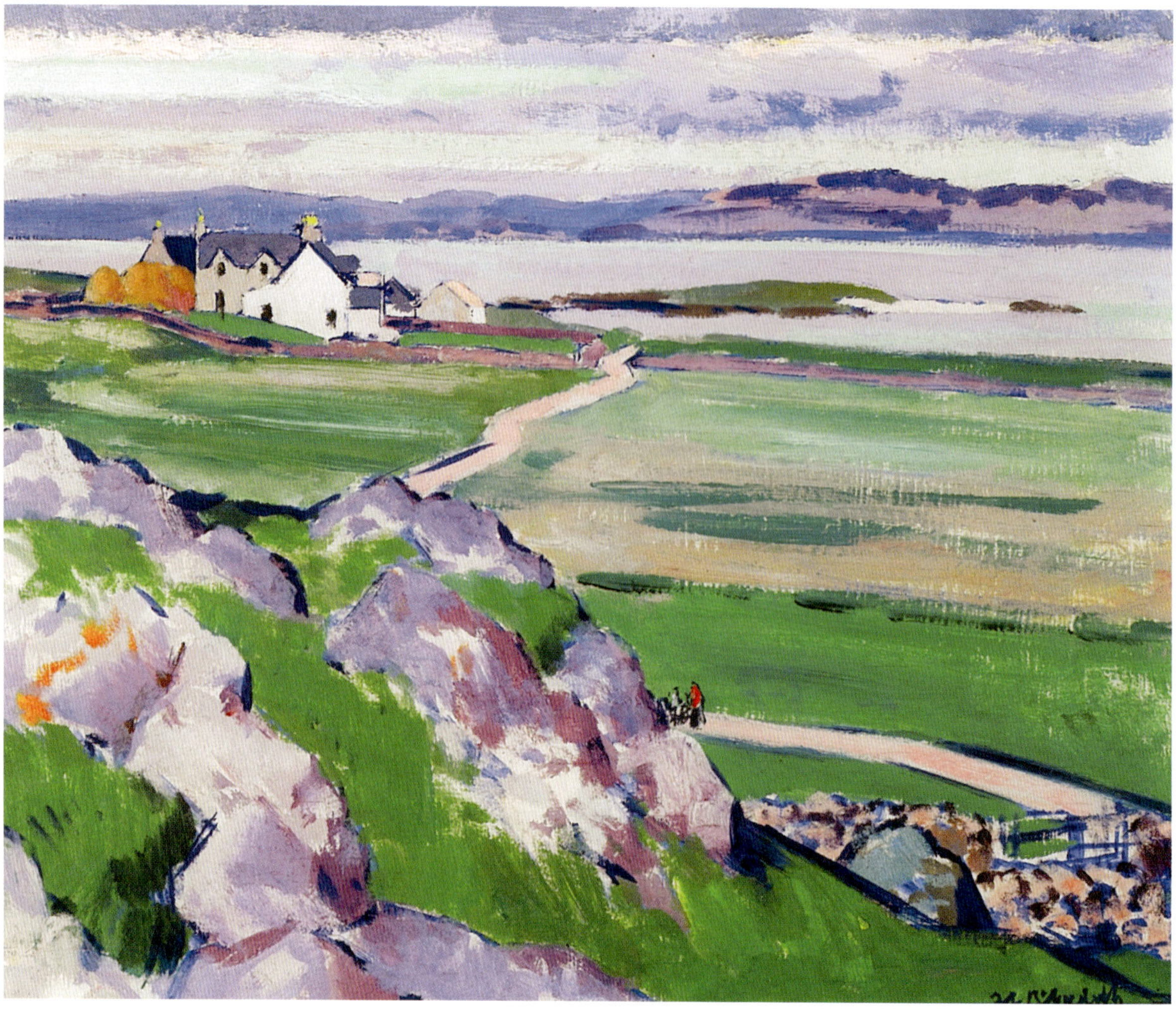

[PLATE 21]

F. C. B. Cadell

Clachanach Croft

Oil 15 x 18

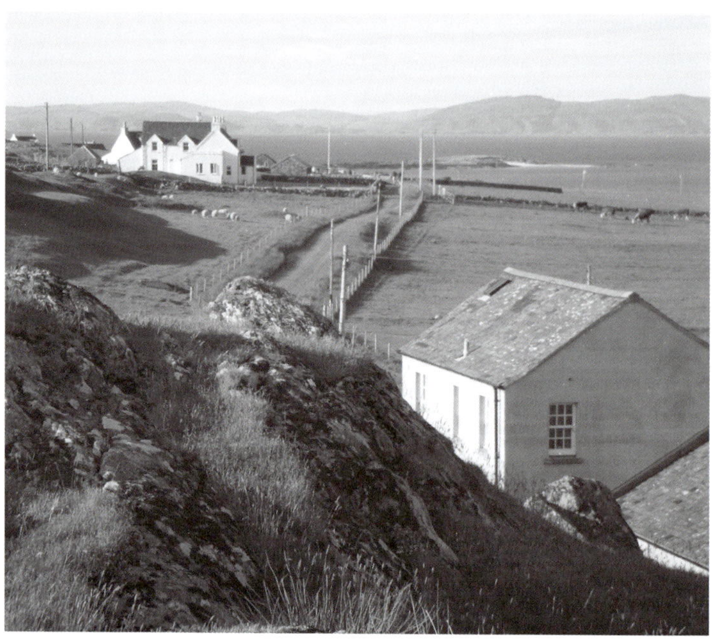

Photograph 2010

Clachanach is the first croft north of the village. Here Cadell has painted it from the same rocky outcrop as Plate 19, and from this elevated position we see beyond the house to Eilean Annraidh, the small island off the northeast corner of Iona, and further, on the horizon, to the island of Ulva, which is on the right, and the hills of northwest Mull on the left.

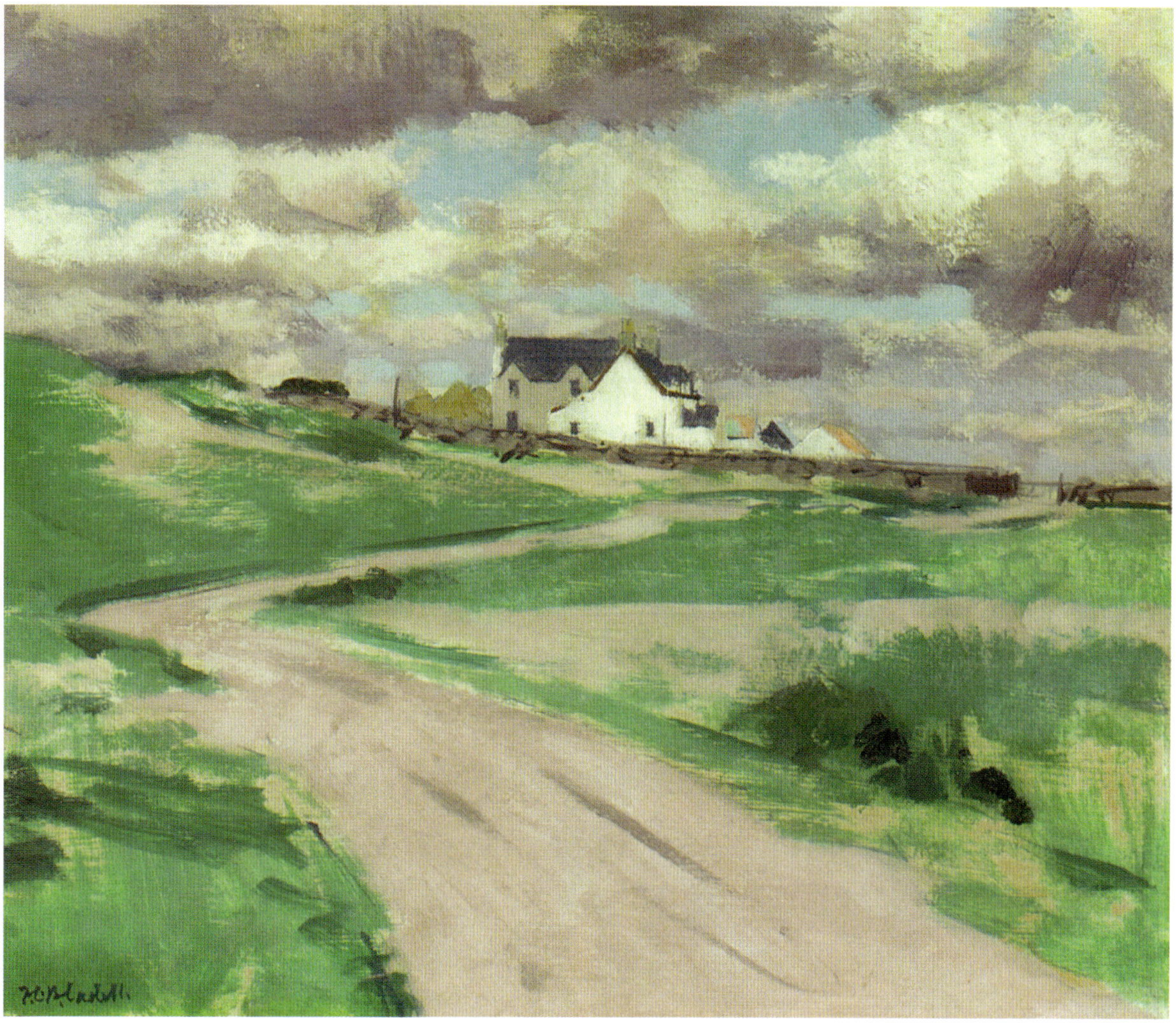

[PLATE 22]
F. C. B. Cadell
Clachanach Croft
Oil 15 x 18

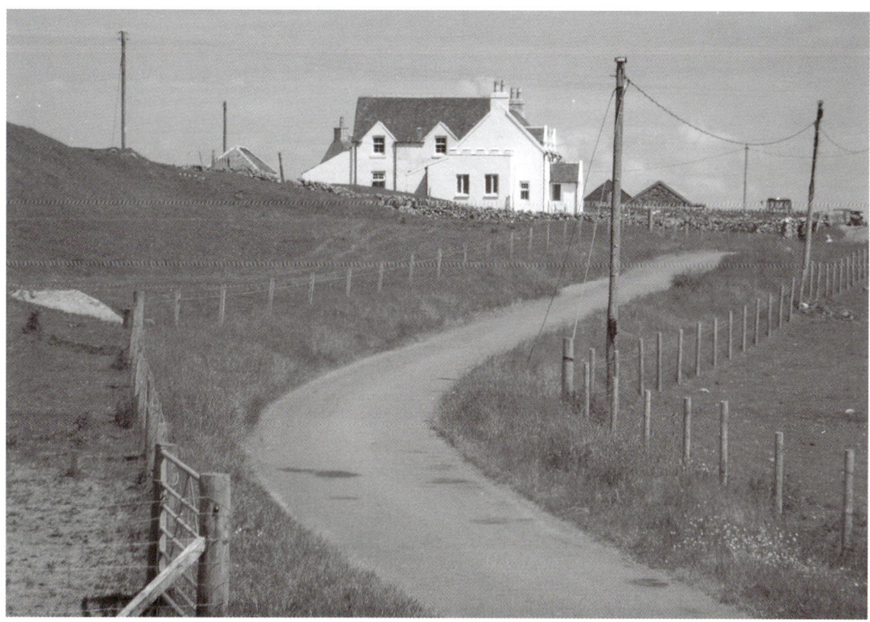

Photograph 2009

Clachanach is a finely proportioned two-storey house with three dormer windows on the road elevation, which remains very much as Cadell painted it. The outbuildings which appear to the right of the house in this picture are the subject of Plates 23 and 24.

[PLATE 23]

F. C. B. Cadell

The Steading, Clachanach

Oil 15 x 18

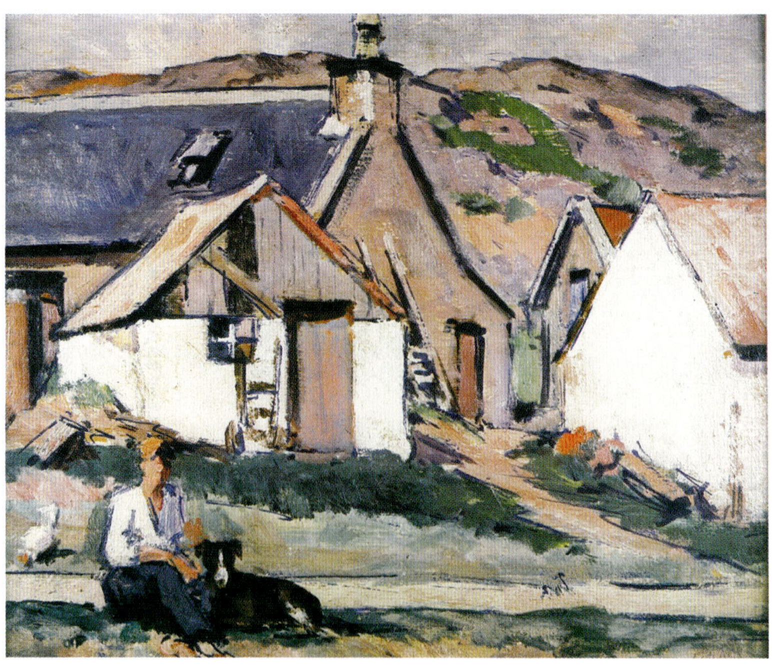

The outbuilding in the left foreground has been demolished; however the outlines of the other buildings remain clearly recognisable.

The same group of buildings appears in Plate 24 painted from a slightly different angle.

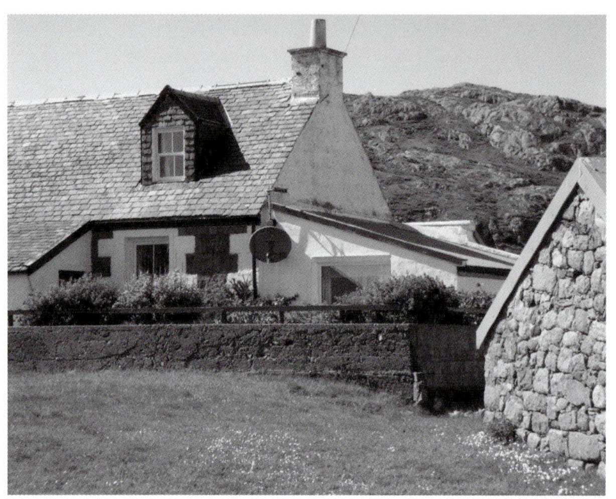

Photograph 2009

[PLATE 24]

F. C. B. Cadell

The Steading, Clachanach

Oil 15 x 18

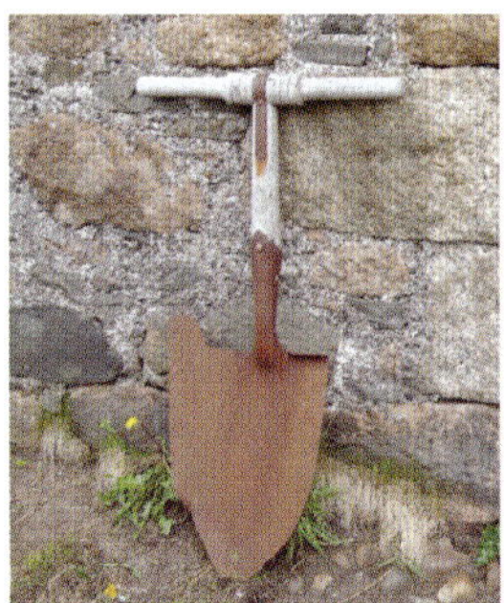

A similar if not the same spade, used for ditching, is still leaning against the wall!

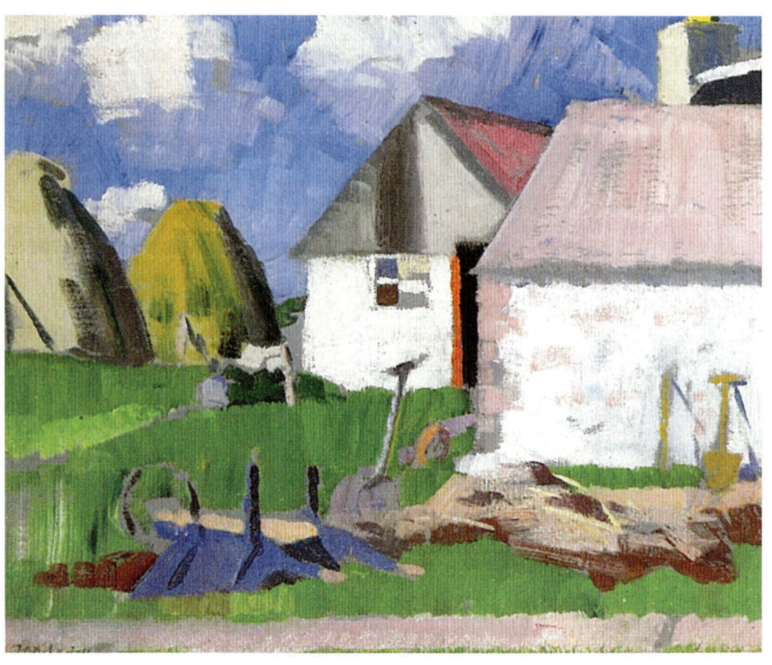

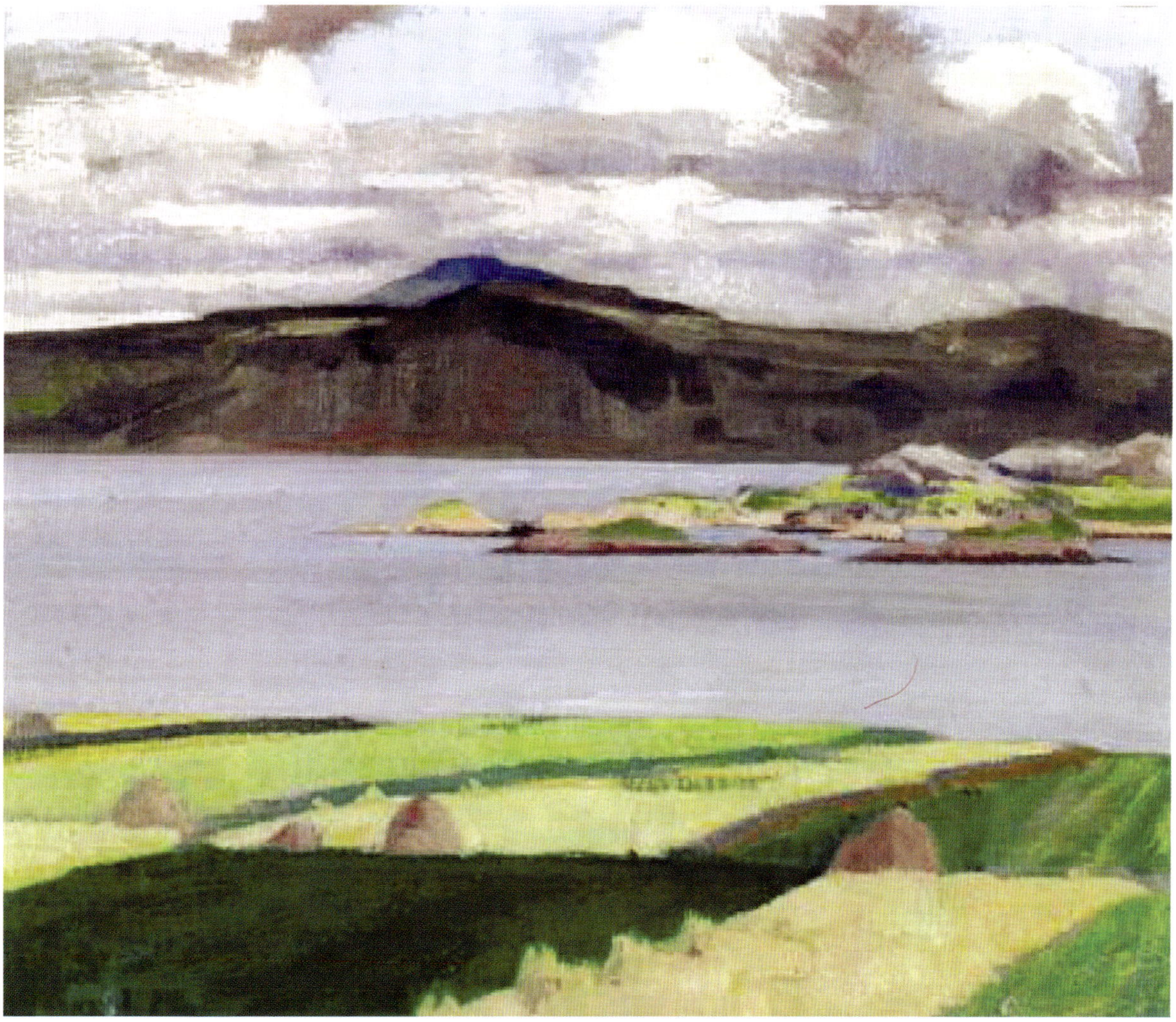

[PLATE 25]
F. C. B. Cadell
Ben More from Clachanach
Oil 15 x 18

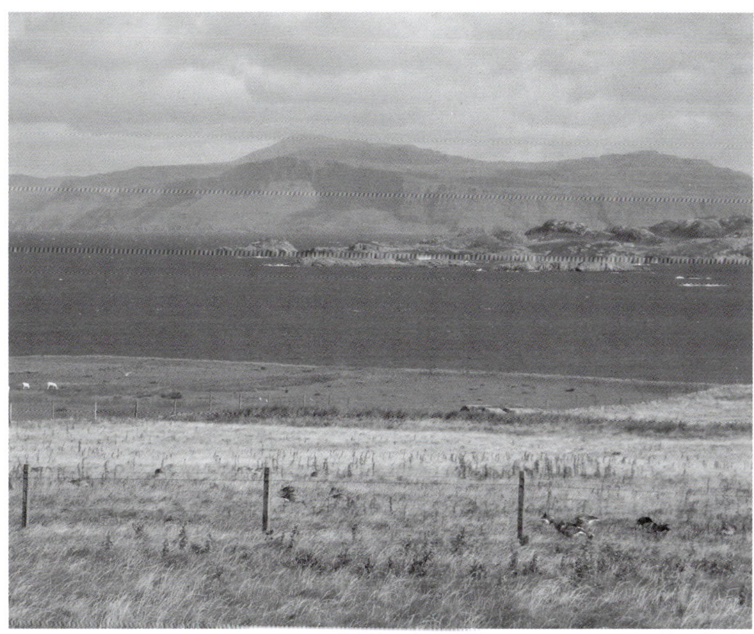

Photograph 2010

The fields in the foreground slope down to the Sound of Iona. The northern end of the Ross of Mull is on the right and Ben More and the Burg are in the distance.

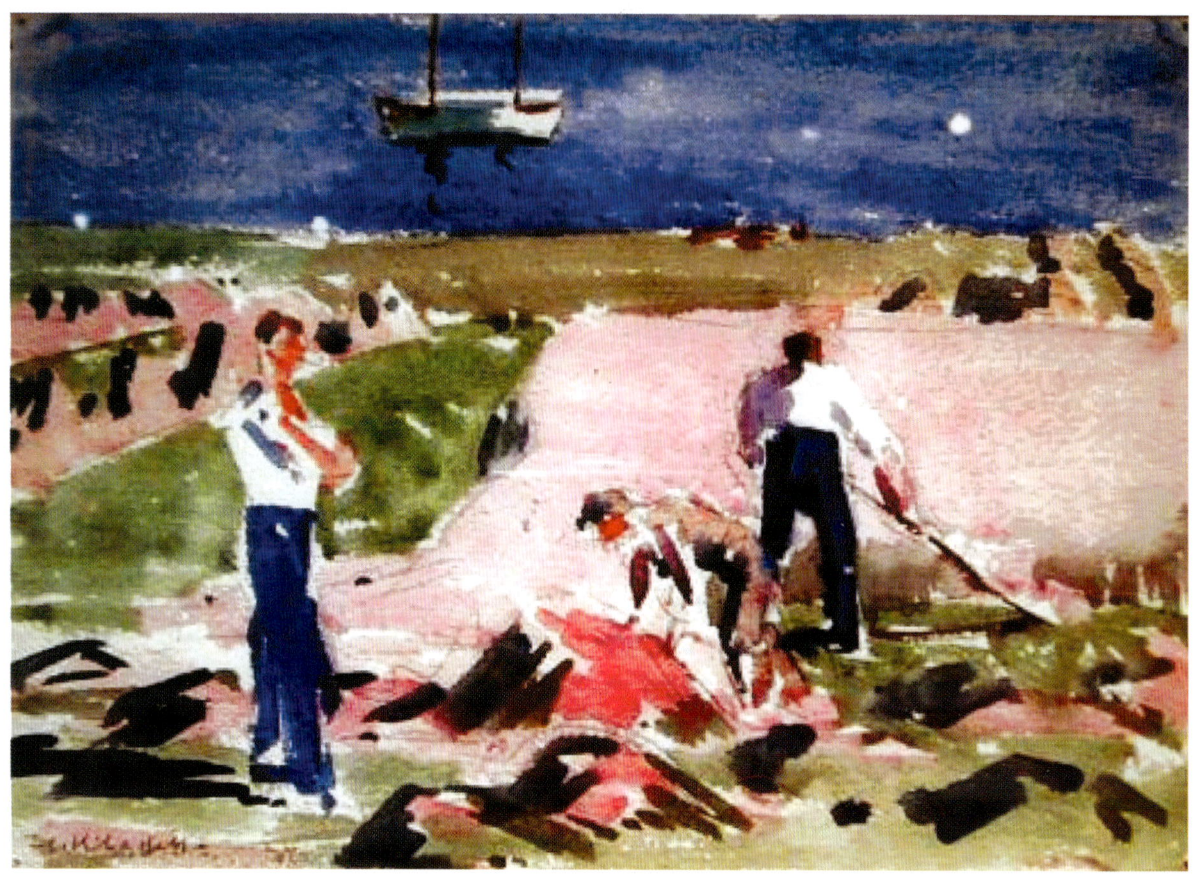

[PLATE 26] **F. C. B. Cadell** *Harvest Time* Watercolour 7 x 10

The farm workers are in the fields which appear in the foreground of the previous painting.

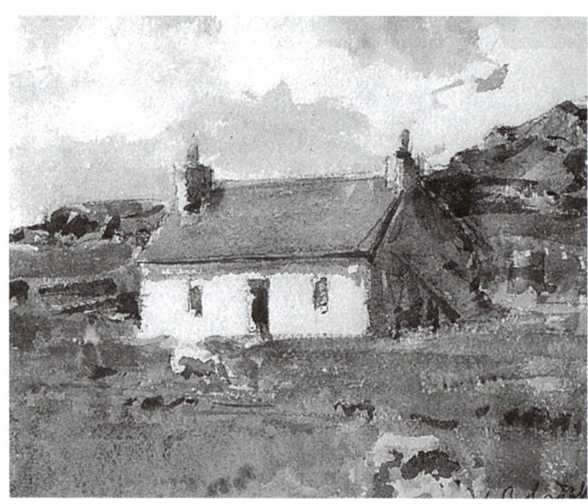

[FIGURE 8]

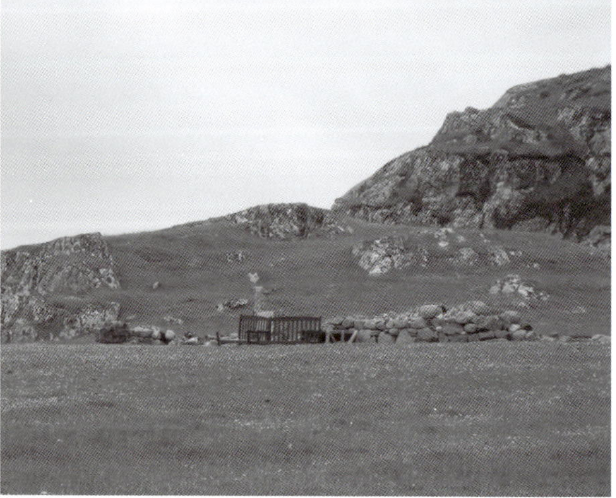

Photograph 2013

The next croft north of Clachanach is Bishop's Walk, situated below Dun I. There is a watercolour by Cadell of a croft in which the profile of the hill in the background corresponds to the southern slopes of Dun I, and so Bishop's Walk is a likely identification (Figure 8). This possibility is further reinforced by the existence of the remains, and outline on the ground, of a building the correct size and position to have been the cottage in the painting. Demolished in the 1980s, it had served as a byre in living memory, but was possibly the original dwelling on the croft, abandoned when the present two-storey house was built.

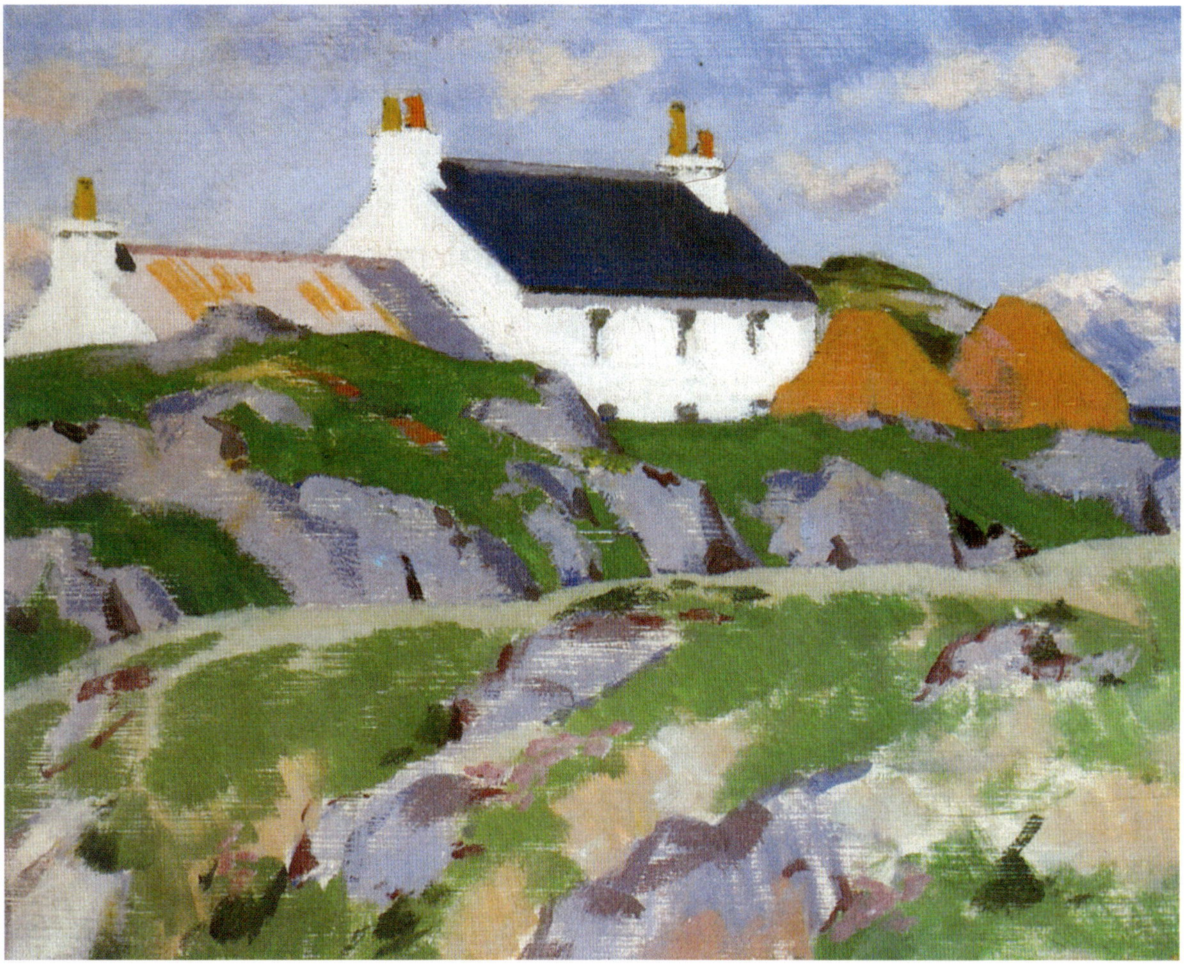

[PLATE 27]
F. C. B. Cadell
Auchabhaich Croft
Oil 15 x 18

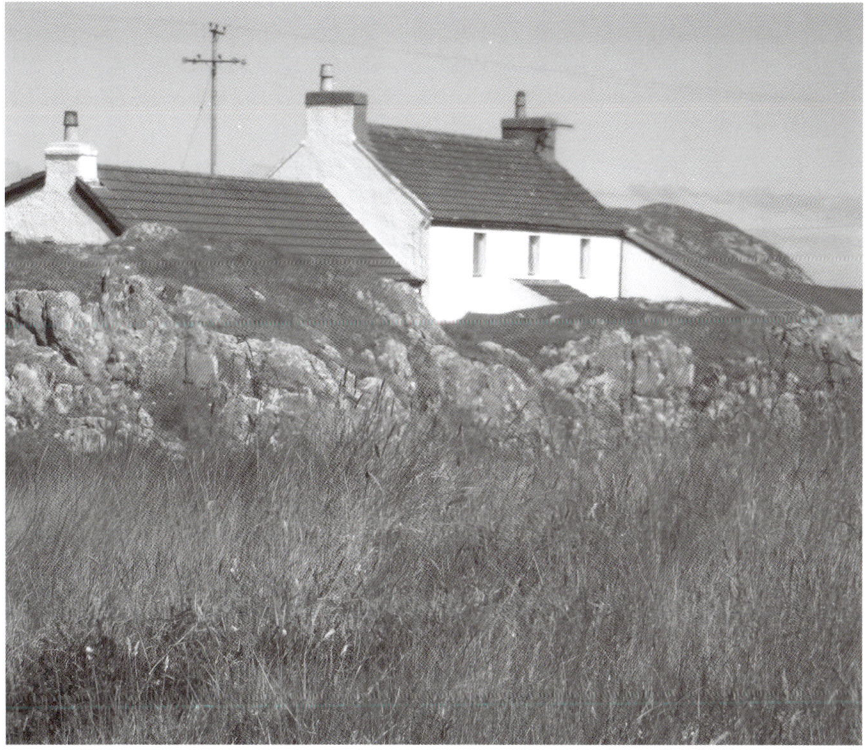

Photograph 2009

Beyond Bishop's Walk there is a bend in the road between two outcrops of rock. The croft Auchabhaich is on the left. The house has been extended on the north side. However this view of it from the outcrop on the right-hand side of the road remains very much as Cadell painted it.

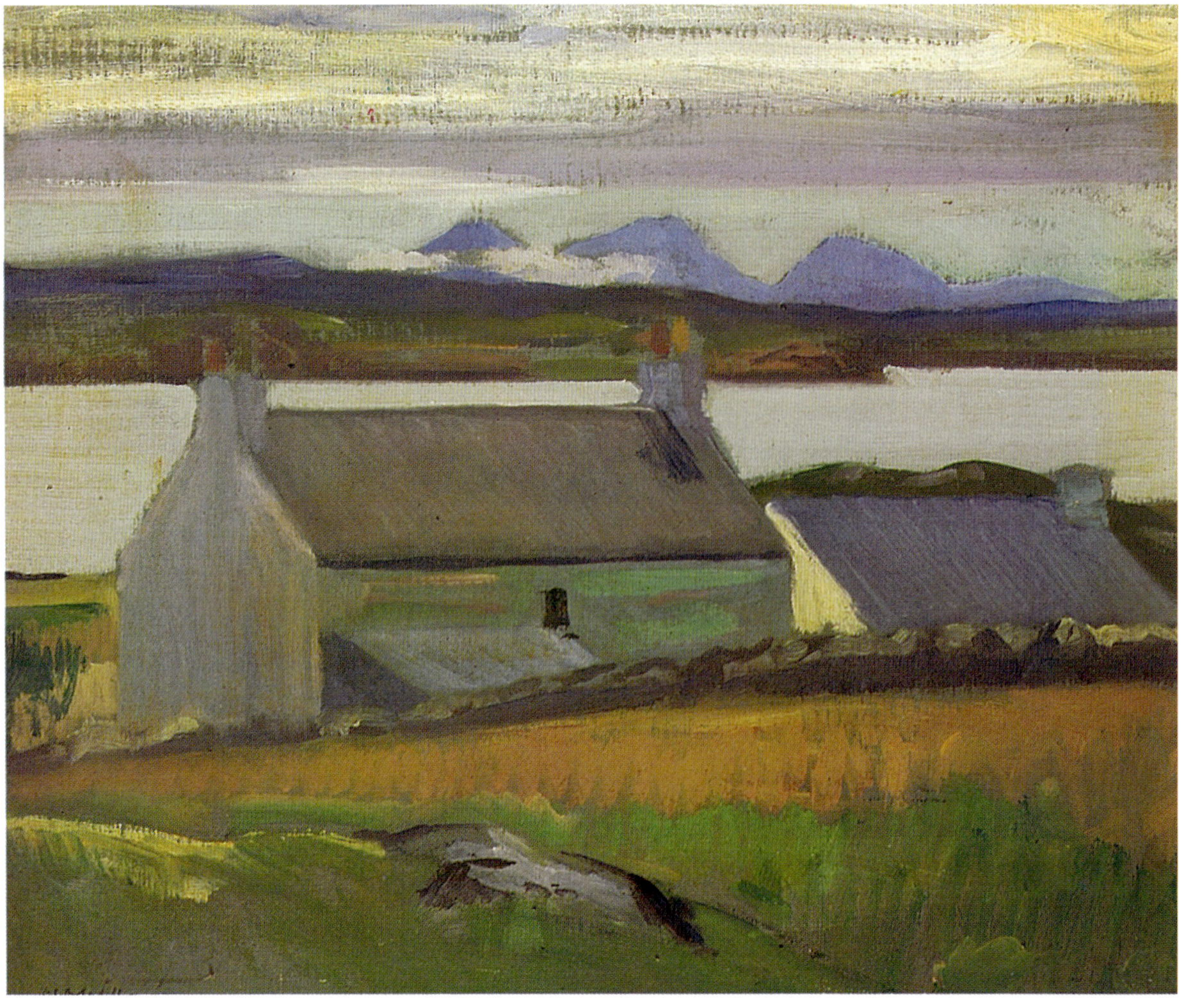

[PLATE 28]
F. C. B. Cadell
Auchabhaich Croft
Oil 15 x 18

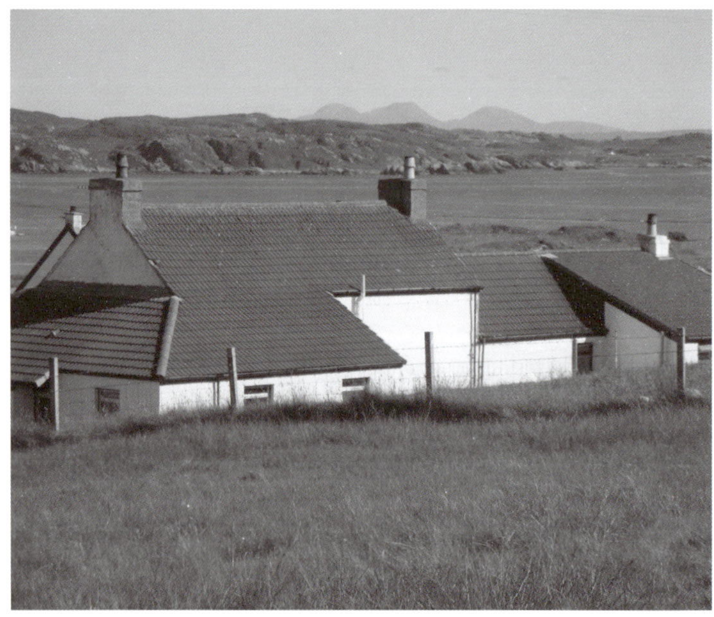

Photograph 2009

This view of the house was painted from the field to the north, and includes the Ross of Mull and the Paps of Jura in the distance.

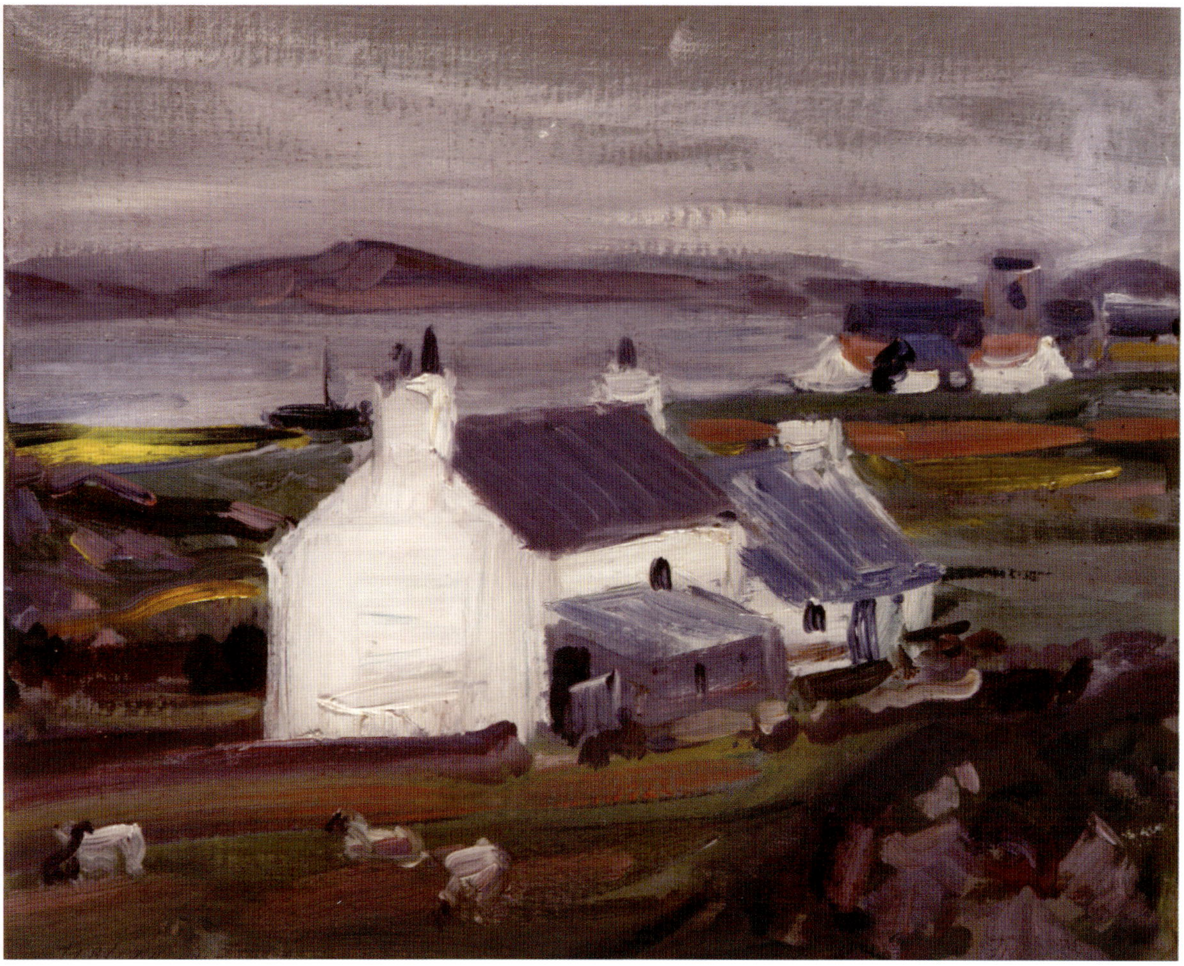

[PLATE 29]
F. C. B. Cadell
Auchabhaich Croft
Oil 15 x 18

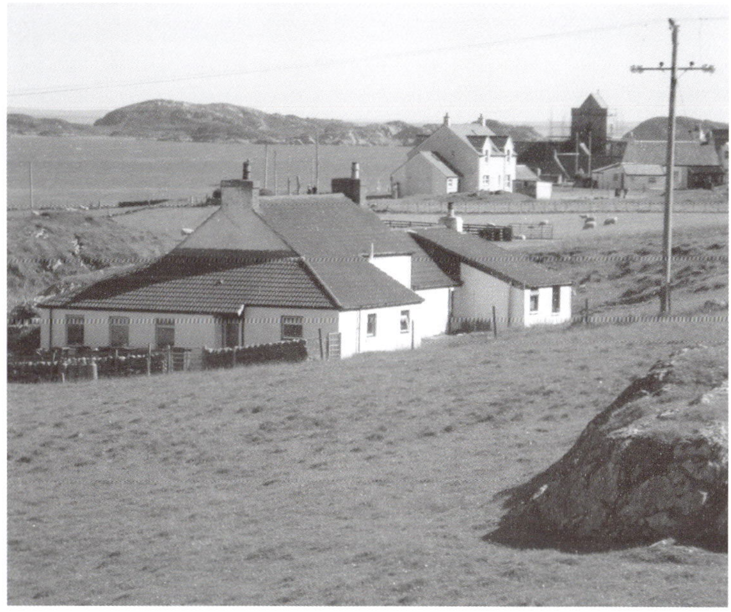

Photograph 2009

This is similar to Plate 28, but here looking south to the Abbey.

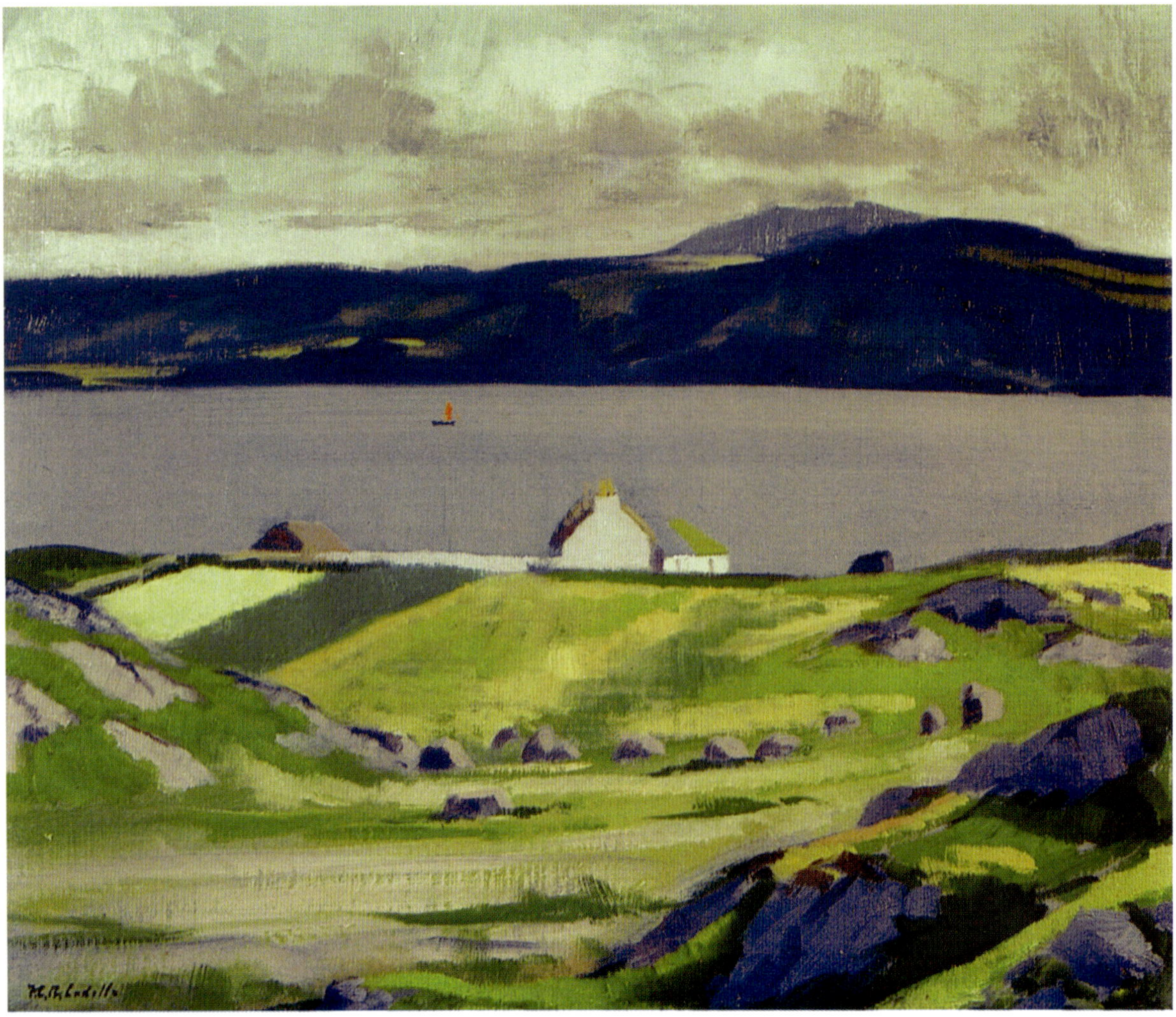

[PLATE 30]

F. C. B. Cadell

Ben More from the slopes of Dun I

Oil 15 x 18

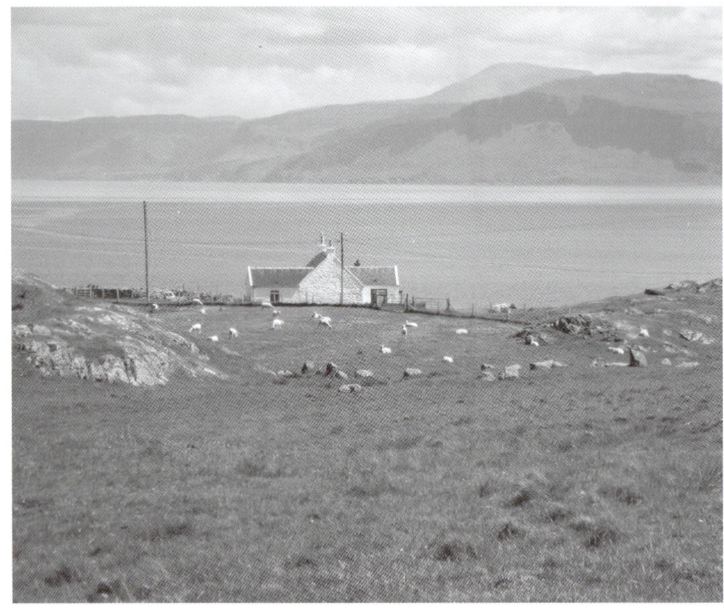

Photograph 2009

Dun I is the highest point on Iona. This picture was painted from the lower slopes looking down to the Cuil Phail croft and the Sound of Iona, with Ben More and the spectacular cliffs of the Burg in the distance.

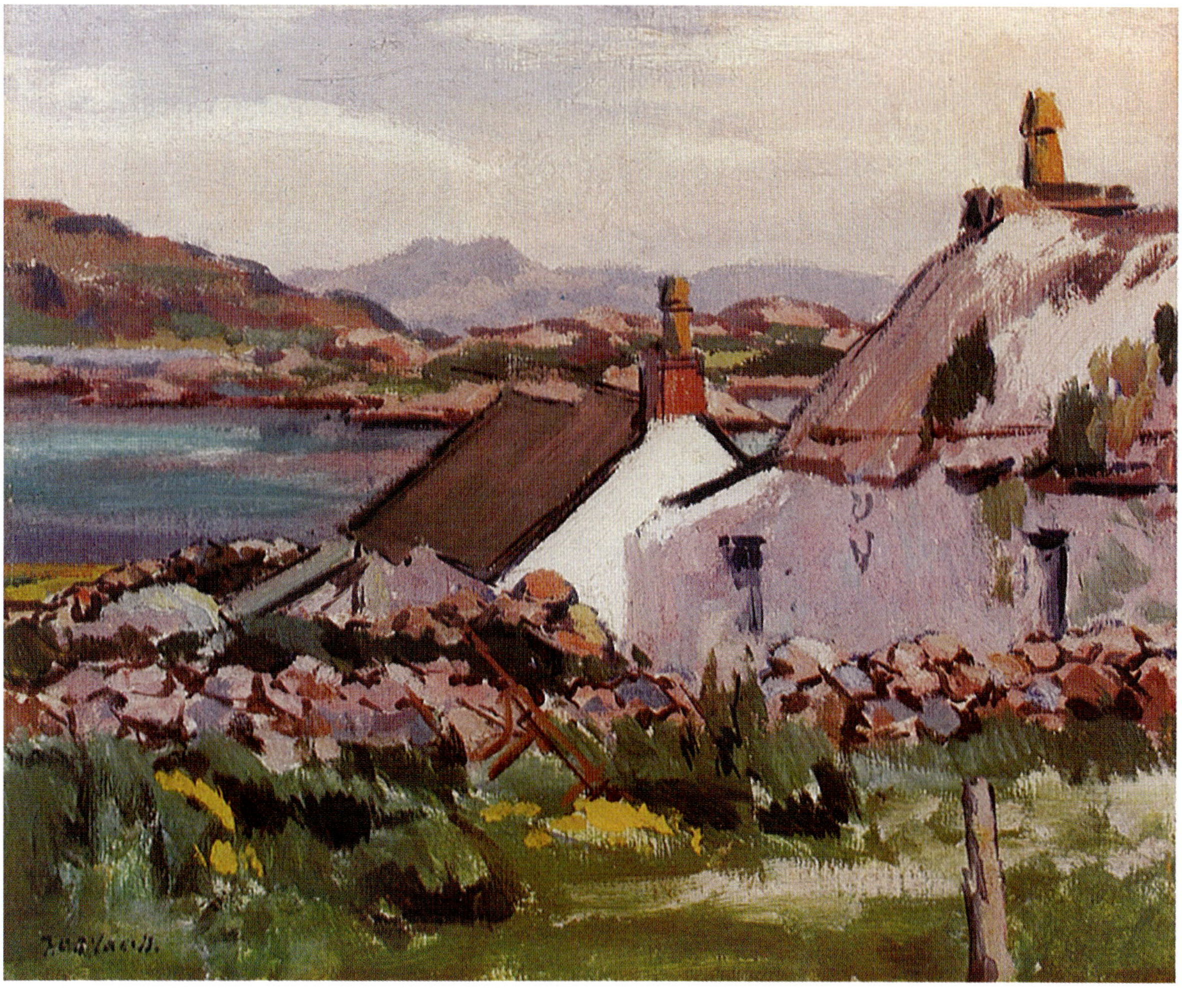

[PLATE 31]
F. C. B. Cadell
Ben Buie from Cuil Phail Croft
Oil 15 x 18

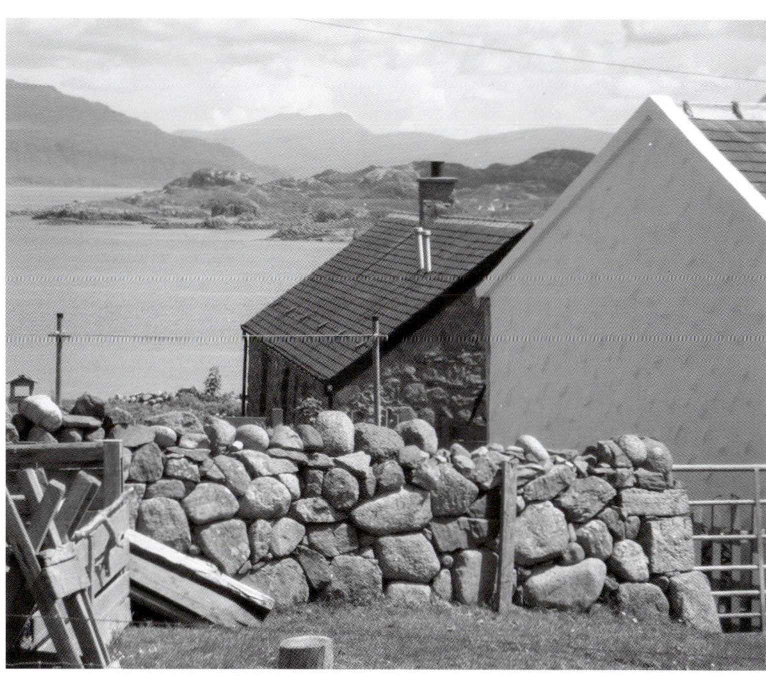

Photograph 2009

Painted from beside the road, this shows the two dwellings on the Cuil Phail croft. The northern end of the Ross of Mull is in the middle distance with Ben Buie beyond.

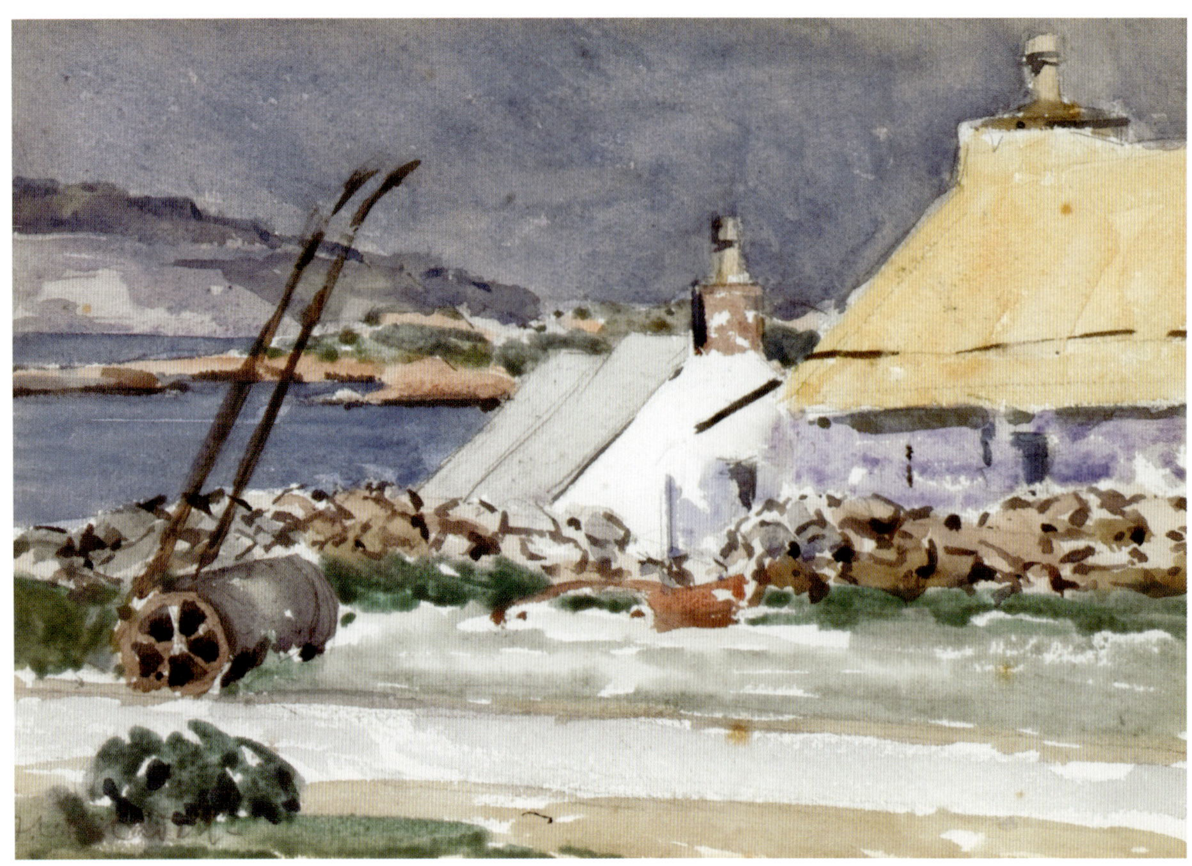

[PLATE 32]
F. C. B. Cadell
Cuil Phail Croft
Watercolour 7 x 10

The composition of this watercolour is similar to the preceding oil painting (Plate 31).

This is also the location of the photograph of Cadell with the croft behind him (Figure 9).

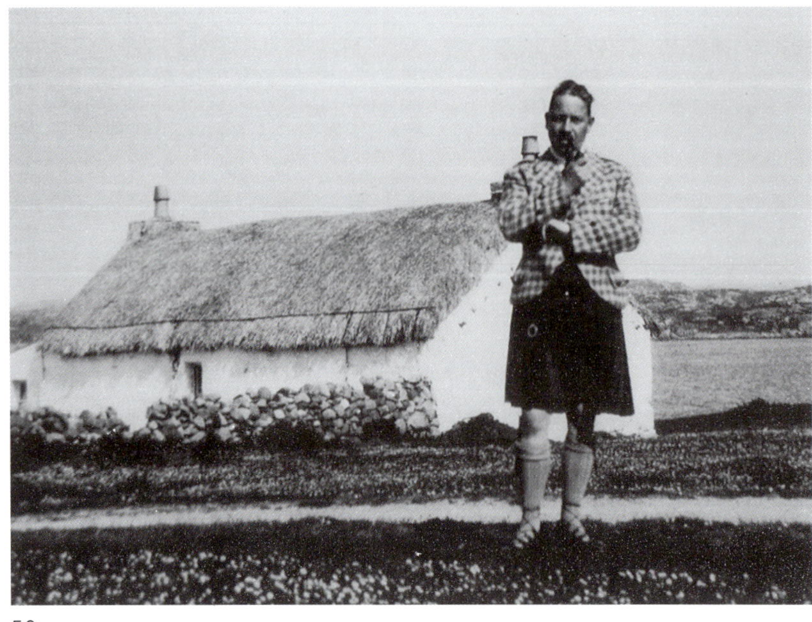

[FIGURE 9]
Cadell at Cuil Phail

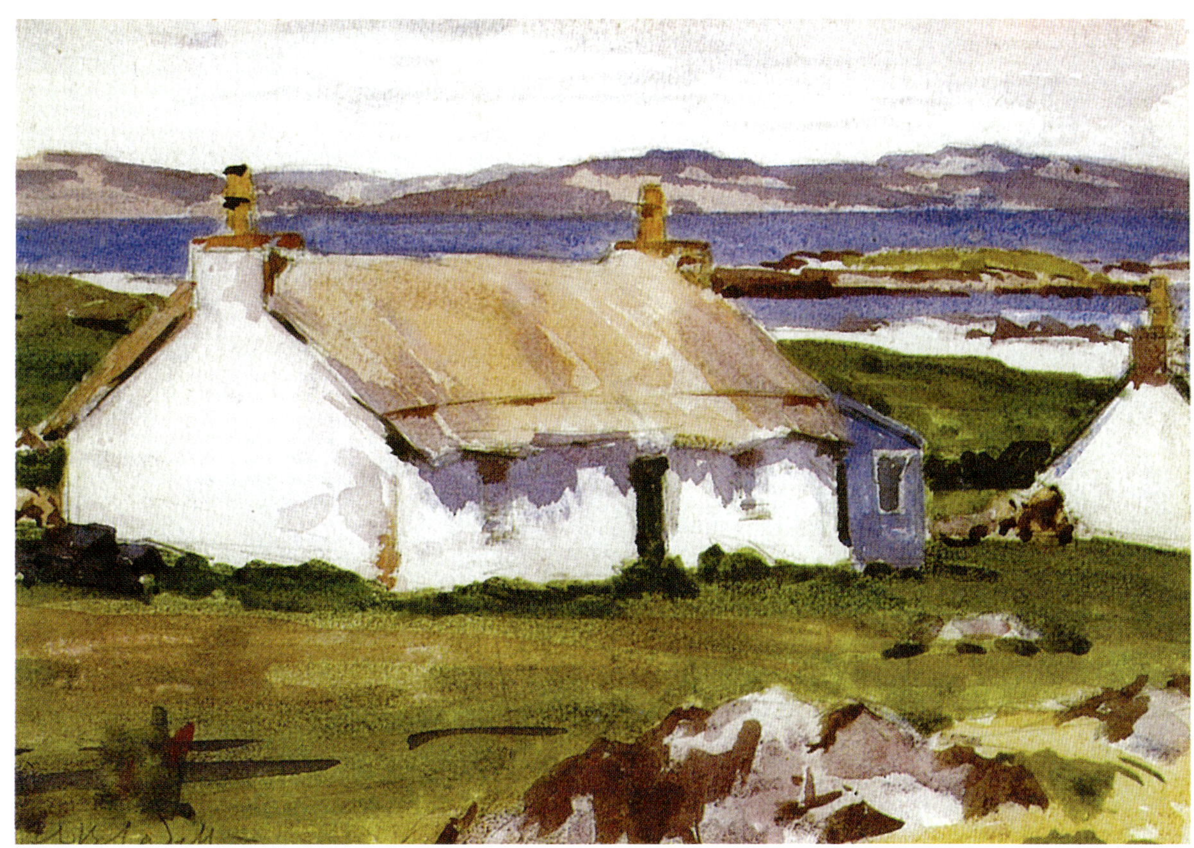

[PLATE 33]
F. C. B. Cadell
Cuil Phail Croft
Watercolour 7 x 10

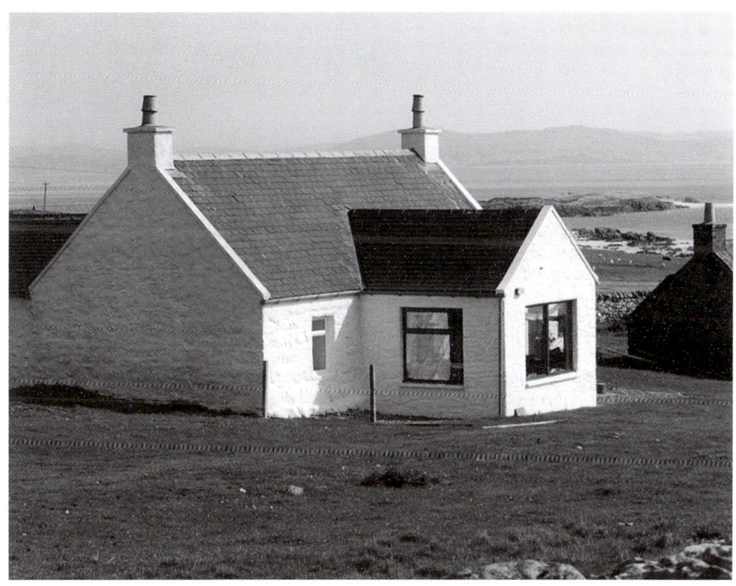

Photograph 2006

Cadell painted this view of the croft many times; Plate 34 is another example. In the middle distance are the sands of the White Strand, with Eilean Annraidh beyond, and in the far distance Ulva and the northwest of Mull.
In more recent years the gable walls of the cottage have been raised, the thatch roof replaced with slates, and the house extended on the north, south and east sides.

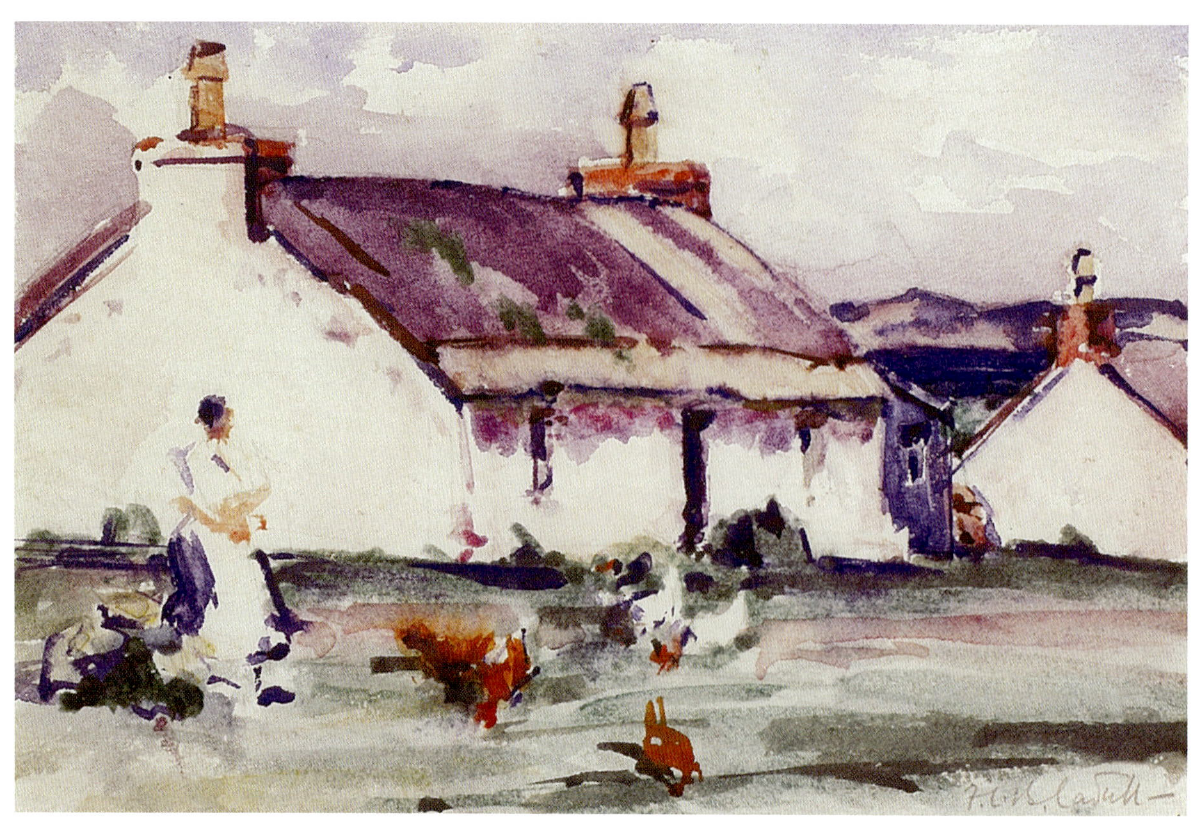

[PLATE 34]
F. C. B. Cadell
Cuil Phail Croft – feeding the chickens Watercolour 7 x 10

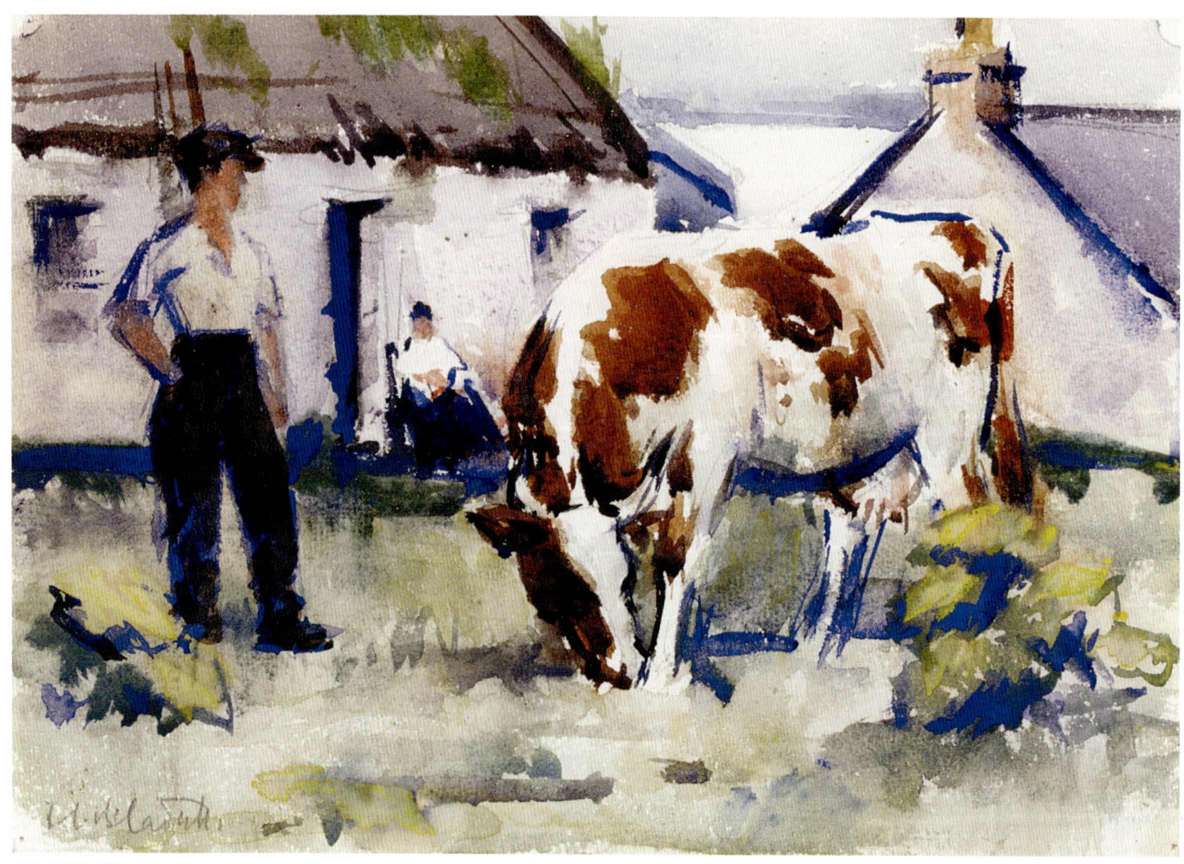

[PLATE 35]
F. C. B. Cadell
Cuil Phail Croft – the brown and white cow Watercolour 7 x 10

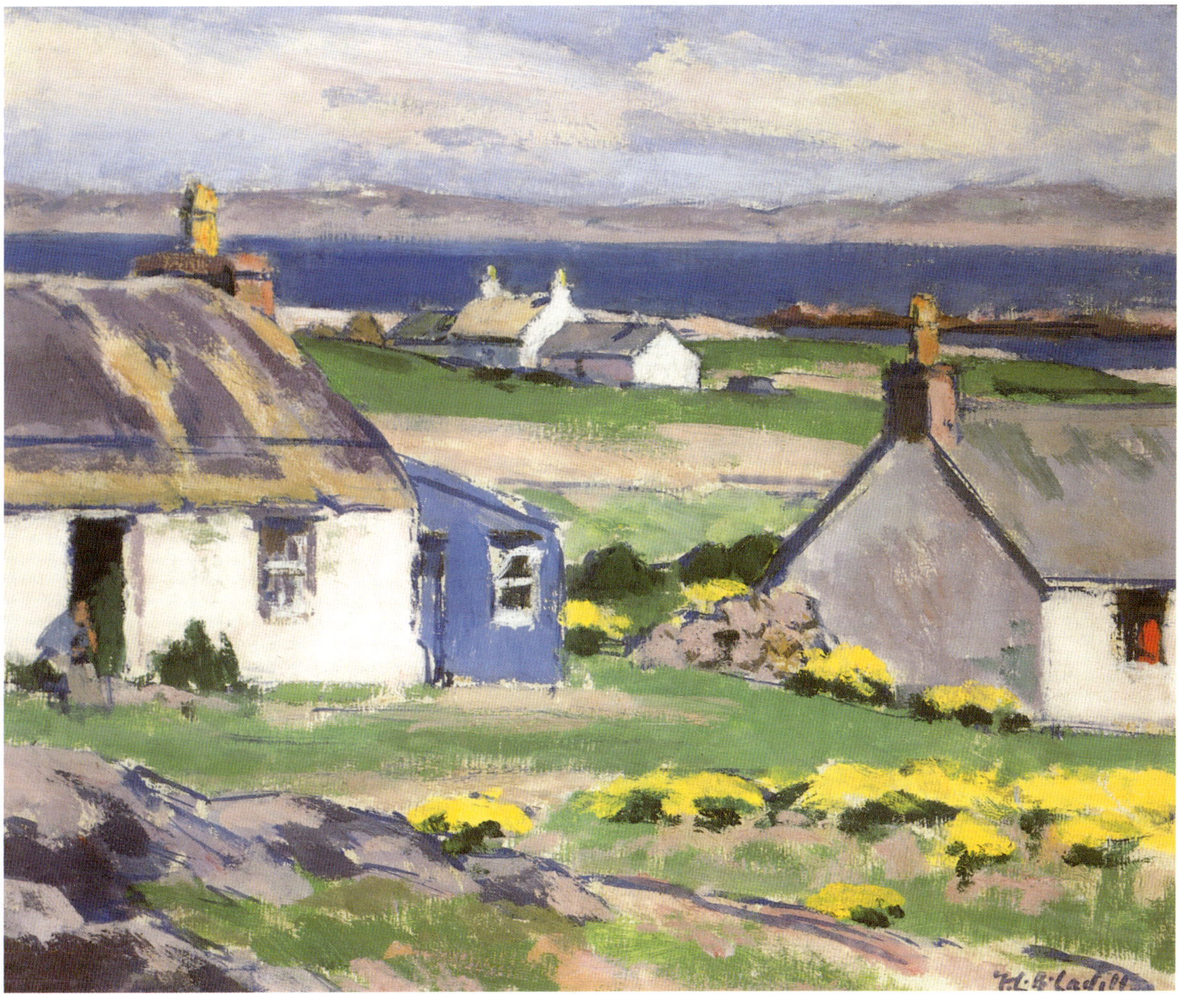

[PLATE 36]
F. C. B. Cadell
Cuil Phail Croft
(The Two Crofts, Iona)
Oil 15 x 18

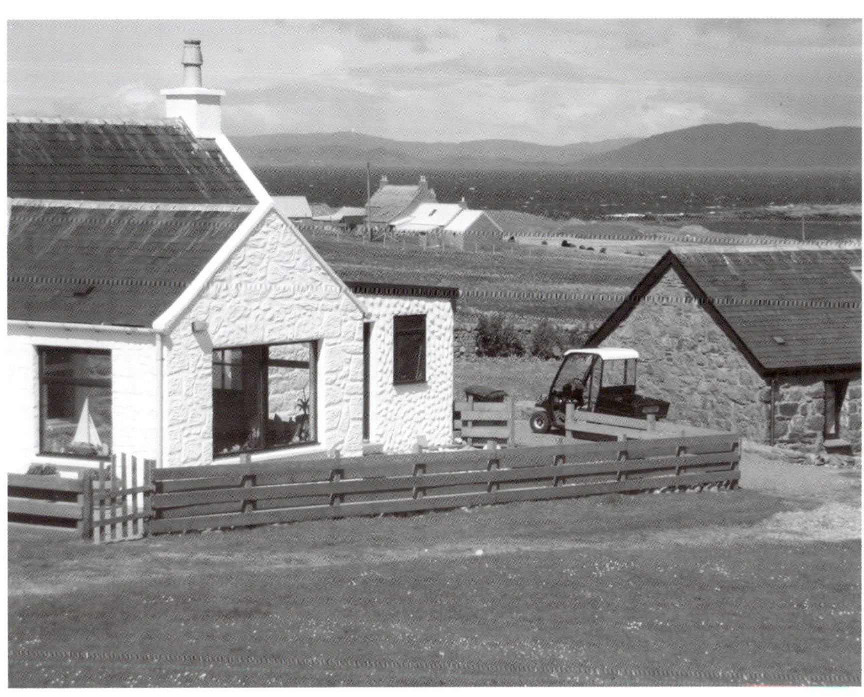

Photograph 2009

The two crofts referred to in the title are Cuil Phail and, in the background, the adjacent croft, Ardionra.

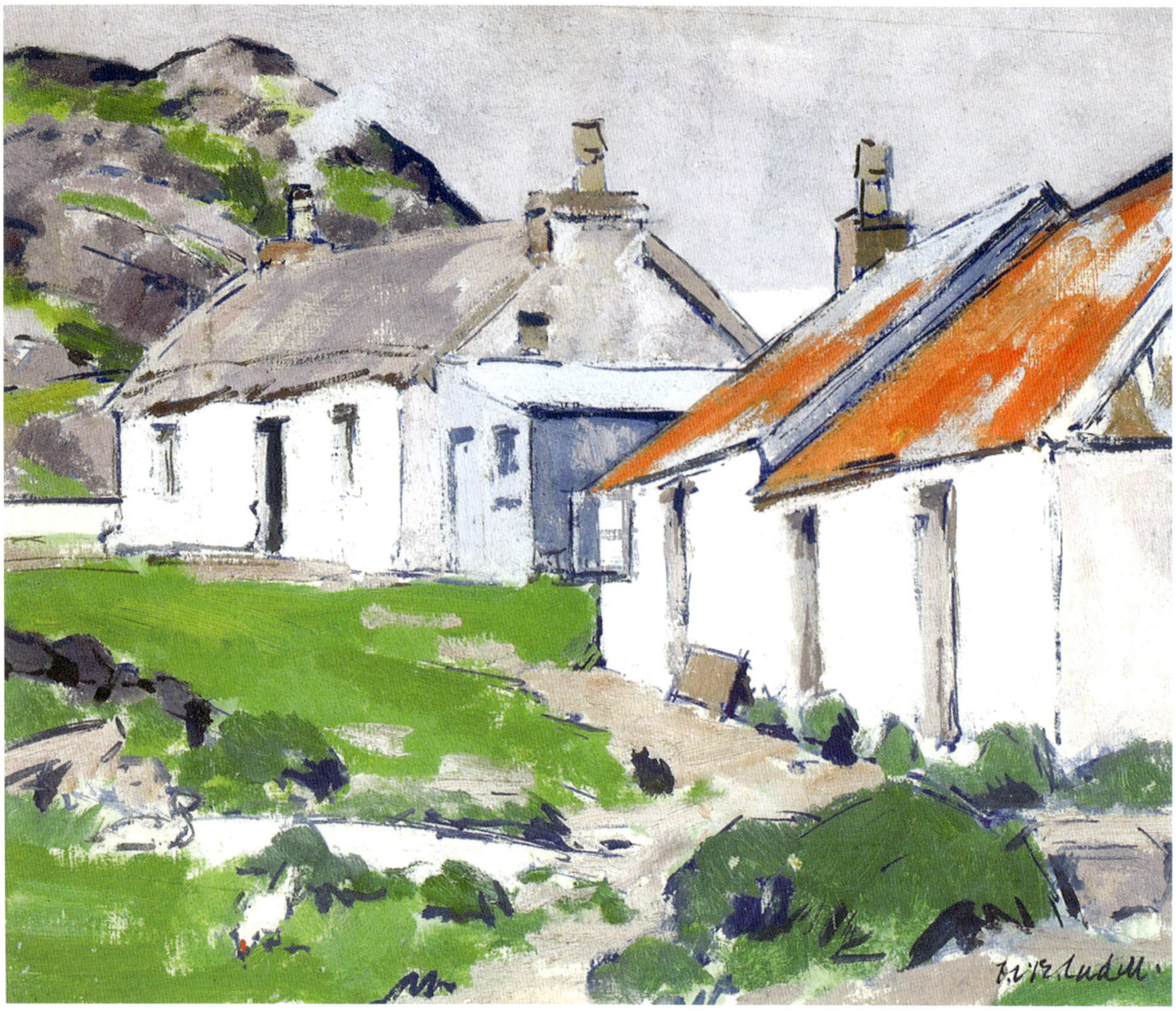

[PLATE 37]
F. C. B. Cadell
Cuil Phail Croft
Oil 15 x 18

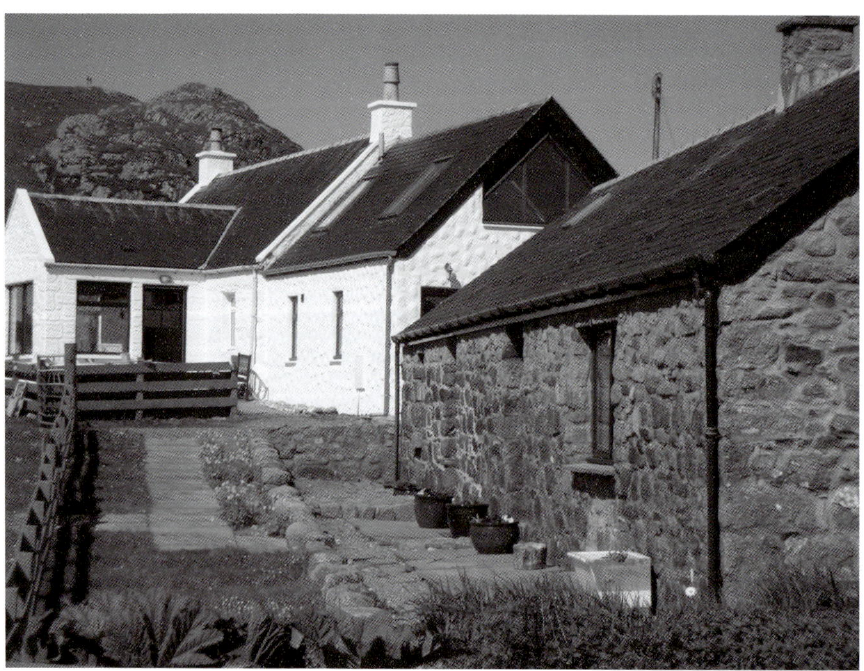

Photograph 2012

This view of the croft is from the east. Dun I is in the background.

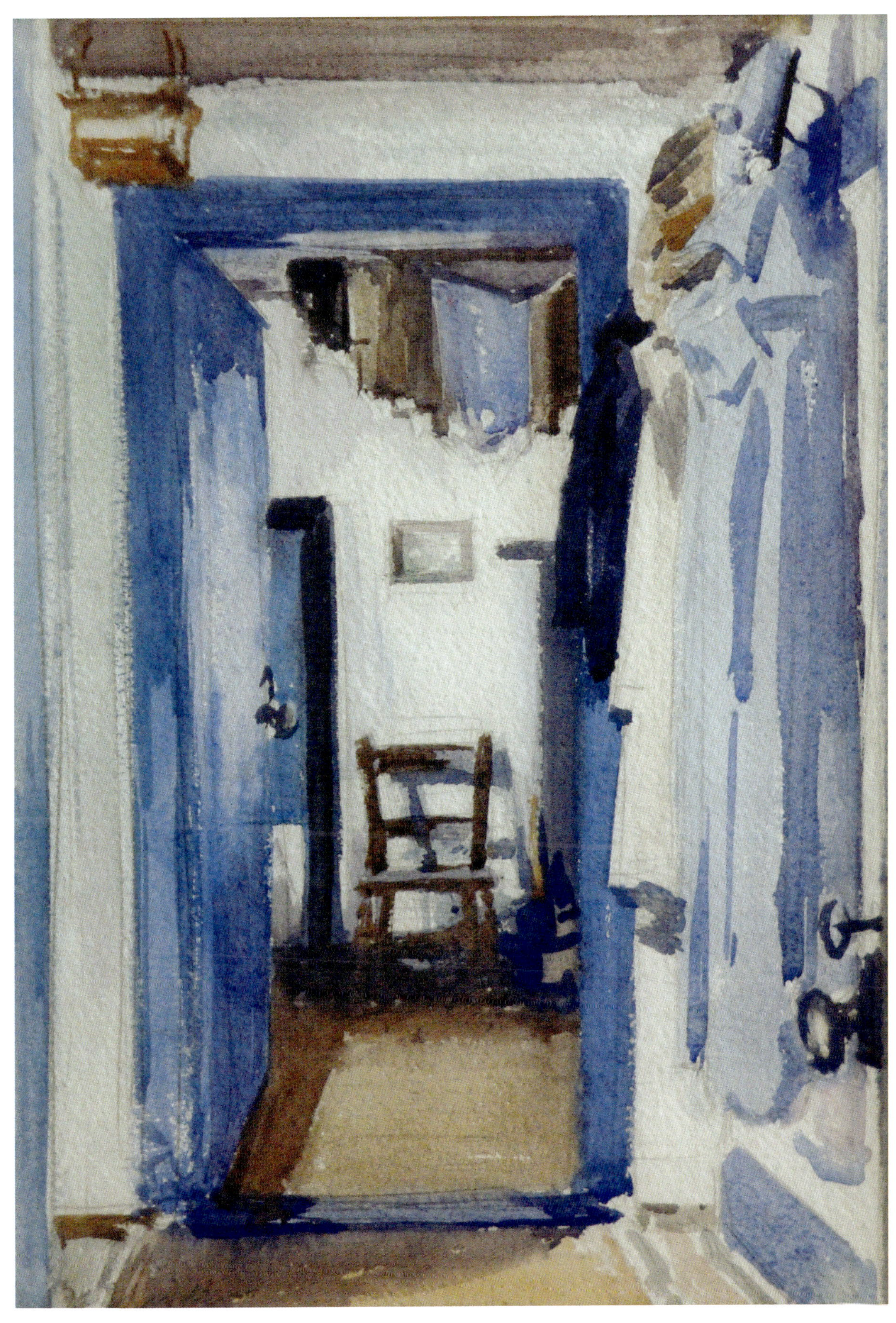

[PLATE 38]

F. C. B. Cadell

Cuil Phail Croft, interior

Watercolour 13 $^{1}/_{2}$ x 9 $^{3}/_{4}$

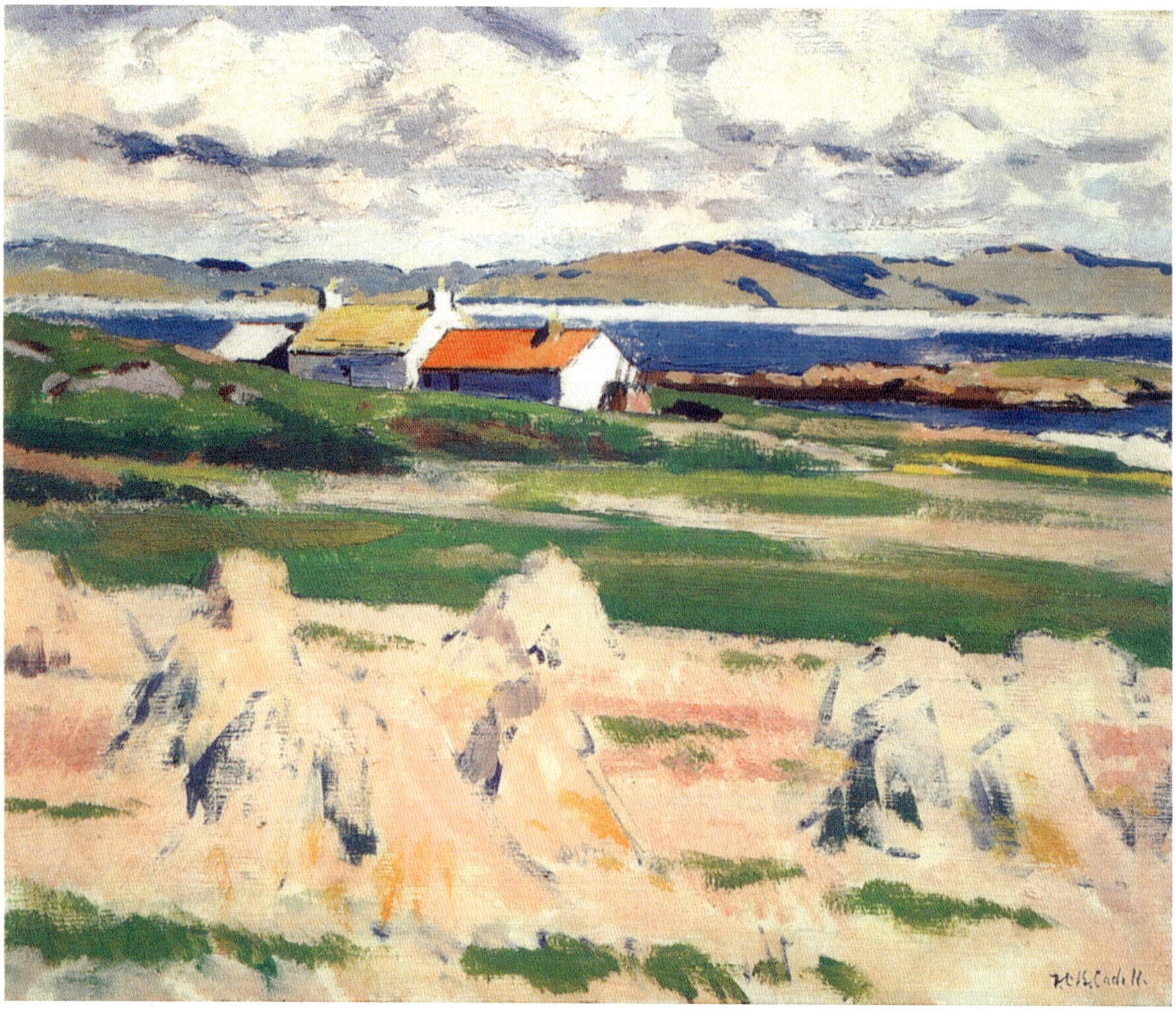

[PLATE 39]
F. C. B. Cadell
Ardionra Croft
(Harvest on the Croft)
Oil 15 x 18

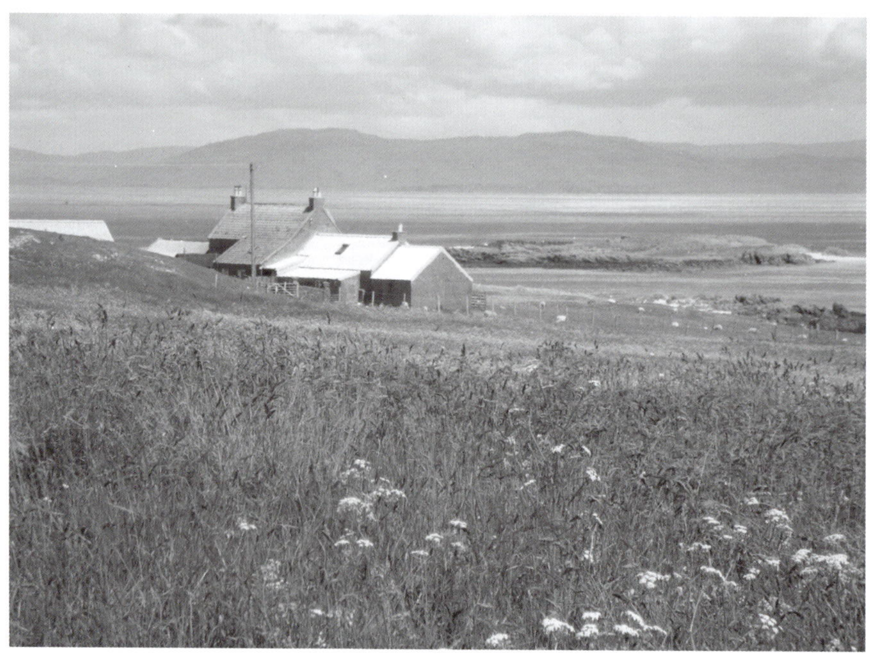

Photograph 2009

Ardionra is the last croft on the right-hand side of the road.

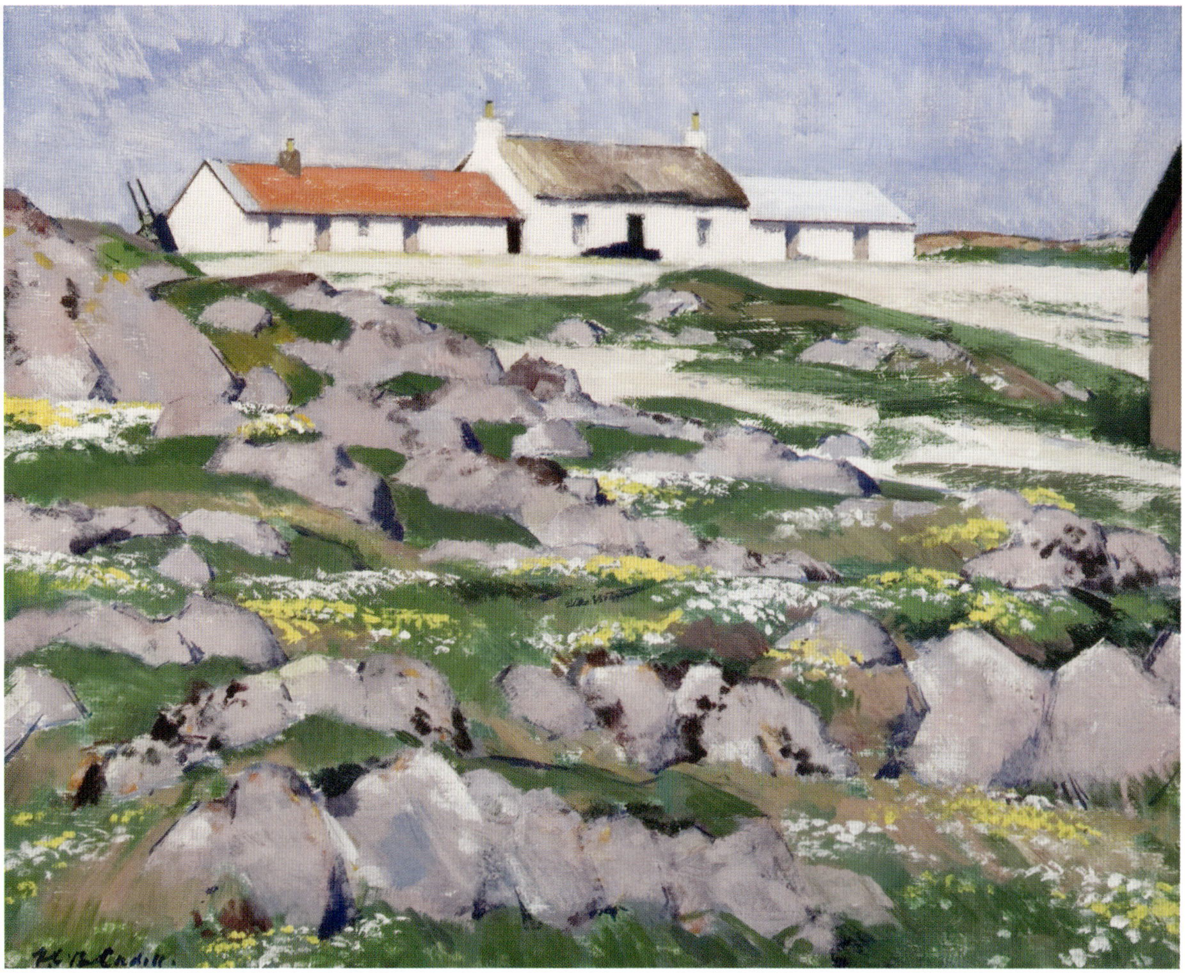

[PLATE 40]
F. C. B. Cadell
Ardionra Croft
Oil 15 x 18

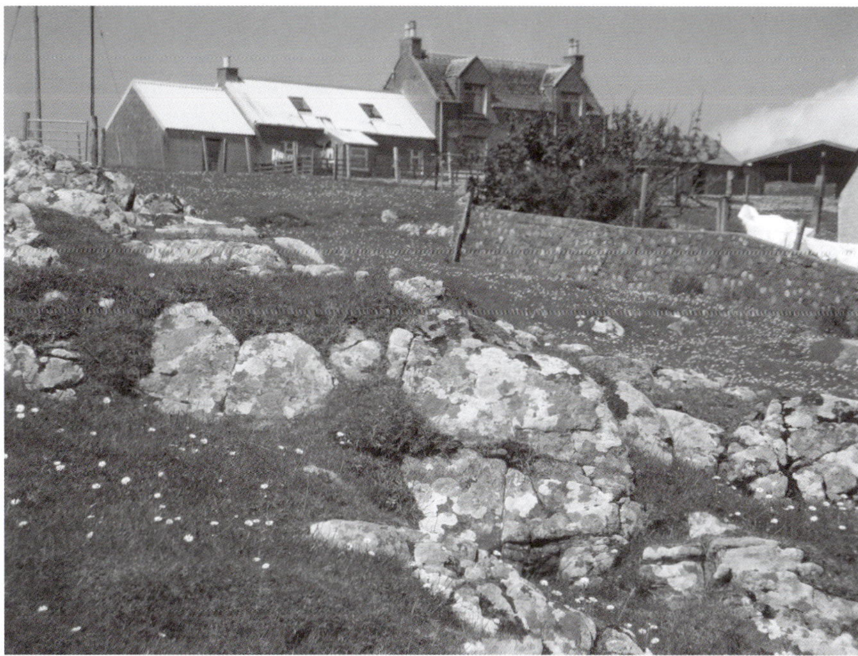

Photograph 2013

This view of Ardionra is seen looking up from almost on the beach, and is most conveniently approached having walked down to the south end of the White Strand (see page 59). The extreme corner of the house Traigh Bhan is included at the right-hand edge of the painting.

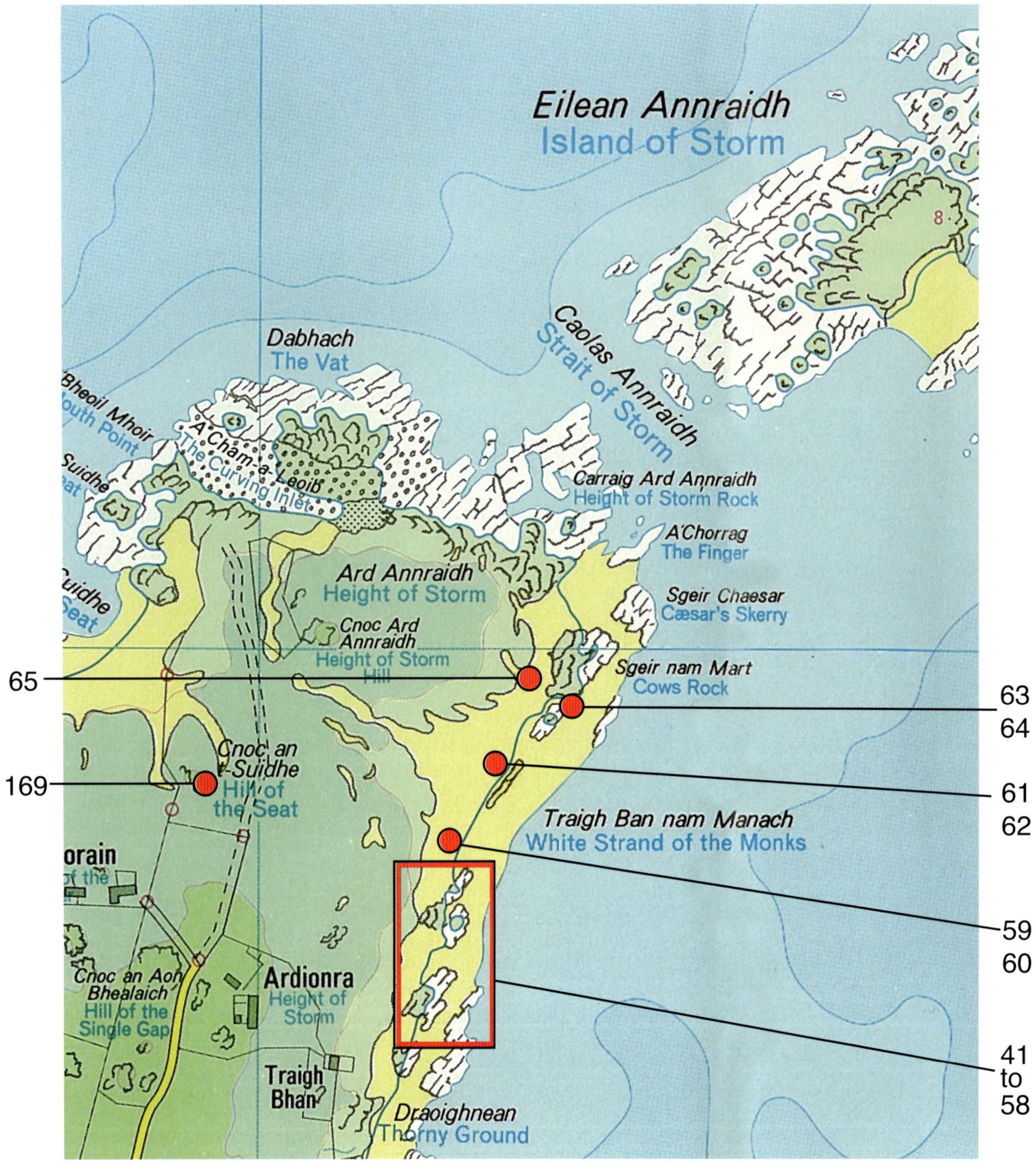

Eilean Annraidh
Island of Storm
Dabhach
The Vat
Caolas Annraidh
Strait of Storm
A'Cham-a-Leoib
The Curving Inlet
Carraig Ard Annraidh
Height of Storm Rock
A'Chorrag
The Finger
Ard Annraidh
Height of Storm
Sgeir Chaesar
Cæsar's Skerry
Cnoc Ard Annraidh
Height of Storm Hill
Sgeir nam Mart
Cows Rock
Cnoc an t-Suidhe
Hill of the Seat
Traigh Ban nam Manach
White Strand of the Monks
Cnoc an Aon Bhealaich
Hill of the Single Gap
Ardionra
Height of Storm
Traigh Bhan
Draoighnean
Thorny Ground

65
63
64
169
61
62
59
60
41
to
58

1/2 Mile (800 metres)

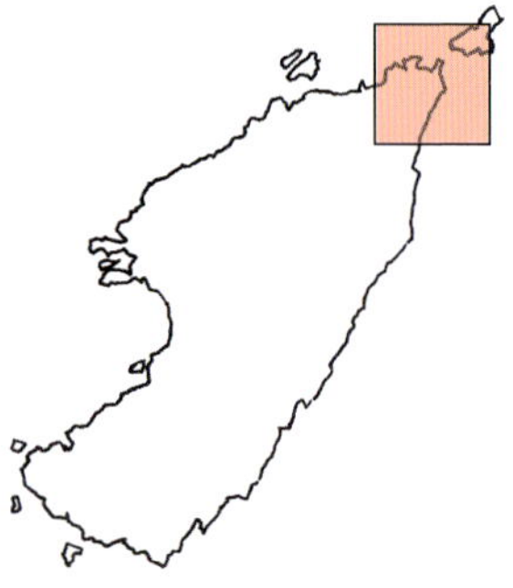

[FIGURE 10]
Locations of paintings illustrated in Chapter 3

3 · THE WHITE STRAND

AT the end of the road a small gate straight ahead gives access to the North End. As soon as one has walked along the track far enough to be clear of the outbuildings of Ardionra, it is possible to turn right and walk due east across the machair down to the shore. At the point of arrival there is an area of exposed rocks on the beach at the southern end of the White Strand. These rocks provide the foreground for many of the paintings (Plates 41 to 58).

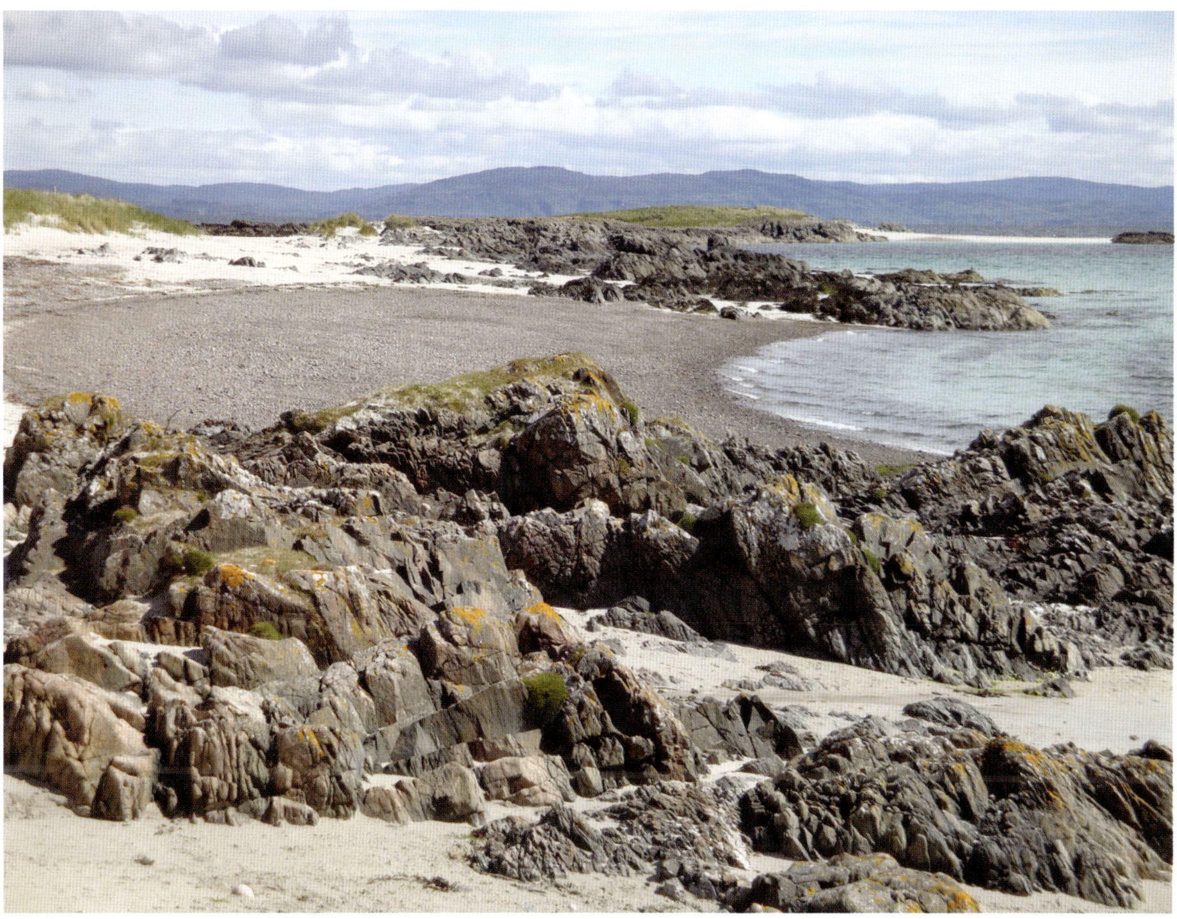

In the view north from this point the Strand is seen curving away to the northeast, ending at Cows Rock, beyond which there is a narrow stretch of water, the Strait of Storm, between Iona and the small rocky island of Eilean Annraidh – Island of Storm. This is crowned with grass above the rocks and has a white sandy beach on the southeast side. This beach is a distinctive feature in many of the paintings, although it should be noted that it is underwater at high tide and therefore would not be seen. In the distance are the twin summits of Ulva, with the hills of northwest Mull beyond.

The shallow waters lying over the white sand give rise to seas of turquoise and emerald with contrasting blueviolet streaks where dark, submerged, patches of seaweed cut off the light reflected from the sand below.

If Cadell and Peploe could stand here today their first question would surely be, "Where has all the sand gone?" For in recent years the beach has looked very different from the time they were on the island. Whether this change is a long-term cyclical event or a permanent loss only time will tell, but the wide expanse of white sand seen in the paintings has gone, leaving a steeply sloping stony beach. Occasionally the stones are covered with a layer of sand sufficient to give a hint of its former appearance.

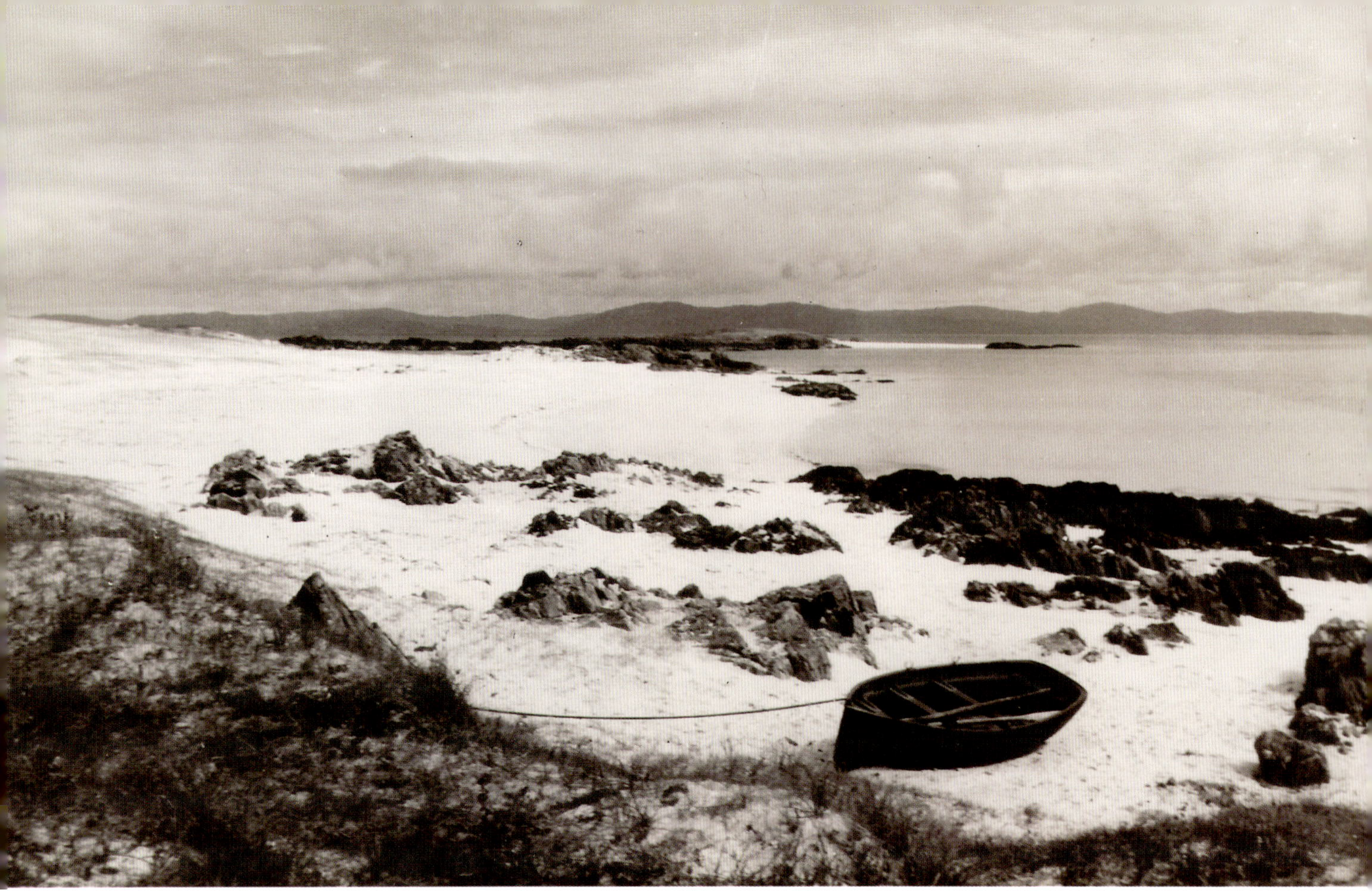

[FIGURE 11] Photograph of the White Strand, by Donald B. MacCulloch in the mid 1920s

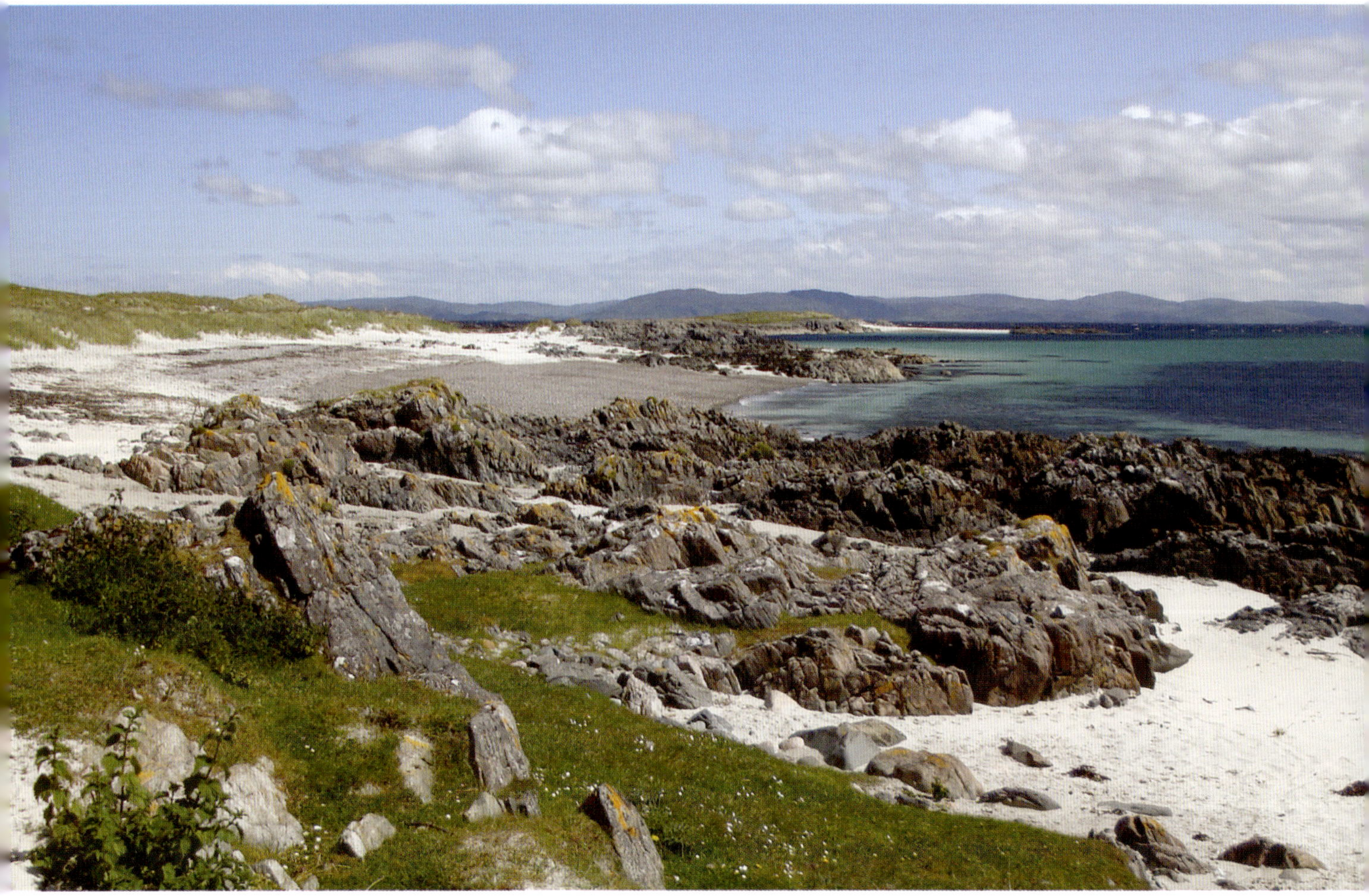

[FIGURE 12] Photograph of the White Strand by the author in 2009

A comparison of the photograph taken in the mid 1920s by Donald B. MacCulloch (Figure 11) with that taken by the author in 2009 (Figure 12) makes this change very clear. The MacCulloch photograph is contemporary with the paintings, and if it is edited to show the same angle as Cadell and Peploe generally painted, one can see the appearance as recorded in their pictures completely confirmed.

One's first thought is that coastal erosion has taken place, and this may be part of the cause. However, careful examination reveals that, whereas the level of the beach is lower, the level of the machair is considerably higher. Grass grows through sand that is blown on to the machair causing the level to rise. So rather than a net loss, it appears that there has been a redistribution of sand from the beach to under the grass of the machair. This can be seen in the photographs and is also confirmed in Cadell's picture *Iona Sound and Ben More* (Plate 169). This was painted from the rocky knoll called Cnoc an t-Suidhe, and shows not only that Cows Rock was visible from there in the 1920s, but also the White Strand itself. However the machair and dunes are high enough now to hide Cows Rock almost completely, and the beach can no longer be seen.

Further evidence of this change is provided by the Ordnance Survey Map of 1900, which shows at that time a continuous sandy beach from the north shore, below Lagandorain, over to the east side and down the White Strand (Figure 13). Subsequent maps prepared during the twentieth century show a gradually increasing area of machair and a corresponding decrease in the area of sand.

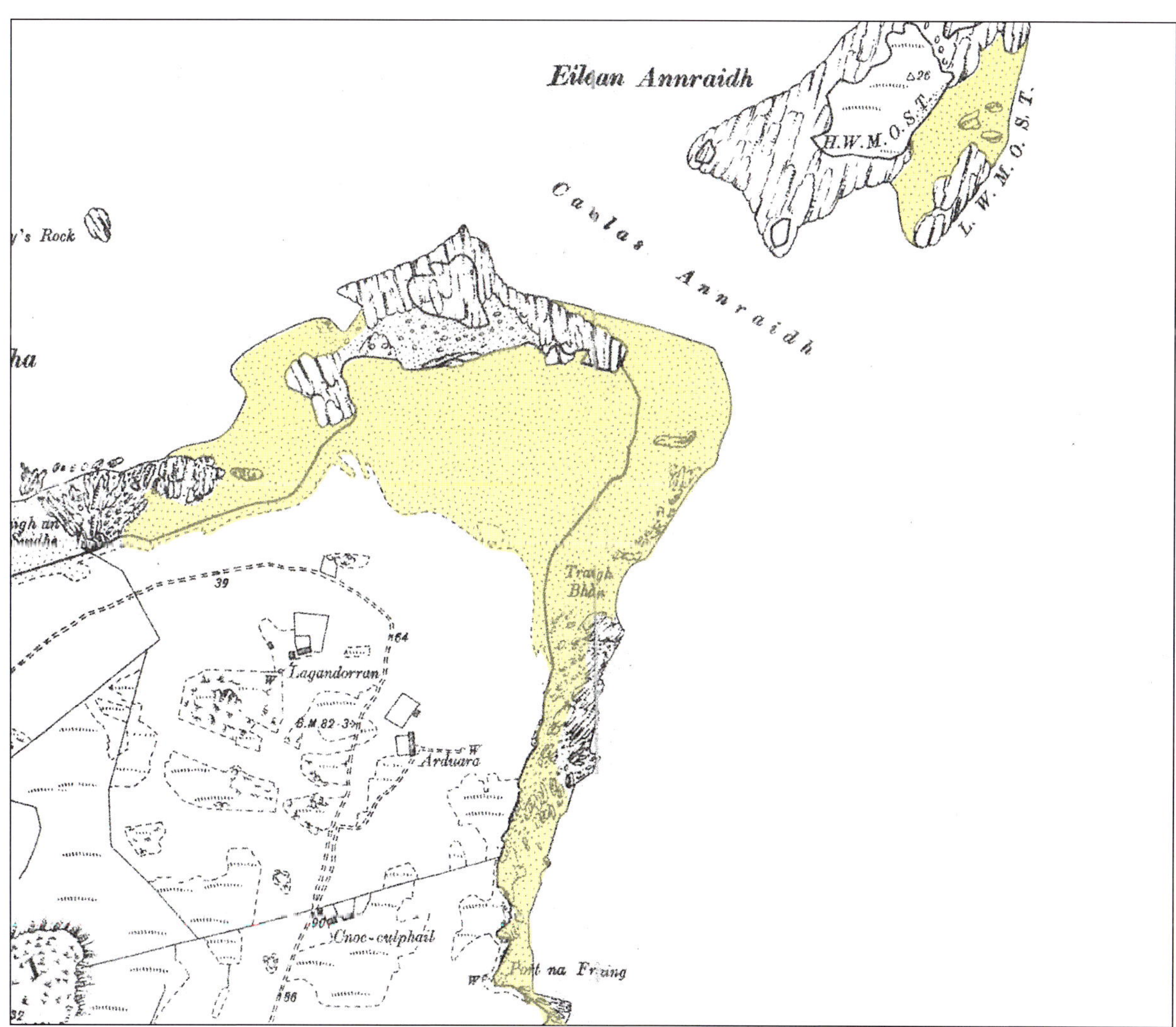

[FIGURE 13] Detail from Ordnance Survey Map Sheet C1V Argyllshire (Islands of Iona and Mull) © Crown copyright 1900

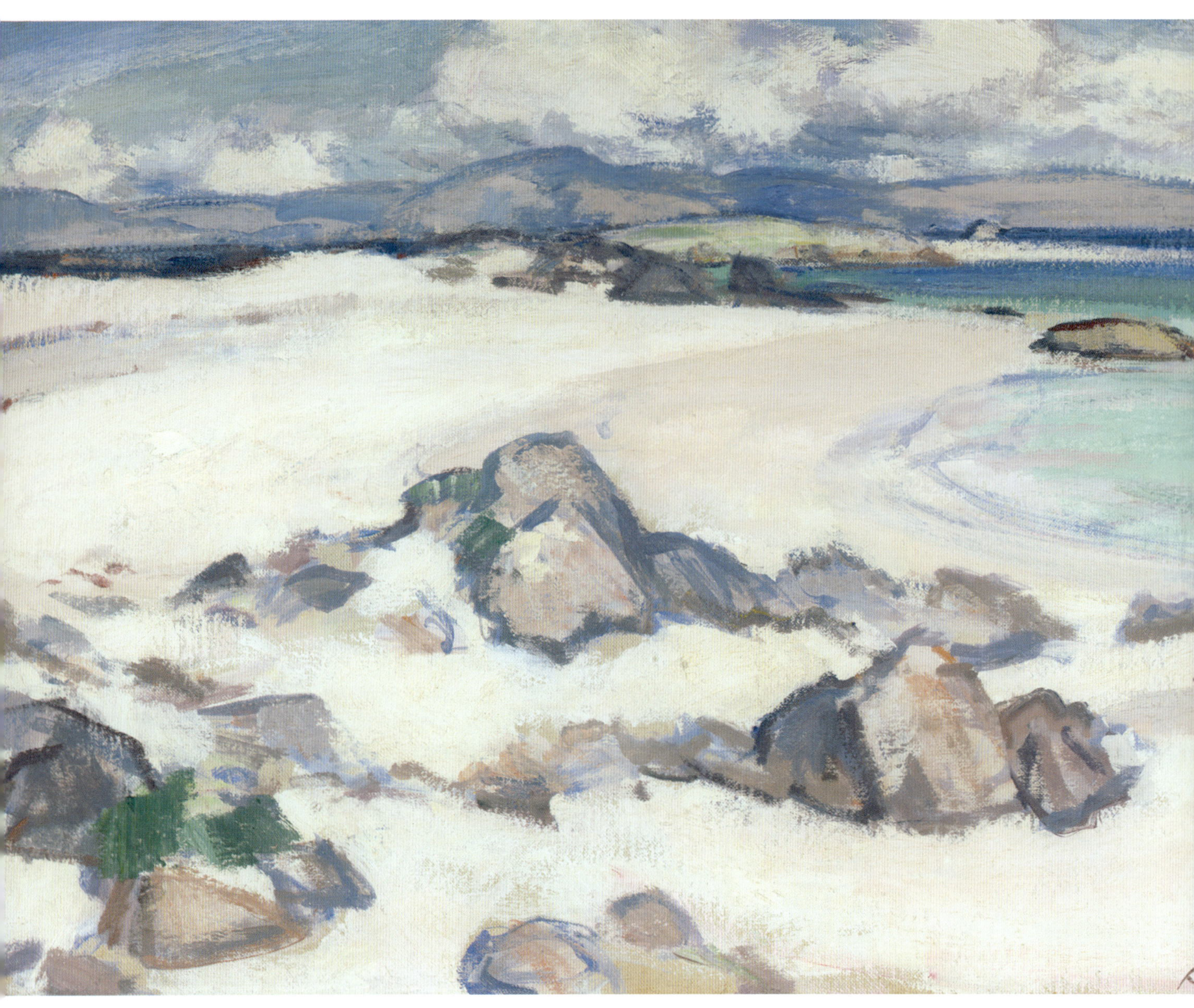

Painted from amongst the rocks at the south end of the White Strand, looking northeast toward Eilean Annraidh and to Ulva on the horizon, this is a subject which Peploe repeated many times. Plates 41 to 50 are a selection from a larger number of works.

A recurring element in paintings of the White Strand, about three quarters of the way along the beach, is a hump-backed rock protruding from the sand; it appears here in the mid-distance at the right edge. Since it lacks a name on the map I shall refer to it as the "Whaleback". This rock appears as an isolated feature in the paintings, but now, as a result of the lower sand level, many other rocks are exposed around it and the Whaleback is rather lost amongst them. Another outcome of the lower sand level is that the sea now advances further inshore. It is clear in the paintings, particularly at low tide, that the beach was wider in the past than it is now.

[PLATE 41]
S. J. Peploe
The White Strand
Oil 18 x 24

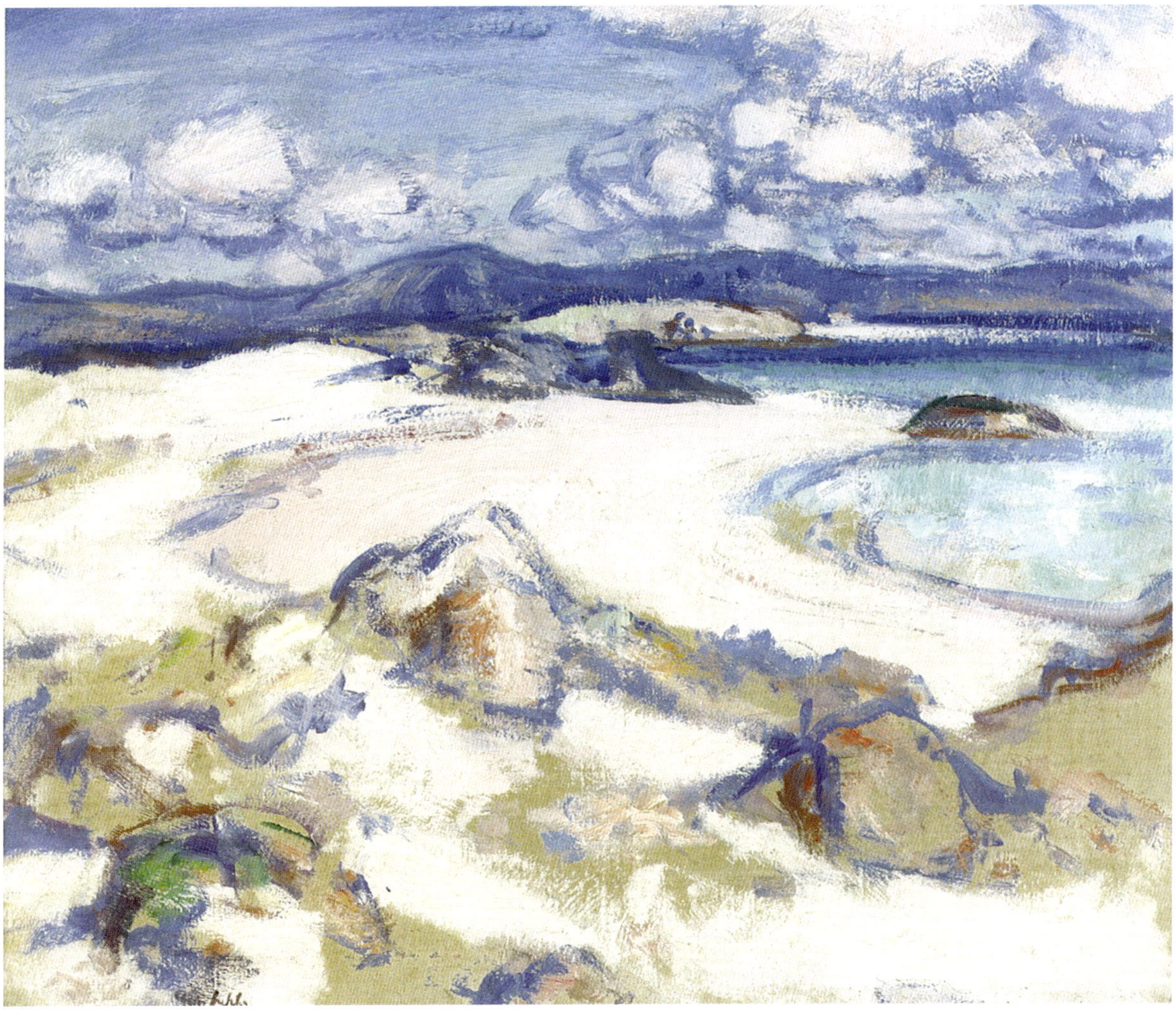

[PLATE 42]

S. J. Peploe

The White Strand

Oil 18 x 22

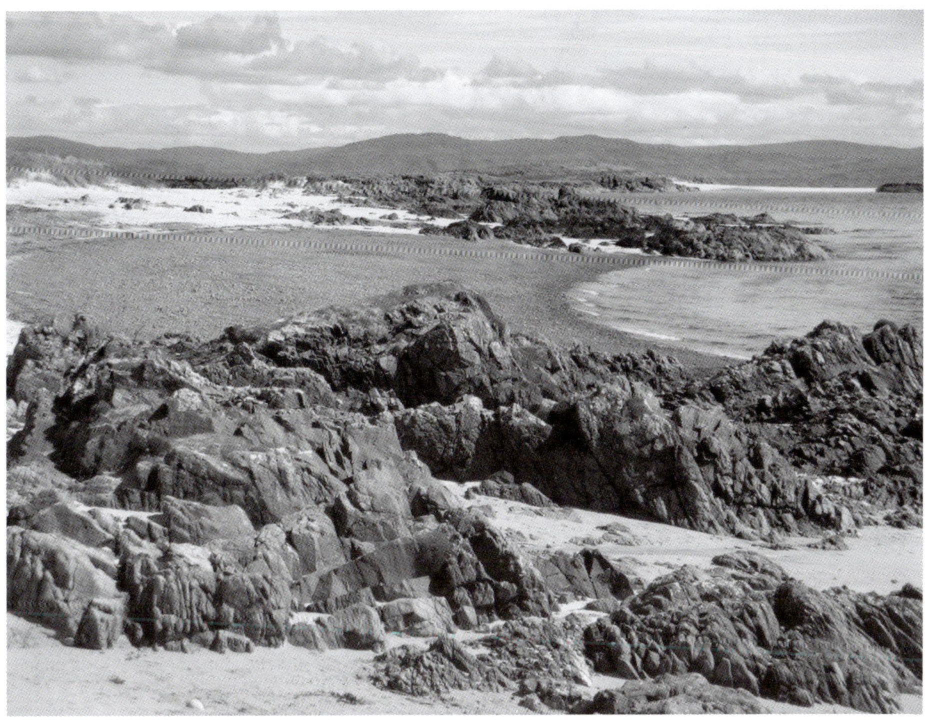

Photograph 2009

This was painted from the same position as Plate 41. The slightly squarer format of this picture has allowed a larger area of sky to be included, but otherwise it is an exact repeat of the subject.

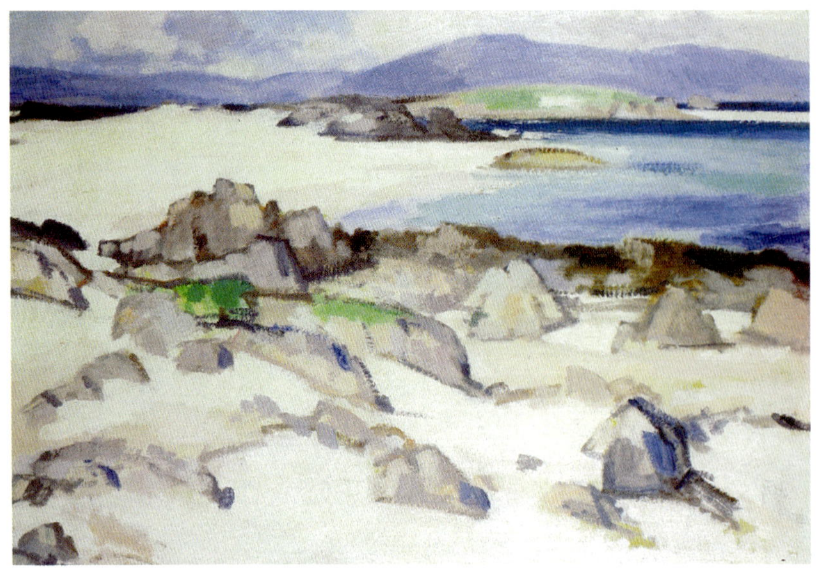

[PLATE 43]
S. J. PEPLOE
The White Strand
Oil 20 x 28

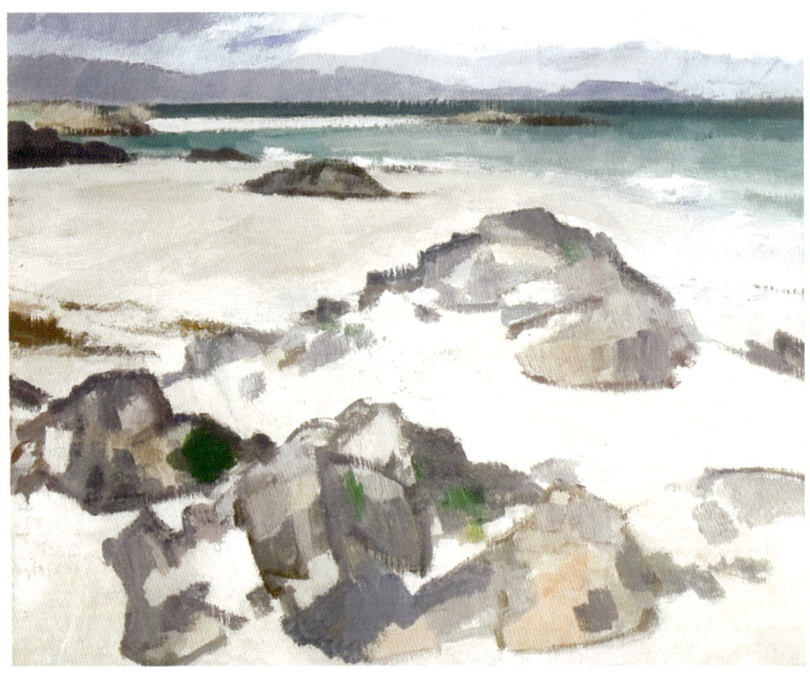

[PLATE 44]
S. J. PEPLOE
The White Strand
Oil 15 x 18

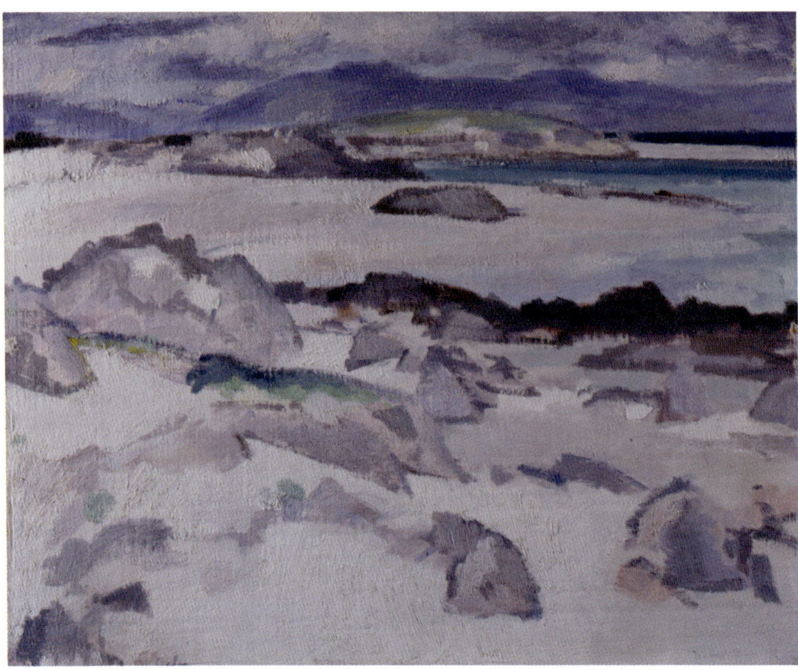

[PLATE 45]
S. J. PEPLOE

IONA LANDSCAPE
The White Strand
Oil 15 x 18

Fife Cultural Trust
(Kirkcaldy Galleries)
on behalf of Fife Council

[PLATE 46]
S. J. PEPLOE

IONA

The White Strand
Oil 20 x 28

Fife Cultural Trust
(Kirkcaldy Galleries)
on behalf of Fife Council

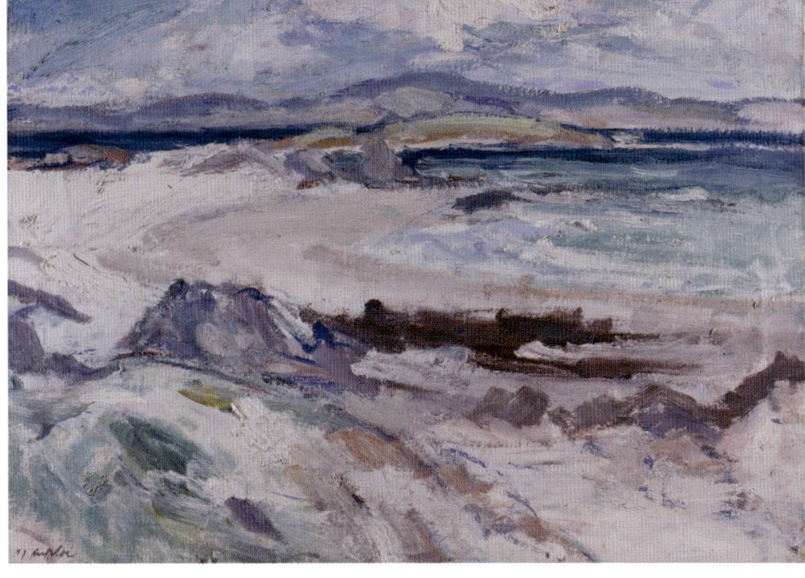

[PLATE 47]
S. J. PEPLOE
The White Strand
Oil 15 x 18

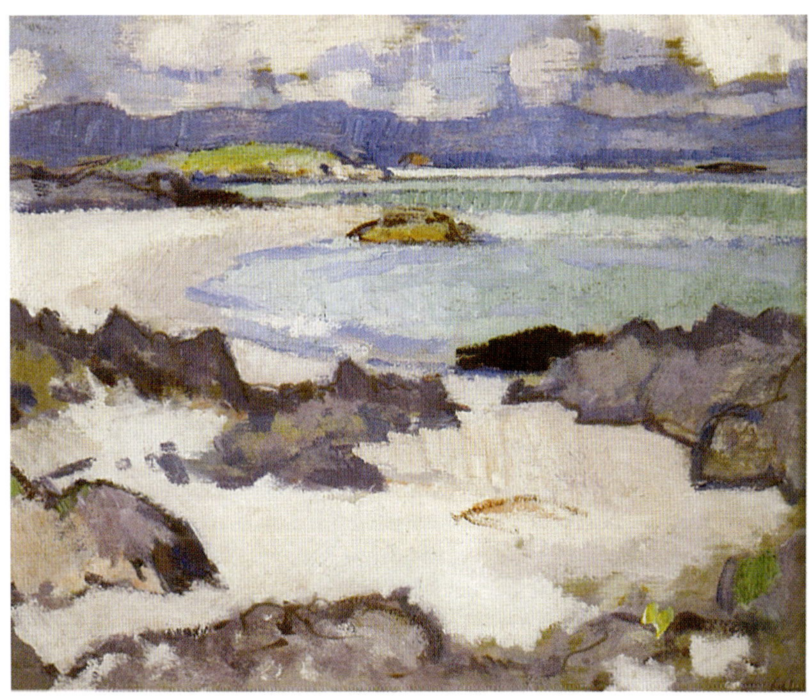

[PLATE 48]
S. J. PEPLOE
The White Strand
(The Rainbow)
Oil 20 x 28

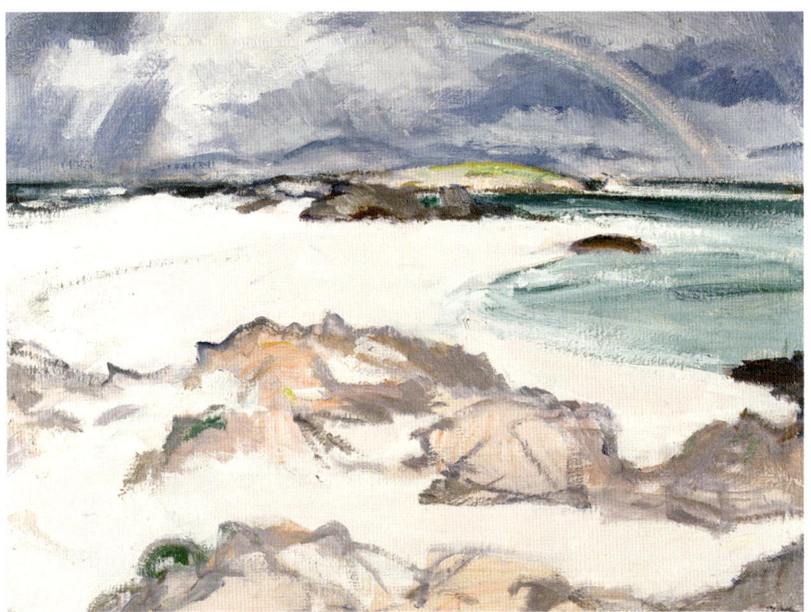

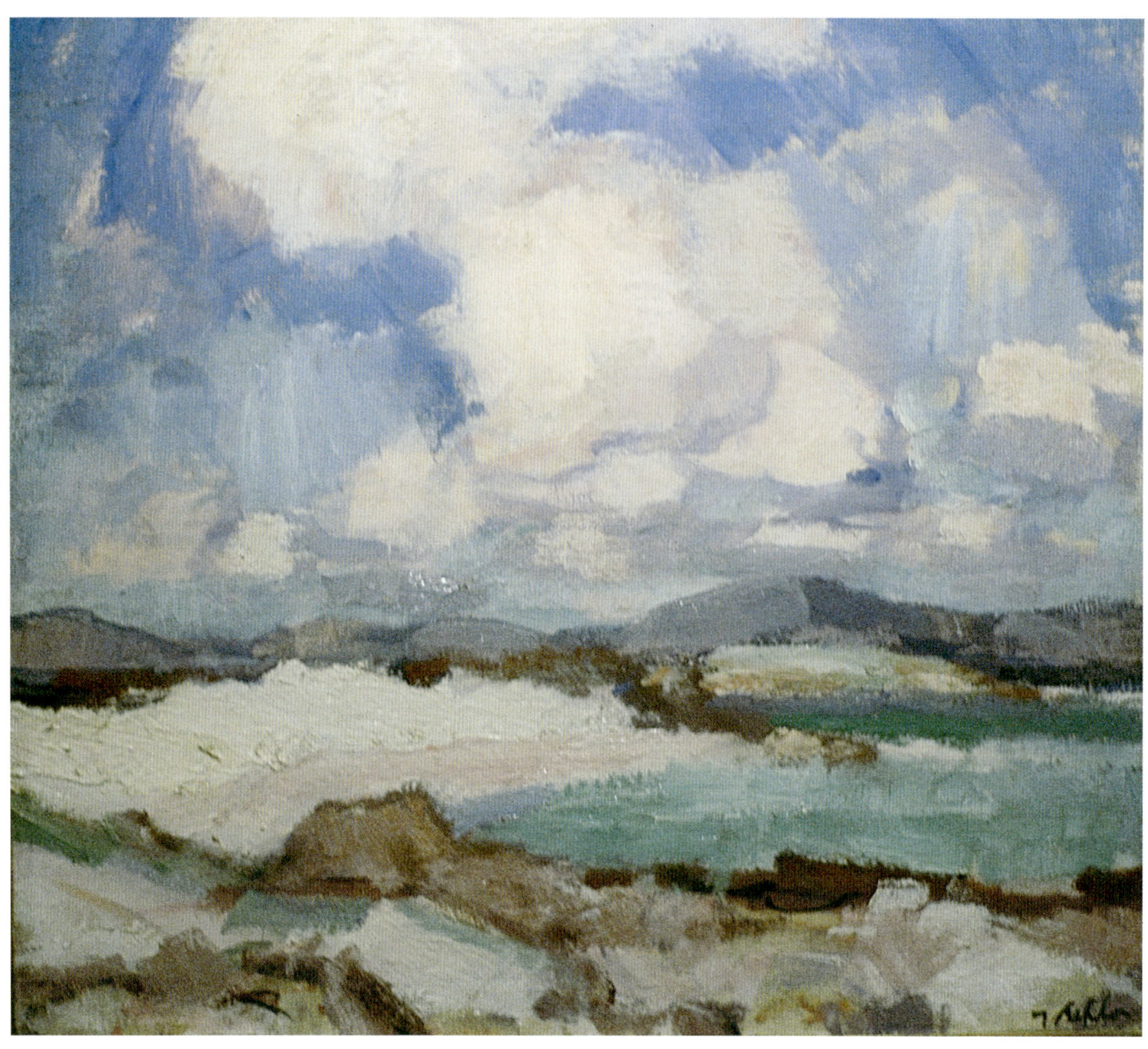

Most of the paintings by both Peploe and Cadell show their preference for a high horizon for this type of subject. This is an exception in which more than half the picture is devoted to the sky. The painting hung in Peploe's home during his lifetime, so must have been a favourite work.

[PLATE 49]

S. J. Peploe

CLOUDS AND SKY, IONA

The White Strand
Oil 16 x 18

The Hunterian, University of Glasgow

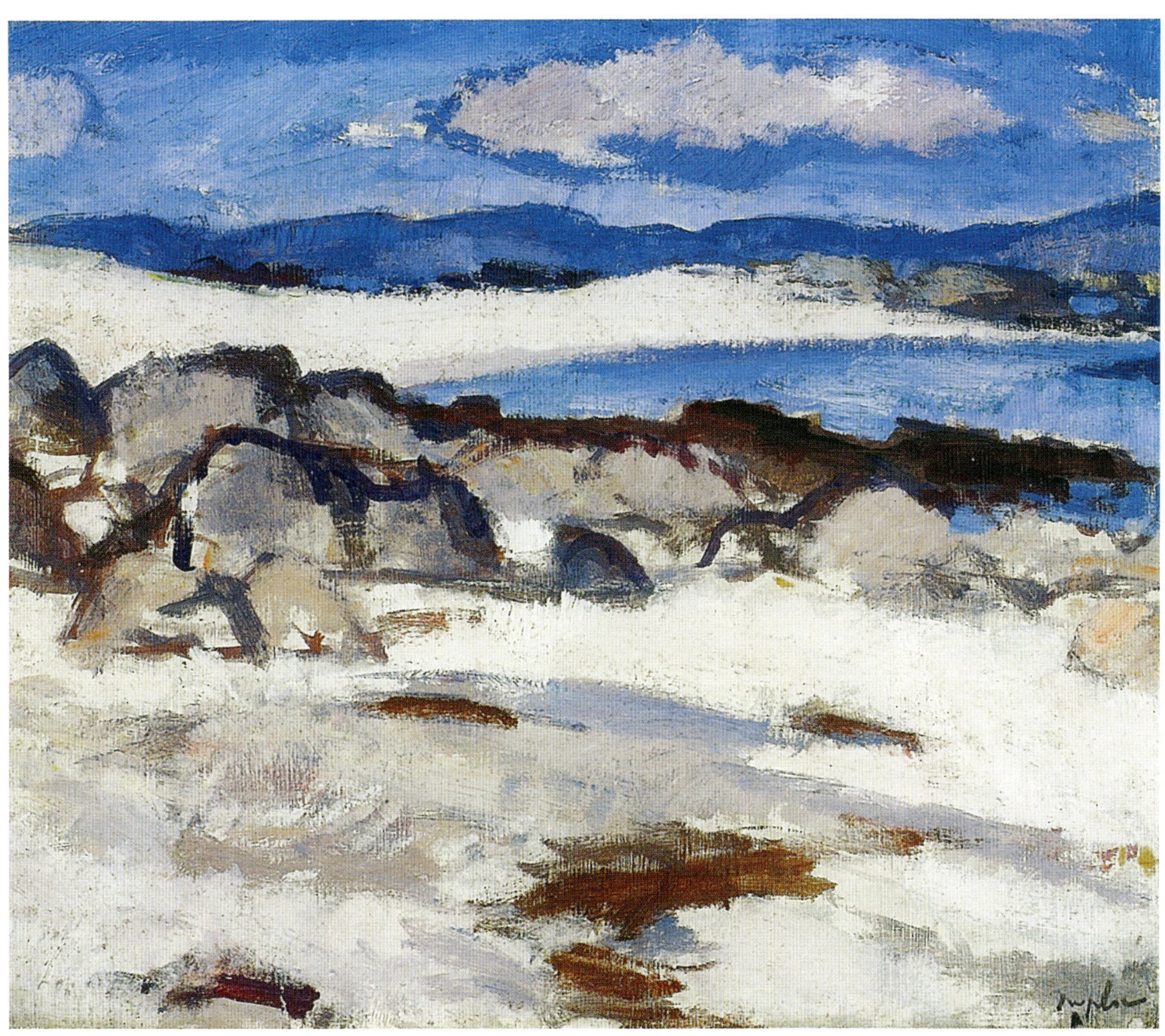

The view in this picture is similar to Plate 49, but with more foreground and less sky. The beach of Eilean Annraidh, which appears in Plates 41 to 49, is just outside the right-hand edge of this picture.

[PLATE 50]
S. J. Peploe
The White Strand (Iona, the Bay)
Oil 15 x 18

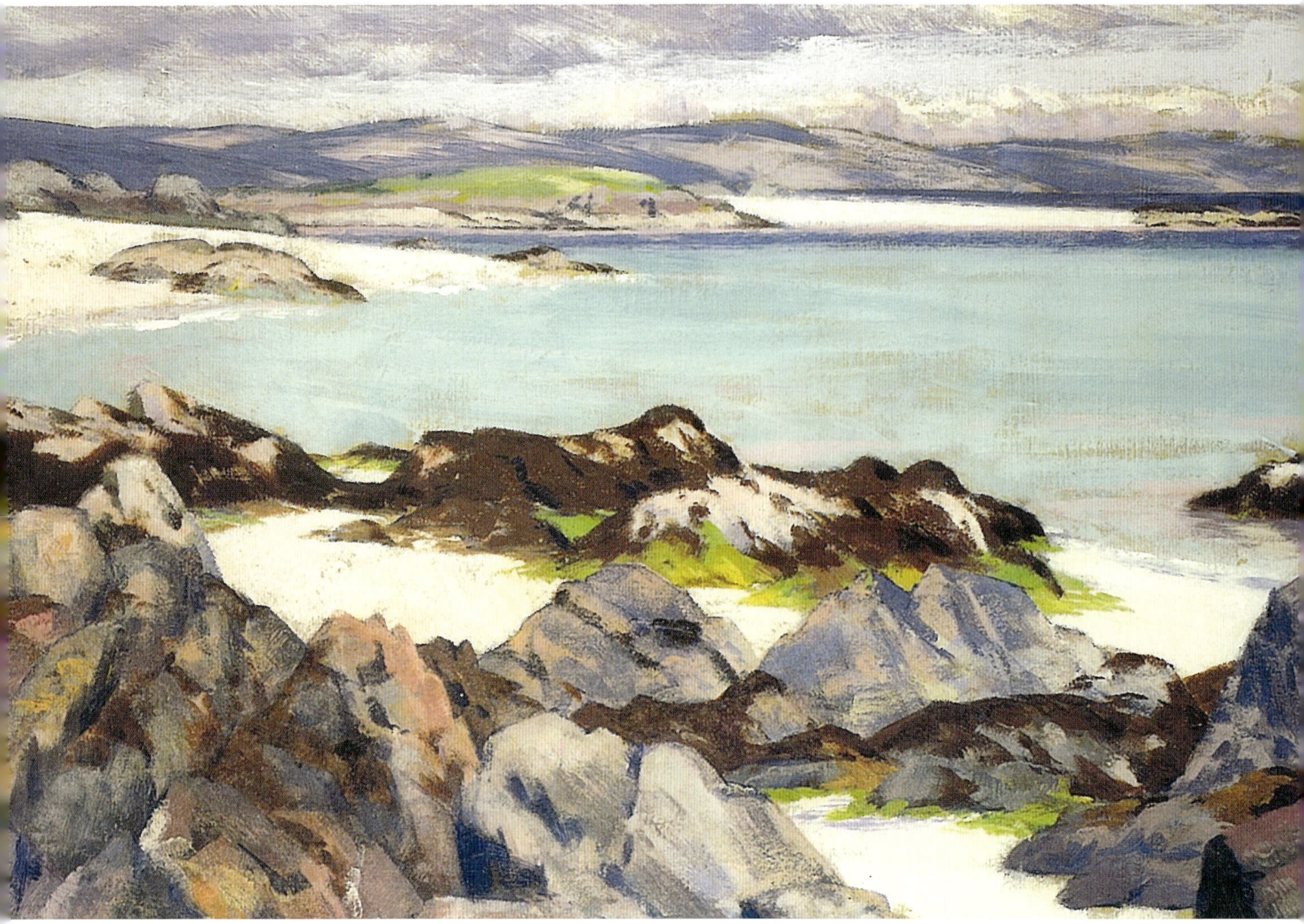

[PLATE 51]
F. C. B. Cadell
The East Bay
Oil 20 x 30

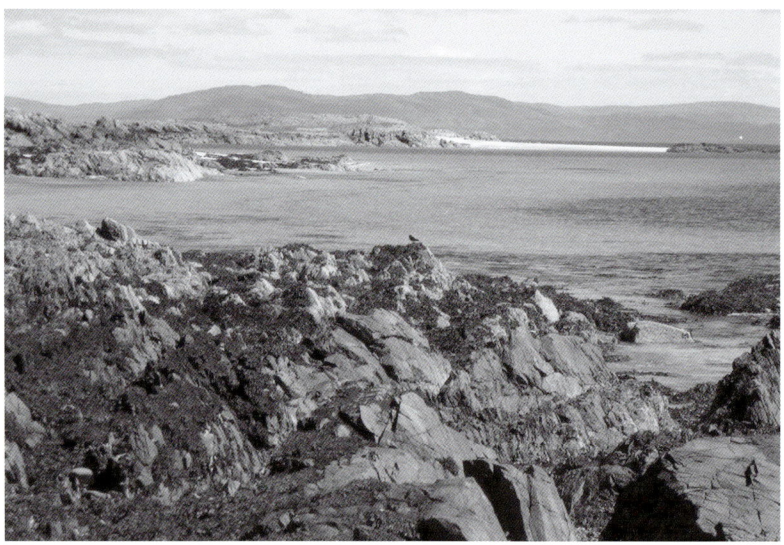

Photograph 2010

Cadell painted this from further out among the rocks than the preceding pictures by Peploe. The Whaleback Rock and part of the White Strand are at the left-hand side, but as may be seen there was no sand in this area when the corresponding photograph was taken. Eilean Annraidh is in the middle distance, with Ulva and northwest Mull in the background.

The foreground rocks have been accurately painted, but it is not easy to appreciate this from the photograph, in the absence of the patches of sand to delineate their upper profiles.

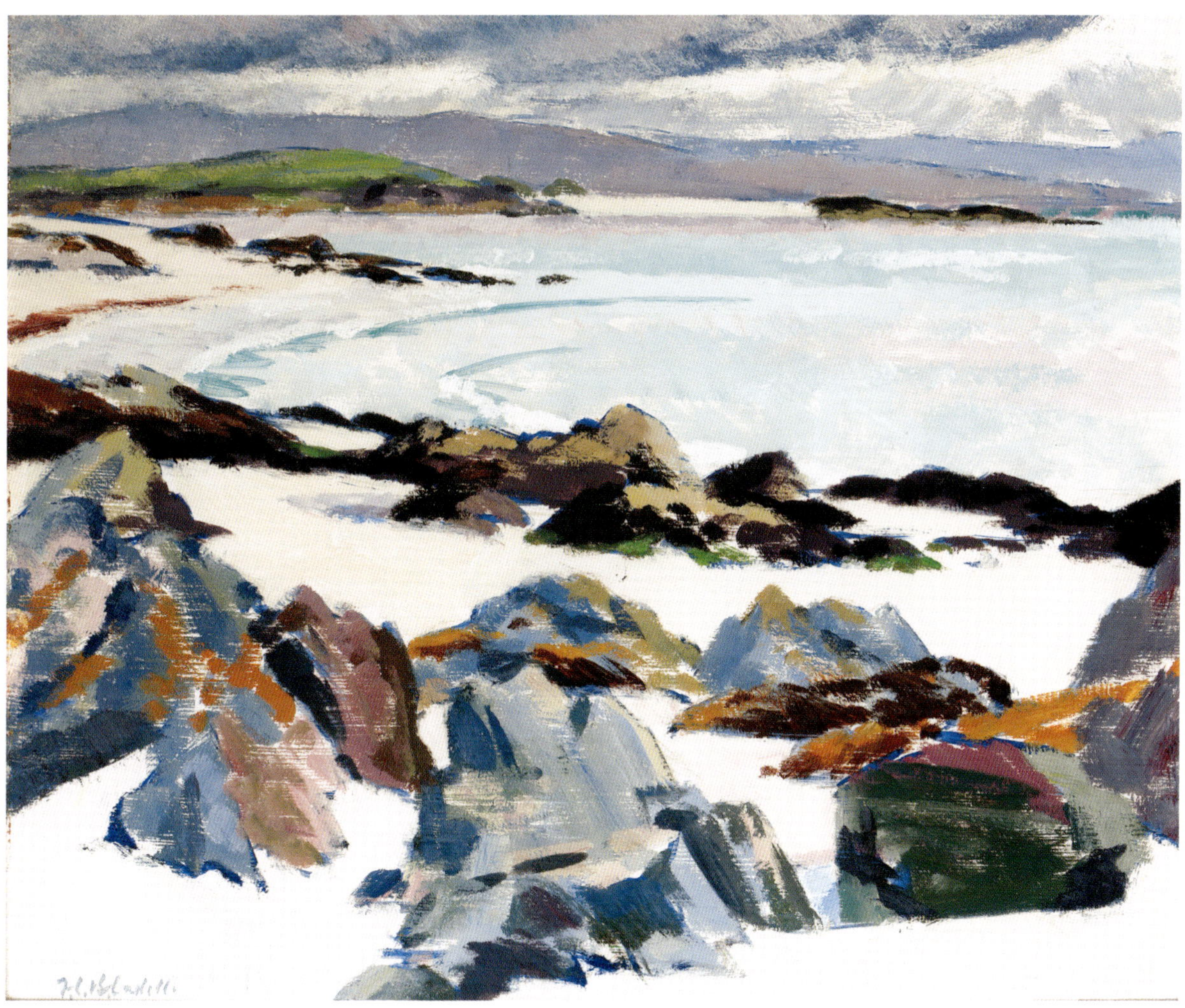

This was painted from the same position as Plate 51, although here, owing to the squarer format, less of the White Strand is seen at the left side, and the Whaleback is cut by the frame.

[PLATE 52]
F. C. B. Cadell
The East Bay
Oil 15 x 18

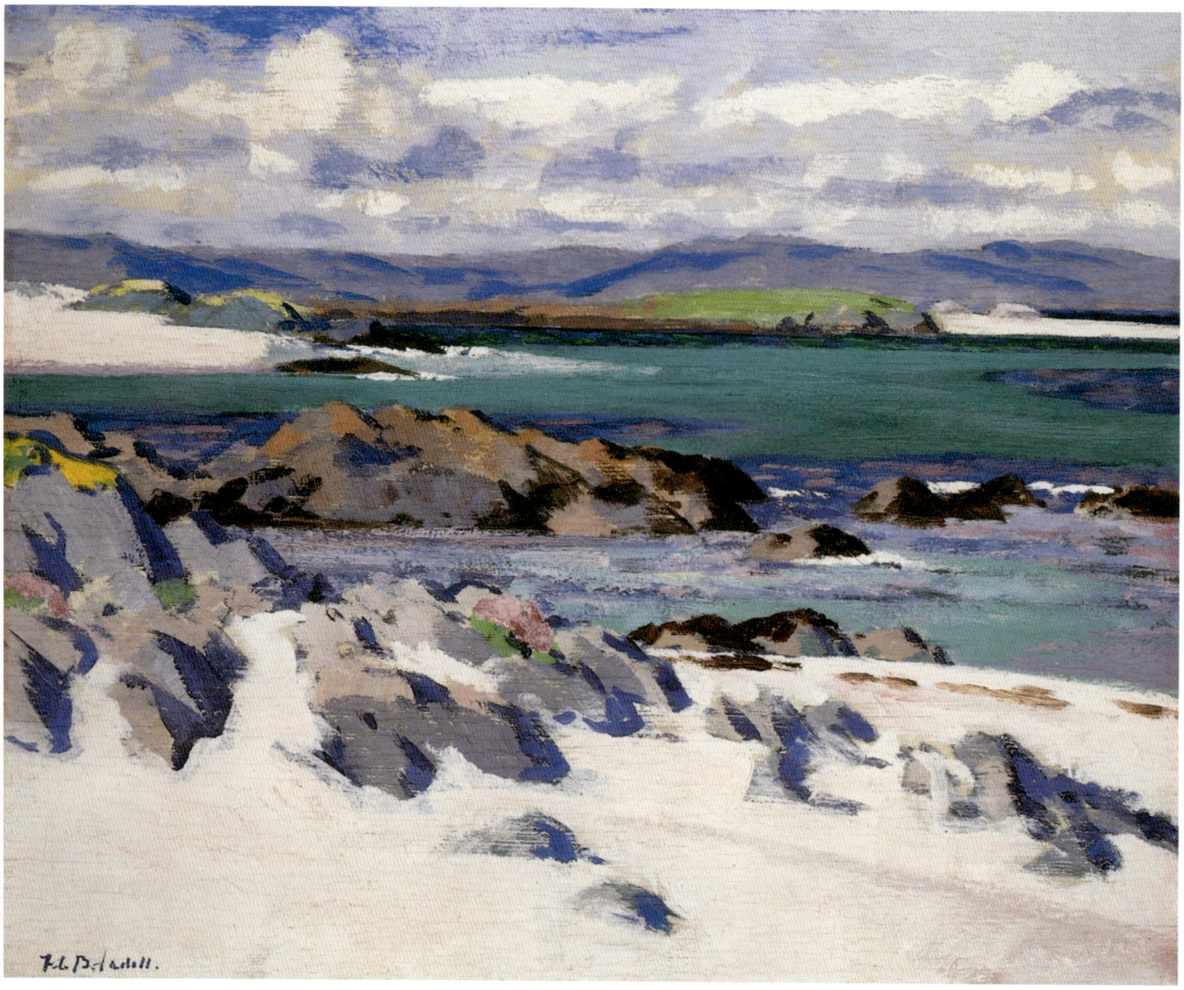

[PLATE 53]
F. C. B. Cadell
The East Bay
Oil 15 x 18

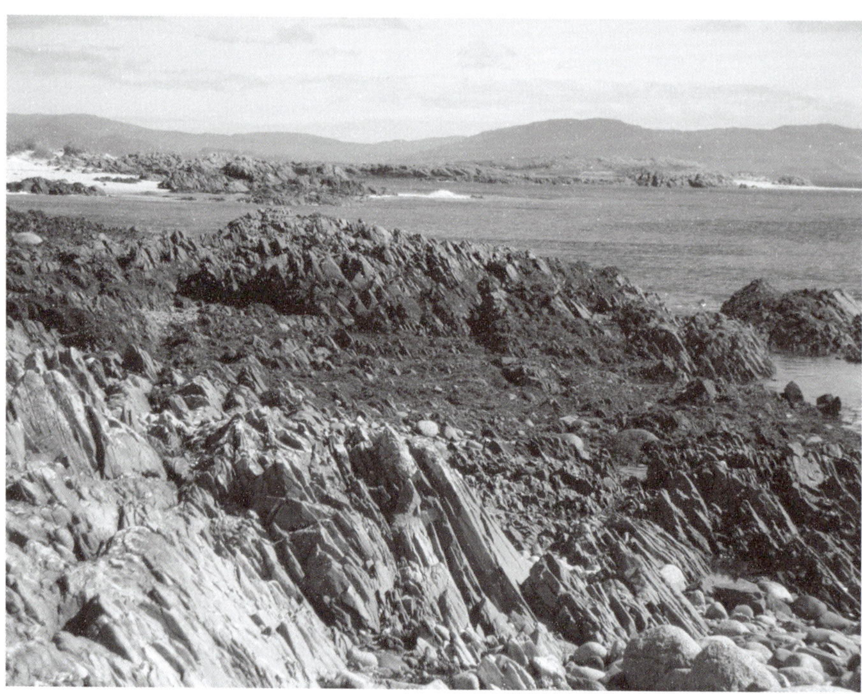

Photograph 2010

The far end of the White Strand is on the left, and the beach of Eilean Annraidh is on the right. This viewpoint is the most southerly of the painting locations illustrated in this chapter.

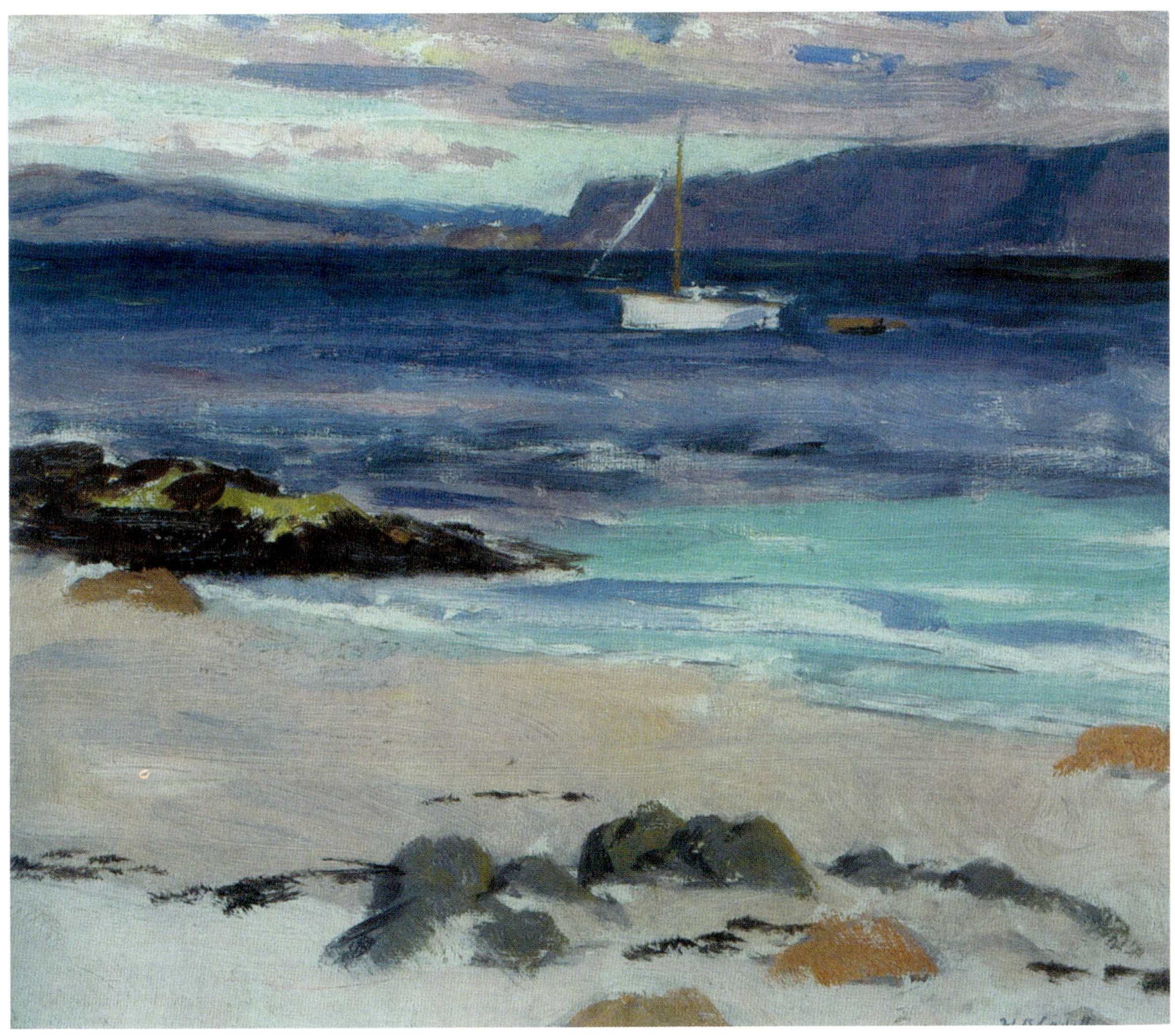

Painted from the south end of the White Strand, this is the view to the northeast, and shows the vertical step of the cliffs at Gribun central on the horizon.

[PLATE 54]
F. C. B. Cadell
Towards Loch na Keal
Oil 15 x 18

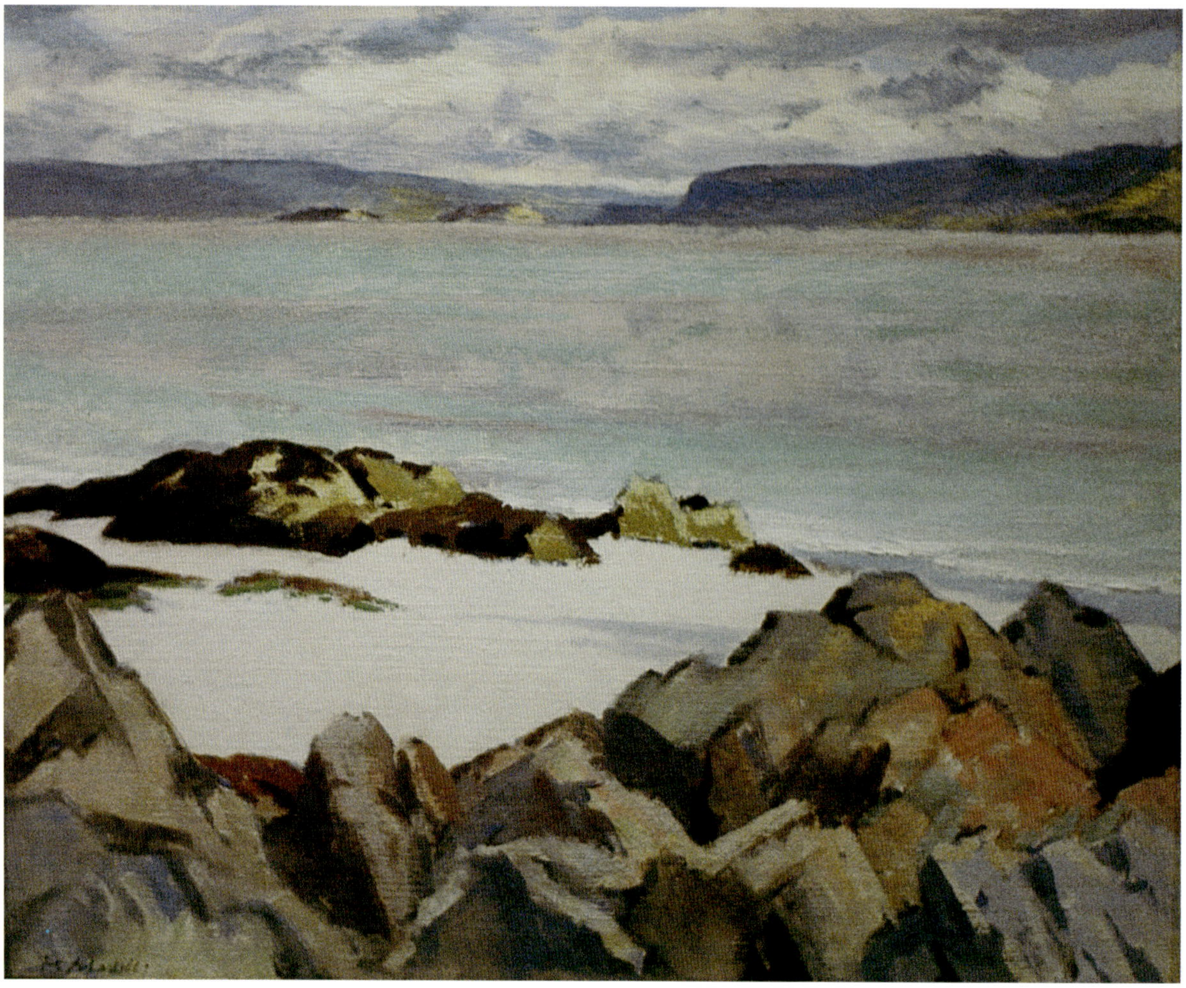

[PLATE 55]

F. C. B. Cadell

IONA, LOCH NA KEAL

Oil 15 x 18

The Hunterian, University of Glasgow

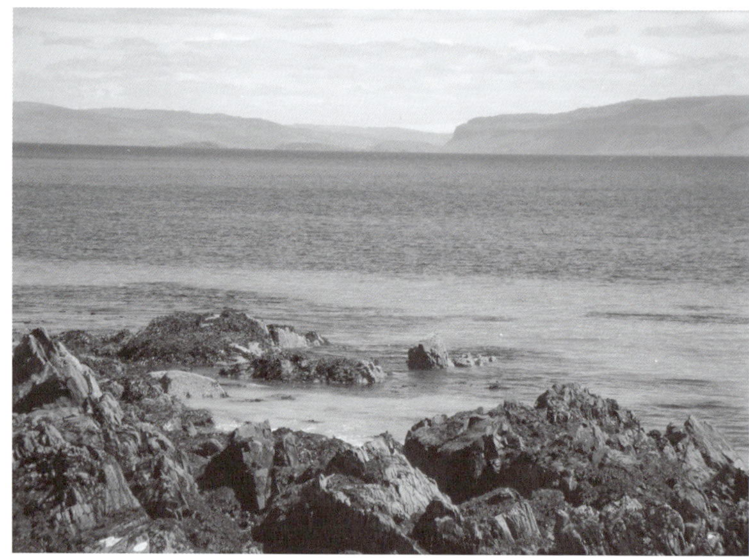

Photograph 2010

As with the preceding picture the cliffs at Gribun are seen almost central on the horizon. To the left of these, from right to left, are the three islands of Eorsa, Inch Kenneth, and Erisgeir. From this angle they appear closely spaced like stepping stones, but are in reality at quite different distances.

The foreground rocks are accurately painted, but with the lower sand levels of recent years they are now more exposed. In the photograph the water is at about the same level as the sand in the painting, which assists recognition.

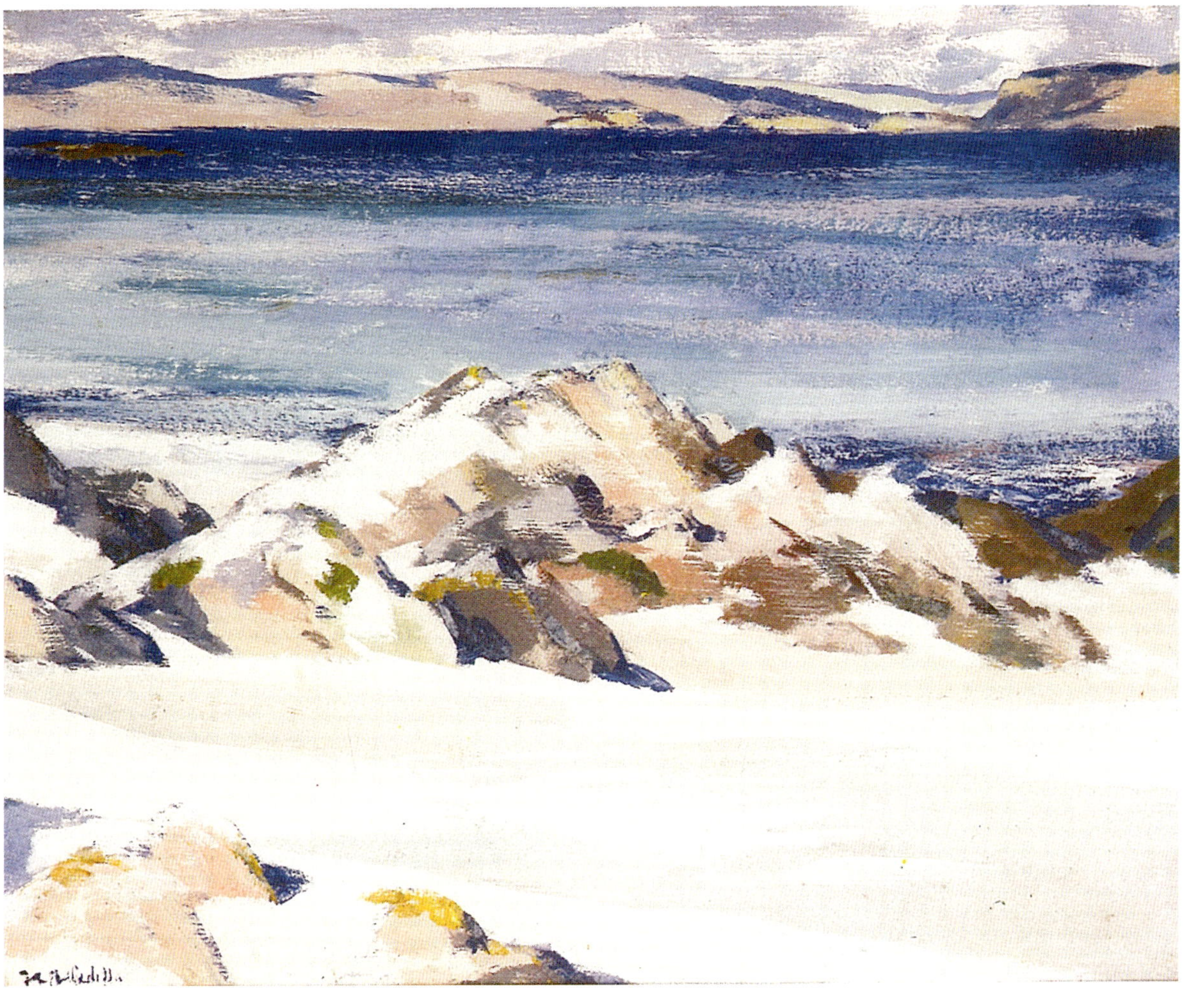

[PLATE 56]
F. C. B. Cadell
Towards Loch na Keal
Oil 15 x 18

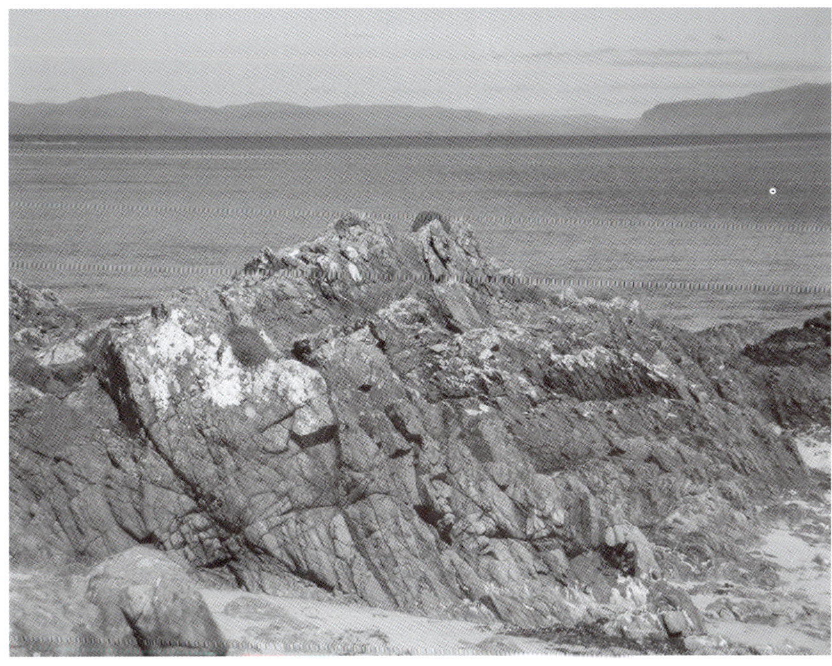

Photograph 2010

Painted from close to Plate 55, this view towards Loch na Keal is a little further round to the north, with the cliffs at Gribun seen near the right-hand side. The same three islands are shown but in this picture Erisgeir is almost exactly central.

The rock in the foreground appears much taller in the photograph than in the painting owing to the lower sand level.

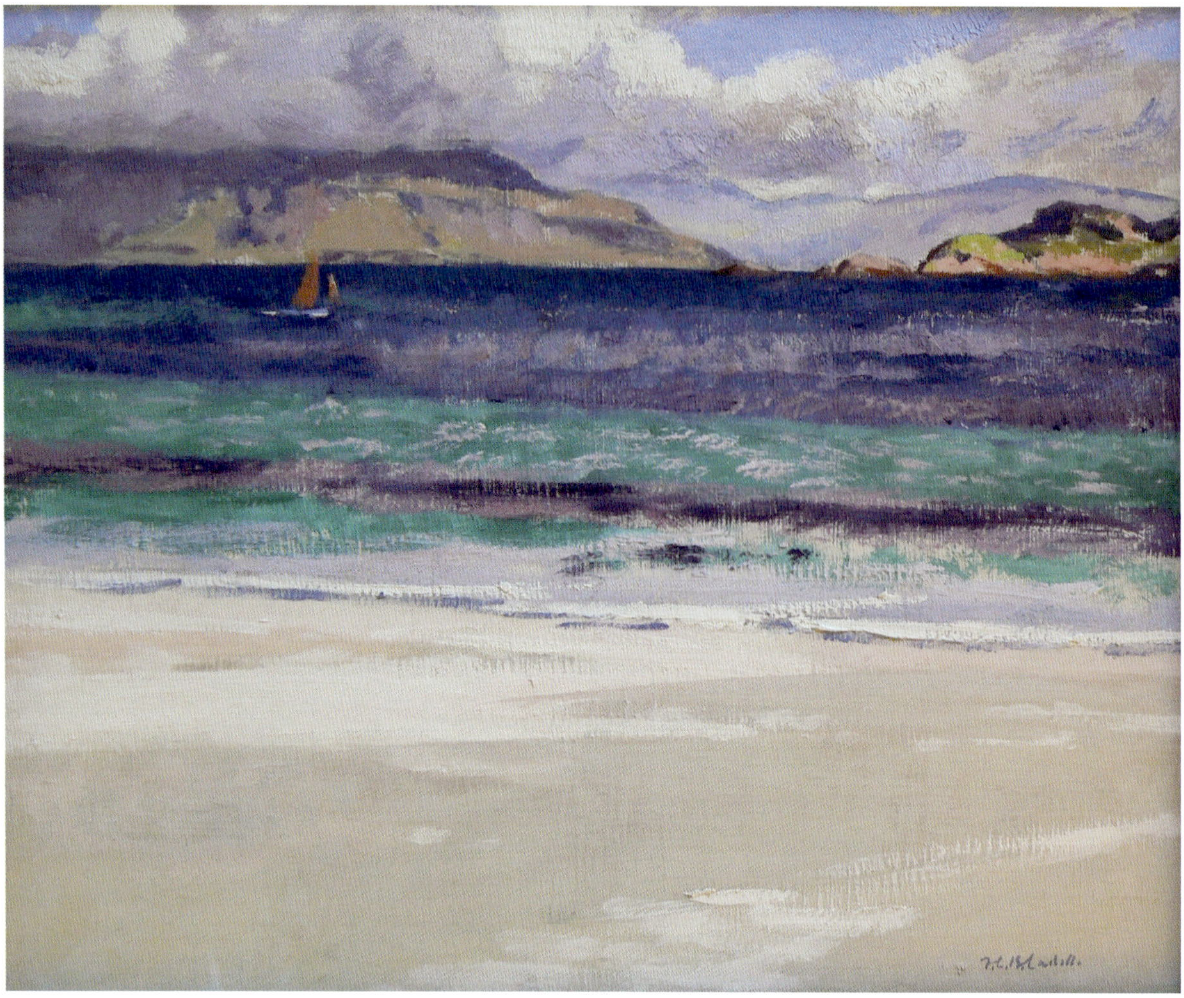

[PLATE 57]

F. C. B. Cadell

Towards Loch Scridain

Oil 15 x 18

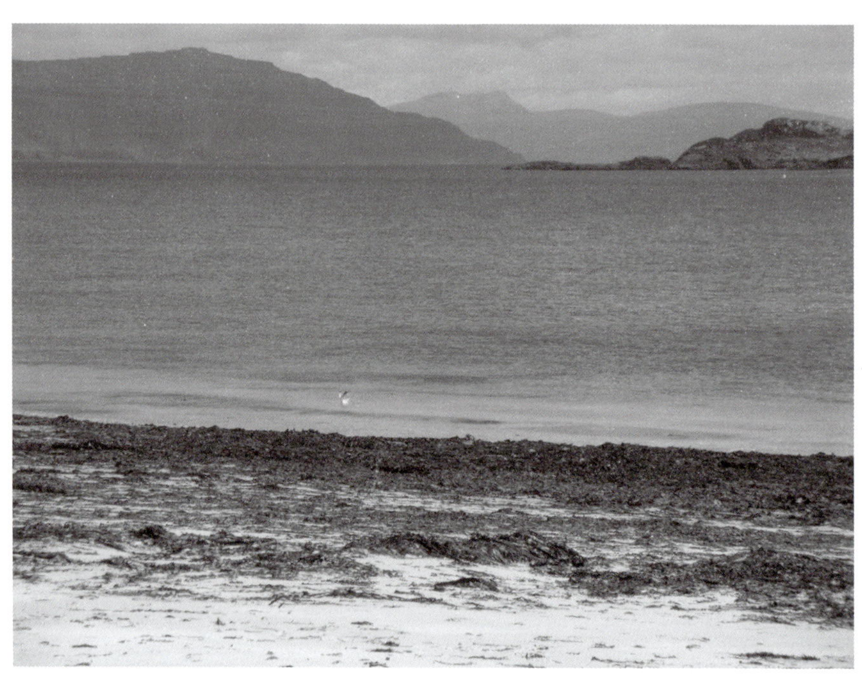

Photograph 2012

Painted from the south end of the White Strand, this is the view almost due east to Loch Scridain, with the south end of the Burg on the left, the Ross of Mull on the right, and Ben Buie central in the far distance, partly obscured by cloud.

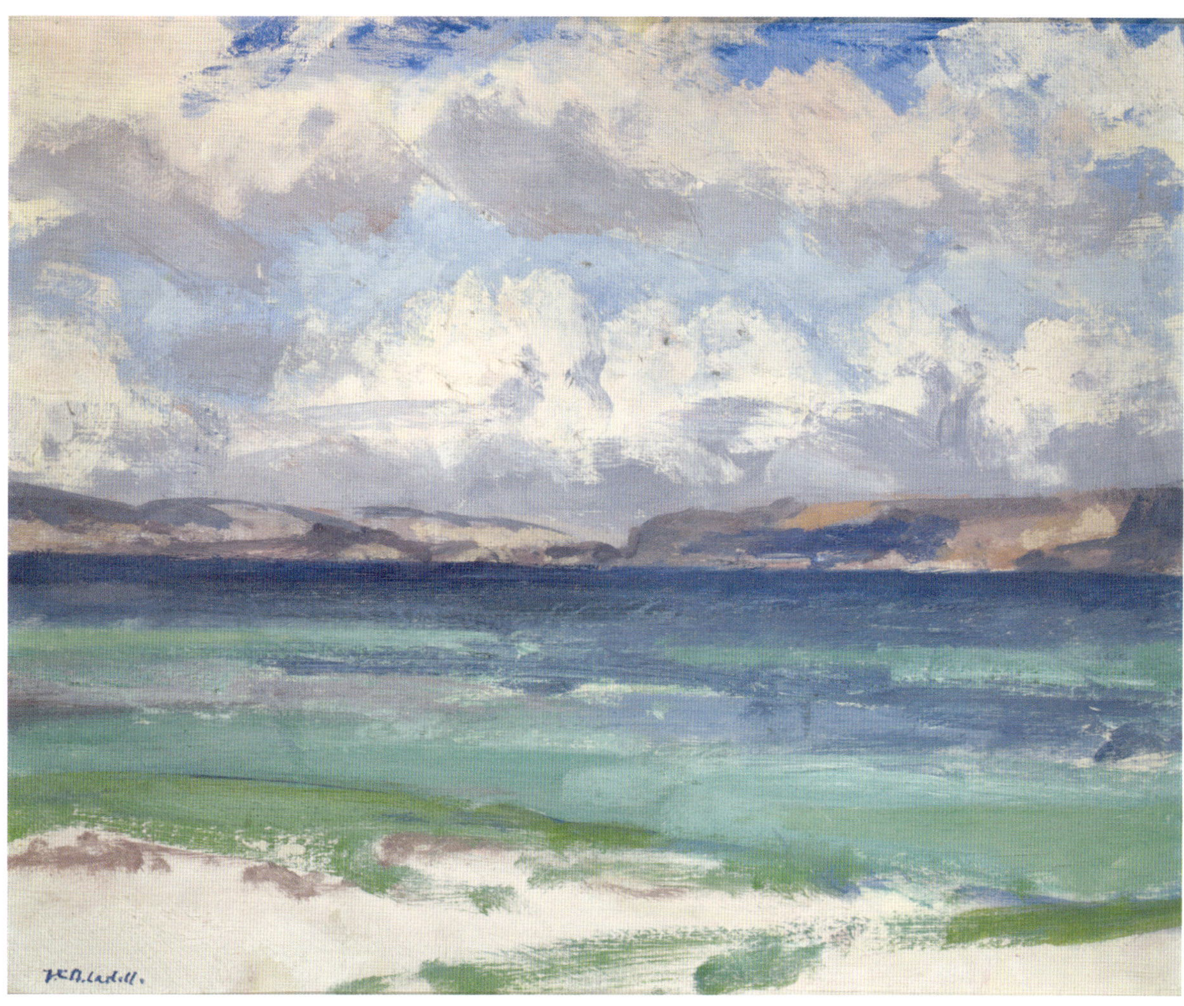

The exact location of this picture is difficult to determine as the profile of the dunes in this area has changed. However it was painted from above the White Strand looking towards Loch na Keal with the vertical step of the cliffs at Gribun in the centre. The picture is notable for its beautifully rendered fairweather cumulus sky which occupies more than half the painting.

[PLATE 58]
F. C. B. Cadell
Towards Loch na Keal
Oil 15 x 18

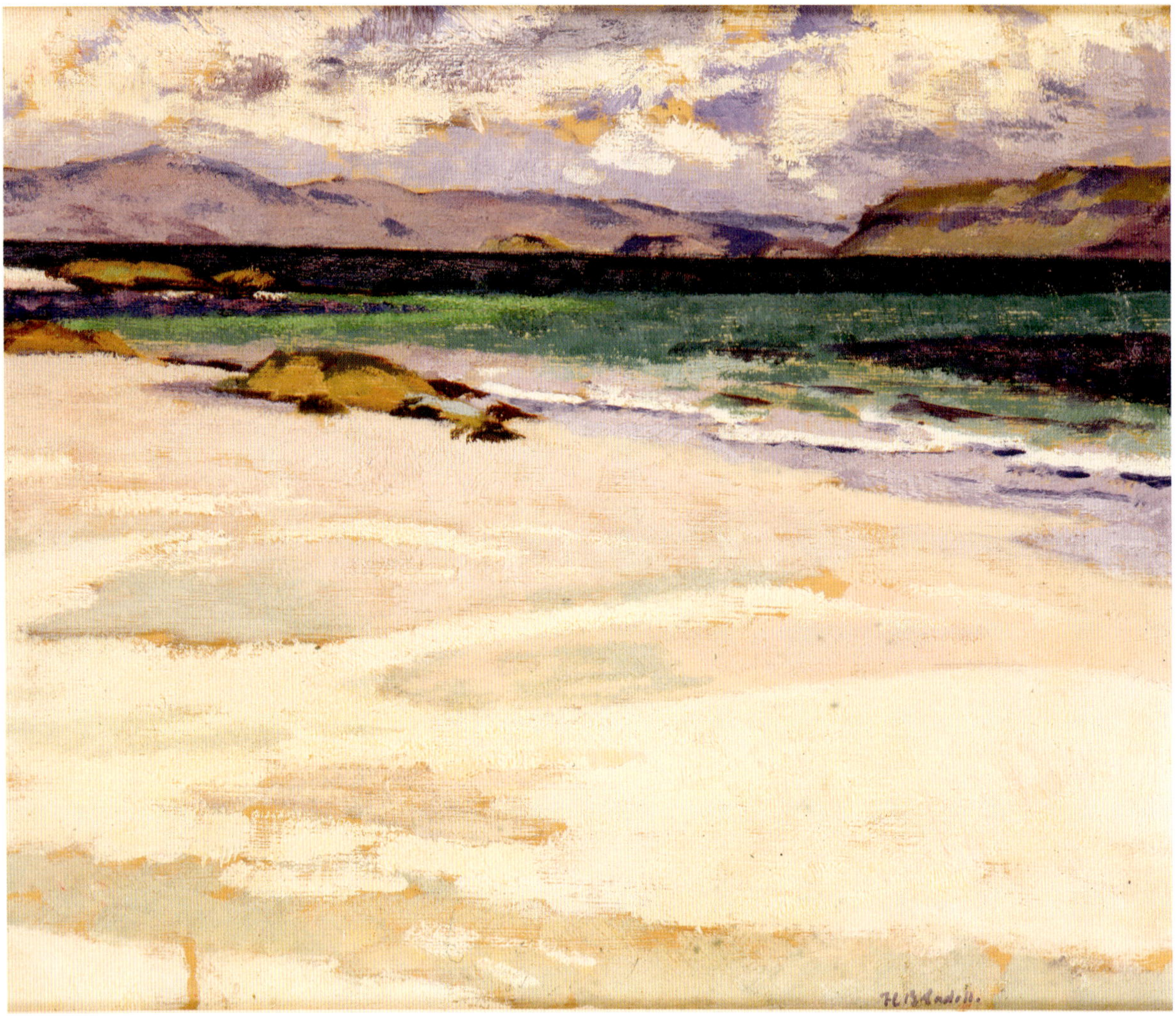

[PLATE 59]
F. C. B. Cadell
The White Strand
Oil 15 x 18

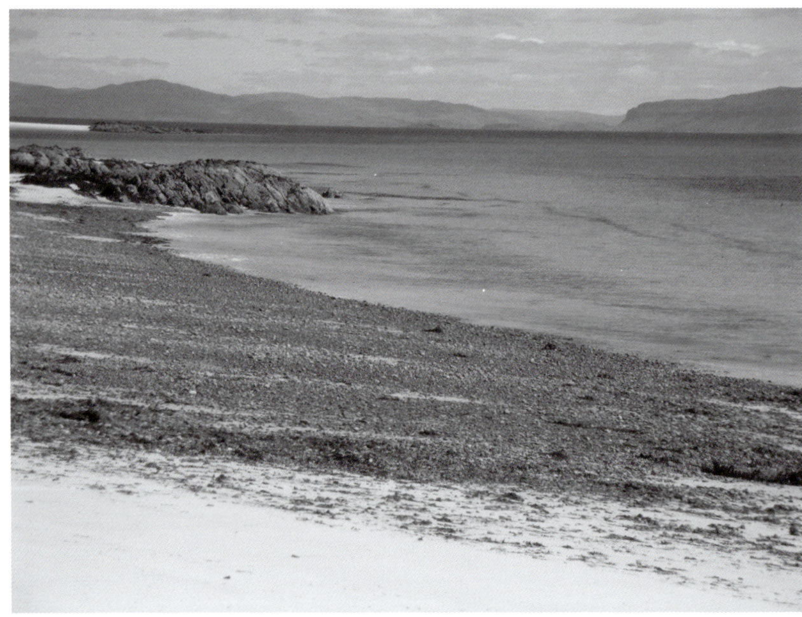

Photograph 2010

The Whaleback Rock is seen at the water's edge left of centre. The distant elements are the same as those in Plate 56. The change in the appearance of the beach is graphically illustrated here by comparing the painting with the recent photograph.

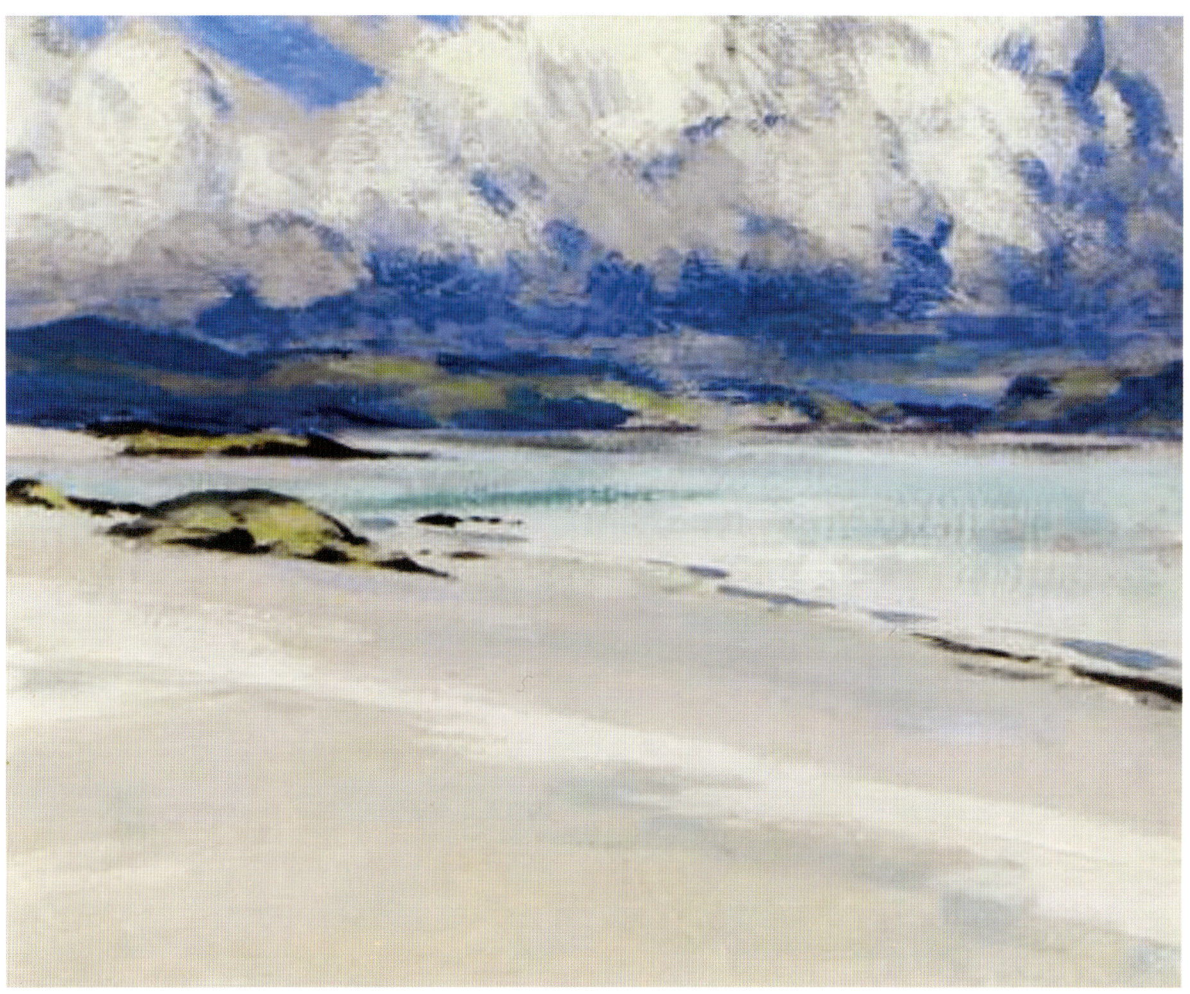

This is the same view as the preceding picture, painted from a short distance along the White Strand. The horizon is lower here and the more active sky plays a more important part in the overall effect. The Whaleback is on the left, with the end of Eilean Annraidh beyond it. The cliffs at Gribun are on the right.

[PLATE 60]
F. C. B. Cadell
The White Strand
Oil 15 x 18

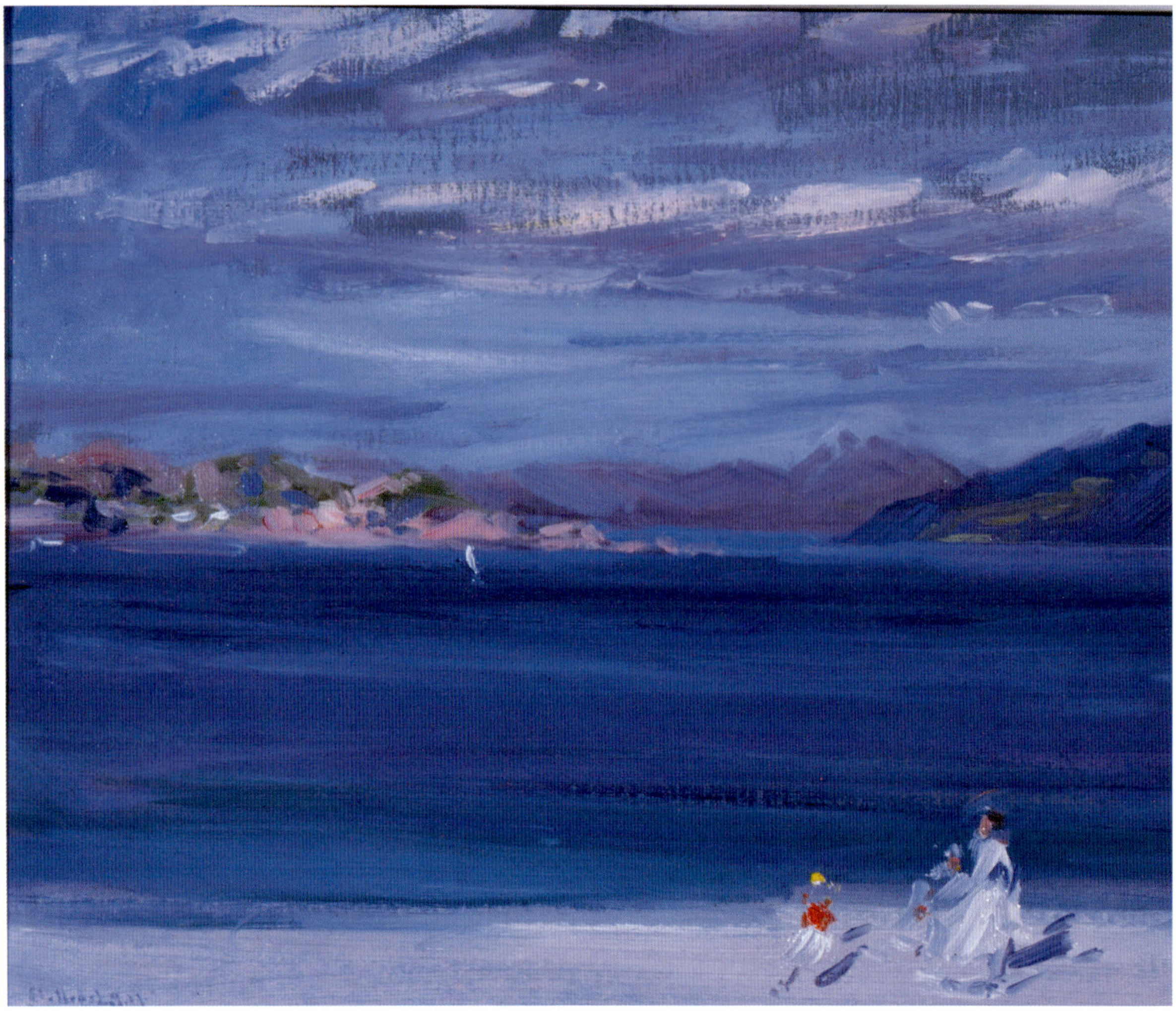

[PLATE 61]

F. C. B. Cadell

Towards Loch Scridain
(The Tail of Mull from Iona)
Oil 15 x 18

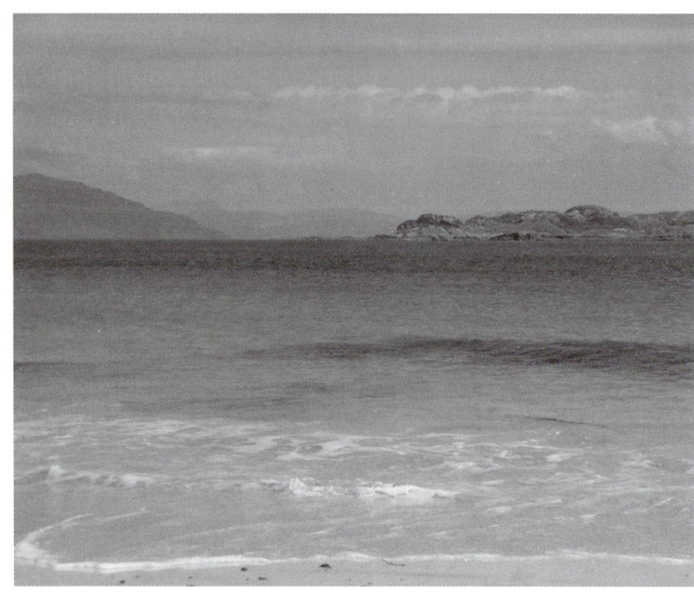

Photograph 2010

Painted from about halfway along the White Strand, this shows the south end of the Burg on the left, and Ben Buie in the distance. The "Tail of Mull" in the title refers to the long slender peninsula of the Ross of Mull, seen here on the right.

This painting shows clearly Cadell's early style of long slashing brushstrokes of quite fluid paint, which he used prior to about 1920.

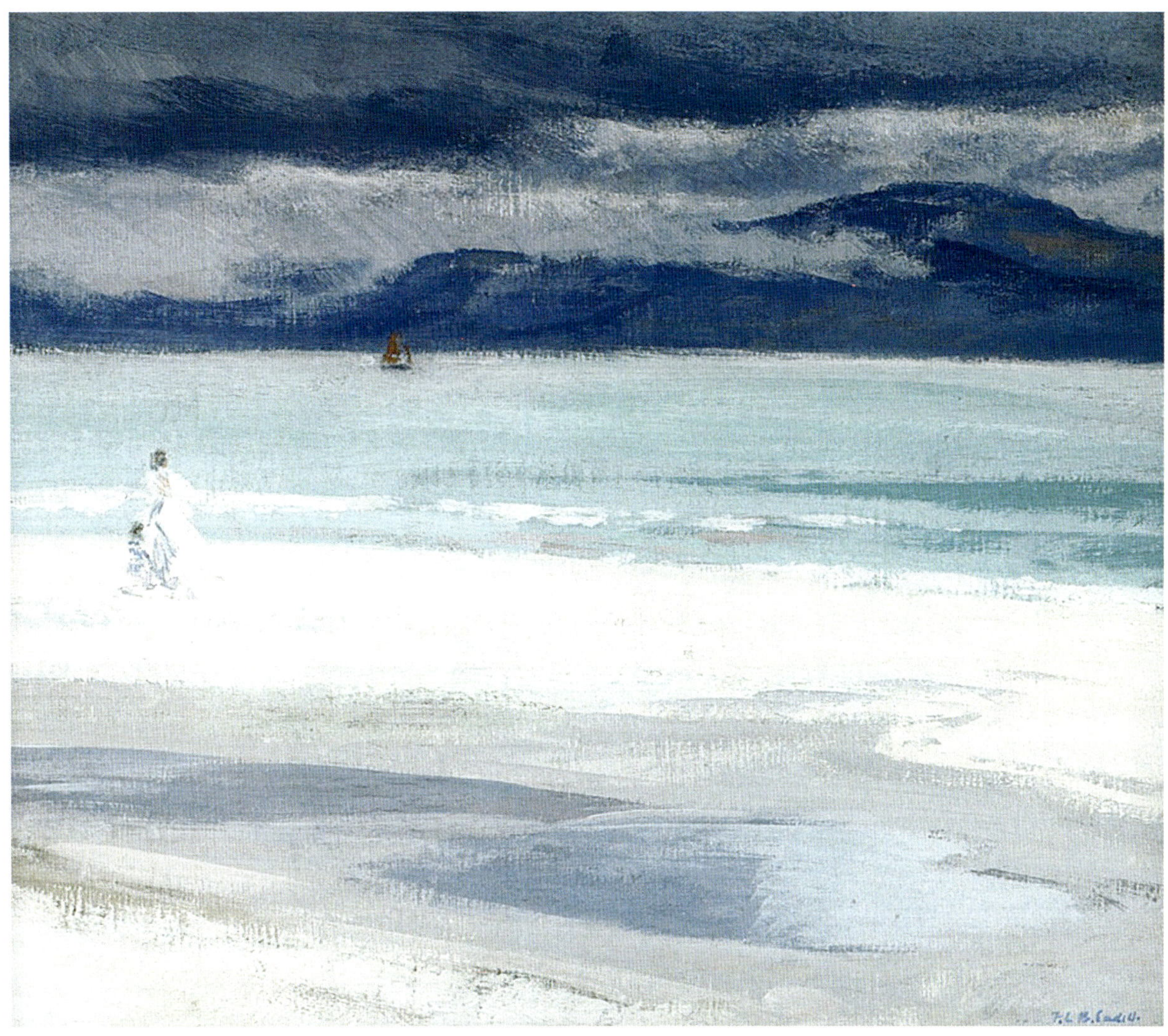

Painted from about the same position as the preceding picture, here the Burg is seen partly shrouded in cloud and in deep shadow, contrasted with the sunlit pale green waters of the Sound.

The low-lying terrain of Iona is often bathed in bright sunshine when the weather is stormy over the high mountains of Mull and the Mainland. In these conditions the colour of the sea is generated by sunlight reflected from the white sandy base of the shallow waters of the Sound, and is independent of the dark sky. This effect is surprising and very beautiful, and occurs not infrequently at this location. Usually the colour of the sea is in some way related, by reflection, to the colour of the sky, but in this picture they are quite different.

[PLATE 62]
F. C. B. Cadell
The Burg from the White Strand
Oil 15 x 18

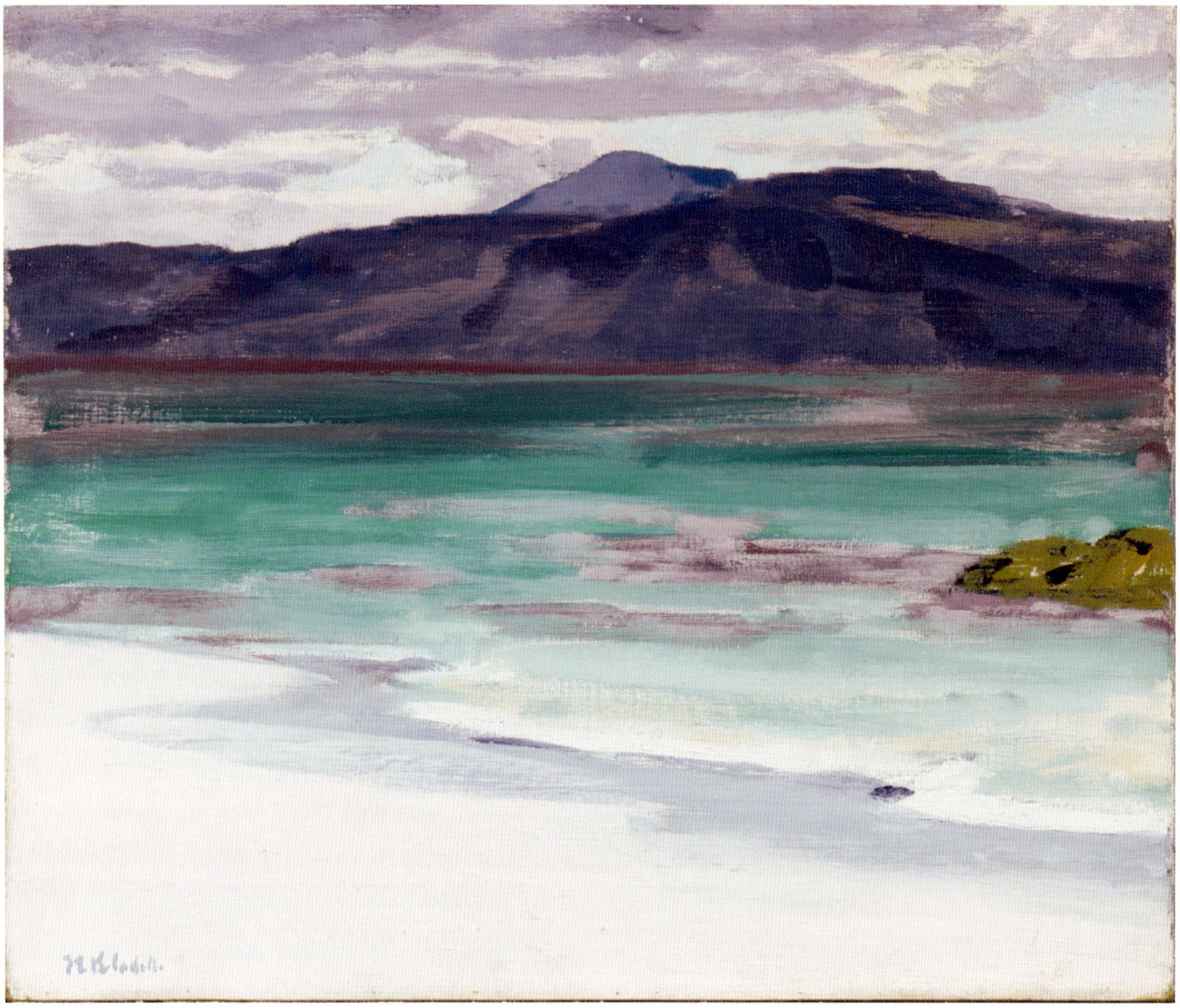

[PLATE 63]
F. C. B. Cadell
The Burg and Ben More from the White Strand
Oil 15 x 18

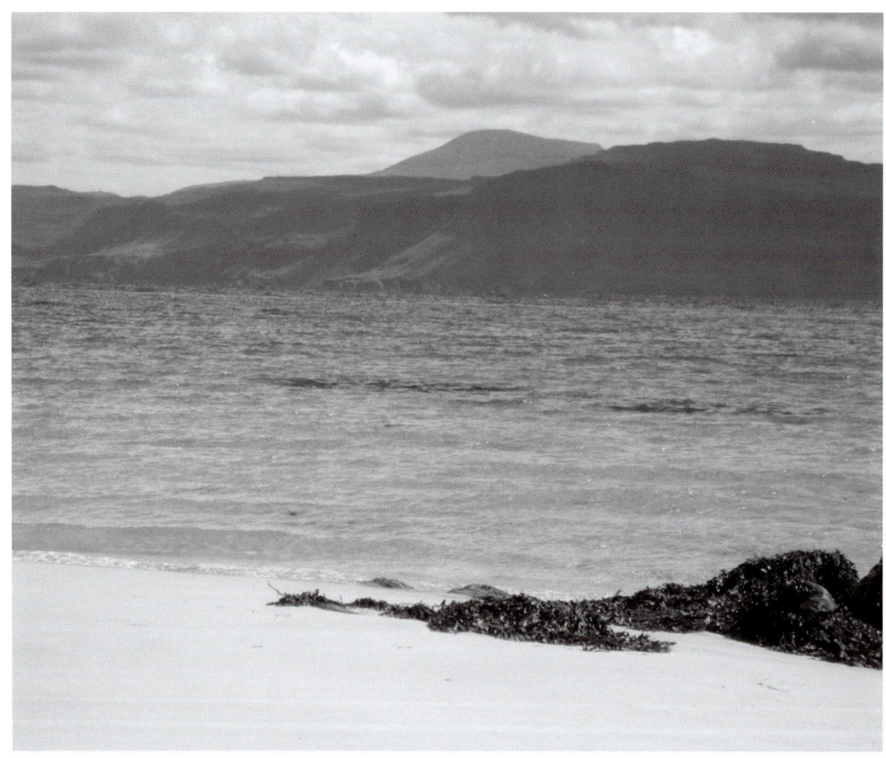

Photograph 2009

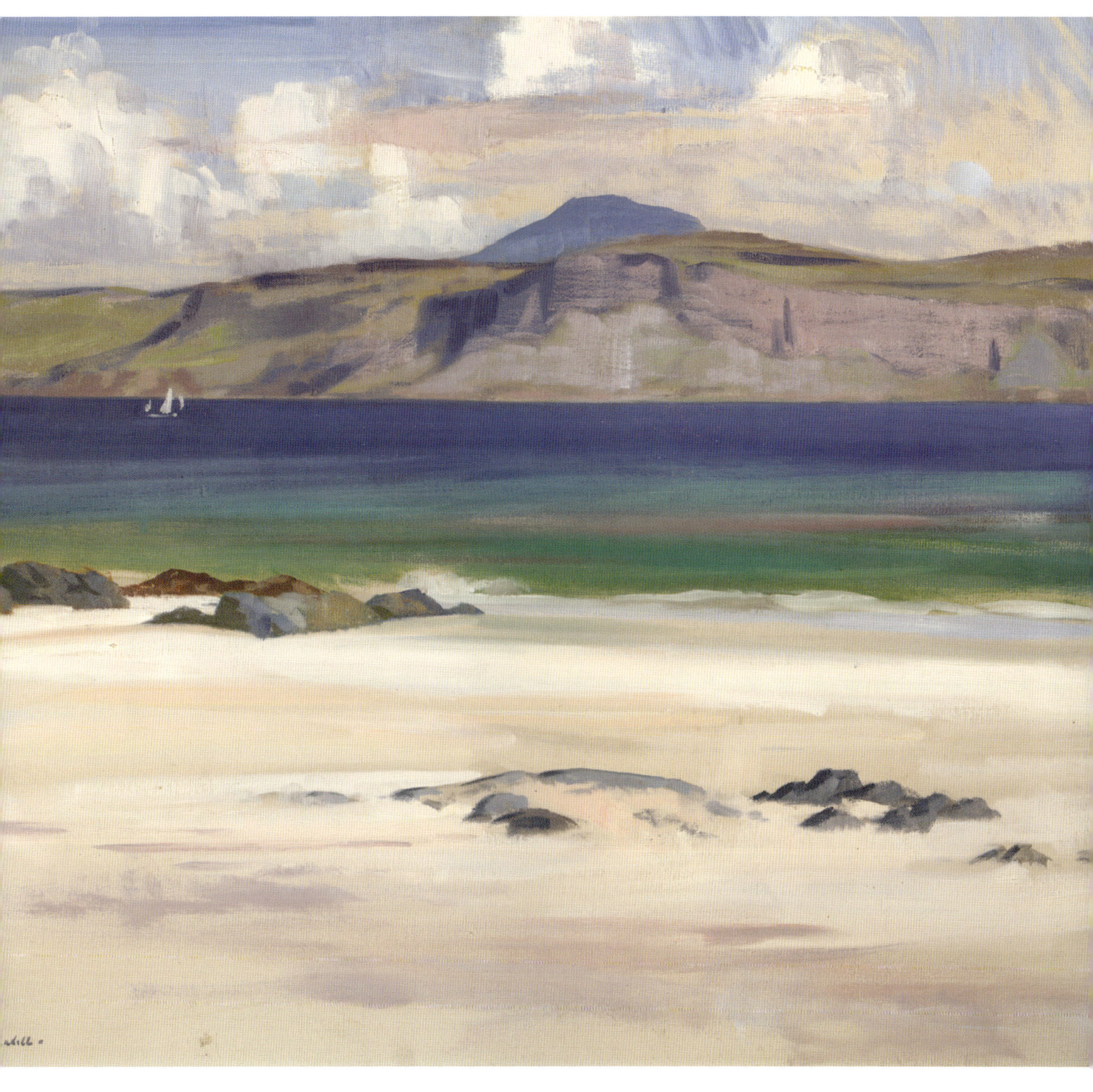

[PLATE 64]

F. C. B. Cadell

The Burg and Ben More
from the White Strand

Oil 25 x 30

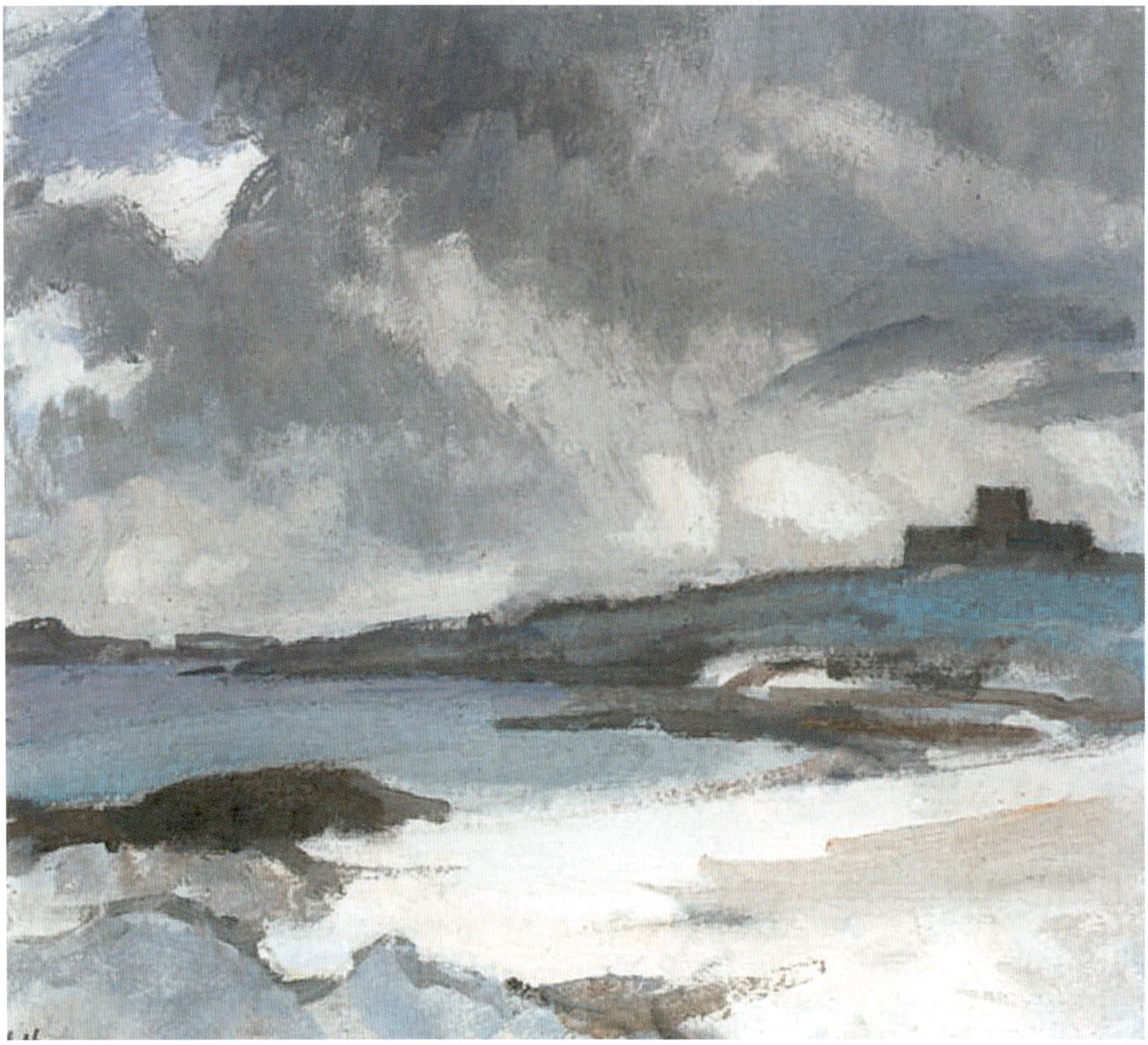

[PLATE 65]

S. J. Peploe

The Abbey from the White Strand

Oil 16 x 20

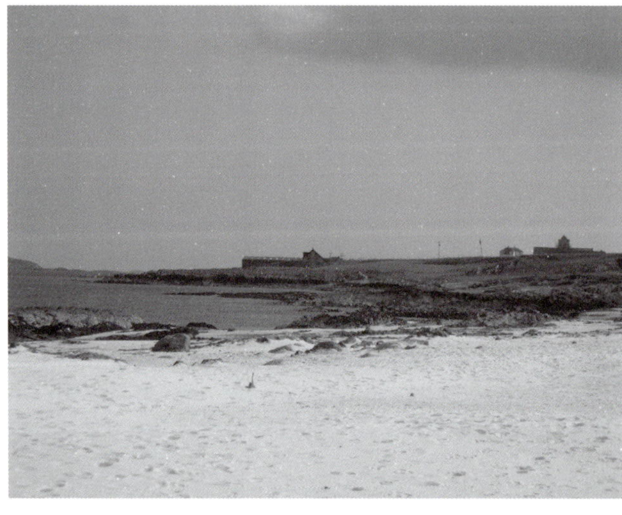

Photograph 2009

This was painted from near Cows Rock looking south along the White Strand. The Abbey is up on the right in the distance.

This is an excellent and very satisfying example of what is frequently called a zig-zag composition. From the centre of the bottom edge of the painting the eye is taken up the rocks diagonally to the left, then back to the right along the shoreline, returning left to the island on the horizon. From here the eye is led up the slope to the Abbey and finally diagonally upwards across the grey band of clouds to the brightly lit patch of sky in the top left corner.

4 · THE NORTH END

THE term "North End" may be used in a general sense, but here I use it more specifically to mean the area from Cows Rock to The Headland. This section of shore, just 200 metres, has been painted more intensively than any other part of Iona, and possibly anywhere in the whole of Scotland.

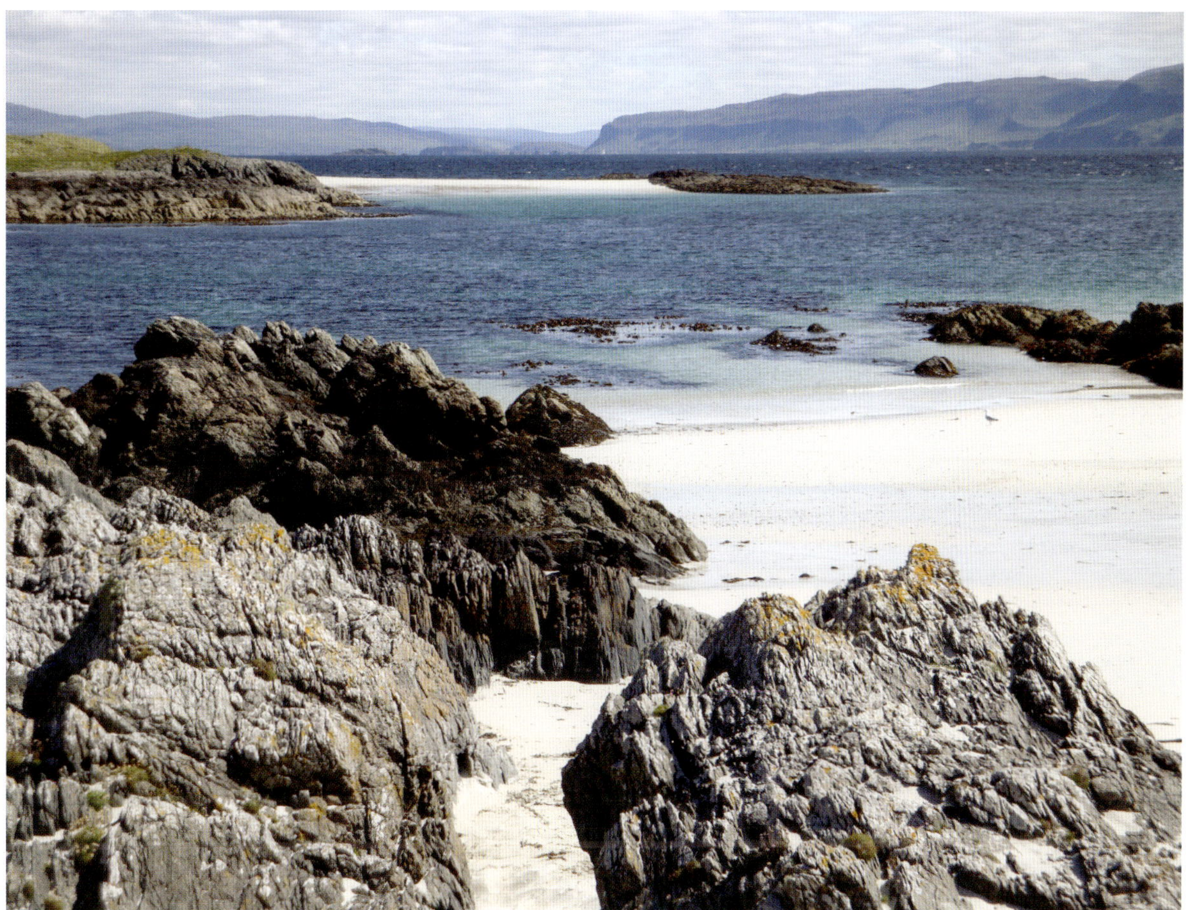

Having walked along the White Strand one arrives first at Cows Rock on the right. The gap between Cows Rock and the dunes leads through to another beach beyond Cows Rock, with a spectacular view to the north (Plate 78). This, the North End Beach, is divided by a rock known as A'Chorrag (The Finger), which is underwater at high tide, but at low tide is revealed as a long slender ridge pointing northeast towards Eilean Annraidh (Island of Storm). In the photograph above, the lower end of the Finger is at the water's edge on the right-hand side, and Eilean Annraidh is in the middle distance.

The Beach is bounded on the north by a rocky headland, which is the extreme northeast corner of Iona, and which includes the conspicuous Cathedral and Pulpit Rocks. The Headland is separated from the mainland of Iona by a cleft known as Mermaids Corridor (Figure 14 overleaf).

As there are so many paintings of this area, for ease of description it is divided into three sections: firstly, Cows Rock (Plates 66 to 91), secondly, the North End Beach (Plates 92 to 118), and lastly, the Headland (Plates 119 to 137).

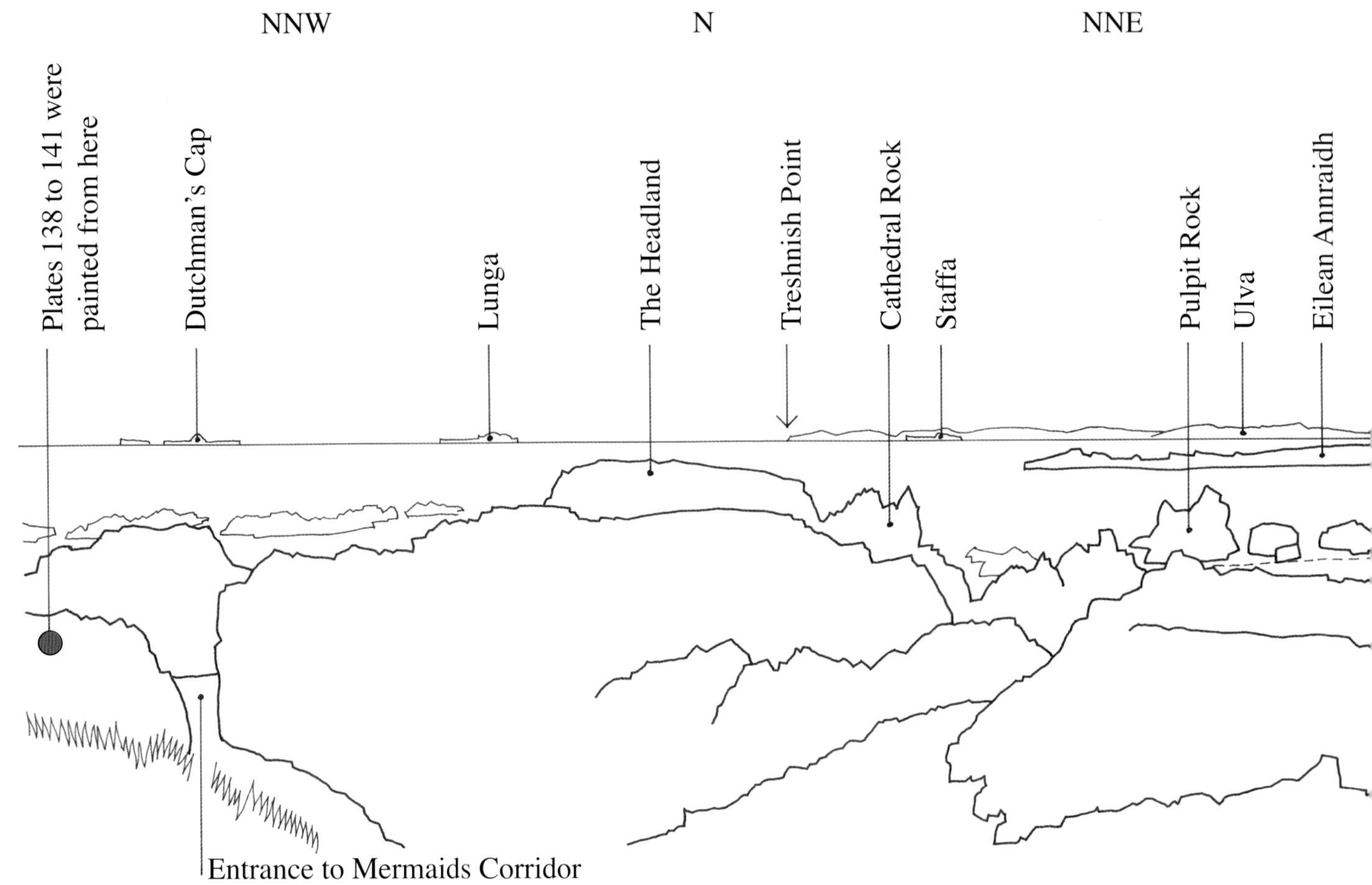

[FIGURE 14]
The Principal Features of the North End

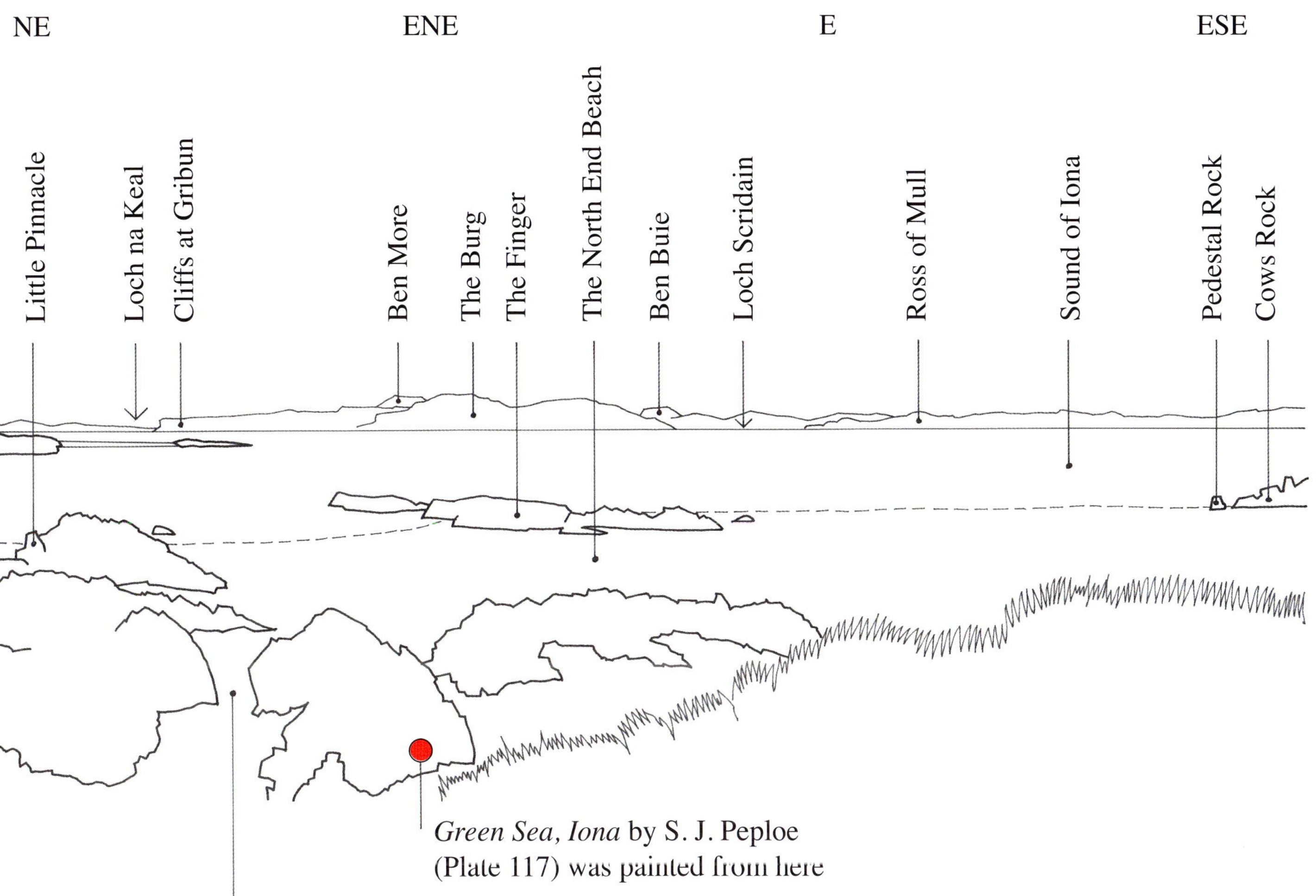
NE
ENE
E
ESE
Little Pinnacle
Loch na Keal
Cliffs at Gribun
Ben More
The Burg
The Finger
The North End Beach
Ben Buie
Loch Scridain
Ross of Mull
Sound of Iona
Pedestal Rock
Cows Rock
Green Sea, Iona by S. J. Peploe
(Plate 117) was painted from here
The Narrow Gap (see Plates 109 to 116)

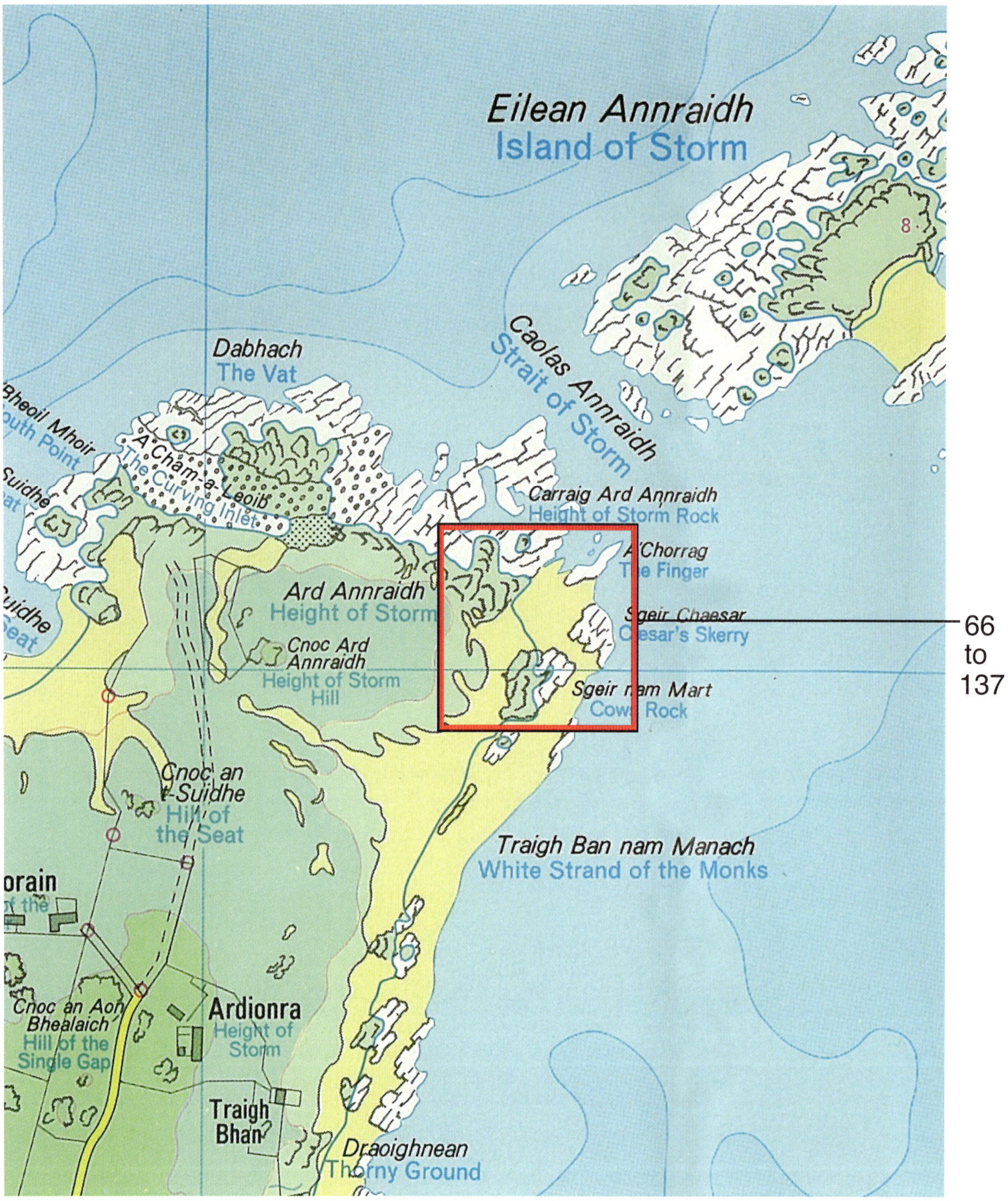

$^{1}/_{2}$ Mile (800 metres)

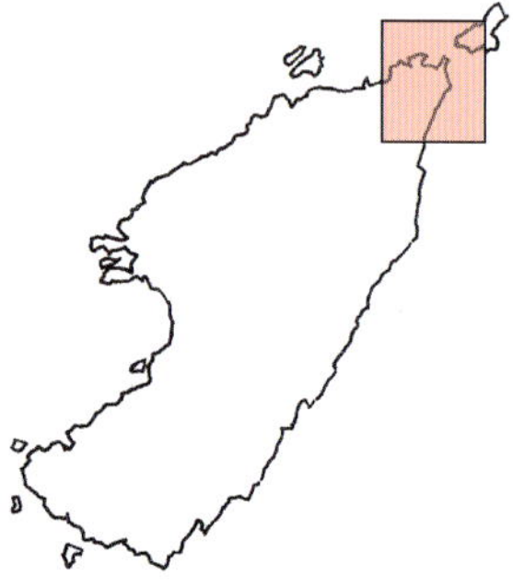

[FIGURE 15]
Locations of paintings illustrated in Chapter 4

COWS ROCK

Cows Rock varies in appearance depending on the state of the sand. Many paintings show considerable amounts of sand on top of the rock, with only the high points protruding, but usually, in recent times, it has been almost clear of sand.

Being raised above the general level of the shore, Cows Rock provides an excellent panoramic view. Clockwise from the north one can see the Treshnish Islands of the Dutchman's Cap and Lunga, then Rhum, Skye, Staffa, the northwest of Mull, Gometra, Ulva, Loch na Keal and its various islands, Gribun, Ben More, The Burg, Loch Scridain and the Ross of Mull.

Cadell painted a number of figure studies of bathers, the model being his manservant, Charles Oliver. The rocks in these studies have the tilted slabby appearance of Cows Rock, and it is likely they were painted in this area. Geologically the rocks are metamorphosed sandstones, mudstones, and shales. The original bedding plane is now tilted up at a steep angle. The east shore of Iona is composed of this type of rock, and one can see the characteristic slope in the rocks down this side of the island. At the North End the near vertical bedding plane gives rise to many interesting formations, including The Finger and Cathedral Rock.

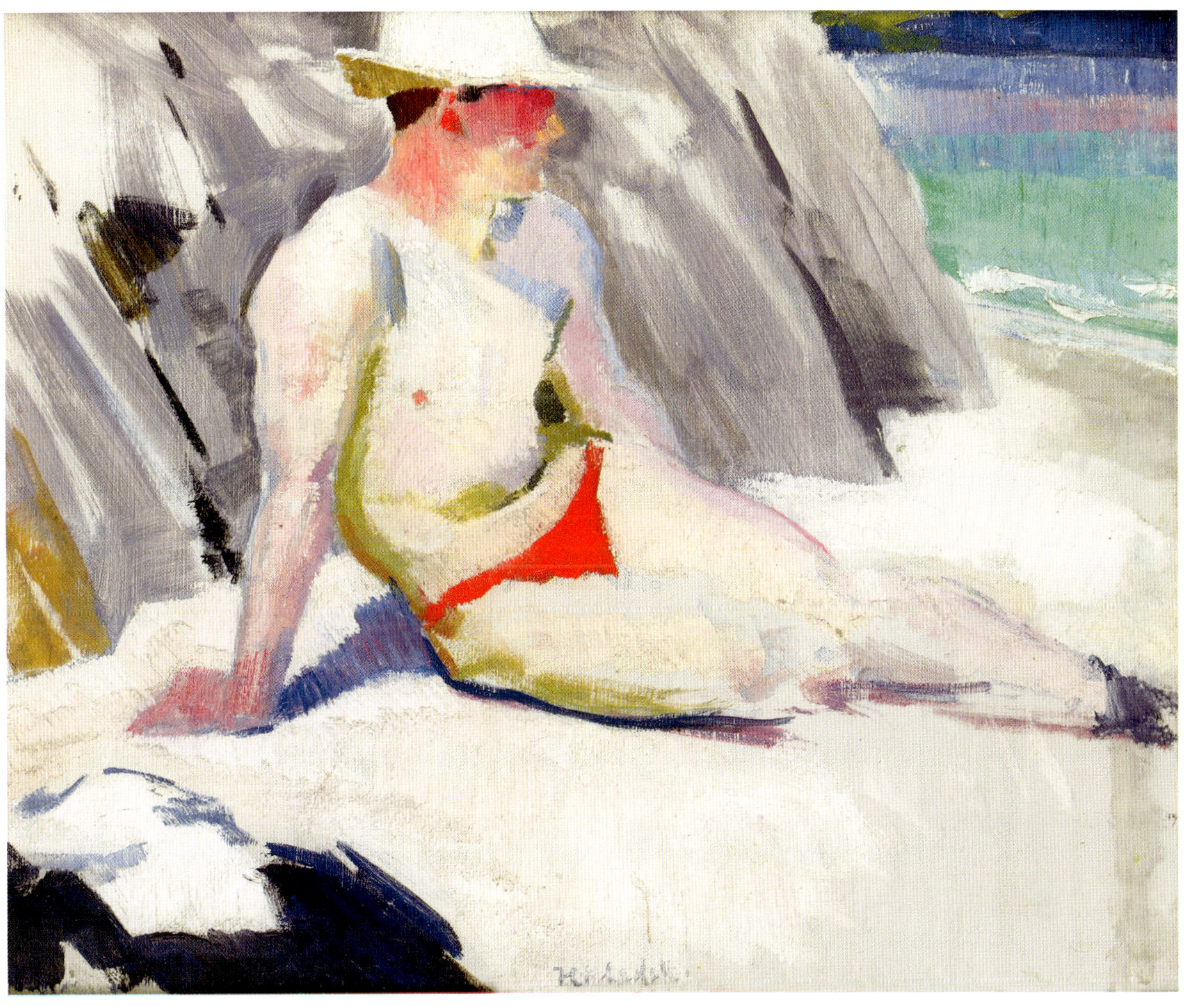

[PLATE 66]
F. C. B. Cadell
Charles Oliver on the beach
Oil 15 x 18

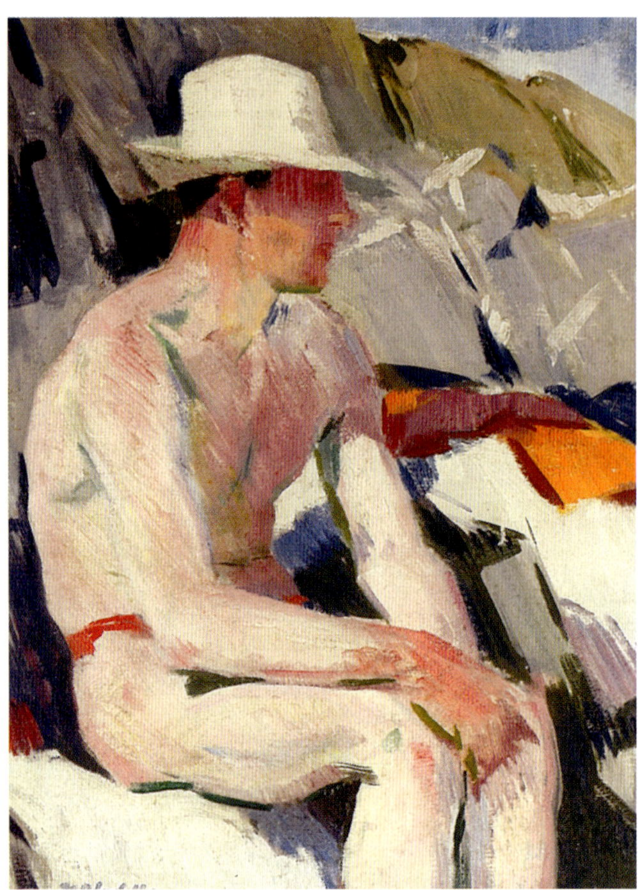

[PLATE 67]
F. C. B. Cadell
Bather
Oil 18 x 15

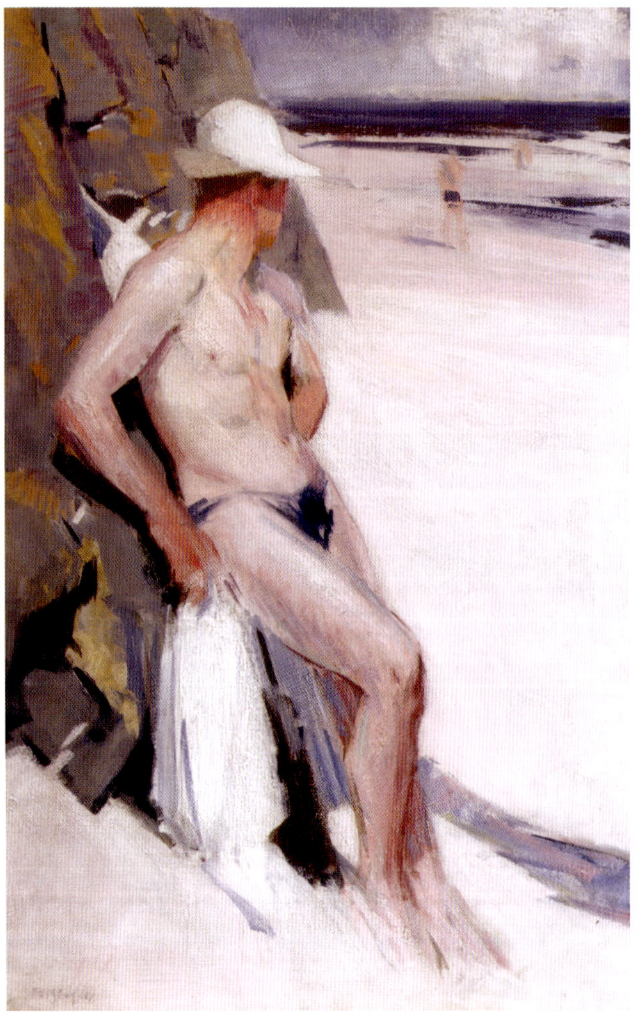

[PLATE 68]
F. C. B. Cadell
Bather
Oil 30 x 20

The subject of the studies of bathers is Cadell's manservant Charles Oliver, who also served as an agent for selling paintings to prospective buyers who were on the island.

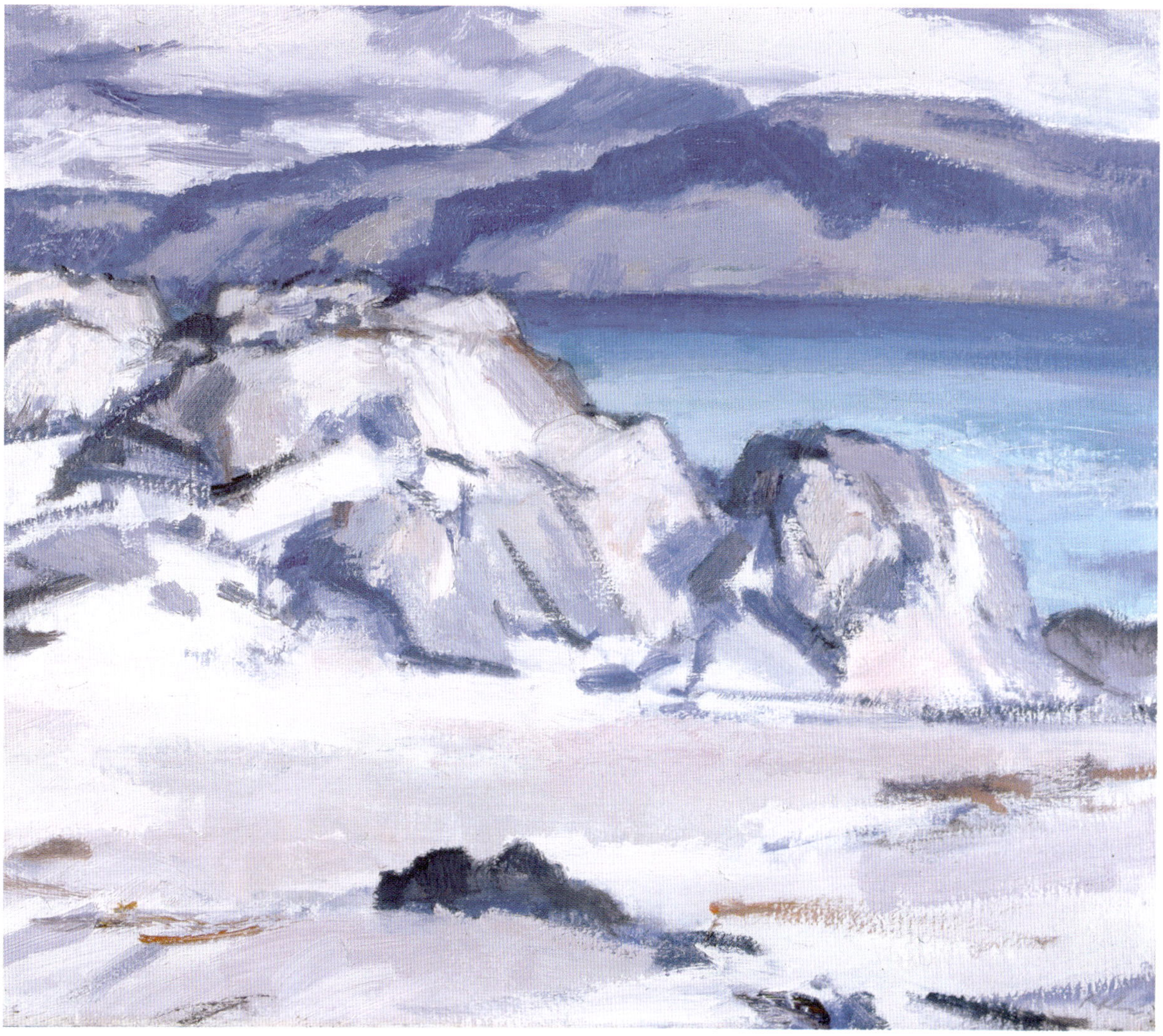

[PLATE 69]

S. J. Peploe

Ben More from Cows Rock

Oil 20 x 24

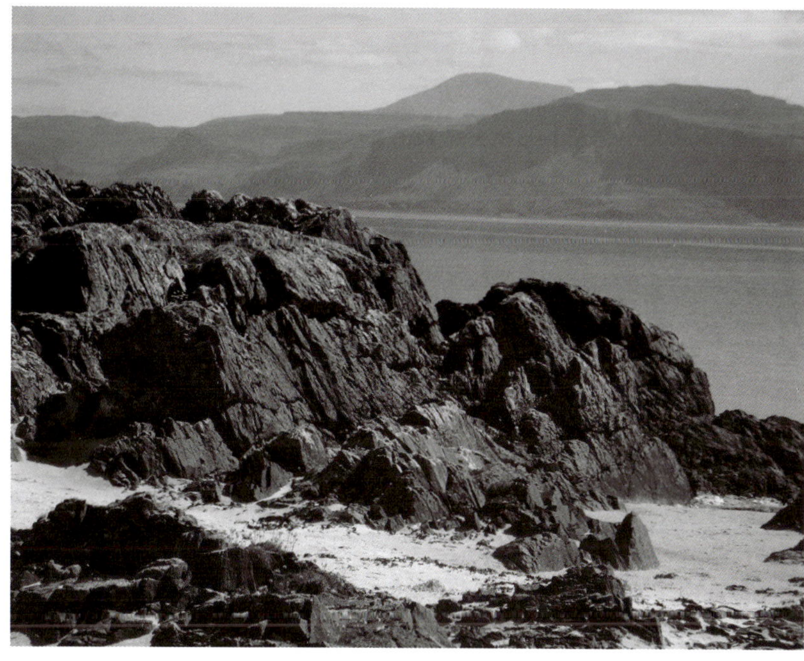

Photograph 2010

The rocks in the foreground are on the south side of Cows Rock, and can be seen on the right as one approaches from along the White Strand. In the distance is the much-painted juxtaposition of the Burg and Ben More.

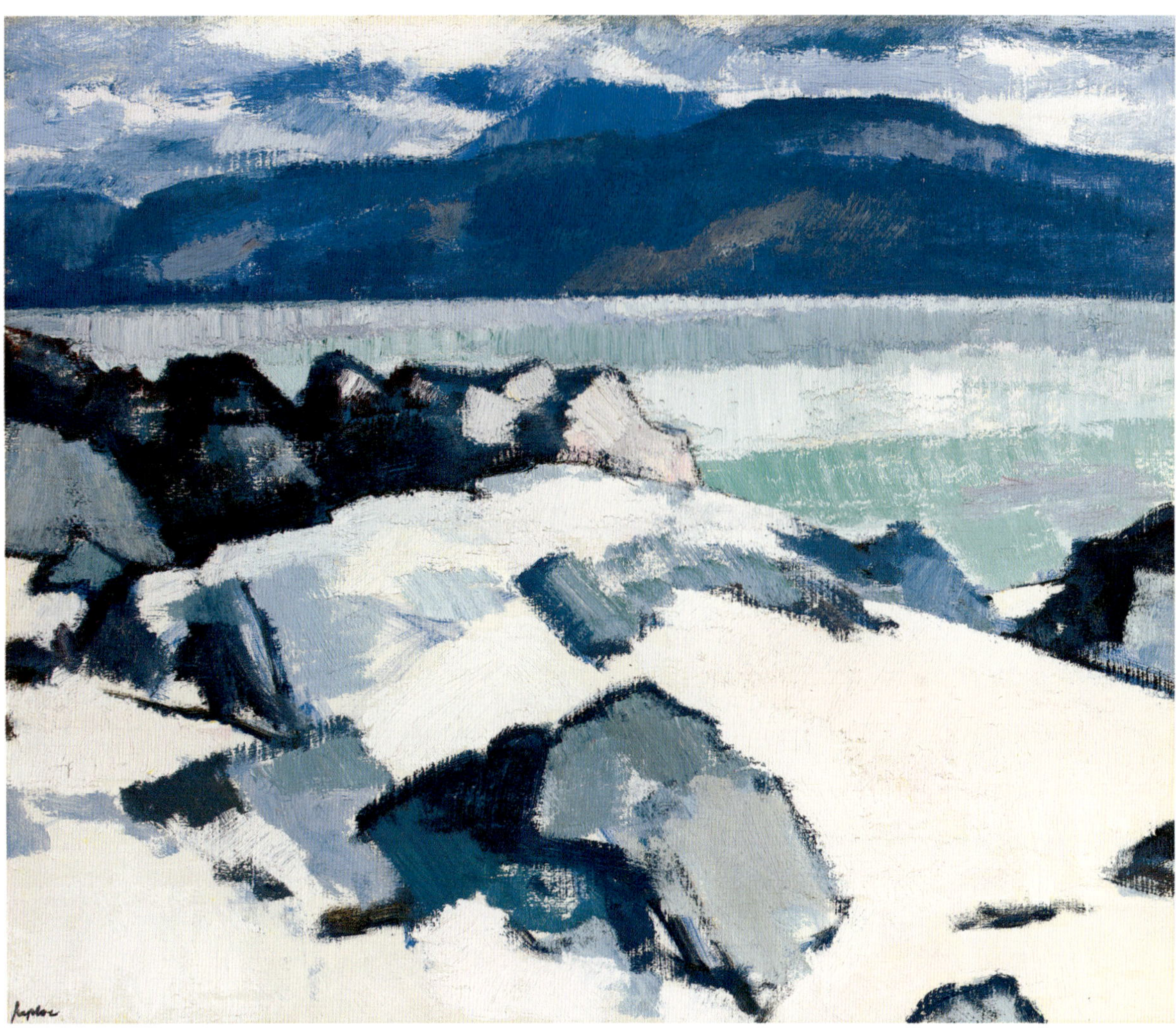

There is a slight shift of viewpoint, but this is essentially the same composition as the preceding picture. The use of a succession of vertical brushstrokes to describe the horizontal bands of the sea is clearly illustrated here. This technique was frequently used by both Cadell and Peploe.

[PLATE 70]

S. J. Peploe

Ben More from Cows Rock

Oil 15 x 18

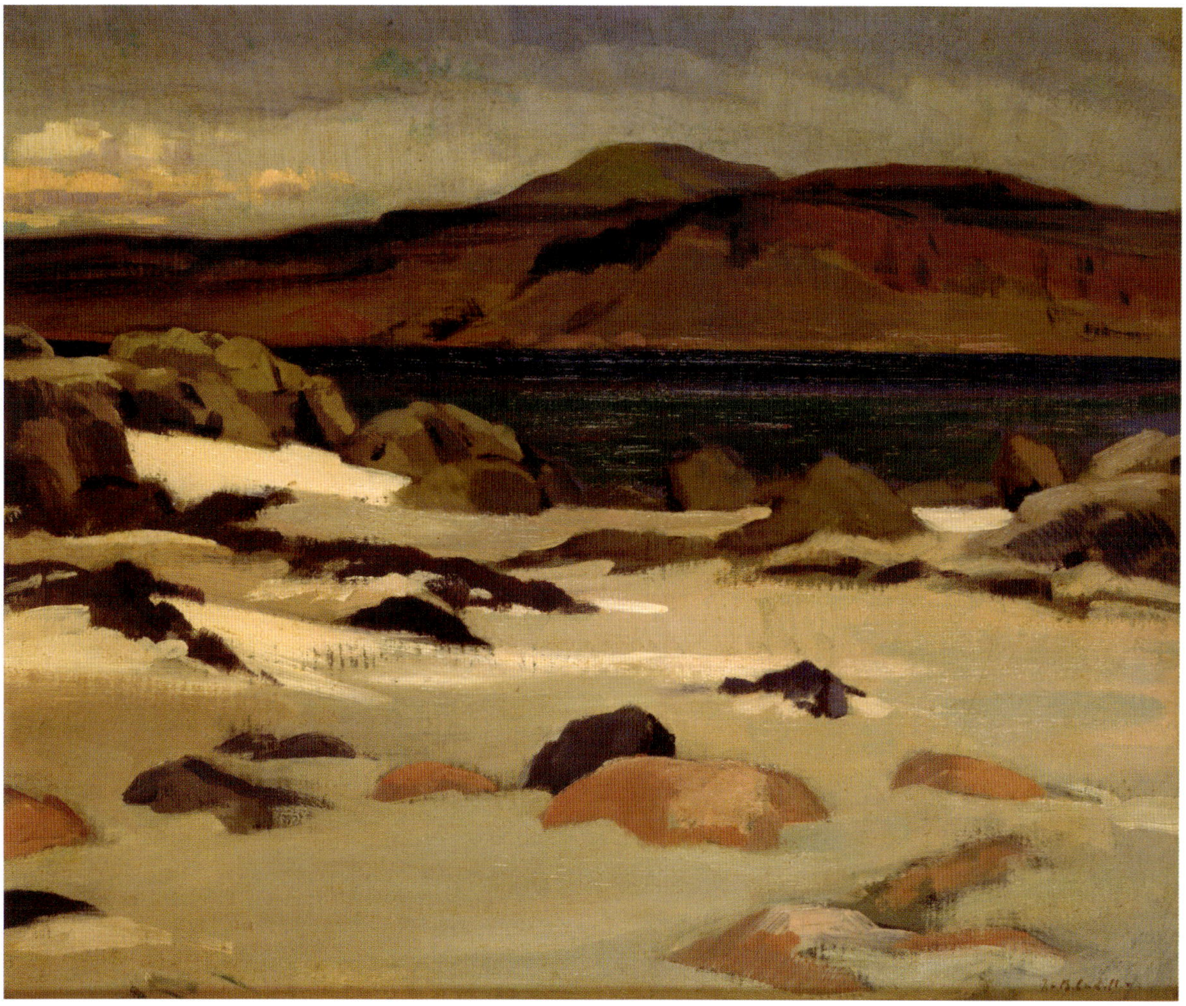

[PLATE 71]
F. C. B. Cadell
Ben More from Cows Rock
Oil 15 x 18

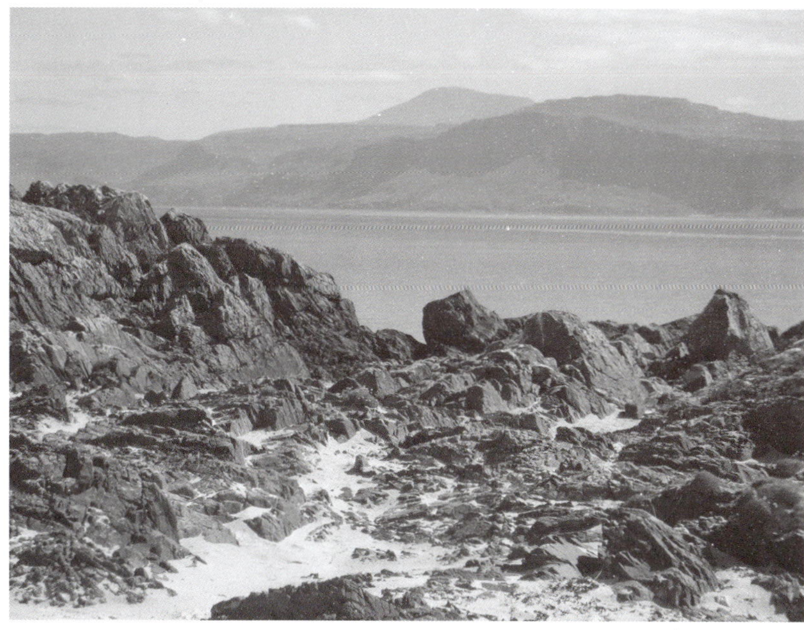

Photograph 2010

This is a similar composition to the two preceding paintings by Peploe, but here Cadell has worked from further back and taken in a wider foreground. The rocks in the left half of this picture are the same as those in the paintings by Peploe.

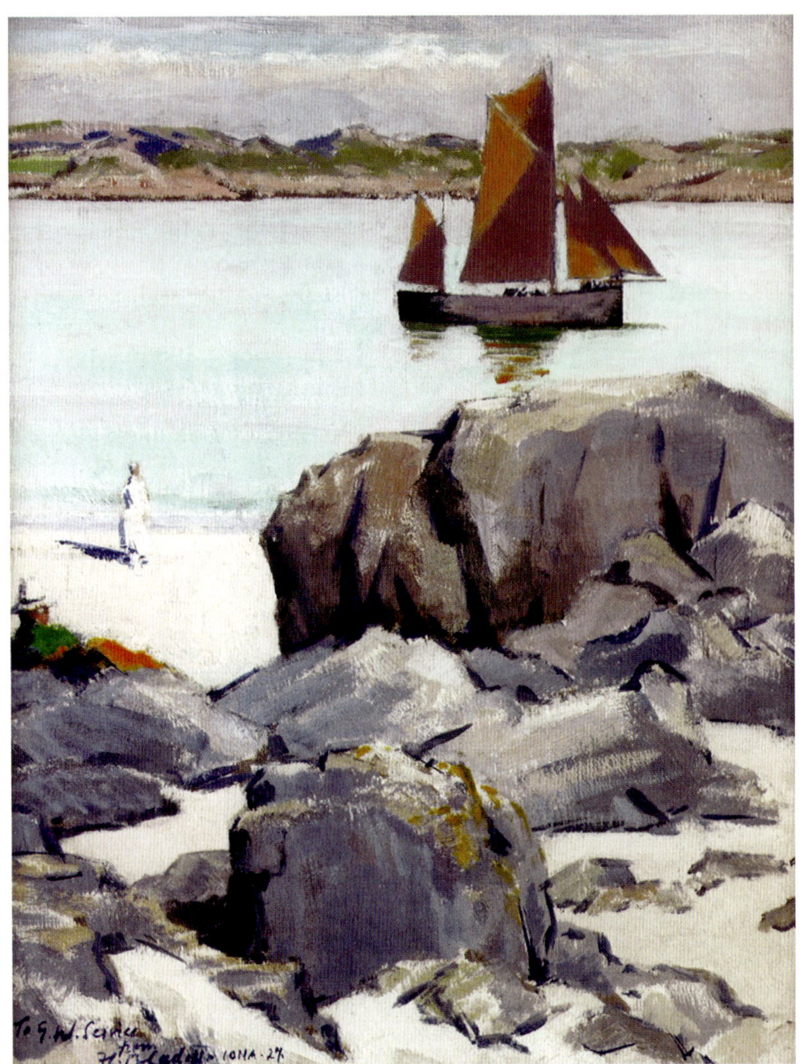

[PLATE 72]
F. C. B. Cadell
Ross of Mull from Cows Rock
Oil 18 x 15

There is a larger version of this subject (24 x18), which Cadell probably painted in the studio working from the picture shown here. This was used for one of the three posters he designed for MacBrayne's Steamers (below left). This process is similar to his use of the painting of the Paddle-steamer Grenadier as a basis for another of the posters (Plates 204 and 205).

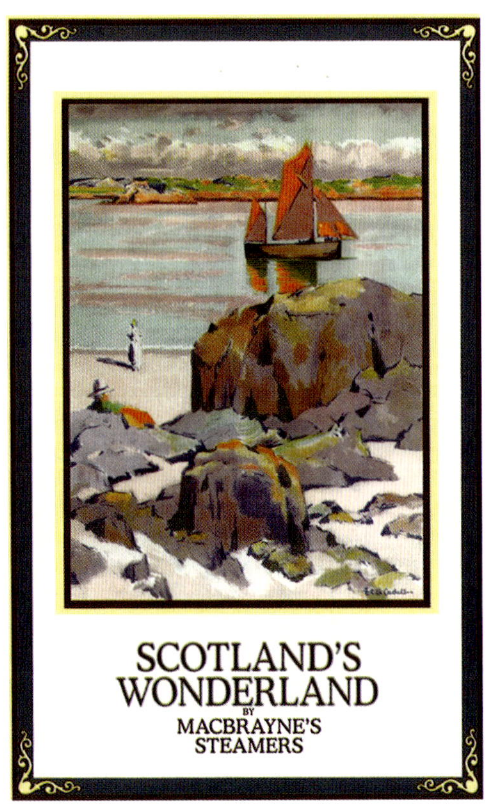

Photograph 2010

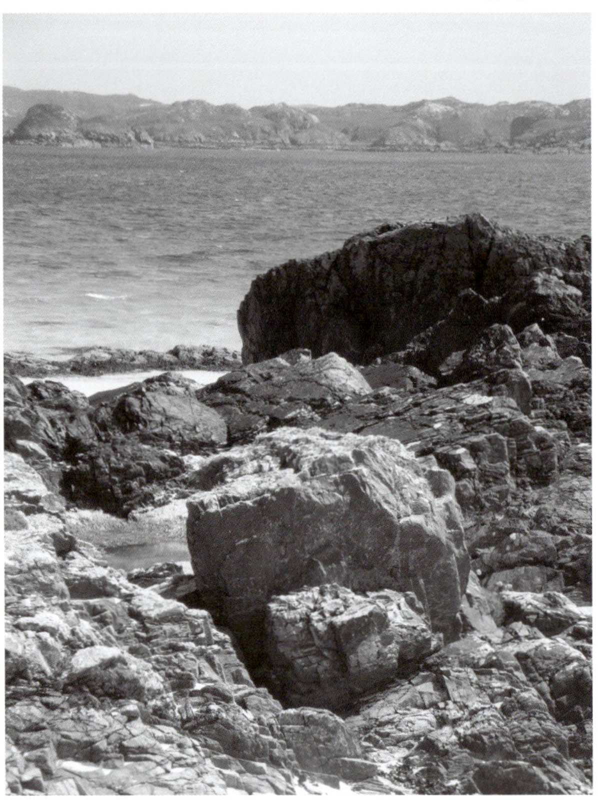

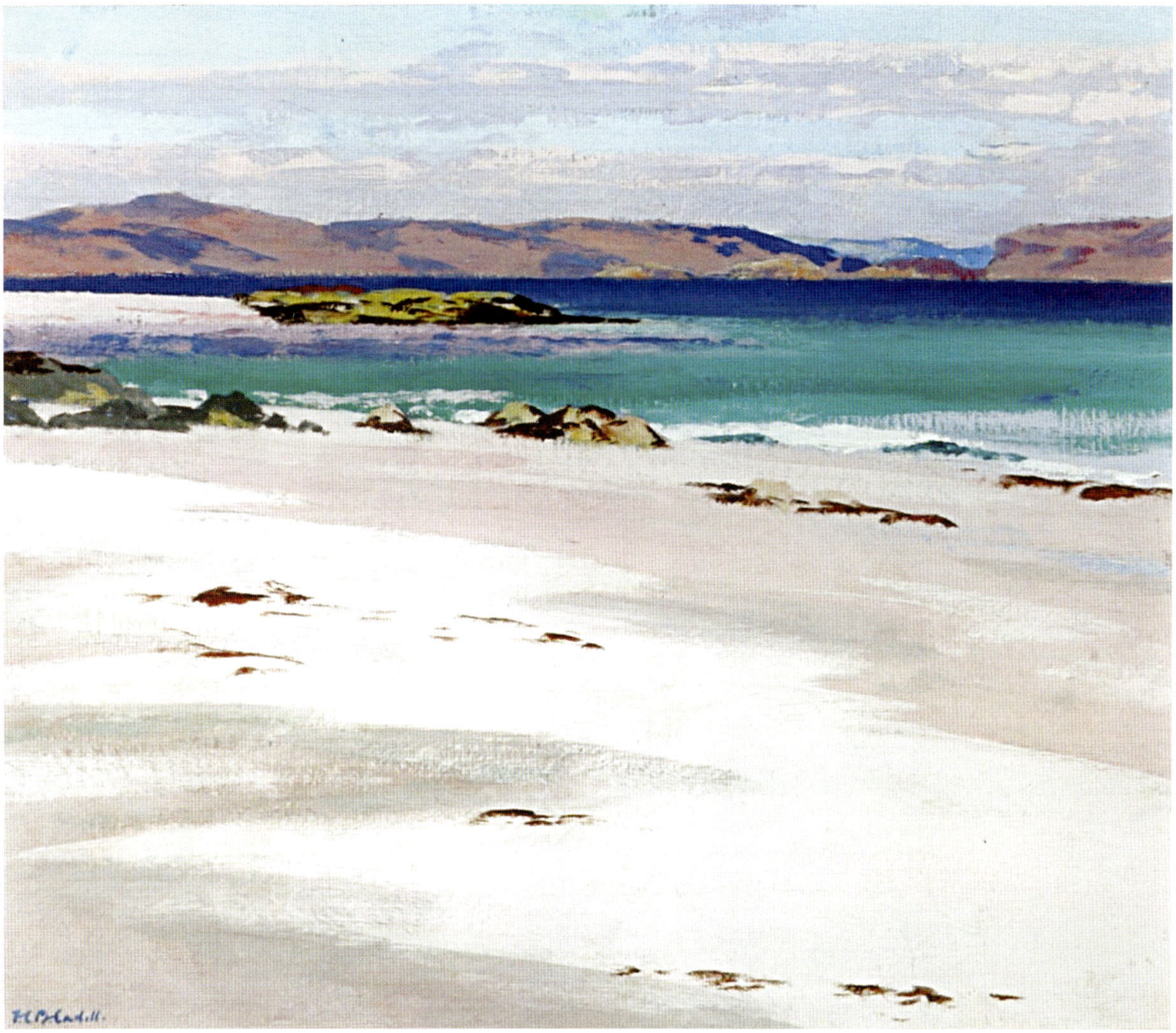

[PLATE 73]
F. C. B. Cadell
Towards Loch na Keal
from near Cows Rock
Oil 15 x 18

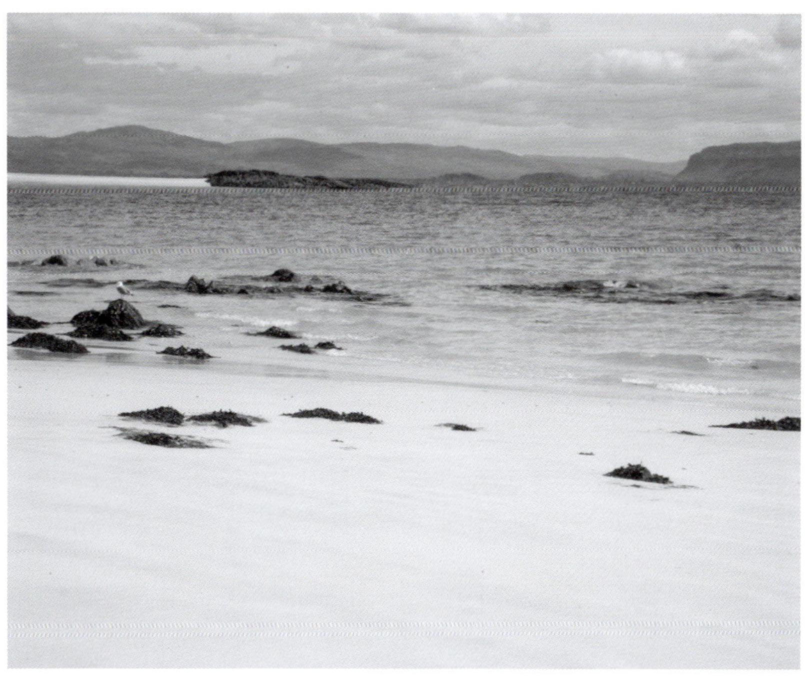

Photograph 2009

The landscape represented in the background is the same as that in Plates 56, 59, and 60, but the foregrounds vary having been painted from different positions along the beach. Here the end of Eilean Annraidh is prominent in the middle distance left of centre.

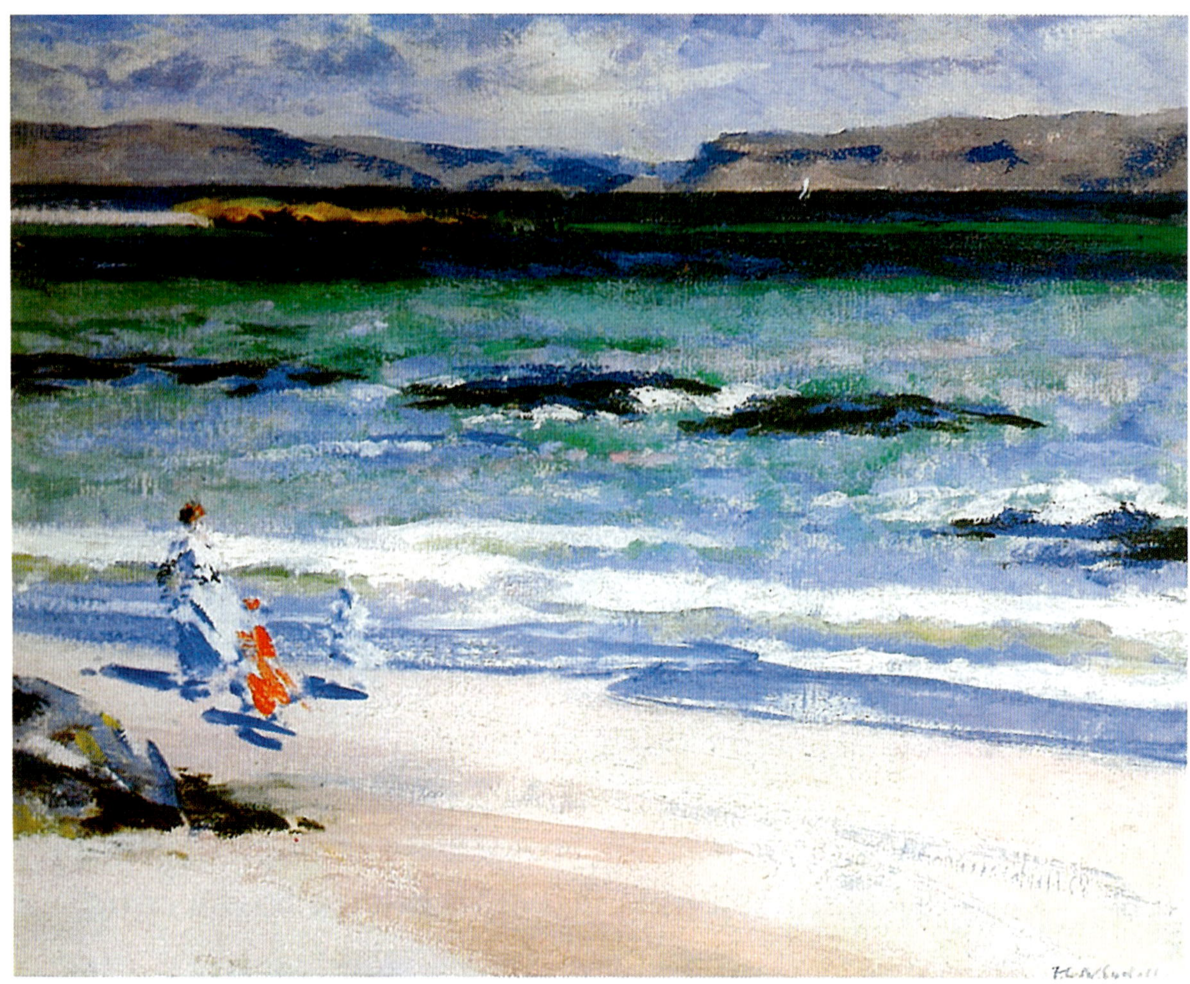

This was painted from close to the same position as the preceding picture, on the beach east of Cows Rock. This area of the beach is underwater at high tide. The southeast end of Eilean Annraidh is in the middle distance on the left. The figures and the yacht are reminiscent of those in Plates 61 and 62 and create a similar lively effect, painted with just a few very deft touches.

[PLATE 74]
F. C. B. Cadell
Towards Loch na Keal from Cows Rock
Oil 15 x 18

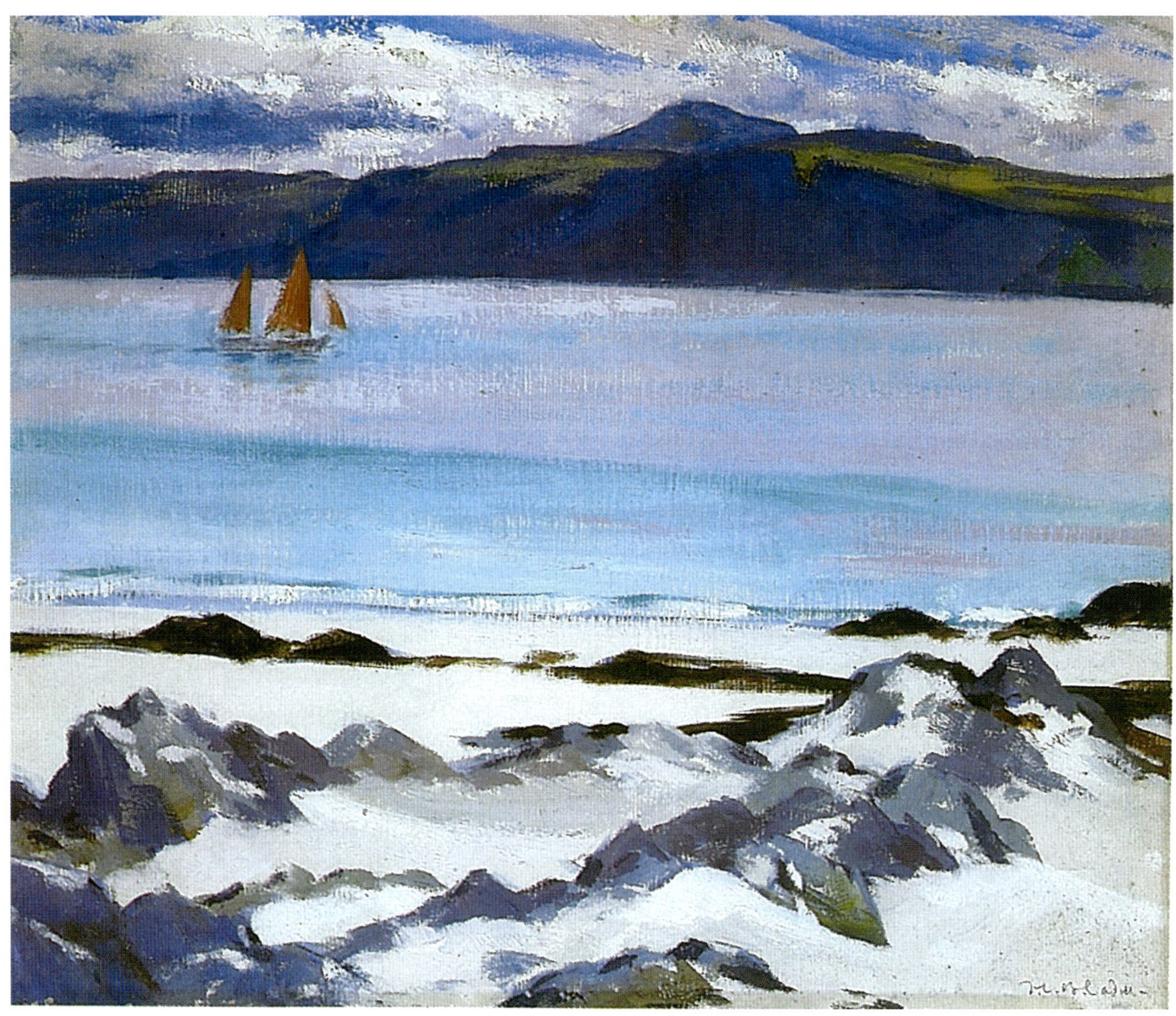

This was painted from the same area of the beach as Plates 73 and 74, but looking towards Ben More, which is just right of centre.

[PLATE 75]
F. C. B. Cadell
Ben More from near Cows Rock
(Red Sail, the Sound of Iona)
Oil 15 x 18

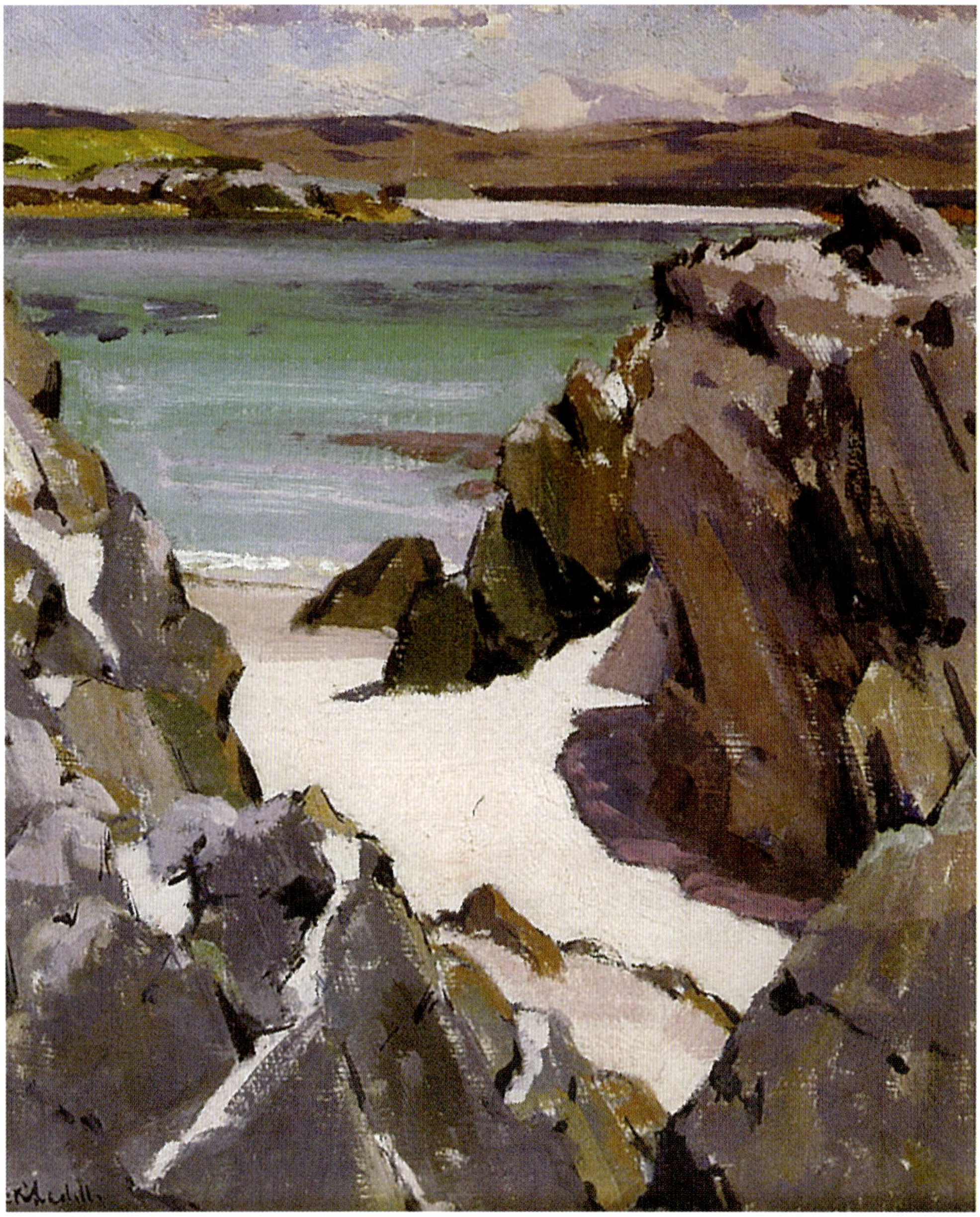

[PLATE 76]

F. C. B. Cadell

Eilean Annraidh from Cows Rock
(Sandy Creek, Iona)
Oil 18 x 15

This deep cleft is an unmistakable feature of Cows Rock, dividing it almost in two from northeast to southwest. The sea comes into the creek at the highest tides. In the mid-distance lies the rocky island of Eilean Annraidh with its sandy beach on the right. Ulva is on the left in the distance with the hills of northwest Mull beyond.

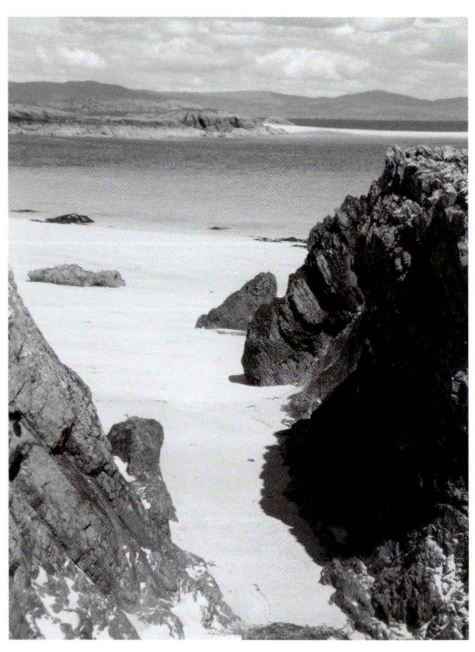

Photograph 2009

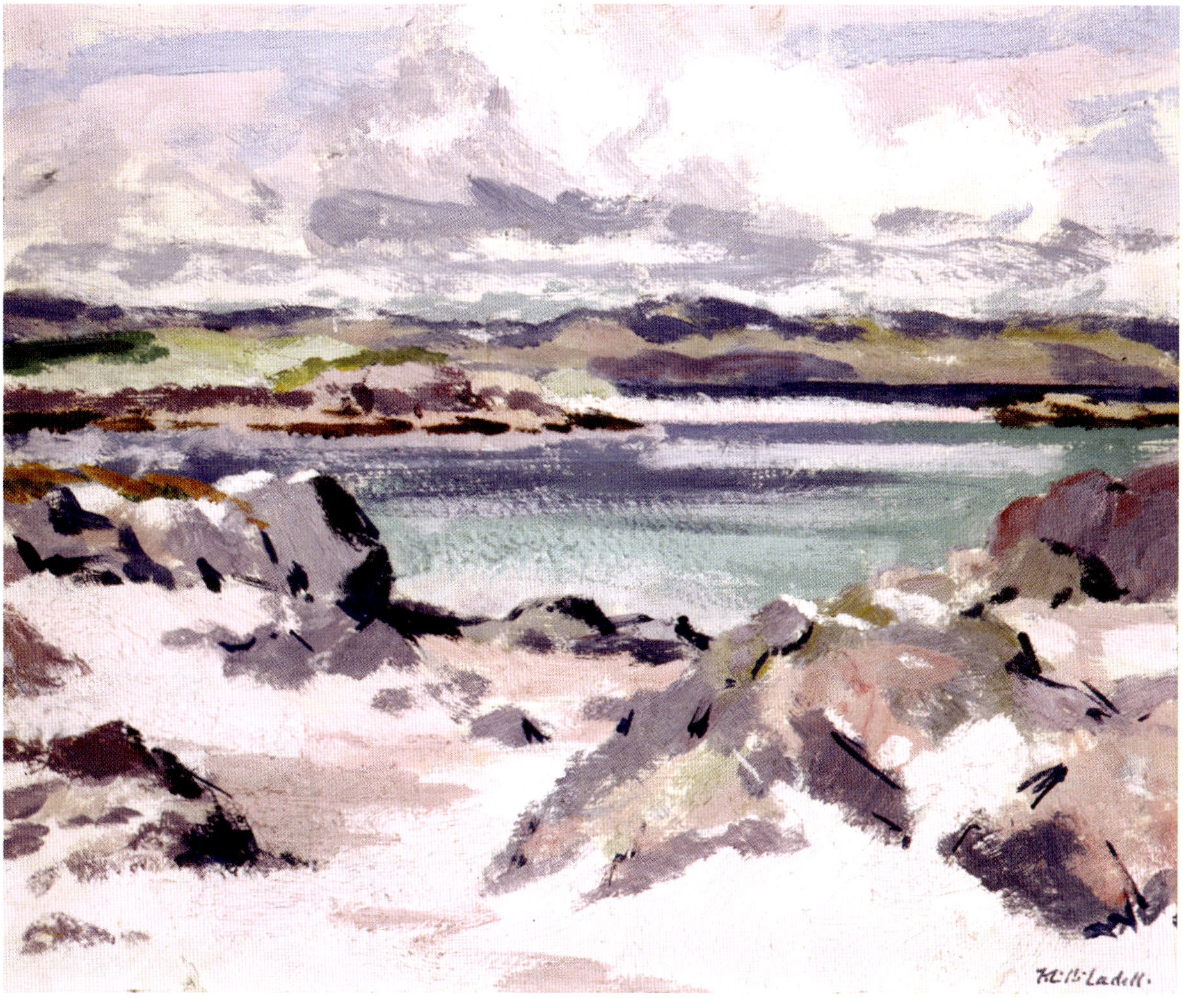

[PLATE 77]
F. C. B. Cadell

IONA

Eilean Annraidh from Cows Rock
Oil 15 x 18

Dundee Art Galleries and Museums

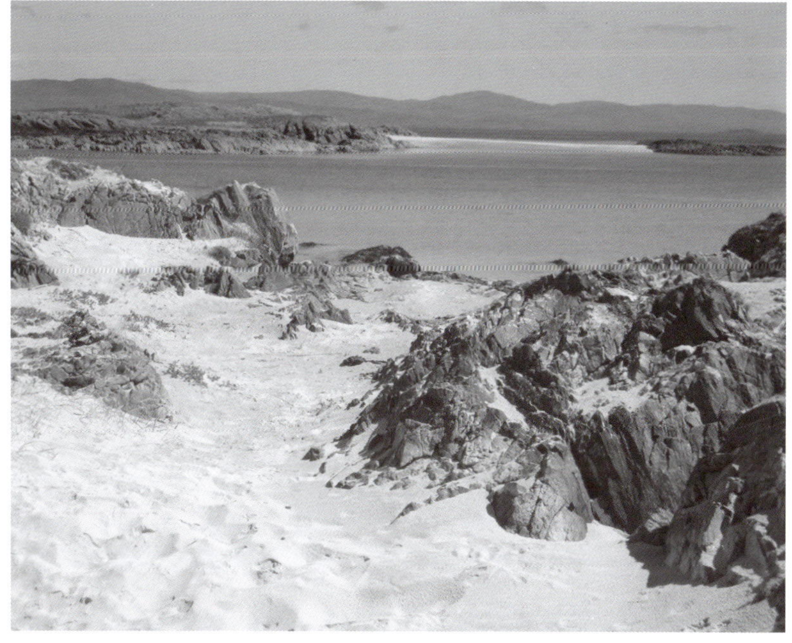

Photograph 2010

Eilean Annraidh is seen here across the Strait of Storm from the top of Cows Rock, much as in *Sandy Creek* (Plate 76), the entrance to which is just below to the right.

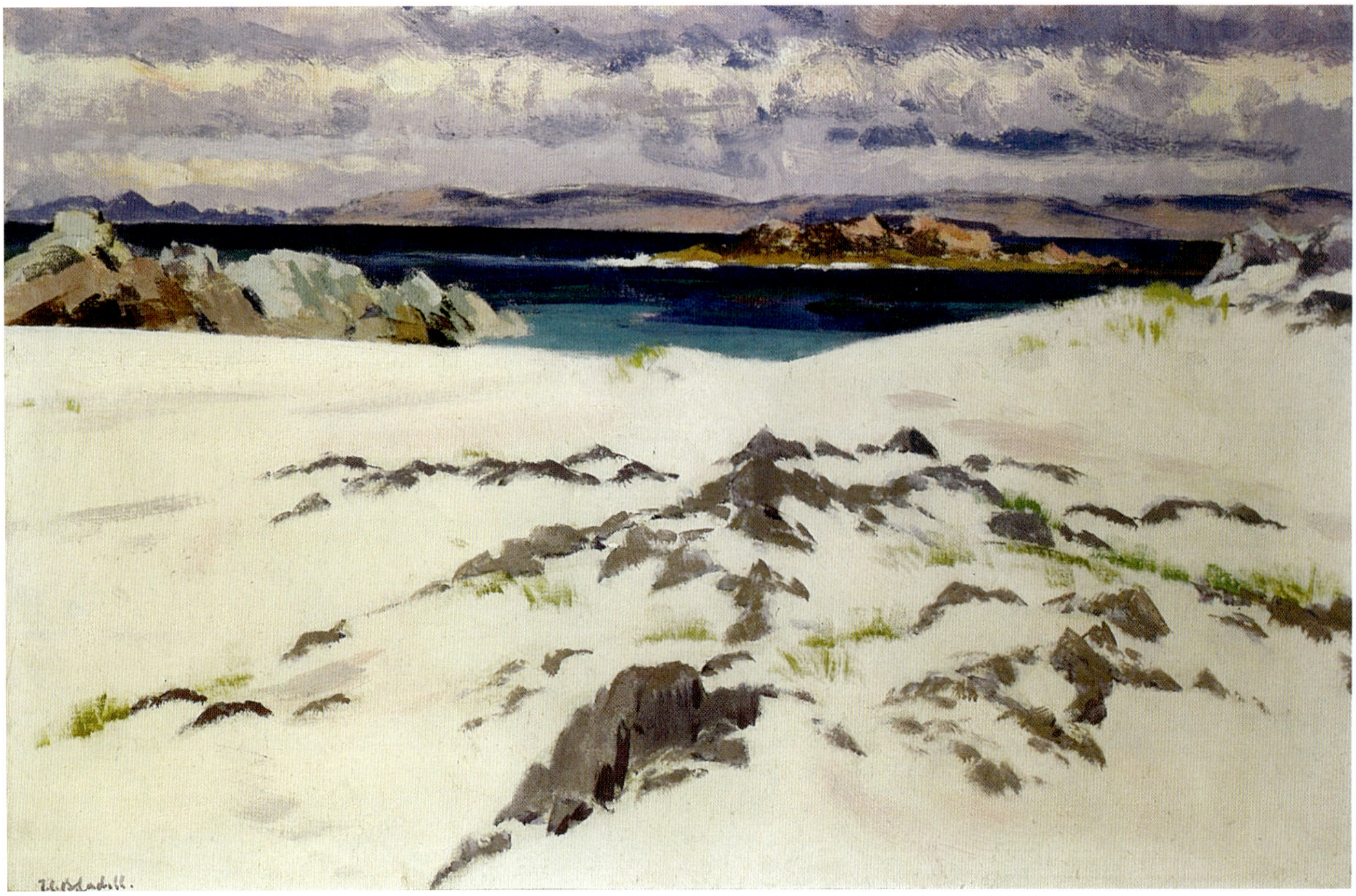

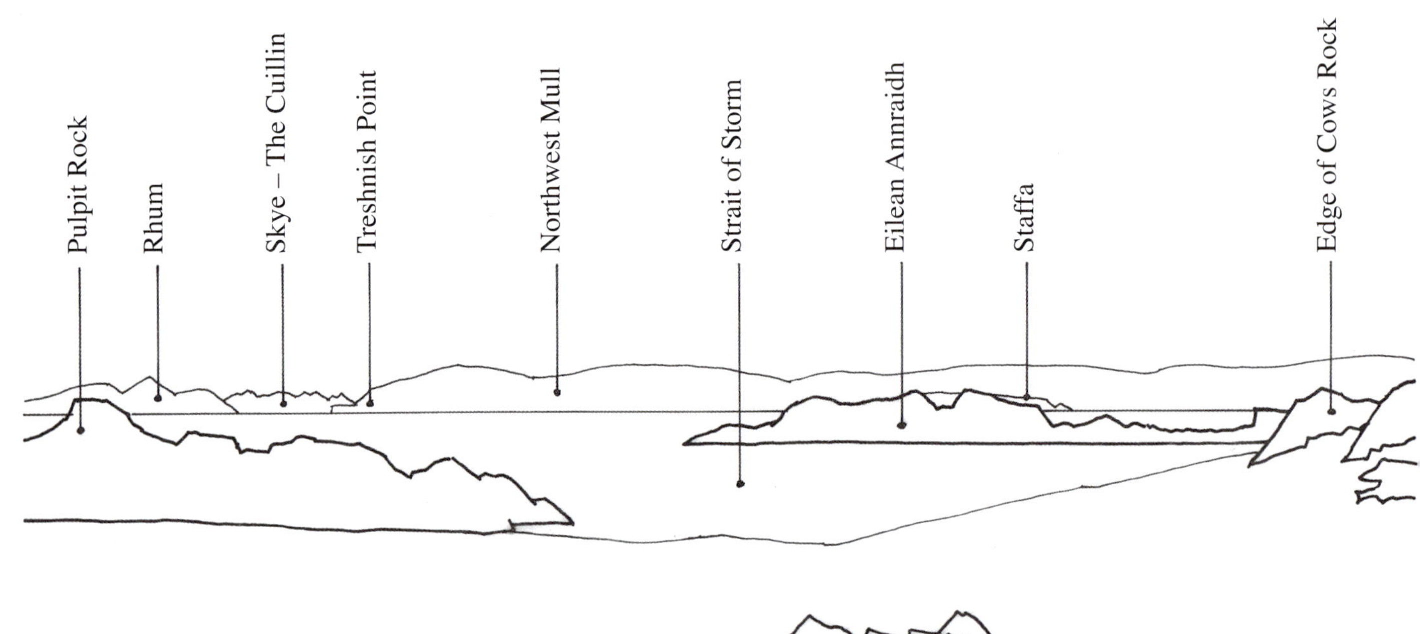

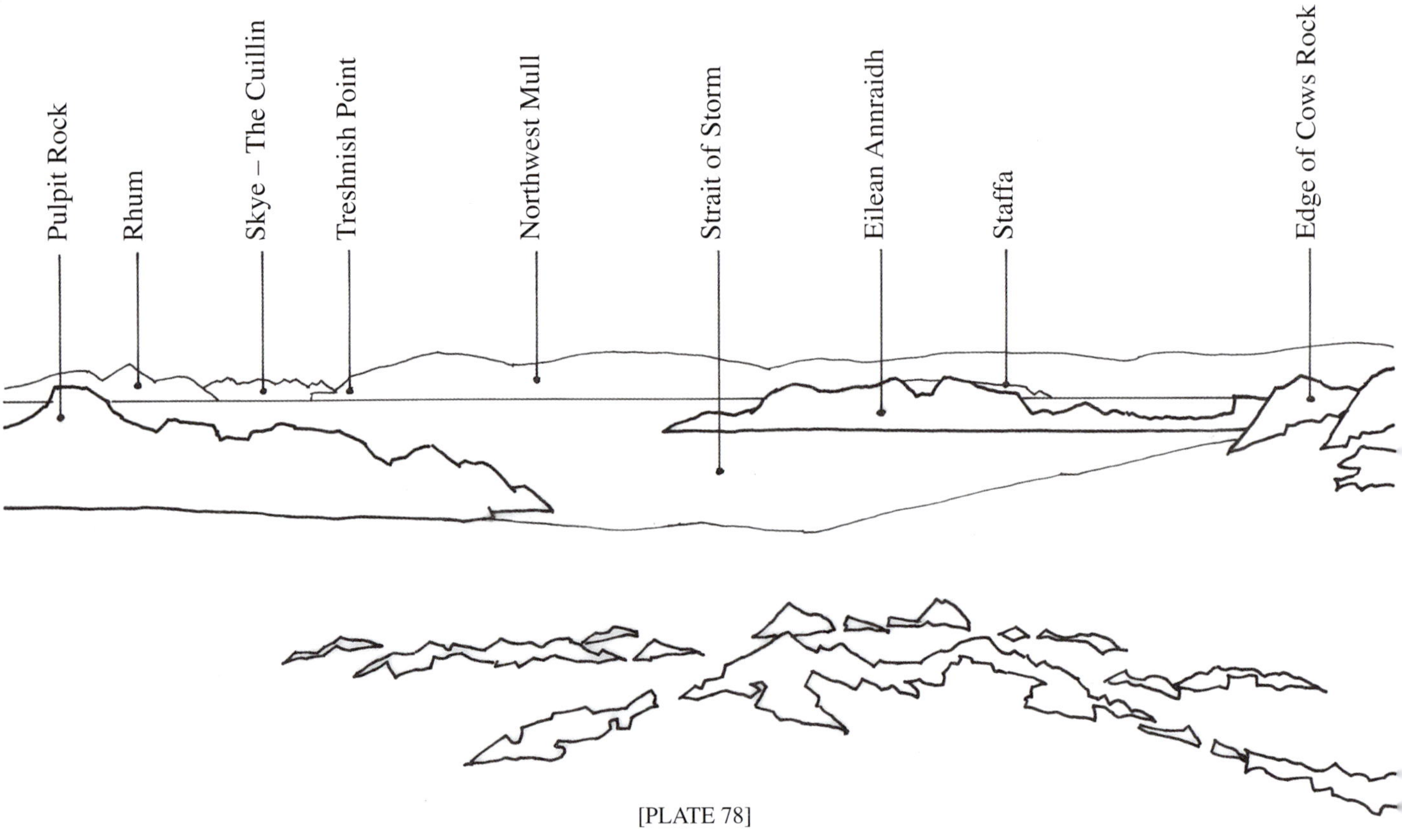

[PLATE 78]

F. C. B. Cadell

The North End (White Sands, Iona)

Oil 20 x 30

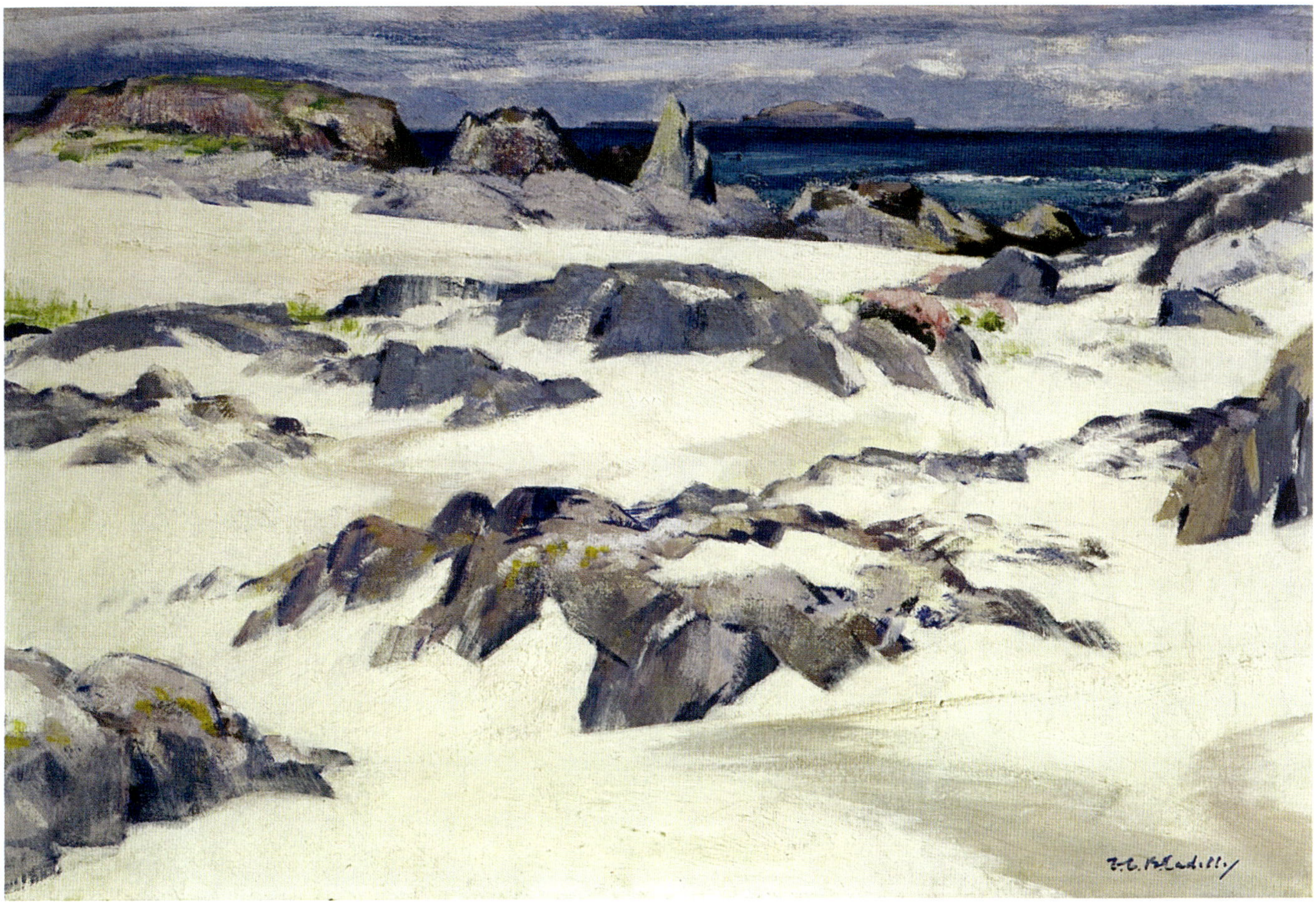

[PLATE 79]
F. C. B. Cadell
Lunga from Cows Rock
(Lunga from Iona)
Oil 20 x 30

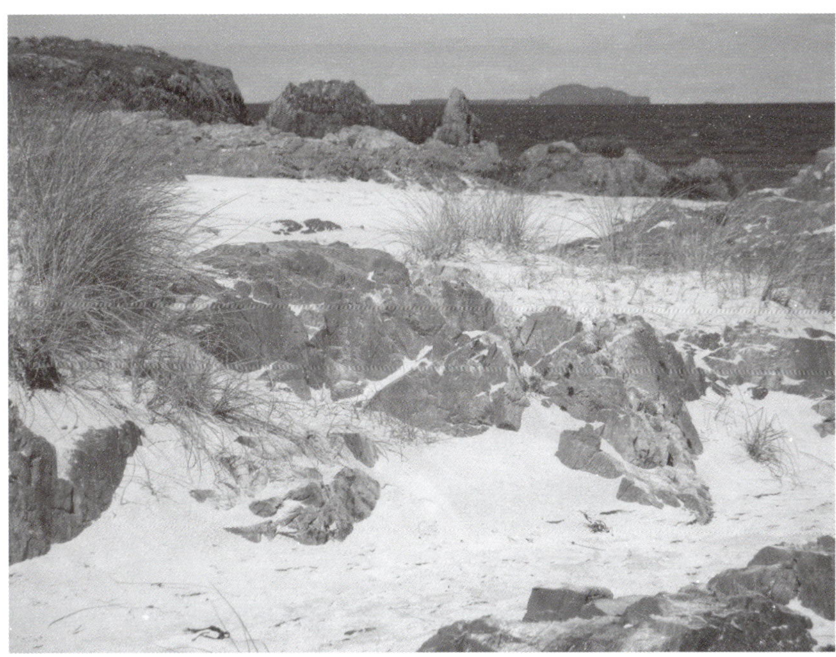

Photograph 2009

Cathedral Rock is central in the middle distance and is partly hiding the island of Lunga on the horizon. The Headland is on the left.

The view in Plate 78 *(opposite)* is slightly east of north, and that in Plate 79 is a little west of due north, but the positions from which Cadell painted these two pictures are only a few metres apart at the northwest corner of Cows Rock.

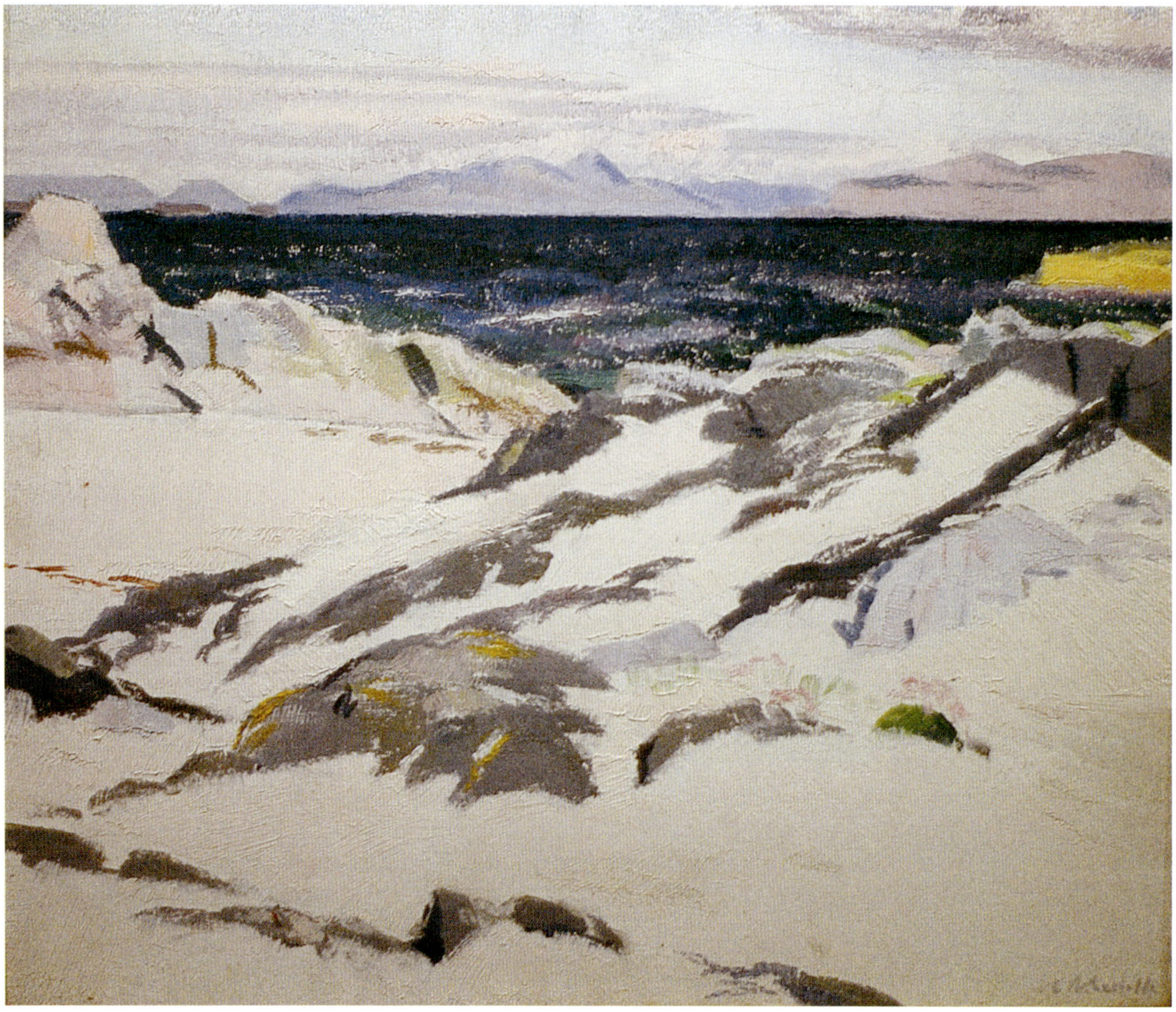

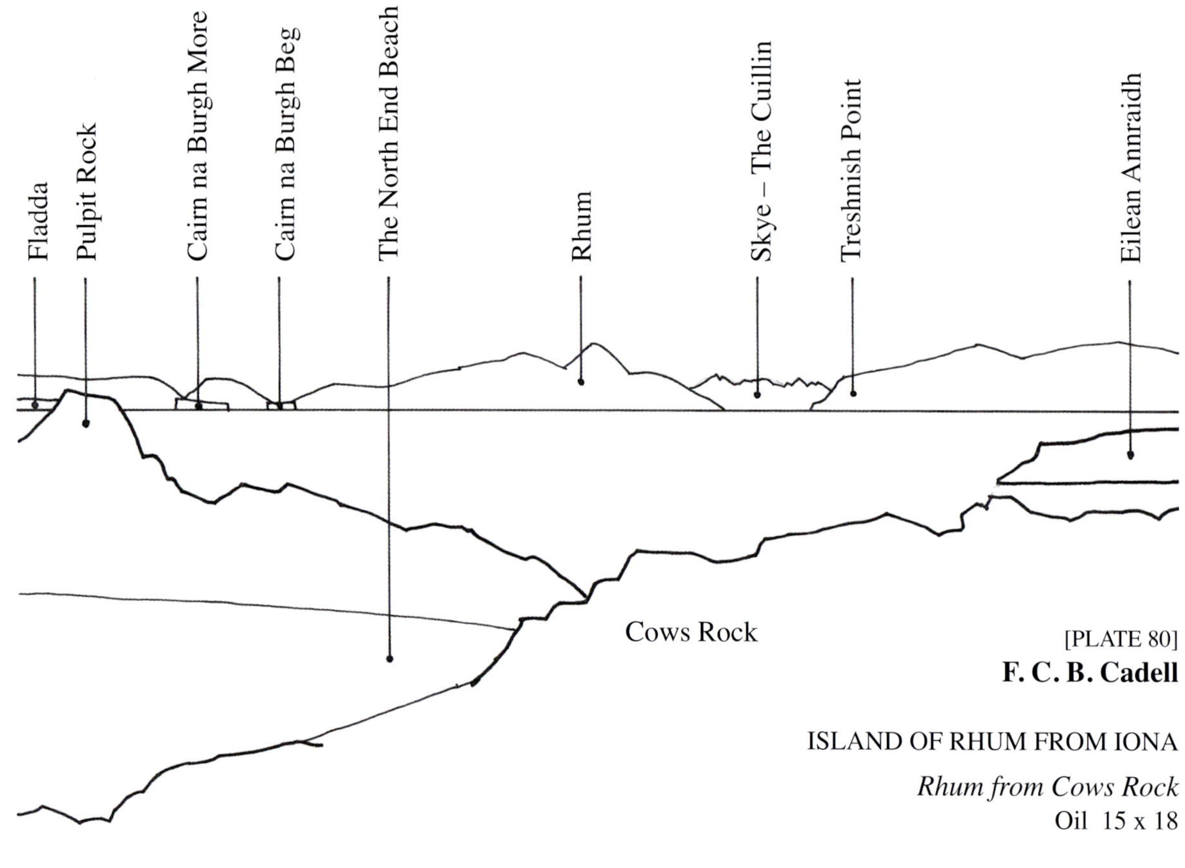

[PLATE 80]

F. C. B. Cadell

ISLAND OF RHUM FROM IONA

Rhum from Cows Rock

Oil 15 x 18

The Hunterian, University of Glasgow

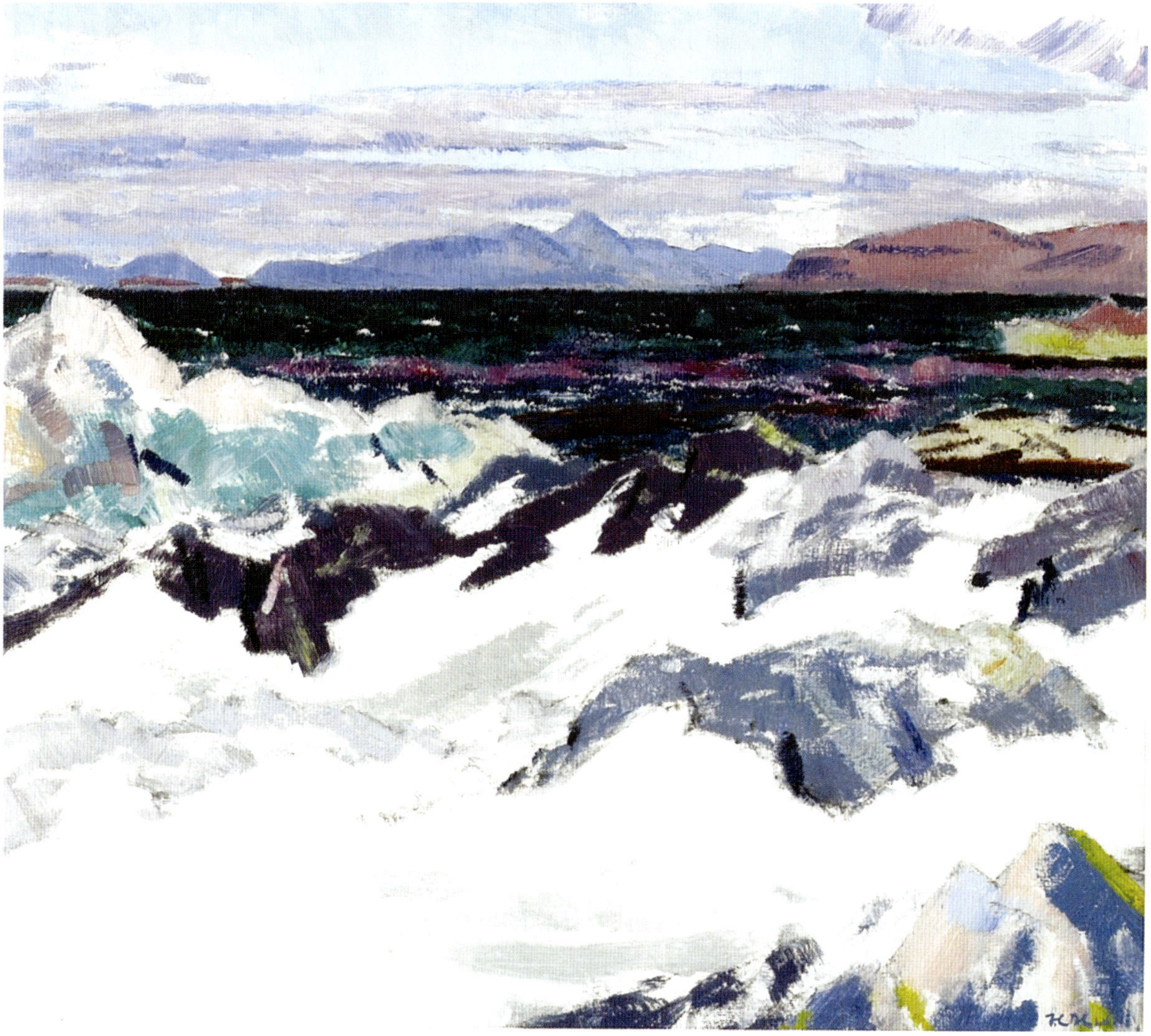

[PLATE 81]

F. C. B. Cadell

Rhum from Cows Rock
(Rhum and Skye from Iona)

Oil 15 x 18

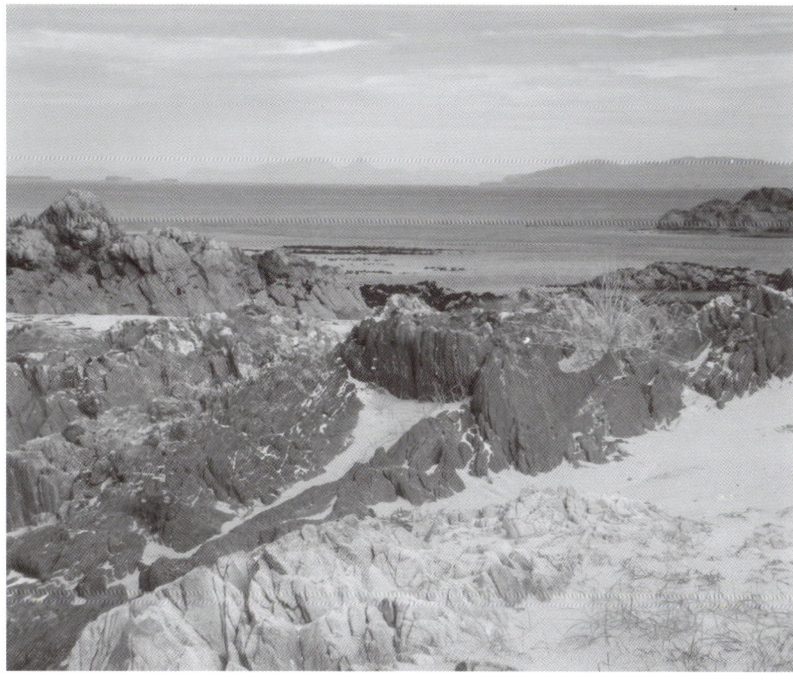

Photograph 2009

Plates 80 and 81 are almost identical compositions and the diagram below plate 80 applies to both paintings.

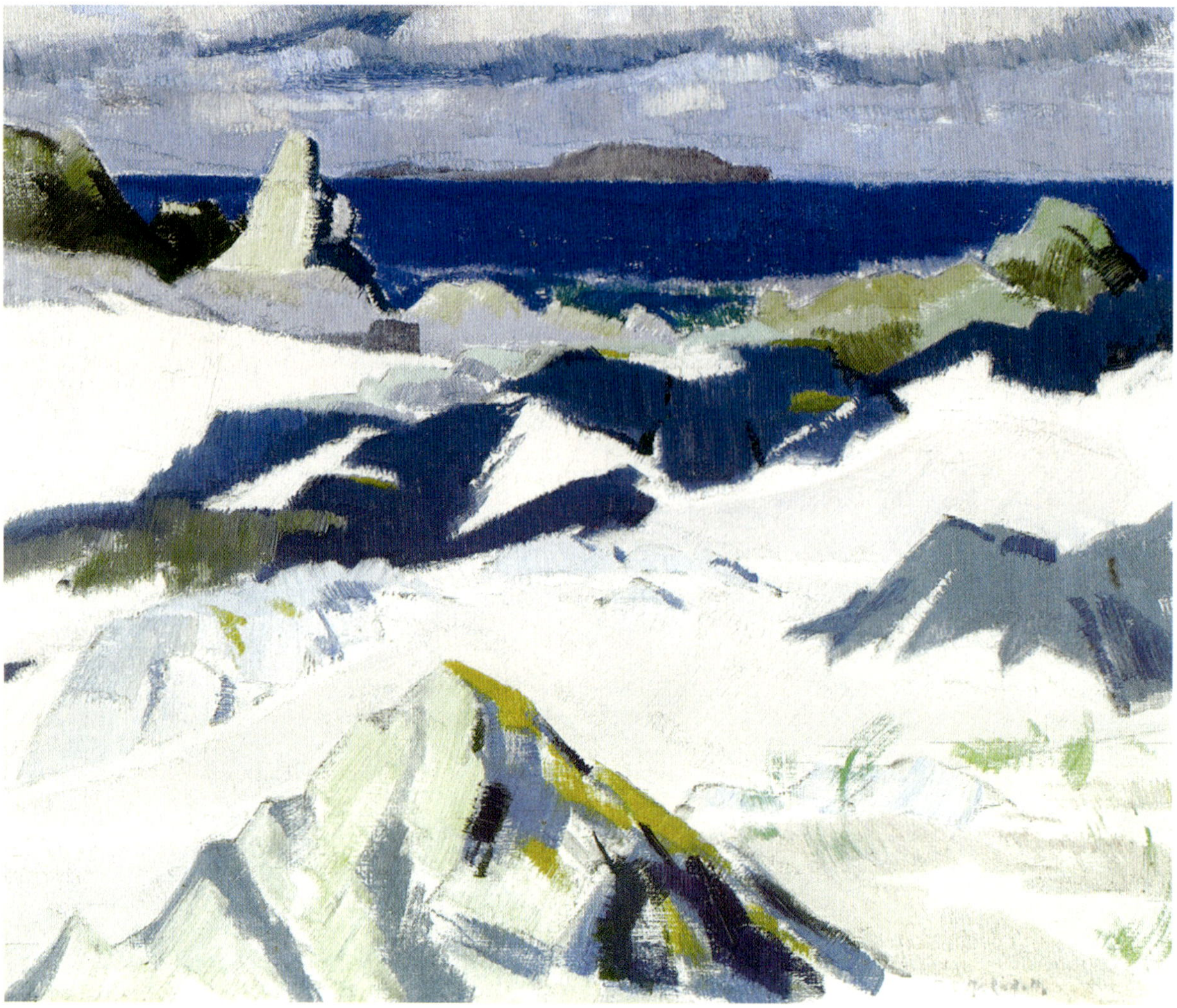

[PLATE 82]

F. C. B. Cadell

Lunga from Cows Rock
(Pulpit Rock, Iona)
Oil 15 x 18

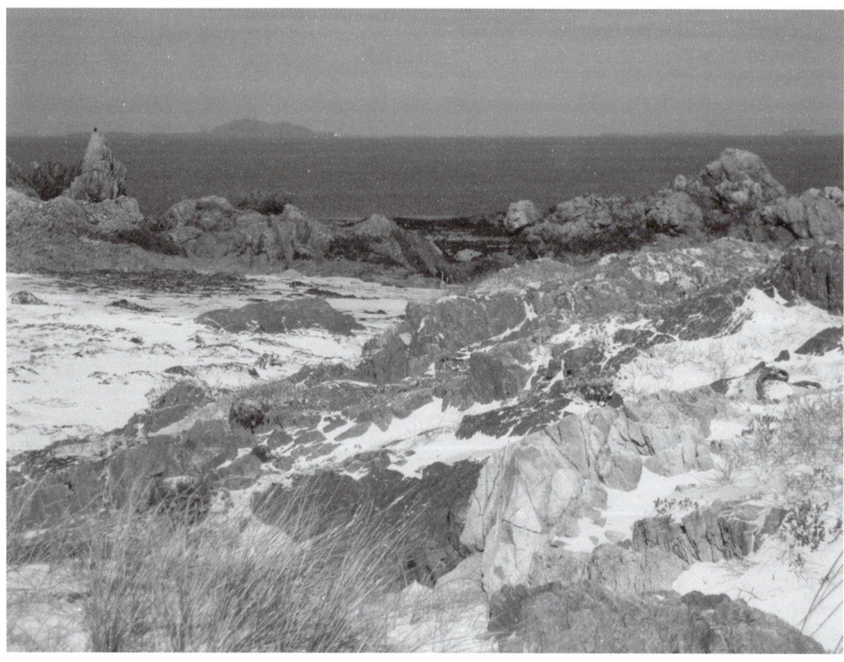

Photograph 2010

Despite the title *Pulpit Rock*, the most obvious feature in the painting is Cathedral Rock on the left; Pulpit Rock is on the right. Lunga is on the horizon. The band of dark blue-grey rock in the foreground also appears in Plates 80 and 81.

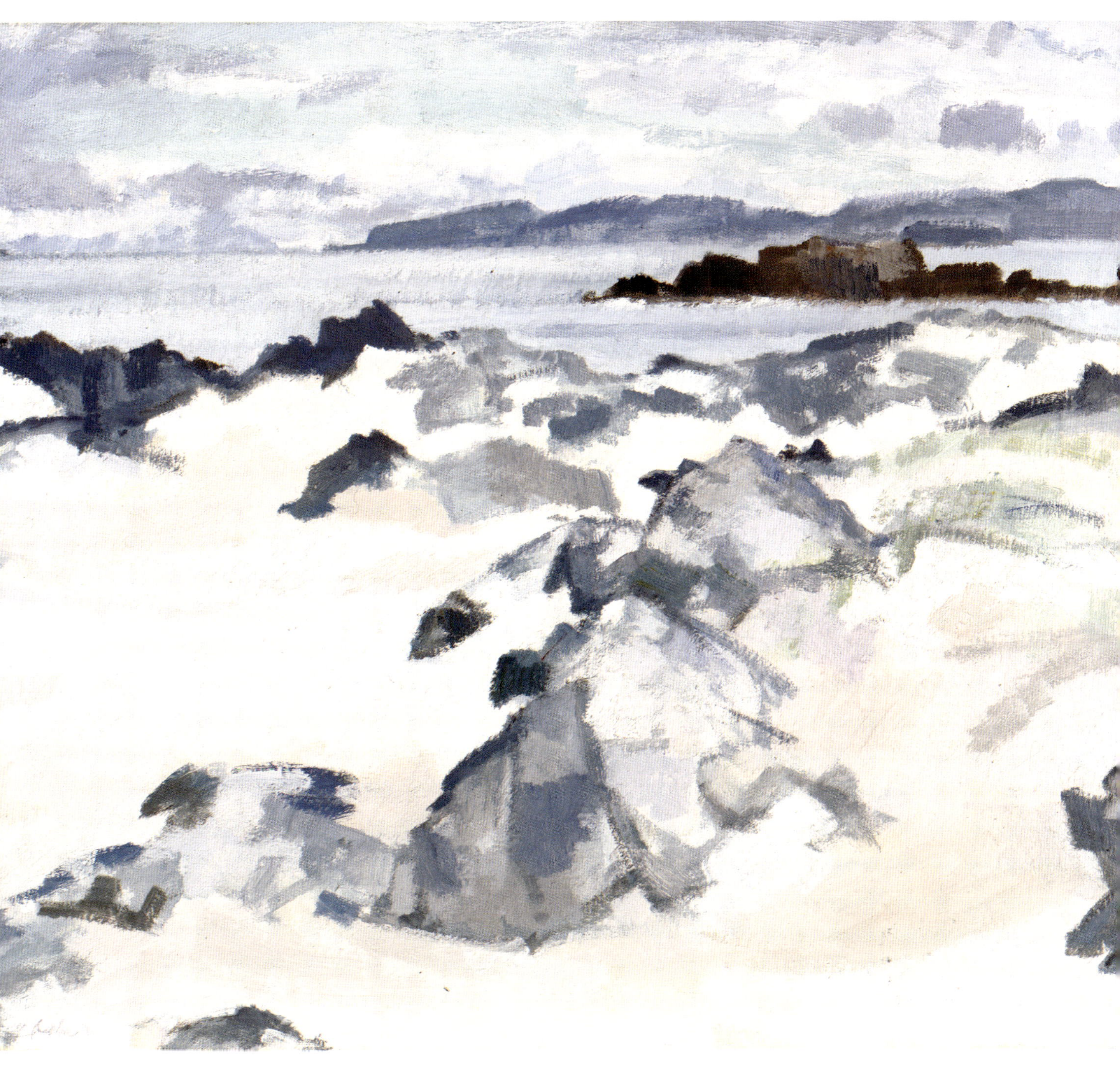

Treshnish Point is on the horizon, left of centre, and the rocky west end of Eilean Annraidh is in the middle distance on the right.

[PLATE 83]
S. J. Peploe

IONA, GREY DAY

Treshnish Point from Cows Rock
Oil 20 x 24

Aberdeen Art Gallery & Museums Collections

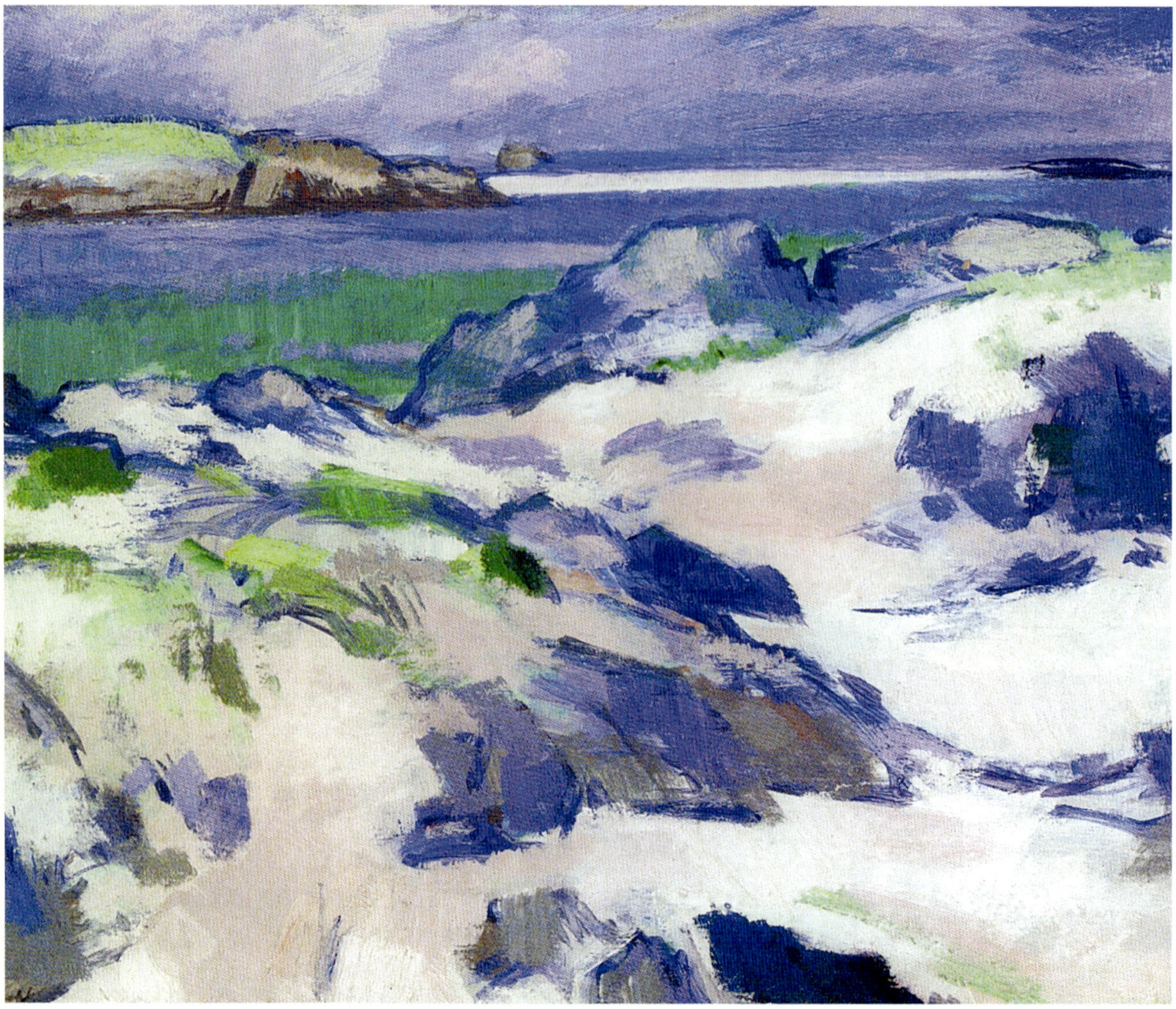

[PLATE 84]
S. J. Peploe
Eilean Annraidh
from Cows Rock
Oil 15 x 18

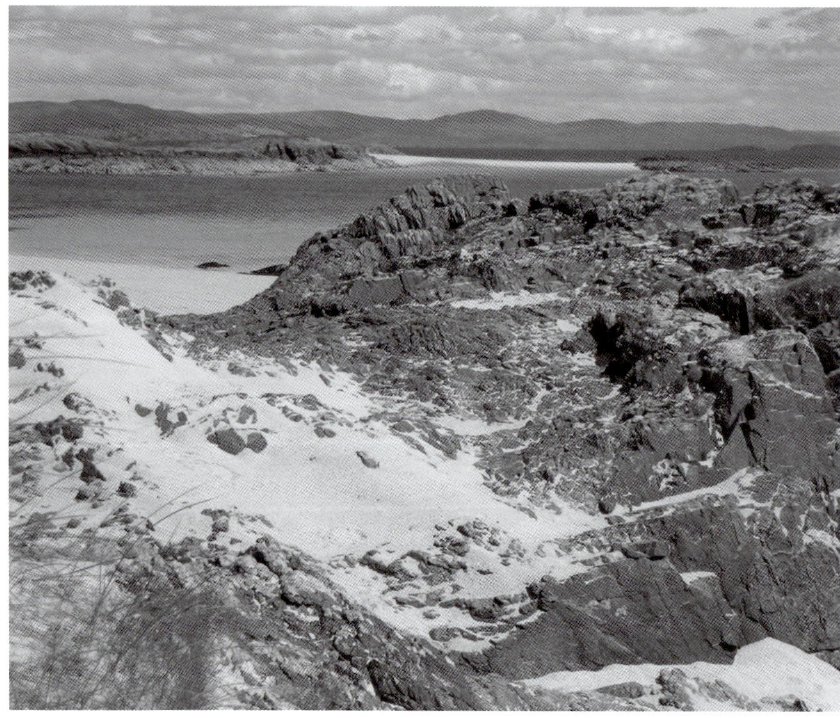

Photograph 2009

There is a painting by Cadell of the same view (Plate 85) and Peploe painted a series of pictures closely related to this subject (Plates 86 to 88).

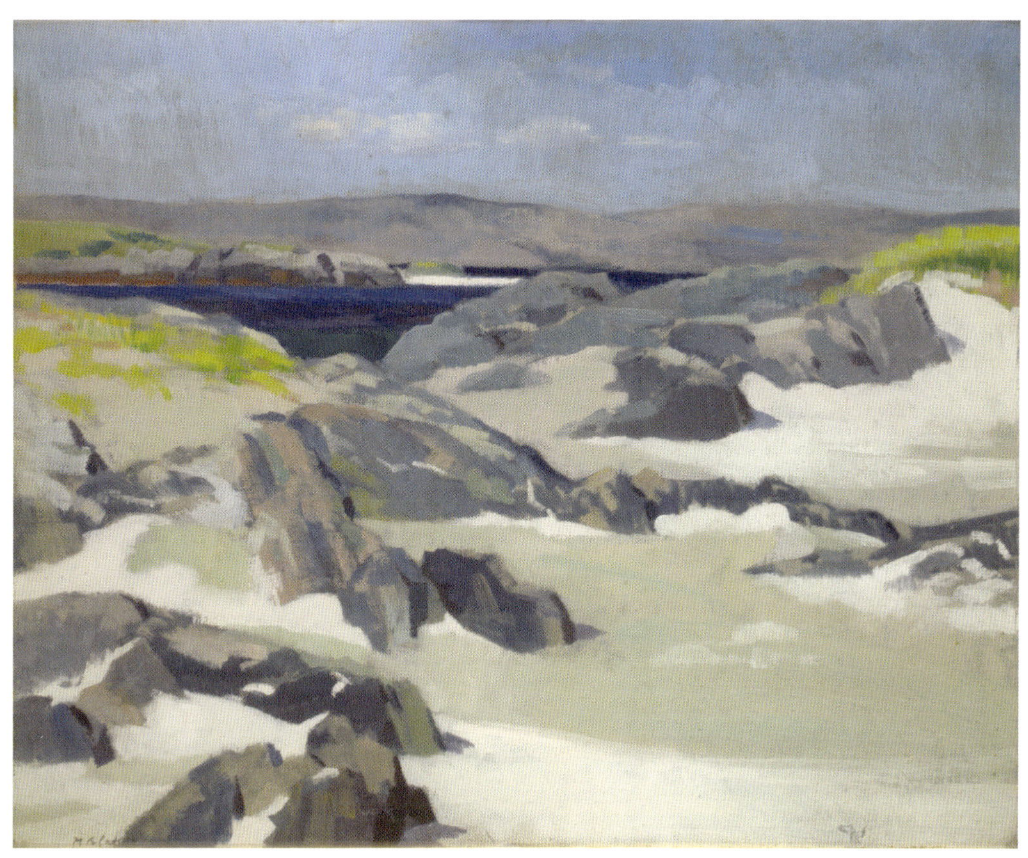

[PLATE 85]
F. B. C. Cadell
Eilean Annraidh from Cows Rock Oil 15 x 18

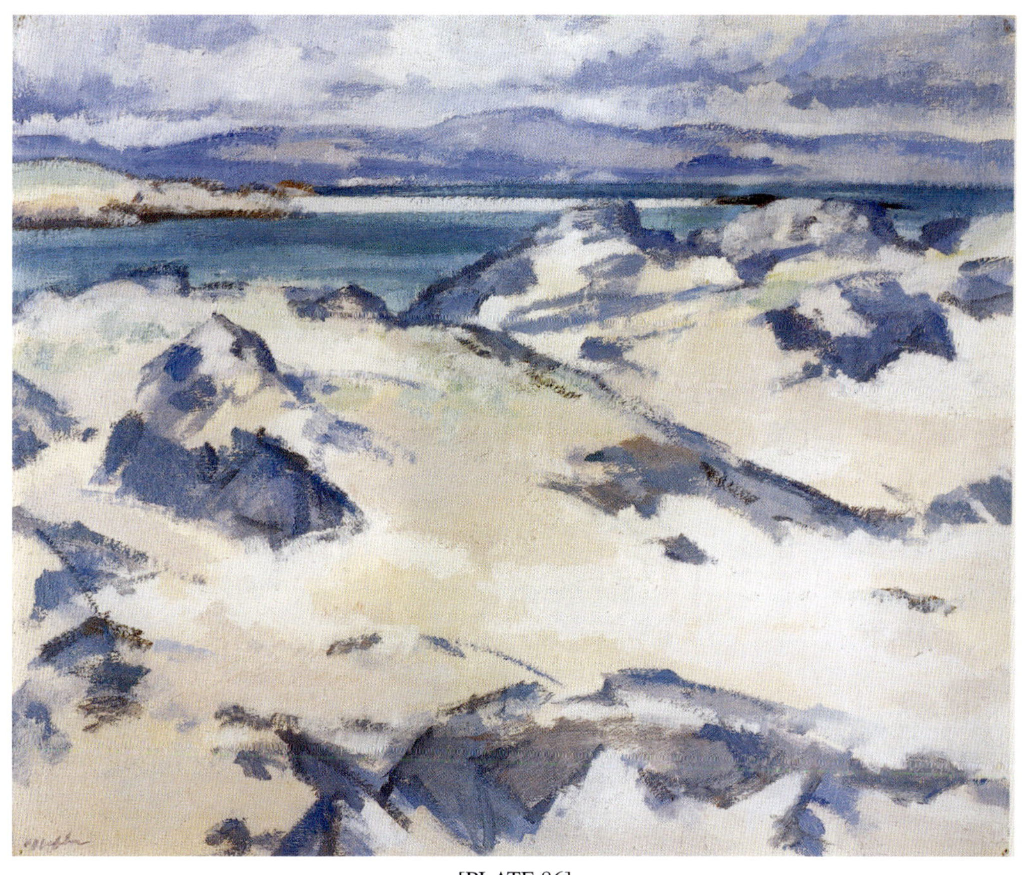

[PLATE 86]
S. J. Peploe
Eilean Annraidh from Cows Rock (White Sands, Iona) Oil 20 x 24

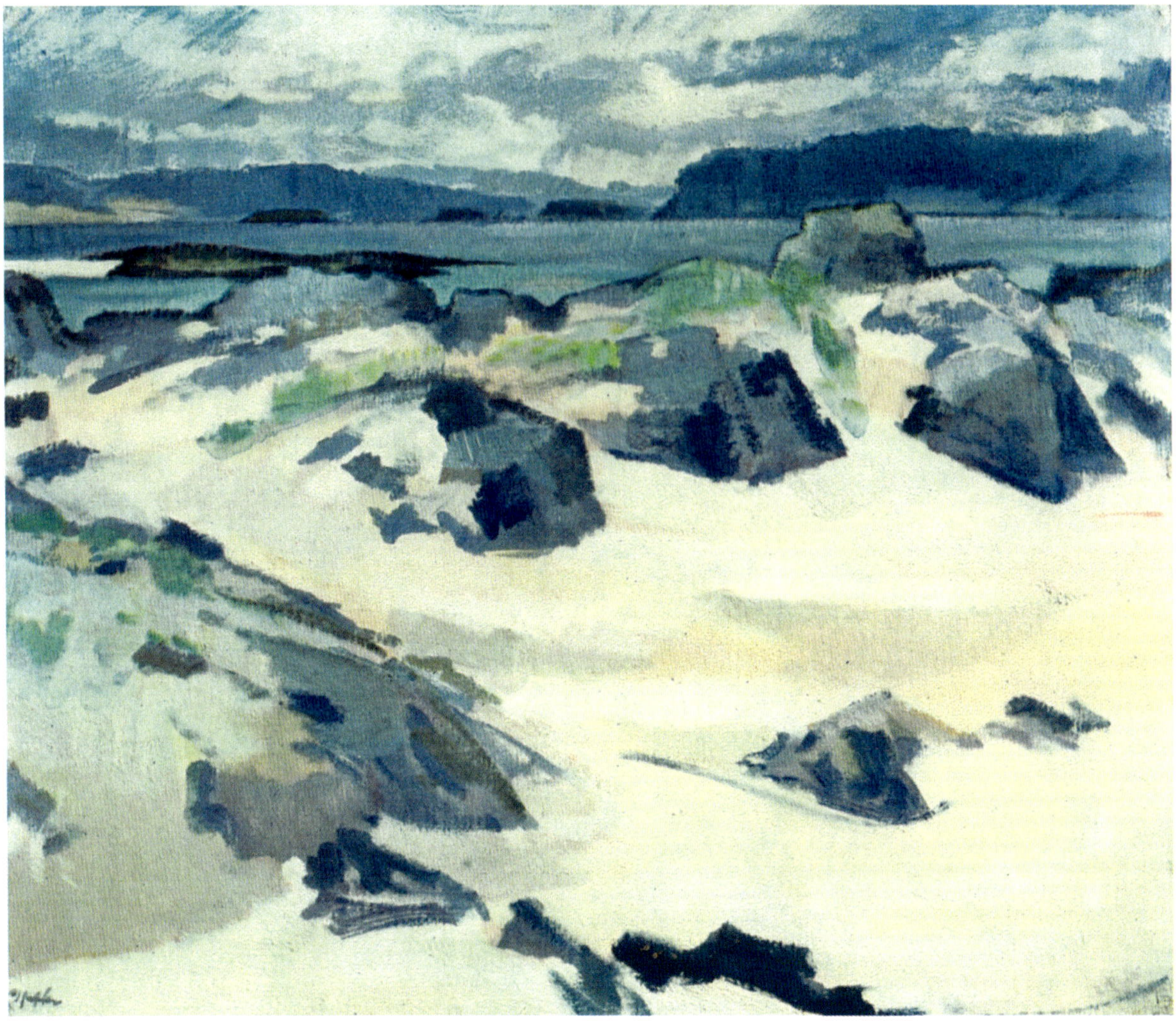

[PLATE 87]

S. J. Peploe

Towards Loch na Keal from Cows Rock (Summer Day, Iona)

Oil 20 x 24

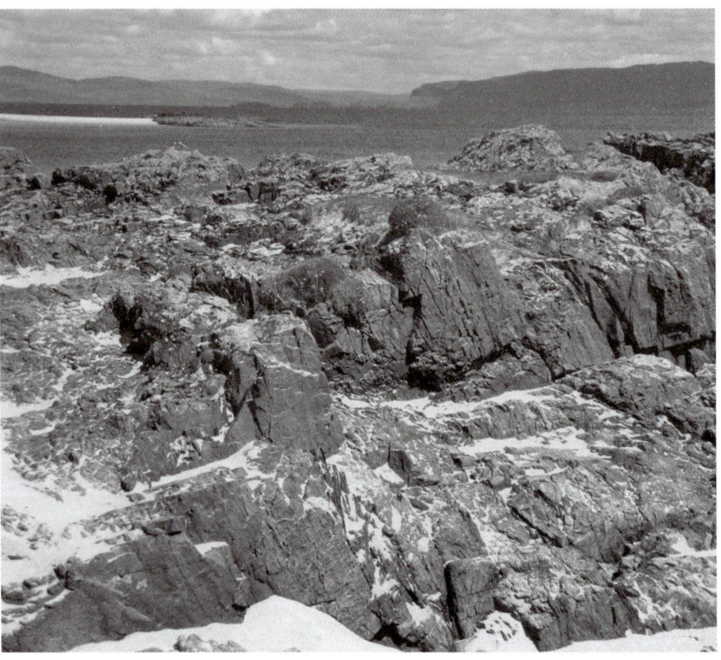

Photograph 2009

Painted from the same position as Plate 86, this is the view a little further to the right. The southeast end of Eilean Annraidh is on the left in the middle distance and the cliffs at Gribun are in the far distance on the right. The islands of Erisgeir, Inch Kenneth and Eorsa are all clearly shown on the horizon; these are identified in the diagram on page 153.

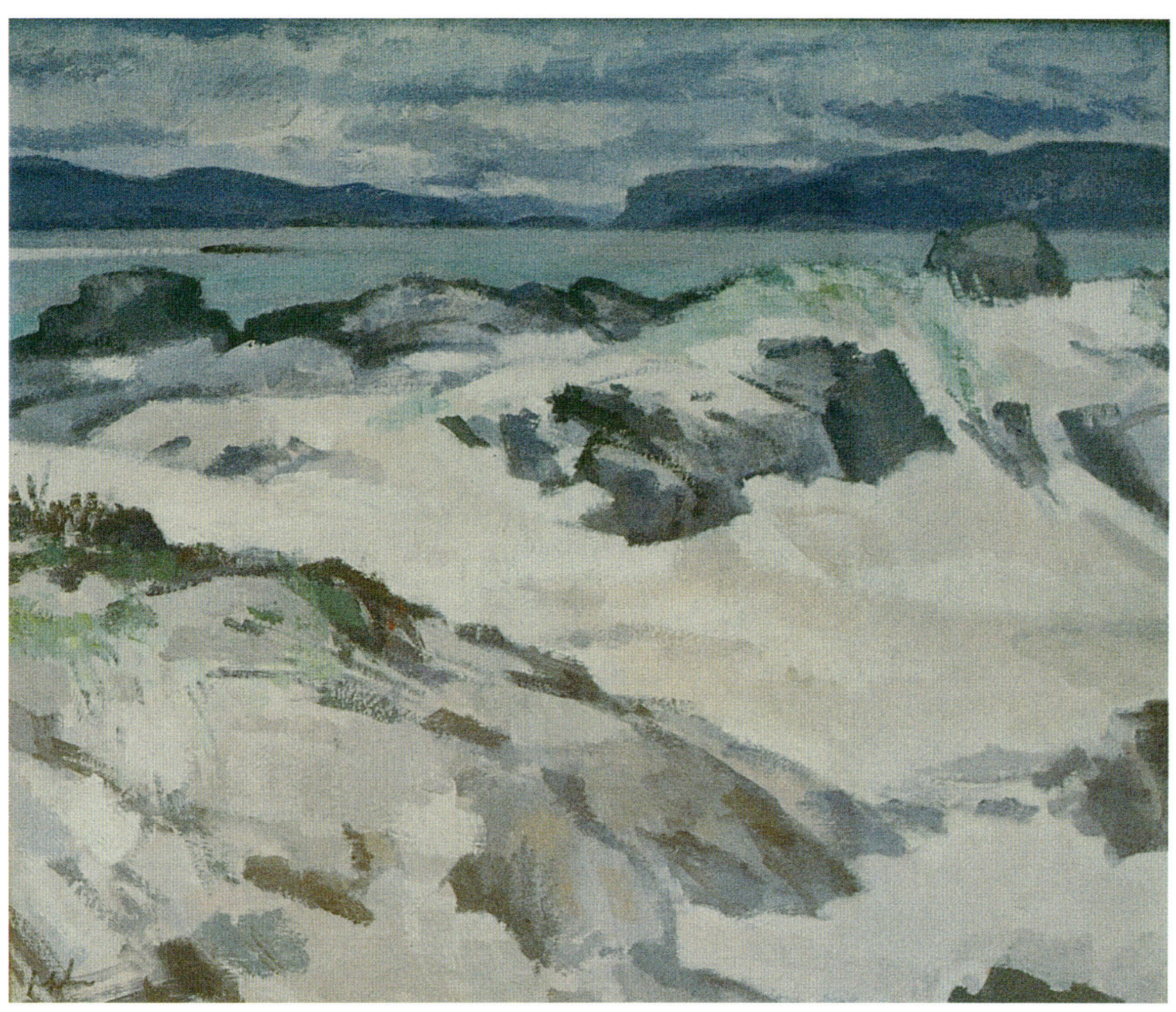

Apart from the minor difference of a higher tide level, which here almost covers Eilean Annraidh, Plates 87 and 88 are almost identical compositions. The sand level is much higher in the paintings than when the corresponding photograph was taken.

[PLATE 88]

S. J. Peploe

Towards Loch na Keal from Cows Rock

Oil 20 x 24

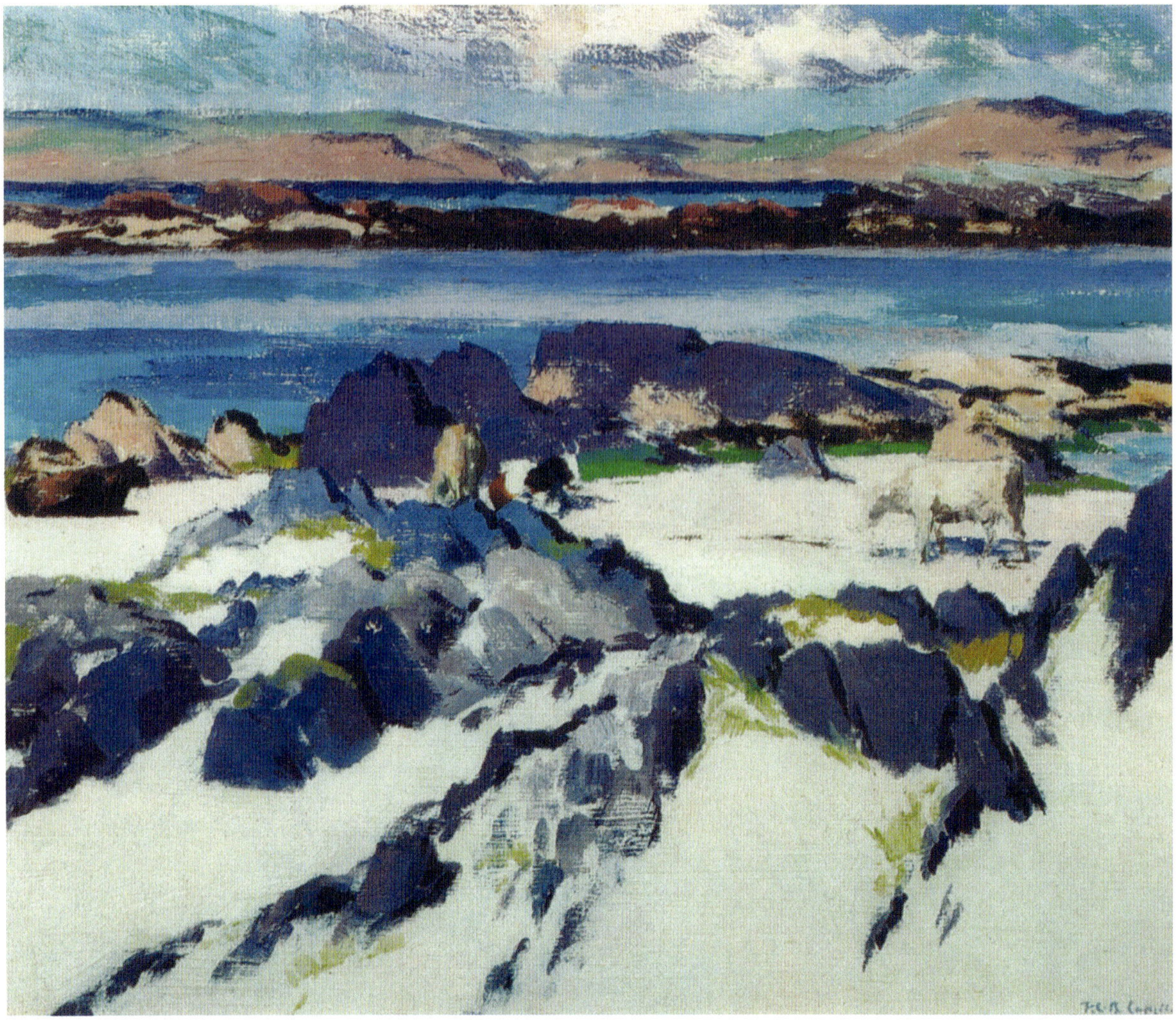

[PLATE 89]

F. C. B. Cadell

Mull from Cows Rock
(Cattle on the Shore, Iona)
Oil 15 x 18

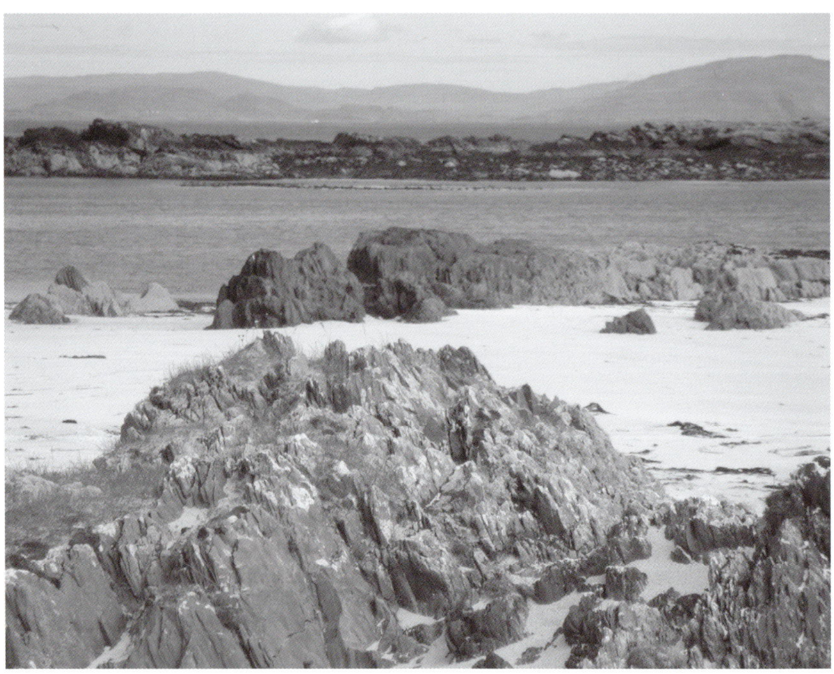

Photograph 2009

The dark rock in the centre of the painting is A'Chorrag – The Finger. Eilean Annraidh is across the full width in the middle distance. The islands of Gometra and Ulva are in the background. Gometra is often difficult to discern against the hills of Mull beyond, but here Cadell has differentiated it with a change of colour.

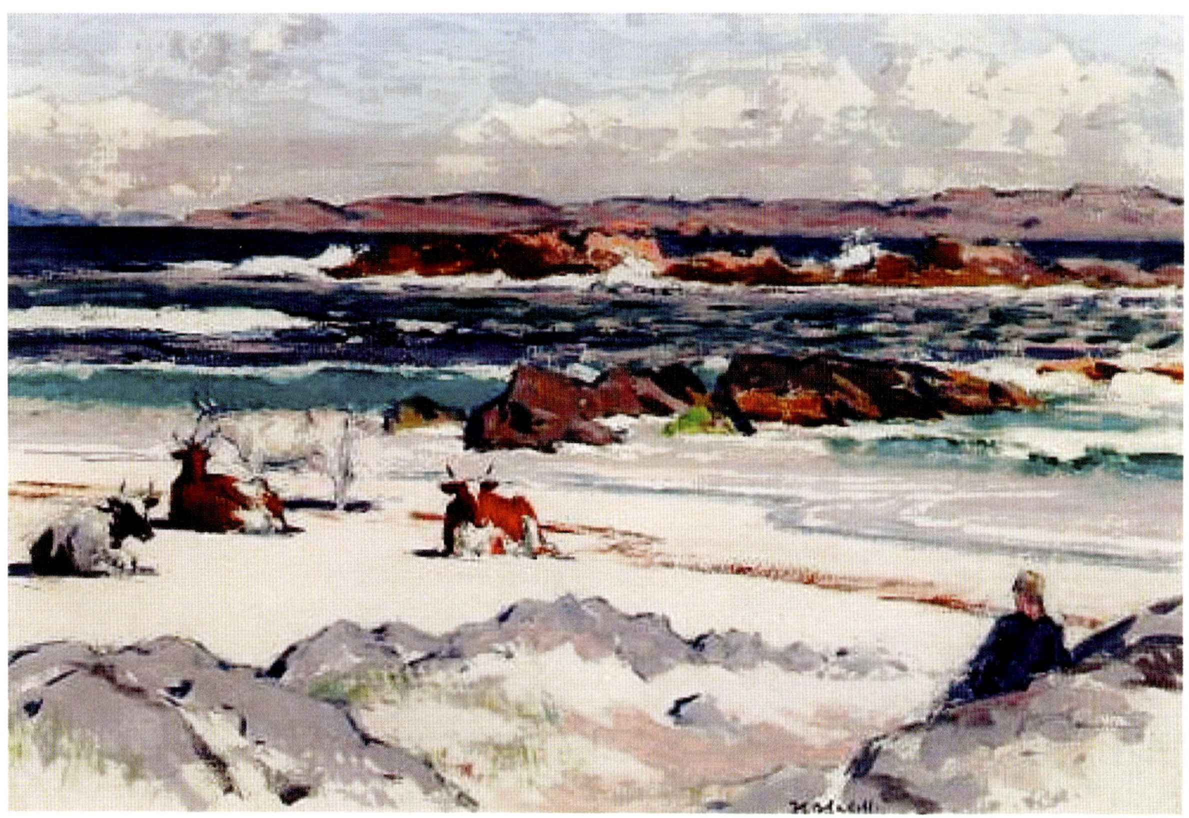

This is similar to Plate 89, but here the wider angle of view includes Treshnish Point, a hint of the Cuillin, and part of Rhum at the left edge of the painting.

[PLATE 90]

F. C. B. Cadell

Northwest Mull from Cows Rock

(Cattle on the Shore, Iona)

Oil

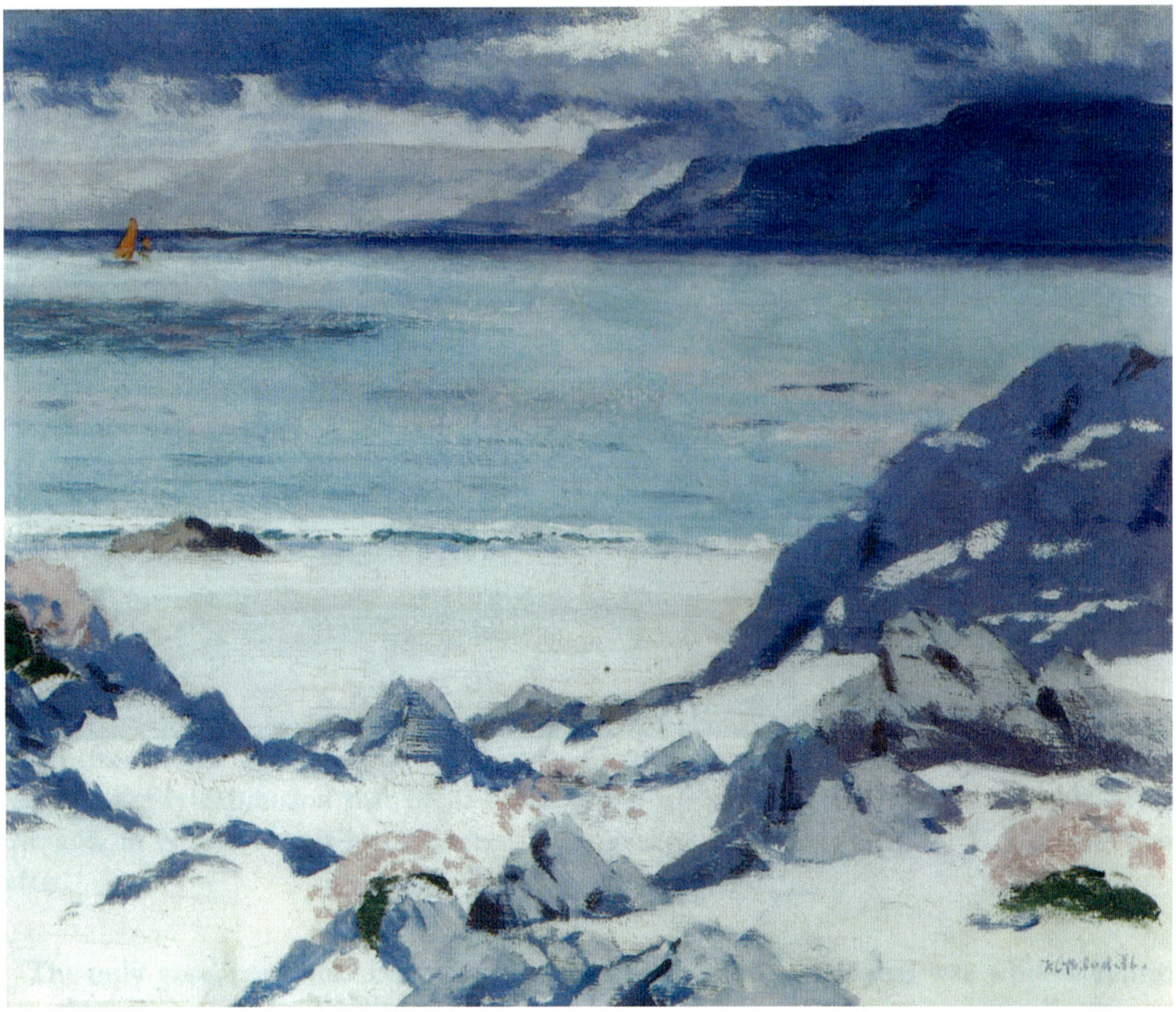

[PLATE 91]
F. C. B. Cadell
Mull from Cows Rock
Oil 15 x 18

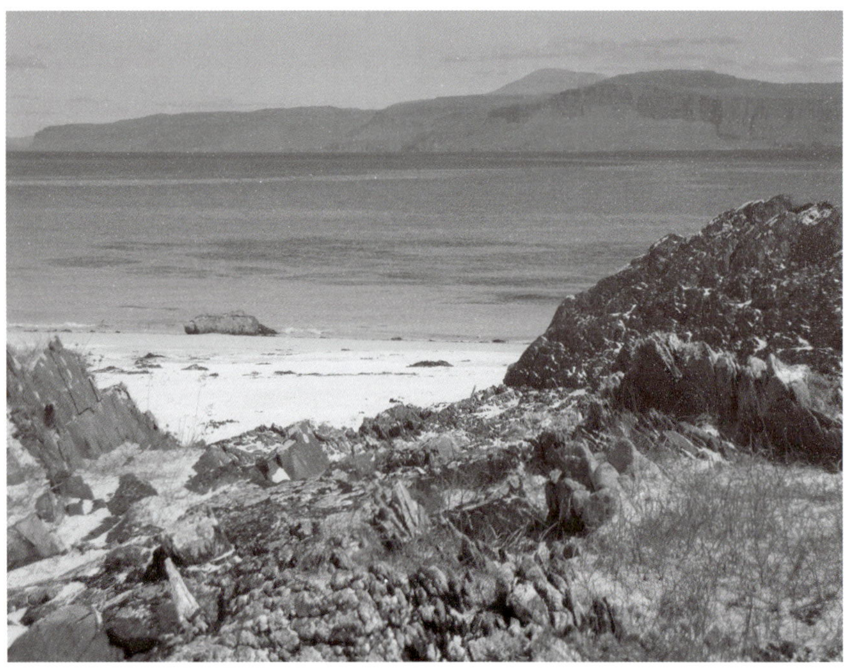

Photograph 2009

Painted from the northwest side of Cows Rock, this is the view to the northeast, with the Burg on the right in deep shadow under heavy clouds. The red sail on the left is only a small touch, but plays an important part in the composition balancing the dark masses on the right.

THE NORTH END BEACH

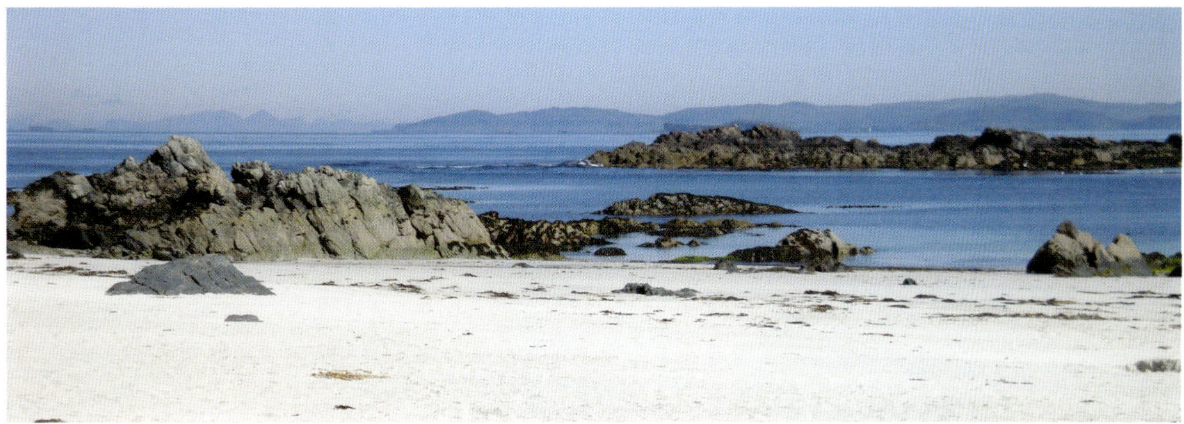

There are many pictures painted from the North End Beach, which lies between Cows Rock and the Headland. Also included in this section are pictures painted from the area of rocks which bound the Beach on the northwest side. Between these rocks and the hillside behind there is a narrow sandy area from where Peploe painted *Green Sea, Iona* (Plate 117). This sandy area leads through to the Mermaids Corridor. As with Cows Rock the views vary in direction from towards Lunga in the north, round to Ross of Mull in the southeast. The paintings towards Loch na Keal, which include Eileann Annraidh in the middle distance, are especially numerous.

Some of the paintings are from below mid-tide level which would indicate a fairly rapid execution of the work unless the artist completed it whilst retreating up the beach as the sea advanced.

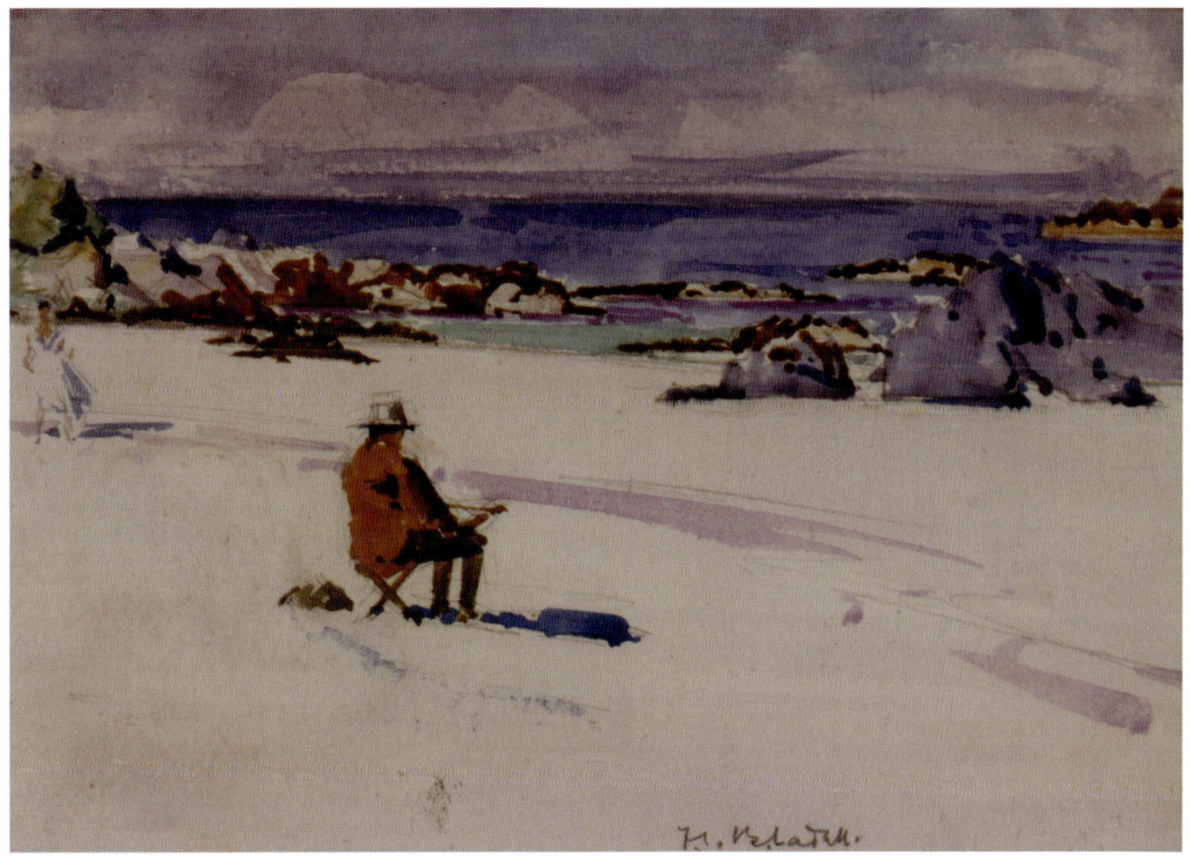

[PLATE 92]

F. C. B. Cadell

A painter at the North End, Iona

Watercolour 7 x 10

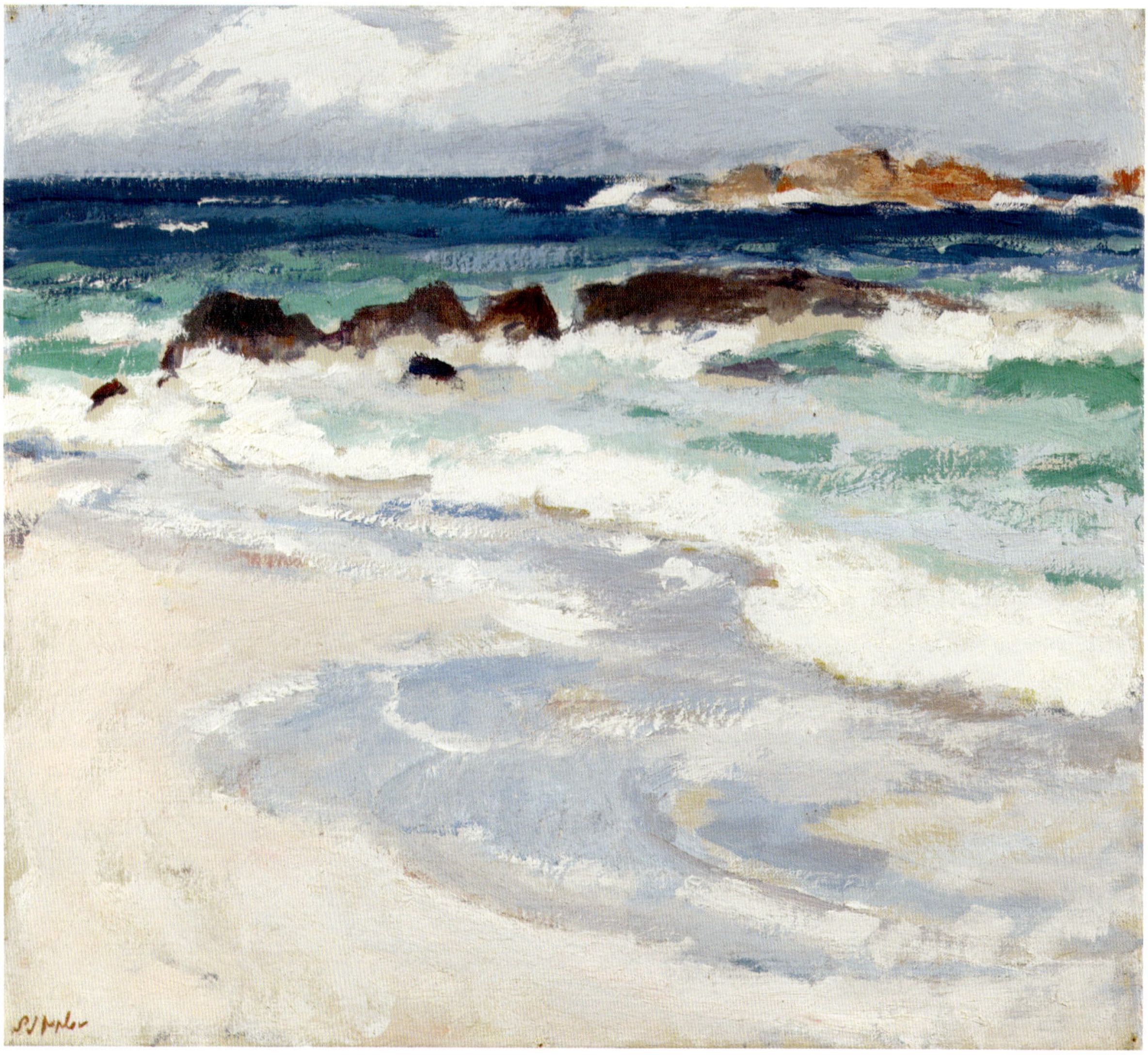

[PLATE 93]

S. J. Peploe

Eilean Annraidh from the North End (Rough Sea, Iona)

Oil 15 x 17 1/2

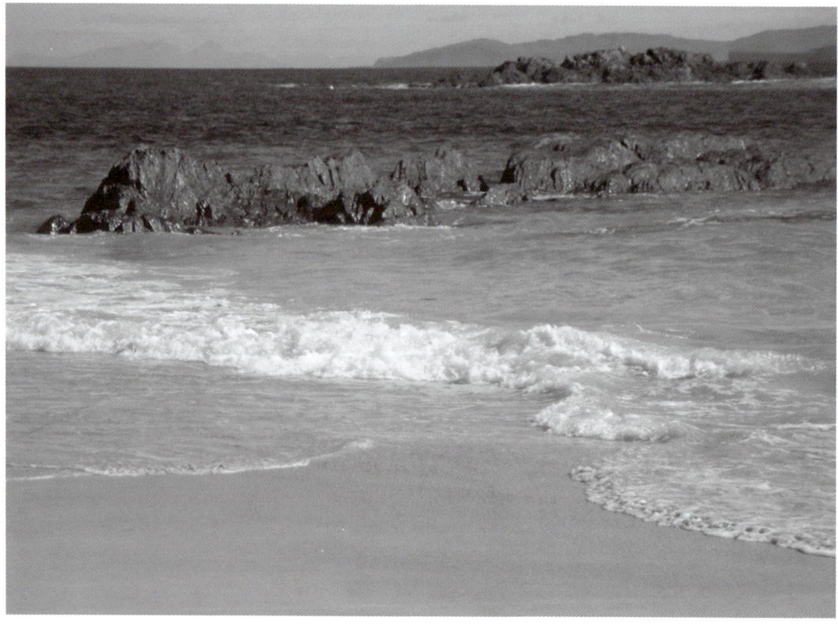

Photograph 2010

The line of dark rocks across the foreground is the Finger; Eilean Annraidh is beyond on the right. This was painted from the beach north of Cows Rock. In the photograph Treshnish Point and a faint image of Rhum are visible on the horizon.

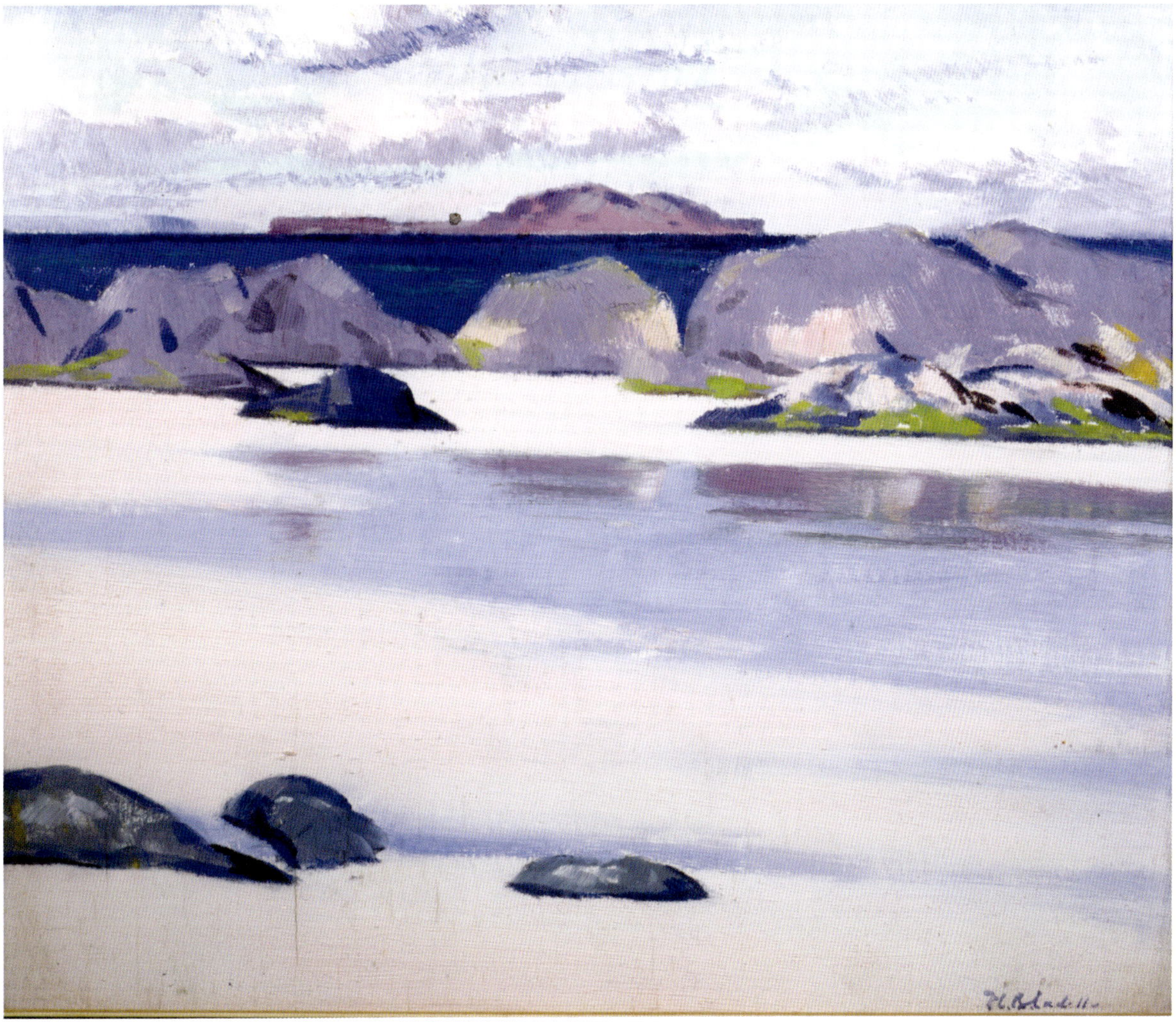

[PLATE 94]

F. C. B. Cadell

Lunga from the North End

Oil 15 x 18

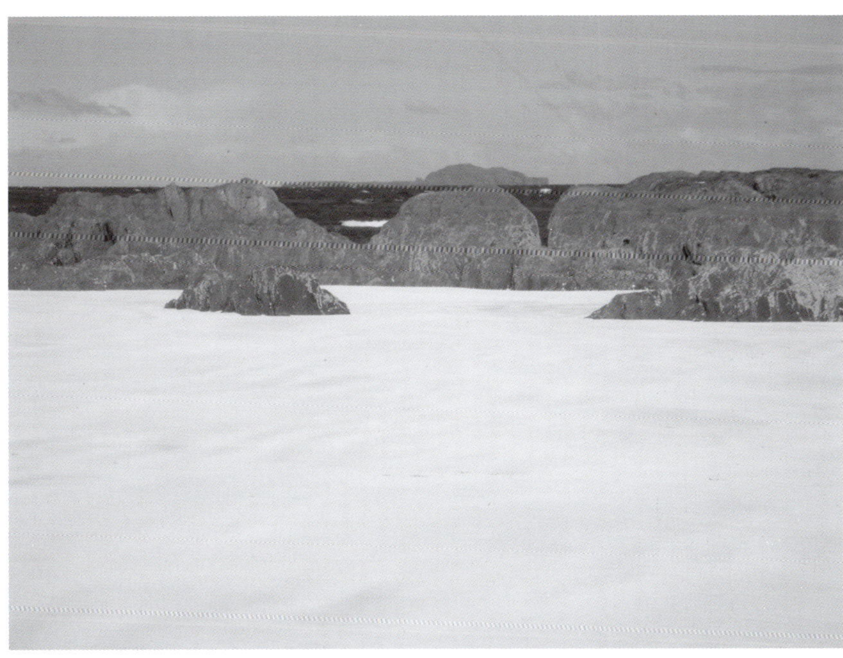

Photograph 2009

Painted at low tide close to Cows Rock, this shows a small section of the Finger across the full width of the picture, with Lunga beyond on the horizon.

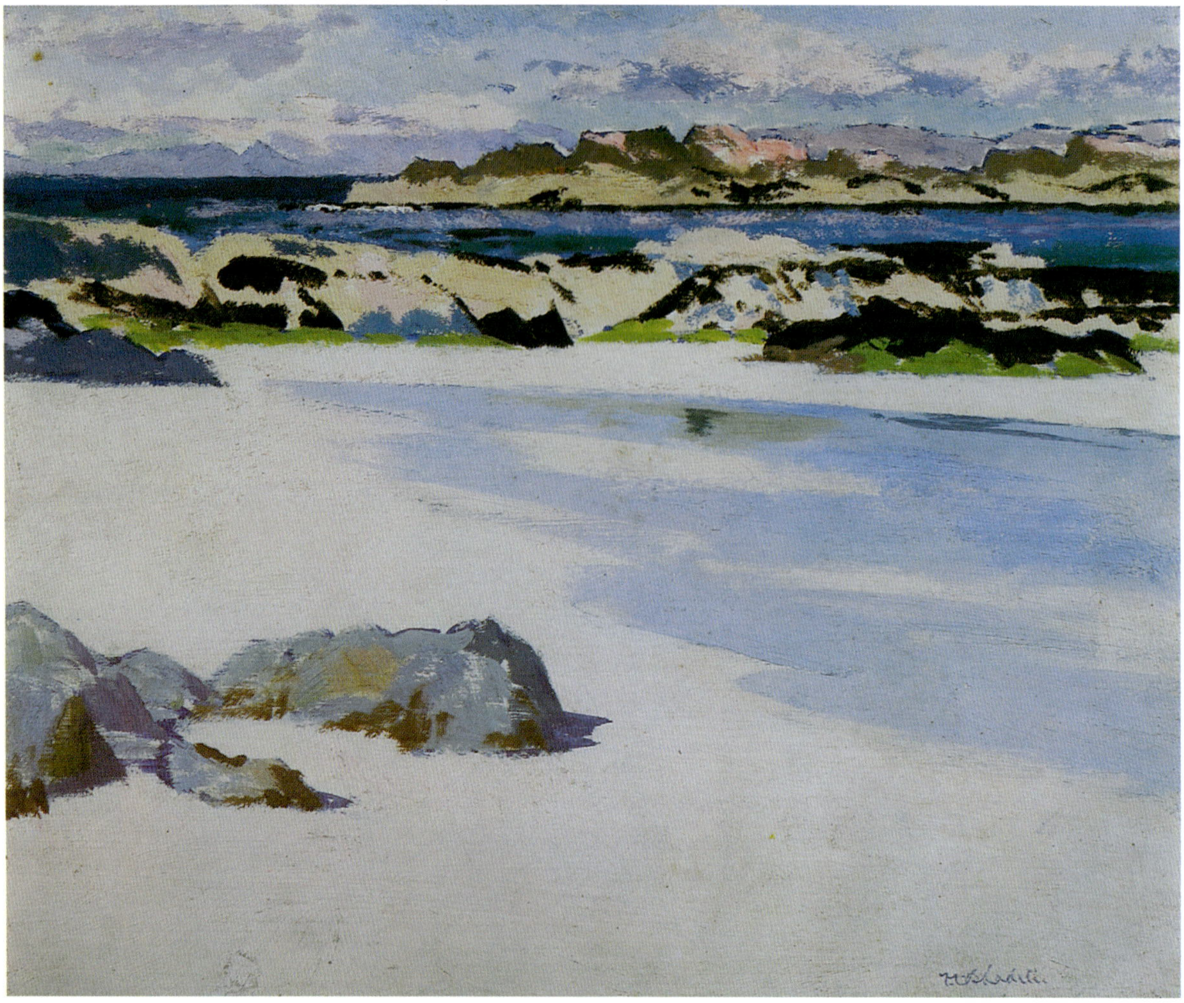

[PLATE 95]

F. C. B. Cadell

Eilean Annraidh
from the North End
(Wet Sands, Iona)
Oil 15 x 18

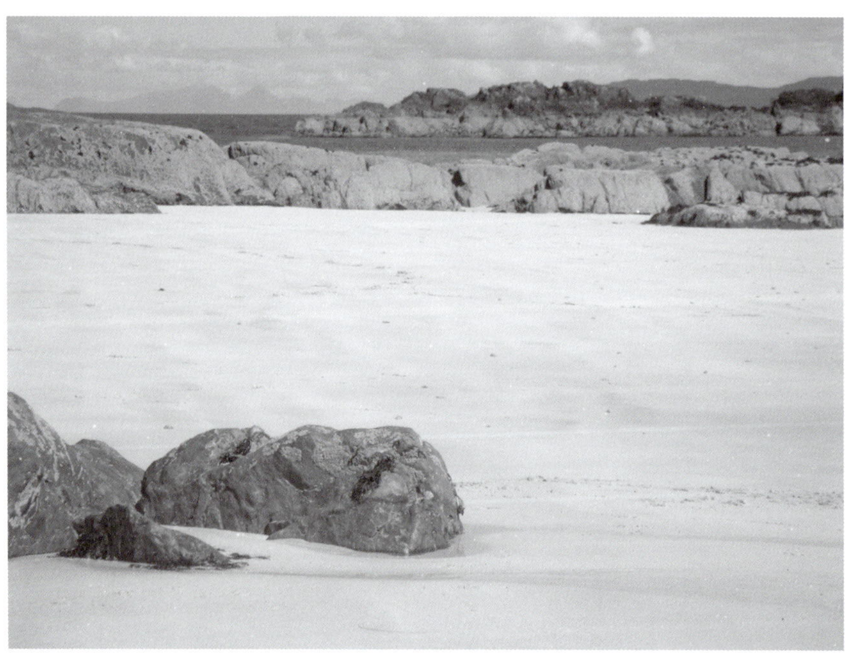

Photograph 2009

This is the lower section of the Finger which is exposed only at low tide. The west end of Eilean Annraidh extends across most of the middle distance from the right, and there is a pale image of Rhum in the distance on the left.

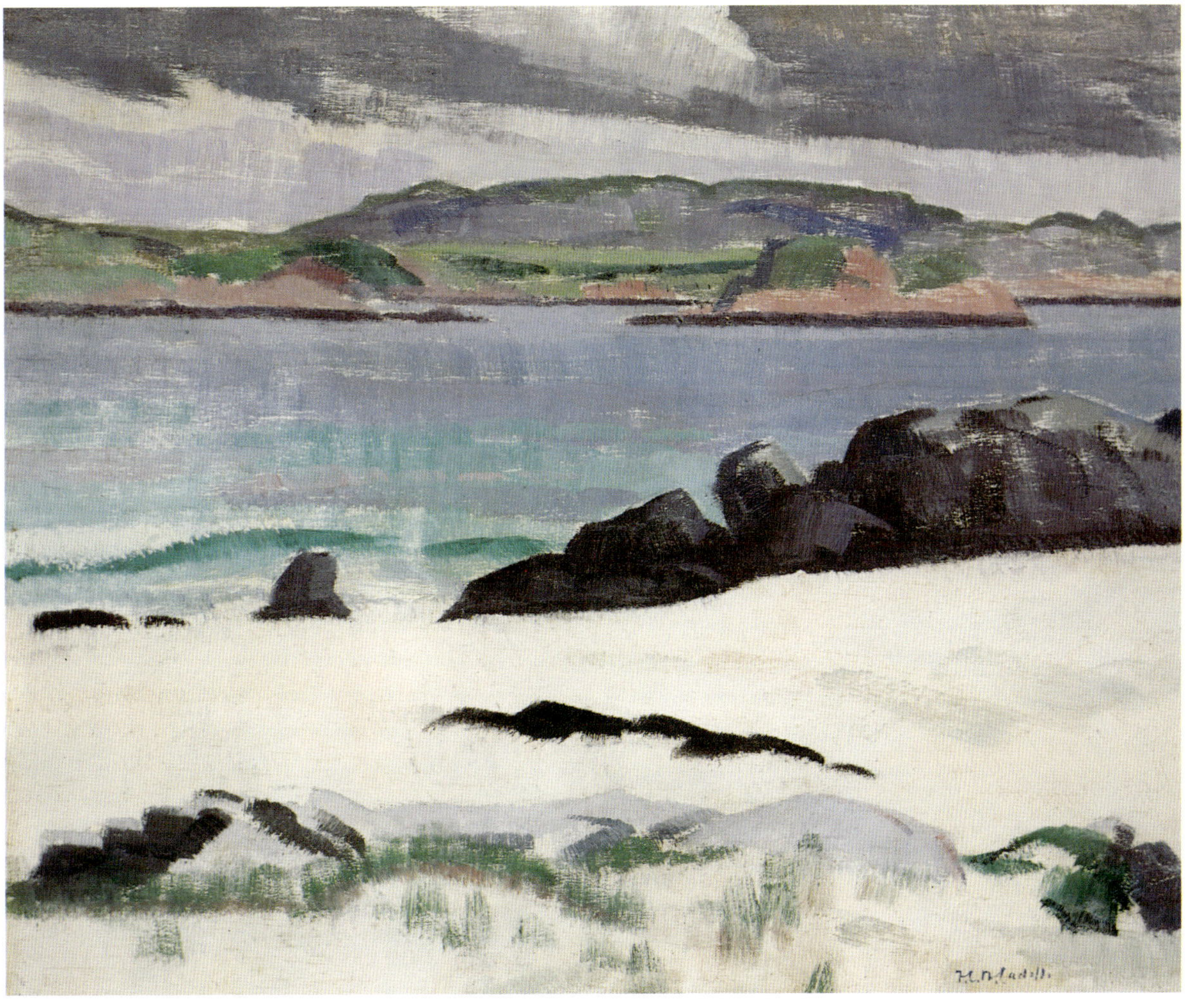

[PLATE 96]
F. C. B. Cadell
Cows Rock
and the Ross of Mull
Oil 15 x 18

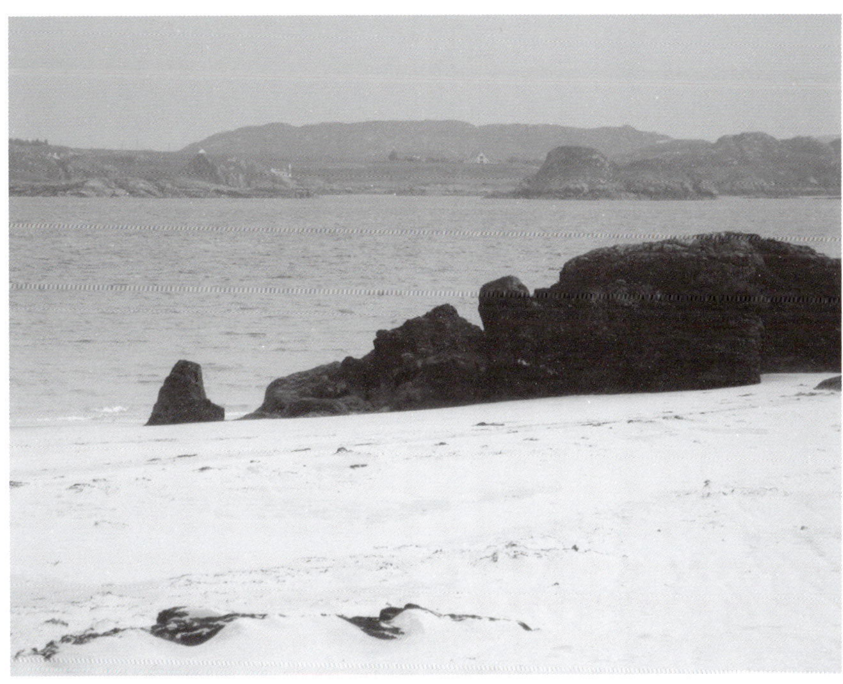

Photograph 2009

This is the northeast corner of Cows Rock. The isolated pillar of rock on the left is in a number of paintings; for identification I shall refer to it as "Pedestal Rock". The entrance to Sandy Creek (Plate 76) is on the right.

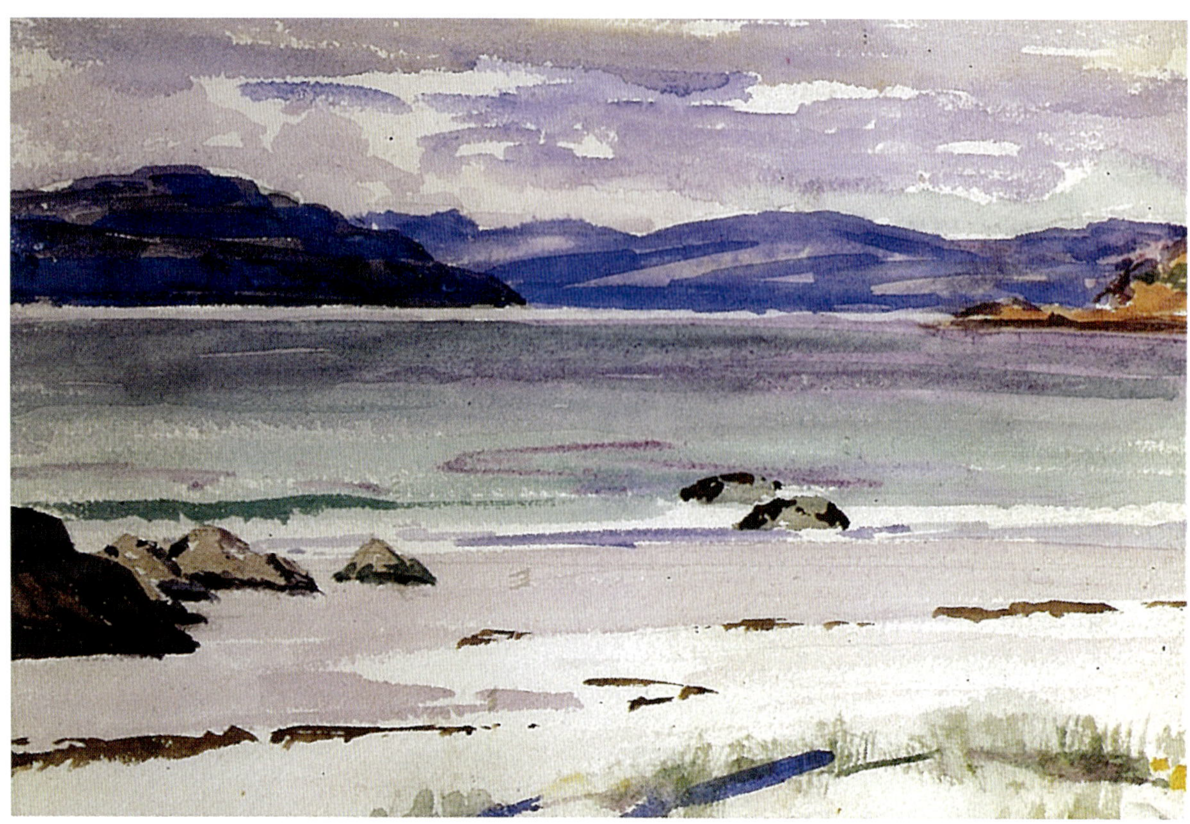

[PLATE 97]
F. C. B. Cadell
Ben Buie
from the North End
Watercolour 8 x 10

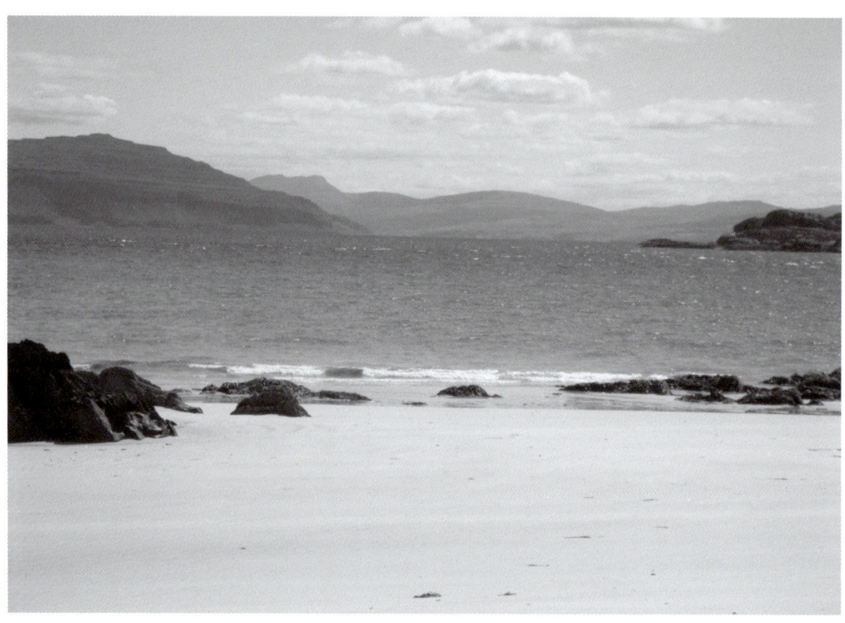

Photograph 2012

This is the view due east to Loch Scridain, with Ben Buie in the distance left of centre. The south end of the Burg is on the left, and the Ross of Mull on the right. The dark rock in the left foreground is the end of the Finger.

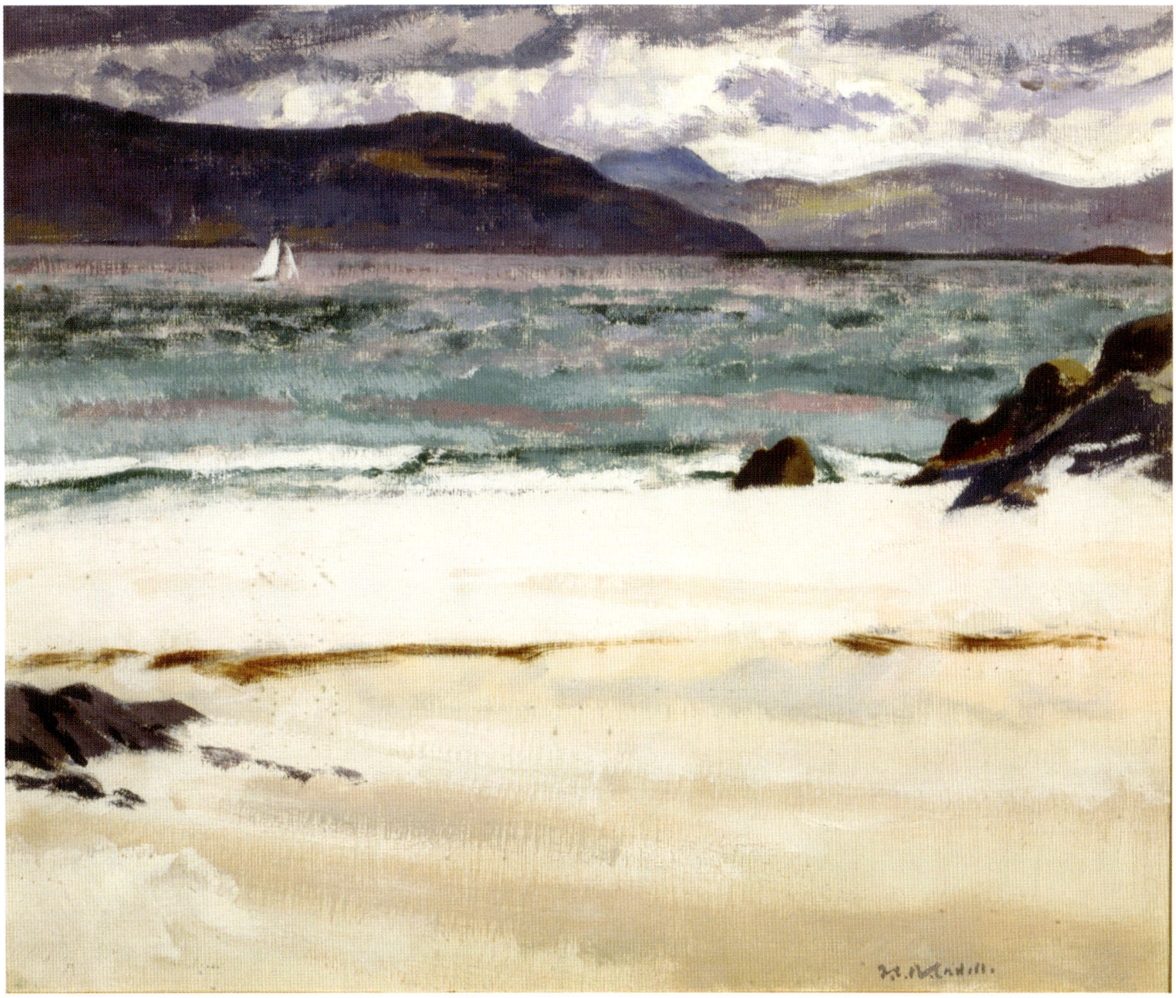

[PLATE 98]
F. C. B. Cadell
Ben Buie
from the North End
Oil 15 x 18

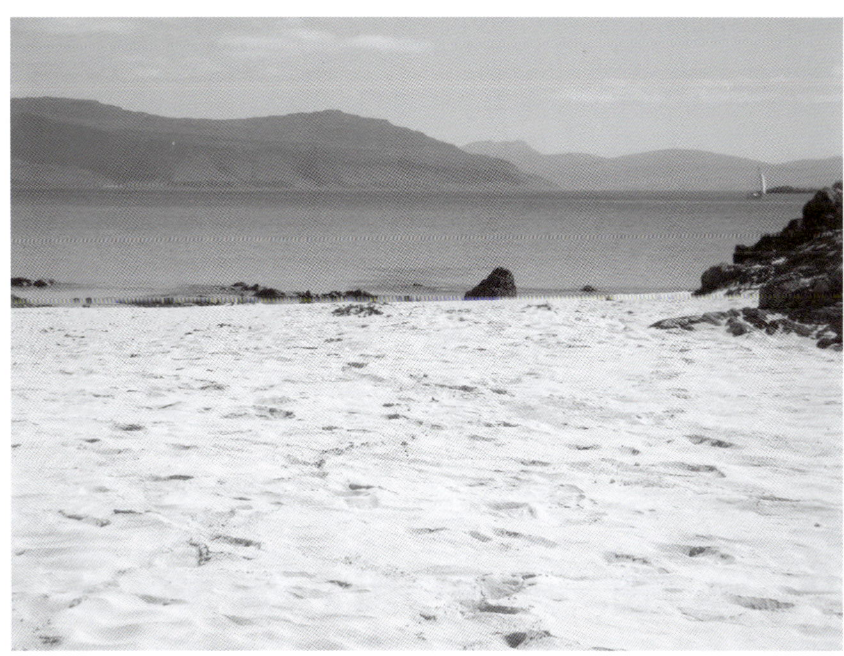

Photograph 2010

This view is similar to that in Plate 97, but was painted from closer to Cows Rock, which is seen at the right-hand side.

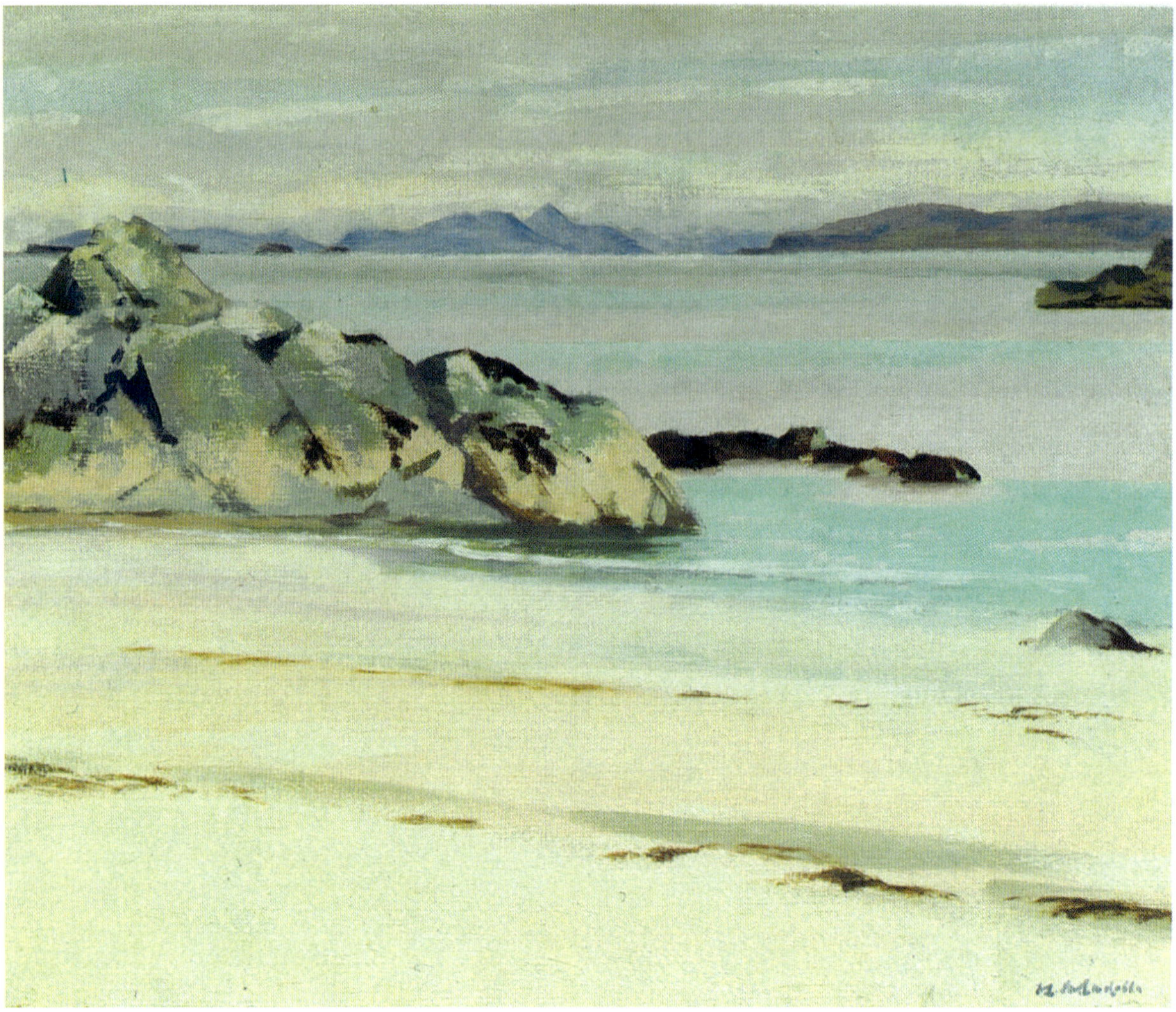

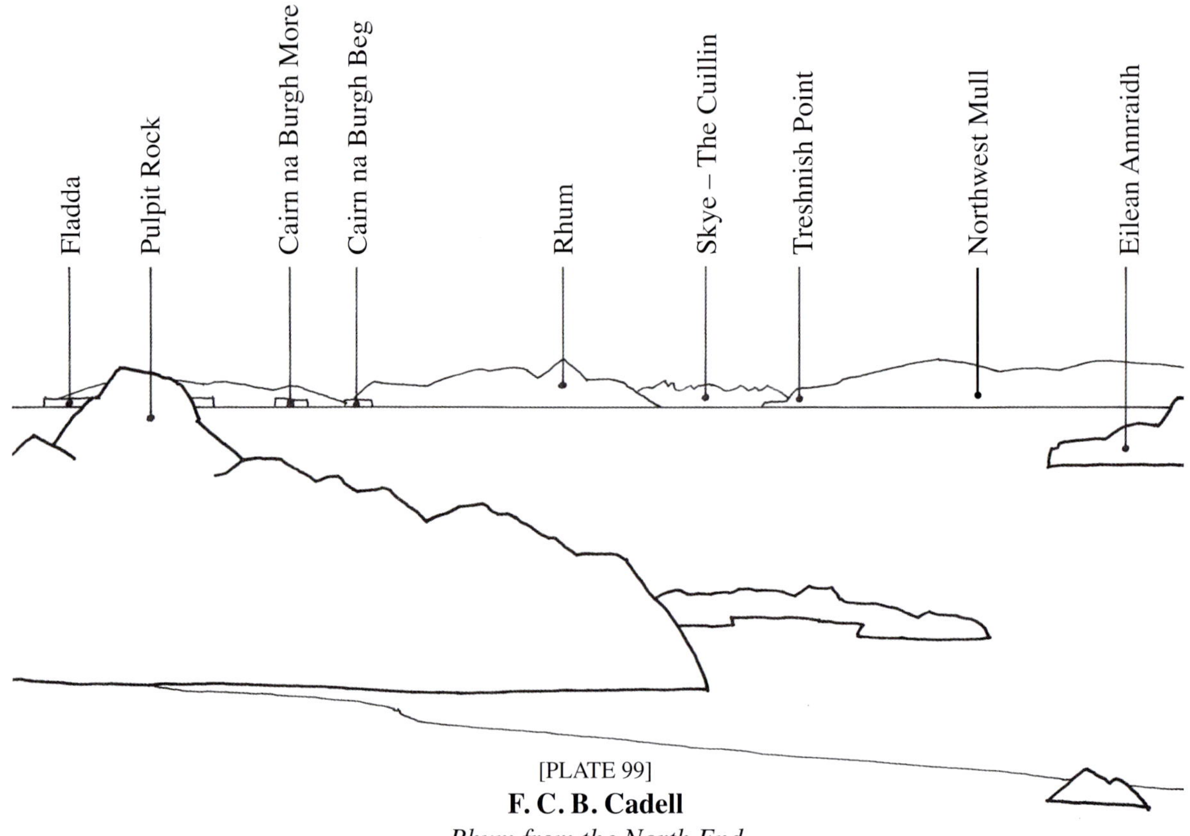

[PLATE 99]

F. C. B. Cadell

Rhum from the North End

Oil 15 x 18

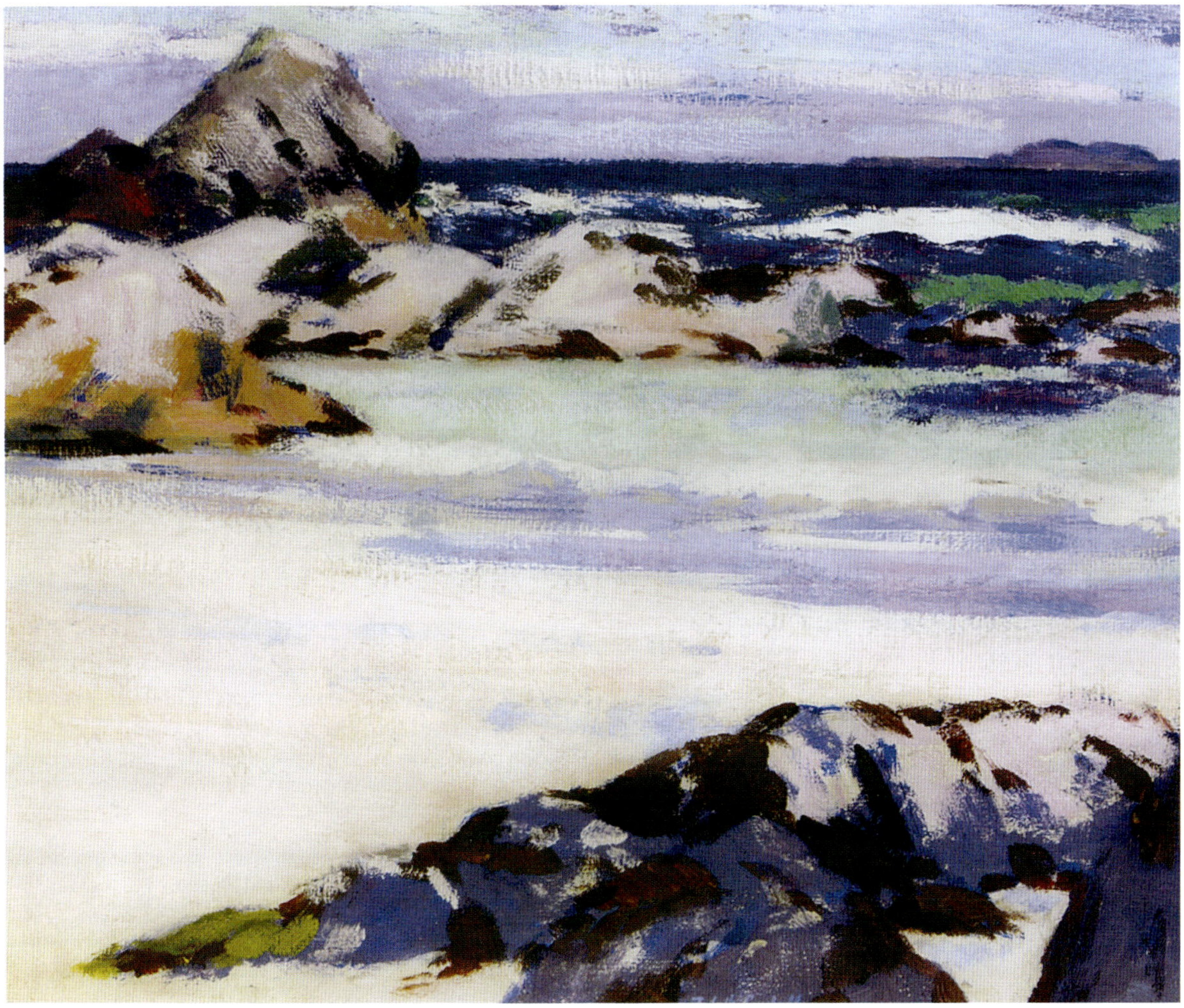

[PLATE 100]

F. C. B. Cadell

Pulpit Rock
(A View from Iona towards Lunga)
Oil 15 x 18

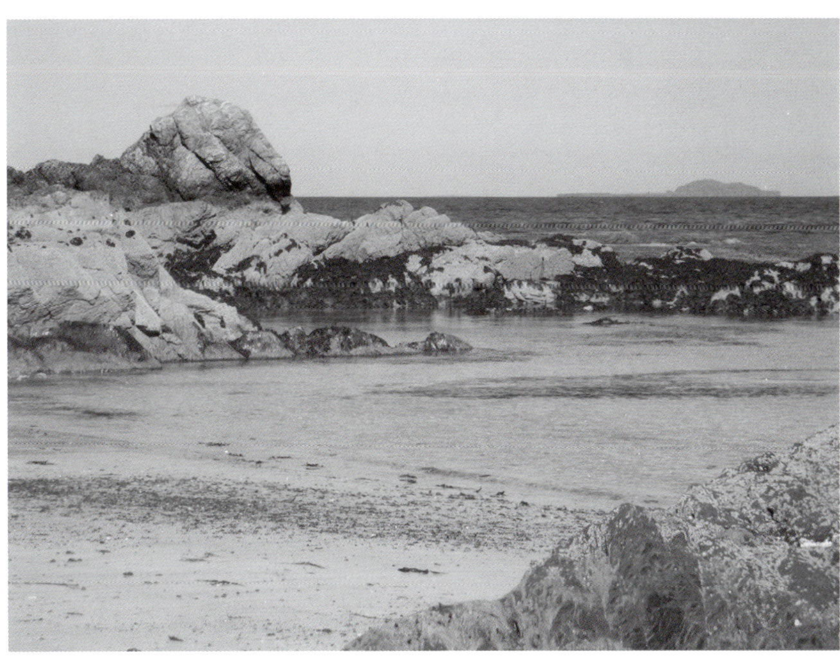

Photograph 2010

Painted from against the northwest face of the Finger, this is the view almost due north to Lunga, on the right at the horizon. Pulpit Rock is prominent at the left-hand side of the painting.

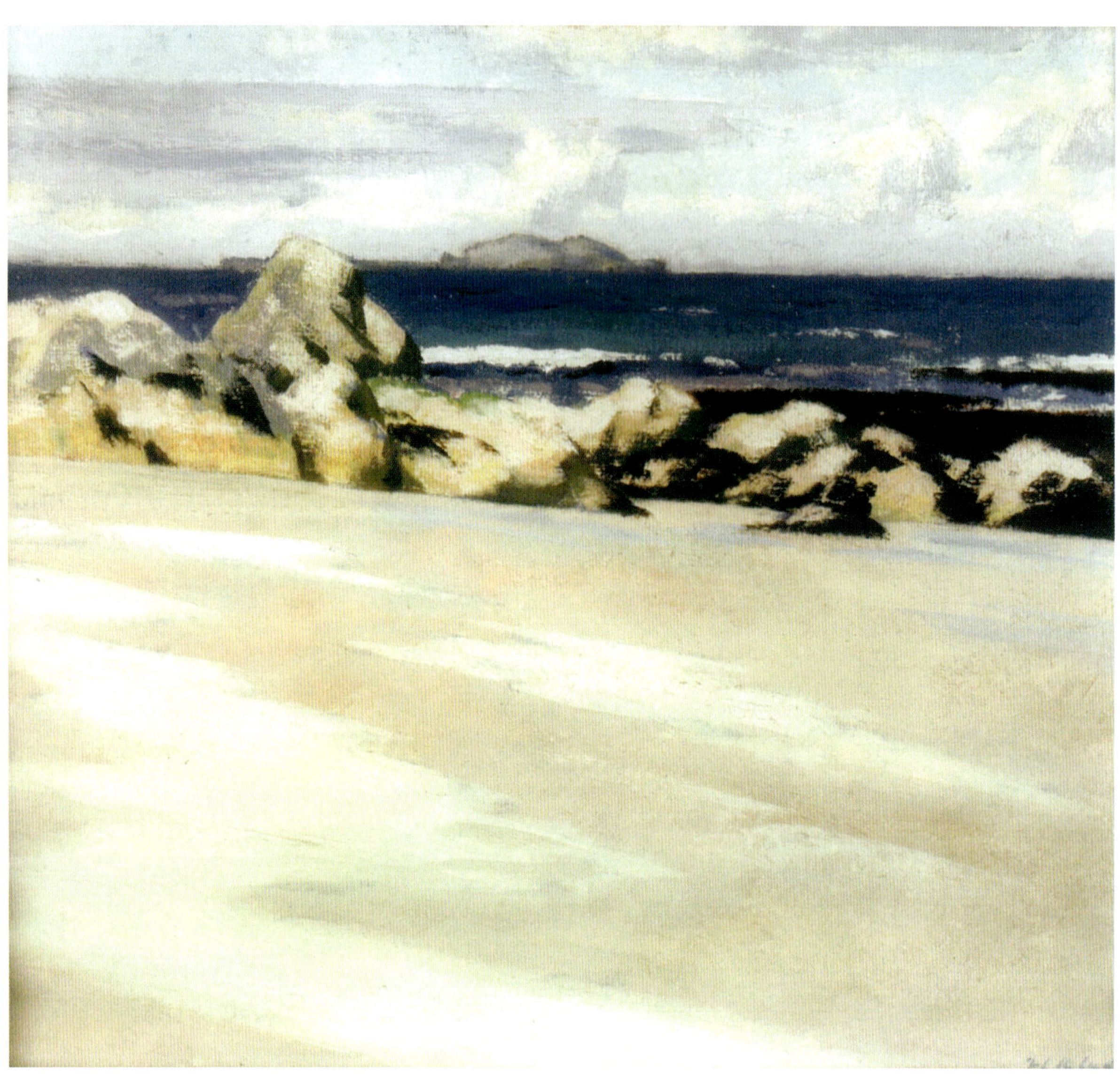

Lunga is placed more centrally than in Plate 100, and is partly hidden by the top of Pulpit Rock.

[PLATE 101]
F. C. B. Cadell
Lunga from the North End
Oil 15 x 18

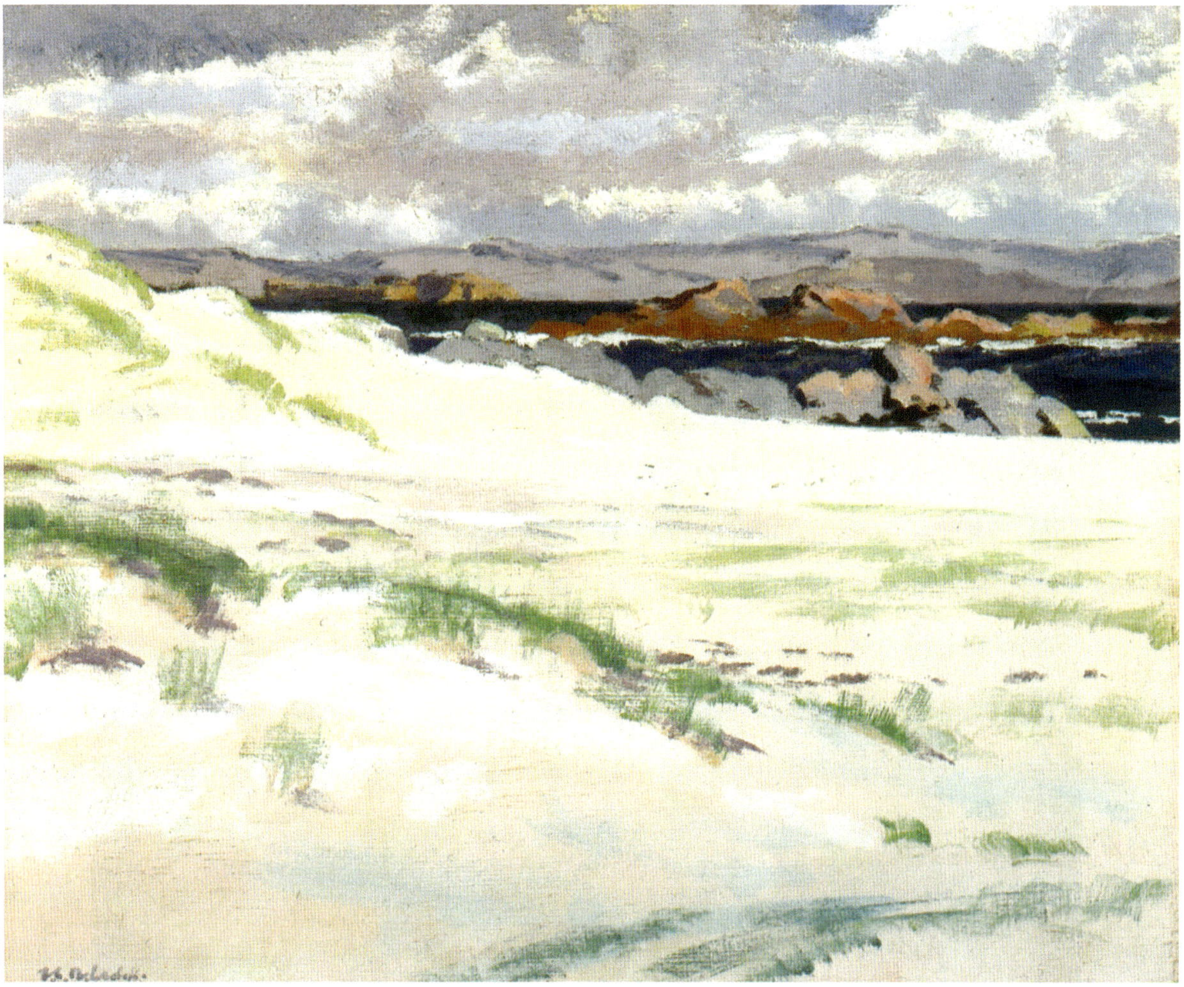

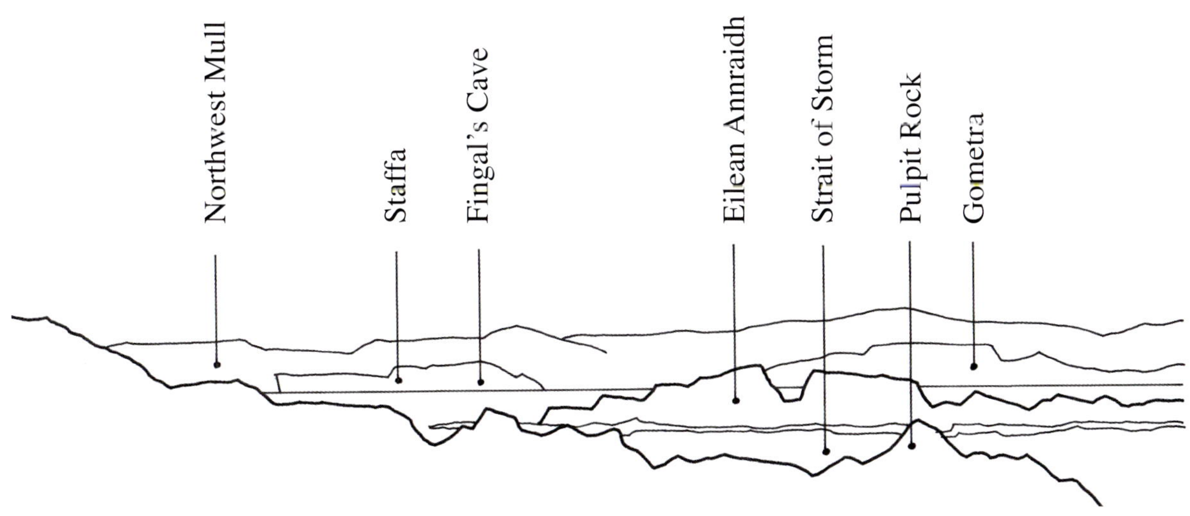

[PLATE 102]

F. C. B. Cadell

Staffa and Eilean Annraidh from the North End

(White Sands, Iona)

Oil 15 x 18

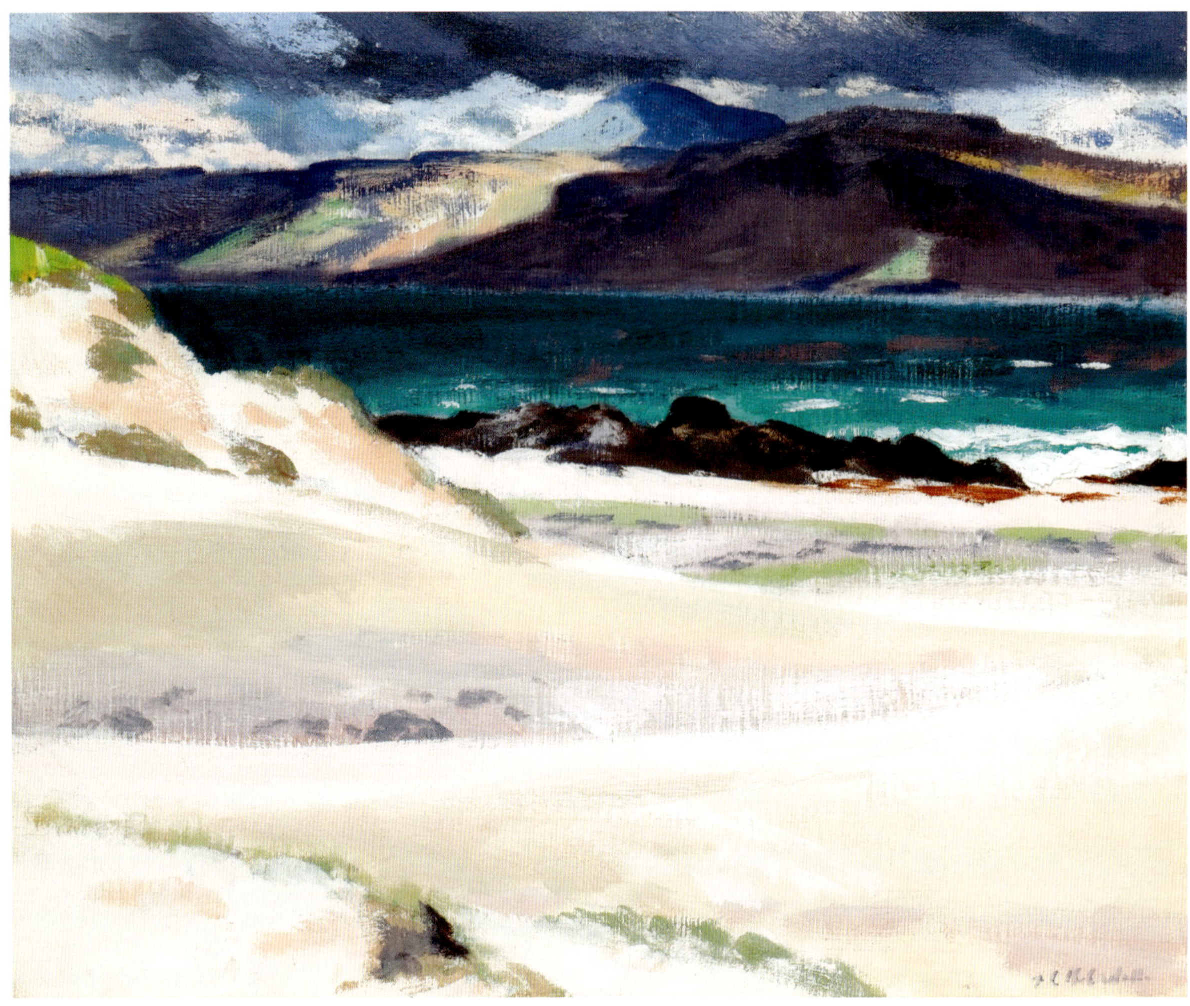

This is the same area of the beach as Plate 102, but here the Finger is also included in this view towards Ben More and the Burg, which are seen in light and shade from passing clouds.

[PLATE 103]
F. C. B. Cadell
Ben More from the North End
Oil 15 x 18

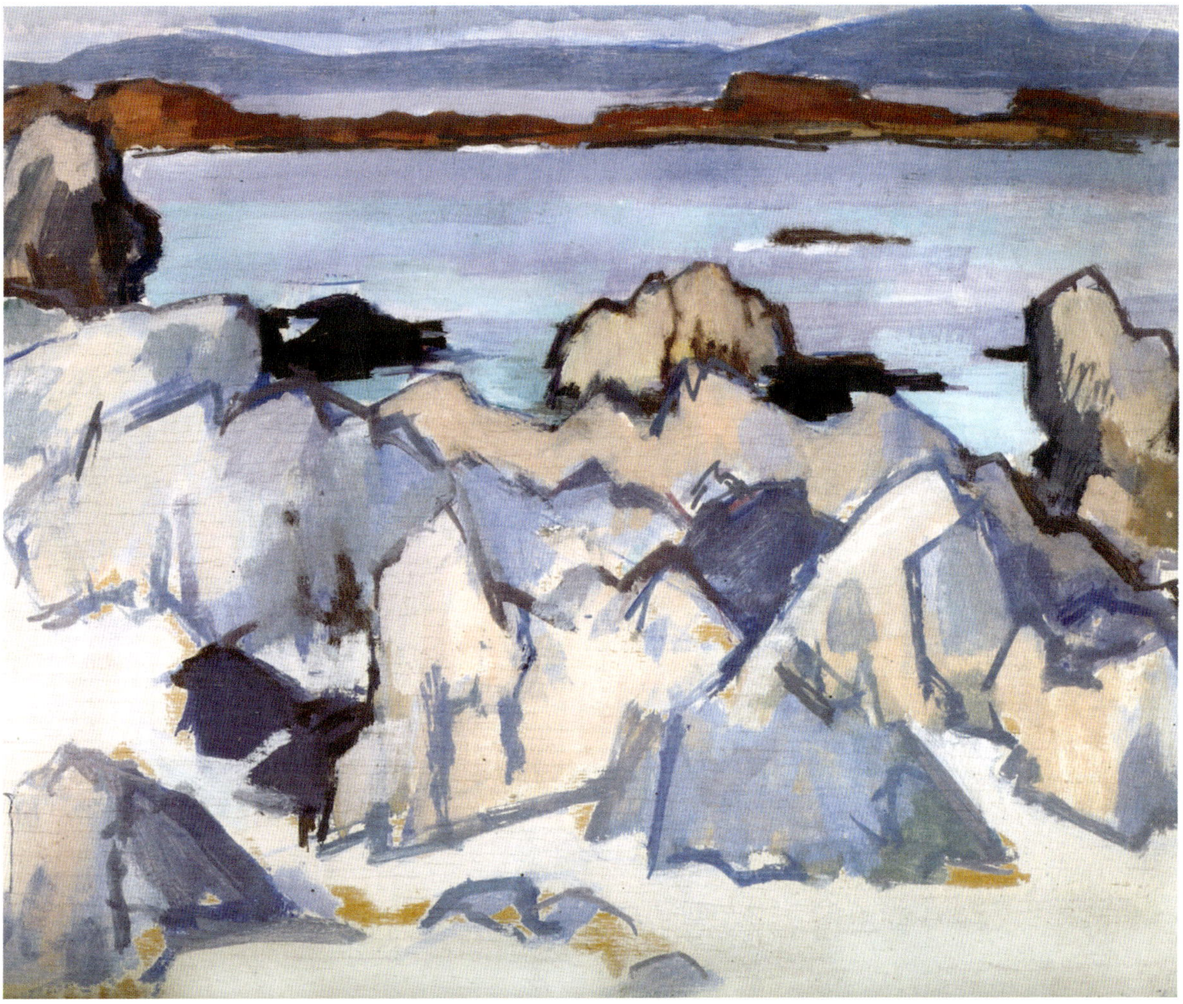

[PLATE 104]

S. J. Peploe

Eilean Annraidh and Ulva from the North End

Oil 13 x 16

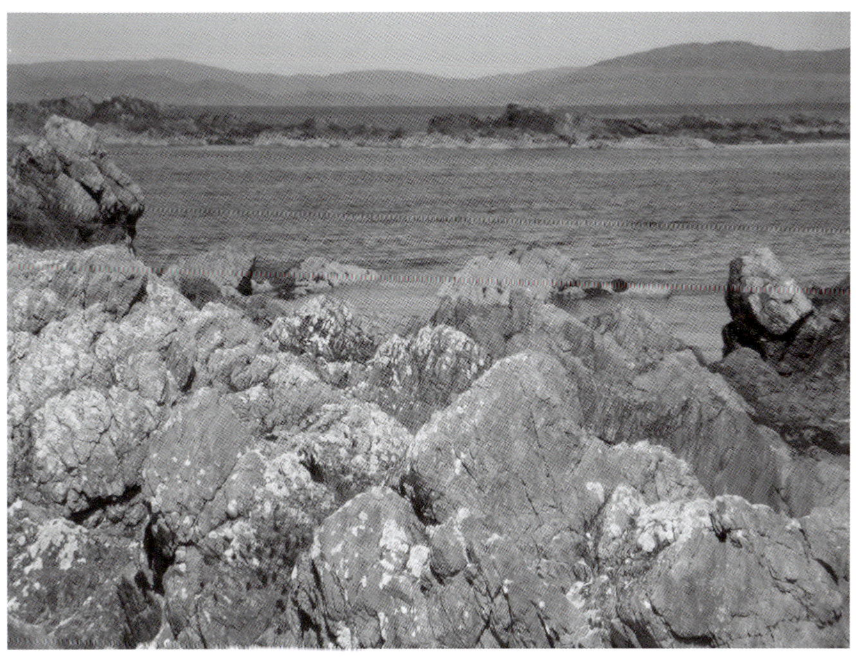

Photograph 2010

Ulva is at the top right, and the western part of Eilean Annraidh is across the whole width of the picture in the middle distance. Pulpit Rock is at the extreme left, and on the right there is a pointed rock which for identification I refer to as the "Little Pinnacle" (see page 85).

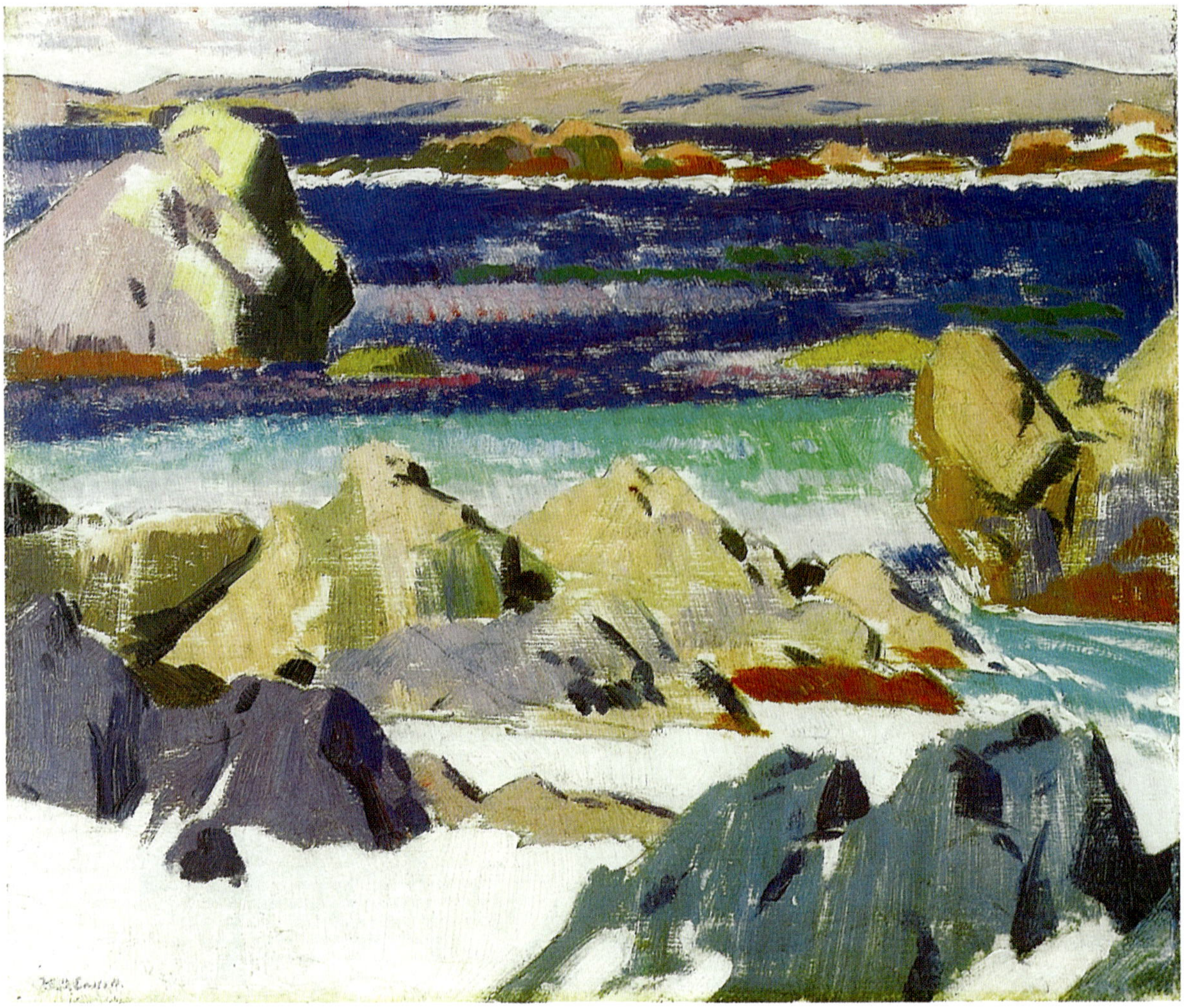

[PLATE 105]

F. C. B. Cadell

EILEAN ANNRAIDH,
ULVA AND STAFFA

Oil 15 x 18

The Hunterian,
University of Glasgow

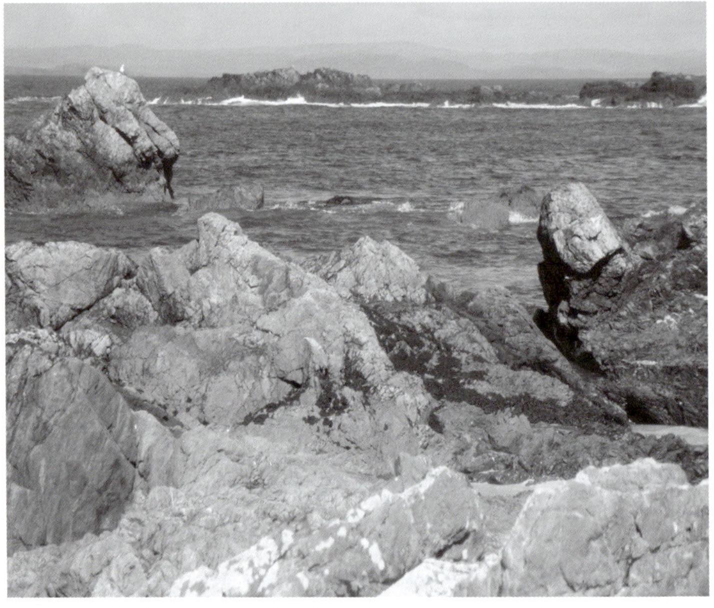

Photograph 2013

Plates 105 and 106 are an example of the two artists having painted the same subject. Both paintings show Pulpit Rock on the left and the Little Pinnacle on the right in the foreground, with the west end of Eilean Annraidh in the middle distance. The tide level is slightly higher in this painting by Cadell than it is in the Peploe. Also Cadell's viewpoint is a little further forward and consequently slightly lower down; the top of Pulpit Rock comes just above the horizon and is partly hiding the island of Staffa in the top left corner of the painting. The hills of northwest Mull are seen in the background.

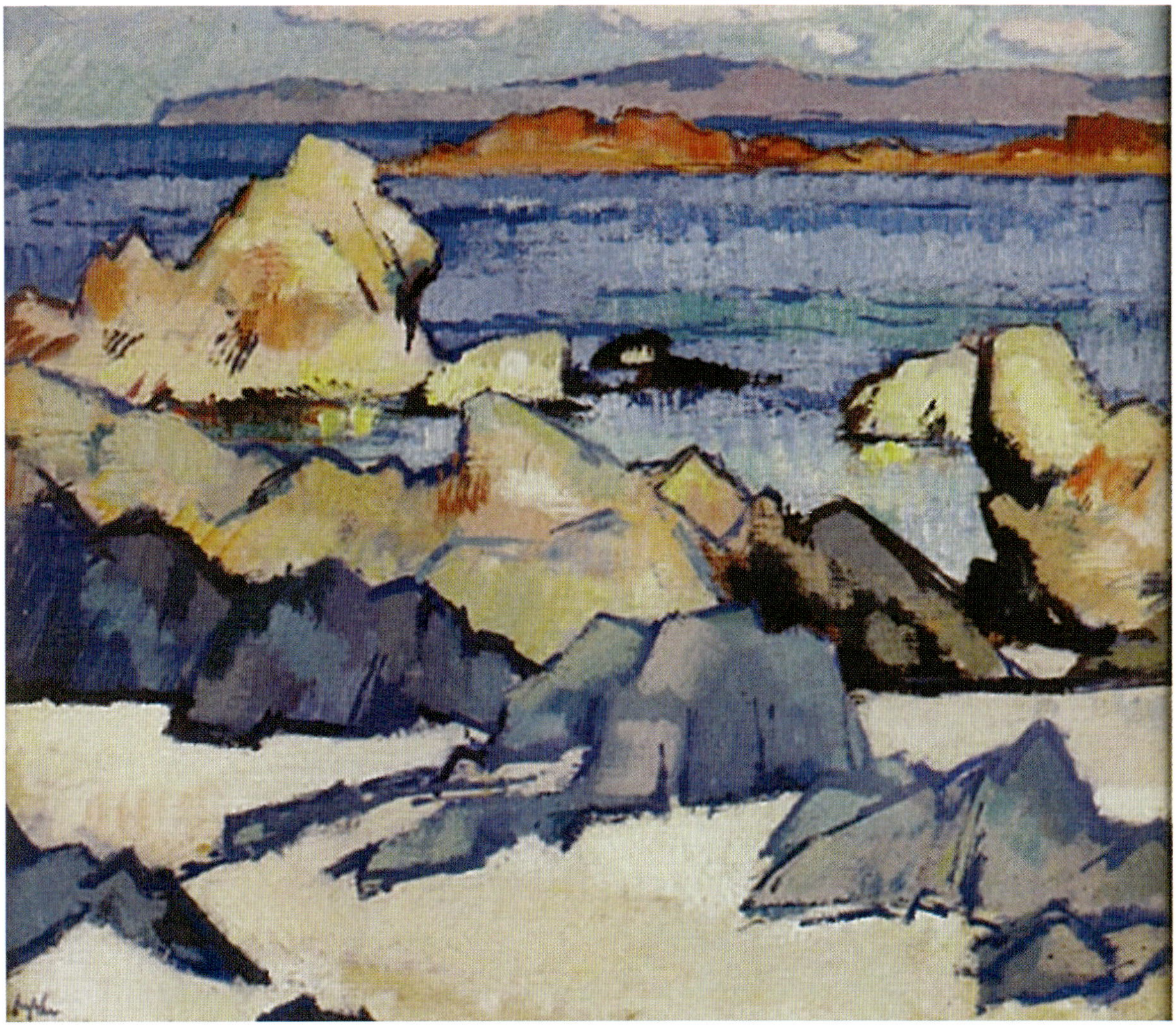

[PLATE 106]

S. J. Peploe

Eilean Annraidh from the North End

Oil 13 x 15

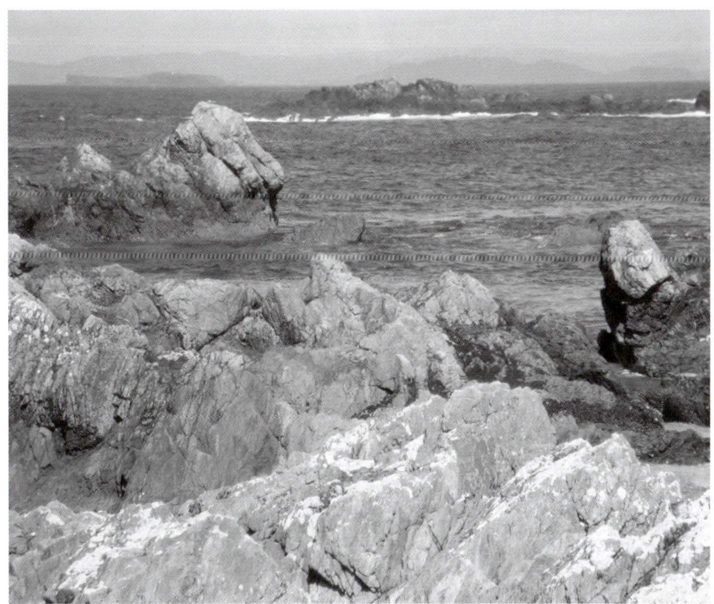

Photograph 2013

As in Plate 105 Pulpit Rock is on the left and the Little Pinnacle on the right. The foreground rocks are painted with such precision that the exact viewpoint can be established beyond any doubt. The sand levels are lower in the photograph, but nevertheless the rocks can be traced quite clearly. The headland in the top left corner appears to be Treshnish Point, with open sea to the left, but is in fact the west end of the island of Staffa. The hills on the right correspond to Gometra and not northwest Mull, which was probably not visible in the conditions prevailing at the time Peploe painted this picture.

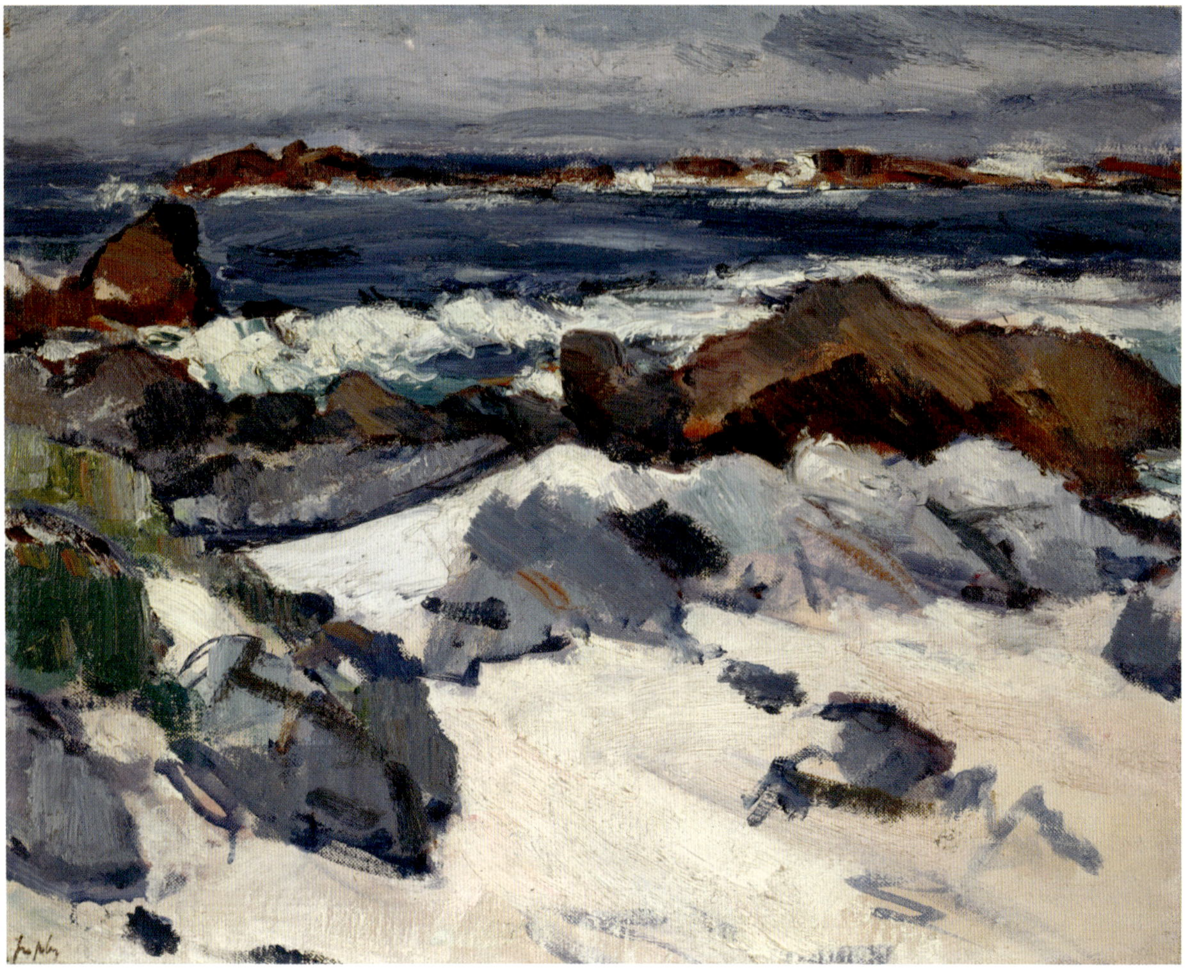

[PLATE 107]

S. J. Peploe

A ROCKY SHORE, IONA

Eilean Annraidh
from the North End
Oil 16 x 20

City Art Centre,
Edinburgh Museums
and Galleries

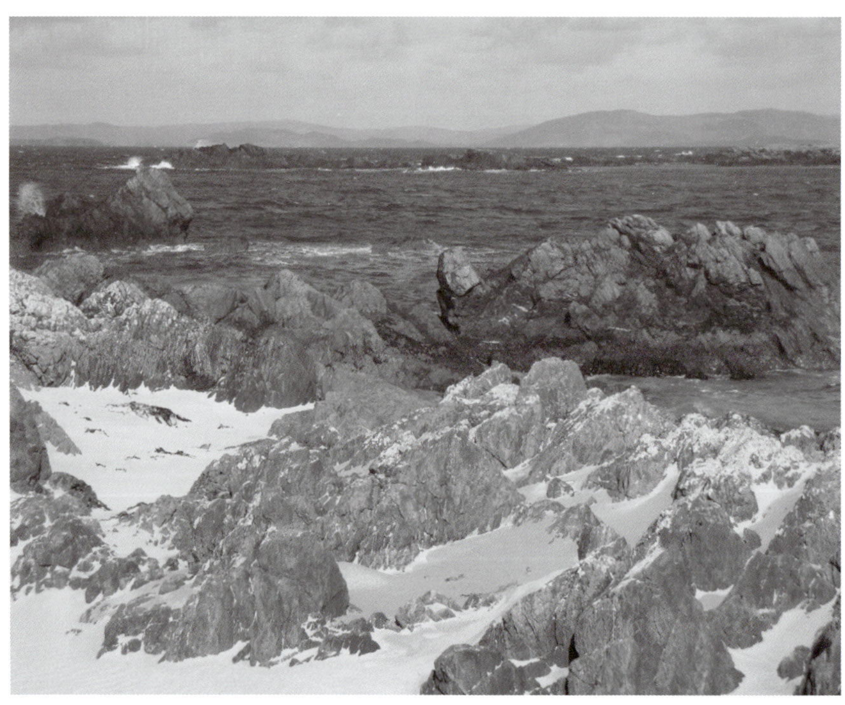

Photograph 2010

This view is to the northeast. The main elements in Plates 104, 105 and 106 feature here also, but in a wider angle composition. Pulpit Rock is on the left and the Little Pinnacle is in the centre. Eilean Annraidh lies across almost the entire width of the painting in the middle distance. Briskly painted, there is a wide range of surface from thinly stained canvas to thick impasto, applied mostly with a brush, but with a knife for the white sand left of centre.

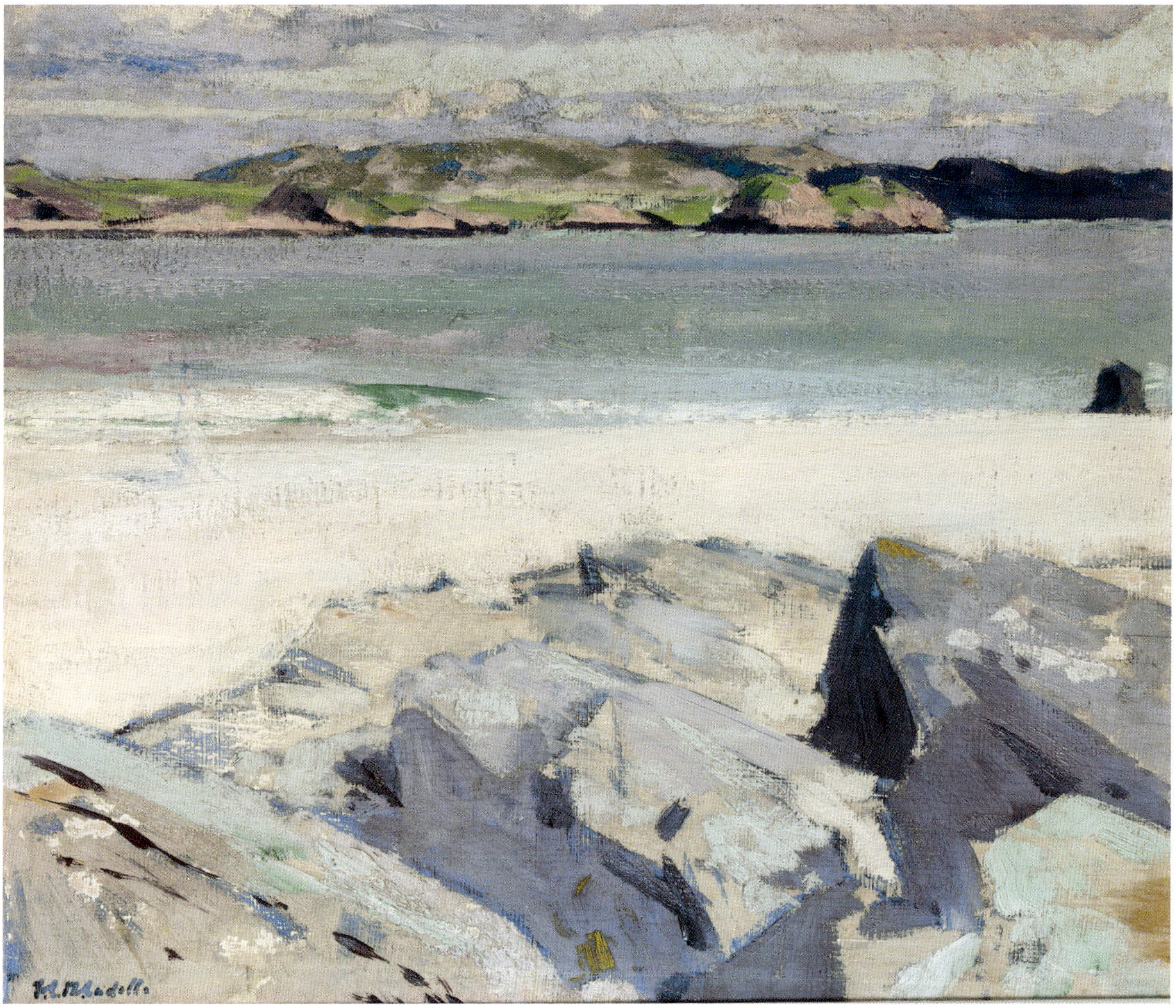

[PLATE 108]
F. C. B. Cadell
Ross of Mull
from the North End
Oil 15 x 18

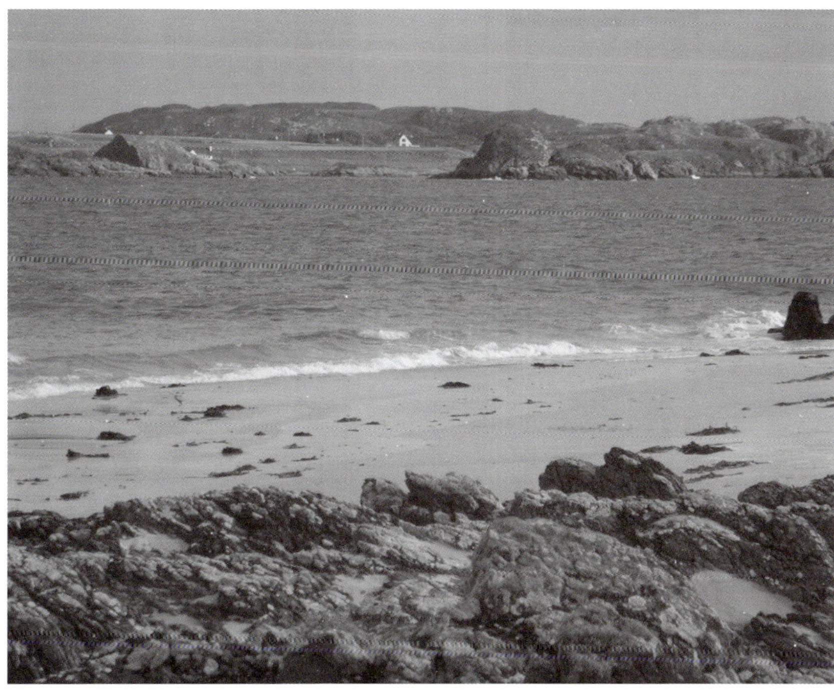

Photograph 2010

Painted from a position close to that of Plate 107, this is the very different view towards the southeast. The isolated rock to the extreme right is Pedestal Rock, the main part of Cows Rock being excluded (see Plate 96).

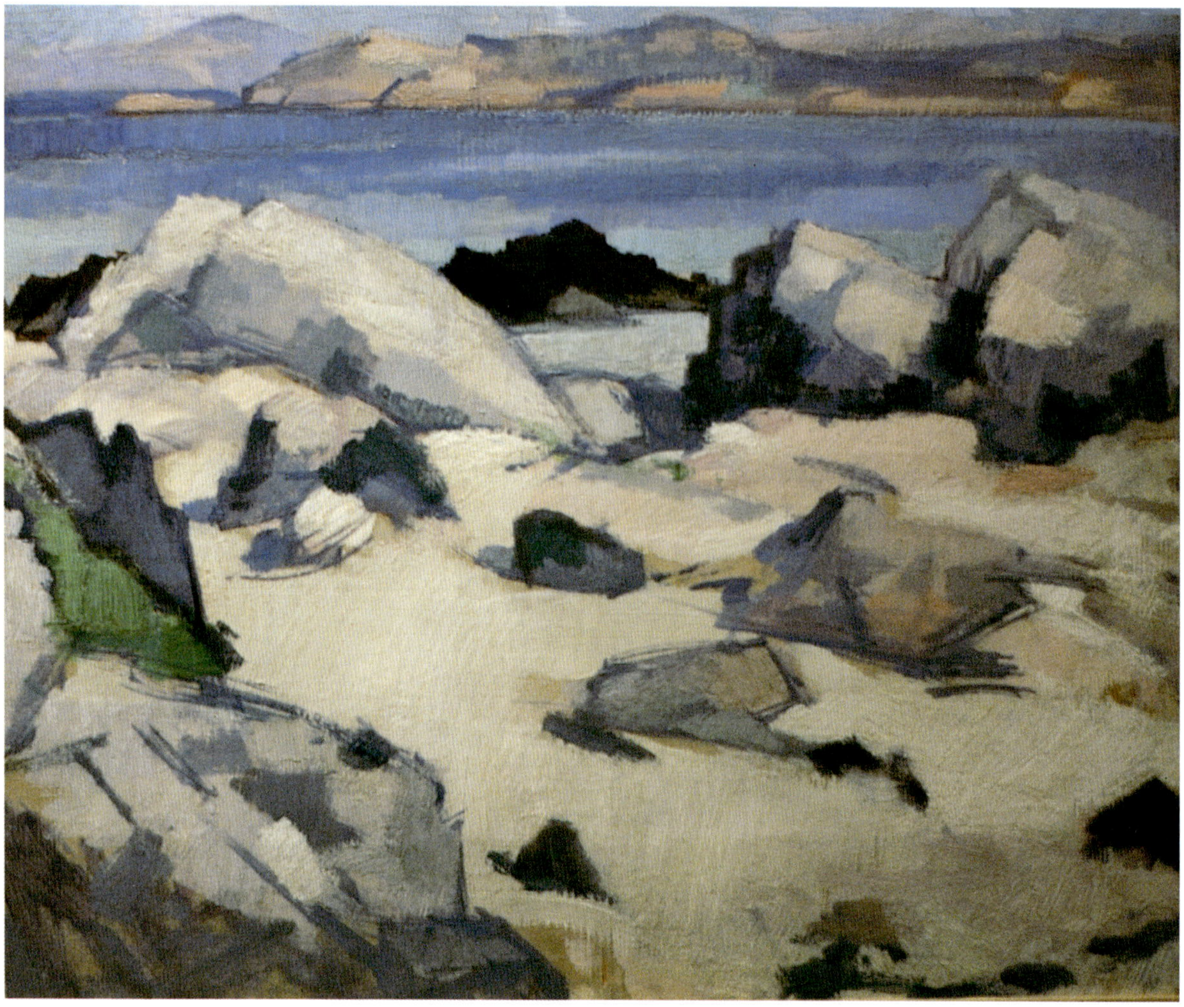

[PLATE 109]

S. J. Peploe

IONA

Ross of Mull
from the North End
Oil 15 x 18

The Hunterian,
University of Glasgow

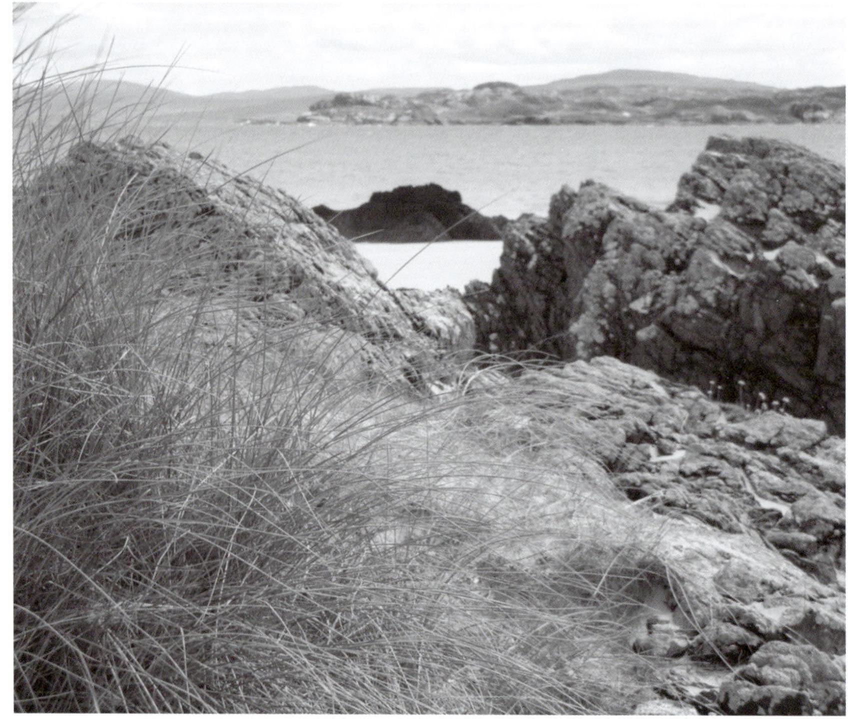

Photograph 2009

The dark rock in the centre is the top end of the Finger. It is seen through a small but obvious break in the rocks, which for identification I refer to as the "Narrow Gap" (see page 85). The Ross of Mull is in the distance with part of Loch Scridain at the left-hand side.

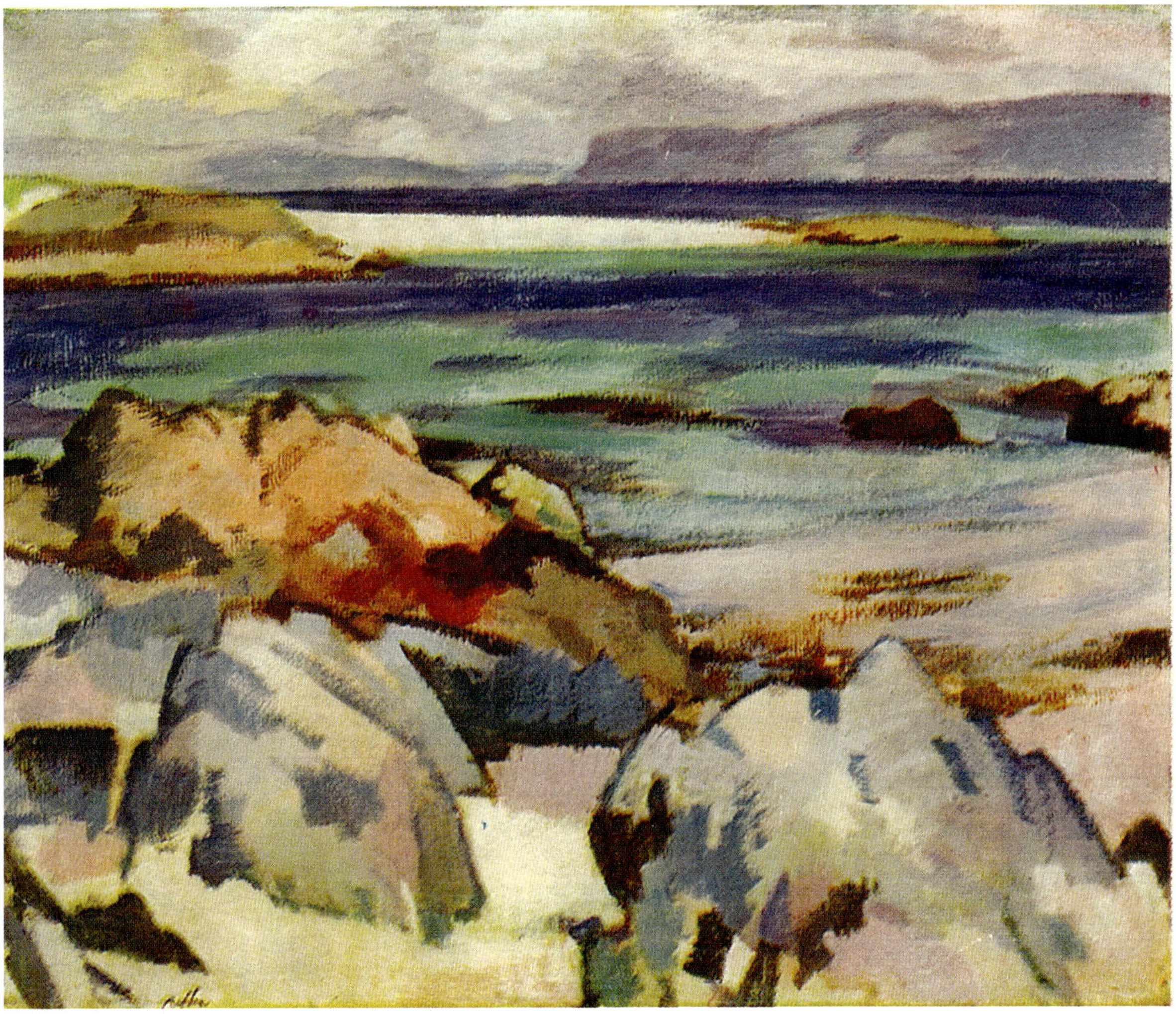

[PLATE 110]

S. J. Peploe

Eilean Annraidh from the North End (Sea and Rocks, Iona)

Oil 20 x 24

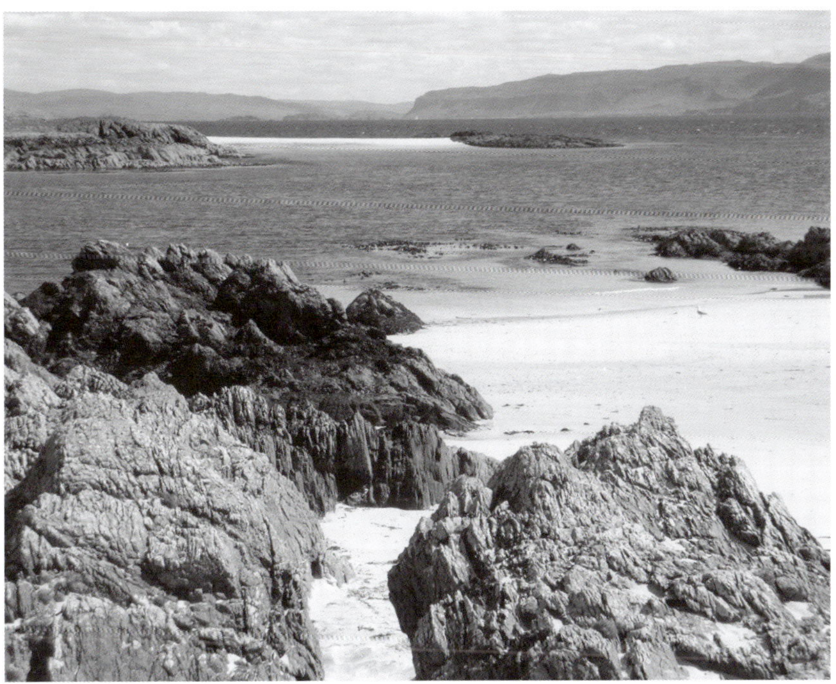

Photograph 2012

The Narrow Gap is central in the foreground. Eilean Annraidh is in the middle distance, and the cliffs at Gribun are in the centre on the horizon.

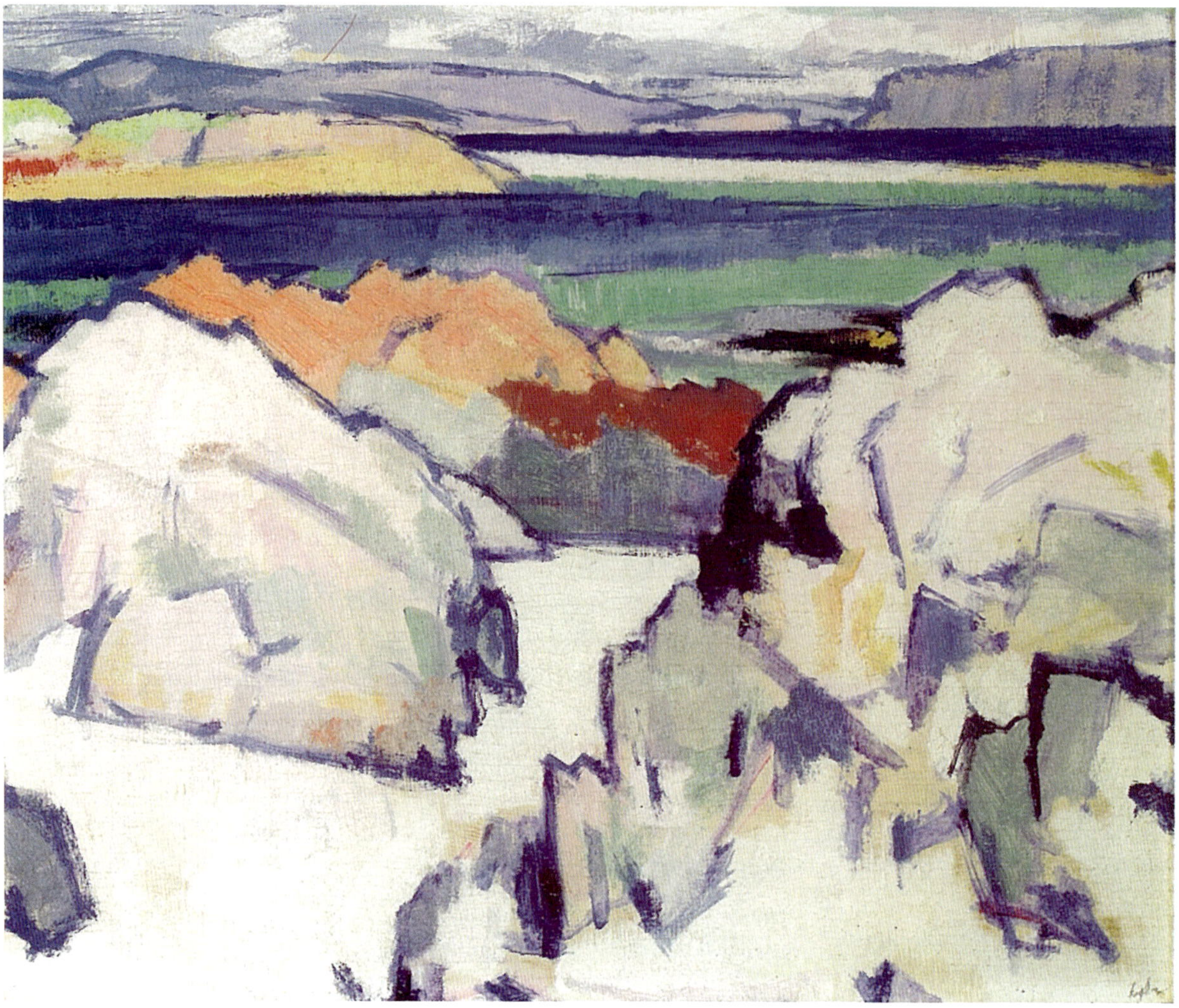

[PLATE 111]
S. J. Peploe
Eilean Annraidh
from the North End
Oil 15 x 18

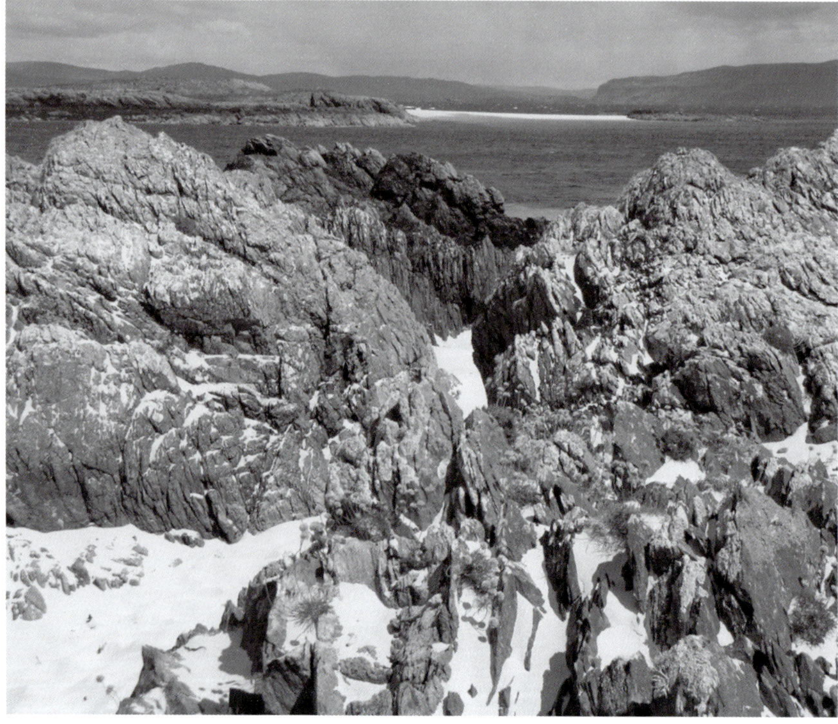

Photograph 2009

This is the same subject as Plate 110, but painted from lower down. From this level the rocks each side of the Narrow Gap are more prominent in the composition.

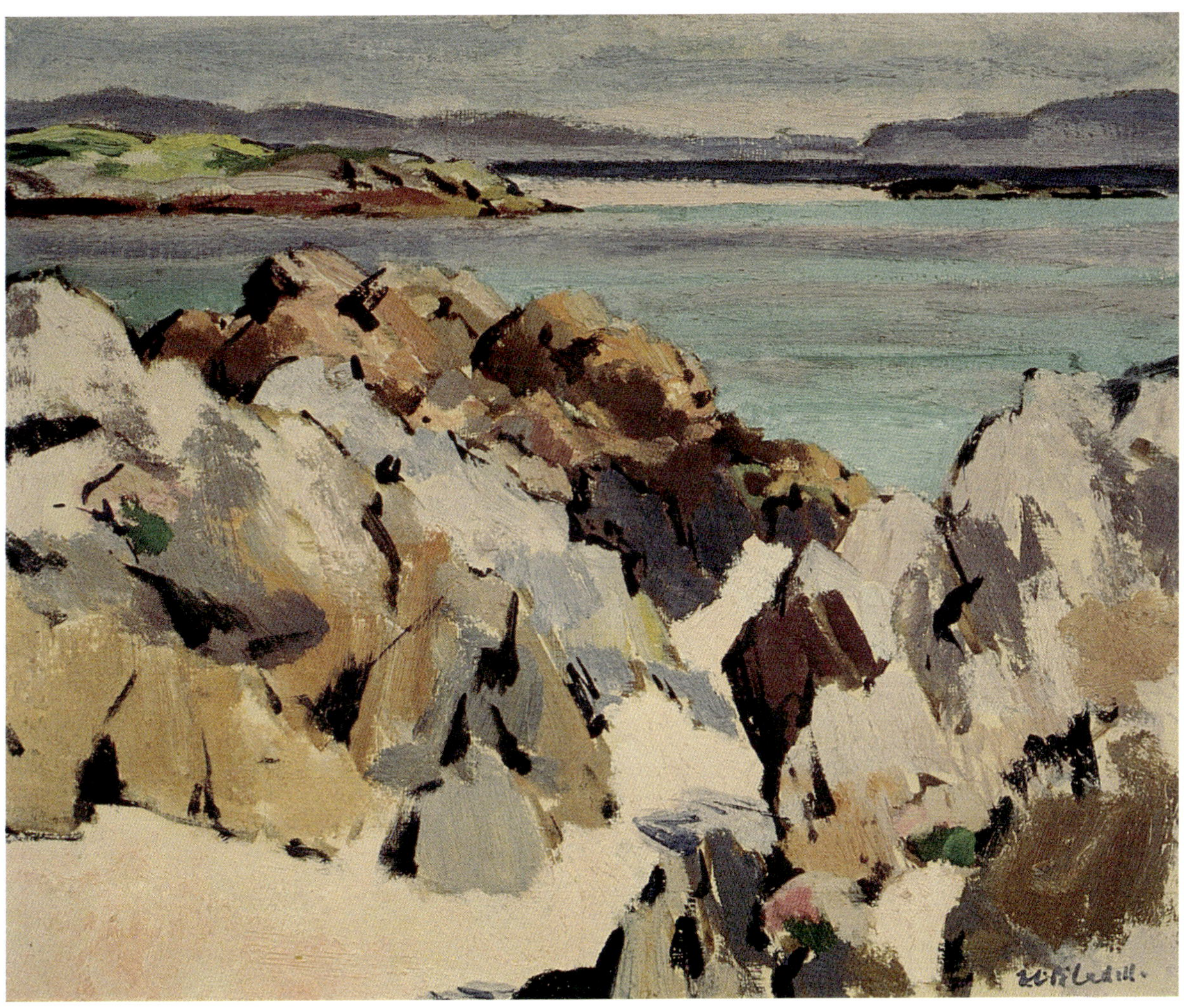

This picture by Cadell was painted from very nearly the same position as the preceding picture by Peploe.

[PLATE 112]
F. C. B. Cadell
Eilean Annraidh from the North End
Oil 15 x 18

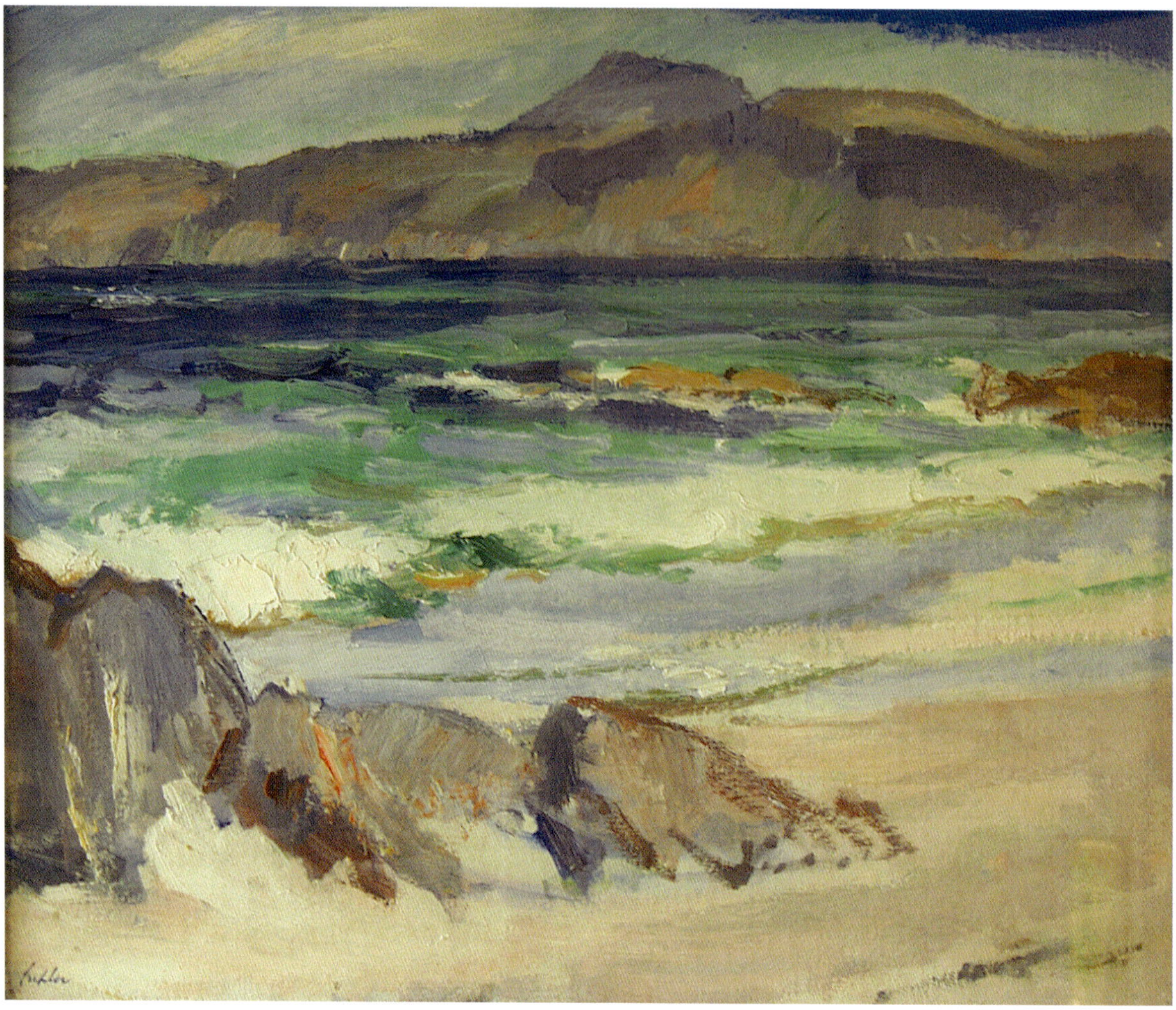

[PLATE 113]

S. J. Peploe

Ben More
from the North End
(The North Wind,
Sound of Iona)
Oil 20 x 24

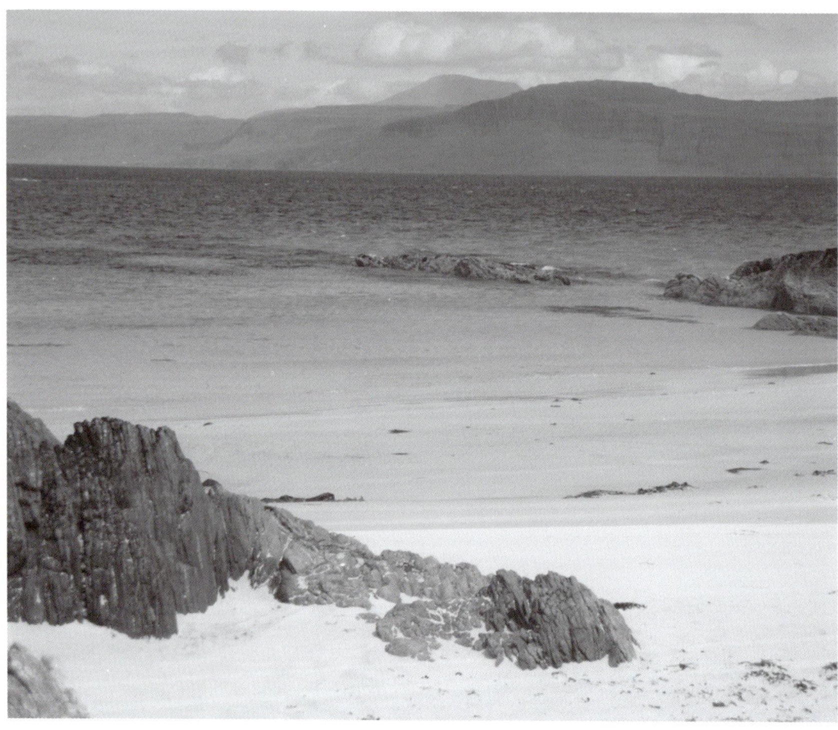

Photograph 2009

This picture was painted from within the Narrow Gap looking towards Ben More and the Burg. The lower end of the Finger is in the middle distance, partly submerged.

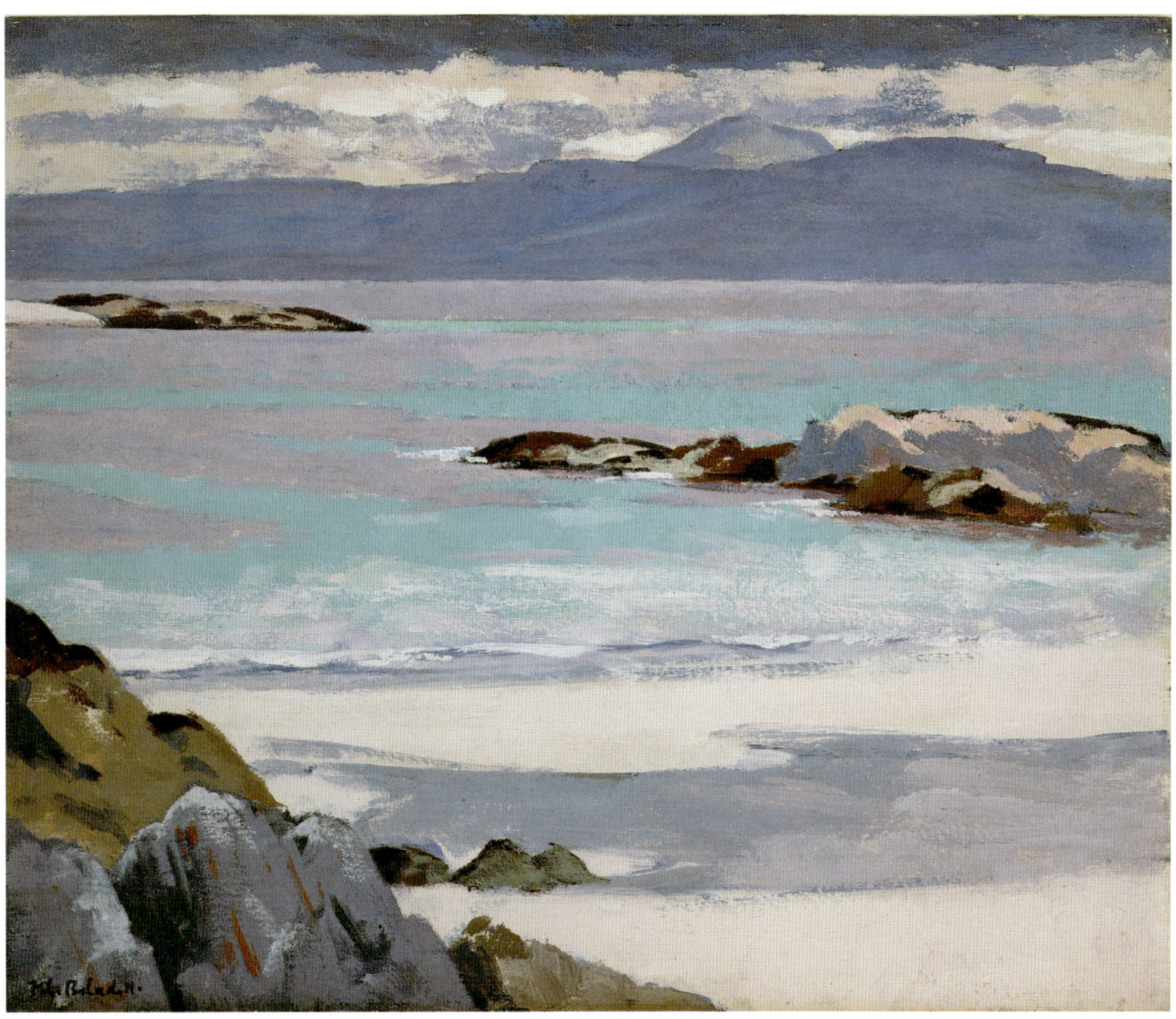

This was painted from the same position as Plate 113, but Cadell has taken a view a little more to the left to include the southeast end of Eilean Annraidh.

[PLATE 114]

F. C. B. Cadell

Ben More from the North End

Oil 15 x 18

[PLATE 115]
S. J. Peploe
Eilean Annraidh from the North End
Oil 15 x 18

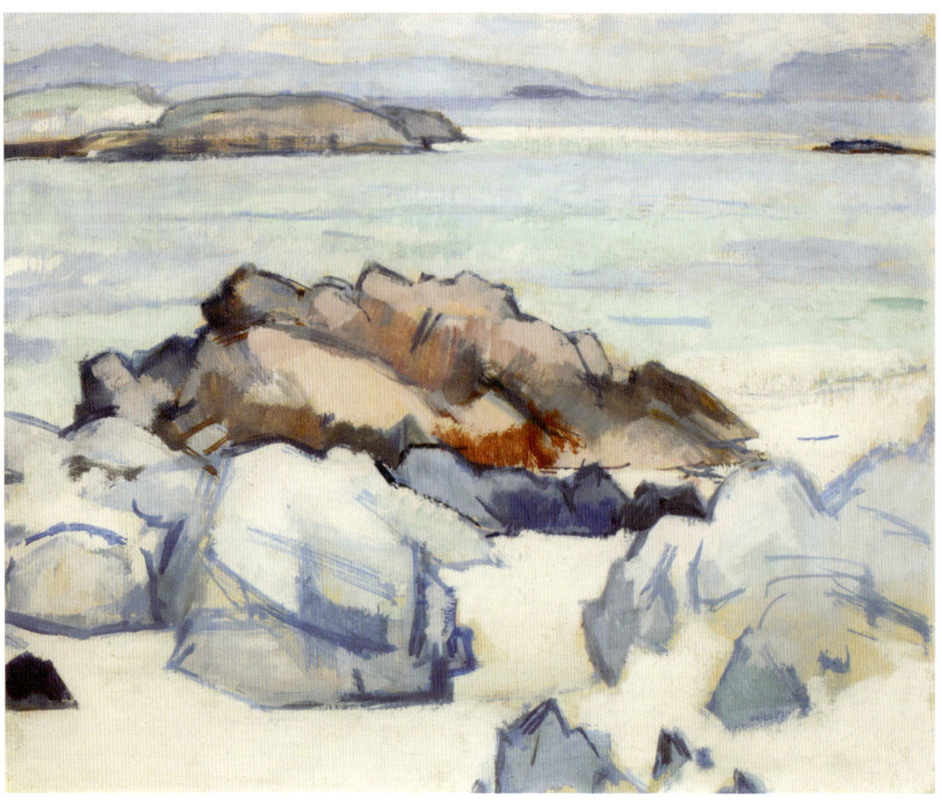

[PLATE 116]
F. C. B Cadell
Eilean Annraidh from the North End
Oil 15 x 18

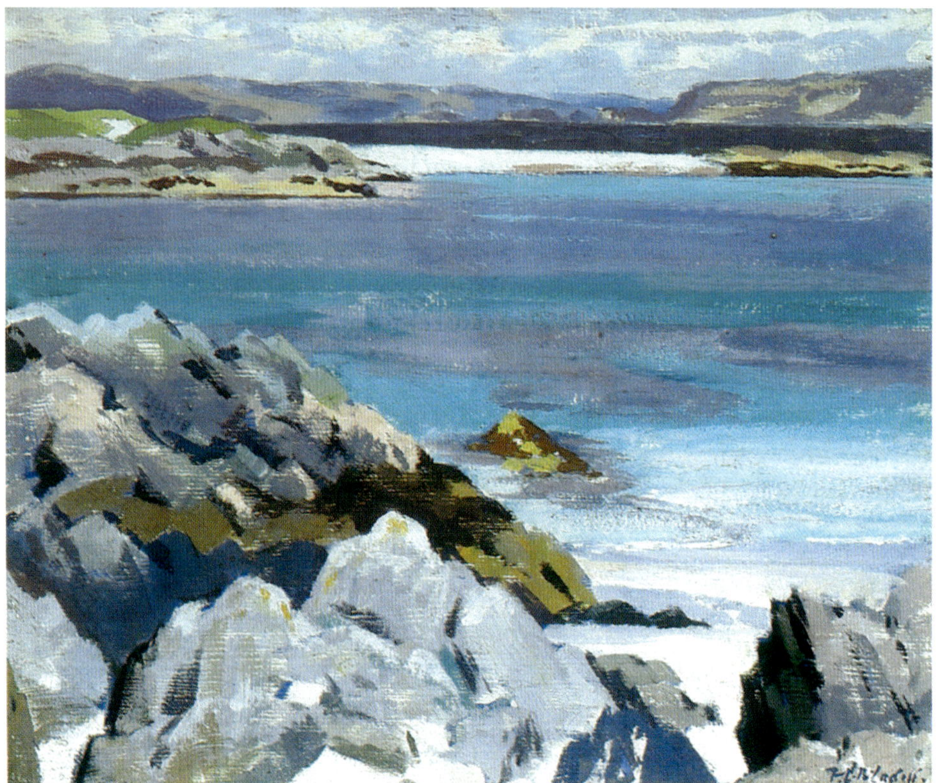

These pictures by Peploe and Cadell are closely related in subject matter. On the horizon in both pictures we see the view towards Loch na Keal with the cliffs at Gribun on the right and the islands of Inch Kenneth and Erisgeir in the centre (see the diagram on page 153). Eilean Annraidh is in the middle distance. The foreground rocks are viewed from slightly different positions, the Narrow Gap being central in the Peploe and at the bottom left corner of the Cadell.

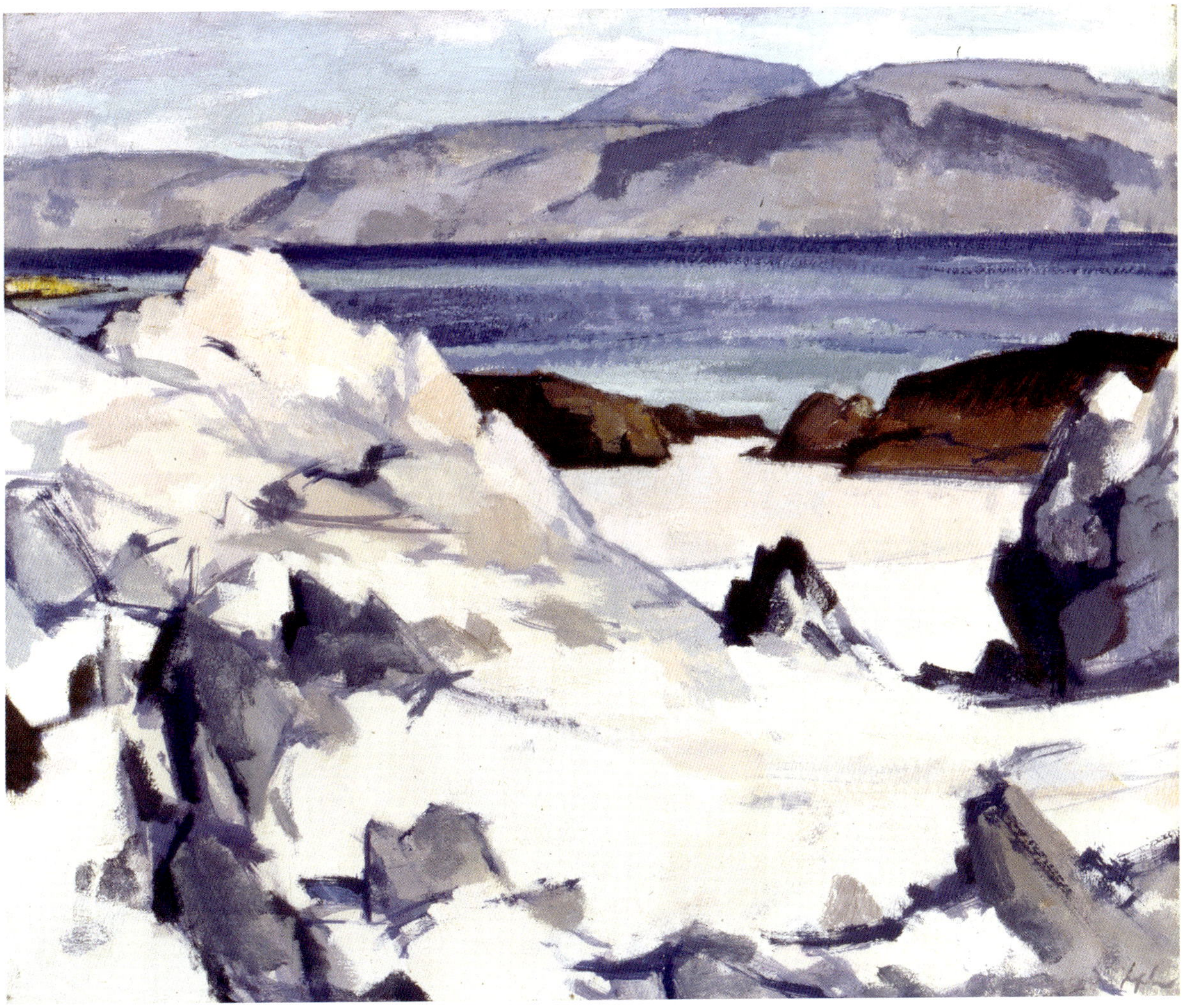

[PLATE 117]

S. J. Peploe

GREEN SEA, IONA

Ben More
from the North End
Oil 20 x 24

The Fleming-Wyfold
Art Foundation

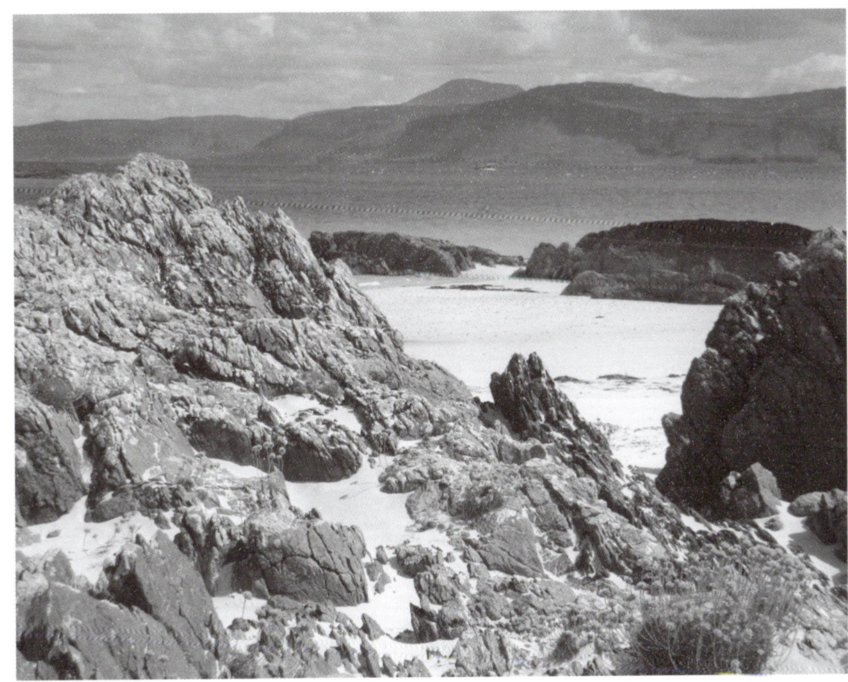

Photograph 2009

The line of dark rocks across the middle of the painting is the Finger, and the tip of Eilean Annraidh just appears at the left-hand side in the middle distance.

The diagram on page 85 indicates the position from which Peploe painted this picture.

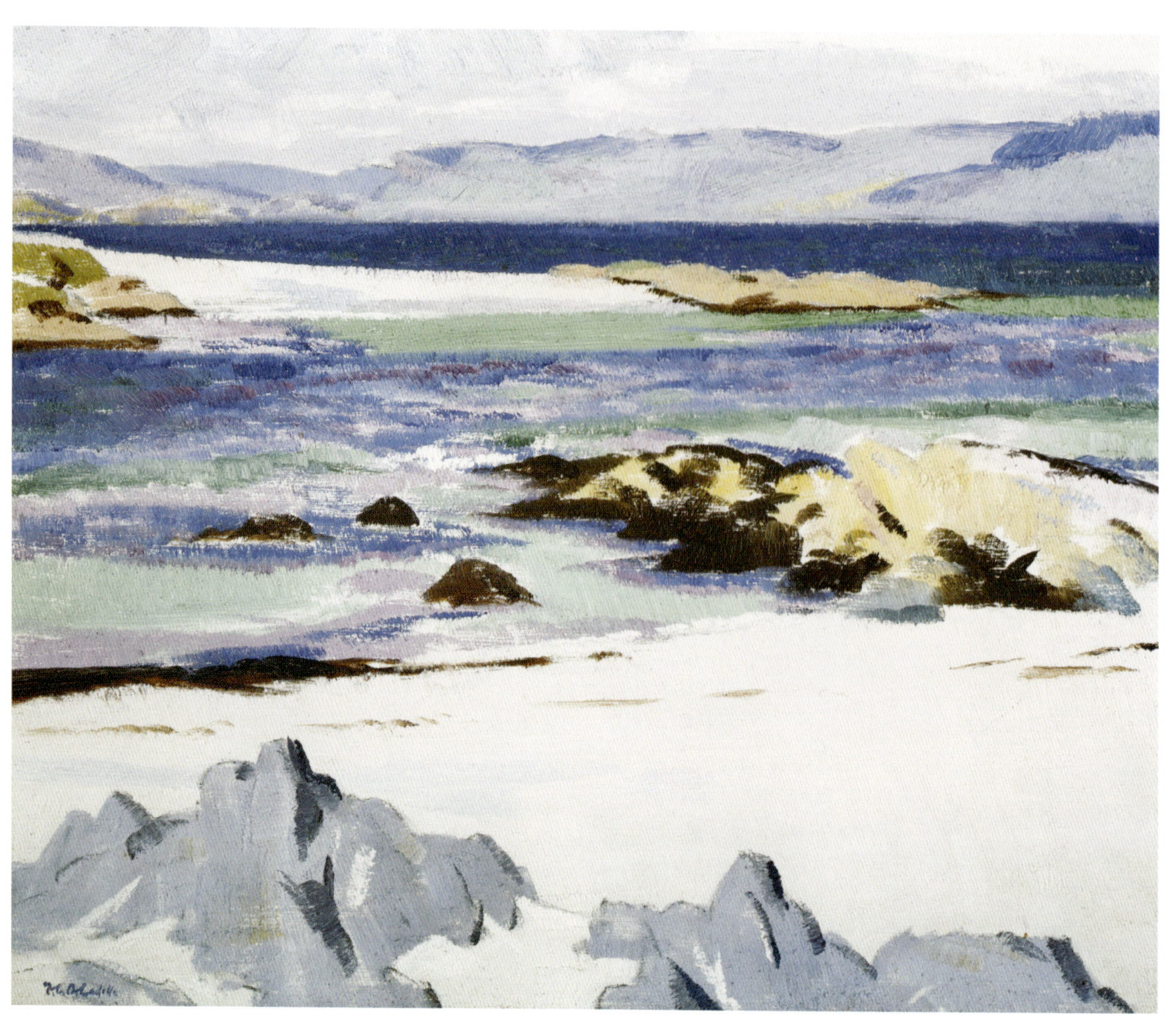

[PLATE 118]

F. C. B. Cadell

Eilean Annraidh from the North End

Oil 15 x 18

THE HEADLAND

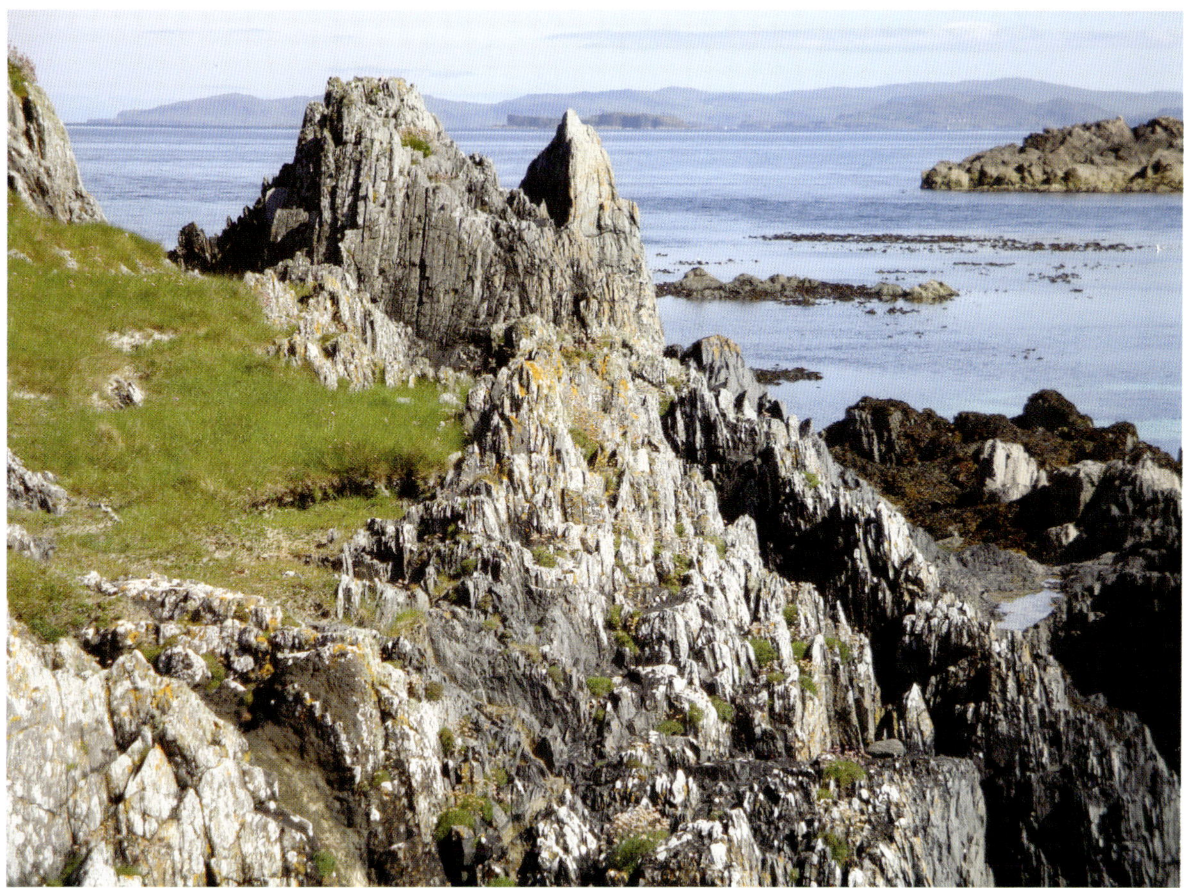

The Headland is the extreme northeast corner of Iona, and the well-known Cathedral Rock is attached to it (above). From here there is a line of pinnacles leading out to Pulpit Rock, with a small bay to the south of them which narrows to a rocky inlet next to Cathedral Rock. This bay appears full of sand in the paintings, but in recent years the rocky base has usually been exposed and when this is covered with wet seaweed the area is not easy to walk into. The pictures in this section were painted on the Headland or from the bay and the surrounding rocks (see page 84).

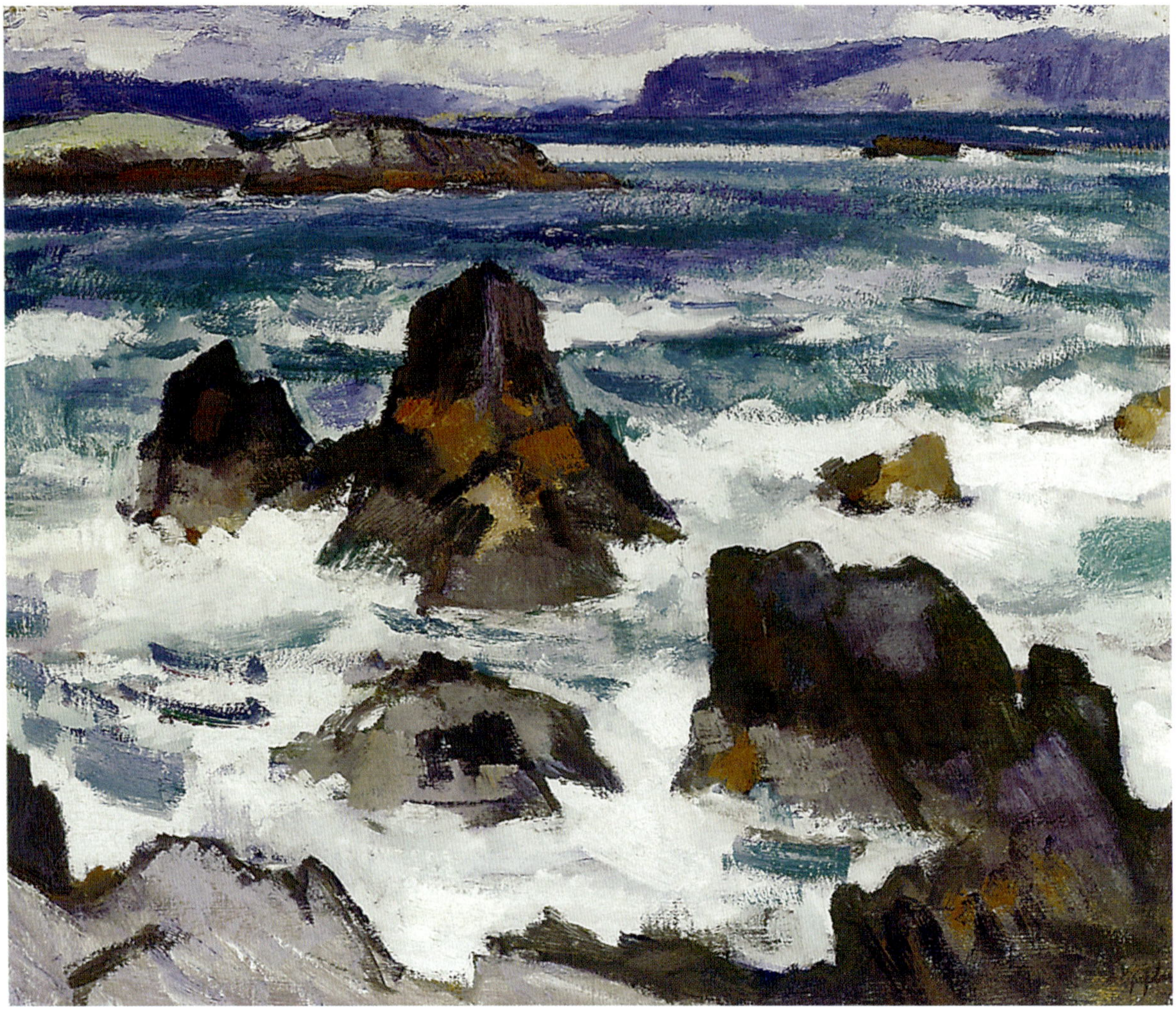

[PLATE 119]

S. J. Peploe

Pulpit Rock
from the Headland
(Rough Day, Iona)
Oil 19 x 23

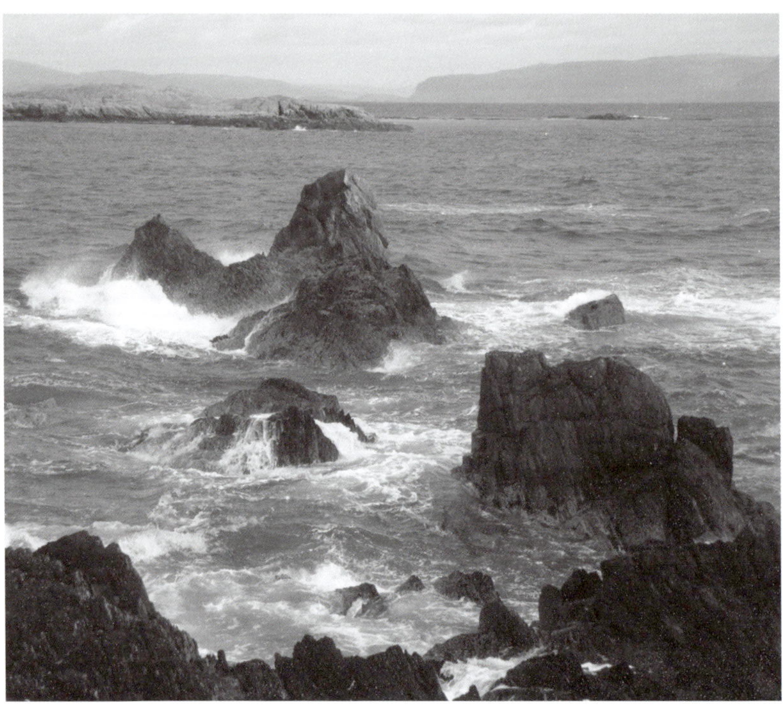

Photograph 2010

Pulpit Rock, as it appears from the beach, is included in many paintings, for example Plates 100, 101, 105, and 106, but here it is seen from the more elevated viewpoint of the Headland. Eilean Annraidh is in the middle distance and the cliffs at Gribun are central on the horizon.

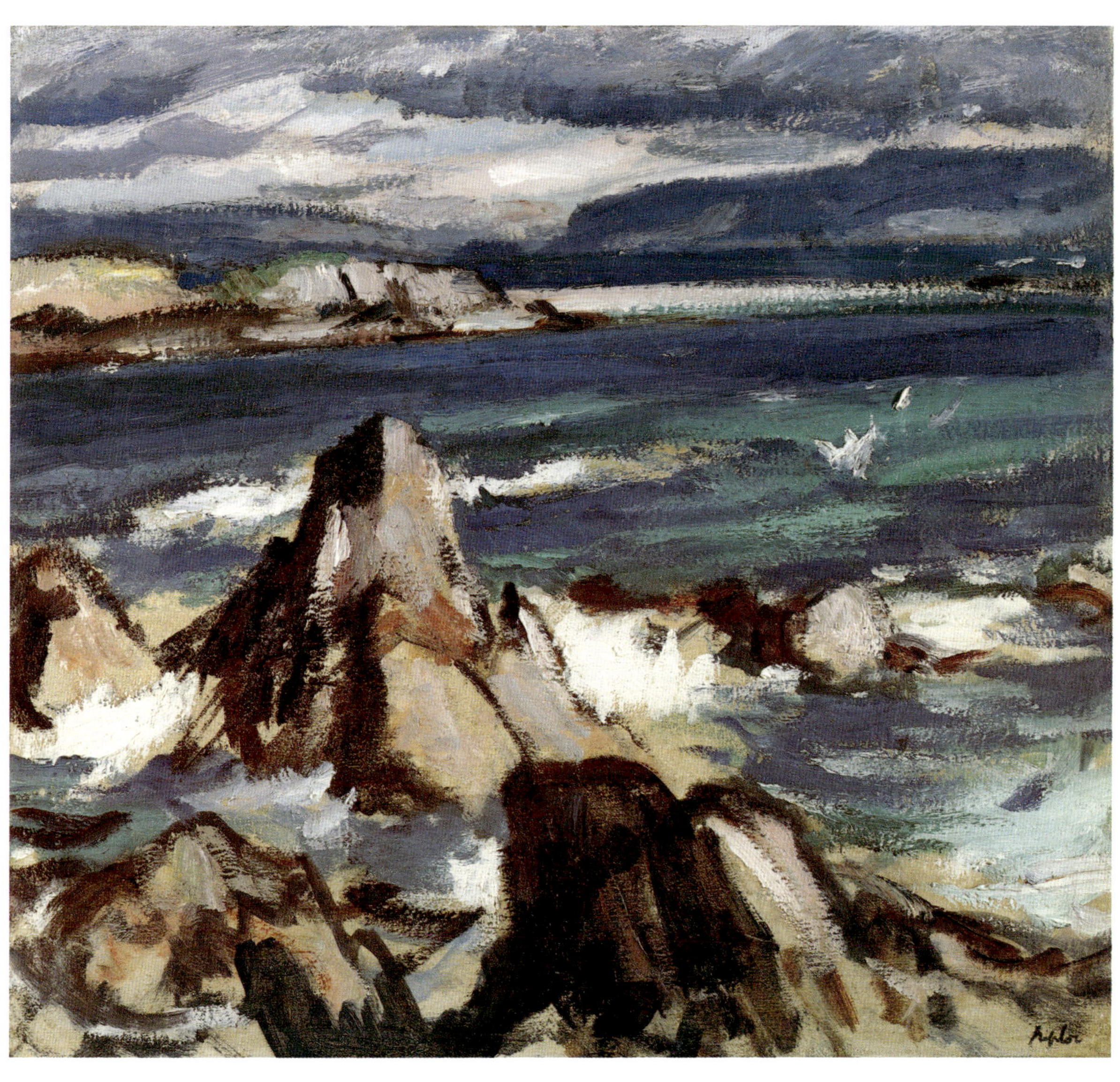

[PLATE 120]

S. J. Peploe

Pulpit Rock from the Headland

(Rocks and Sea)

Oil 20 x 22

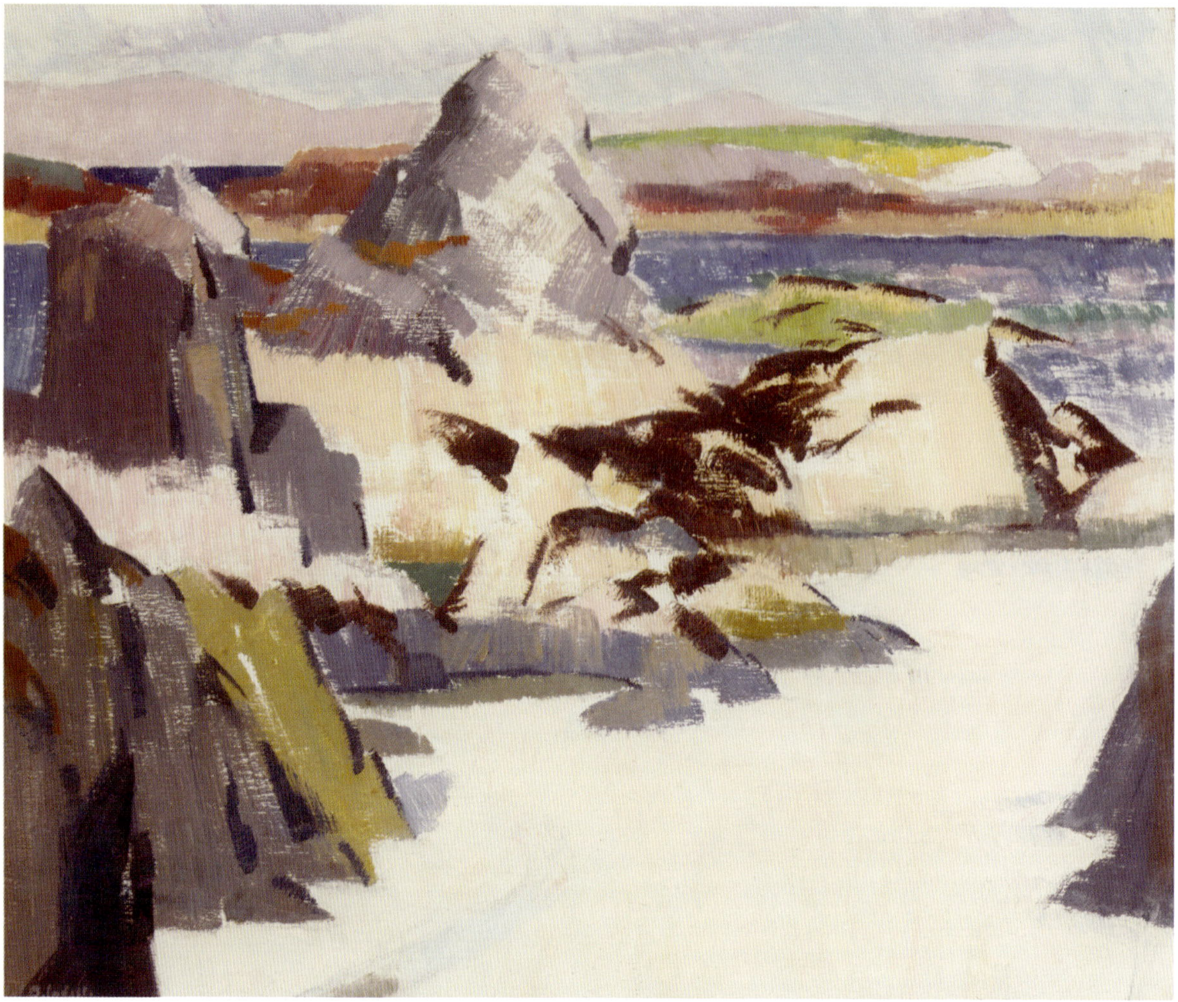

[PLATE 121]

F. C. B. Cadell

Pulpit Rock

Oil 15 x 18

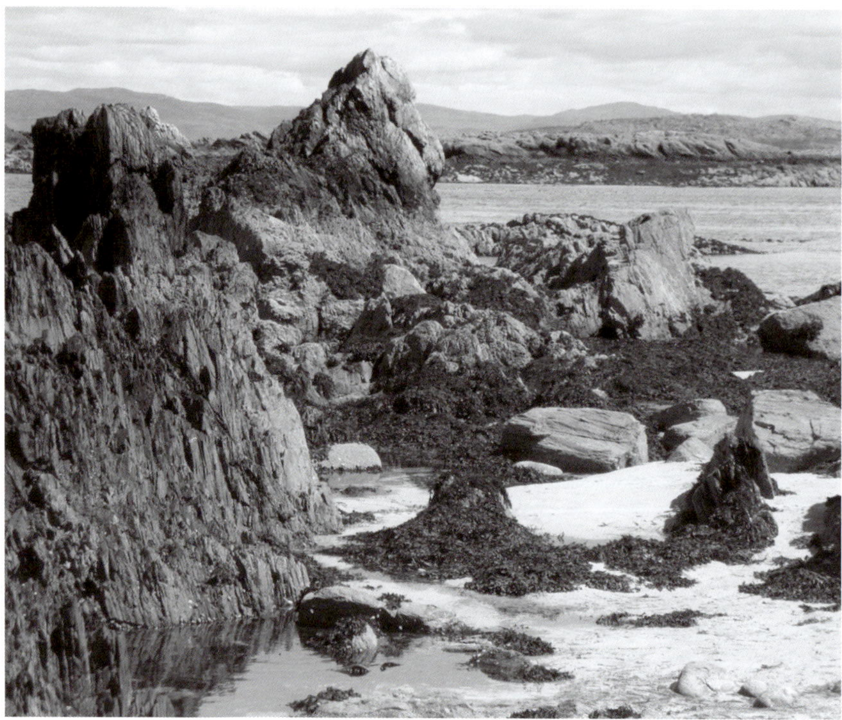

Photograph 2009

Painted from the inlet beside Cathedral Rock, this shows Pulpit Rock in the centre and the line of pinnacles leading out towards it on the left. The central section of Eilean Annraidh is in the background.

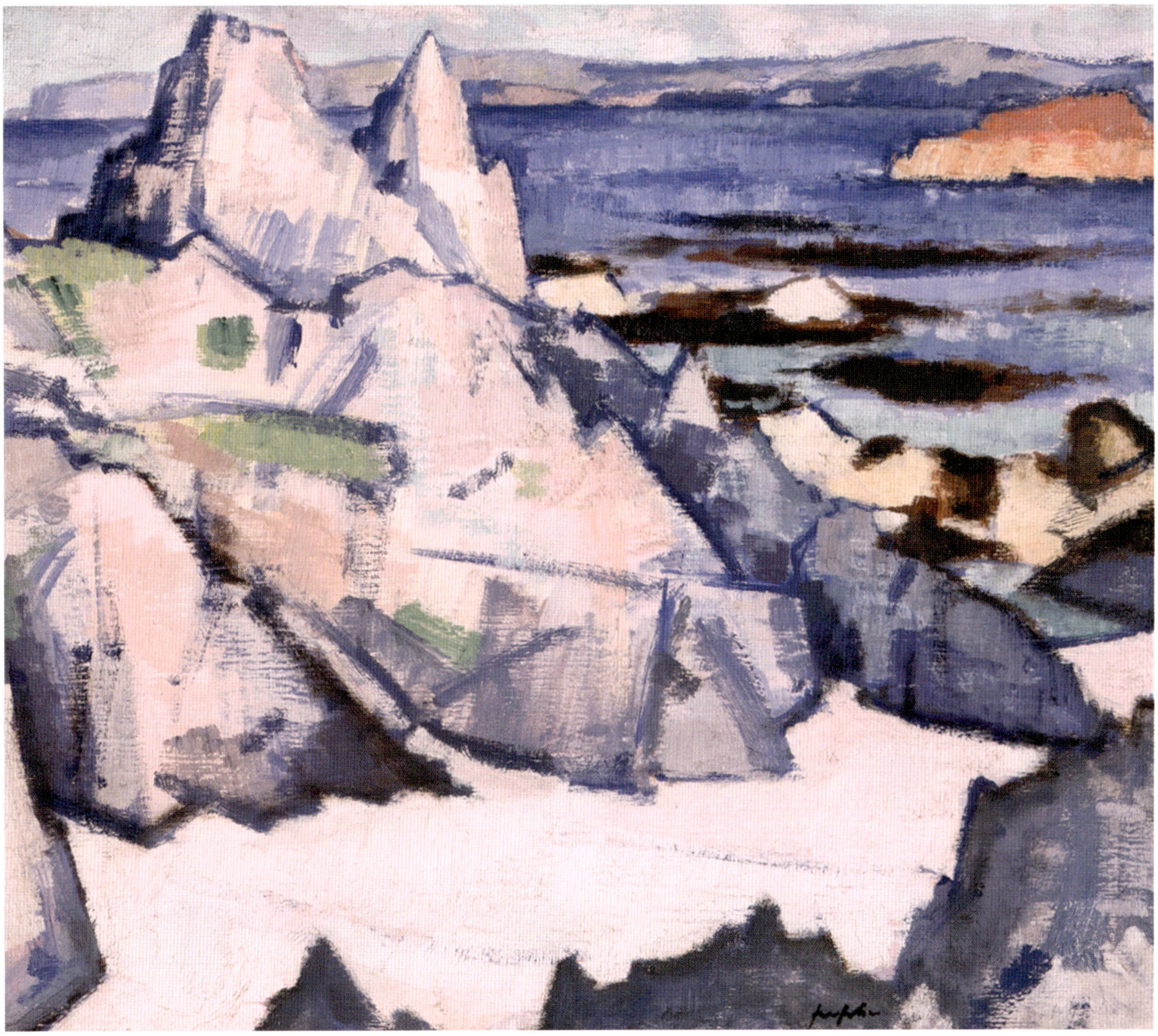

[PLATE 122]

S. J. Peploe

CATHEDRAL ROCK
Oil 15 x 18

Aberdeen Art Gallery
& Museums Collections

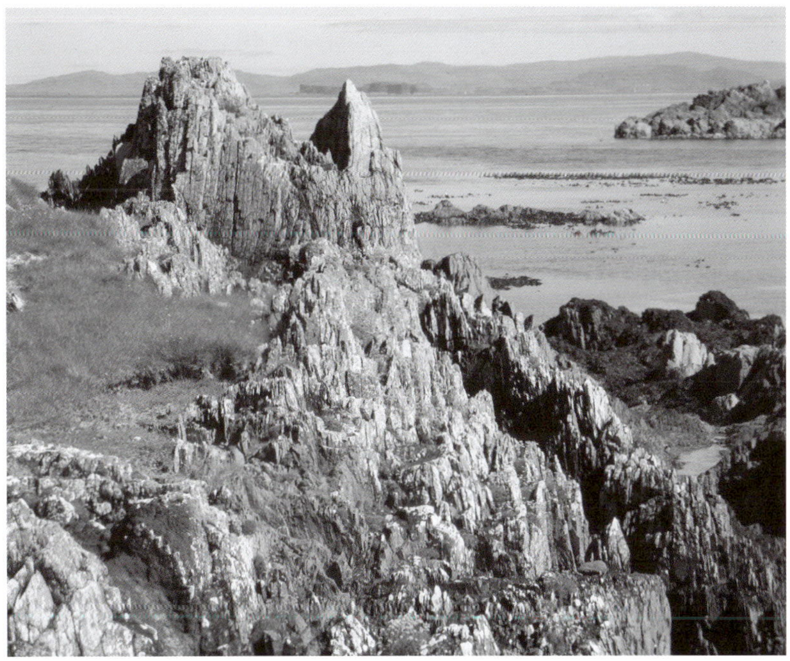

Photograph 2010

Staffa is on the horizon, partly hidden by the tip of Cathedral Rock, with the hills of northwest Mull beyond. The west end of Eilean Annraidh is in the middle distance on the right. Plates 119 and 120 were painted from the grassy ledge on the left.

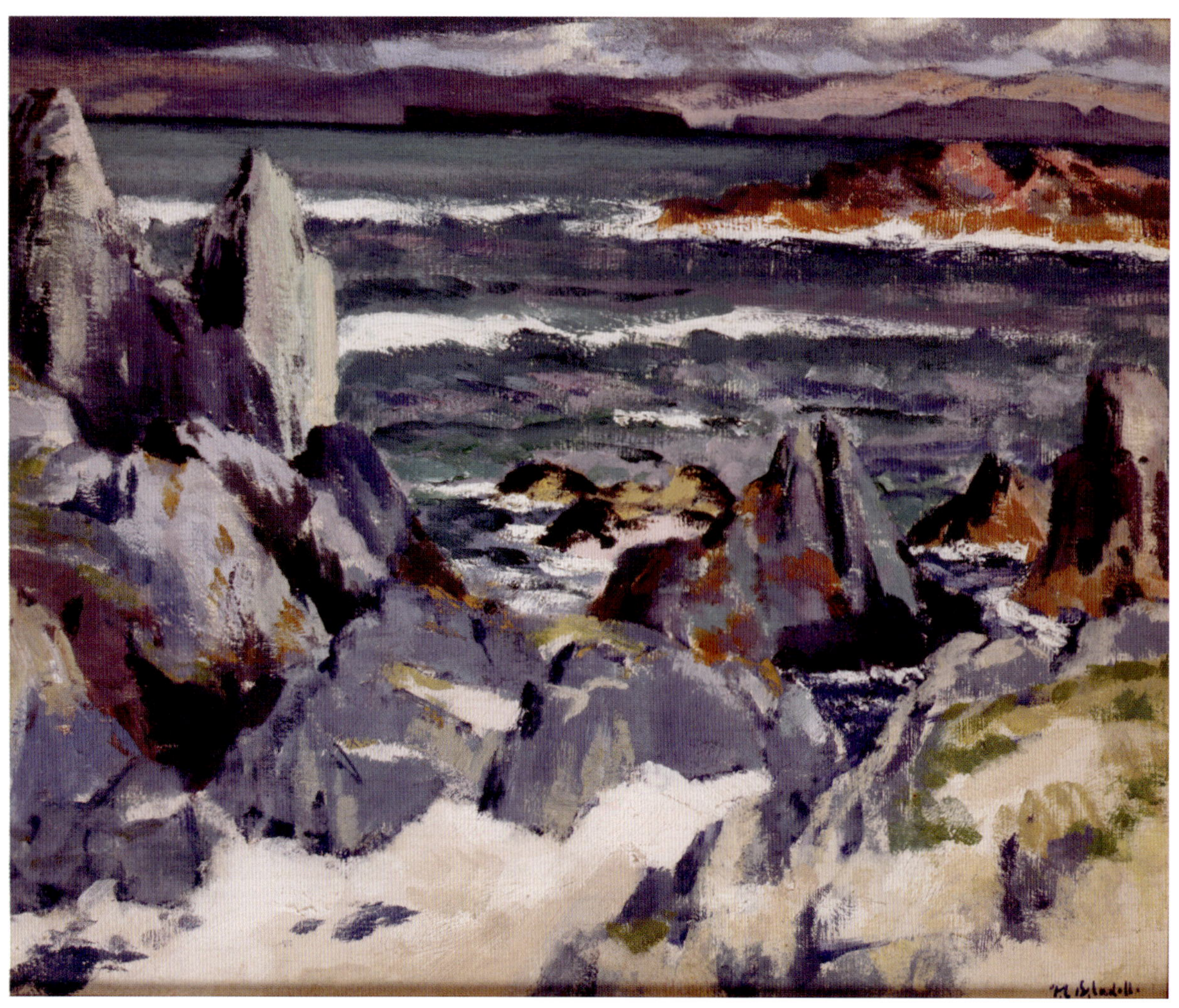

Staffa is central on the horizon and Gometra can be seen to the right. The west end of Eilean Annraidh is in the middle distance on the right hand side.

[PLATE 123]

F. C. B. Cadell

Cathedral Rock

Oil 15 x 18

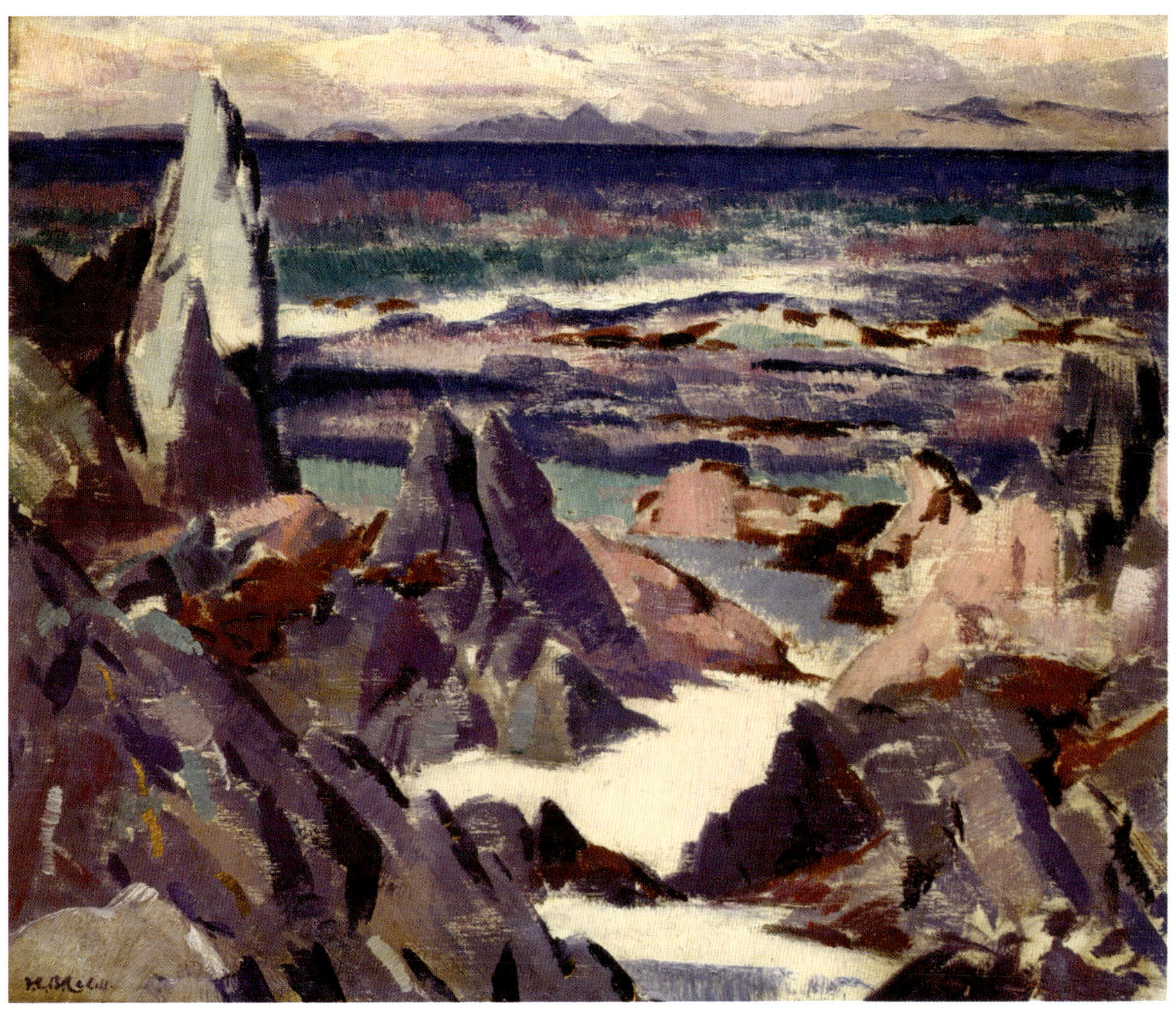

The distance to the island of Rhum, seen here on the horizon, is approximately forty-five miles, and to the Cuillin on Skye about sixty miles. When the weather is clear enough for Rhum to be visible, the island becomes a focus of attention despite its great distance. Here, as in Plates 80, 81, 99 and 165, Cadell has placed it centrally on the horizon.

[PLATE 124]
F. C. B. Cadell
Cathedral Rock
(Rhum from Iona)
Oil 15 x 18

[PLATE 125]
F. C. B. Cadell
Cathedral Rock
Oil 15 x 18

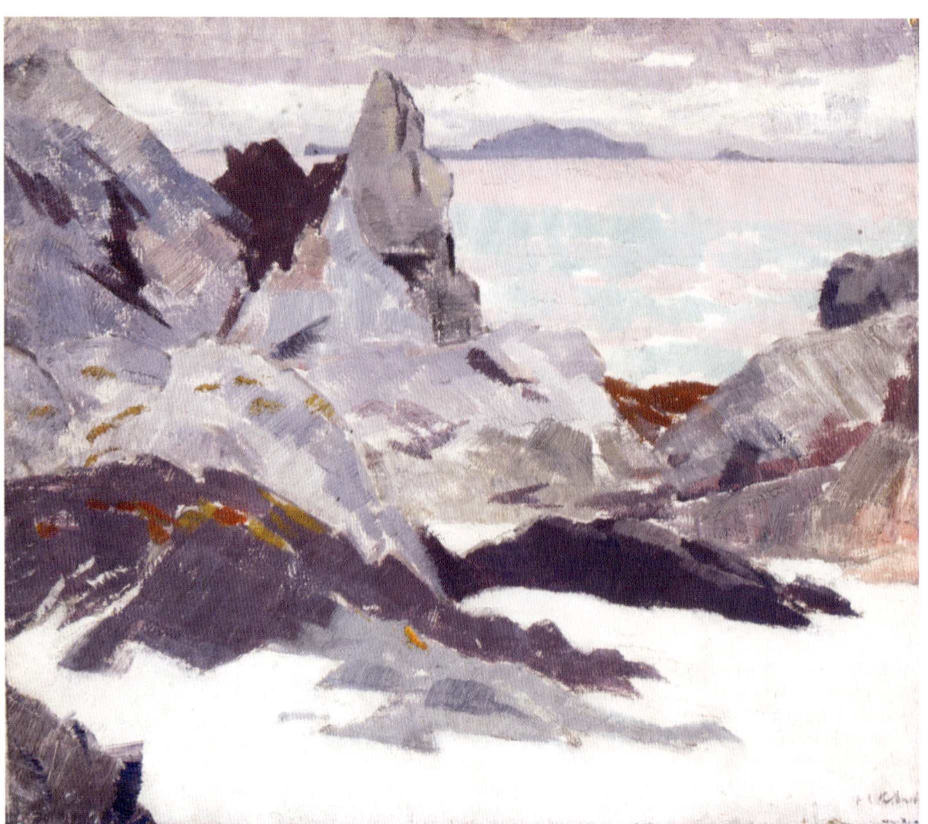

[PLATE 126]
F. C. B. Cadell

LUNGA FROM IONA

Cathedral Rock
Oil 15 x 18

The Hunterian,
University of Glasgow

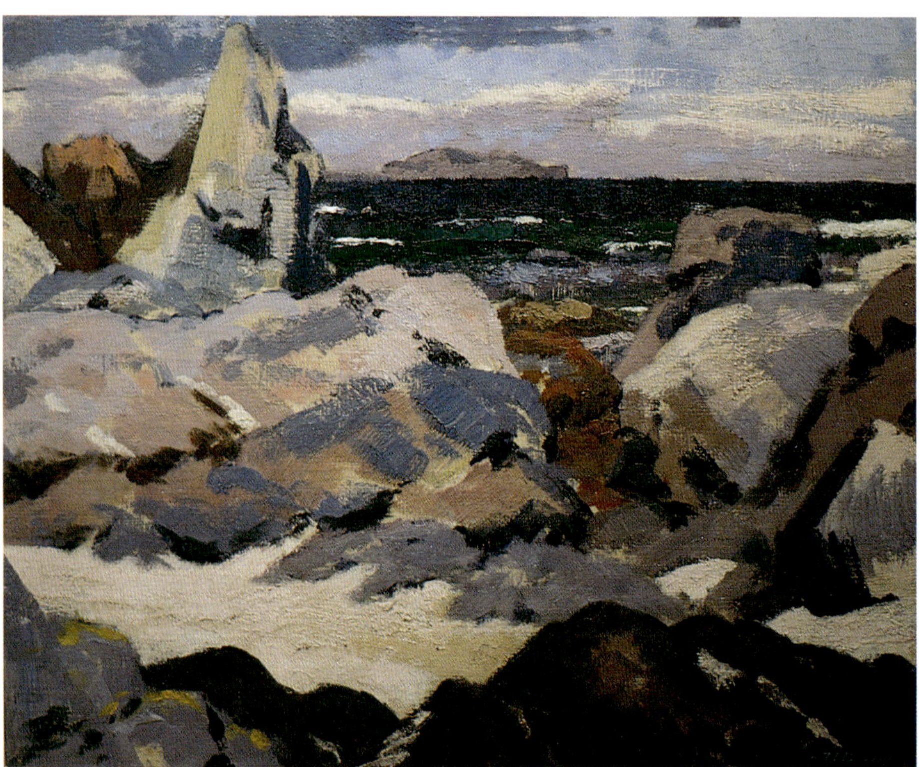

Plates 125 and 126 are similar compositions with Lunga central on the horizon, but their atmospheric effects are very different. In Plate 125 the pale grey sea and soft light are descriptive of a quiet overcast day, whereas in Plate 126 the intense colour and dark sea with white wave crests are typical of the clear bright days that often occur when the wind is northerly.

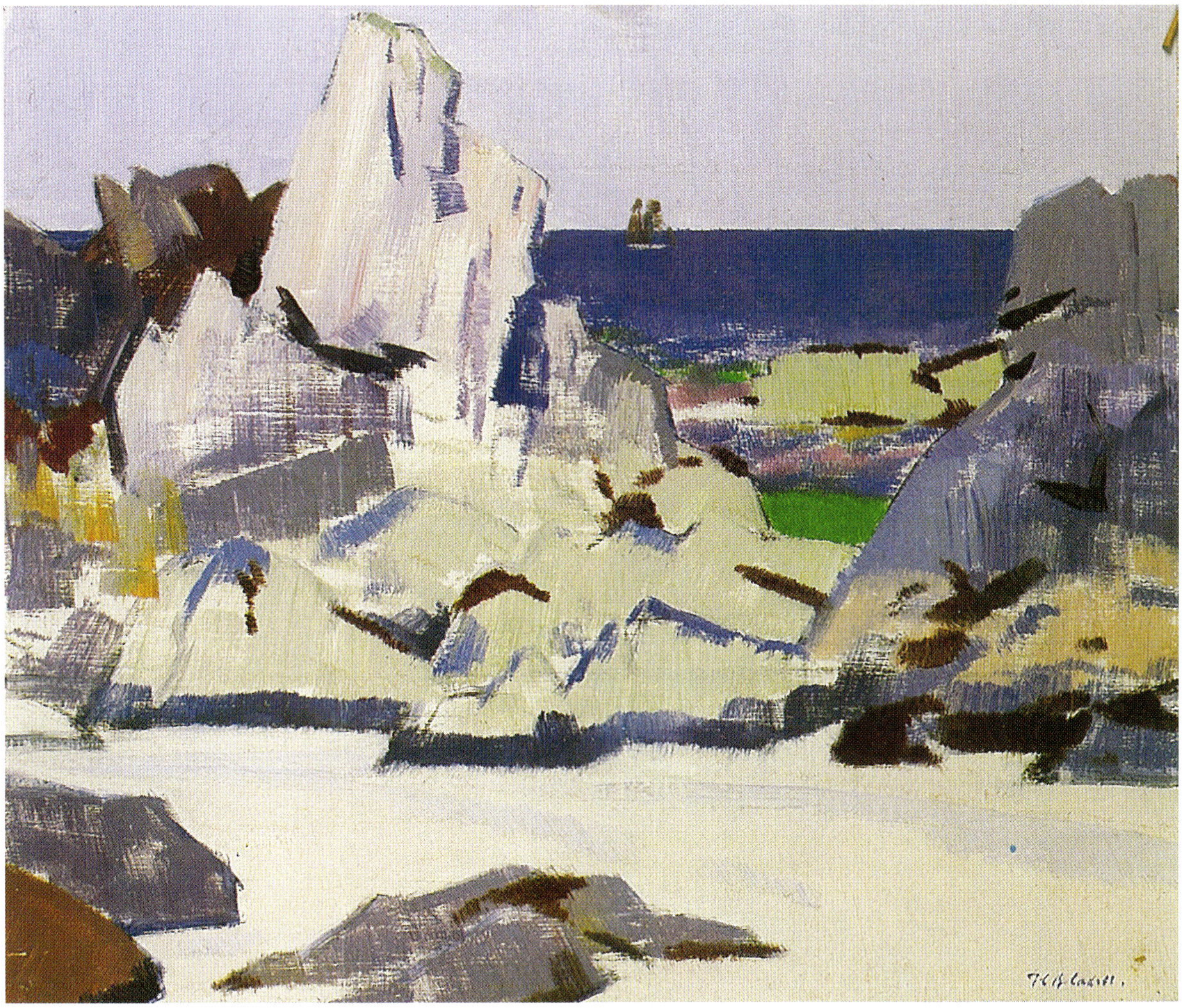

[PLATE 127]
F. C. B. Cadell
Cathedral Rock
Oil 15 x 18

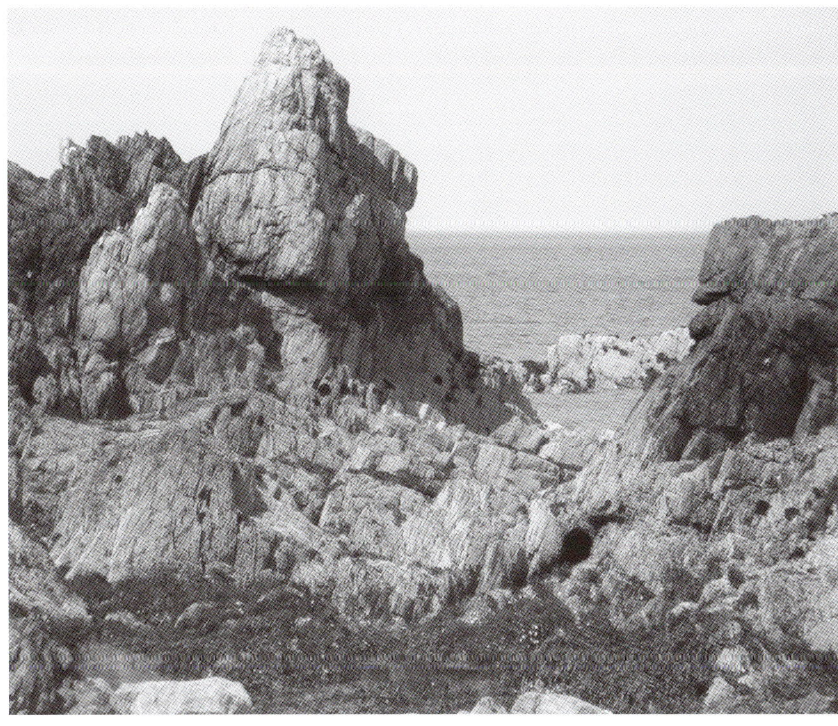

Photograph 2009

The brushwork in this painting is loose and sketchy, yet as will be seen by comparing it with the photograph, there is precise observation of form and detail.

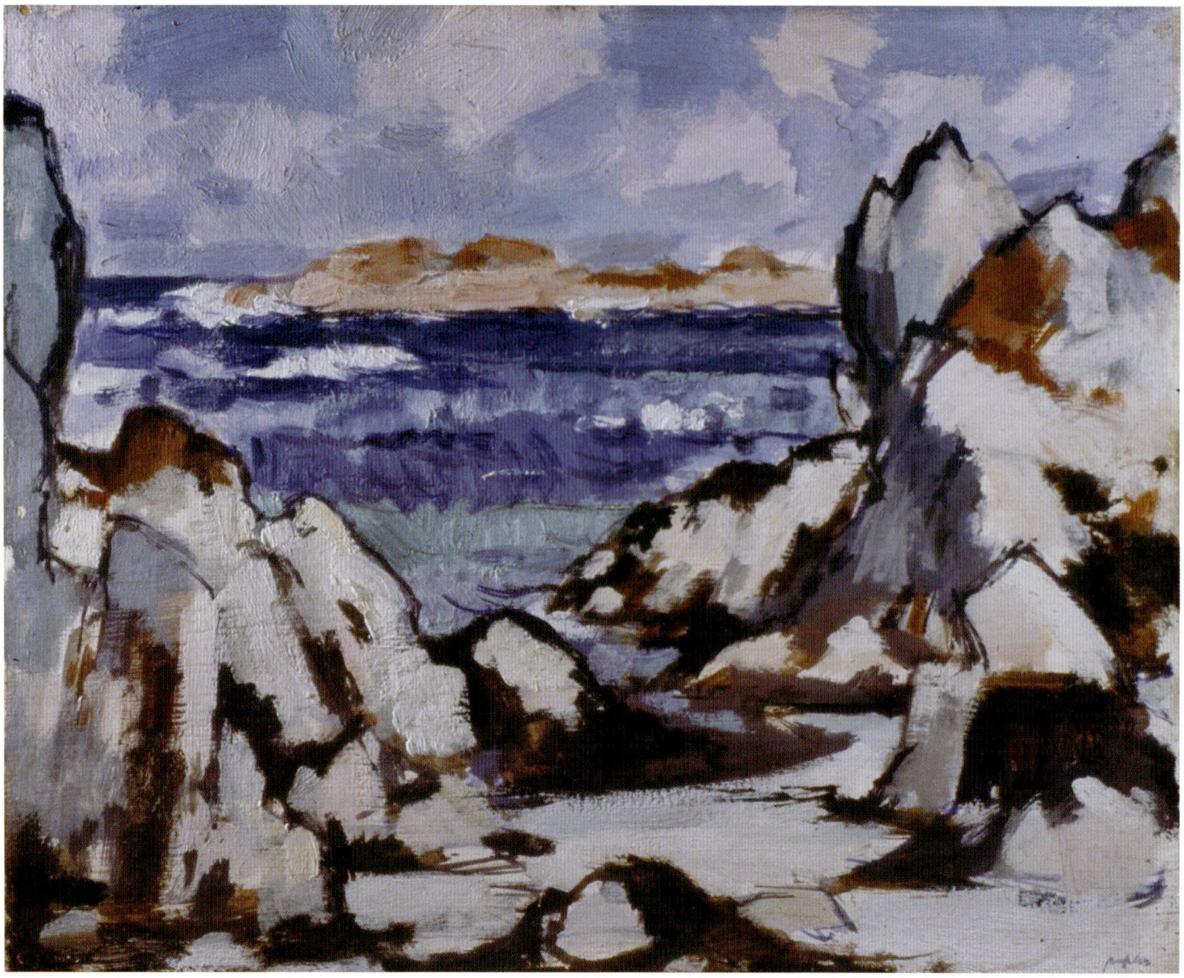

[PLATE 128]

S. J. Peploe

THE CATHEDRAL ROCKS

Towards Eilean Annraidh

Oil 14 x 17

Fife Cultural Trust
(Kirkcaldy Galleries)
on behalf of Fife Council

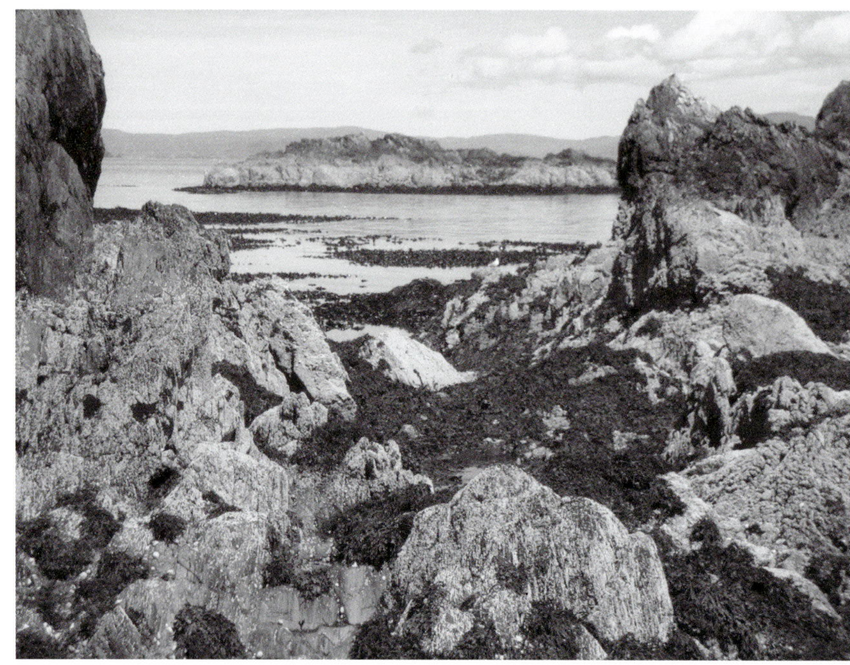

Photograph 2009

The Cathedral Rock itself is out of view to the left. The west end of Eilean Annraidh is seen through the gap between the last pinnacle and Pulpit Rock, which is on the right.

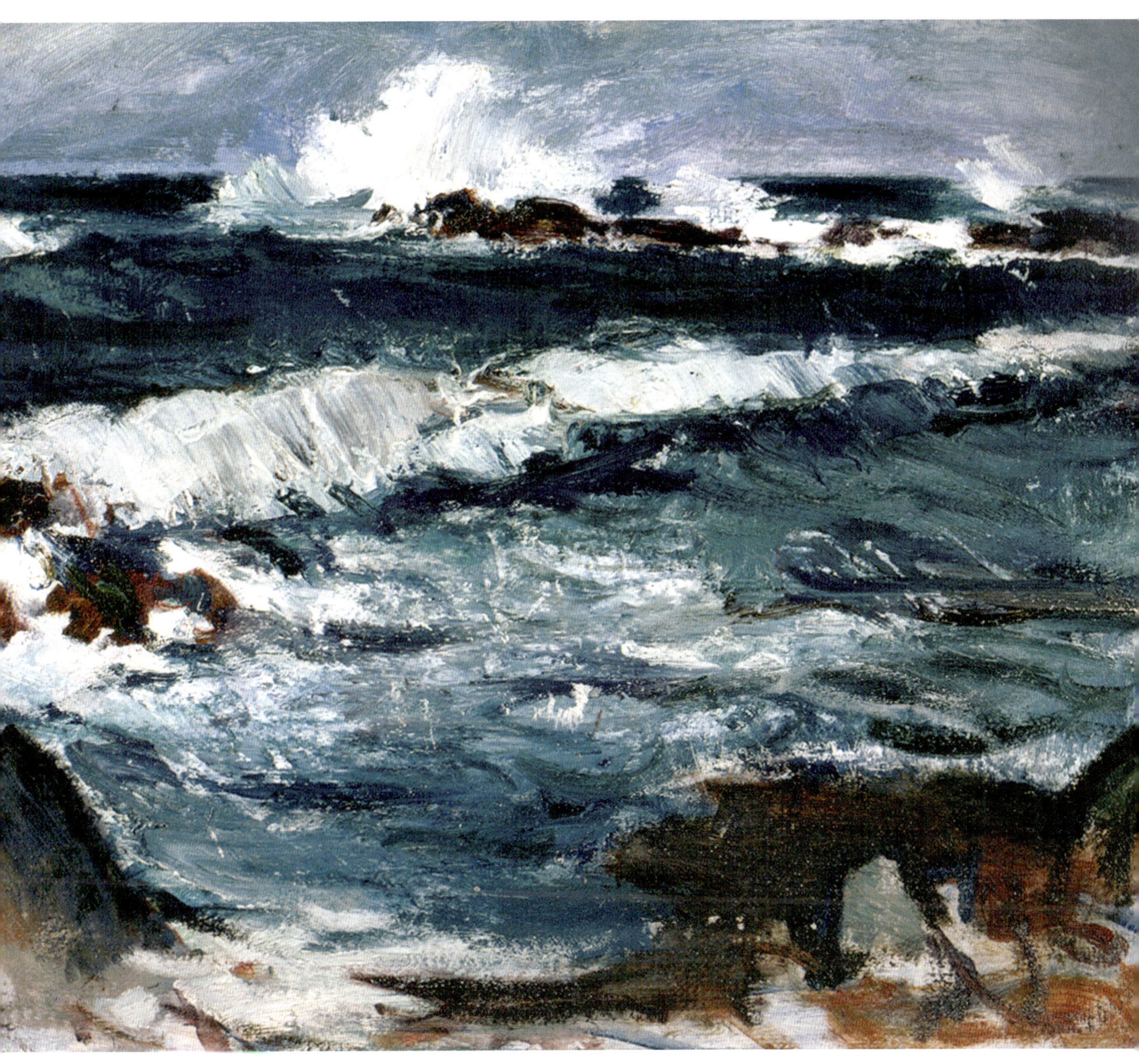

Eilean Annraidh is almost submerged under a high tide and heavy seas.

[PLATE 129]

S. J. Pcploc

STORMY WEATHER, IONA

Eilean Annraidh from the North End

Oil 20 x 24

Aberdeen Art Gallery & Museums Collections

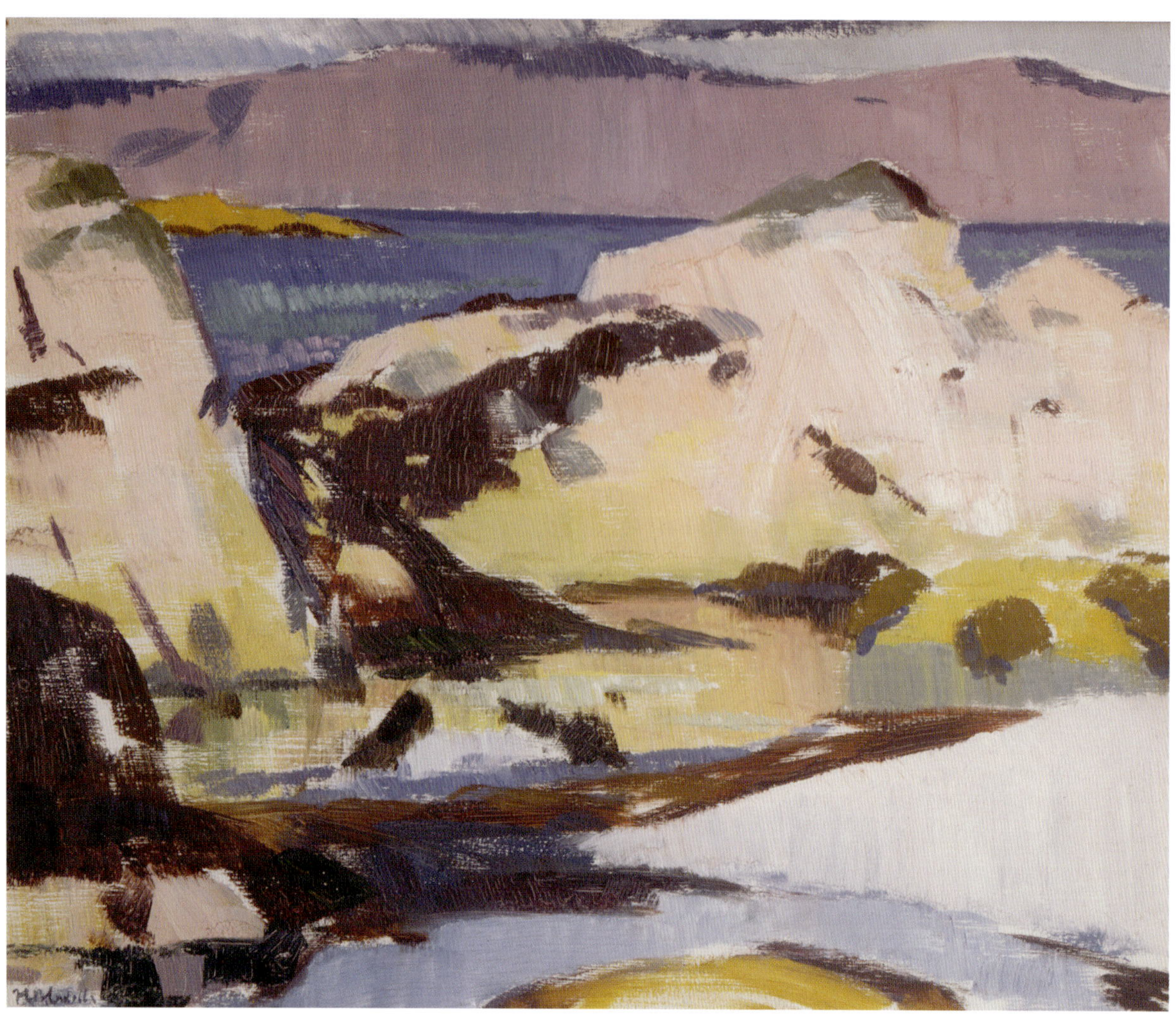

These rocks are at the base of Pulpit Rock. The Burg is across the top of the painting and the southeast end of Eilean Annraidh is in the upper left emerging from behind the foreground rock.

[PLATE 130]
F. C. B. Cadell
Rocks at the North End
(Low Tide, Iona)
Oil 15 x 18

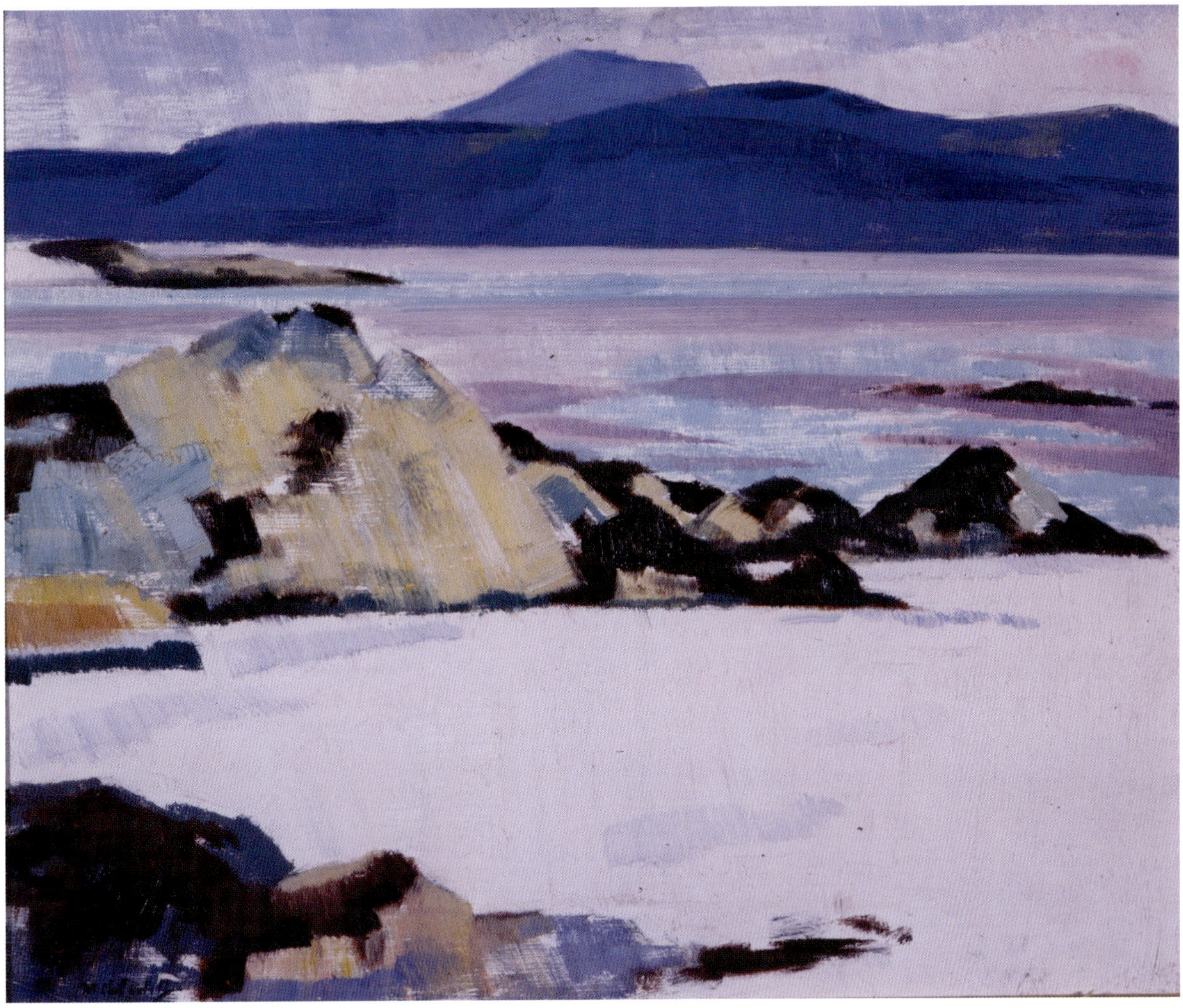

[PLATE 131]
F. C. B. Cadell
Ben More
from the North End
Oil 15 x 18

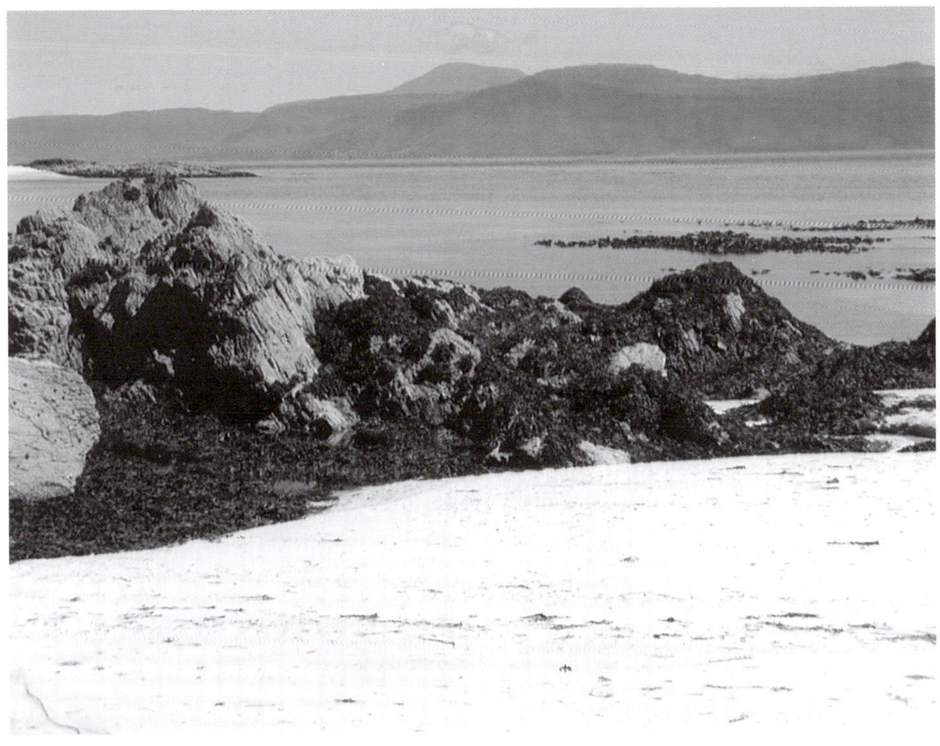

Photograph 2009

Painted from close to Plate 130, but a little further back, this picture includes a wider view of the Sound. Ben More is central in the distance.

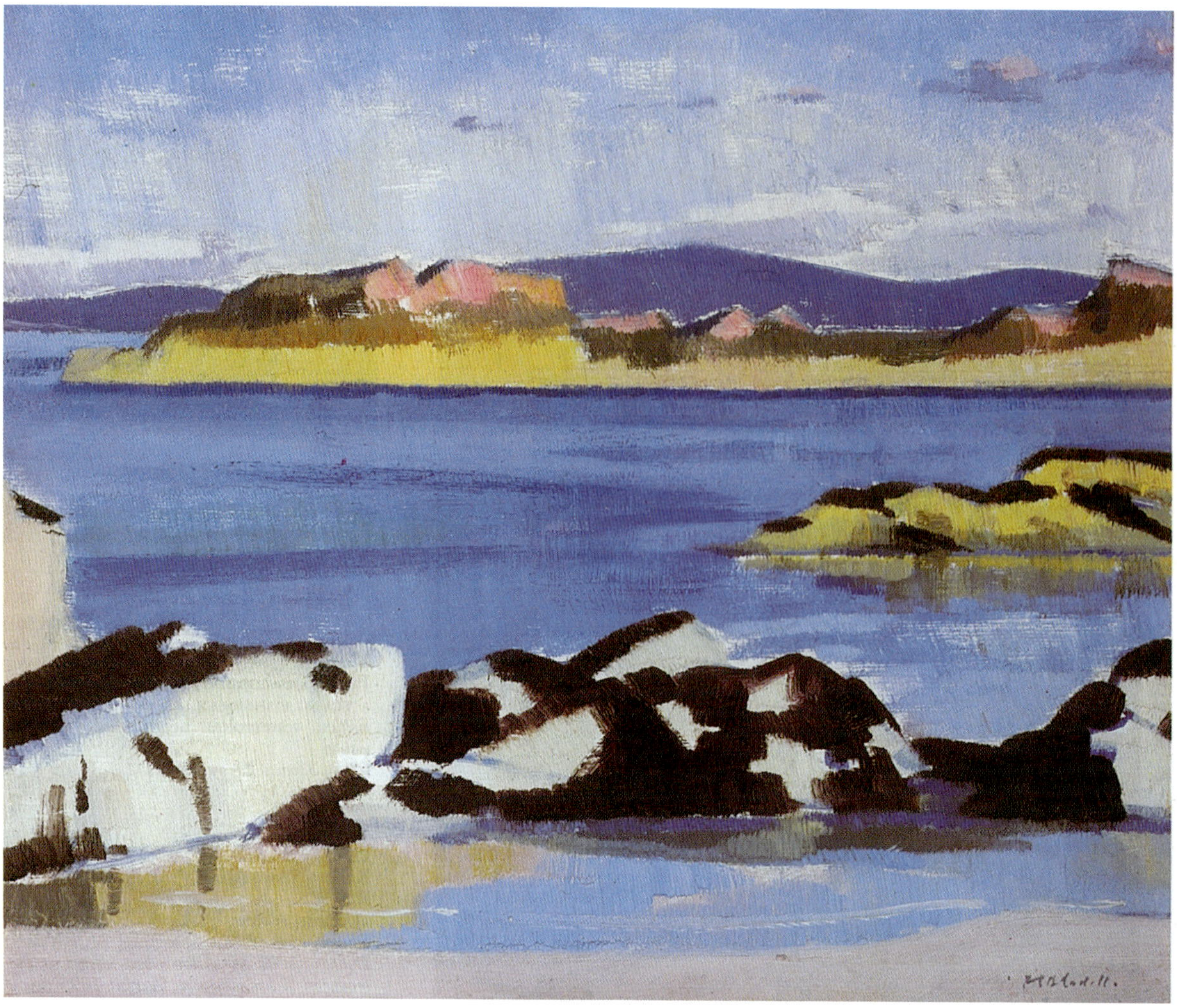

[PLATE 132]

F. C. B. Cadell

Eilean Annraidh
from near Pulpit Rock
Oil 15 x 18

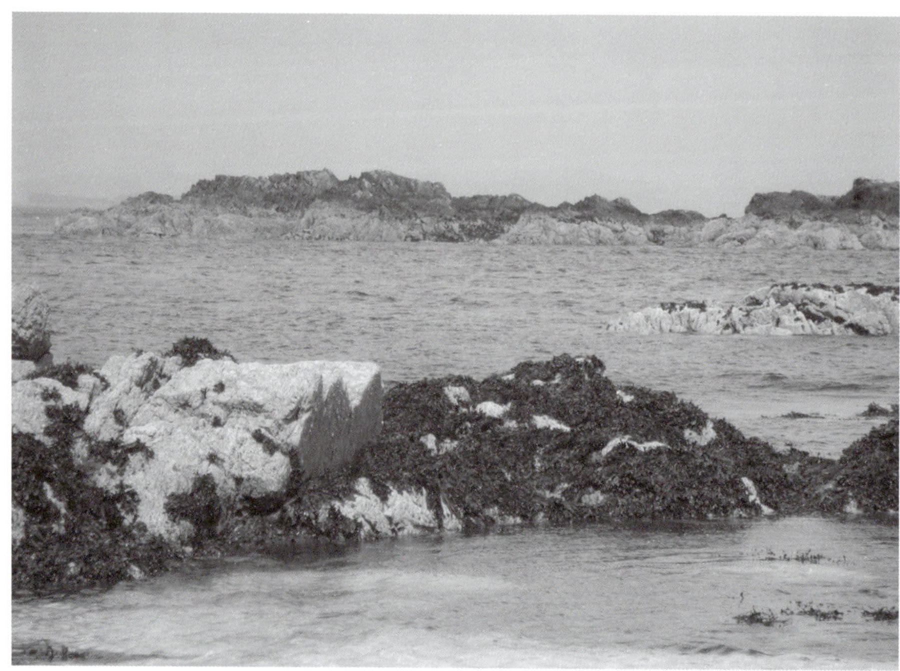

Photograph 2009

The foreground rocks are on the east side of Pulpit Rock. The west end of Eilean Annraidh is across the full width of the painting in the middle distance.

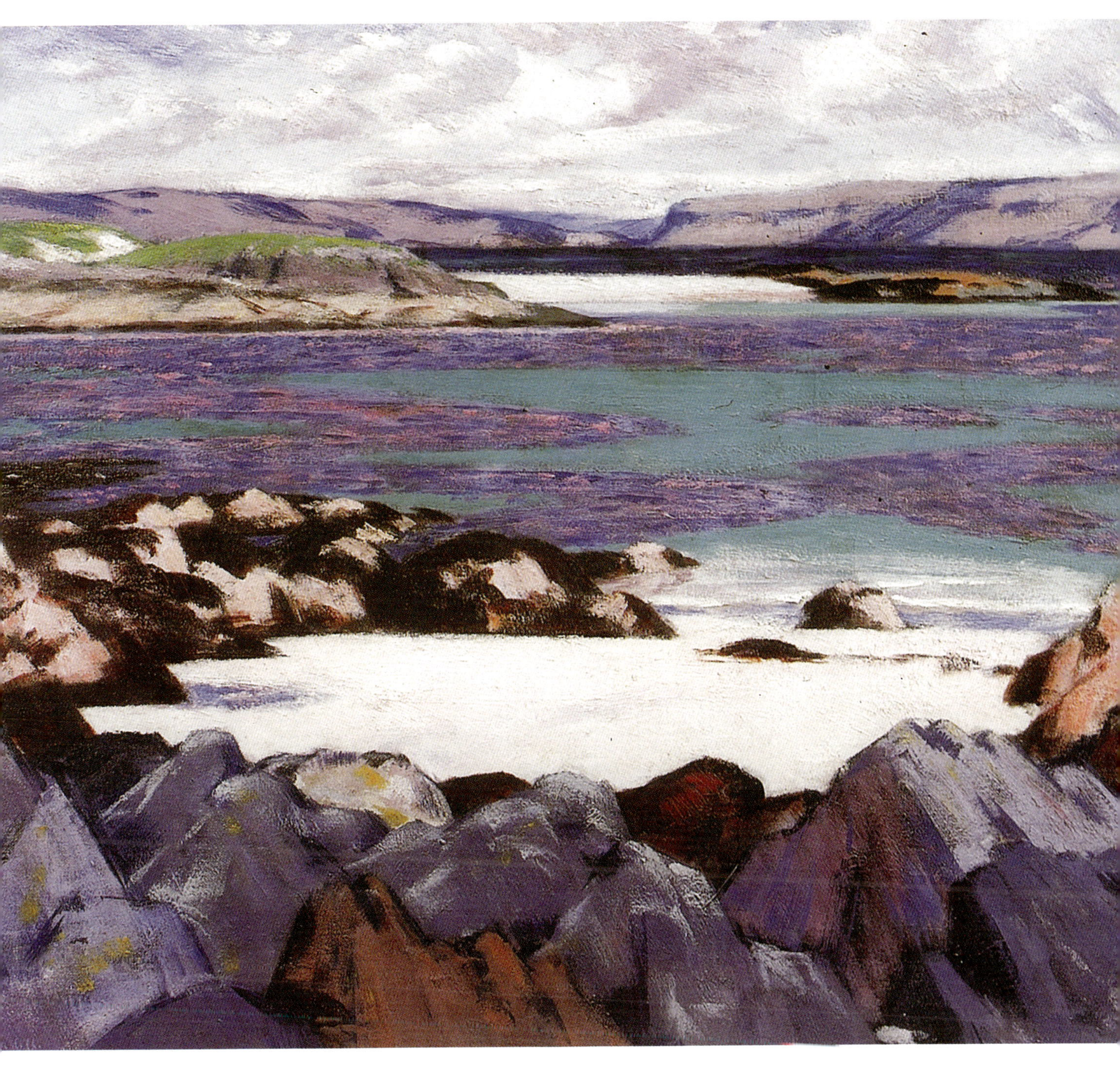

[PLATE 133]

F. C. B. Cadell

Eilean Annraidh from the North End

Oil 25 x 30

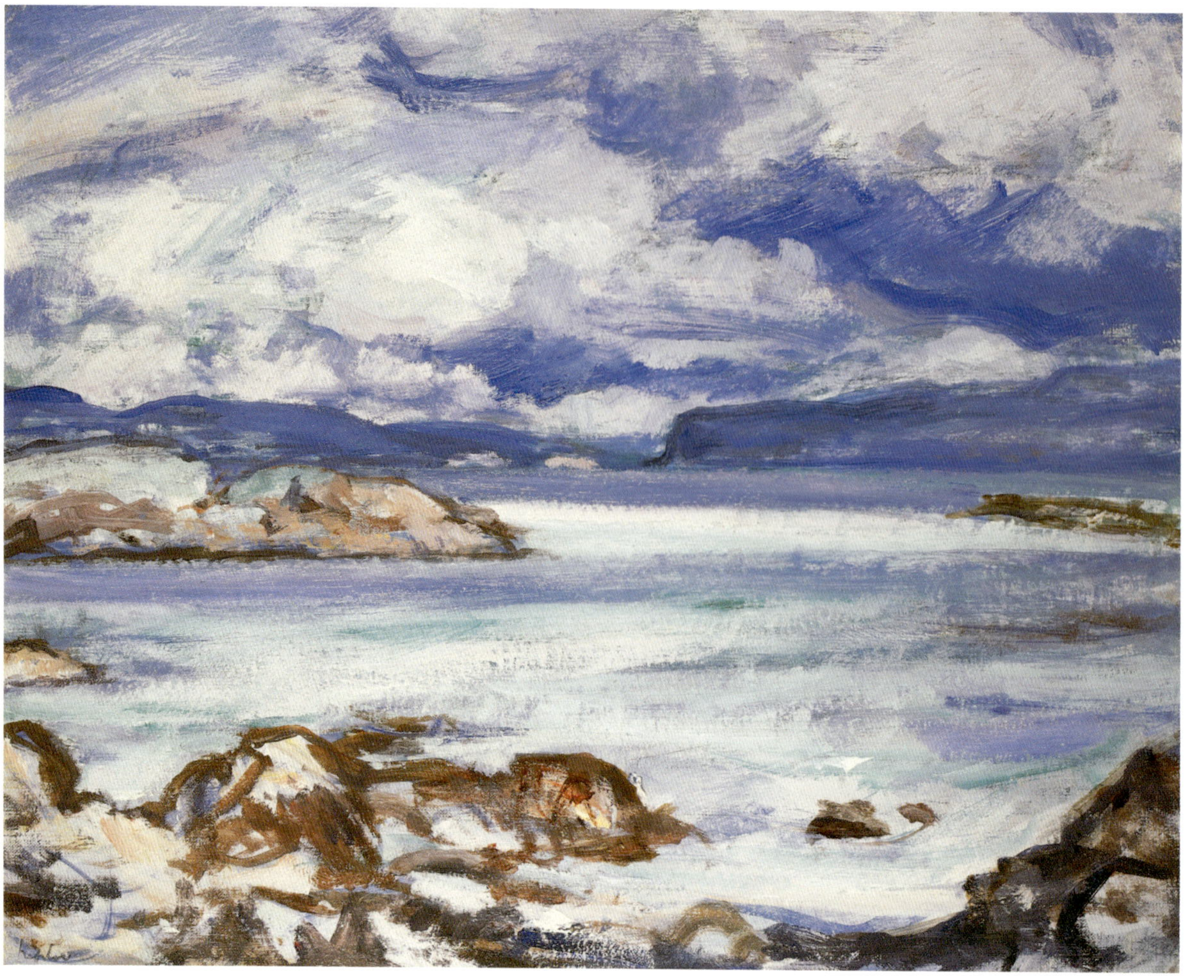

[PLATE 134]
S. J. Peploe
Eilean Annraidh
from the North End
(Iona, a Cloudy Sky)
Oil 18 x 22

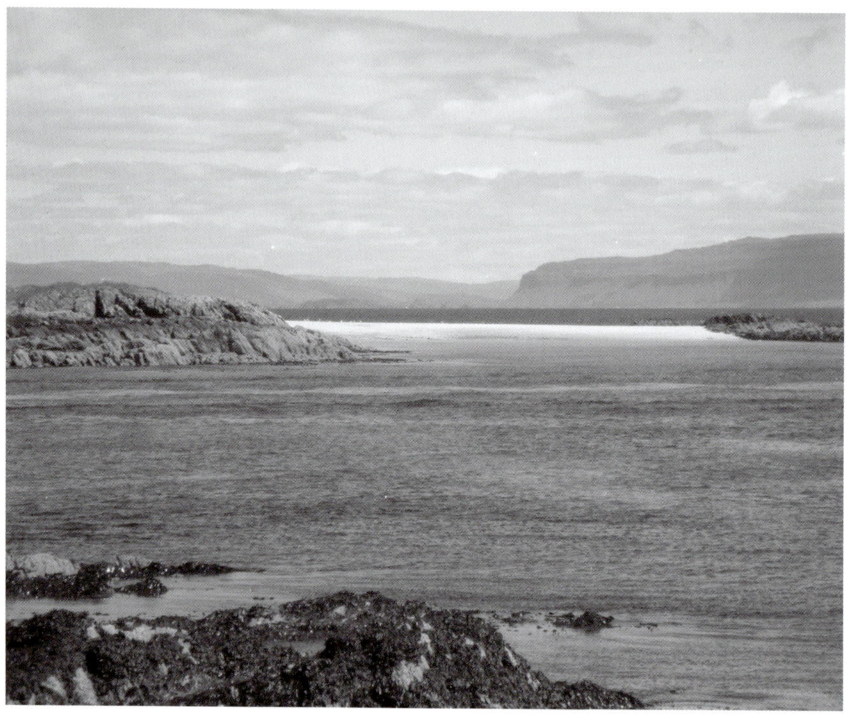

Photograph 2009

Plates 133 to 135 represent the same view towards Loch na Keal. The foregrounds vary, having been painted from slightly different viewpoints, but the distant elements are the same in each, and are identified in the diagram opposite.

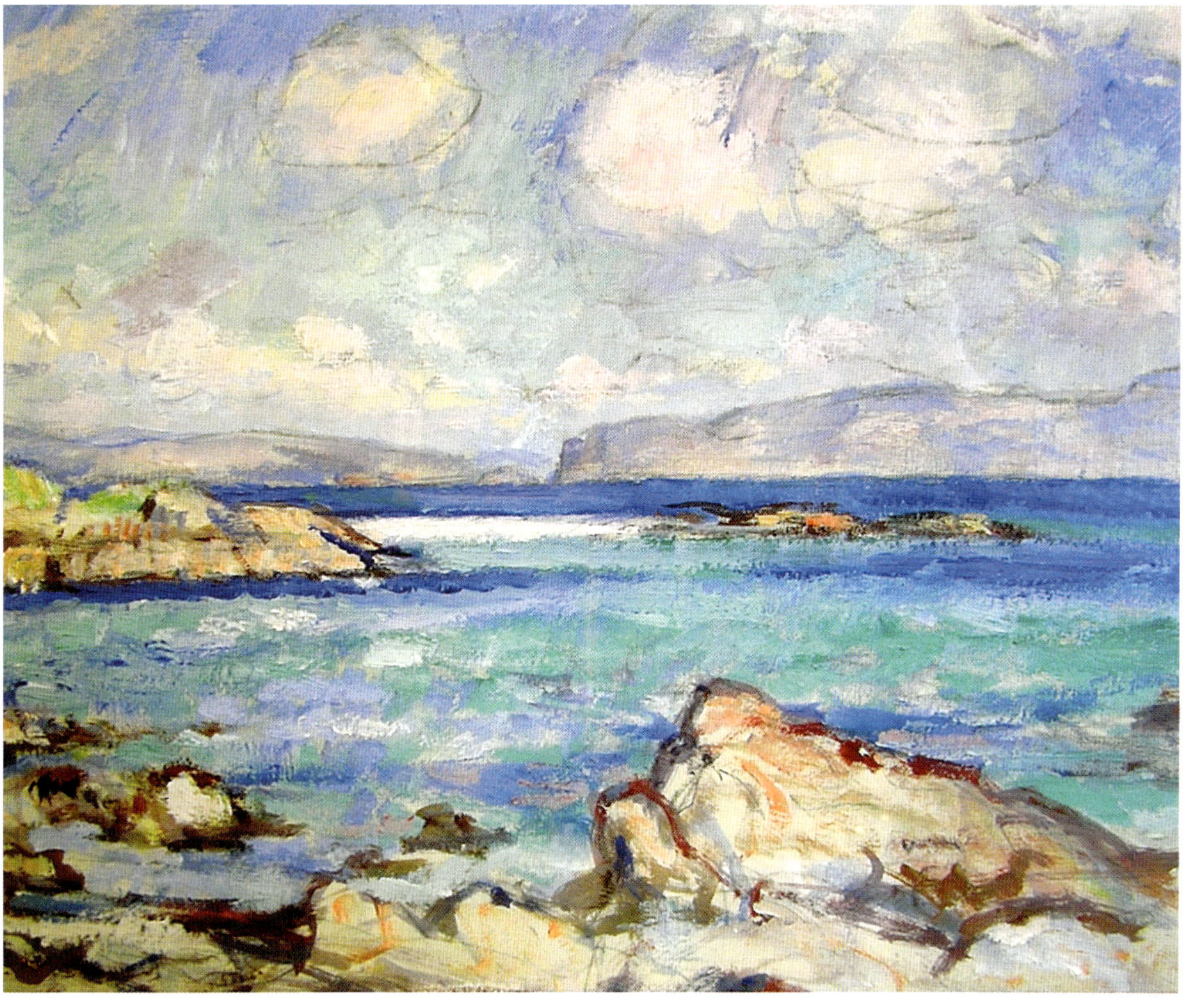

[PLATE 135]
S. J. Peploe
Eilean Annraidh from the North End
Oil 18 x 22

The Little Pinnacle is just right of centre near the bottom edge of the painting.

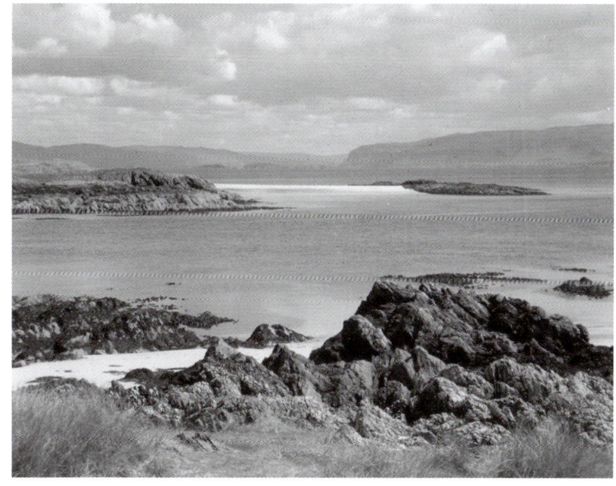

Photograph 2012

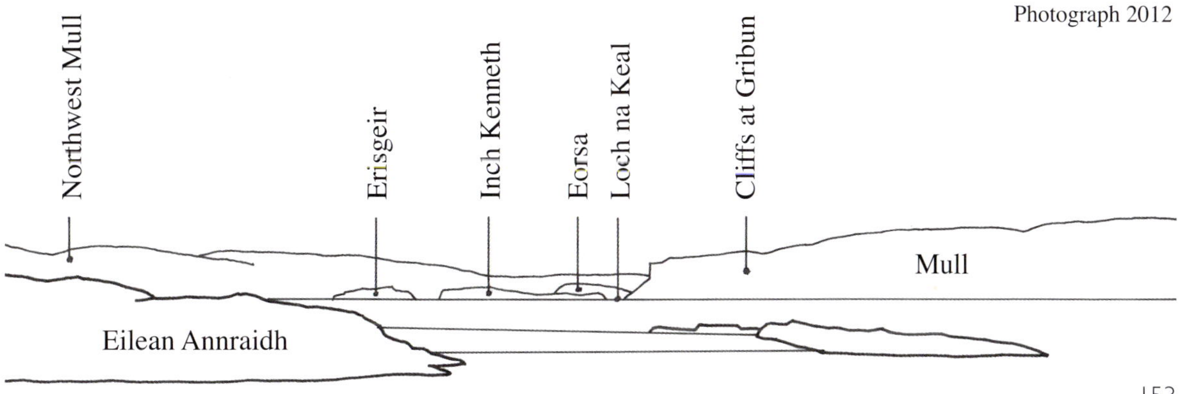

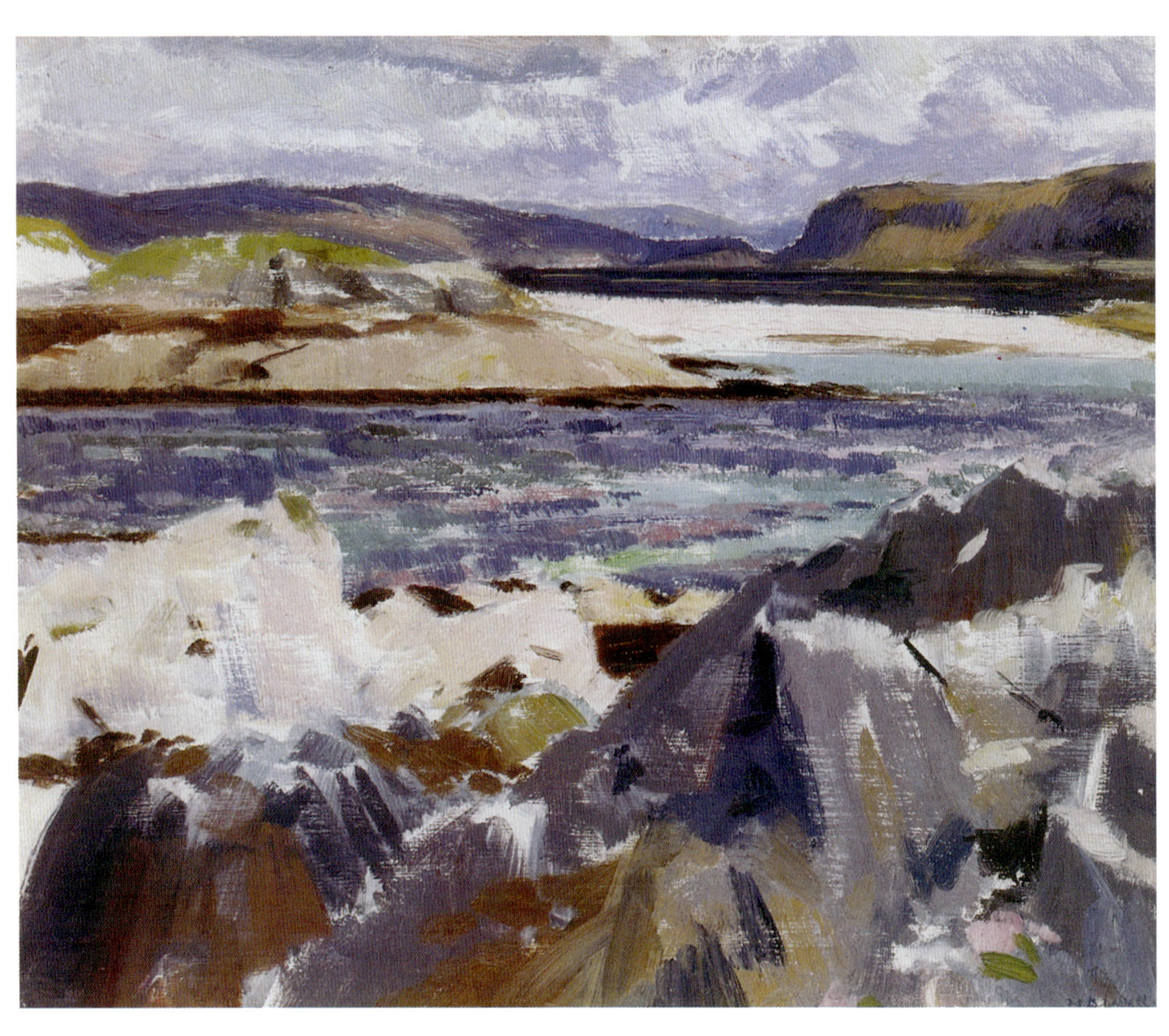

[PLATE 136]
F. C. B. Cadell
Eilean Annraidh
from the North End
Oil 15 x 18

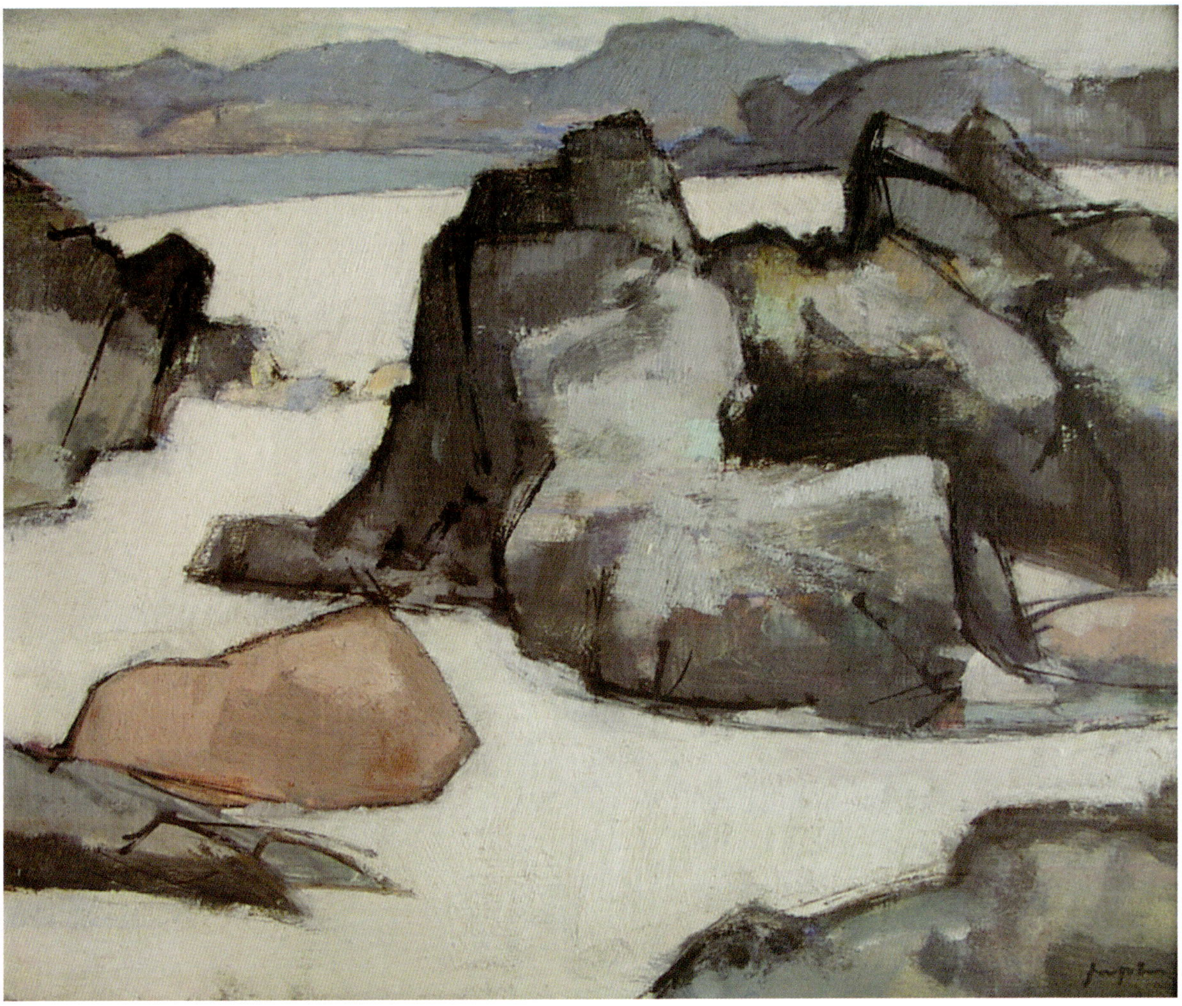

[PLATE 137]

S. J. Peploe

Rocks at the North End

Oil 15 x 18

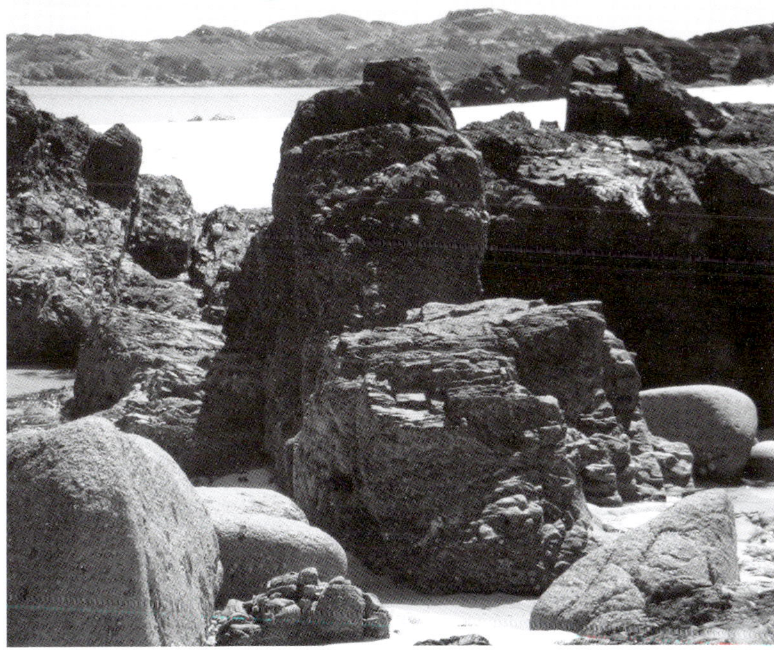

Photograph 2009

The Little Pinnacle is just out of sight on the left. Cows Rock is in the top right corner, partly hidden by the foreground rocks, and the Ross of Mull is in the background.

The level of the sand is lower in the photograph than the painting, but one can still see that the rocks have been accurately recorded.

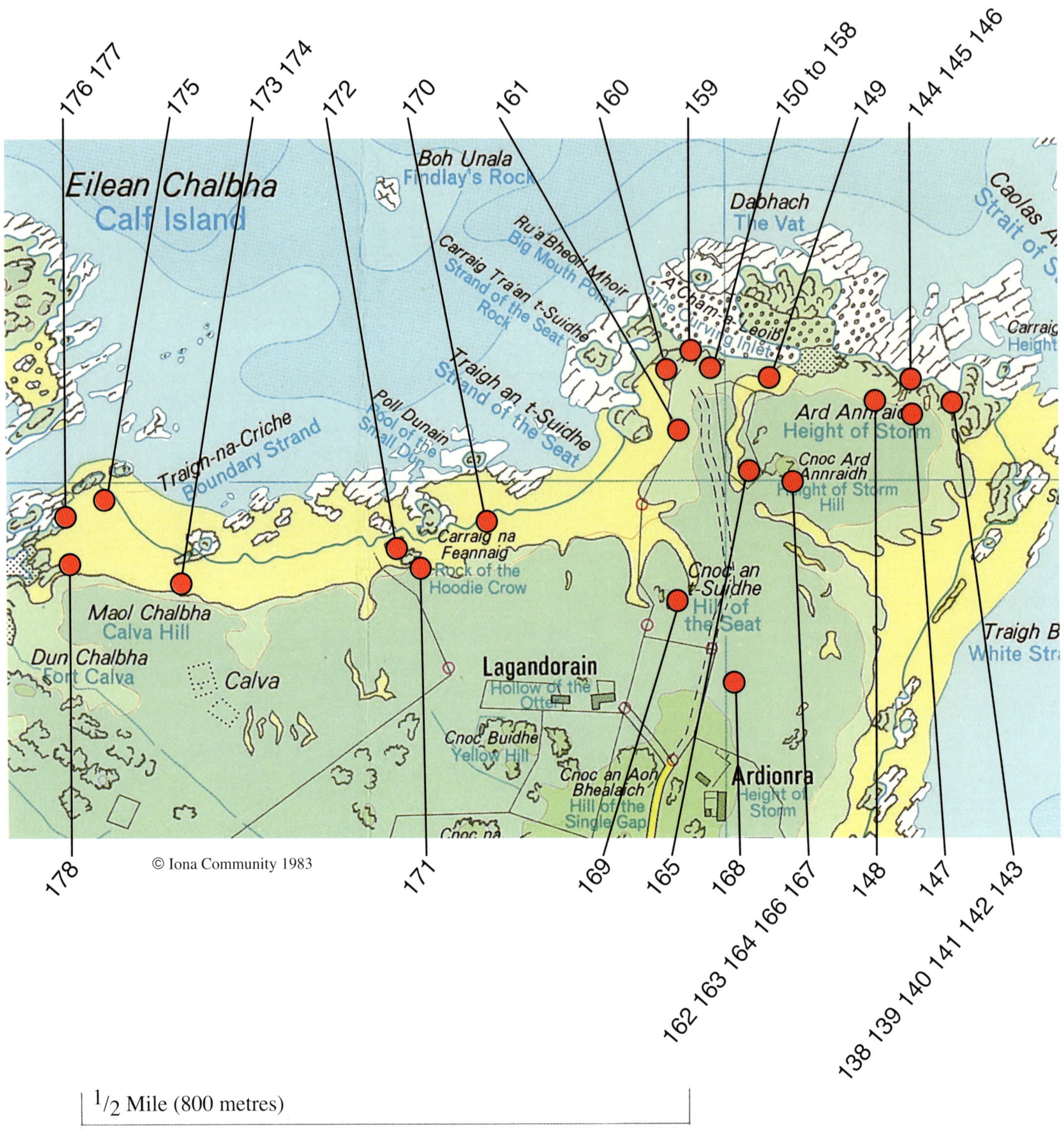

176 177
175
173 174
172
170
161
160
159
150 to 158
149
144 145 146

Eilean Chalbha
Calf Island
Boh Unala
Findlay's Rock
Ru'a Bheoil Mhoir
Big Mouth Point
Carraig Tra'an t-Suidhe
Strand of the Seat
Rock
Dabhach
The Vat
A' Cham-Leoib
The Curving Inlet
Caolas
Strait of
Carraig
Height
Traigh an t-Suidhe
Strand of the Seat
Poll Dunain
Pool of the
Small Dun
Traigh-na-Criche
Boundary Strand
Ard Annraidh
Height of Storm
Cnoc Ard
Annraidh
Height of Storm
Hill
Carraig na
Feannaig
Rock of the
Hoodie Crow
Cnoc an
t-Suidhe
Hill of
the Seat
Maol Chalbha
Calva Hill
Dun Chalbha
Fort Calva
Calva
Lagandorain
Hollow of the
Otter
Cnoc Buidhe
Yellow Hill
Cnoc an Aon
Bhealaich
Hill of the
Single Gap
Ardionra
Height of
Storm
Traigh B
White Str

178

171
169
165
168
162 163 164 166 167
148
147
138 139 140 141 142 143

1/2 Mile (800 metres)

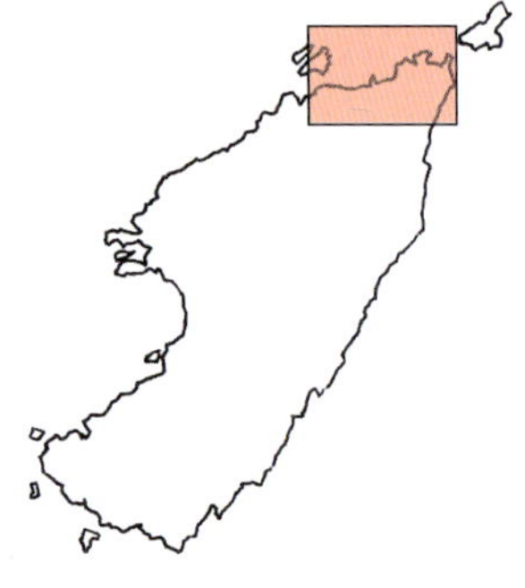

[FIGURE 16]
Locations of paintings illustrated in Chapter 5

5 · FROM MERMAIDS TO CHALBHA

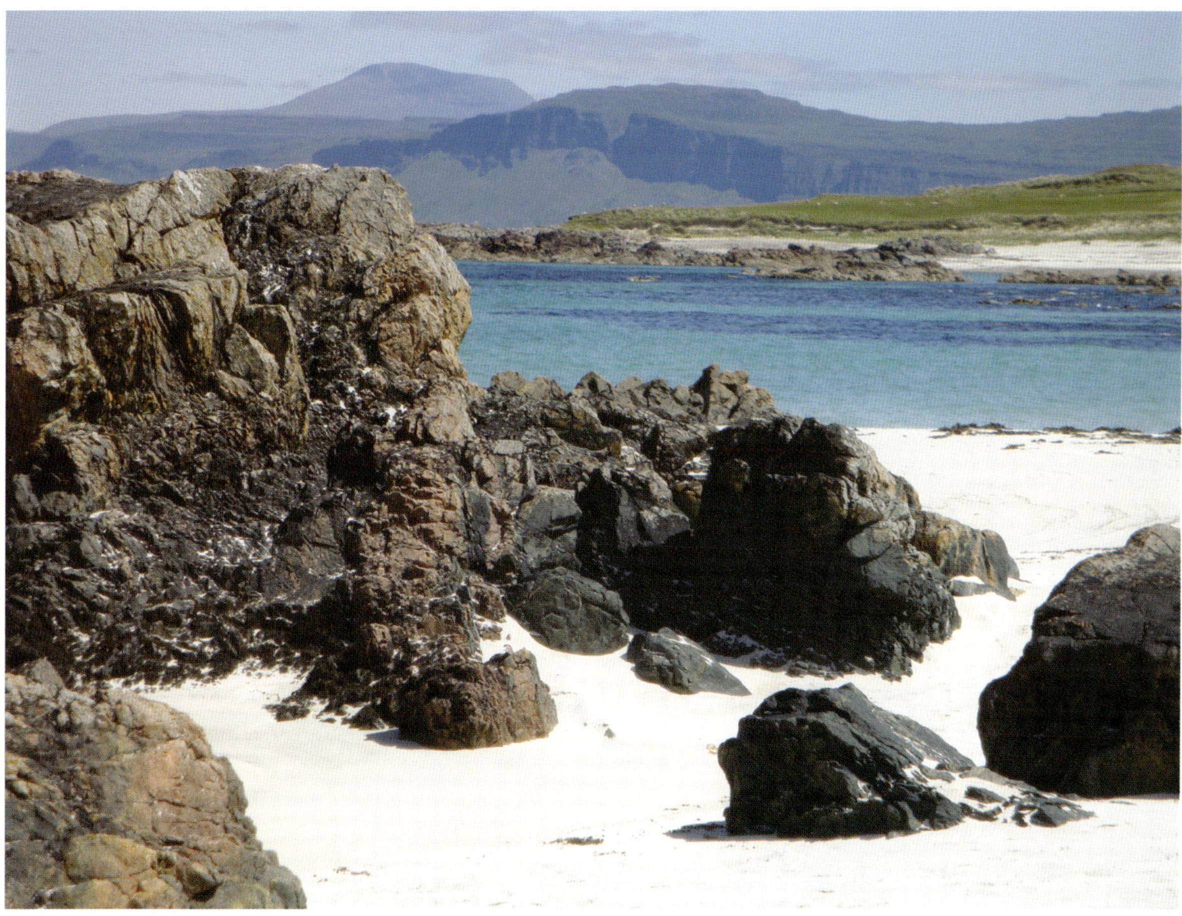

BEFORE proceeding to describe the paintings along the north shore, from Mermaids to Chalbha, it is worth noting that, at the Headland, as we turn from the east shore to the north shore, we also cross a geological boundary. The foreground rocks in the paintings in the previous two chapters are Torridonian. These are metamorphosed sandstones and mudstones. The original bedding plane now stands almost vertical and gives rise to features such as the Finger and Cathedral Rock. These rocks tend to be various shades of grey, but the colour is enlivened by pale green and yellow lichens and, in early summer, by pink thrift.

However, the rocks on the north shore are Lewisian Gneiss and are richly coloured with bands of pink, grey, and green with fine green-yellow veining. These beautiful rocks are the most ancient in Britain having been formed about 2,700 million years ago. In contrast as we look across the Sound of Iona towards the Burg on Mull we see the eroded remains of a landscape formed by volcanic activity only about 65 million years ago, which is very recent in geological terms. The successive flows of lava can still be seen in the terraces across the Burg and also in the remarkable outlines of the Dutchman's Cap, Lunga and Staffa.

Mermaids Corridor is the obvious deep cleft which separates the Headland from the mainland of Iona, and the name has led to this area being known simply as "Mermaids". Plates 138 to 141 were painted from the rock ledges above Mermaids (see page 84).

Plates 142 to 146 were painted at shore level at Mermaids. It is clear from the paintings, and contemporary descriptions, that in the past there was a sufficient depth of sand in the Corridor to have enabled Cadell and Peploe to walk easily to these painting spots. However, in recent years, with no sand in this area, the approach now involves scrambling over rocks, wet seaweed, and through tidal pools. Given that these locations become submerged under a considerable depth of water at high tide, the reader may wish to view them from the safety of higher ground.

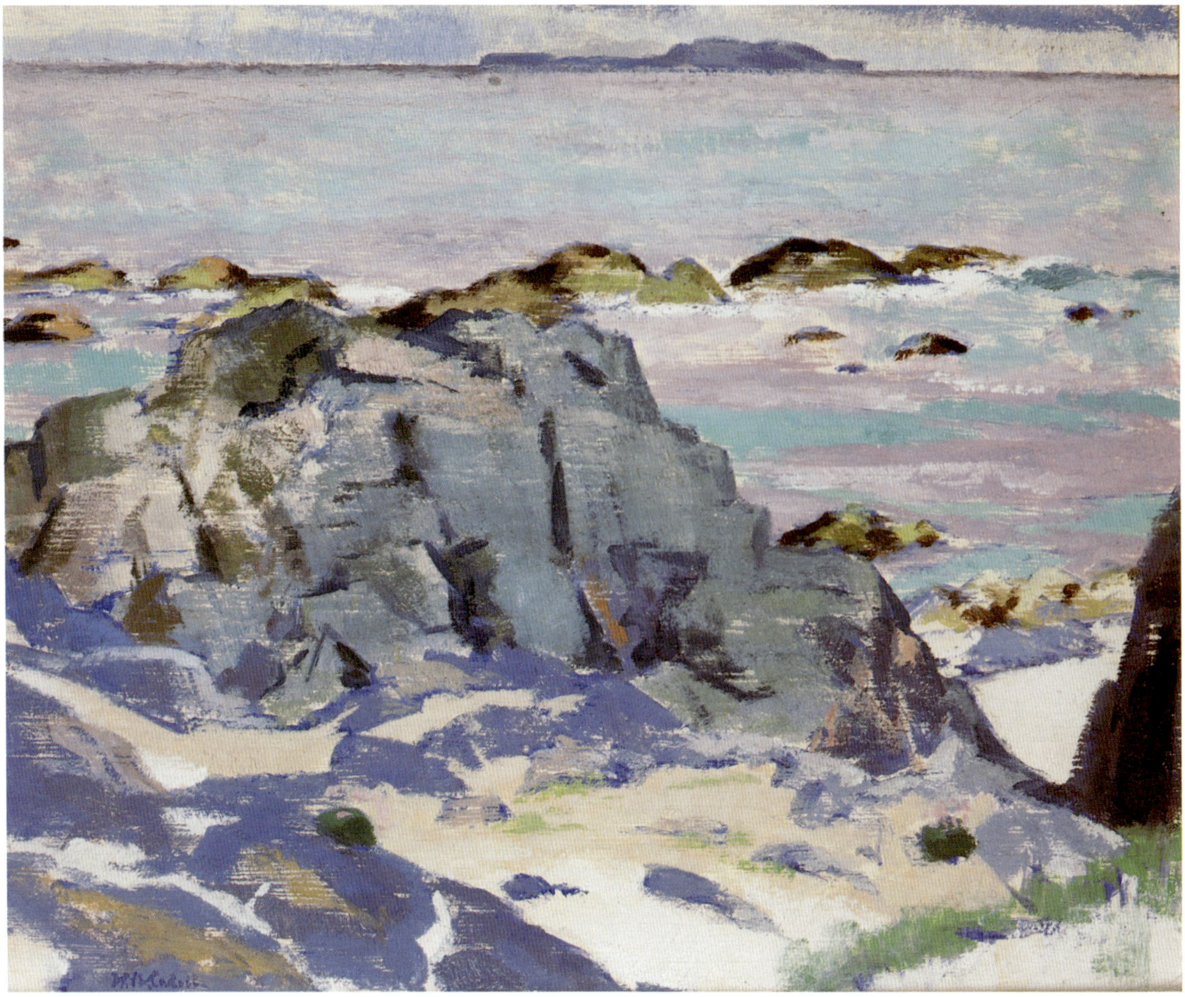

[PLATE 138]

F. C. B. Cadell

Lunga from above
Mermaids

Oil 15 x 18

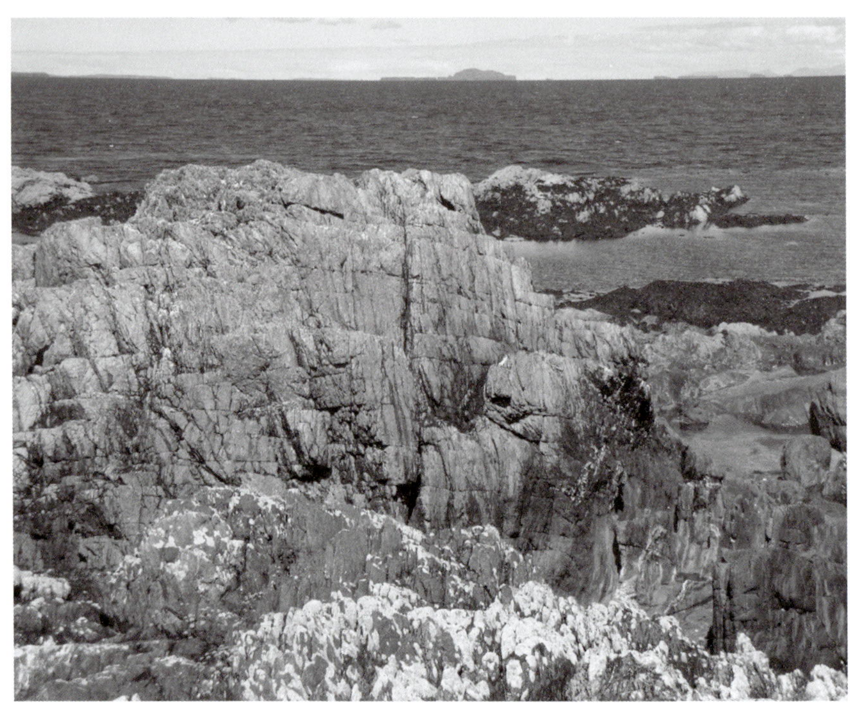

Photograph 2009

[PLATE 139]
F. C. B. Cadell
Lunga from above Mermaids
Watercolour

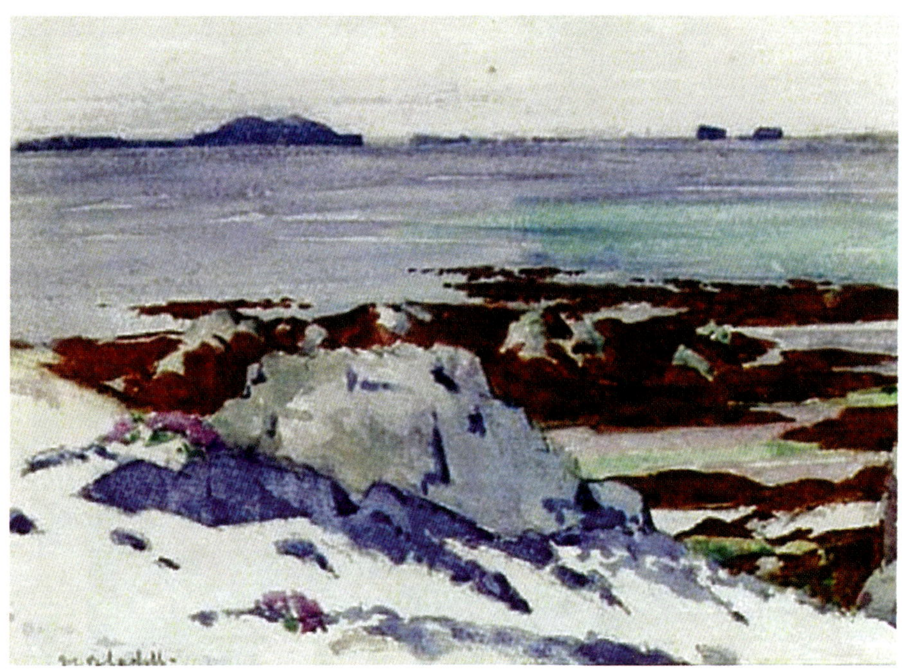

The foreground of this watercolour is similar to that of the preceding oil painting. There is a slight shift of viewpoint and here the island of Lunga is on the left-hand side with some of the smaller Treshnish Isles to the right.

[PLATE 140]
F. C. B. Cadell
Dutchman's Cap from above Mermaids
Watercolour

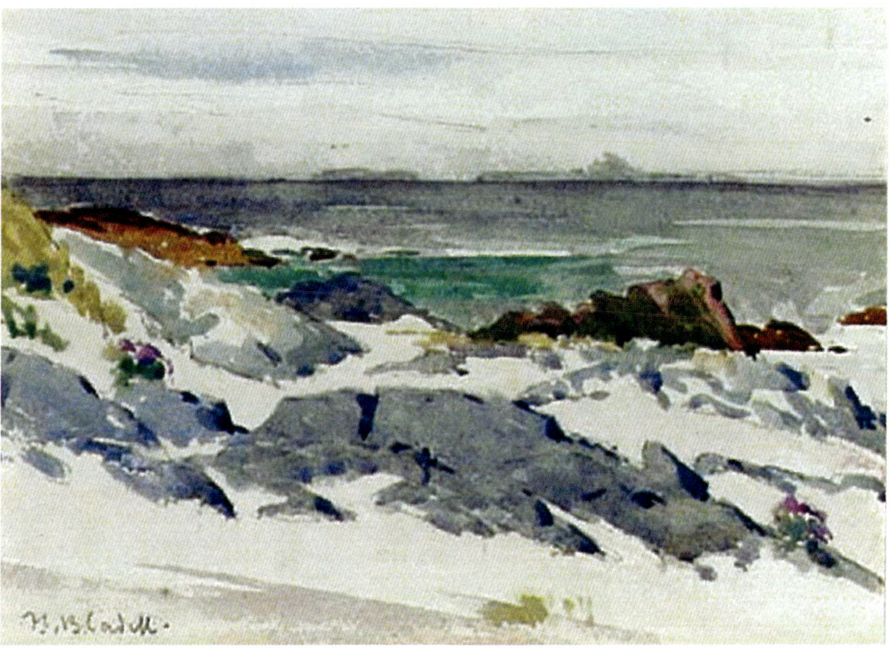

Painted from further back than Plate 139, this view is further to the west and shows the islands of Bac Beag and Bac Mor, more frequently referred to as the Dutchman's Cap, on the horizon. The foreground here is similar to the oil painting that follows.

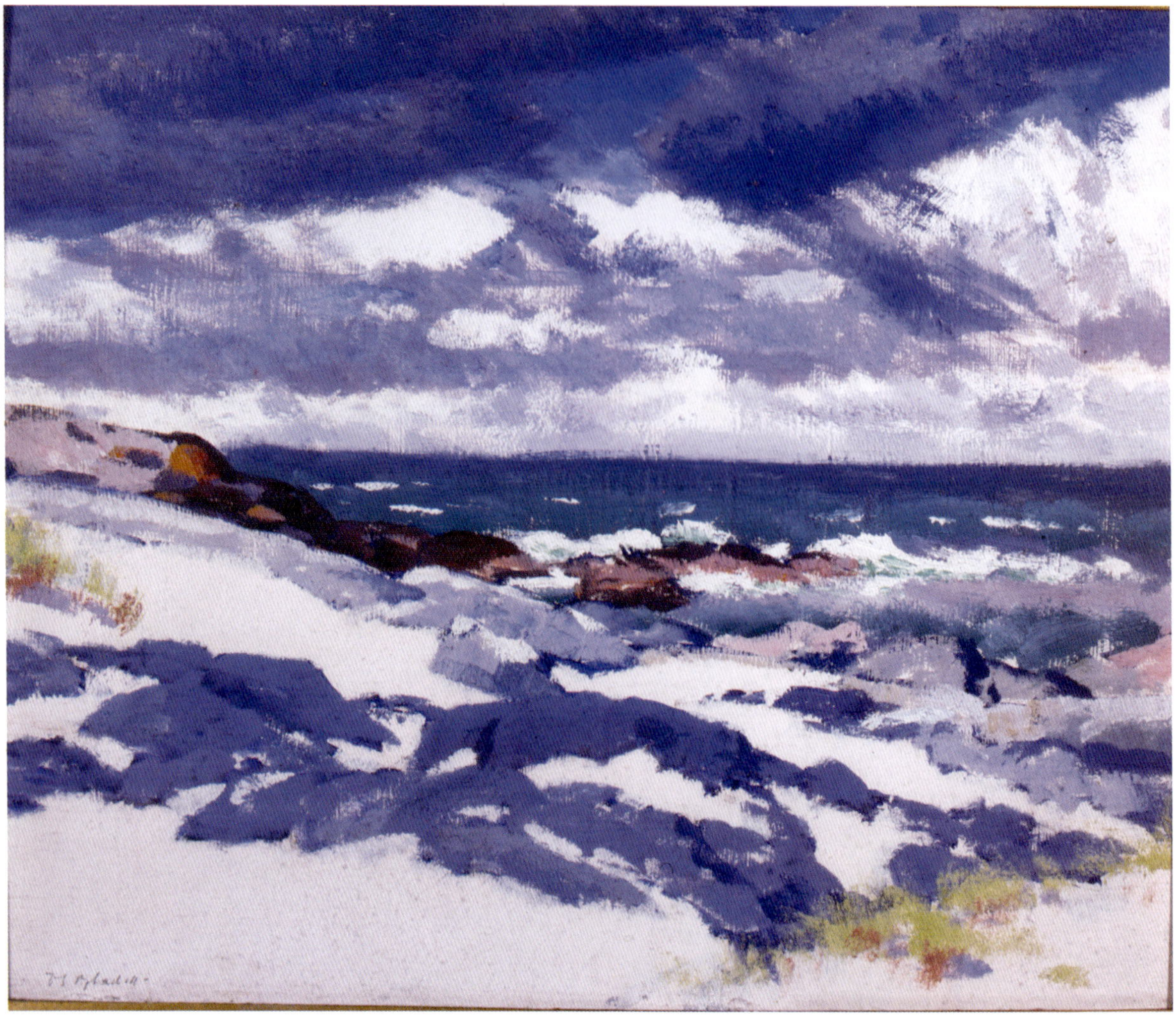

[PLATE 141]

F. C.B. Cadell

Above Mermaids

Oil 15 x 18

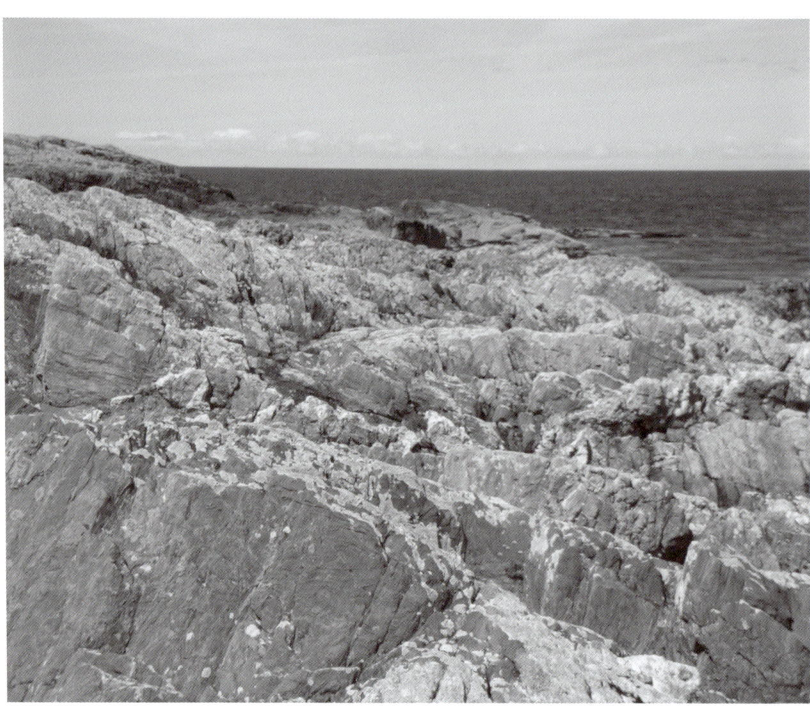

Photograph 2009

Unusually Cadell has chosen a motif with an empty horizon; the Dutchman's Cap is just out of view to the right. He has recorded the change in rocks, referred to at the beginning of this chapter, from the blue grey of the Torridonian in the foreground to the warmer coloured Lewisian Gneiss beyond,

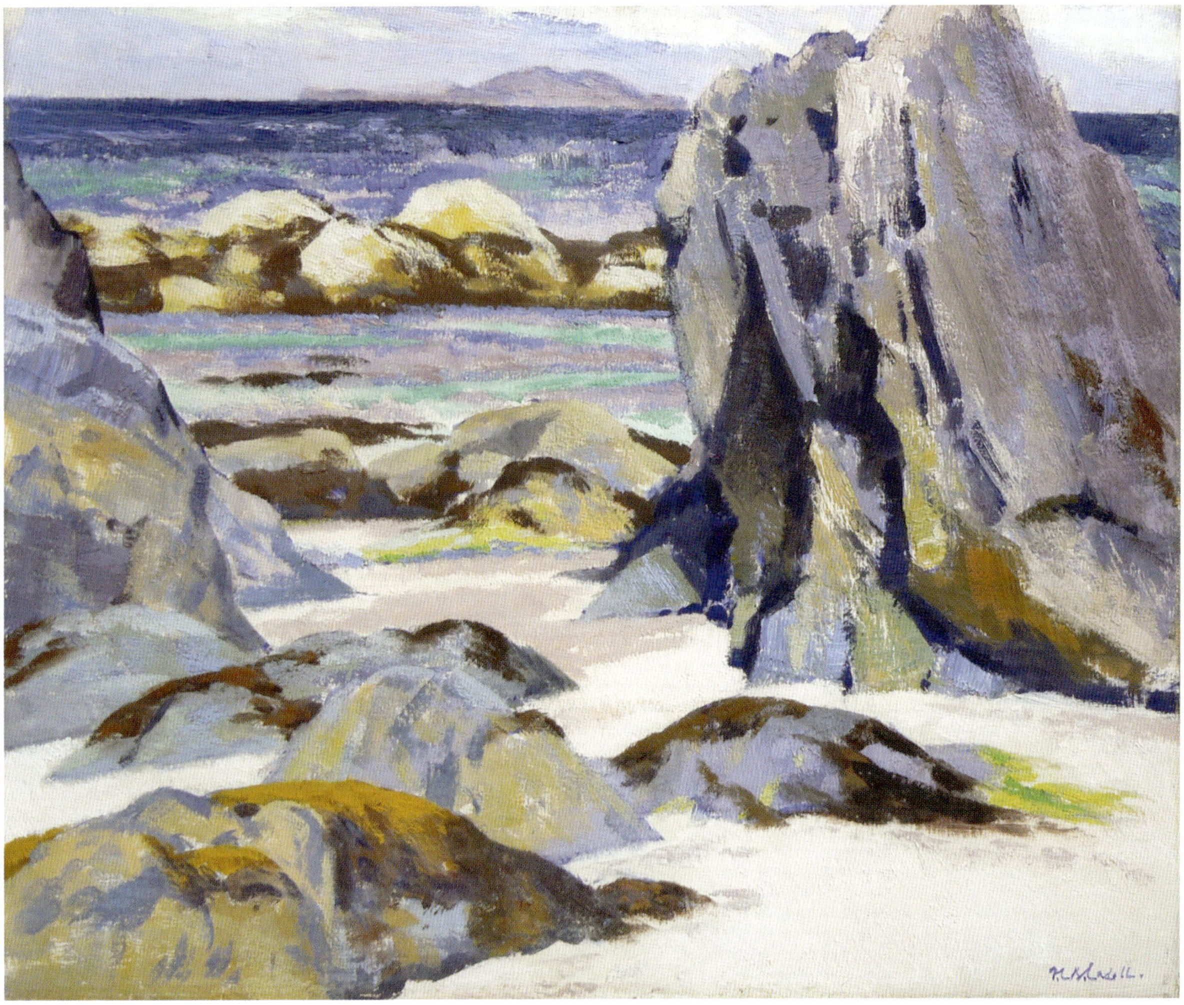

[PLATE 142]

F. C. B. Cadell

Lunga from Mermaids

Oil 15 x 18

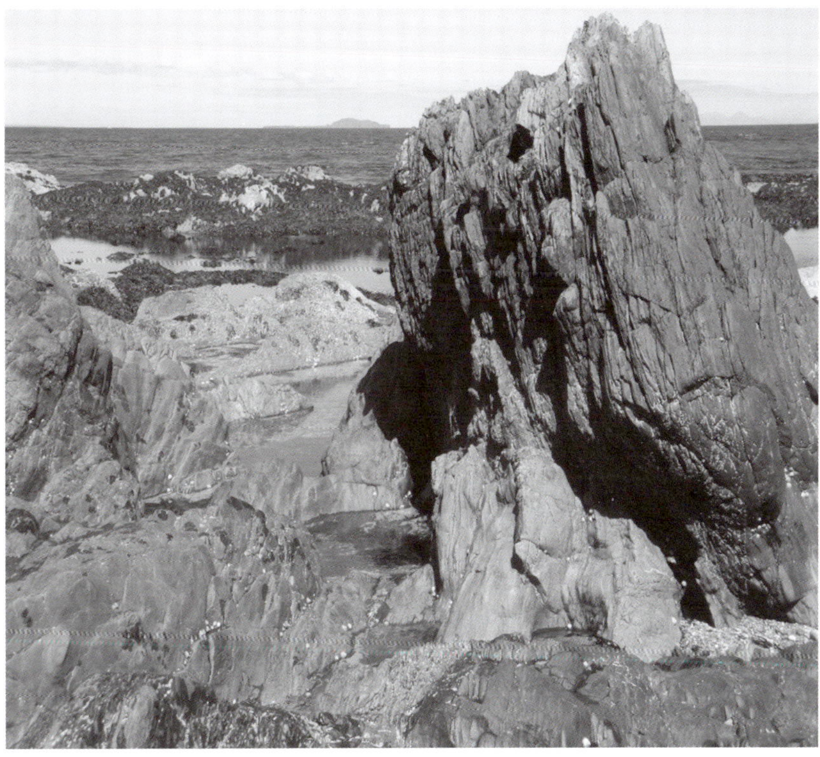

Photograph 2010

The large rock on the right is mostly underwater at high tide. As noted on page 157, this location is difficult to reach, but is easily seen from the ledges above.

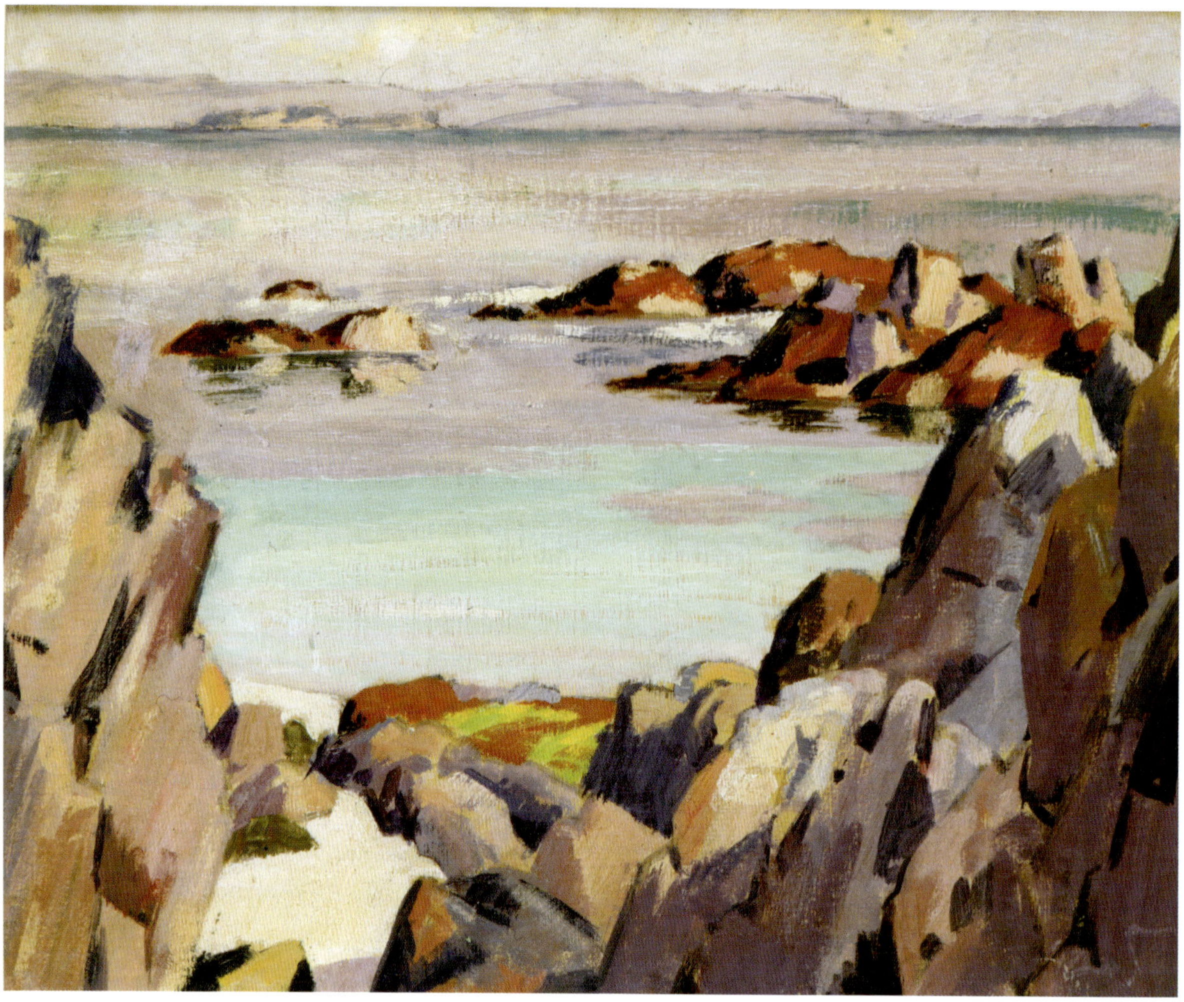

[PLATE 143]
F. C. B. Cadell
Staffa from Mermaids
Oil 15 x 18

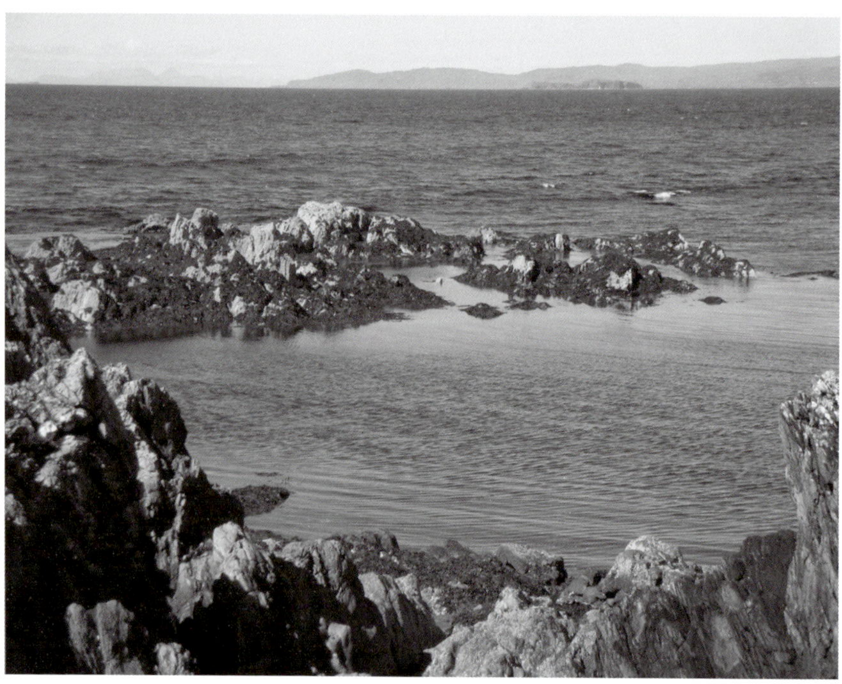

Photograph 2010

This was painted through a gap in the rock wall which encloses the Corridor, and shows Rhum on the horizon on the left, and Staffa on the right seen against the hills of northwest Mull.

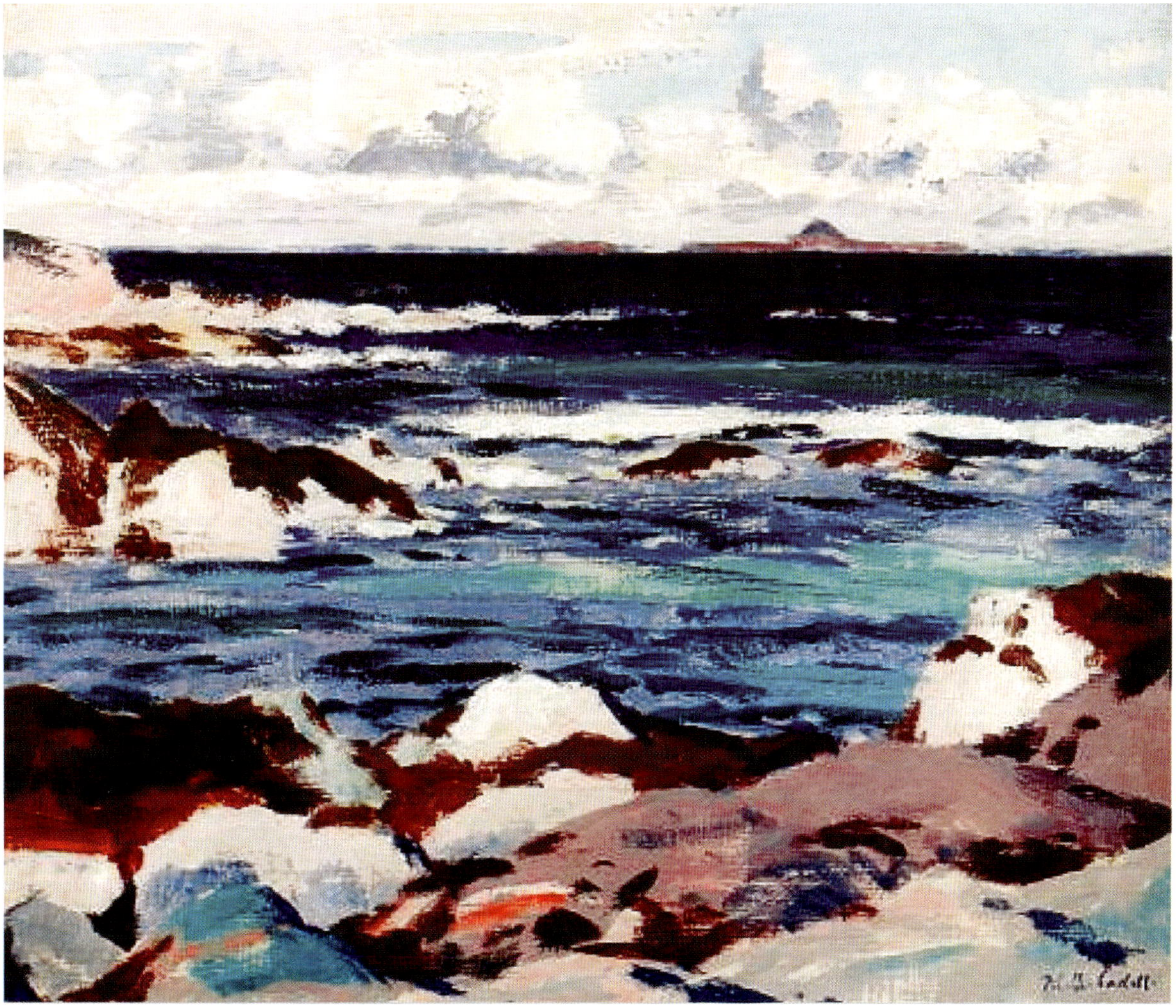

[PLATE 144]

F. C. B. Cadell

The Dutchman's Cap from Mermaids

Oil 15 x 18

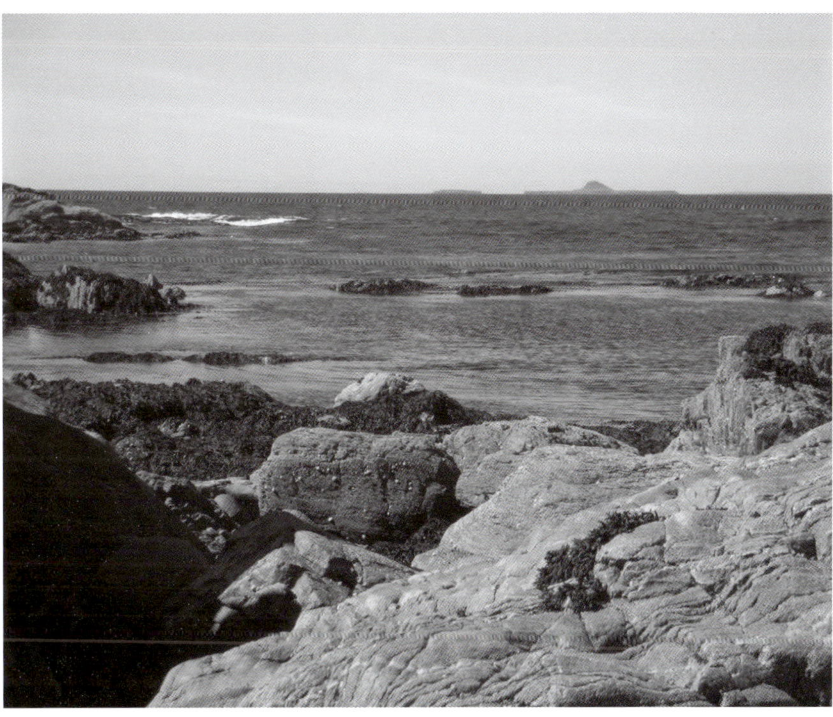

Photograph 2010

Plates 144 to 146 were painted from the small beach at the west end of Mermaids Corridor. As already noted (page 157) access to this area is awkward.

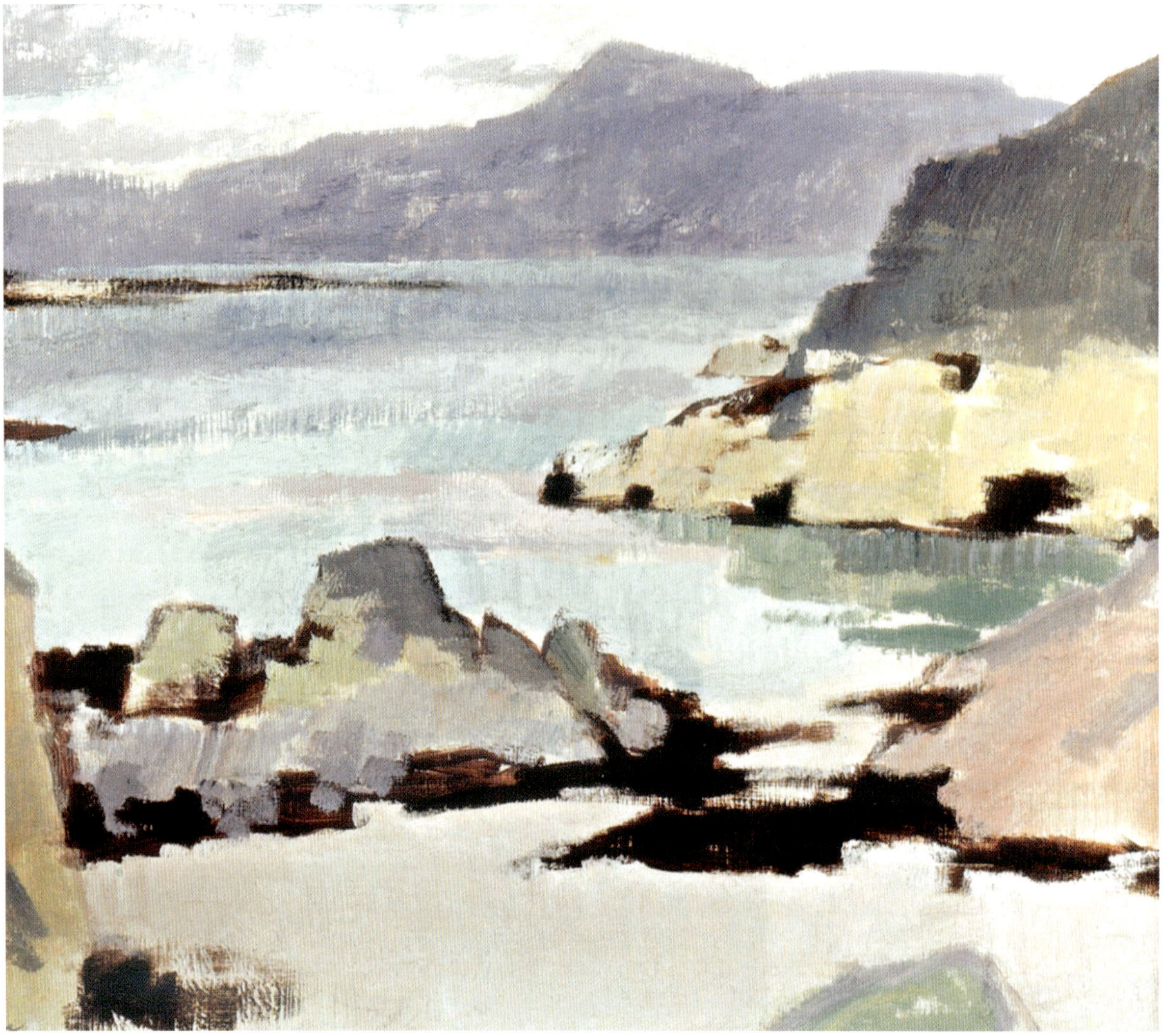

[PLATE 145]

S. J. Peploe

Ben More from Mermaids

Oil 15 x 18

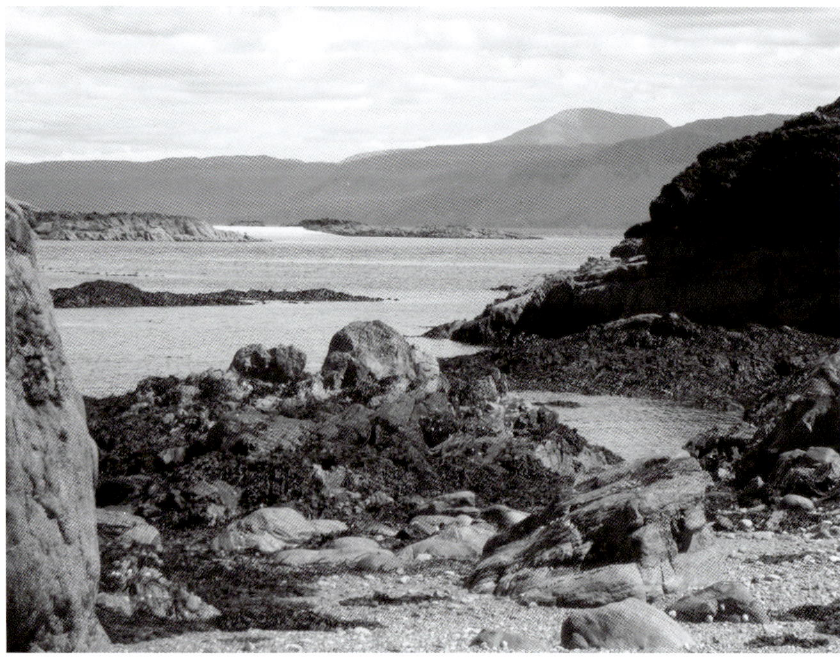

Photograph 2009

This was painted from nearly the same place as Cadell's picture of the Dutchman's Cap (Plate 144) but here Peploe has chosen the view towards Mull and Ben More. The mass of rock on the right is the Headland.

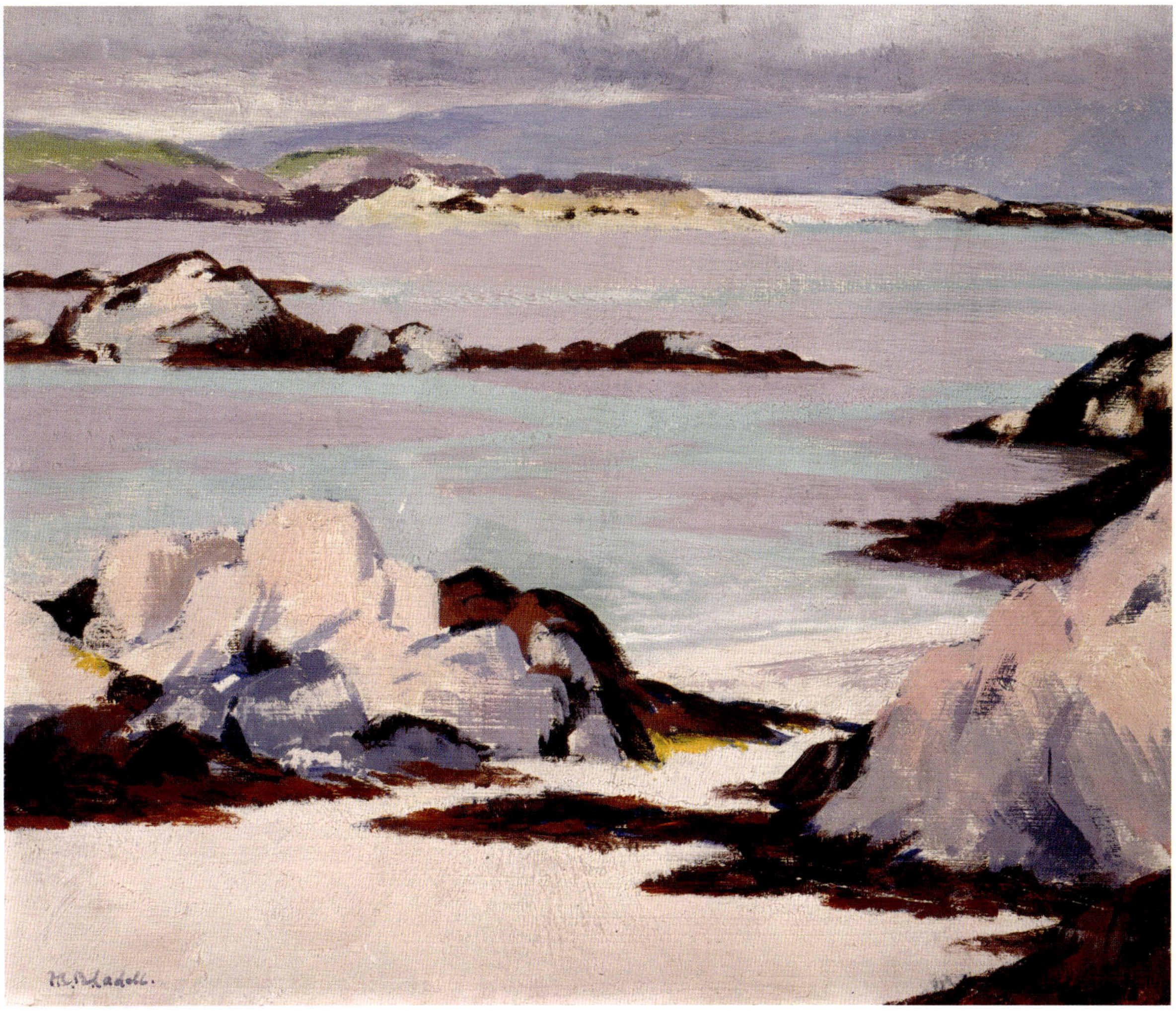

[PLATE 146]

F. C. B. Cadell

IONA

Eilean Annraidh
from Mermaids
Oil 15 x 18

City Art Centre,
Edinburgh Museums
and Galleries

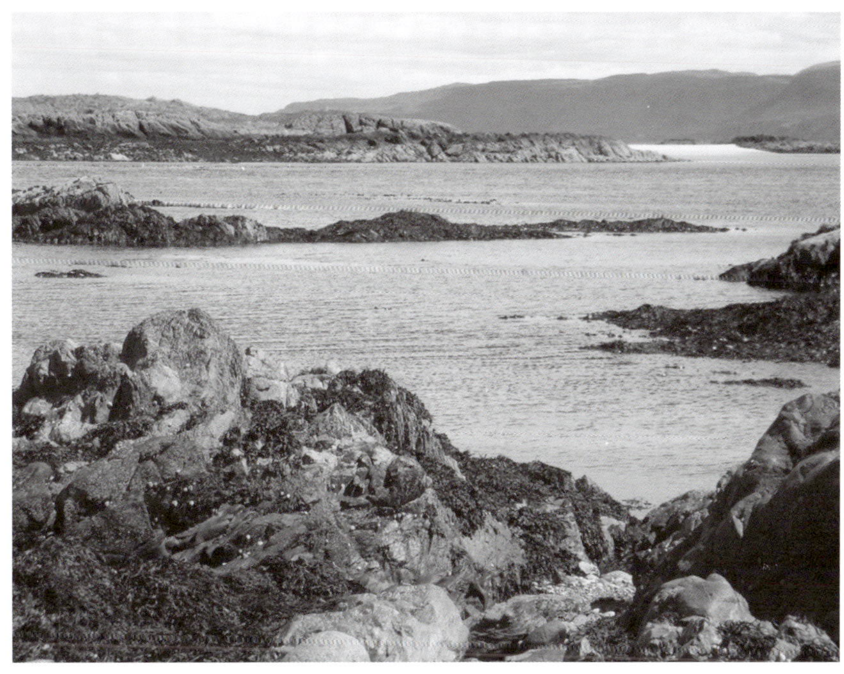

Photograph 2010

The foreground rocks are the same as those in the preceding painting by Peploe, but this view by Cadell is further to the left; Eilean Annraidh is across the entire width of the painting in the middle distance. The tip of the Headland is at the right-hand edge.

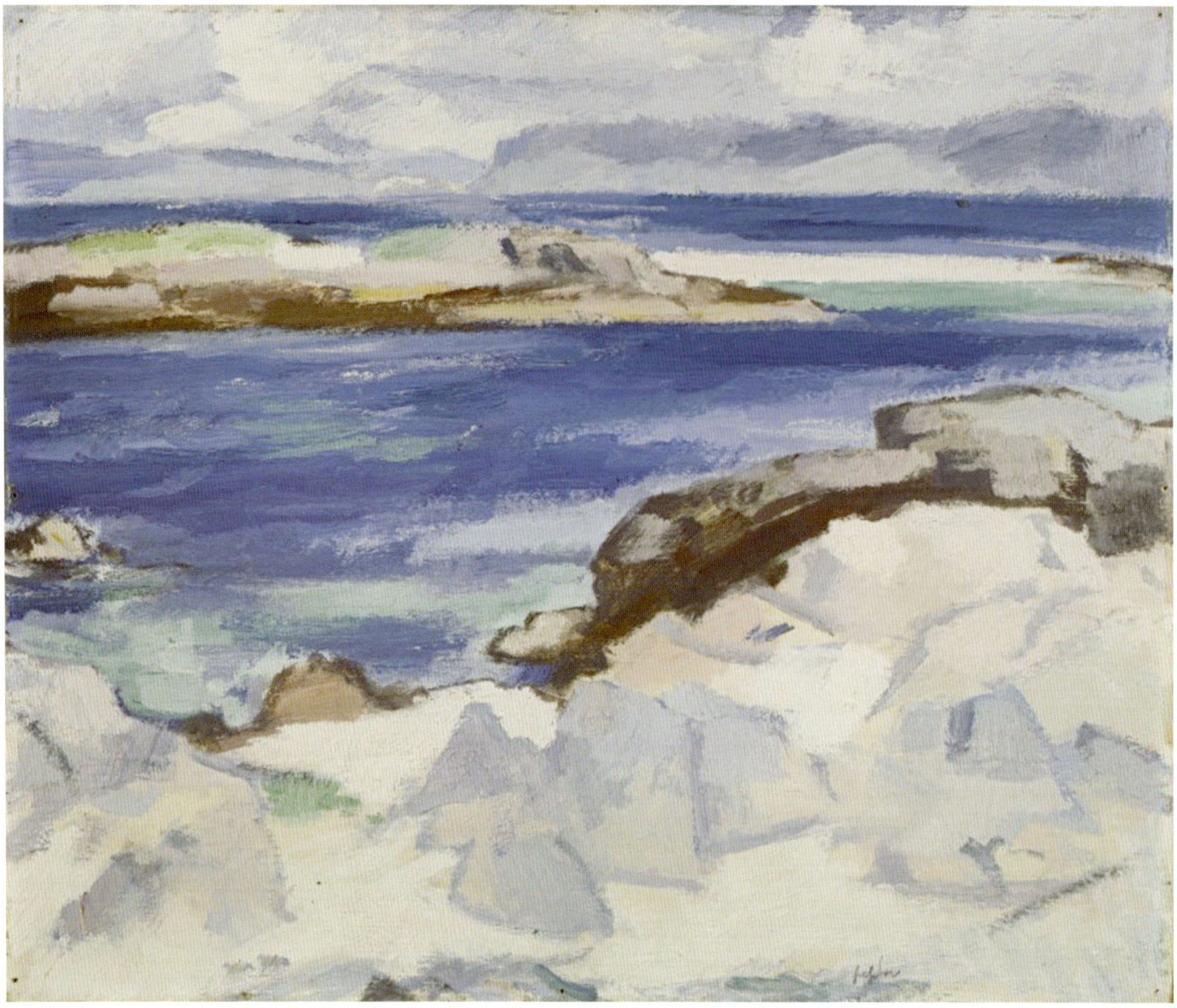

[PLATE 147]

S. J. Peploe

IONA

Towards Mull from Ard Annraidh
Oil 15 x 18

The Scottish National Gallery of Modern Art, Edinburgh

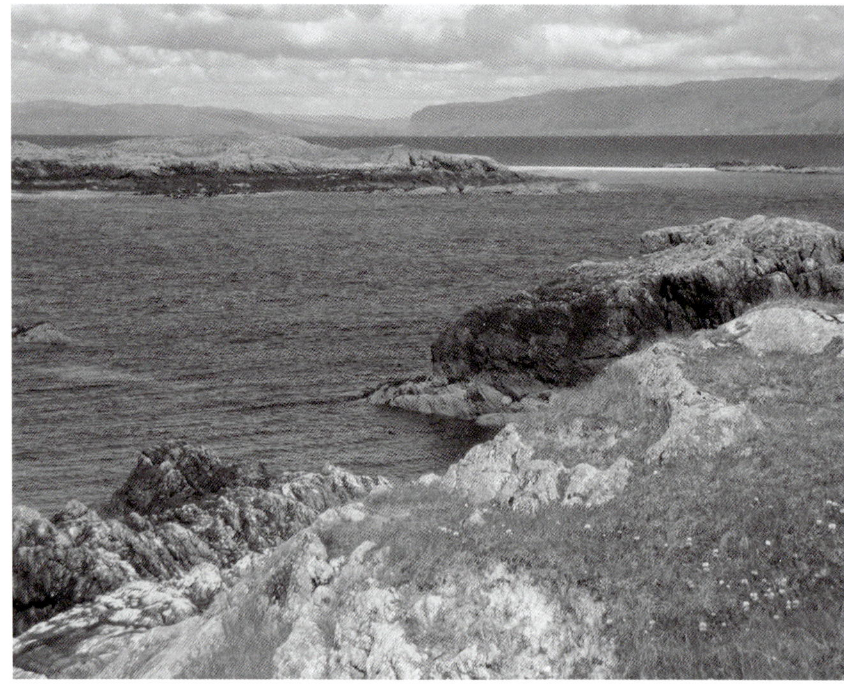

Photograph 2010

Ard Annraidh (Height of Storm) is the high ground above Mermaids. This view is towards the northeast and includes the cliffs at Gribun central in the far distance. Eilean Annraidh (Island of Storm) occupies the full width of the painting in the middle distance and the Headland is in the foreground on the right.

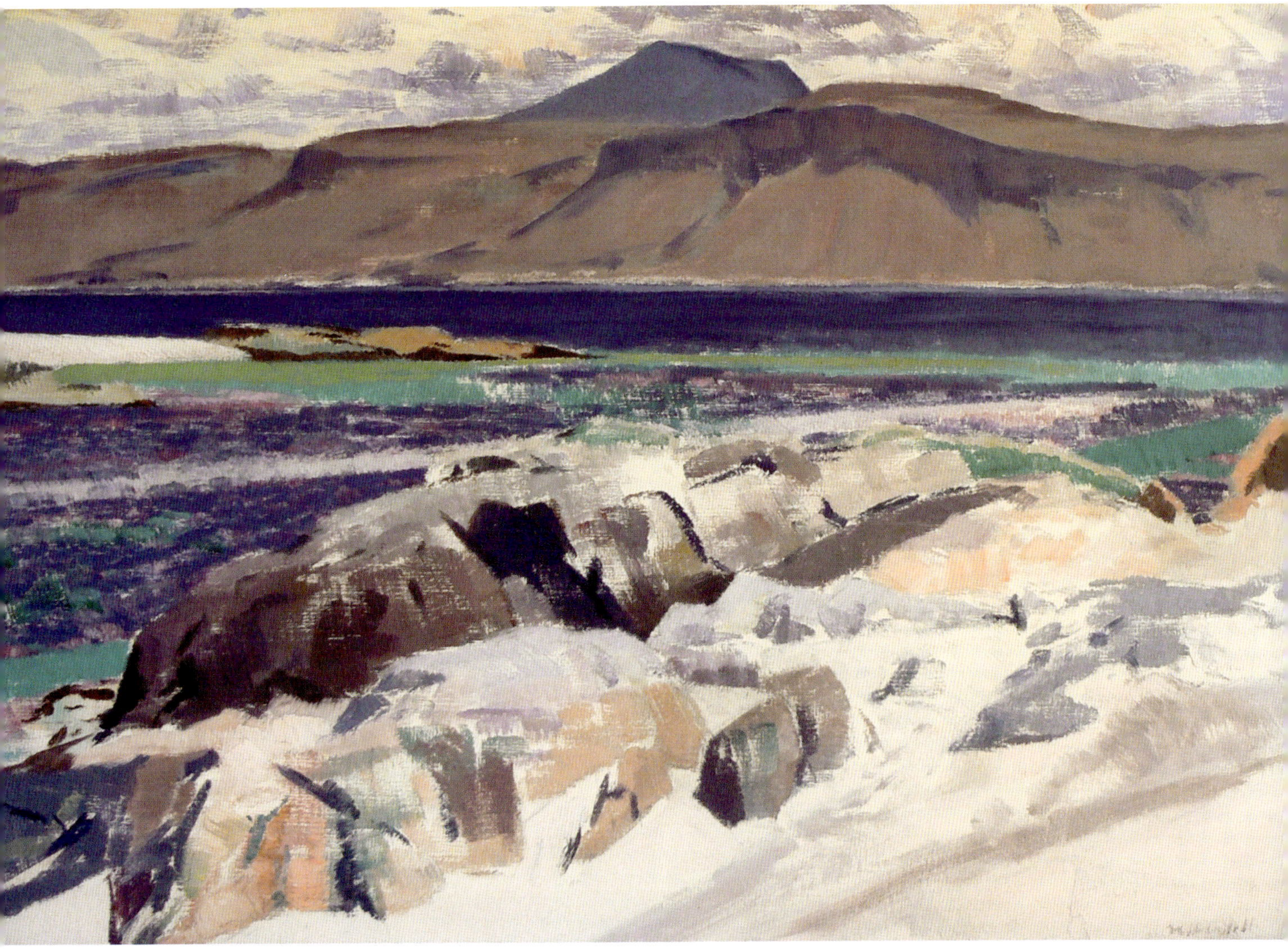

[PLATE 148]
F. C. B. Cadell
Ben More
from Ard Annraidh
Oil 20 x 30

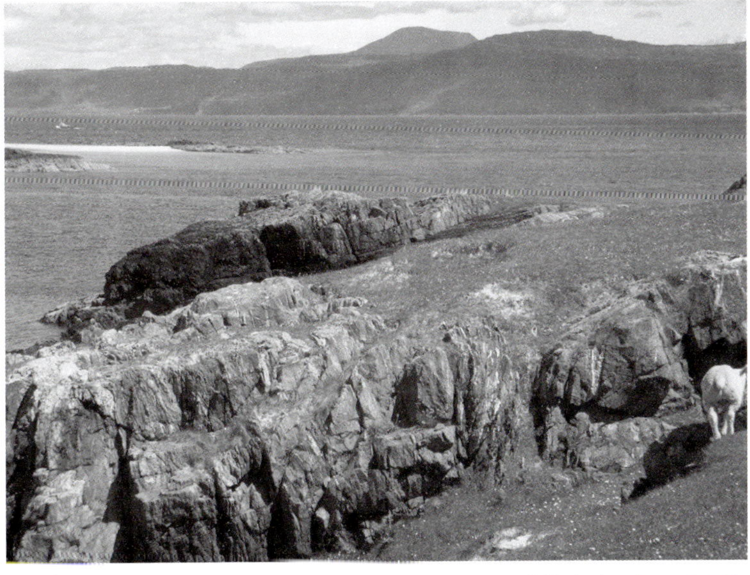

Photograph 2009

The Headland is left of centre in the foreground. The southeast end of Eilean Annraidh is in the middle distance on the left, and Ben More is central in the far distance. The gully in the immediate foreground ends in a rocky scramble down to the small beach where Plates 144 to 146 were painted.
The gully is full of sand in the painting which would have provided Cadell and Peploe with easy access to those locations. Comparison with the recent photograph shows the considerable loss of sand that has taken place.

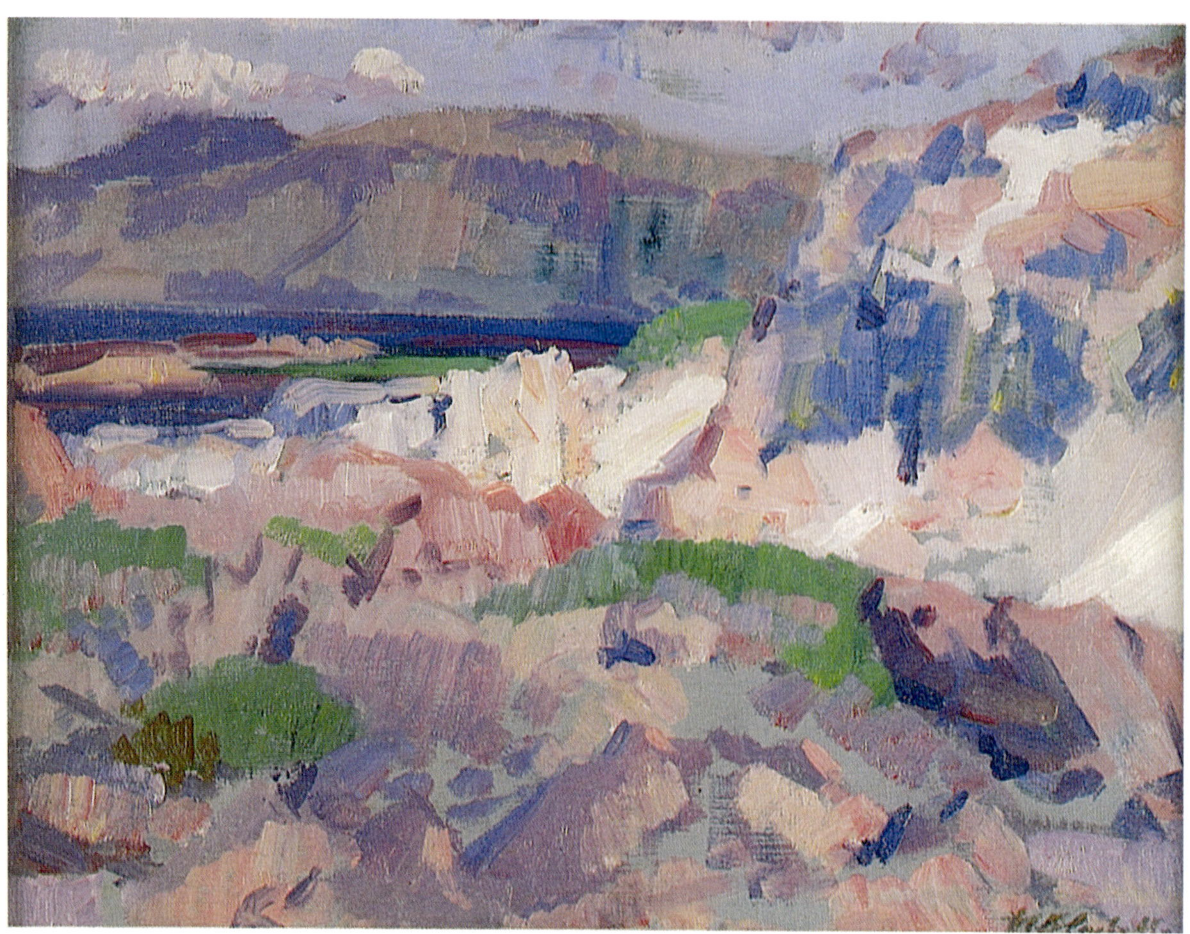

[PLATE 149]
F. C. B. Cadell
The Burg from below Ard Annraidh
Oil 15 x 18

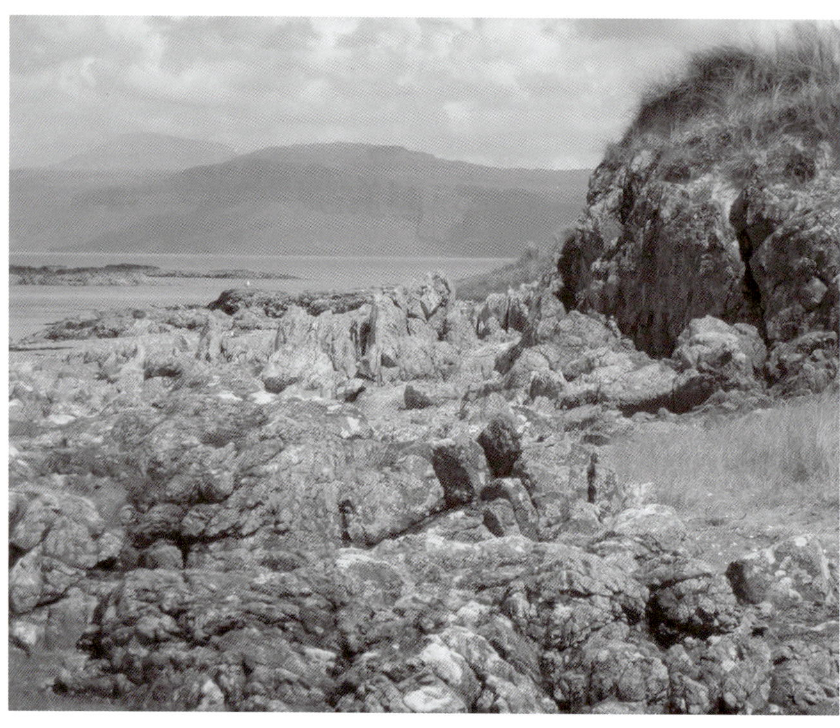

Photograph 2009

A short walk to the west from the location of the previous painting, there is a grassy slope which leads down onto the shore close to some standing rocks known as the Monks' Rocks, below a little cliff, all of which are in the foreground of this painting.
Part of Eilean Annraidh appears in the middle distance on the left and the Burg and Ben More are in the far distance.

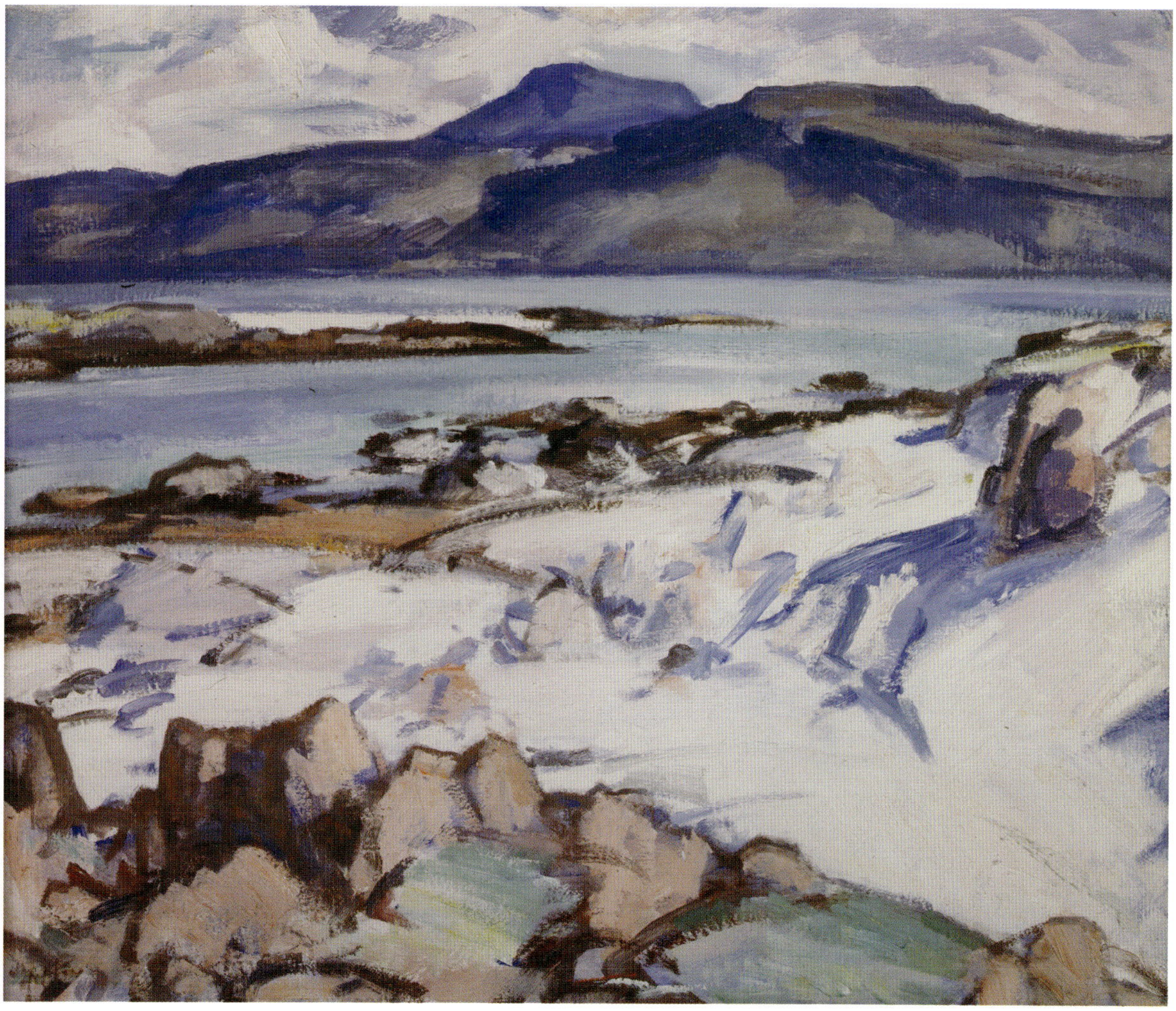

[PLATE 150]

S. J. Peploe

BEN MORE FROM IONA

Ben More
from the North Shore
Oil 25 x 30

Fife Cultural Trust
(Kirkcaldy Galleries)
on behalf of Fife Council

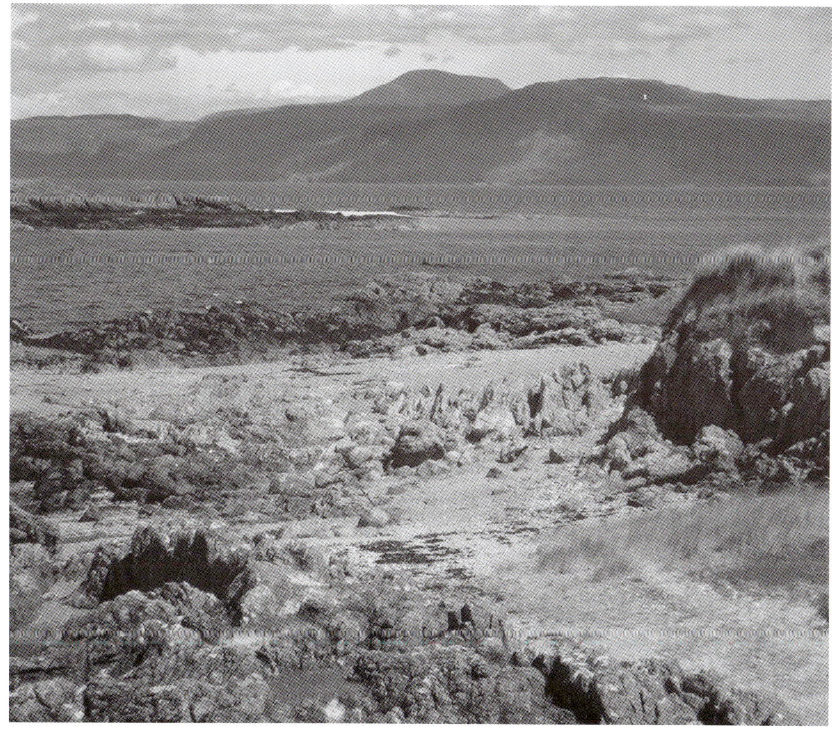

Photograph 2009

This is one of the most celebrated views on Iona, and was painted many times by both Cadell and Peploe (Plates 151 to 157).

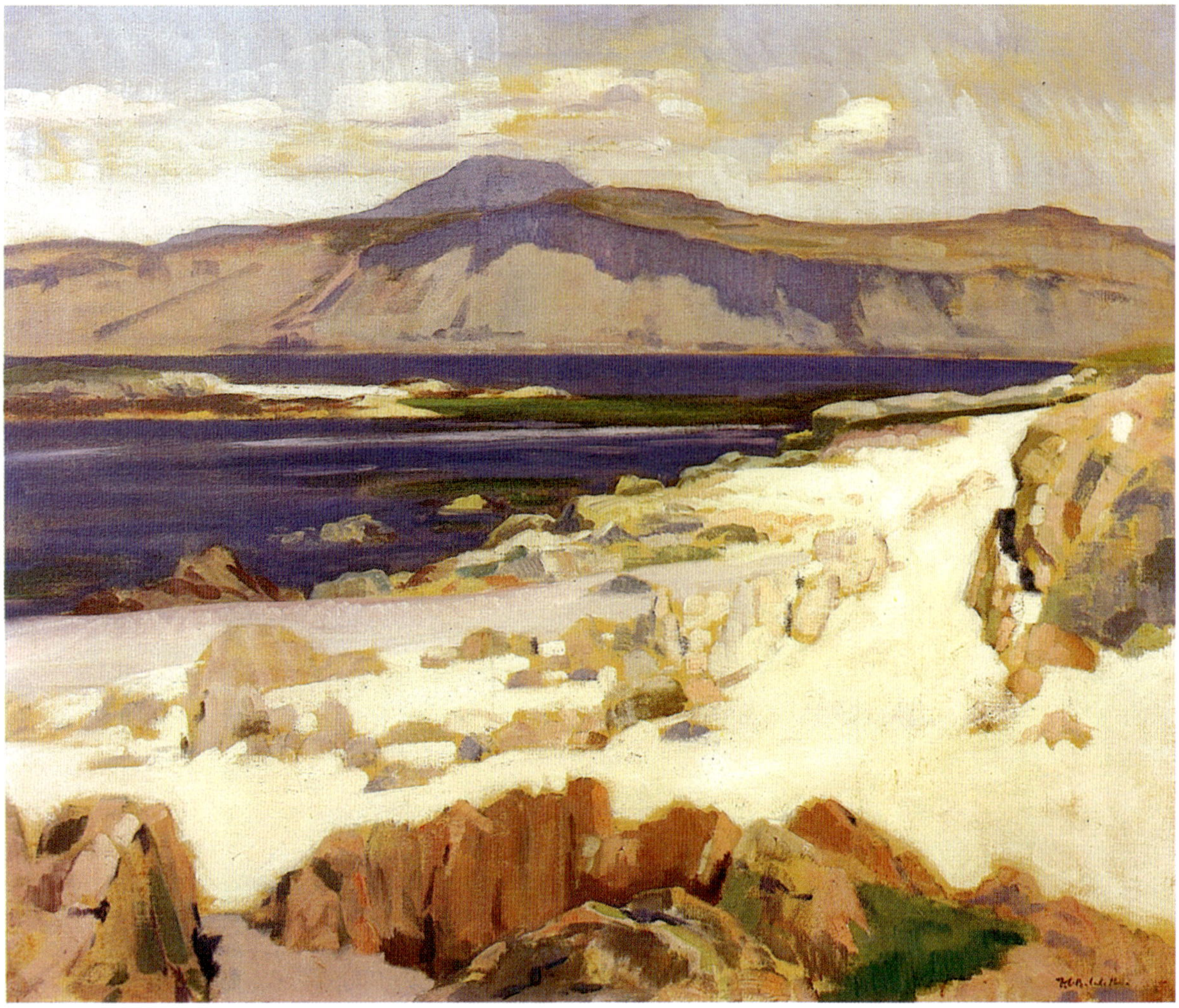

[PLATE 151]
F. C. B. Cadell
Ben More from the North Shore
Oil 25 x 30

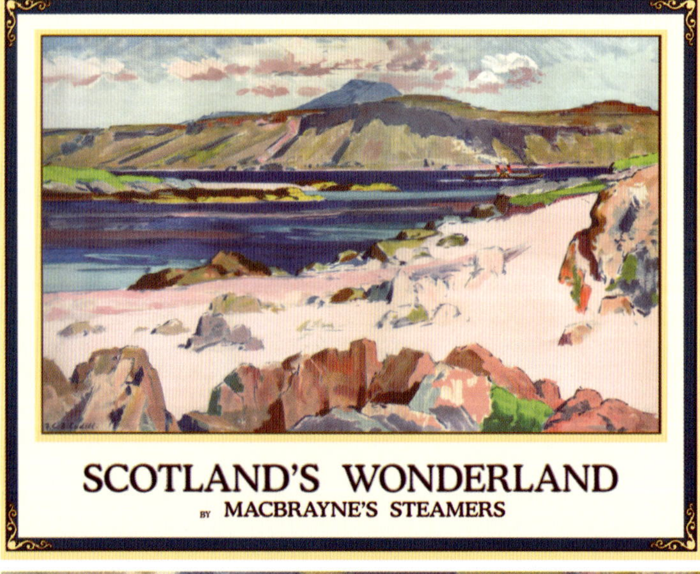

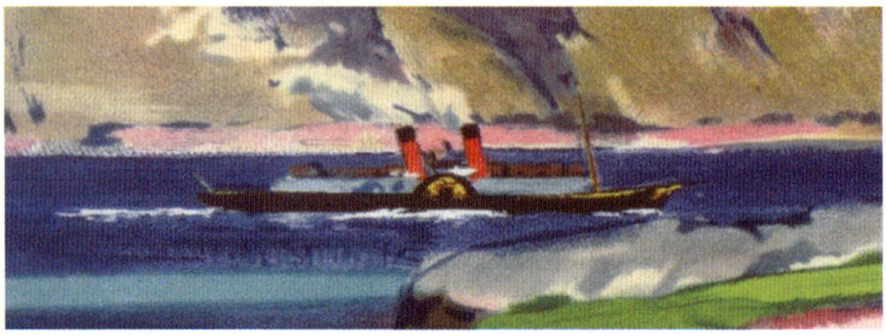

With the addition of the paddlesteamer Grenadier, this version of the subject by Cadell was the basis of one of his three posters for MacBrayne's Steamers.

[PLATE 152]
F. C. B. Cadell
Towards Mull
from the North Shore
Watercolour 15 x 18

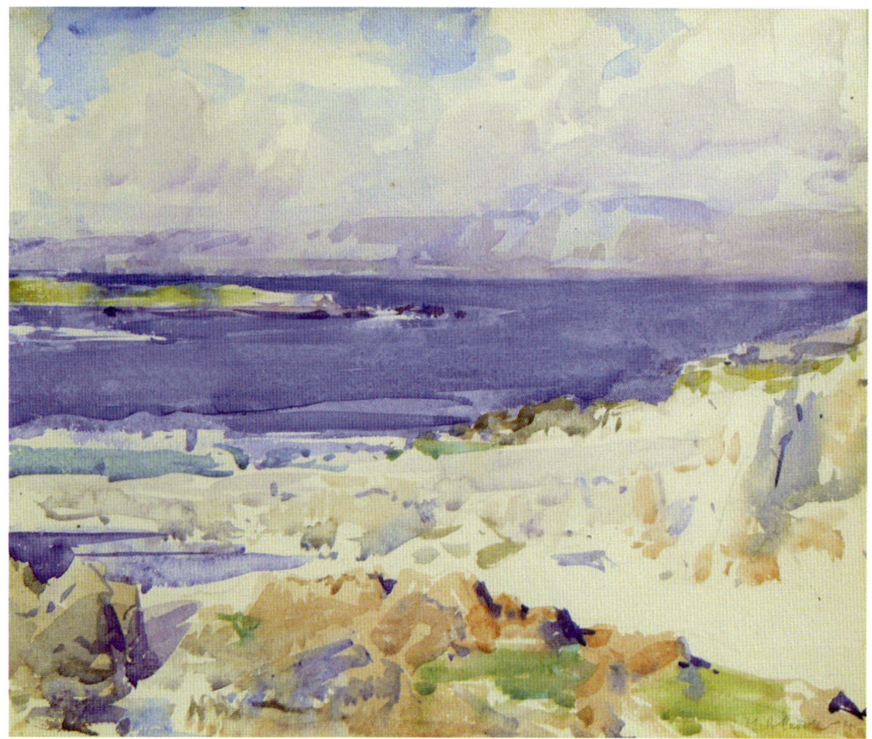

This is the same view as Plate 151, although here Ben More is partially obscured by cloud and the Burg is seen through haze. The same rocks appear in the foreground of the two paintings; however in this picture the shadows indicate a late afternoon light. The tide is high enough for the sea to appear in Curving Inlet on the left just beyond the rocks.

[PLATE 153]
F. C. B. Cadell

BEN MORE FROM IONA

Ben More
from the North Shore
Oil 15 x 18

The Hunterian,
University of Glasgow

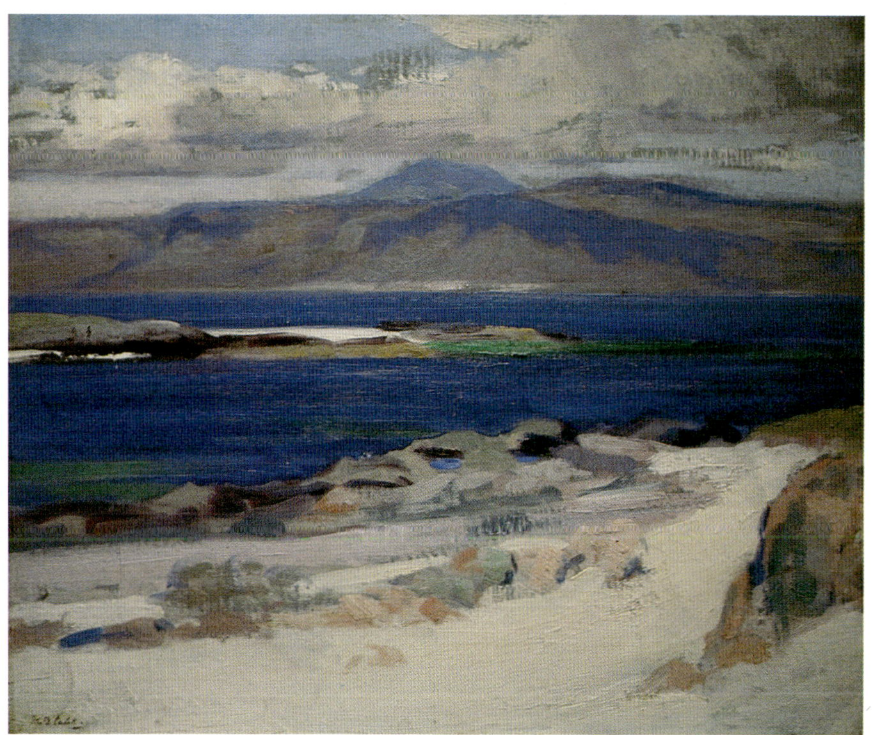

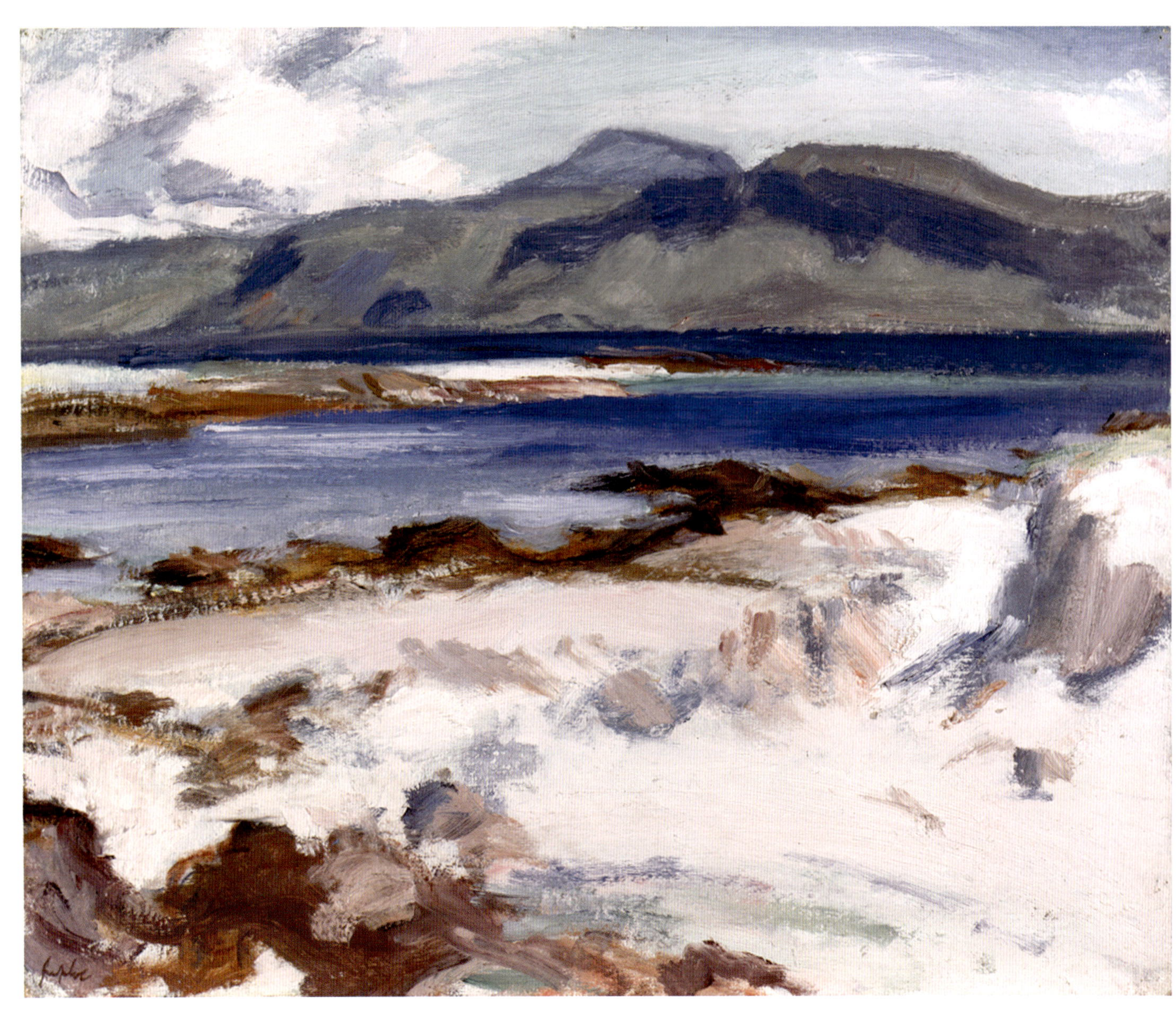

[PLATE 154]
S. J. Peploe

BLUE SEA, IONA

Ben More from the North Shore
Oil 20 x 24

Aberdeen Art Gallery & Museums Collections

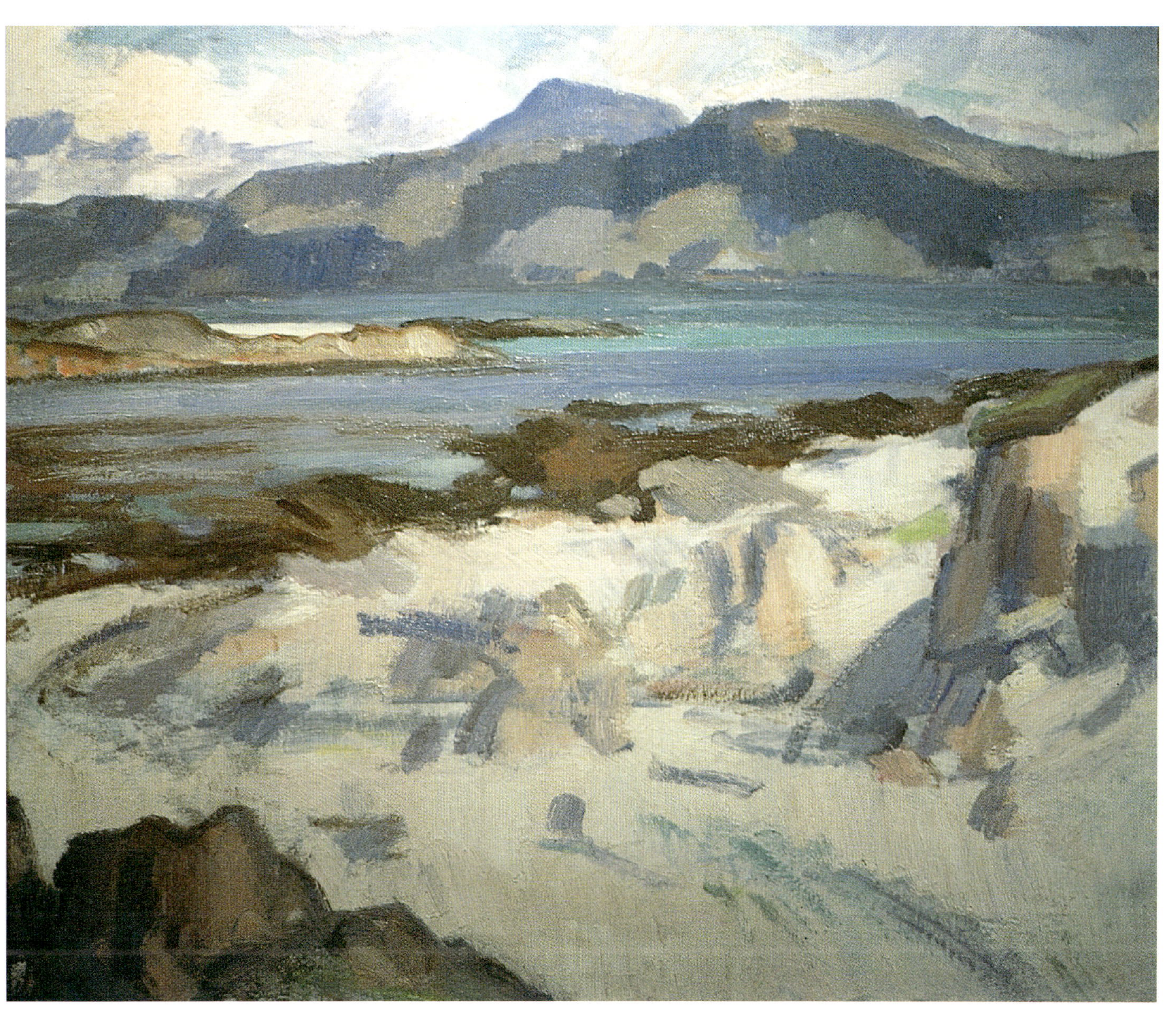

[PLATE 155]

S. J. Peploe

BEN MORE

Ben More from the North Shore
Oil 25 x 30

The Hunterian, University of Glasgow

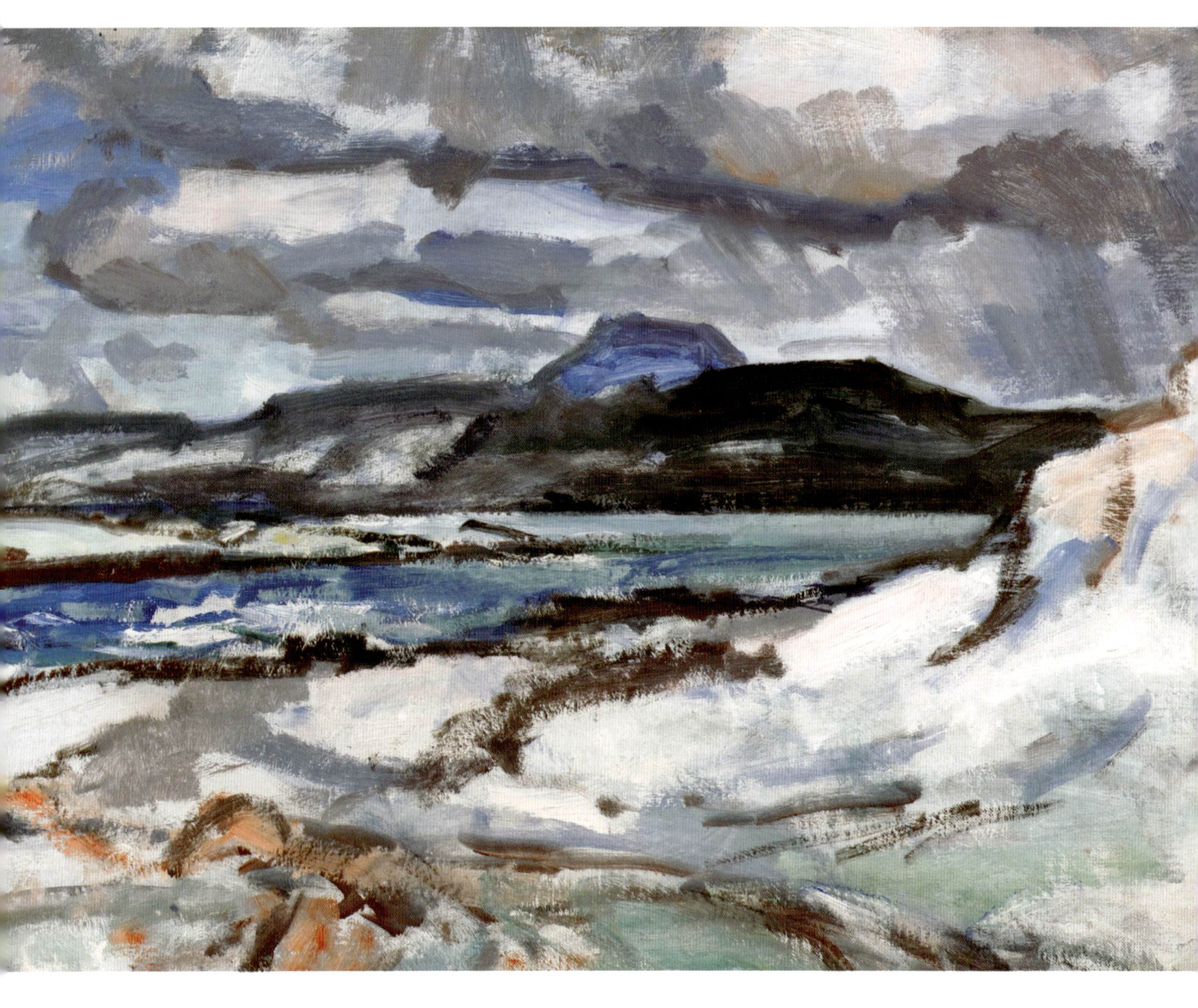

[PLATE 156]

S. J. Peploe

Ben More from the North Shore

(Blue Day, Iona)

Oil 20 x 28

[PLATE 157]
S. J. Peploe
Ben More from the North Shore
Oil 20 x 28

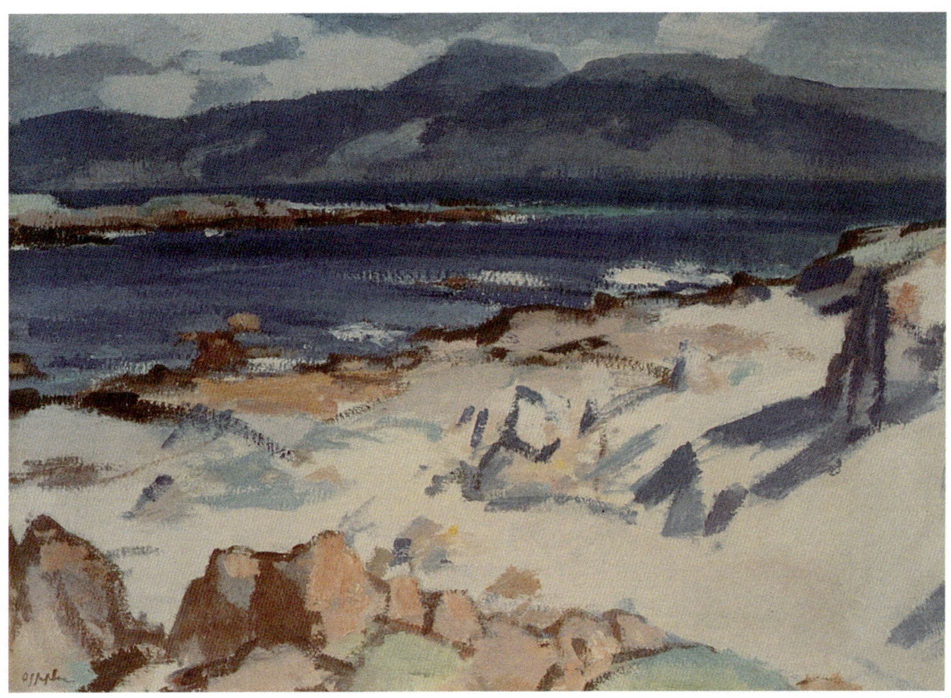

[PLATE 158]
F. C. B. Cadell
The Burg from the North Shore
Oil 15 x 18

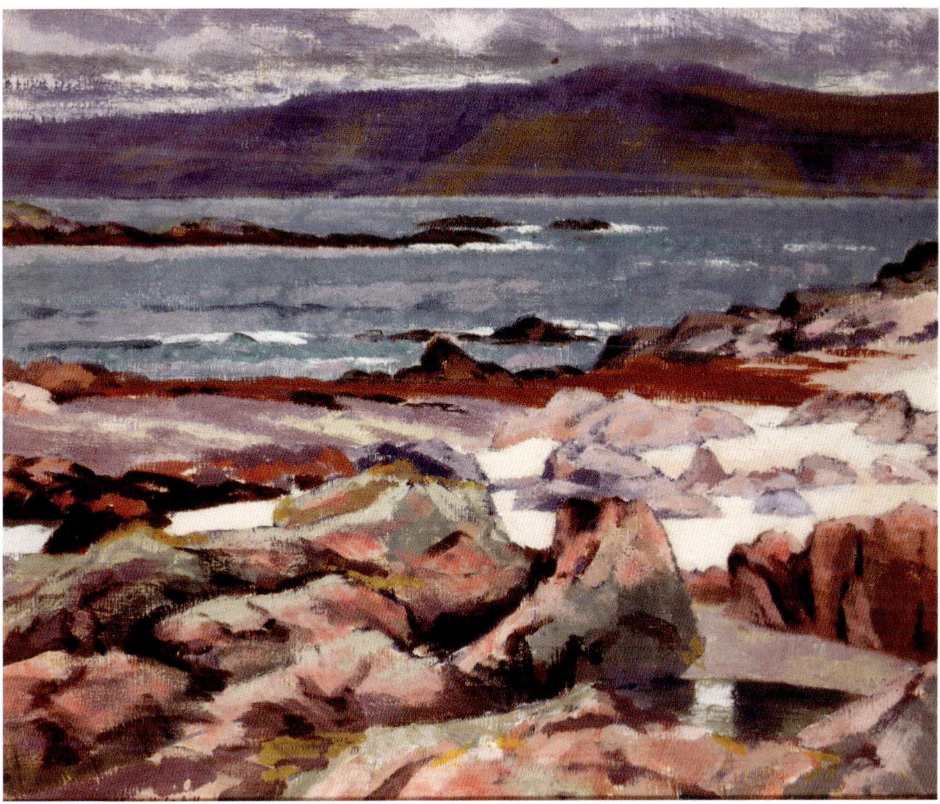

There is a slight shift of viewpoint, but this is essentially the same motif as Plates 150 to 157. However with Ben More lost in cloud, the exclusion of the little cliff on the right, and a high tide that leaves only the highest parts of Eilean Annraidh visible, the subject takes on a less familiar appearance.

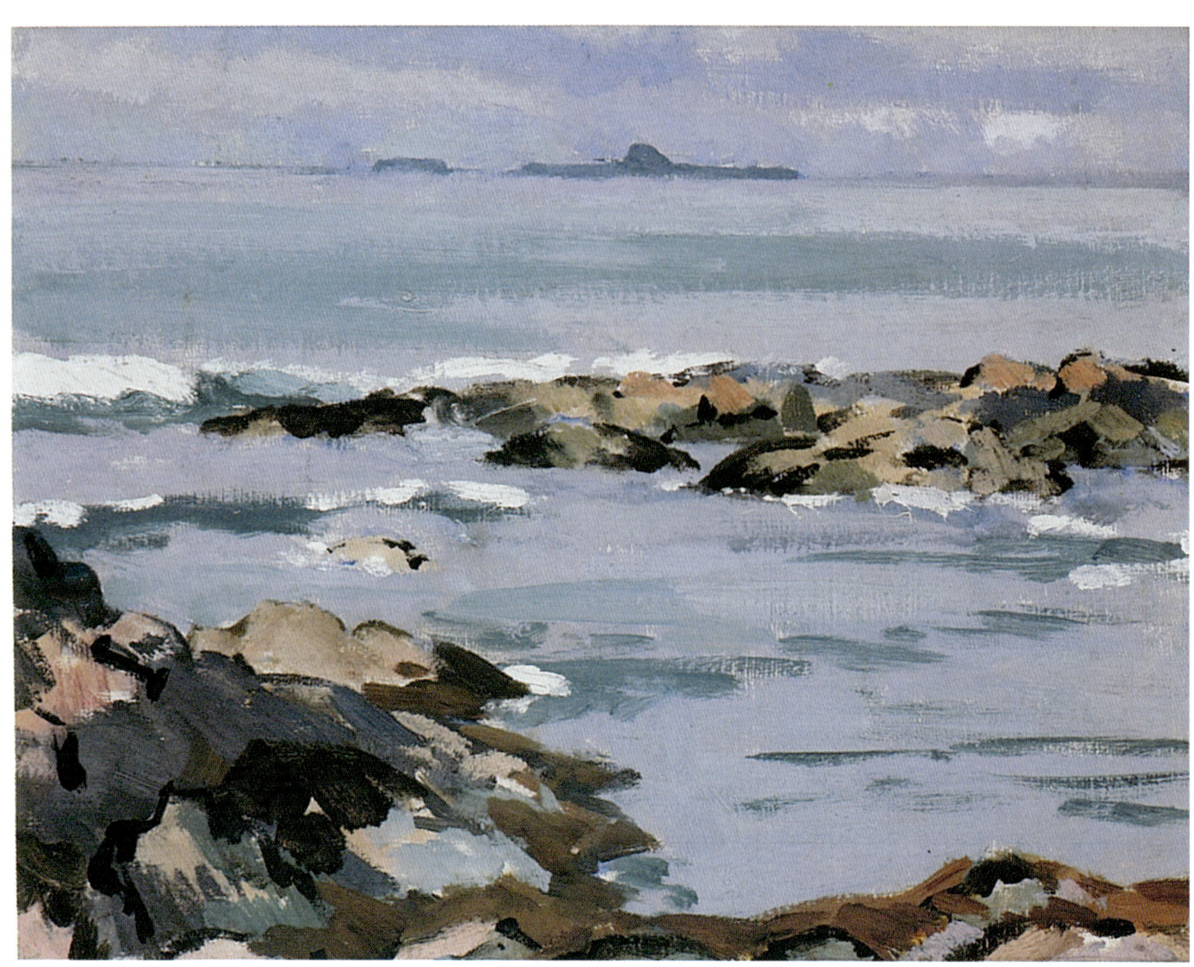

[PLATE 159]
F. C. B. Cadell
The Dutchman's Cap from the North Shore
Oil 15 x 18

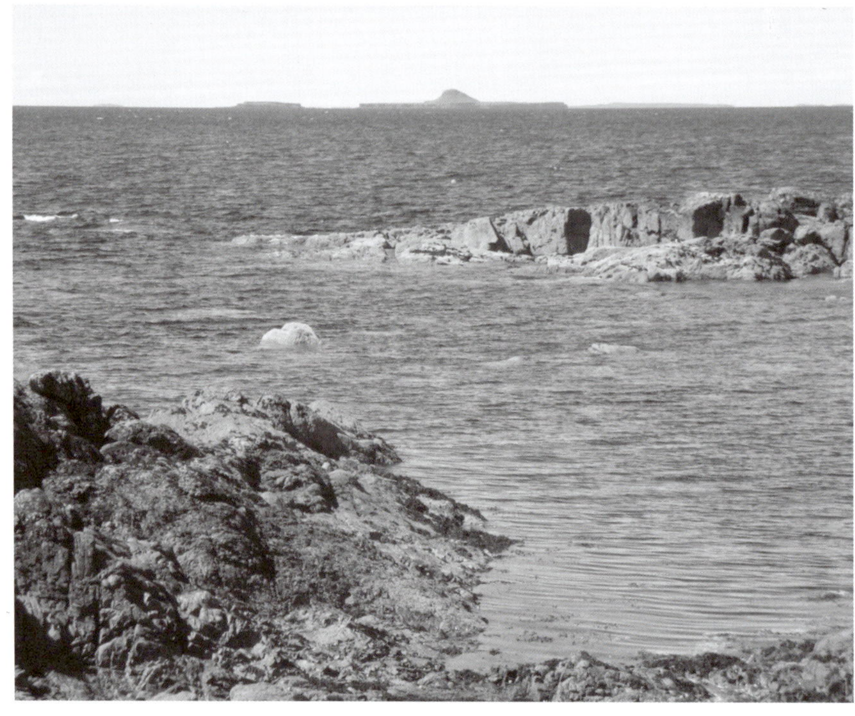

Photograph 2009

Just below where Plates 150 to 157 were painted, there is a rock platform facing north, from where Cadell painted this view of the Dutchman's Cap. The bay in the foreground is known as A Cham-a-Leoib, or The Curving Inlet.

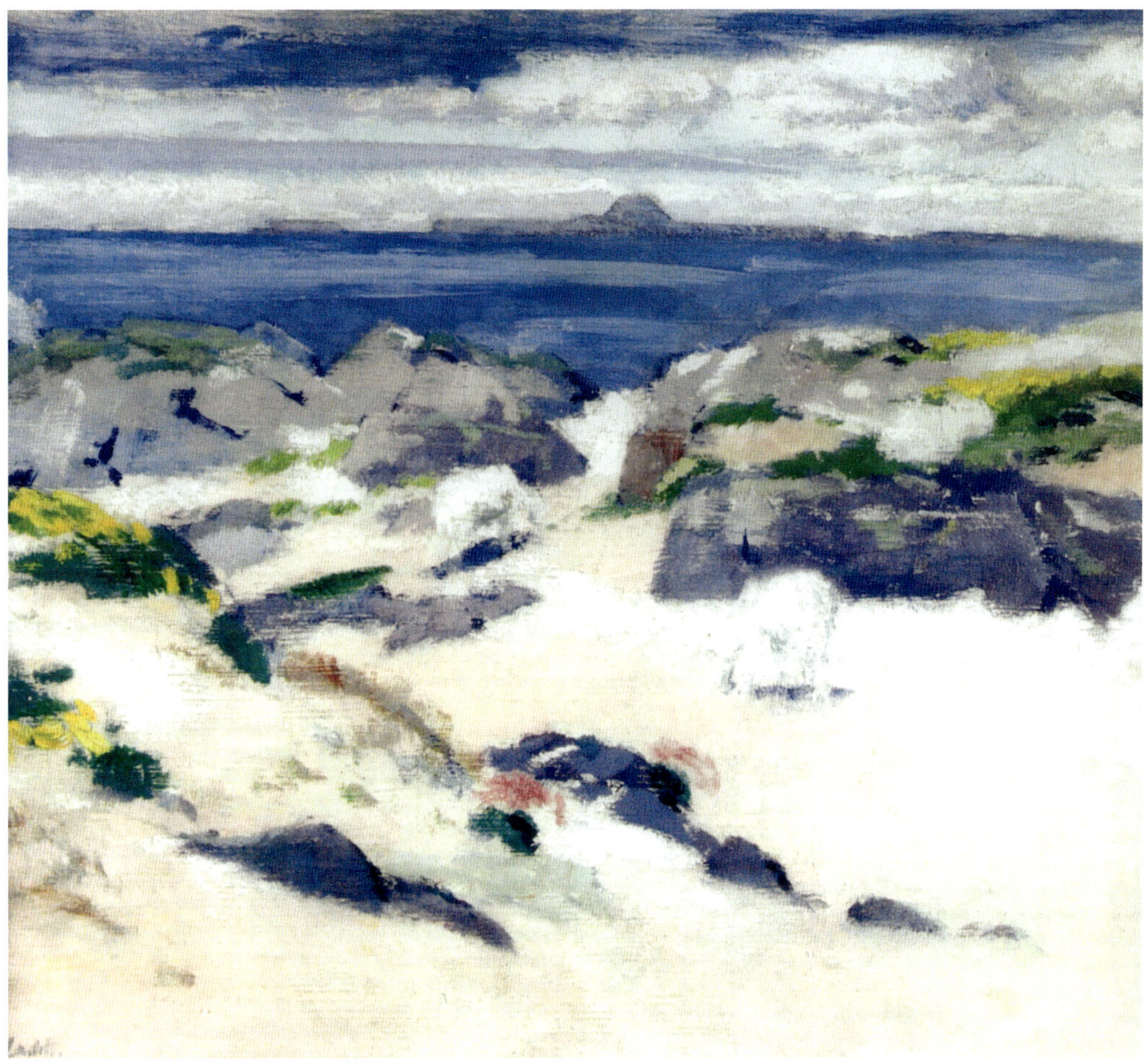

The distinctive profile of the Dutchman's Cap on the horizon is easy to identify, but the foreground is now unrecognisable; the sandy trough in the painting was used to dispose of the accumulated rubbish on the island, and was grassed over in about 1980. The rocks on the left in the middle distance are known as Ru'a Bheoil Mhoir, or Big Mouth Point.

[PLATE 160]
F. C. B. Cadell
The Dutchman's Cap from the North Shore
Oil 14 x 17

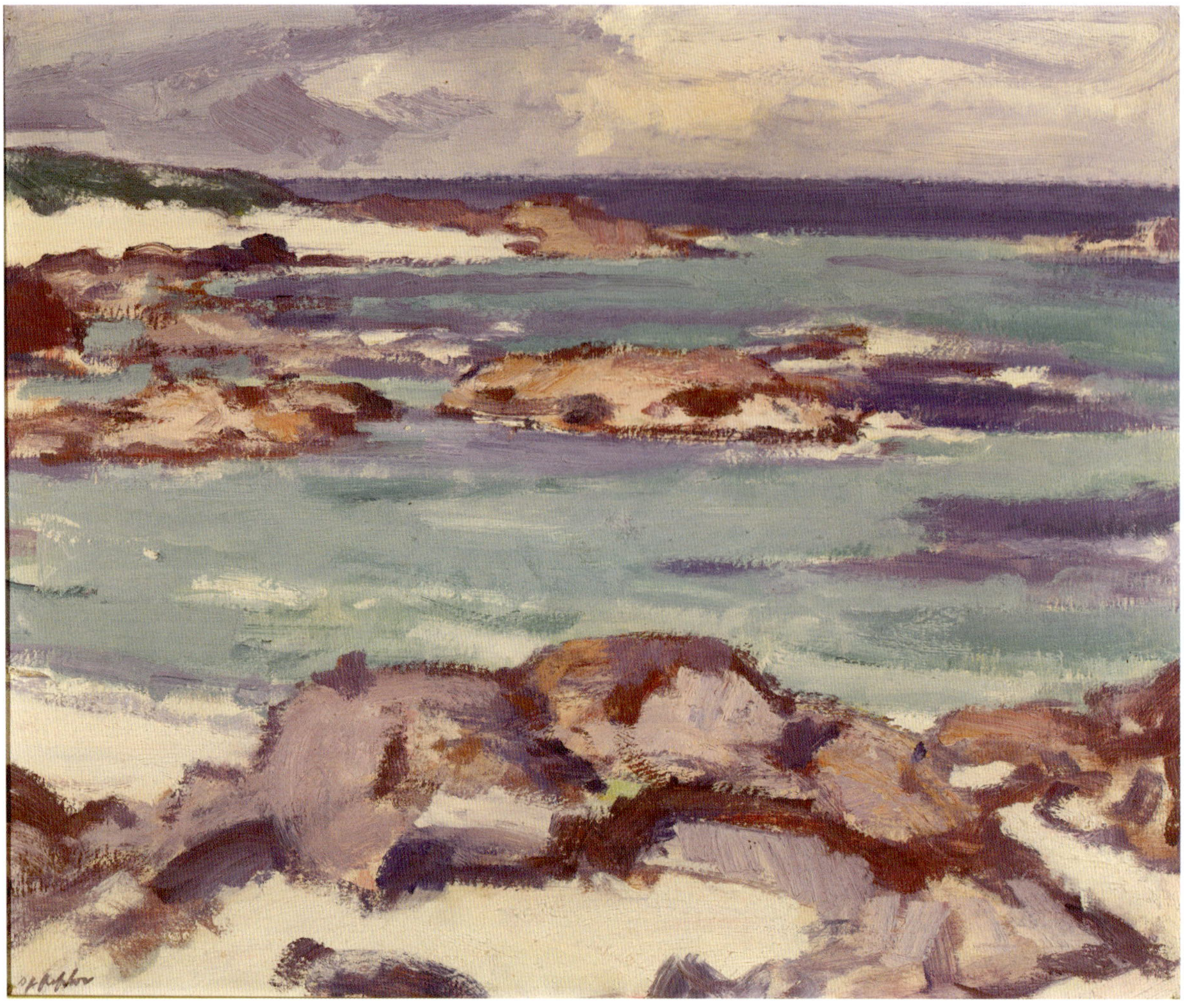

[PLATE 161]
S. J. Peploe
The North Shore
Oil 18 x 22

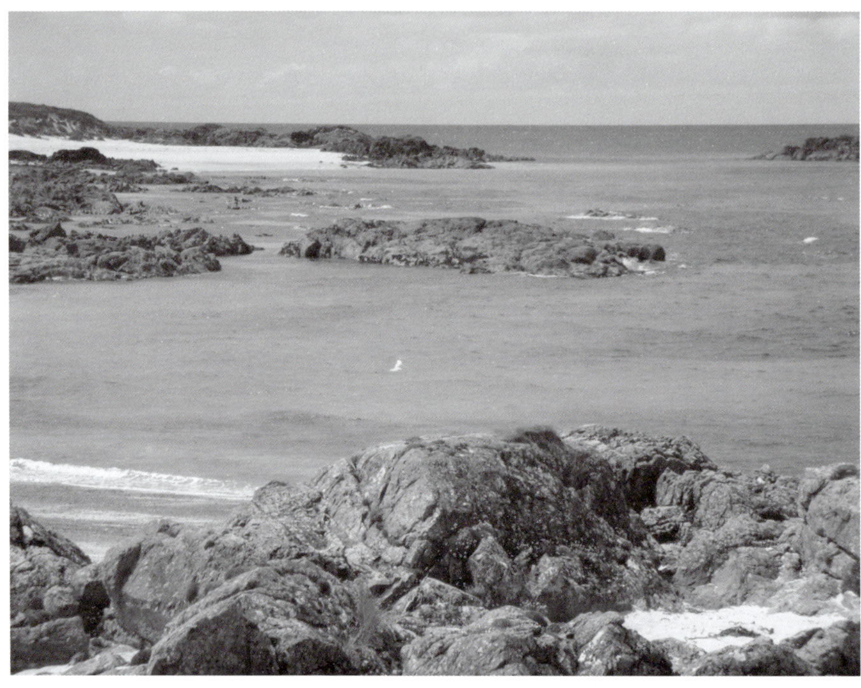

Photograph 2009

This is the view due west along the North Shore. The white beach in the distance on the left is Traigh-na-Criche, and opposite on the right is the edge of the island Eilean Chalbha.

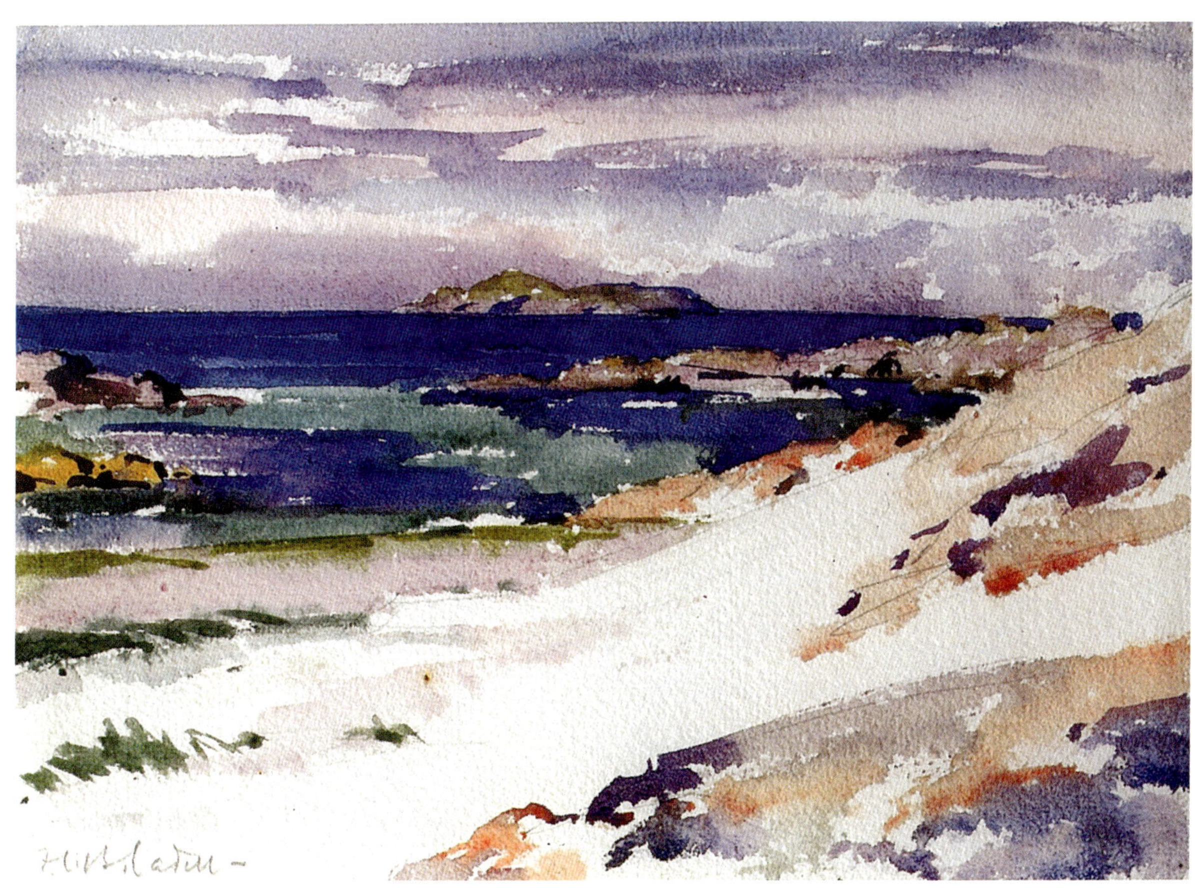

[PLATE 162]
F. C. B. Cadell
Reidh Eilean from Cnoc Ard Annraidh
Watercolour 7 x 10

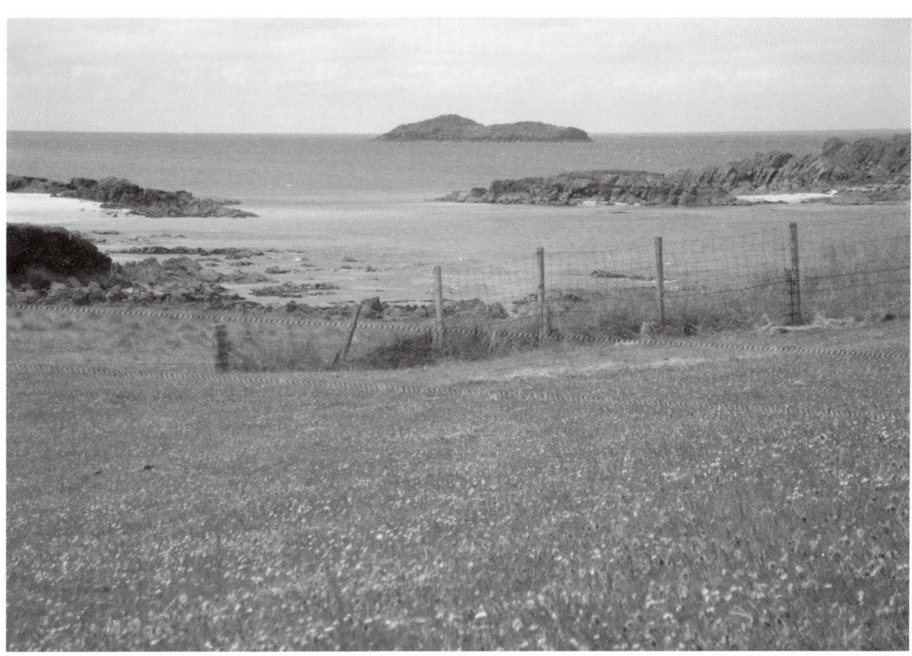

Photograph 2009

Reidh Eilean is central on the horizon, and Eilean Chalbha is in the middle distance on the right.

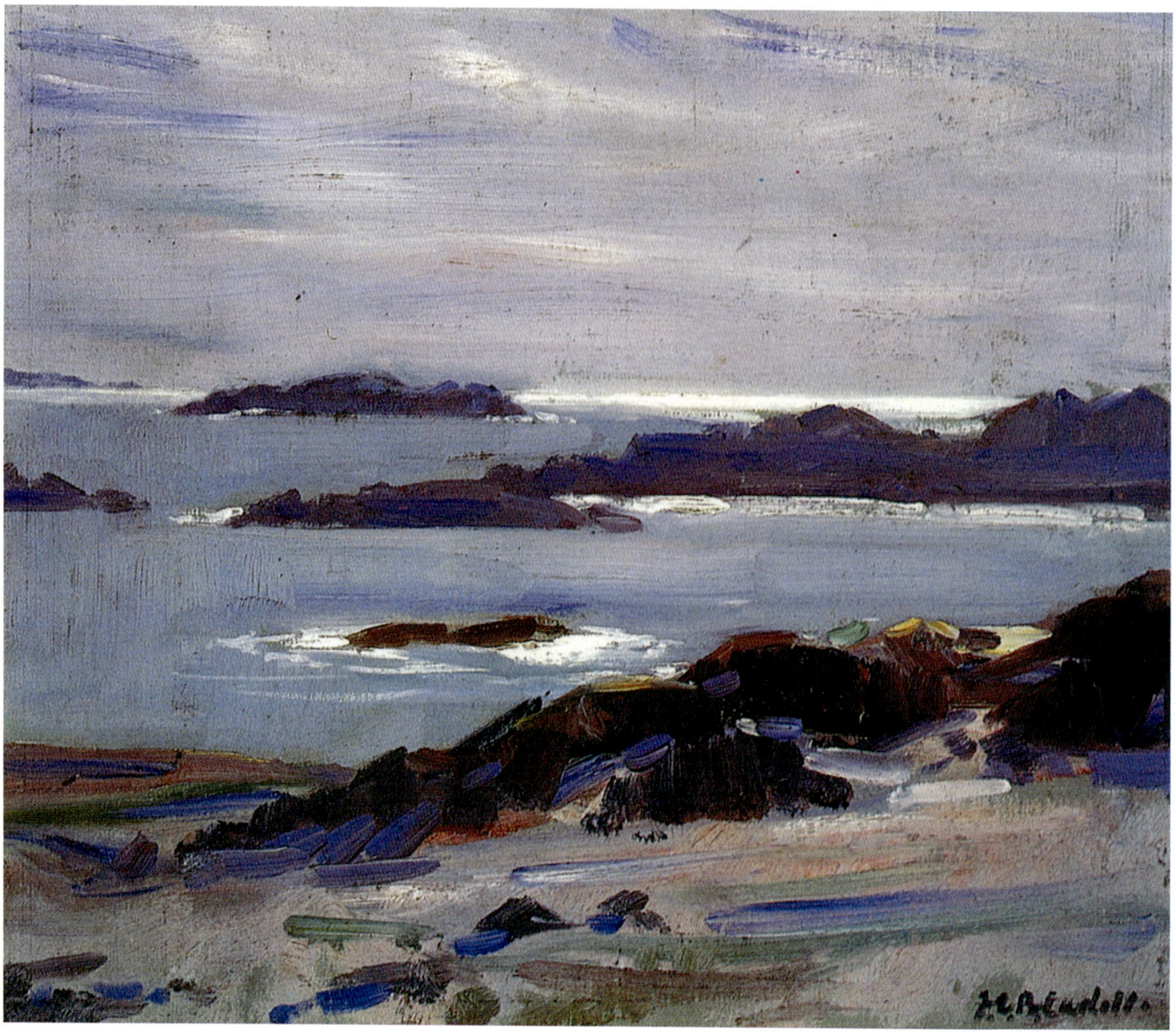

[PLATE 163]

F. C. B. Cadell

Reidh Eilean
and Eilean Chalbha
from Cnoc Ard Annraidh
(On the West Coast)
Oil 15 x 18

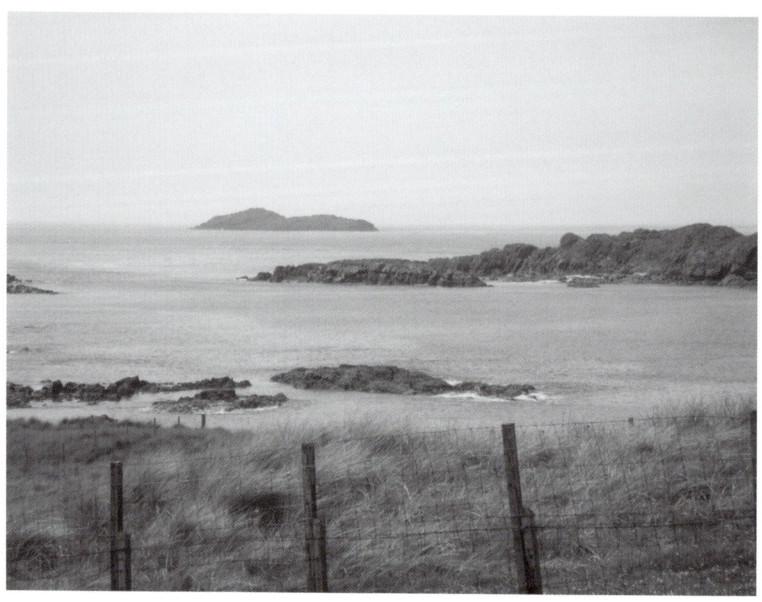

Photograph 2013

This view is slightly further to the right from the preceding picture; Reidh Eilean is now seen left of centre and more of Eilean Chalbha is included on the right.
Although Cadell painted in a wide range of weather conditions, very few pictures depict a particularly early or late time of day. Here he has recorded the dazzling light reflected in the sea towards the west northwest as the sun descends towards the horizon, at around 7pm to 8pm in the summer.

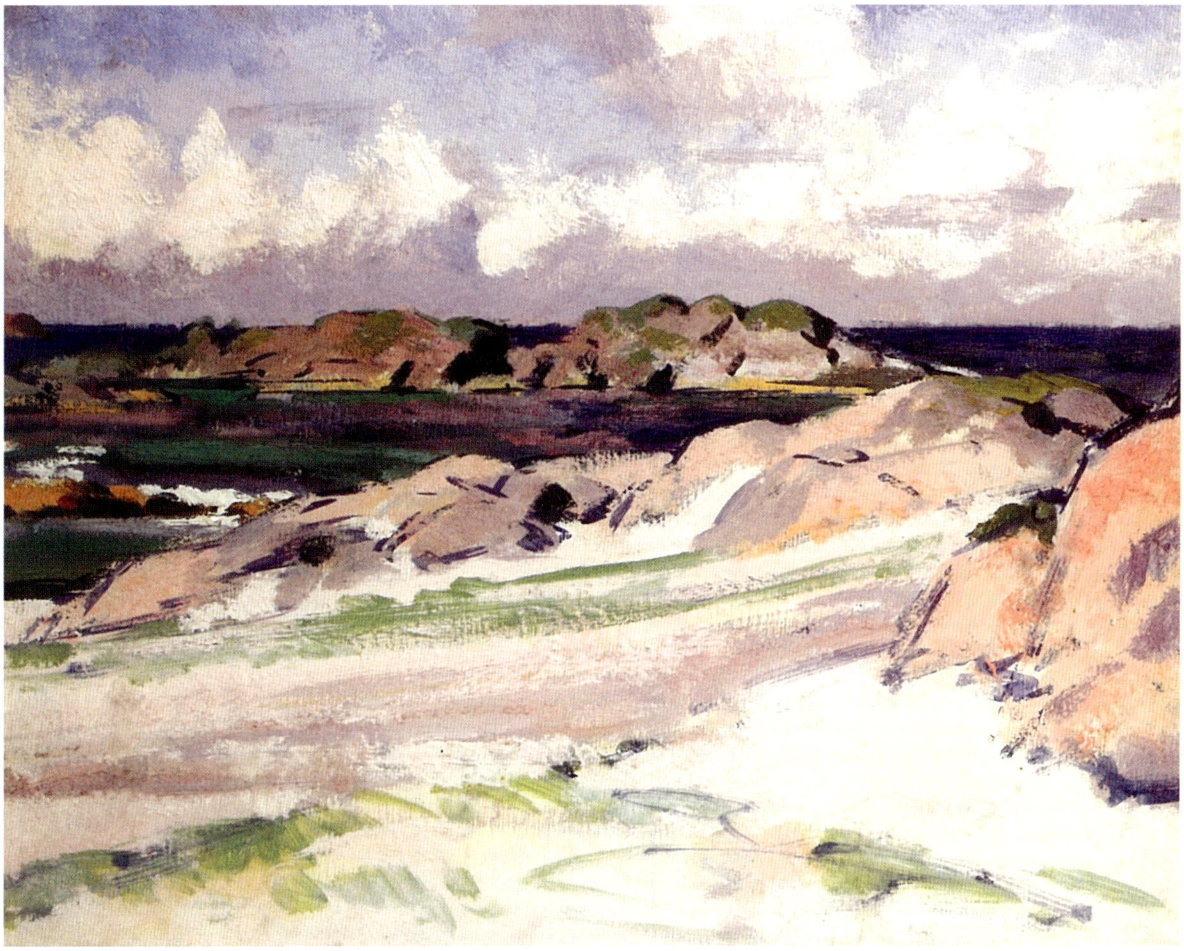

[PLATE 164]
F. C. B. Cadell
Eilean Chalbha from Cnoc Ard Annraidh
Oil 15 x 18

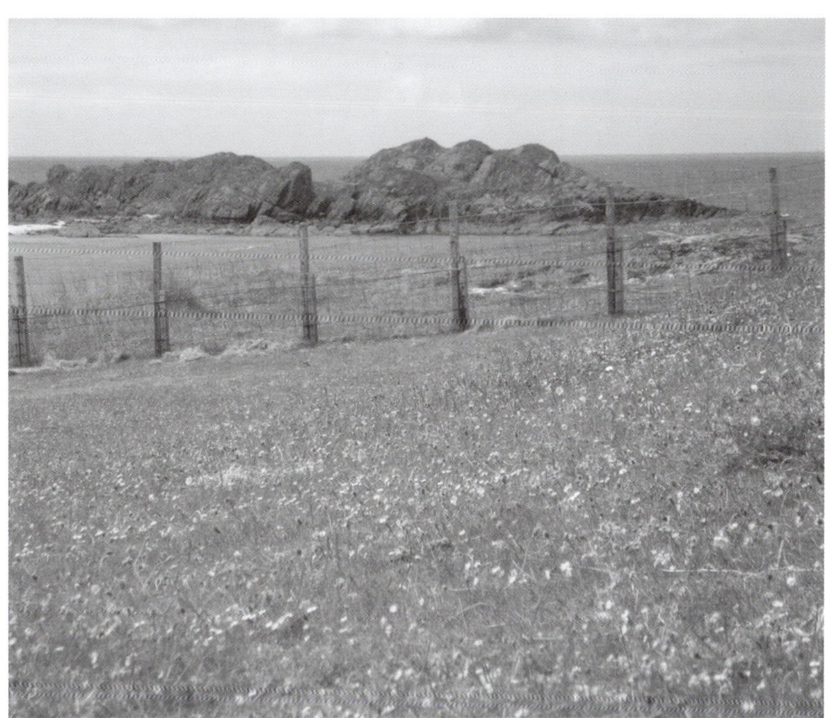

Photograph 2009

The foreground rocks in Cadell's painting now only just break the surface here and there through the present higher ground level. The grass has become more established, and the mixed foreground of rock, grass, and white sand has disappeared.

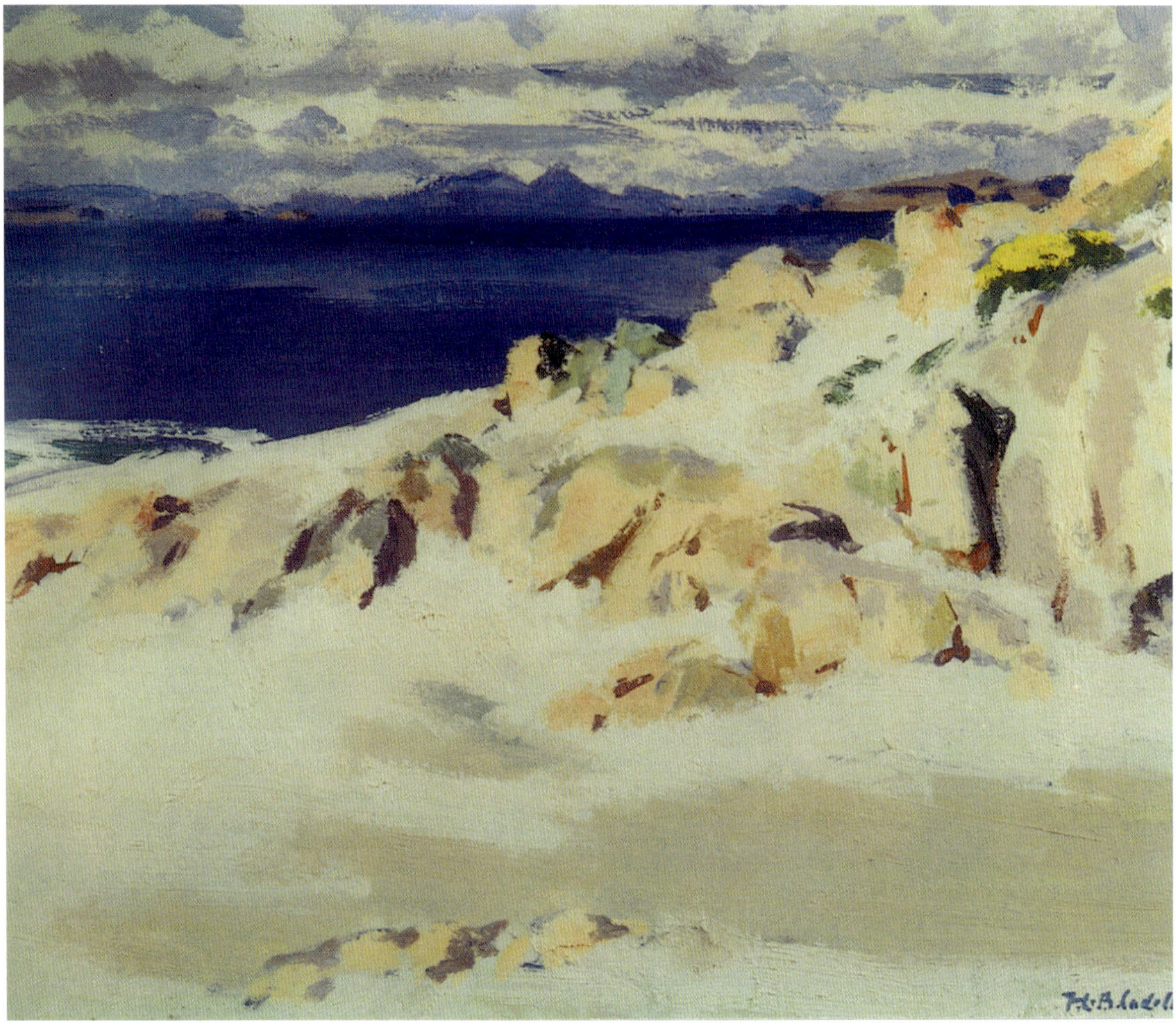

[PLATE 165]
F. C. B. Cadell
Rhum from
Cnoc Ard Annraidh
(Pink Rocks, Iona)
Oil 15 x 18

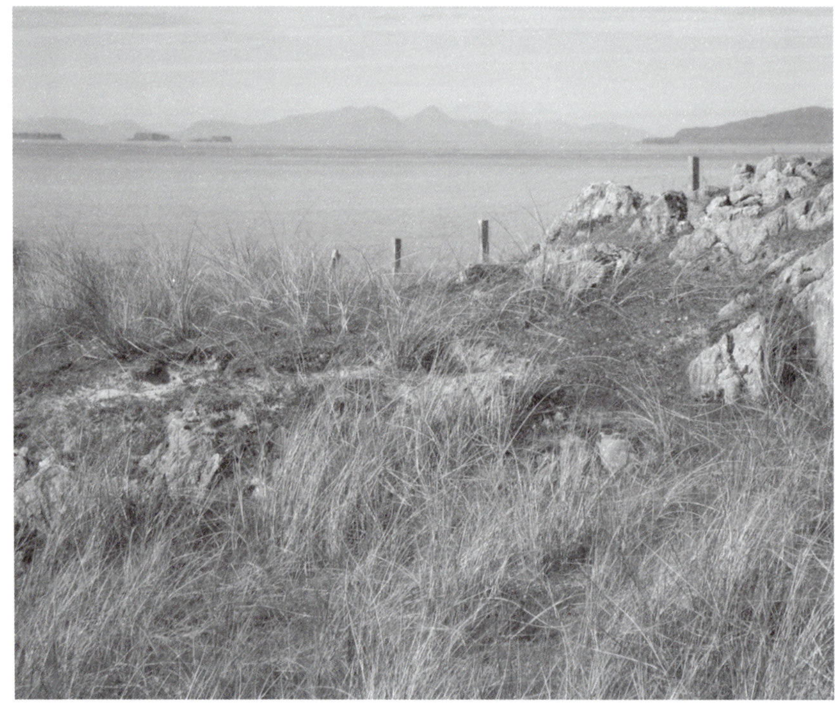

Photograph 2009

As with the gully in Plate 160, the sandy recess in this painting was also used for landfill of rubbish, and grassed over. Only the tops of the pink rocks on the right remain visible above the raised ground level.

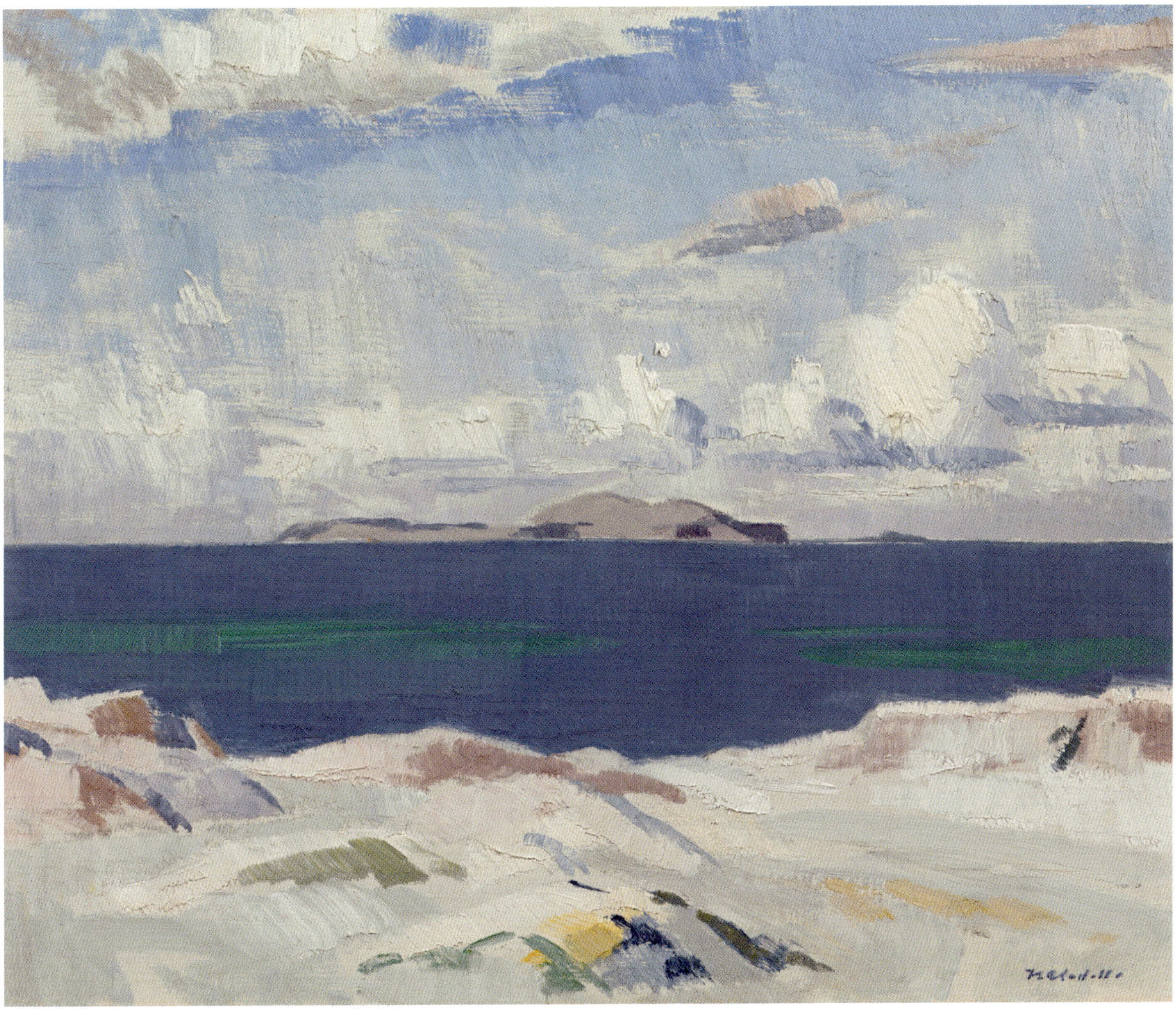

[PLATE 166]
F. C. B. Cadell
Lunga from
Cnoc Ard Annraidh
Oil 15 x 18

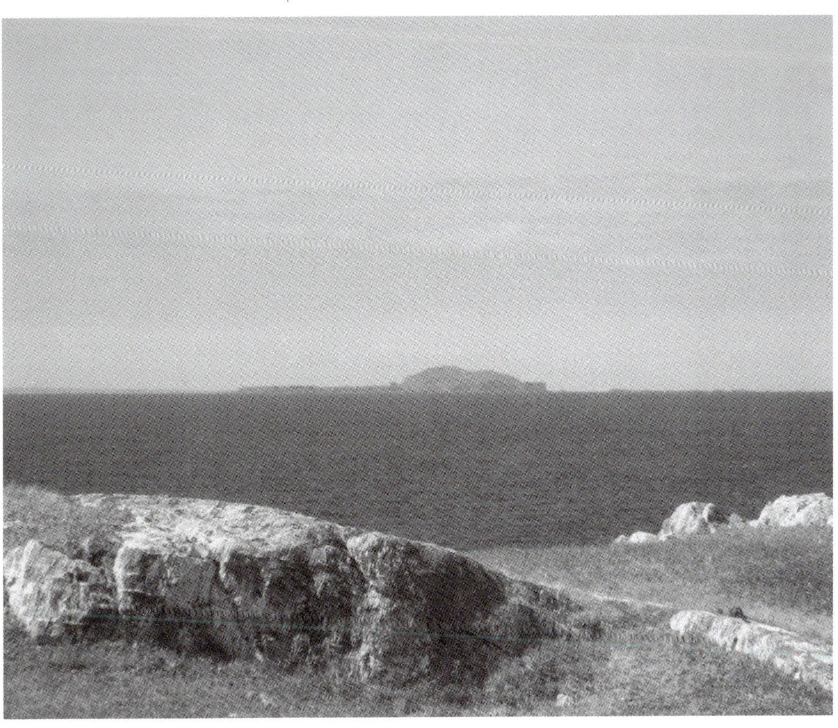

Photograph 2012

This is one of very few Iona paintings by either artist in which more than half the picture is devoted to the sky, here rendered by Cadell with great spontaneity.

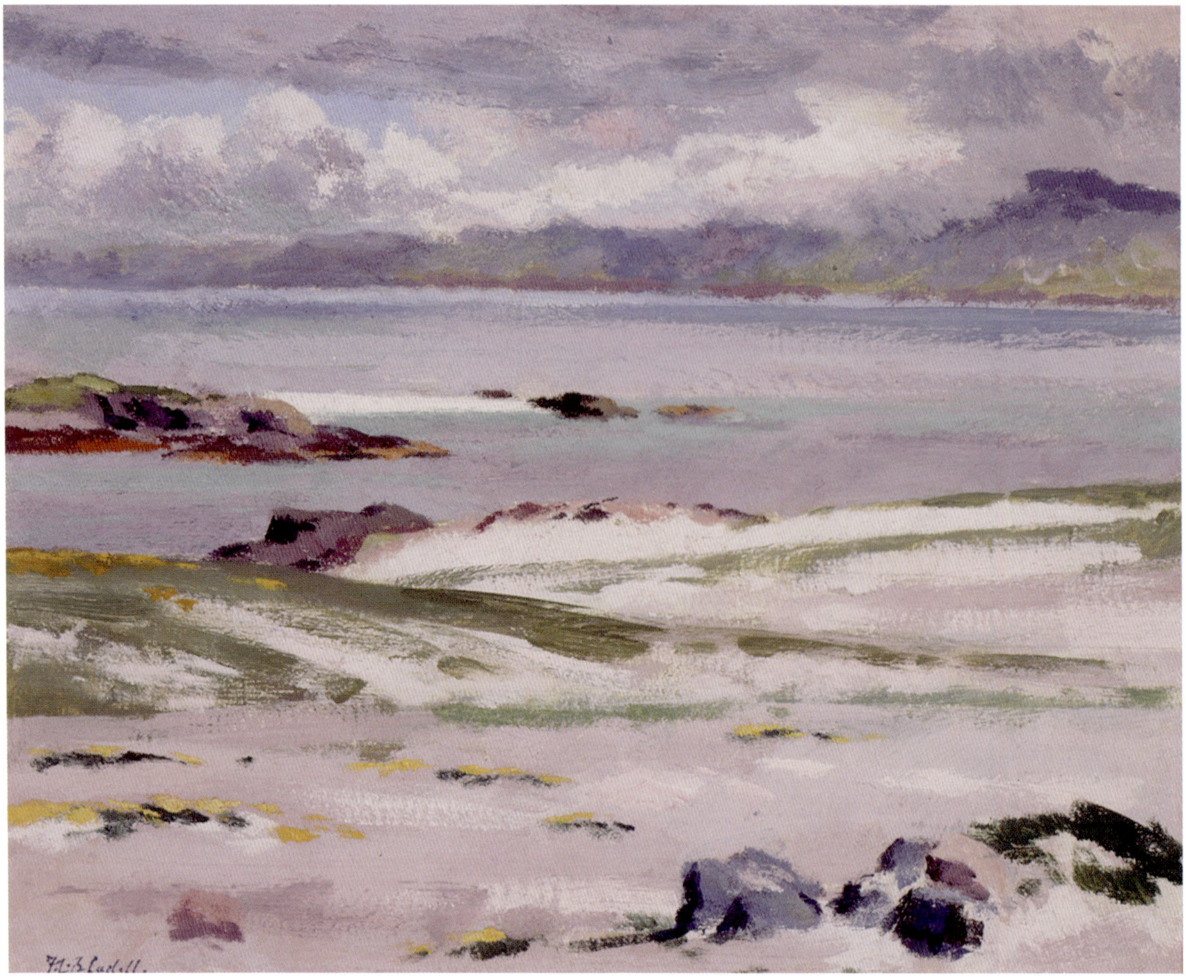

[PLATE 167]
F. C. B. Cadell
Towards Mull from Cnoc Ard Annraidh
Oil 15 x 18

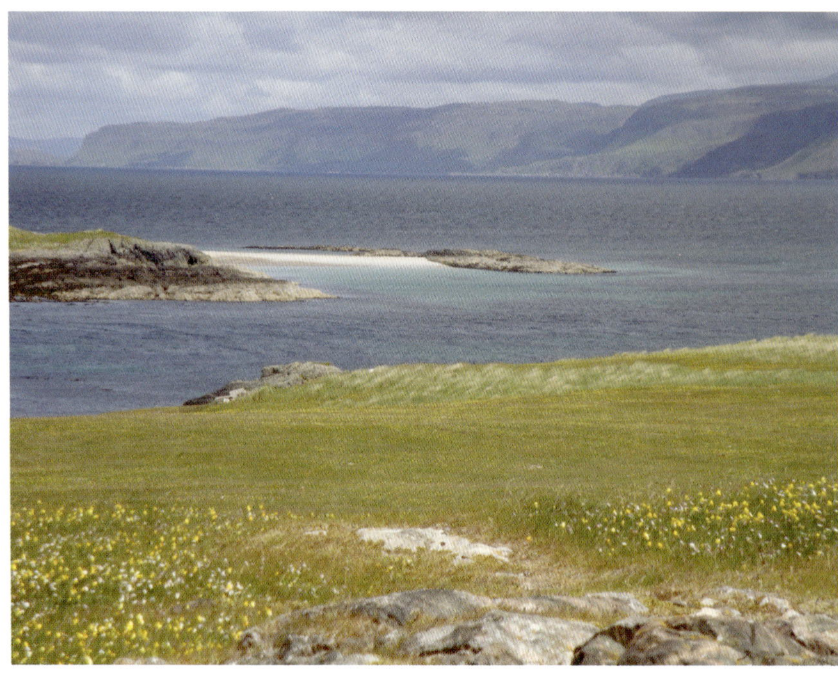

Photograph 2009

Eilean Annraidh is in the middle distance on the left, and the rocks of the Headland are seen on the left just above the grass and sandy slopes of the foreground.

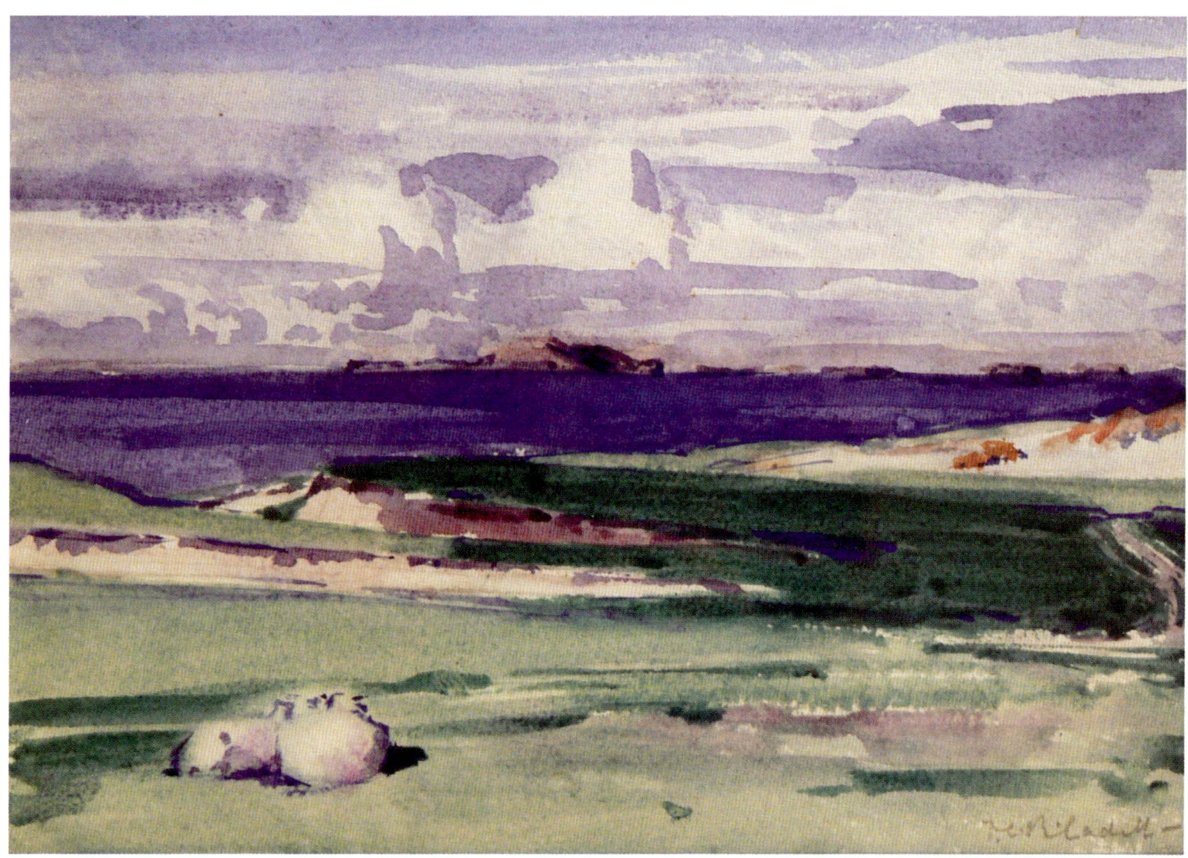

[PLATE 168]
F. C. B. Cadell
Lunga from the North End Machair

Watercolour 7 x 10

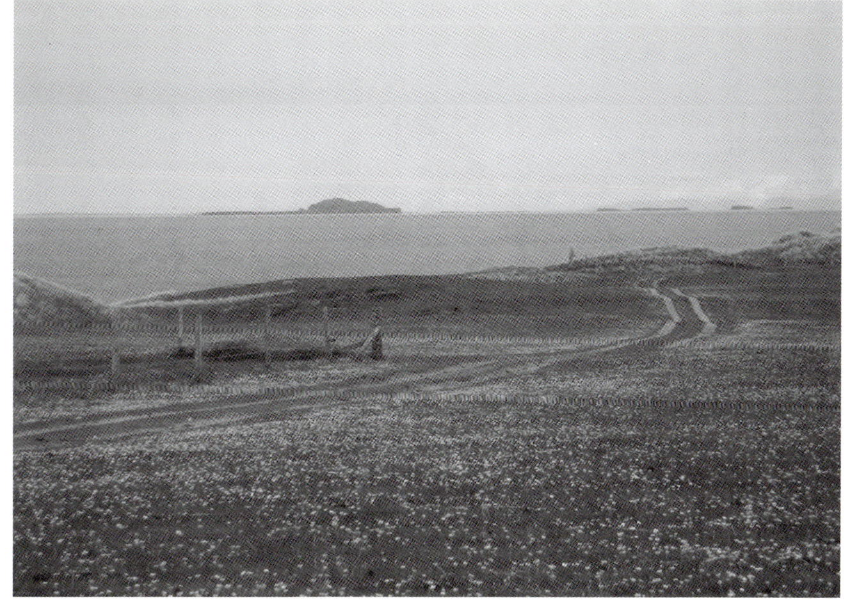

Photograph 2013

This shows Lunga central on the horizon with the smaller Treshnish Islands on the right. The sandy slope on the right in the middle distance is rising up to the top of Cnoc Ard Annraidh, from where Plates 162 to 167 were painted.

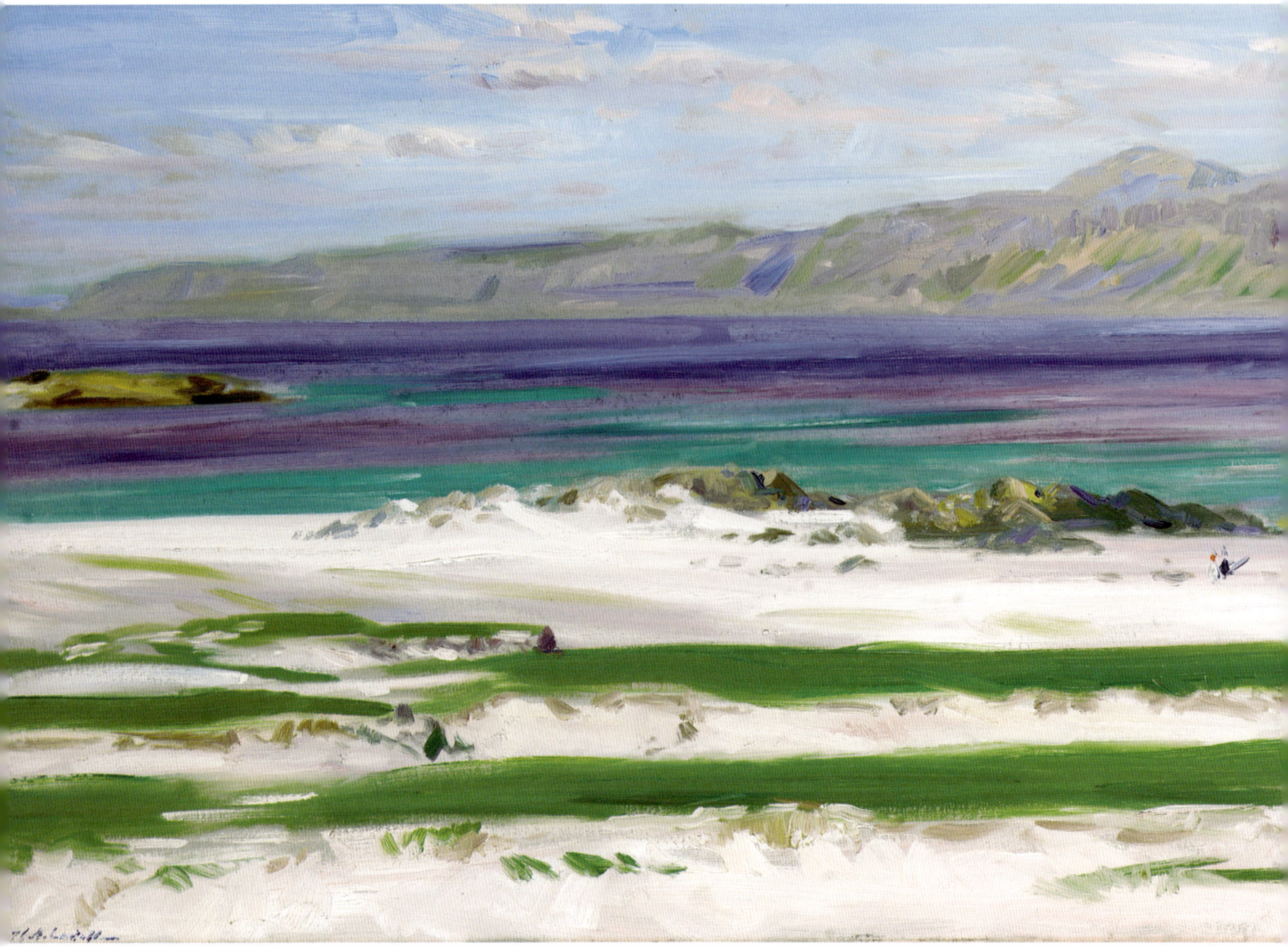

[PLATE 169]
F. C. B. Cadell
Mull from
Cnoc an t-Suidhe
(Iona Sound
and Ben More)
Oil 20 x 30

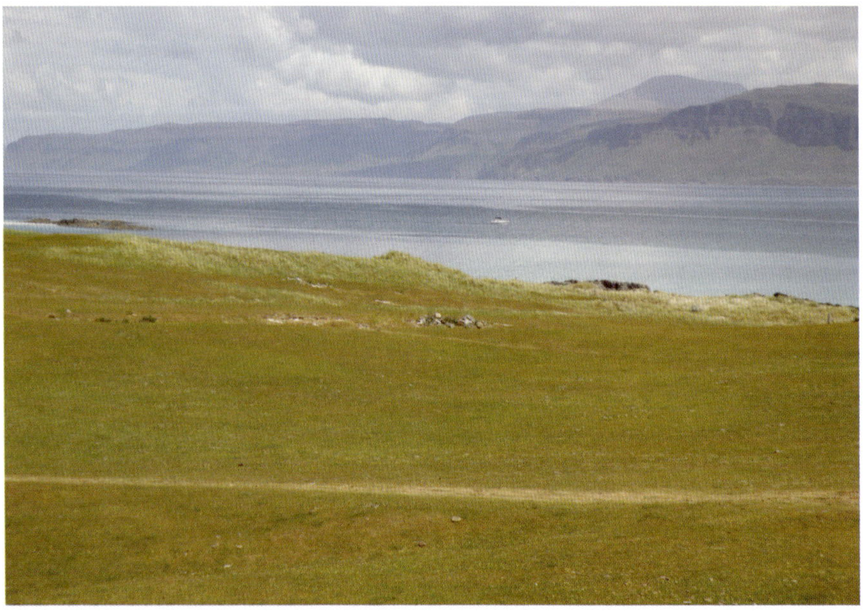

Photograph 2009

The change in ground level as seen by comparing the painting with the photograph is striking, and has been referred to at the beginning of chapter 3 (page 61).

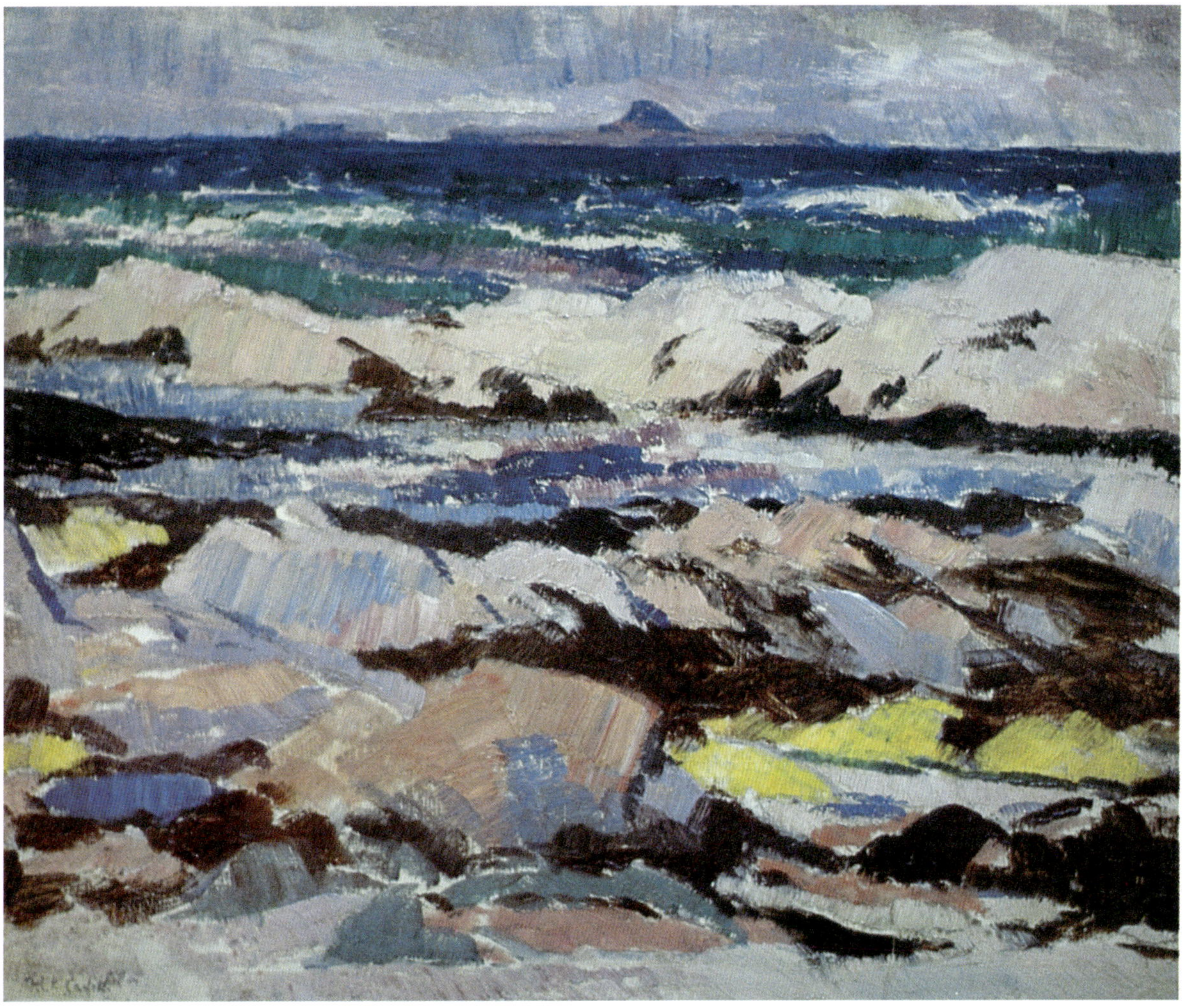

[PLATE 170]

F. C. B. Cadell

THE DUTCHMAN'S CAP

(The Dutchman's Cap from the North Shore)
Oil 15 x 18

Art Gallery and Museum,
Kelvingrove, Glasgow

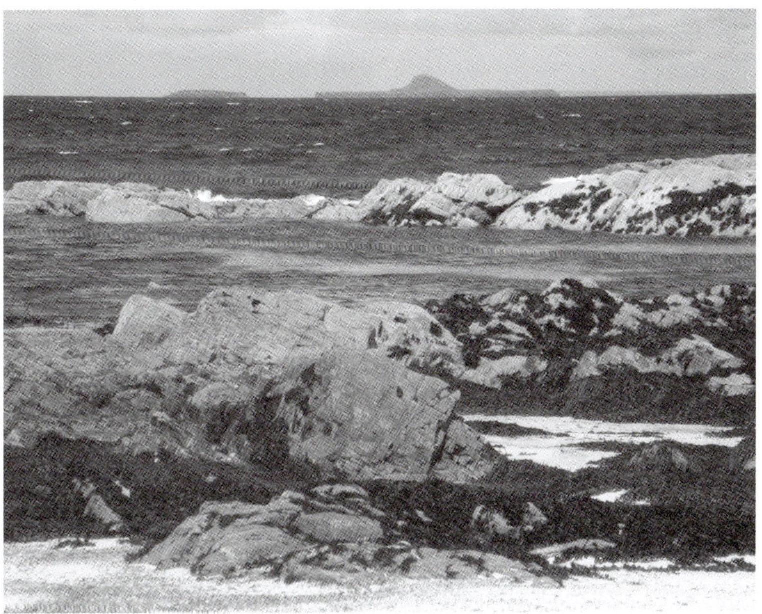

Photograph 2009

This was painted from the beach a short distance east of the Rock of the Hoodie Crow. This part of the shore is generally referred to as Lagandorain Beach.

The foreground is very freely painted and would appear abstract if it were not seen in the context of a seascape. However, comparison with the photograph will show that the brushmarks have a clear correspondence to observed reality.

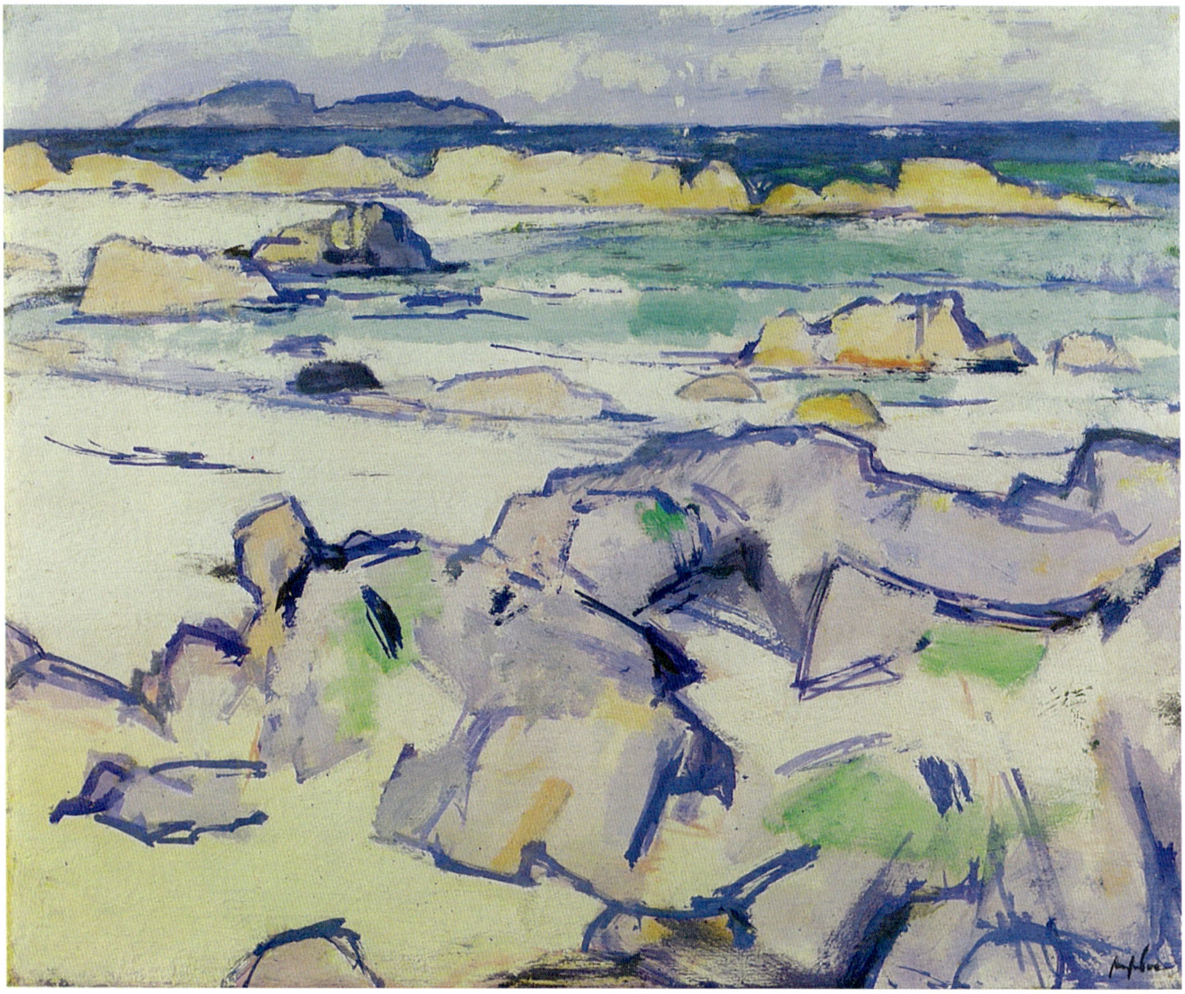

[PLATE 171]
S. J. Peploe
The North Shore at Chalbha (A Windy Day, Iona)
Oil $13\frac{1}{2}$ x 16

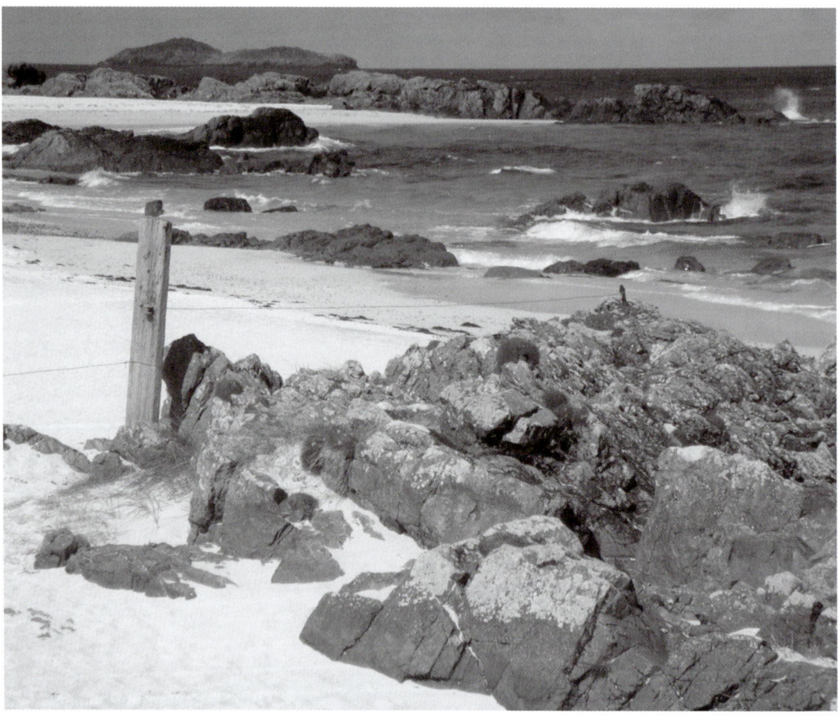

Photograph 2009

This is the north shore west of the Rock of the Hoodie Crow, and the view is westwards along the beach to the island of Reidh Eilean on the horizon.

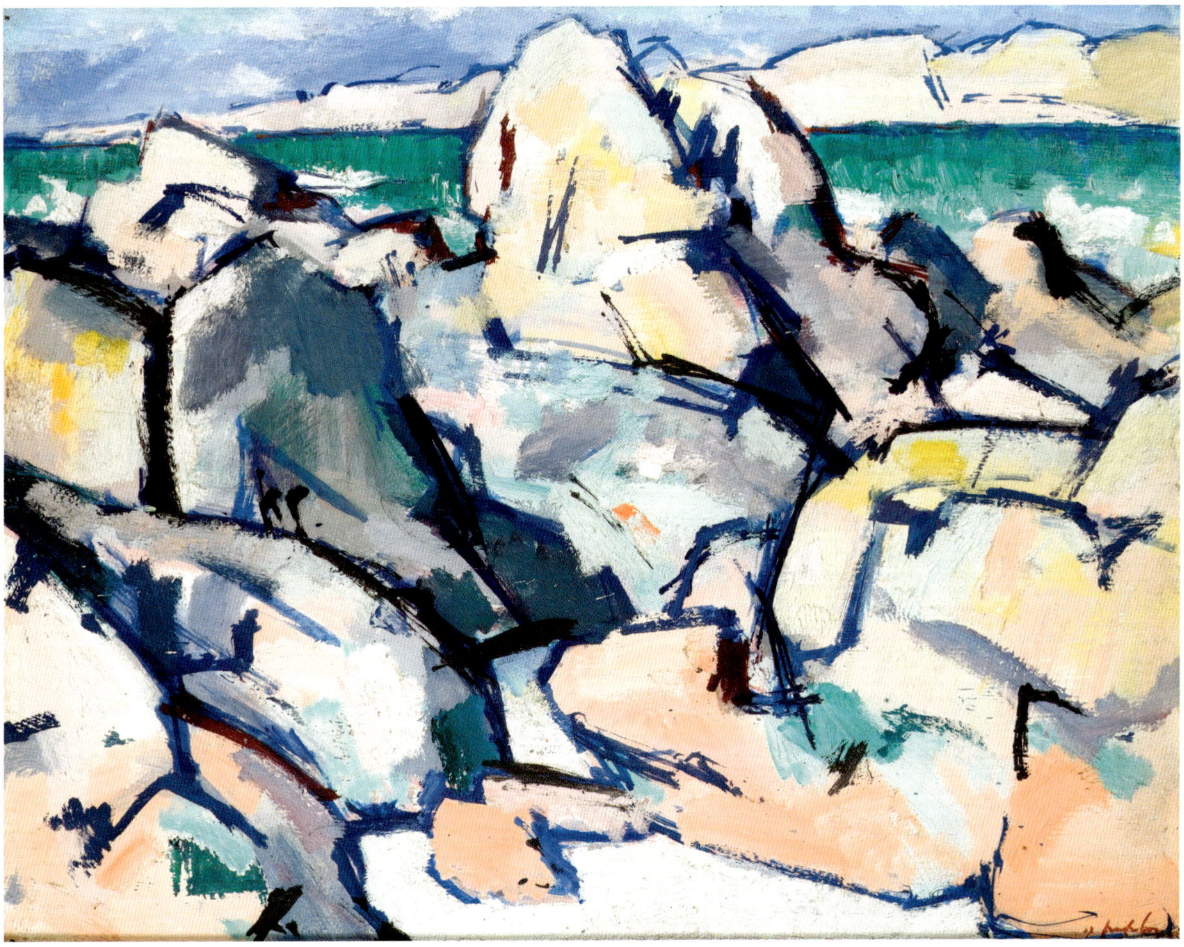

[PLATE 172]

S. J. Peploe

Rocks on the North Shore

Oil $12^{1}/_{2}$ x 16

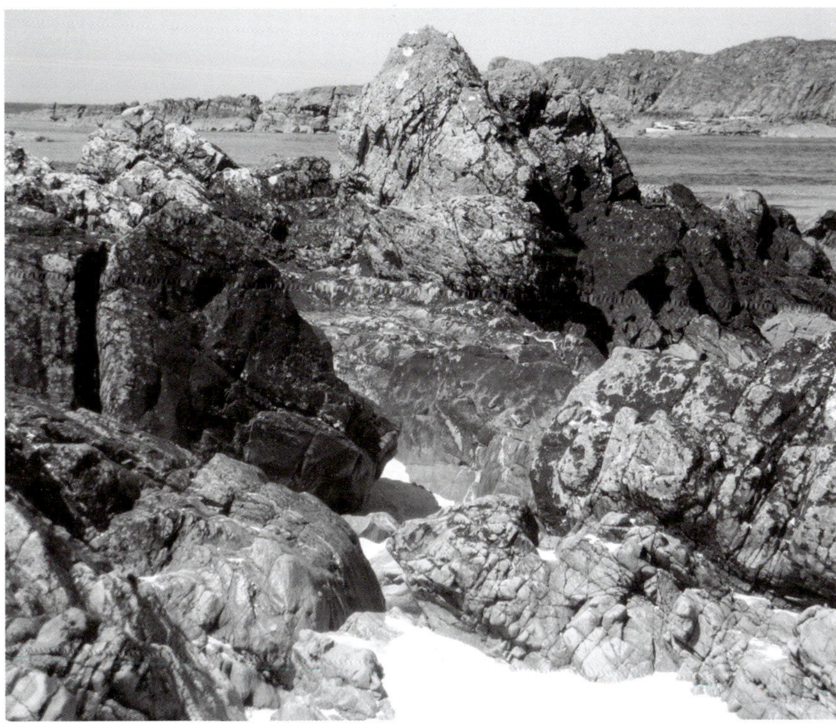

Photograph 2010

This was painted only a few metres away from Plate 171, but looking in a northwesterly direction with Eilean Chalbha in the background.

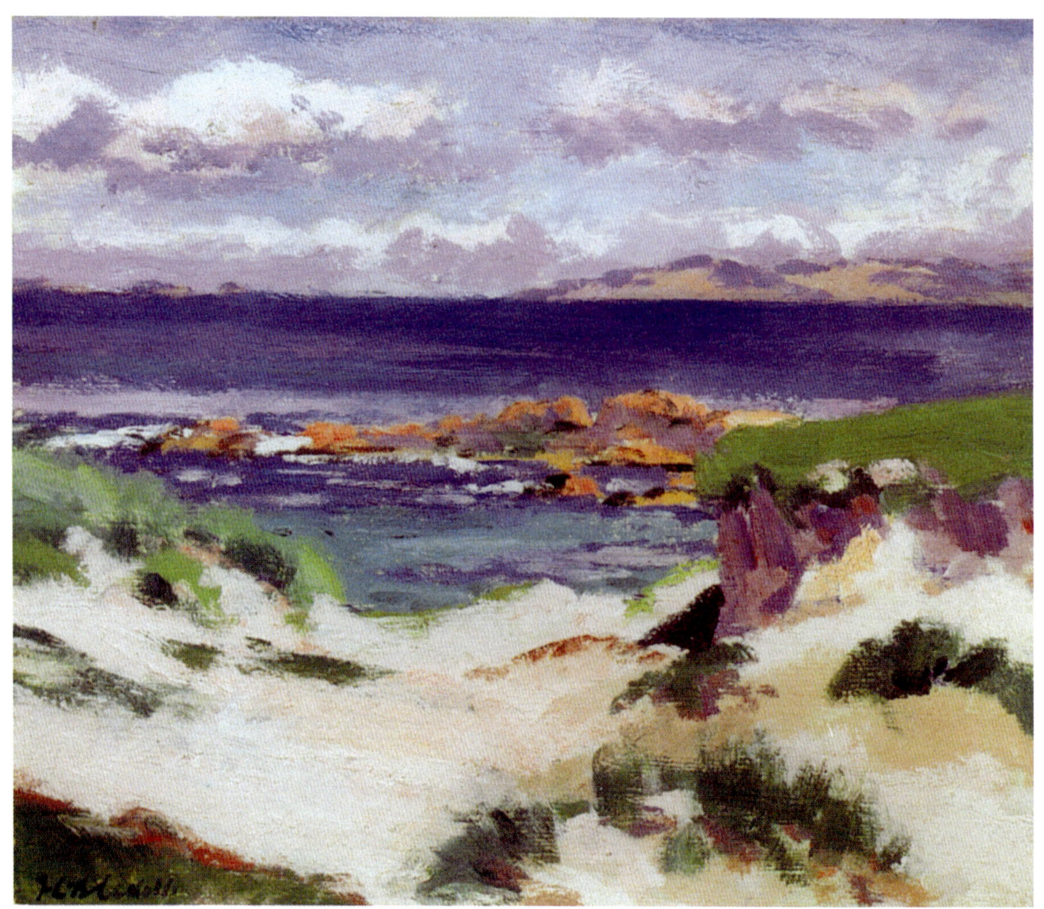

[PLATE 173] **F. C. B. Cadell** *Treshnish Point from the beach at Chalbha* Oil 14 x 17

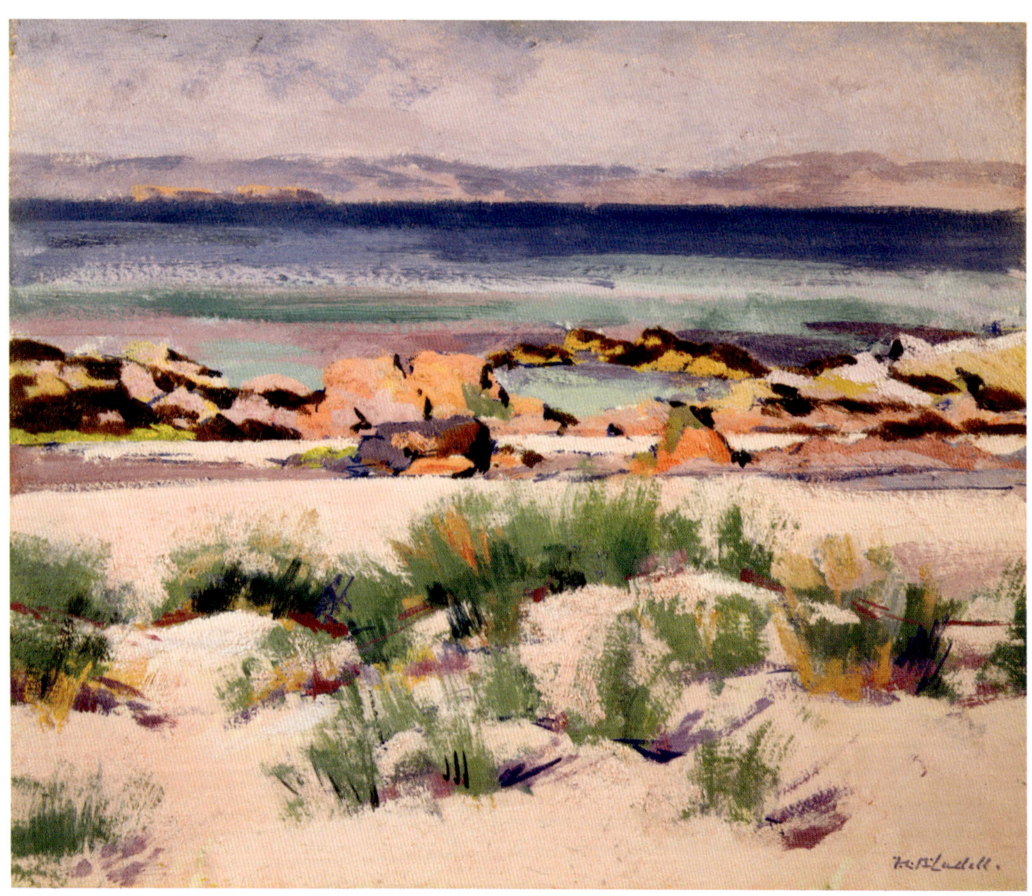

[PLATE 174] **F. C. B. Cadell** *Staffa and Mull from the beach at Chalbha* Oil 15 x 18

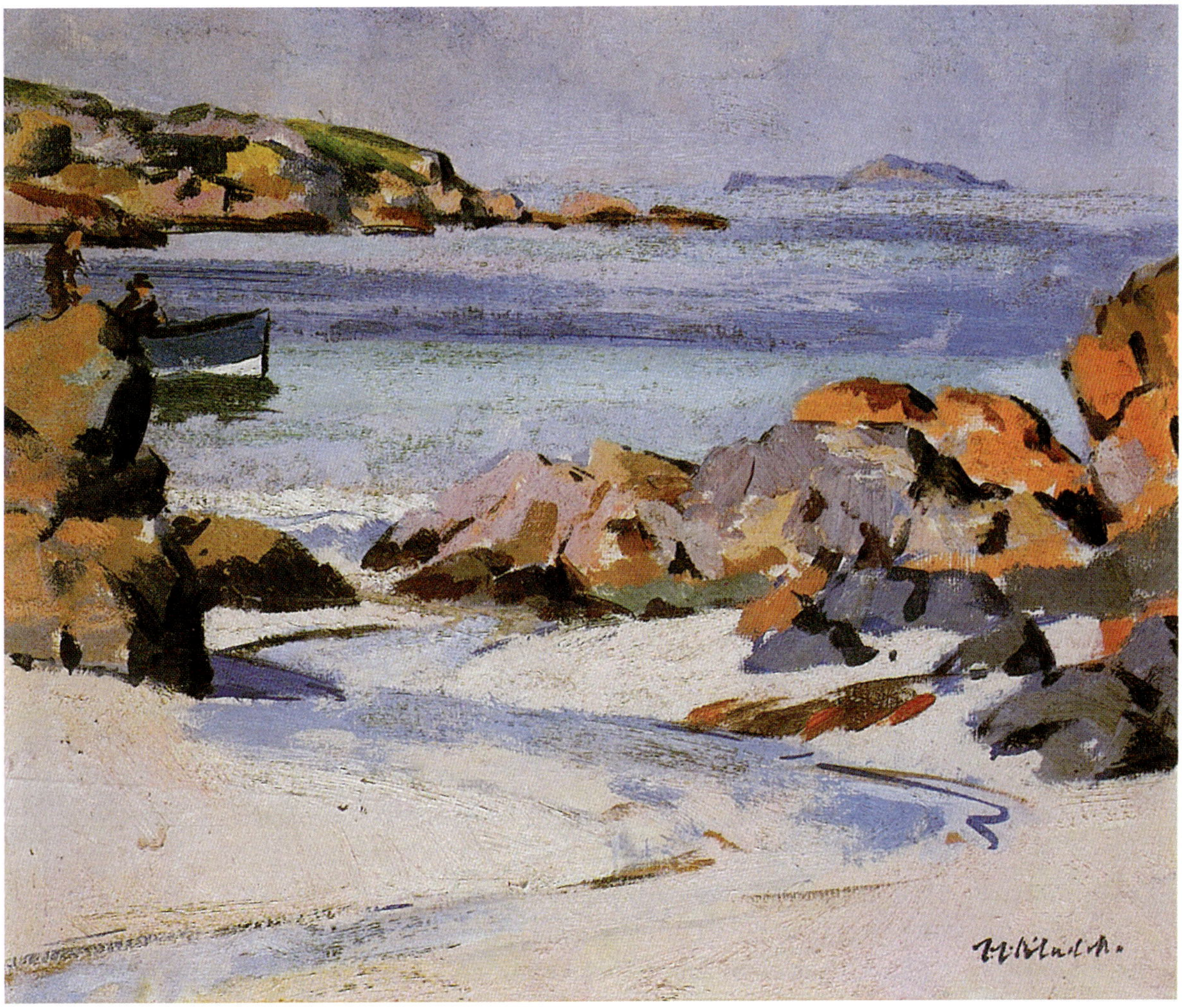

[PLATE 175]
F. C. B. Cadell
Lunga from the beach at Chalbha (Offshore, Iona)
Oil 15 x 18

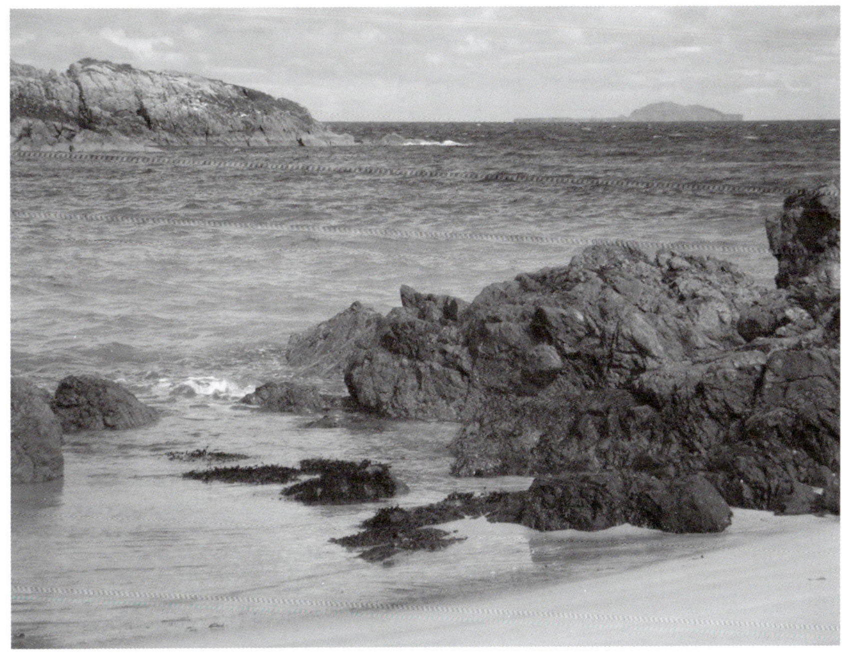

Photograph 2009

Plates 175 to 178 were painted amongst the rocks which form the west boundary of the sands at Chalbha.

In Plate 175 the view is due north to Lunga on the horizon. The east side of Eilean Chalbha is in the middle distance on the left.

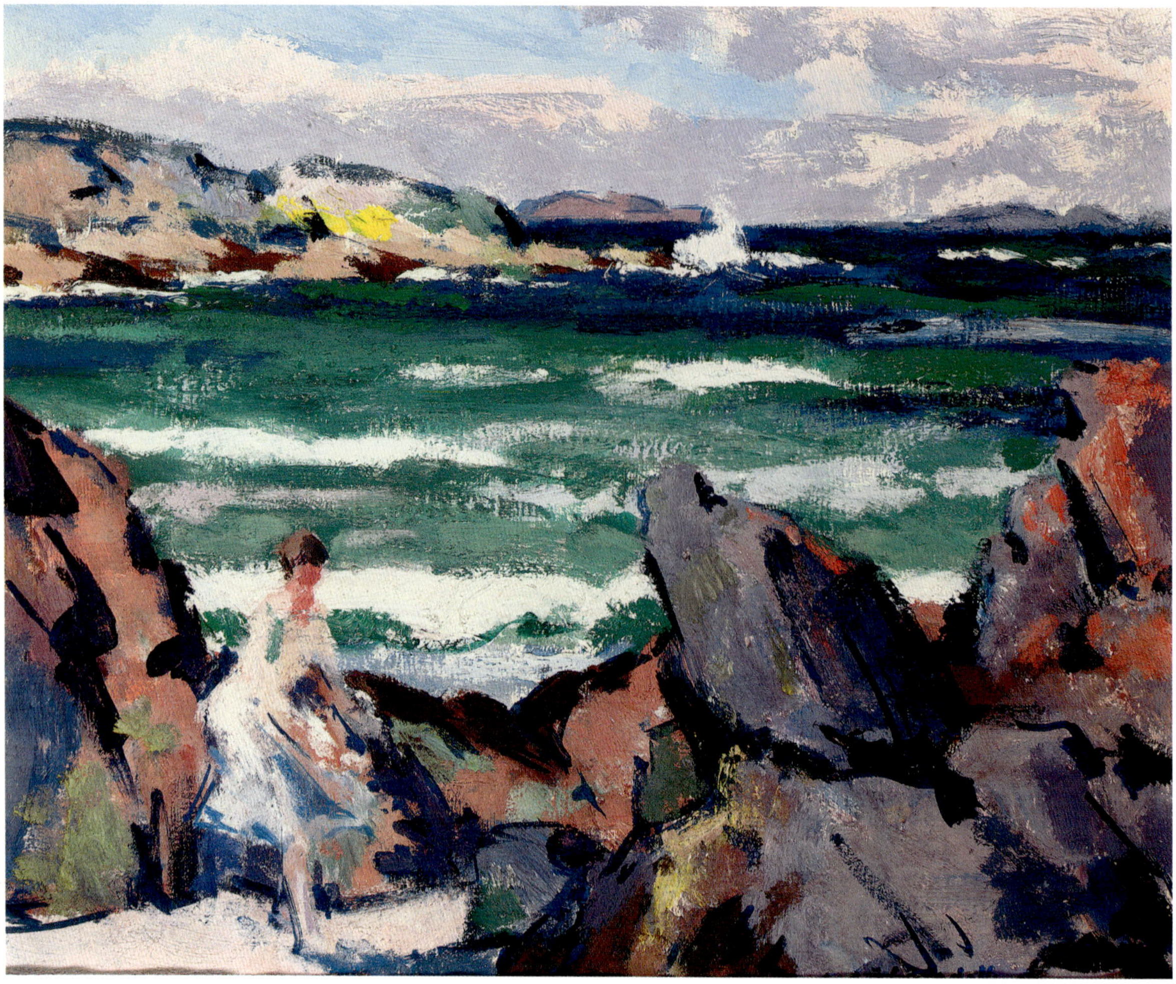

[PLATE 176]
F. C. B. Cadell
Lunga from the beach at Chalbha (North Wind, Iona – The Bather)
Oil 15 x 18

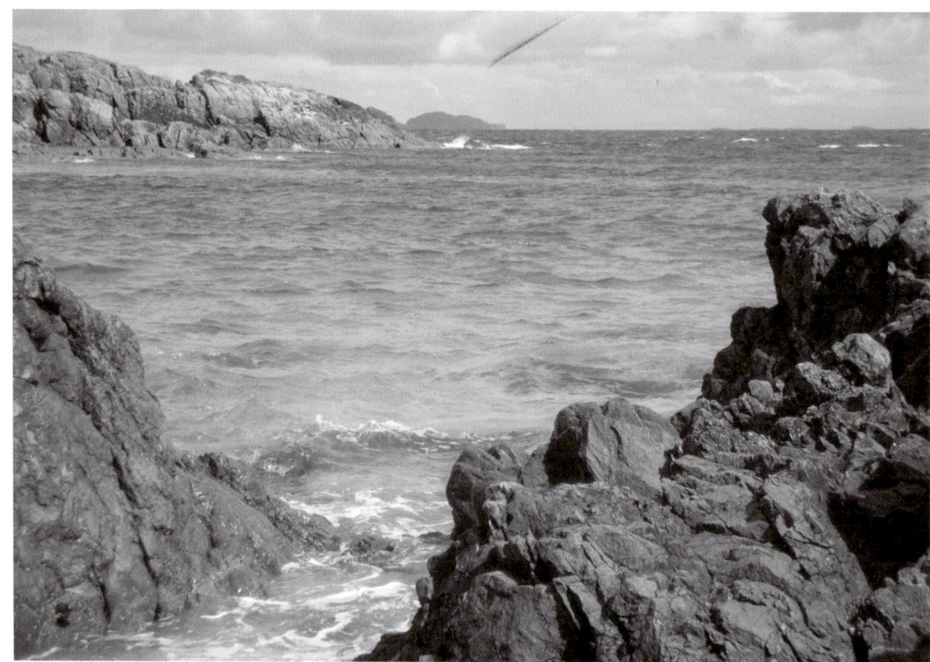

Photograph 2009

This is a similar composition to Plate 175 except here Lunga is partly hidden by Eilean Chalbha.

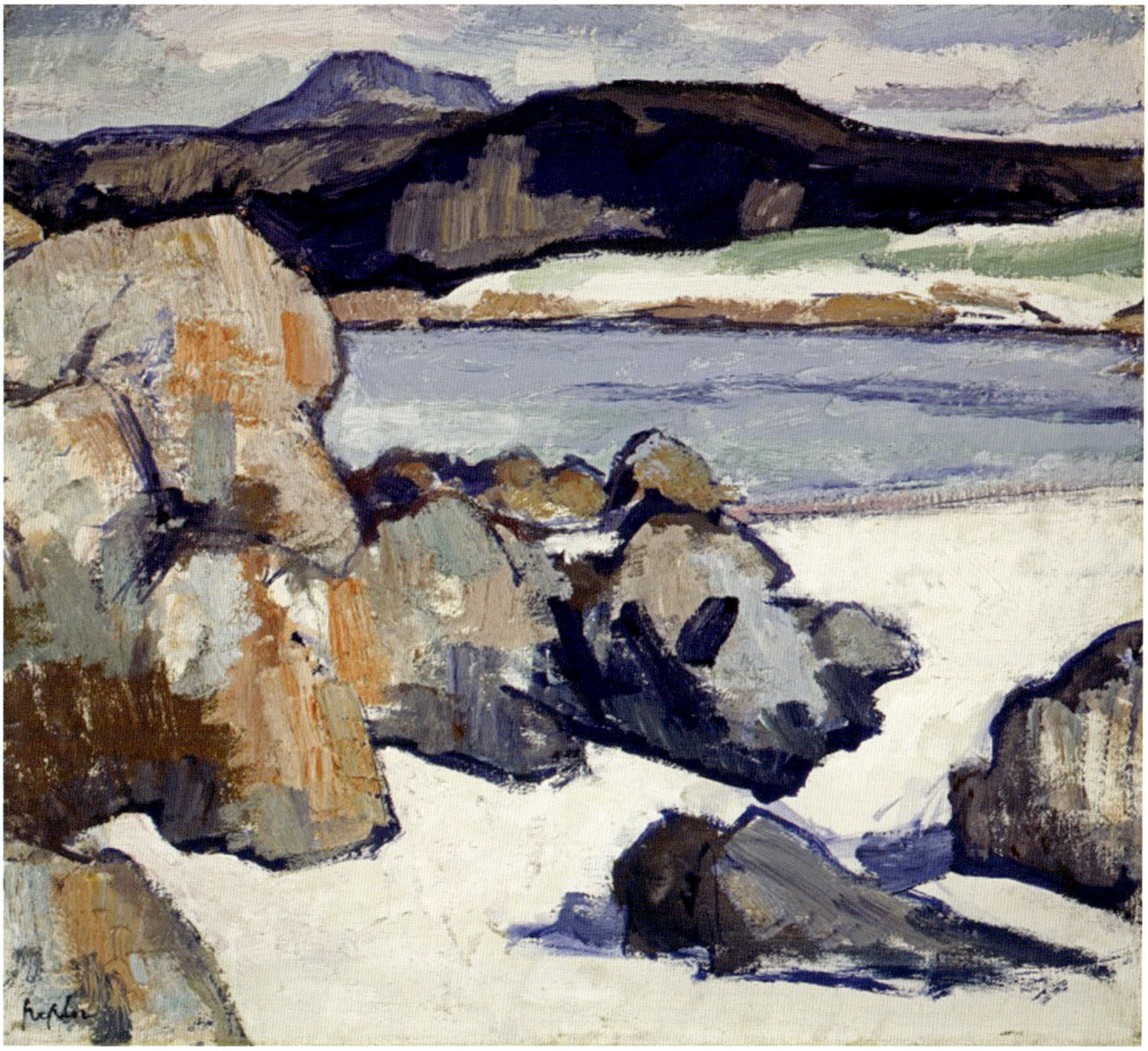

[PLATE 177]

S. J. Peploe

IONA LANDSCAPE, ROCKS

(Ben More from Chalbha)
Oil 16 x 18

Scottish National Gallery
of Modern Art, Edinburgh

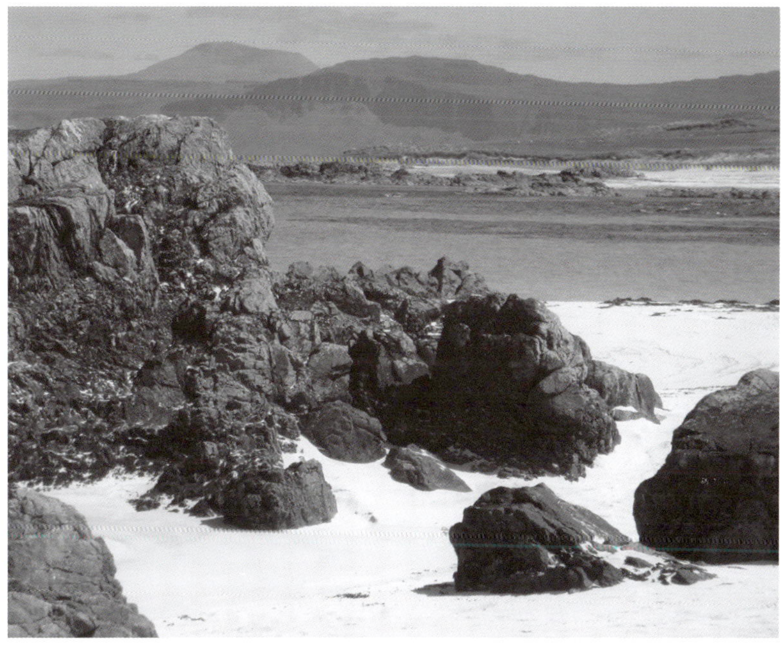

Photograph 2010

The beach in the foreground on the right is Traigh-na-Criche. The familiar outlines of Ben More and the Burg are in the distance with the northeast corner of Iona in front of them sloping up to the top of the Cnoc Ard Annraidh.

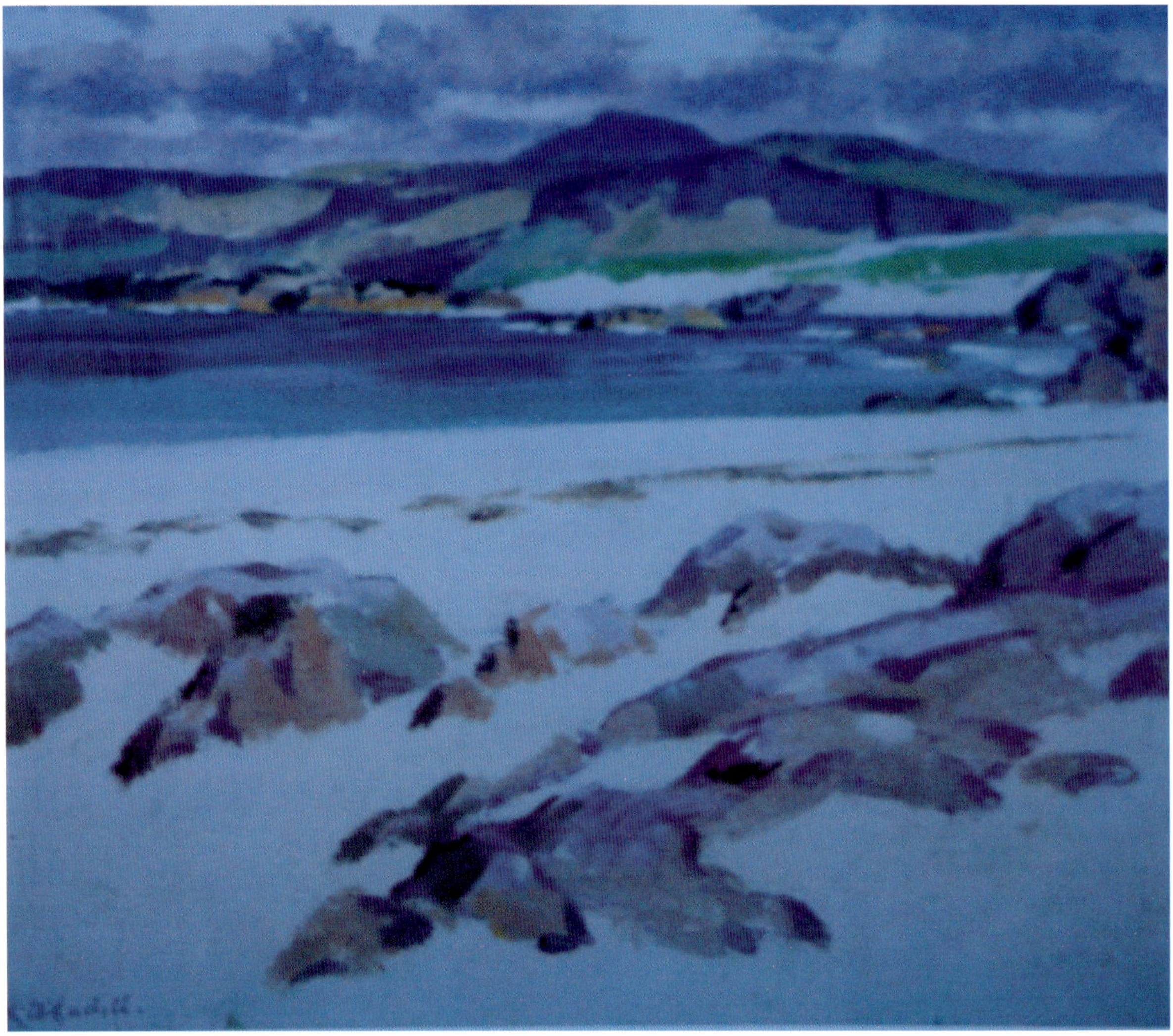

[PLATE 178]
F. C. B. Cadell
Ben More from Chalbha
Oil 15 x 18

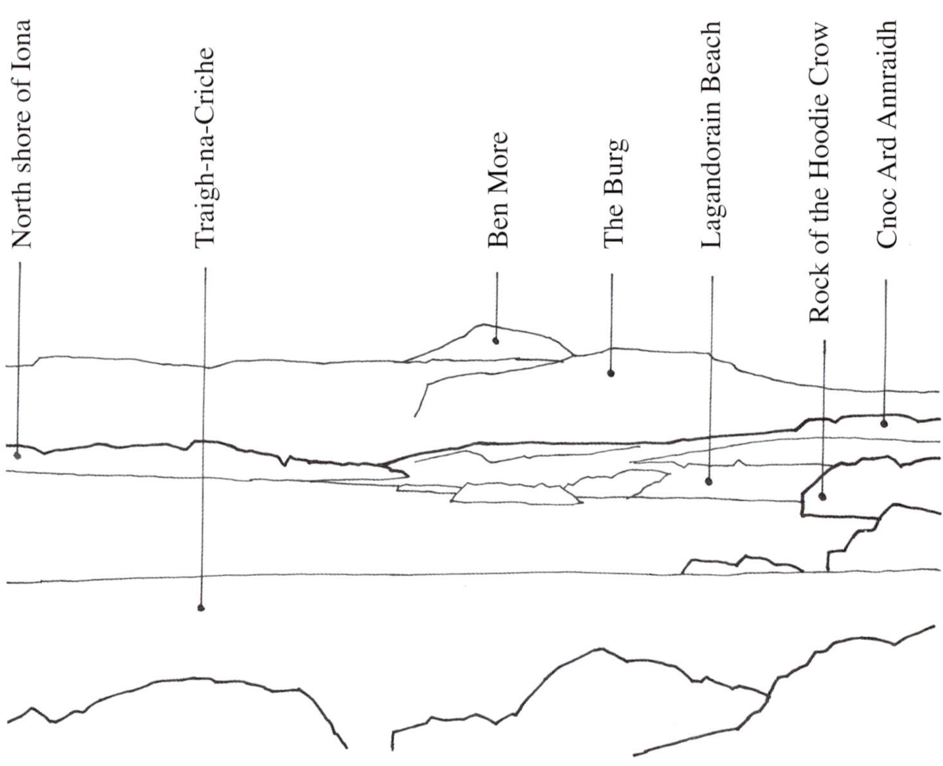

The pink rocks in the foreground are at the west end at the beach at Chalbha, close to the dunes.

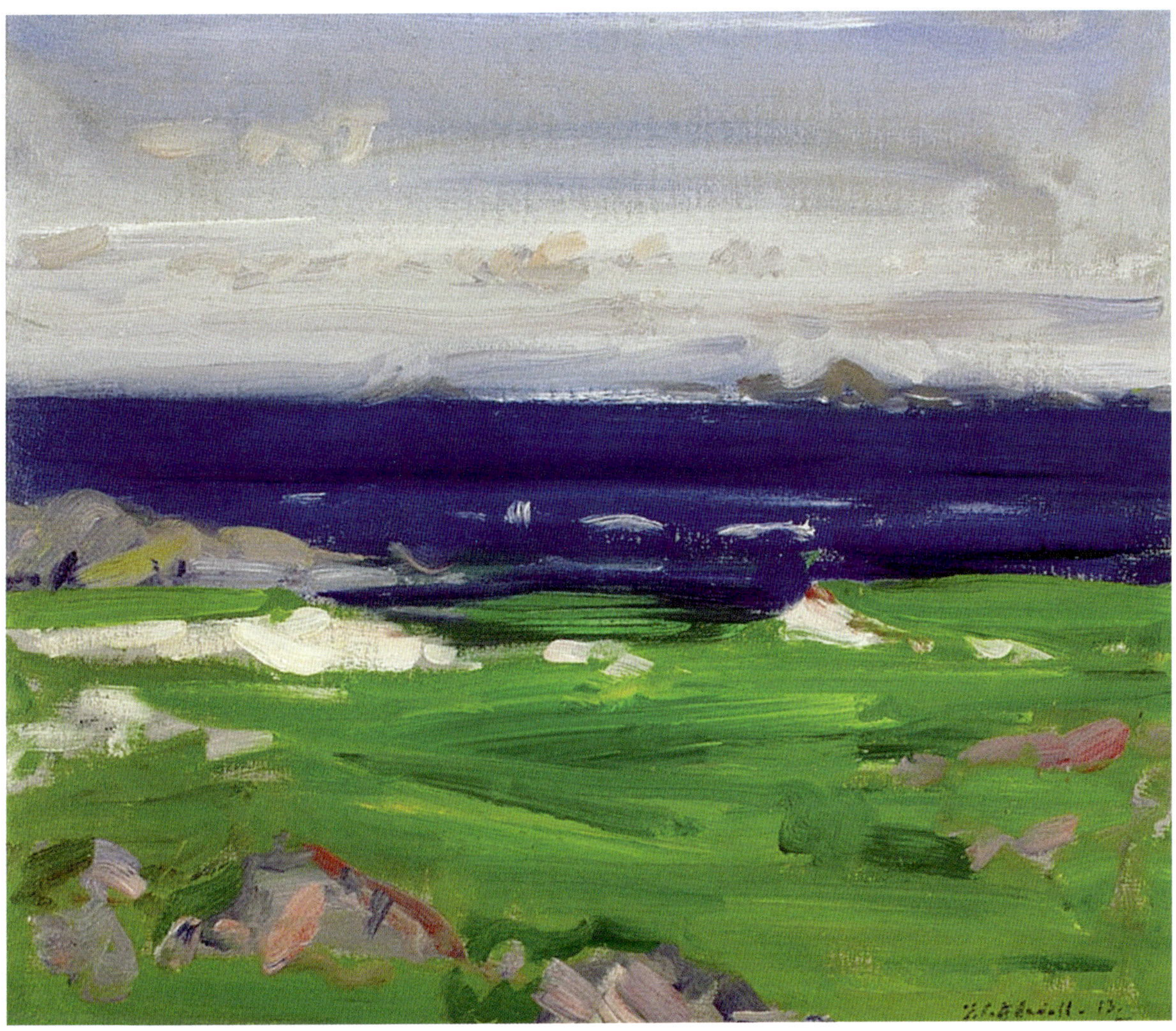

From the location of the preceding picture it is possible to climb onto the dunes above Chalbha to the location of this painting. This work is an example of Cadell's early style using long brushstrokes of fluid paint; it is dated 1913 (see also Plate 61).

From here it is possible to walk back to the end of the road along the top of the dunes, and this provides a fine elevated view of the north shore and distant islands.

[PLATE 179]
F. C. B. Cadell
View from above the dunes at Chalbha
Oil 15 x 18

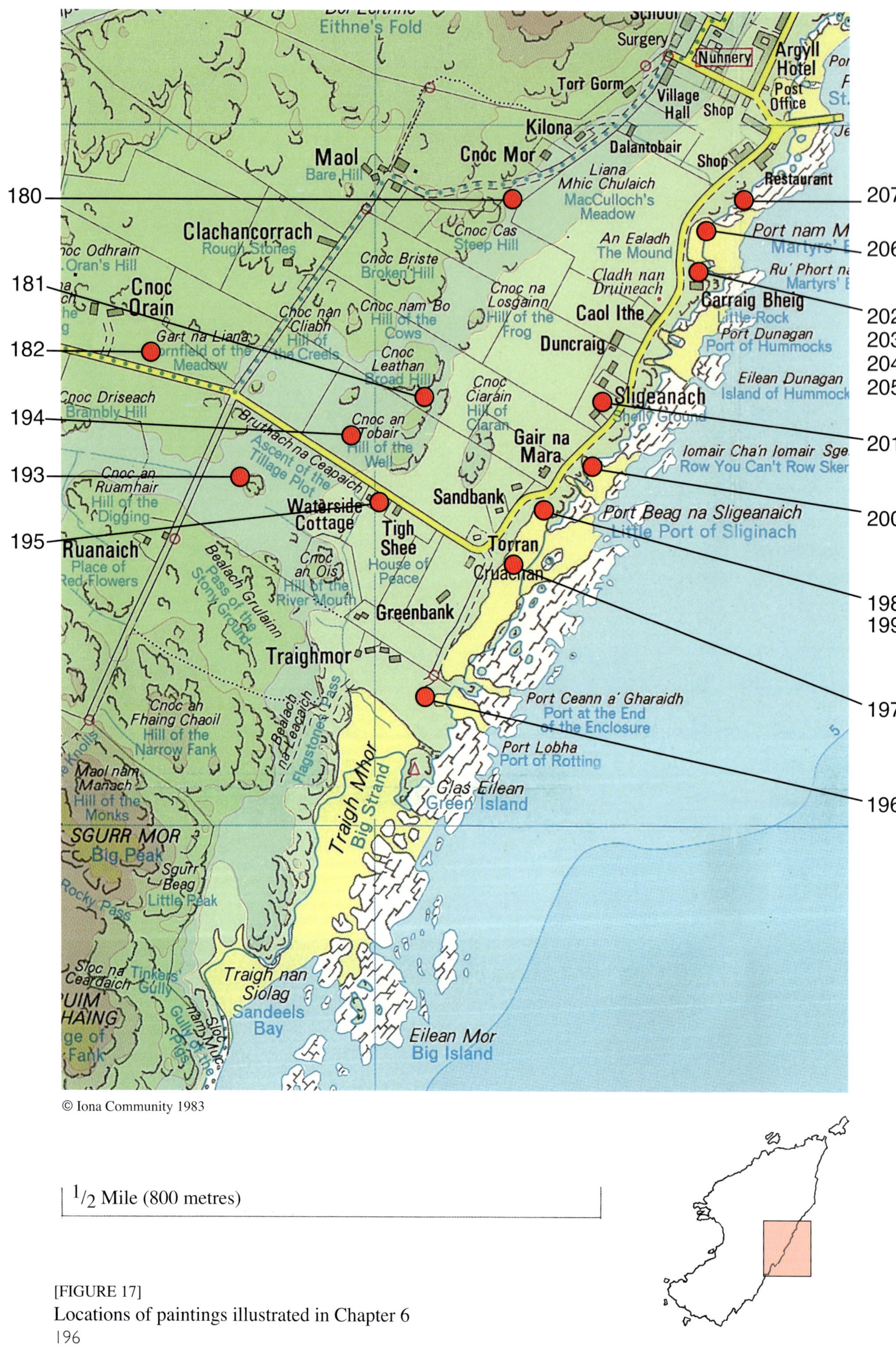

[FIGURE 17]
Locations of paintings illustrated in Chapter 6

6 · PORT BHAN AND THE ISLAND SOUTH OF THE VILLAGE

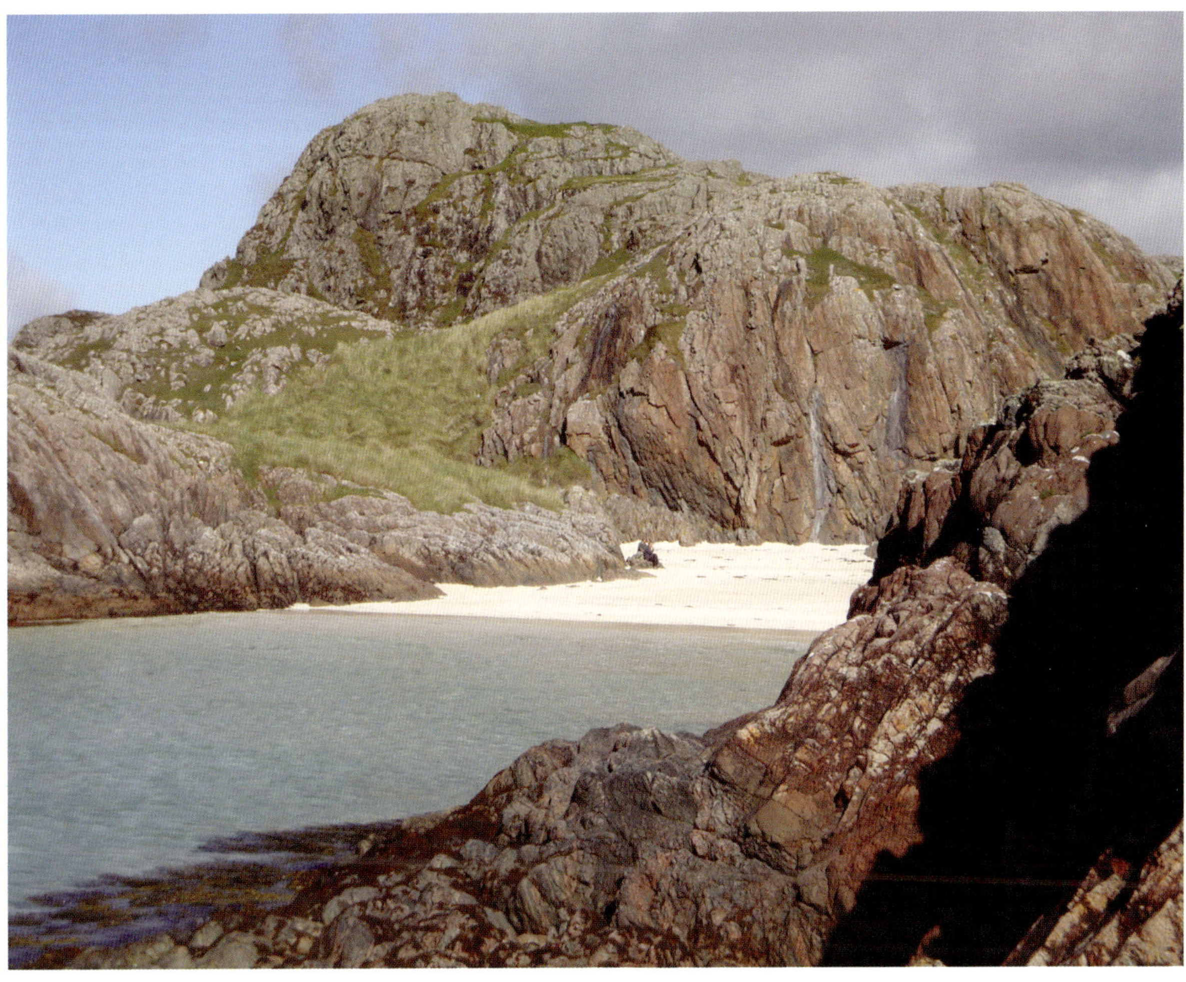

A SECOND circular walk starting and ending at the jetty takes in the paintings on the west coast, Port Bhan, the Marble Quarry, and the area south of the Village. All the paintings in this chapter are by Cadell, a further indication of Peploe's preference for the north of the island.

Most of the painting locations in this chapter appear in Figure 17 opposite. A separate map, Figure 18 (page 203), shows the locations of pictures in the Port Bhan area. The Marble Quarry does not appear in this large-scale map, but its position is shown on the smaller scale map which details the route for the walk (Figure 5, page 17).

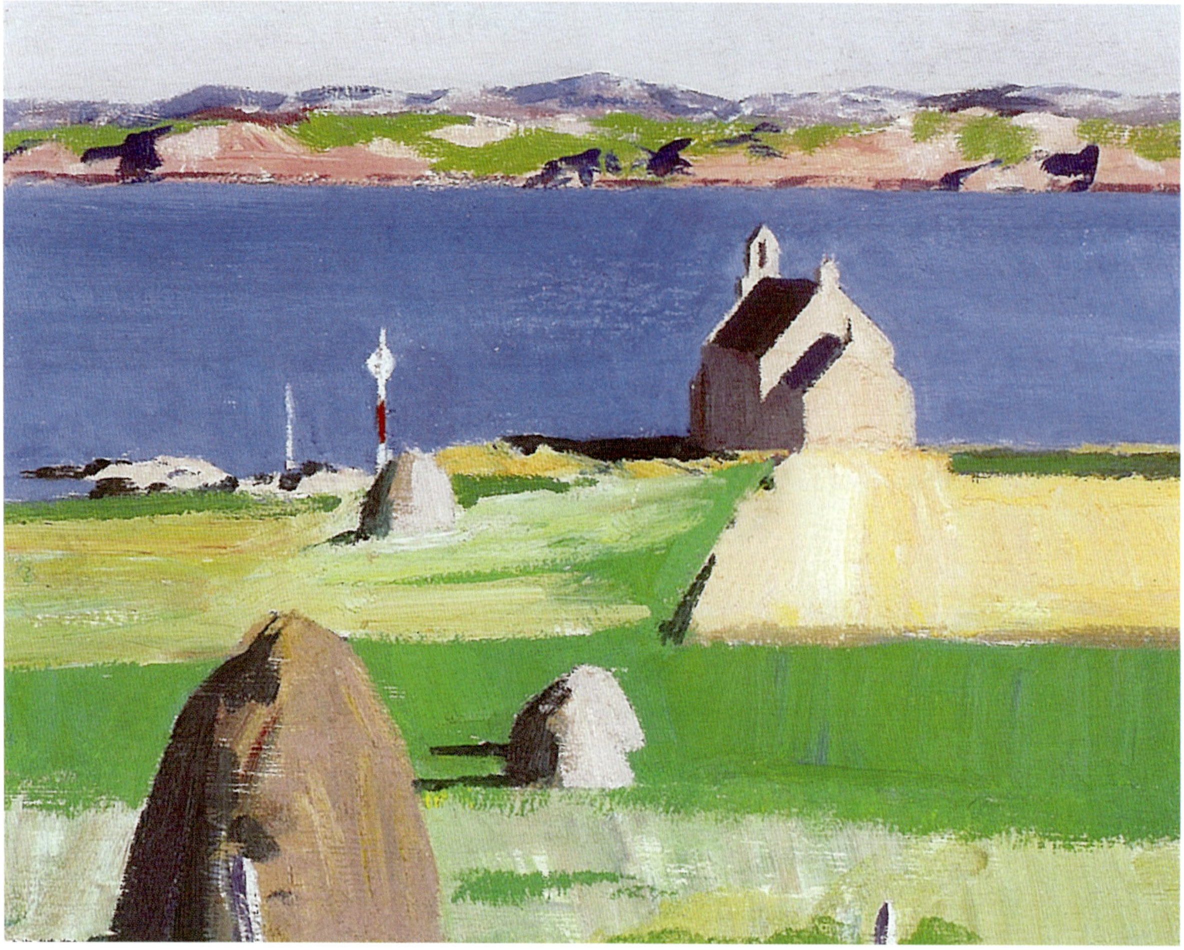

[PLATE 180]
F. C. B. Cadell
The Free Church
Oil 15 x 18

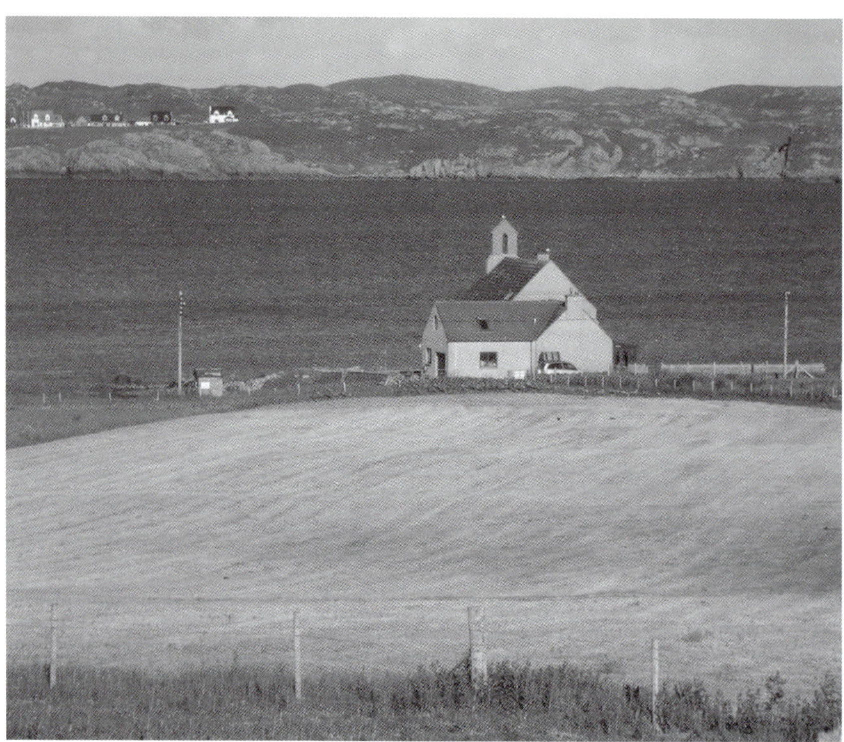

Photograph 2009

By walking up from the Jetty, turning left at the Library, and passing Village Hall, one soon arrives at the first subject. *The Free Church, Iona* was painted from where the track begins to steepen. The church was built on a rocky promontory, donated as the land could serve no other purpose. Now converted into a dwelling, it is one of the most spectacularly sited houses on Iona.

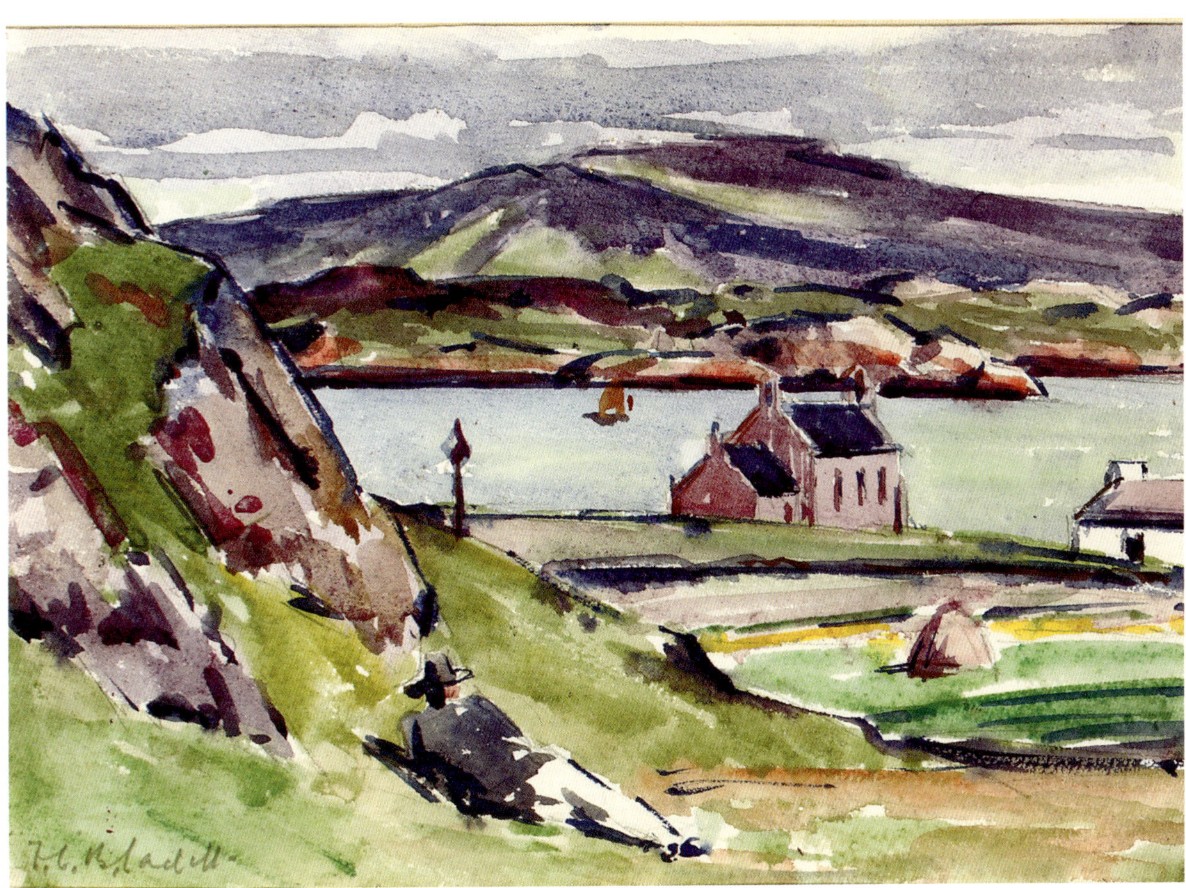

[PLATE 181]
F. C. B. Cadell
The Free Church
(Figure and Kirk)
Watercolour 7 x 10

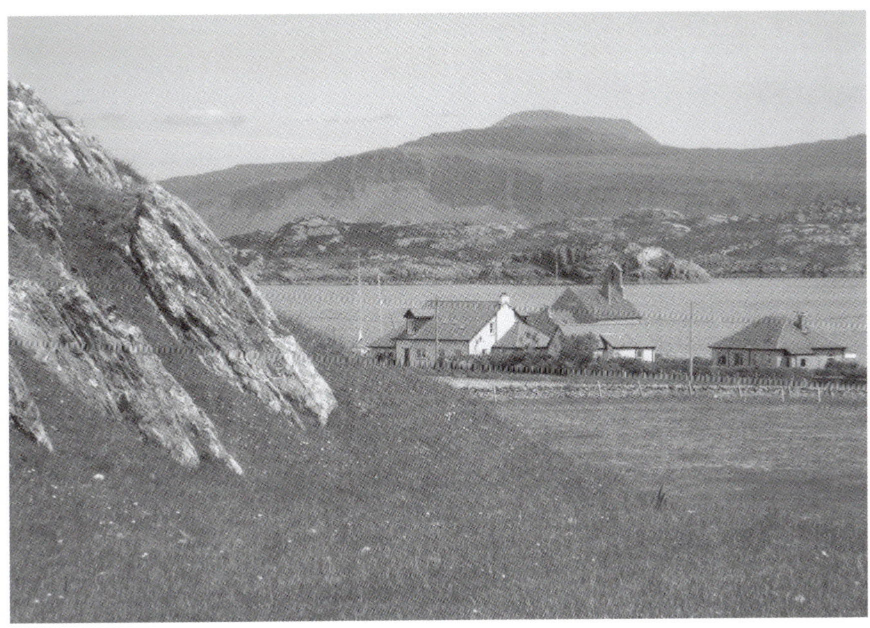

Photograph 2009

From the location of Plate 180 the track continues uphill to Maol, the farm at the top of the hill. Beyond here the track turns down to the left. The location of Plate 181 is in a field on the left of the track. The rock outcrop on the left of the painting is called Cnoc Leathan. The church has become partly hidden by later houses. The Ross of Mull and the Burg are in the background.

In the photograph, Ben More is also visible beyond the Burg.

Lower down, the track crosses the road at a junction known as Four Roads, where a turn to the right leads along the road to The Machair and the painting locations on the west shore of Iona.

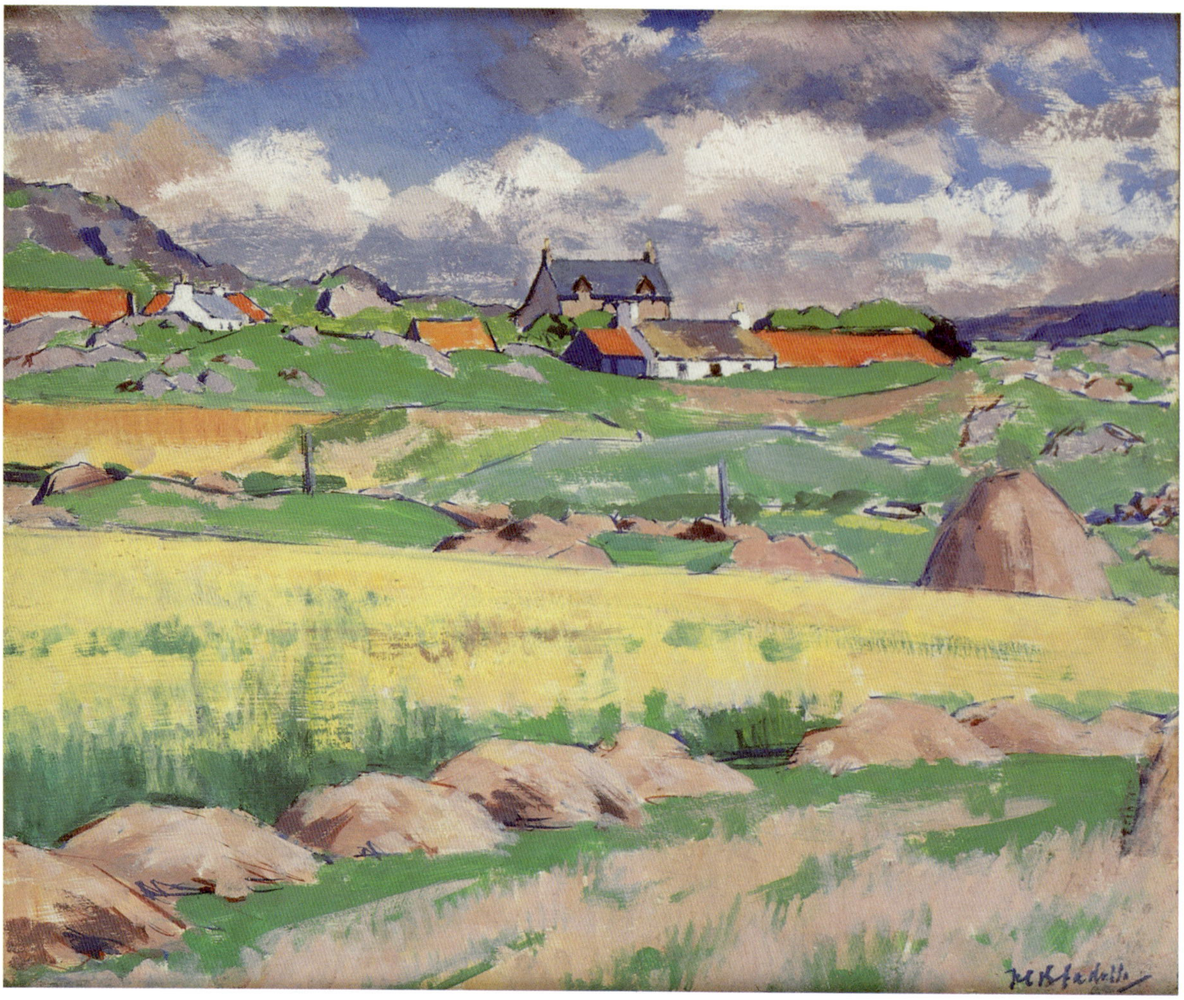

[PLATE 182]
F. C. B. Cadell
Clachan Corrach
(The Clachan)
Oil 15 x 18

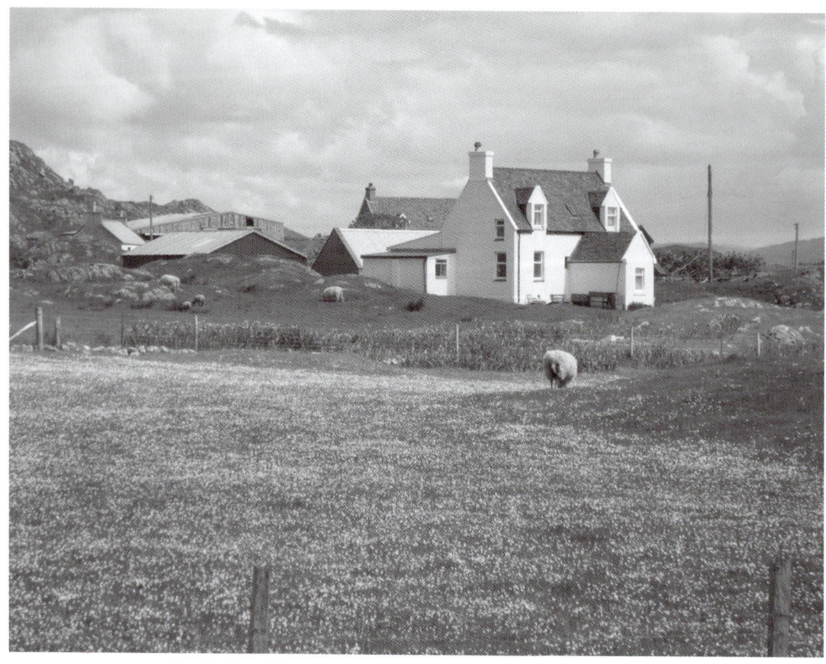

Photograph 2009

A short distance from the Four Roads one has this view back towards the northeast which includes Clachan Corrach Croft with the house at Maol on the skyline. The small white-walled cottage just right of centre in the painting is the original Clachan Corrach dwelling. The present two-storey house seen in the photograph was built in 1928.

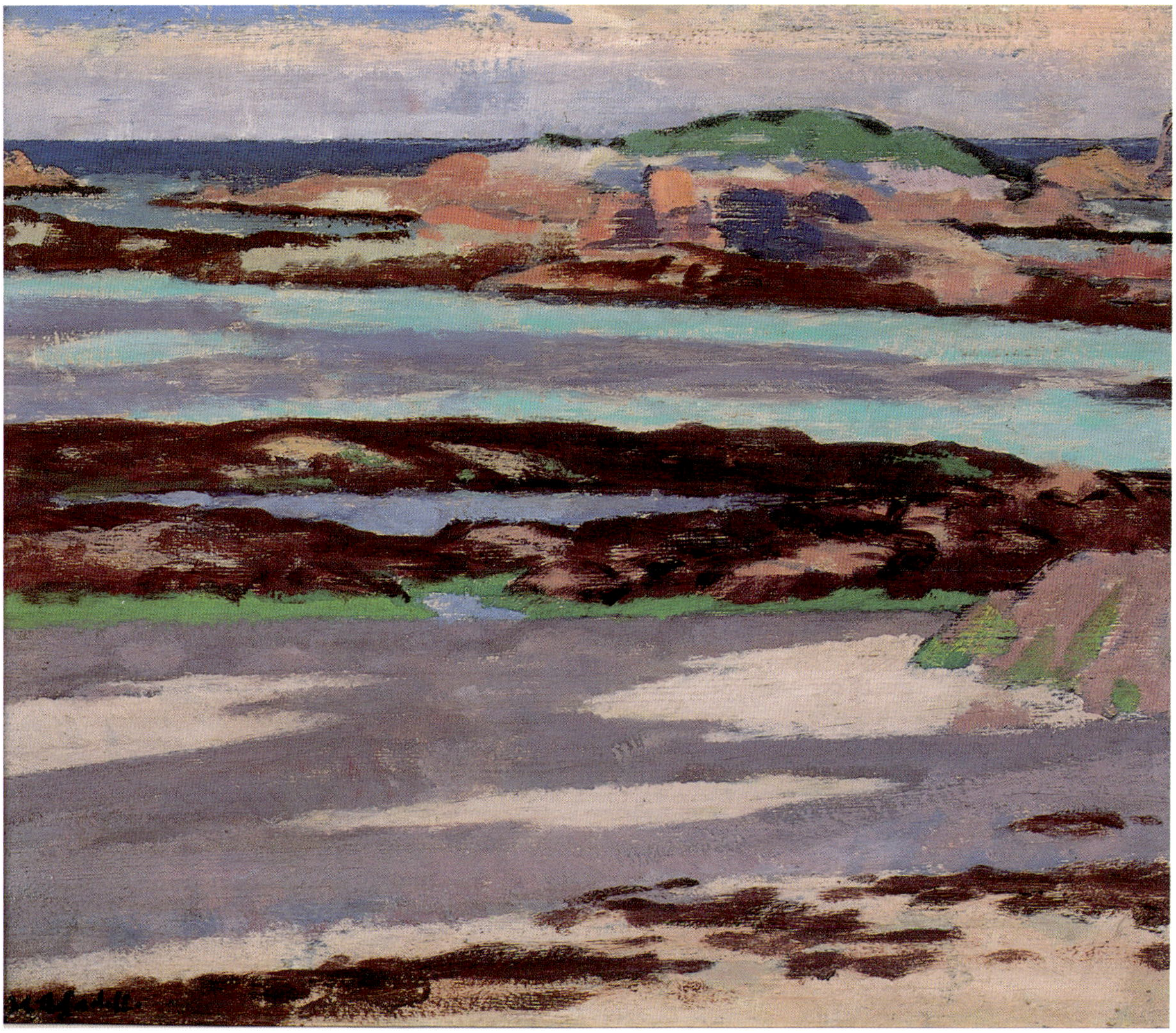

[PLATE 183]

F. C. B. Cadell

Eilean nan Slat,

Bay at the Back of the Ocean

Oil 15 x 18

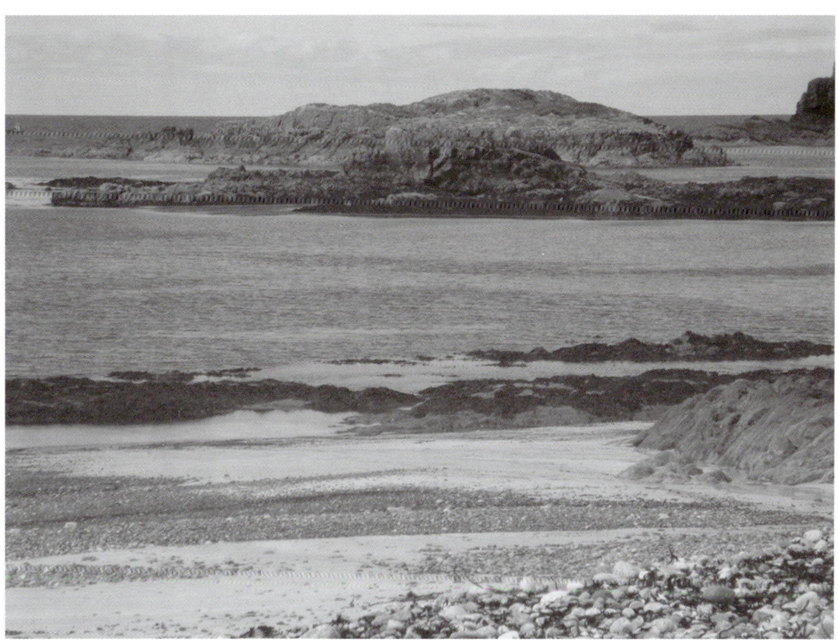

Photograph 2009

At the end of the road there is a gate which leads onto The Machair. The track straight ahead arrives at the shore at the place where Cadell painted this view of the Bay. The vertical rock step at the right-hand edge of the painting is the end of Eilean Didil.

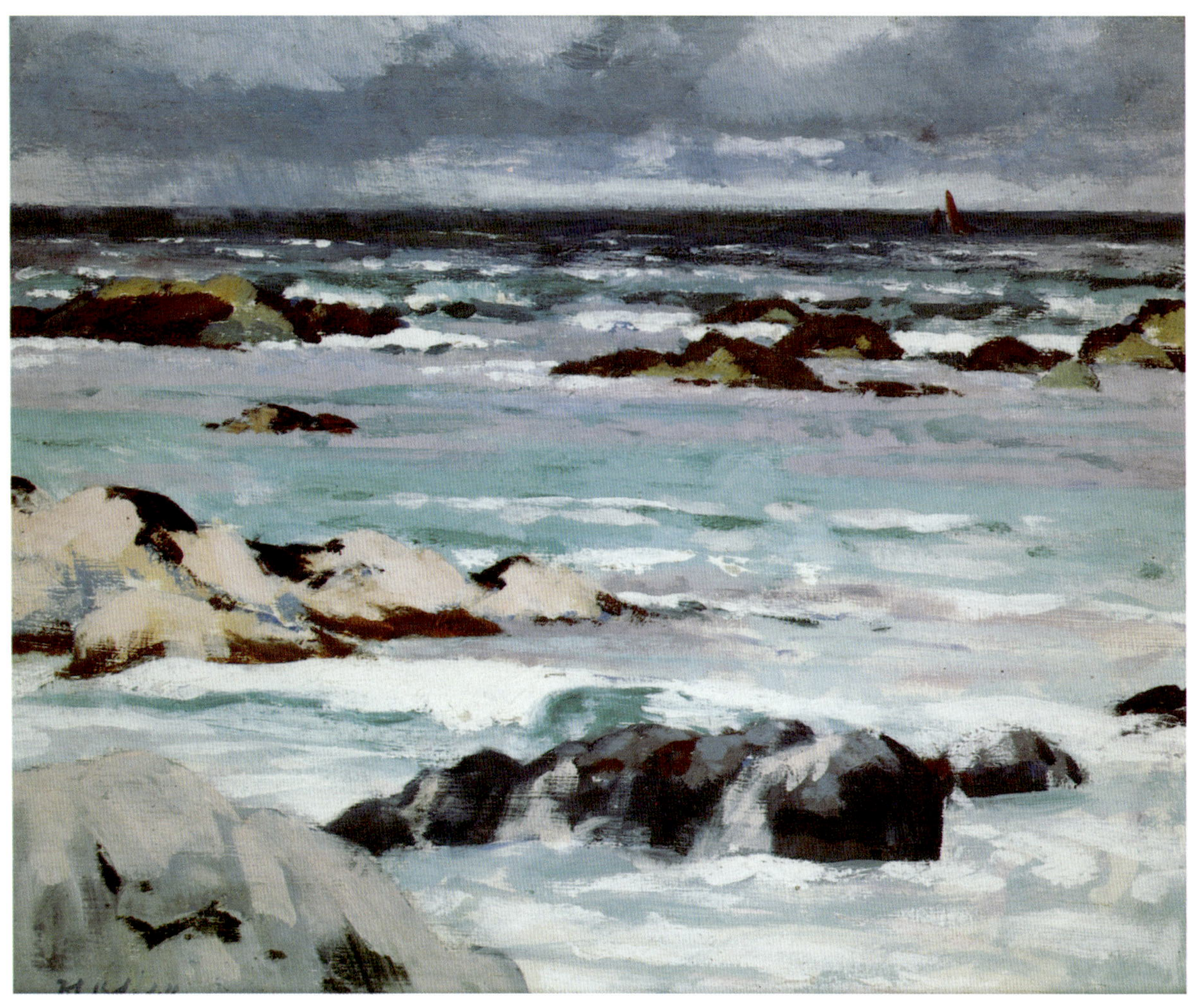

There is insufficient information to be certain of the location of this painting, but the original title inscribed on the back of the panel suggests a view west from the southern end of the Bay at the Back of the Ocean. The likelihood of this is further confirmed by the absence of any islands on the horizon.

[PLATE 184]
F. C. B. Cadell
Looking West from the South, Iona
Oil 15 x 18

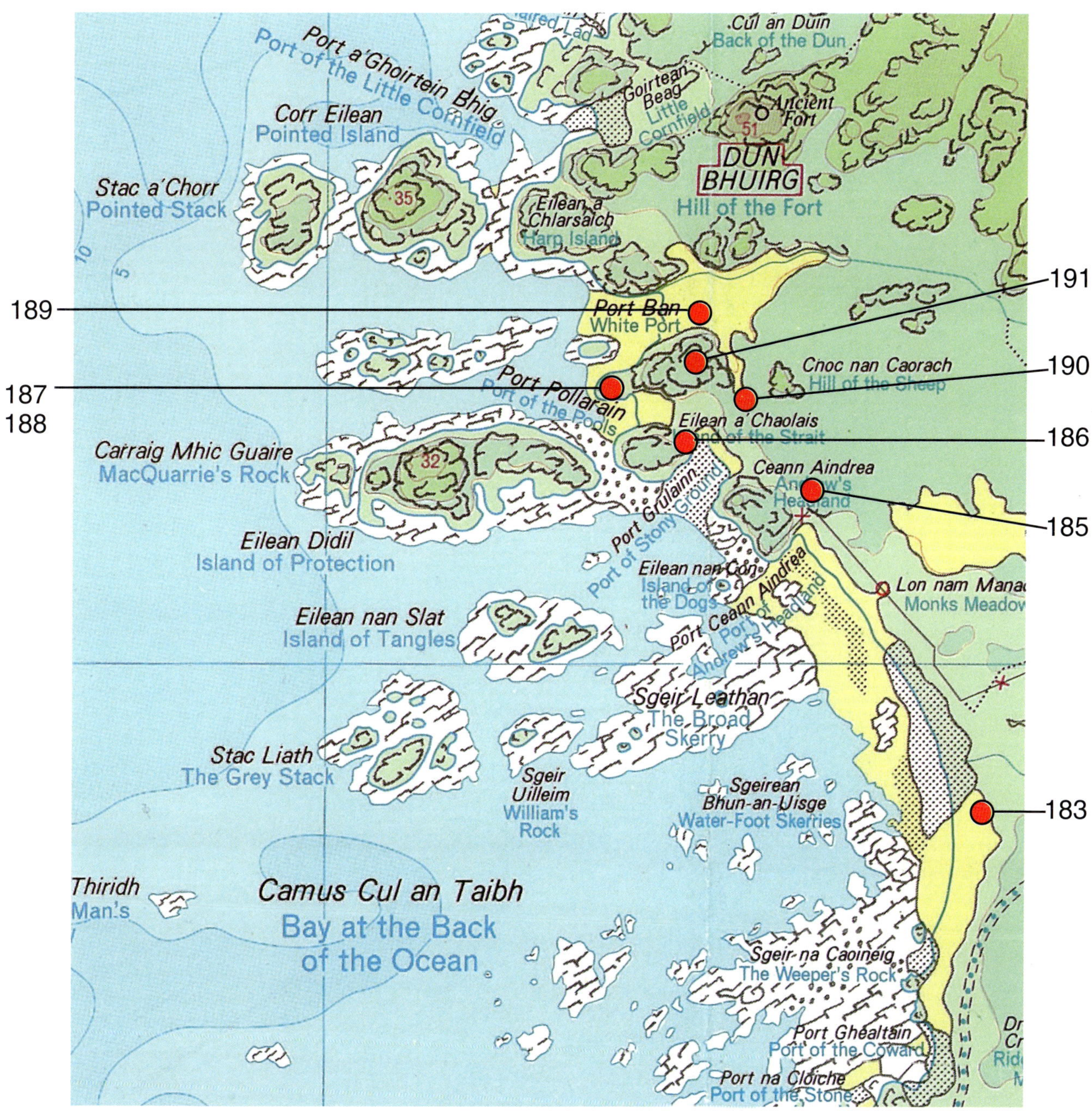

Port a'Ghoirtein Bhig
Port of the Little Cornfield
Cul an Duin
Back of the Dun
Goirtean Beag
Little Cornfield
Ancient Fort
51
Corr Eilean
Pointed Island
DUN BHUIRG
Hill of the Fort
Stac a'Chorr
Pointed Stack
35
Eilean a Chlarsaich
Harp Island
189
191
Port Ban
White Port
Cnoc nan Caorach
Hill of the Sheep
190
187
188
Port Pollarain
Port of the Pools
Eilean a'Chaolais
Island of the Strait
186
Carraig Mhic Guaire
MacQuarrie's Rock
32
Ceann Aindrea
Andrew's Headland
185
Port Grulainn
Port of Stony Ground
Eilean Didil
Island of Protection
Eilean nan Con
Island of the Dogs
Lon nam Manac
Monks Meadow
Port Ceann Aindrea
Port of Andrew's Headland
Eilean nan Slat
Island of Tangles
Sgeir Leathan
The Broad Skerry
Stac Liath
The Grey Stack
Sgeir Uilleim
William's Rock
Sgeirean Bhun-an-Uisge
Water-Foot Skerries
183
Thiridh
Man's
Camus Cul an Taibh
Bay at the Back of the Ocean
Sgeir na Caoineig
The Weeper's Rock
Port Ghealtain
Port of the Coward
Port na Cloiche
Port of the Stone

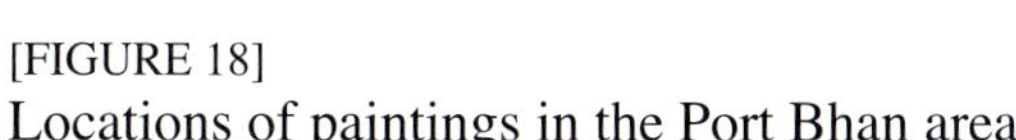

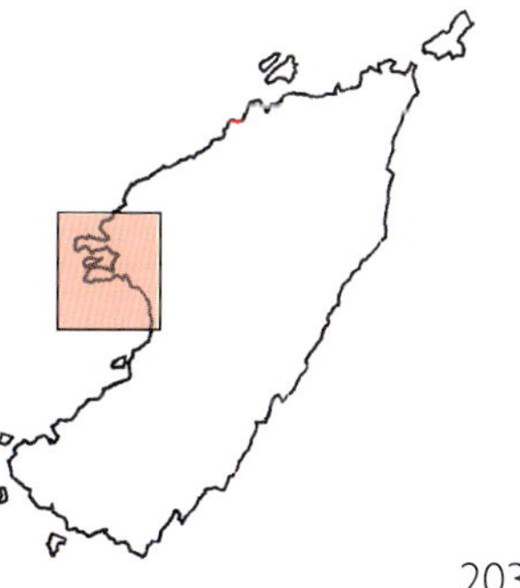

[FIGURE 18]
Locations of paintings in the Port Bhan area

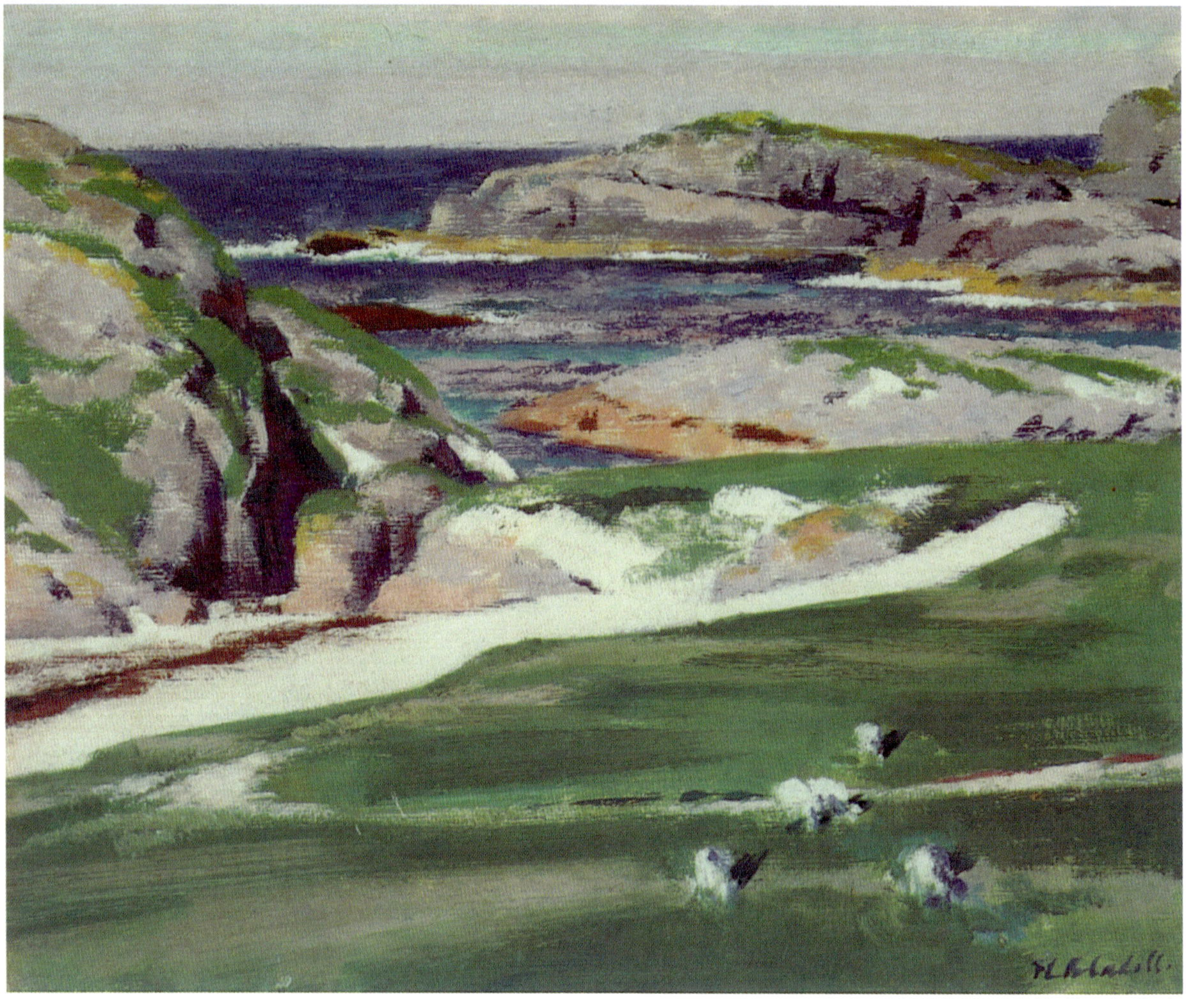

[PLATE 185]

F. C. B. Cadell

Port Bhan from above
Port Grulainn
(Port Bhan, Iona)
Oil 15 x 18

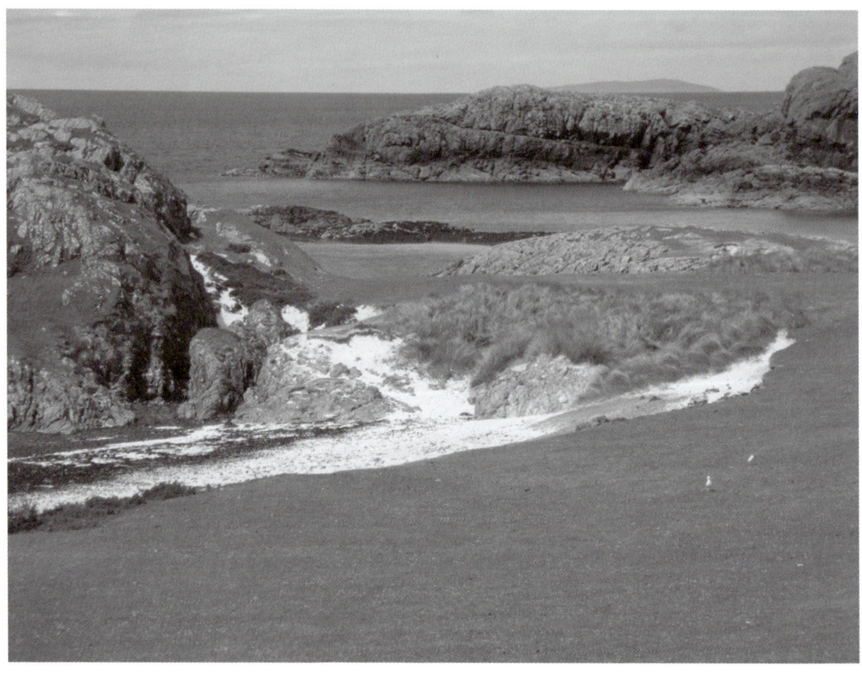

Photograph 2009

This was painted from the top of a little crag on the right of the approach to Port Bhan from The Machair. The headland is Stac a'Chorr, on the north side of Port Bhan.

The island on the horizon in the photograph is Tiree.

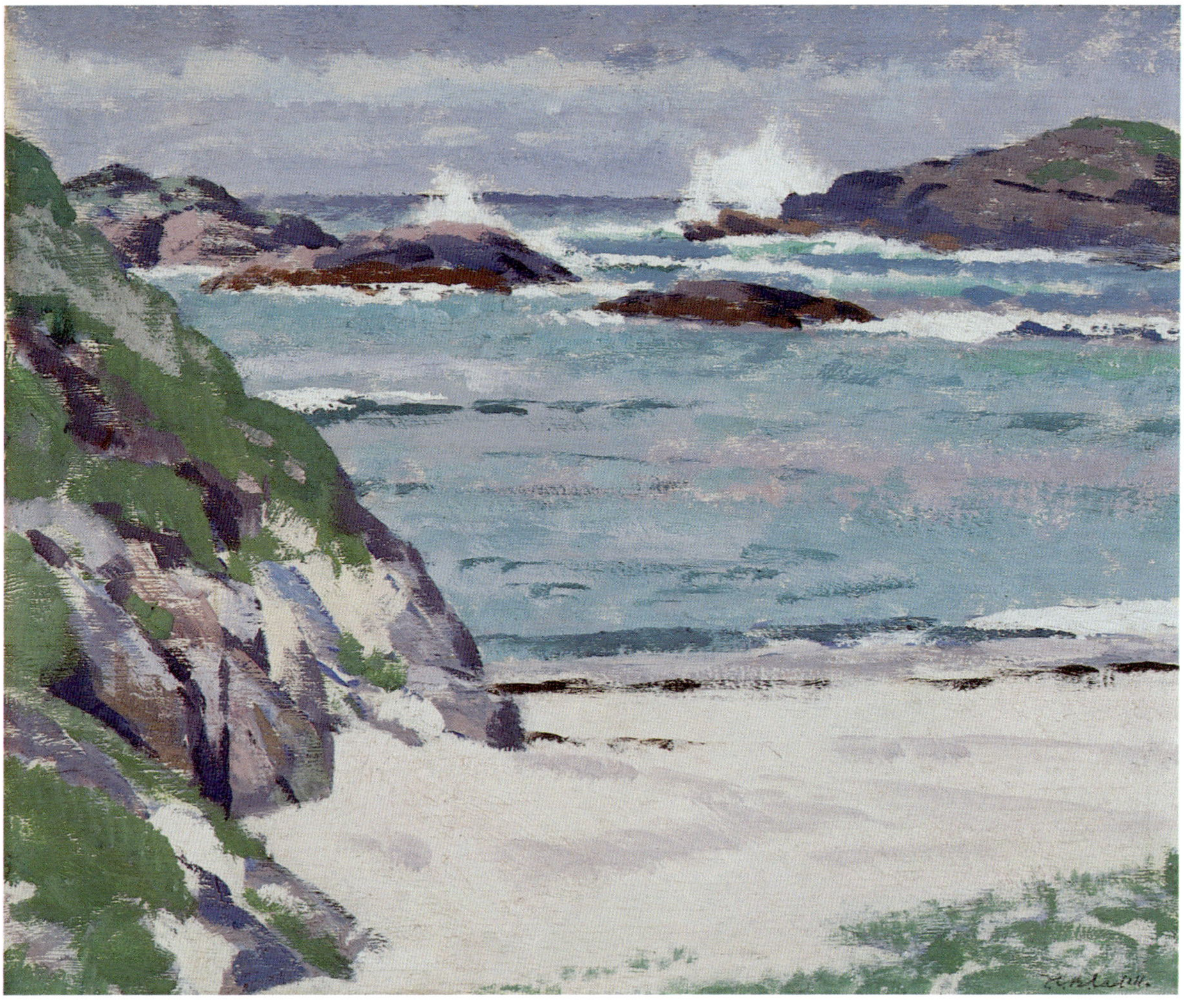

[PLATE 186]

F. C. B. Cadell

Port Pollarain

Oil 16 x 20

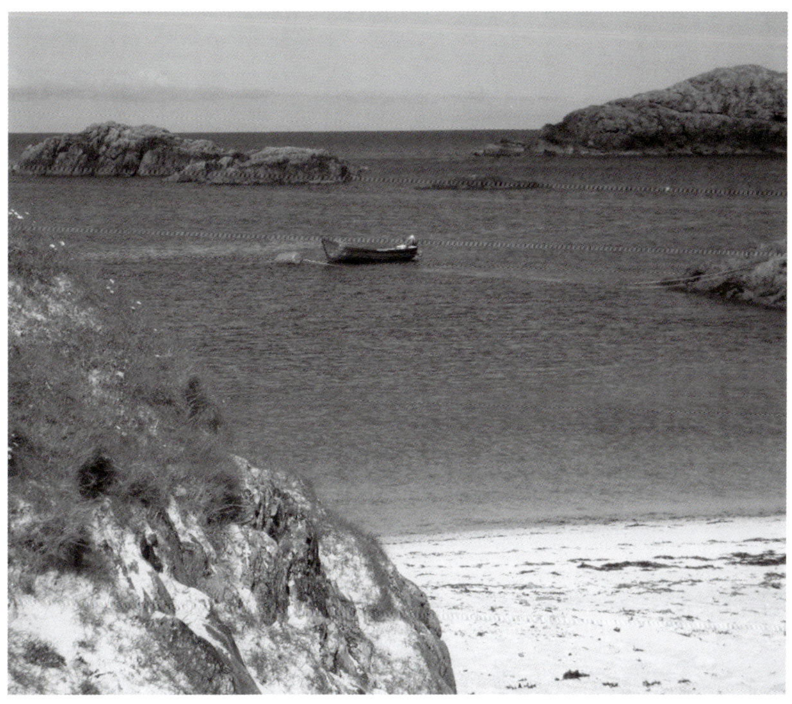

Photograph 2009

Port Pollarain is the small bay to the south of Port Bhan. The headland on the right is Stac a'Chorr which is on the north side of Port Bhan.

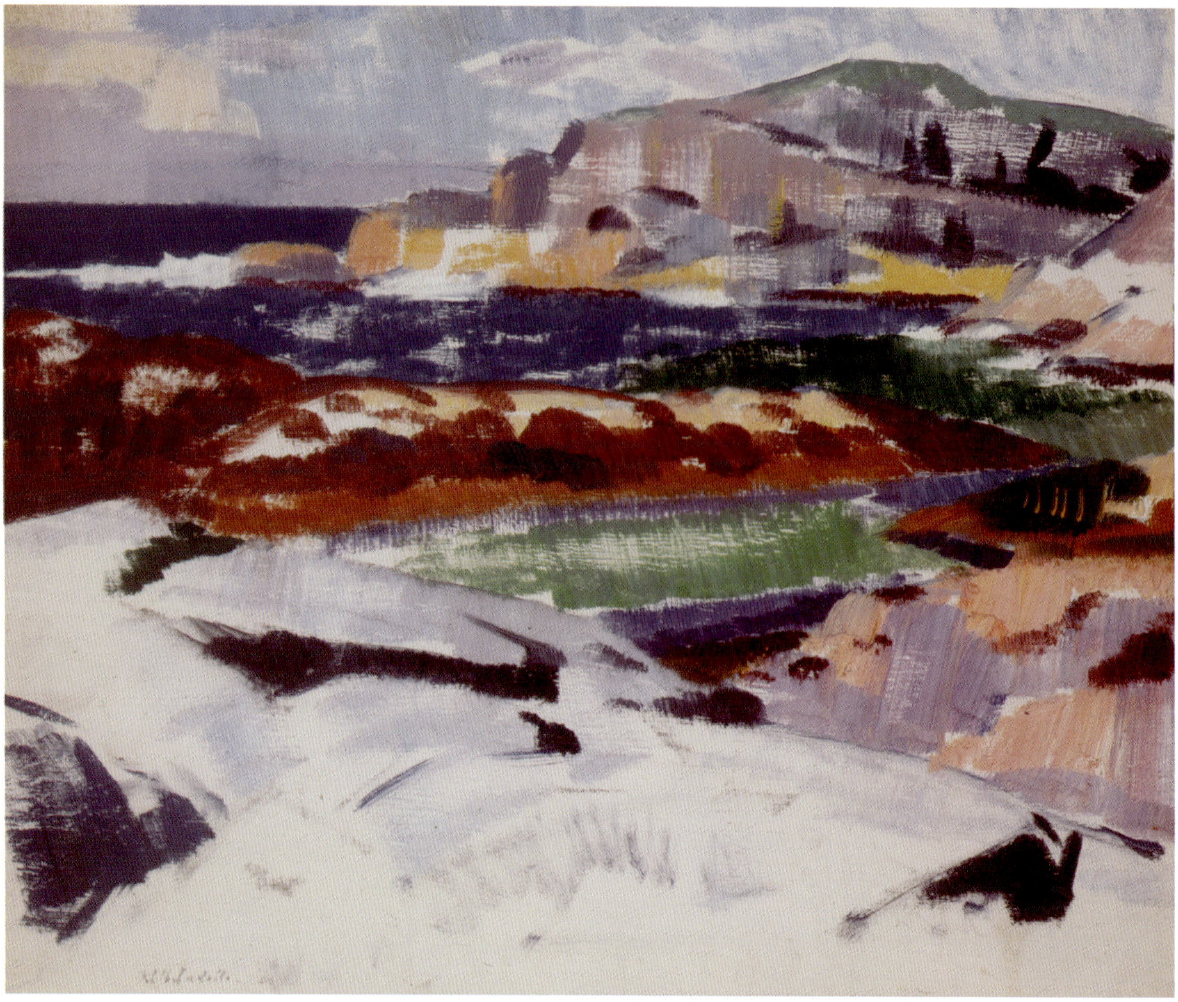

[PLATE 187]

F. C. B. Cadell

Stac a' Chorr, Port Bhan

Oil 15 x 18

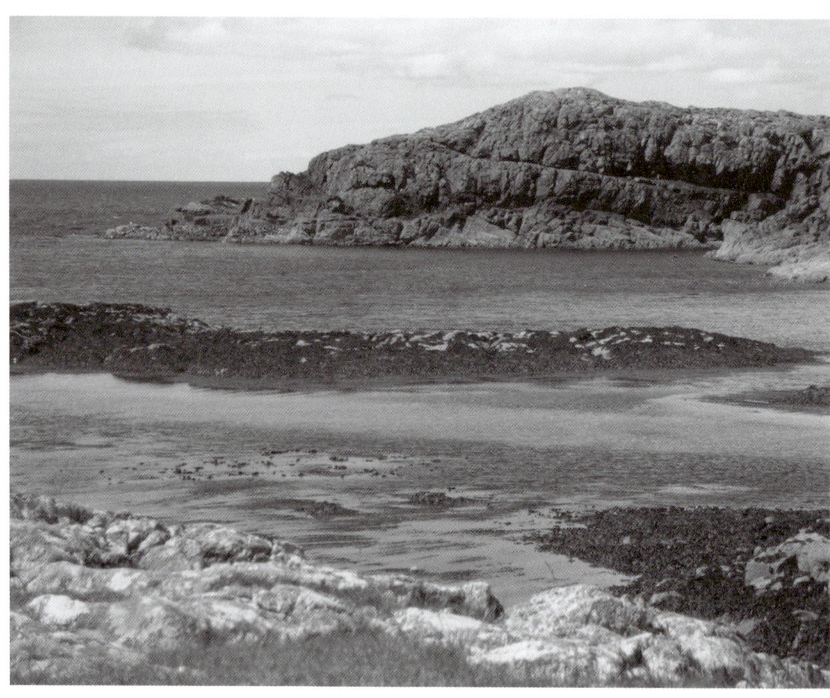

Photograph 2009

Plates 187 and 188 were painted from the peninsula that separates Port Pollarain from Port Bhan. From here it is possible, at low tide, to walk down onto the beach of Port Bhan, but once the sea reaches the steeper rocks it is necessary to go round via Port Pollarain.

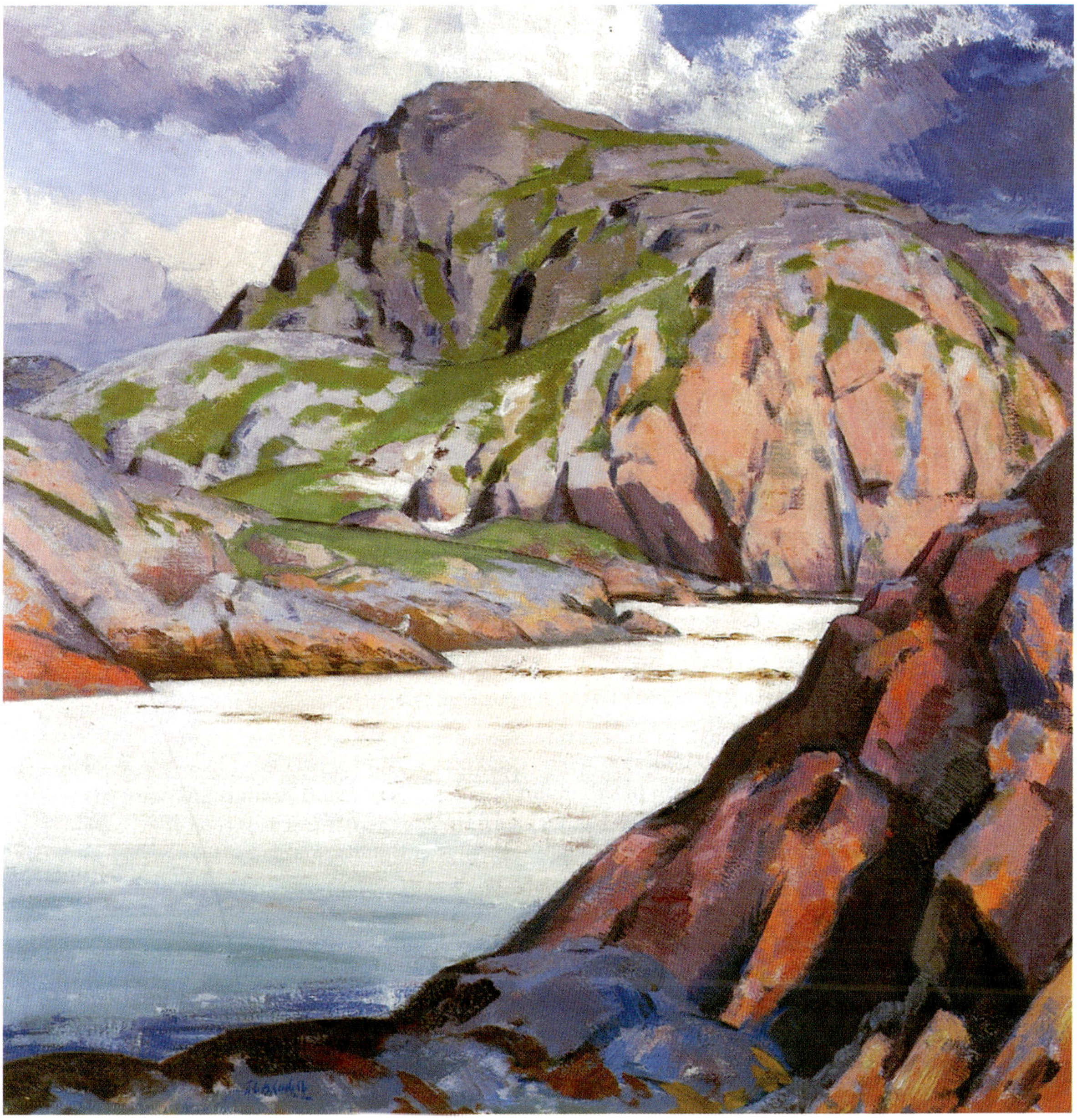

[PLATE 188]

F. C. B. Cadell

Dun Bhuirg from Port Bhan

Oil 30 x 30

This is probably the best-known view of Port Bhan.

Dun Bhuirg, Hill of the Fort, is seen here beyond the bay of Port Bhan. Despite being only 51 metres high, Dun Bhuirg is a prominent feature in this part of the island. It has an overhanging rockface on the northwest side and is very steep on the other faces.

The pink crag on the right above the end of the beach is the subject of Plate 190.

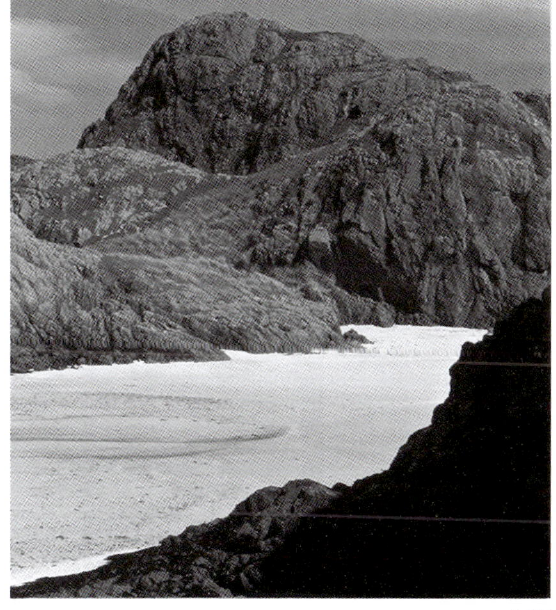

Photograph 2009

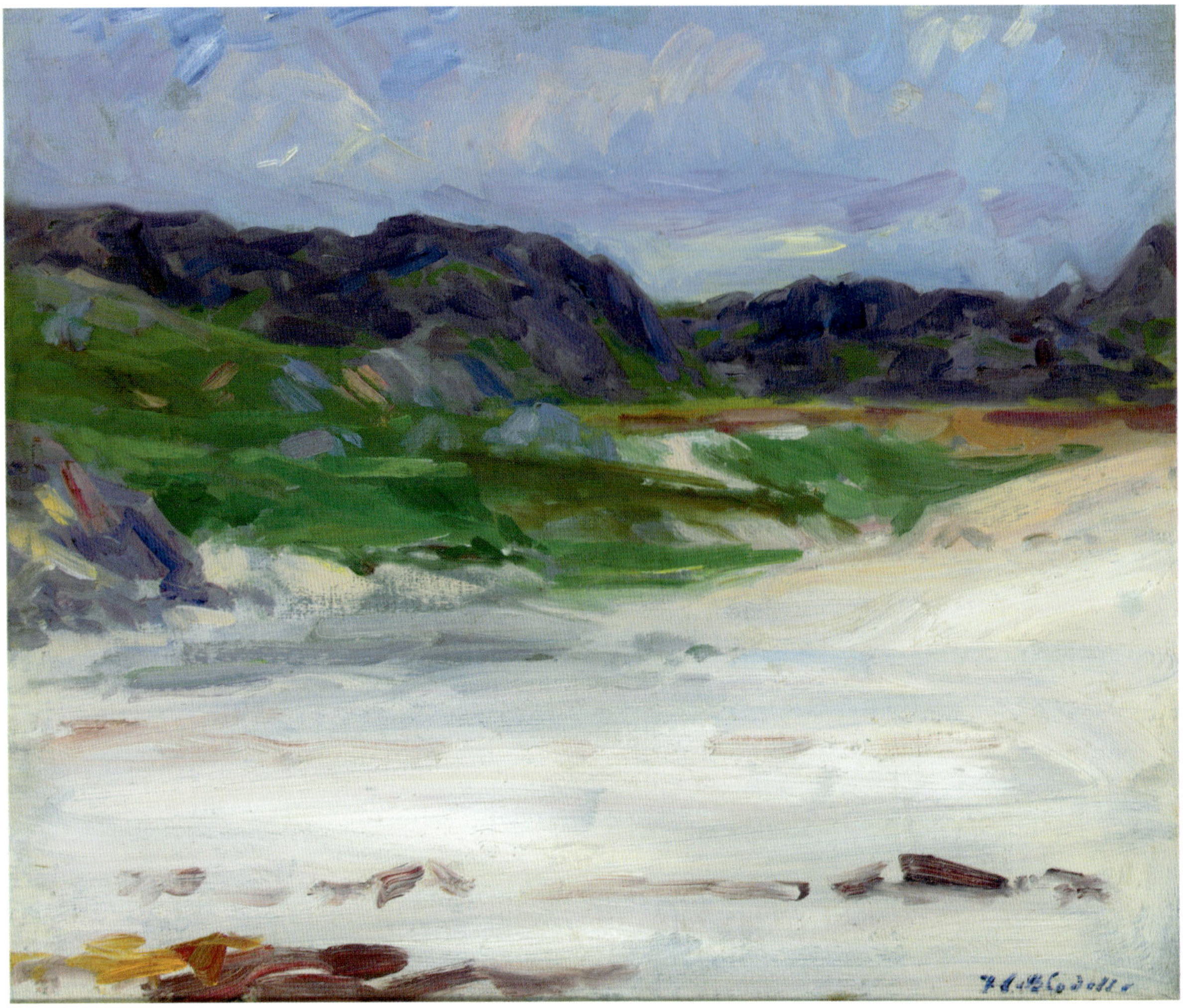

[PLATE 189]

F. C. B. Cadell

Port Bhan

Oil 15 x 18

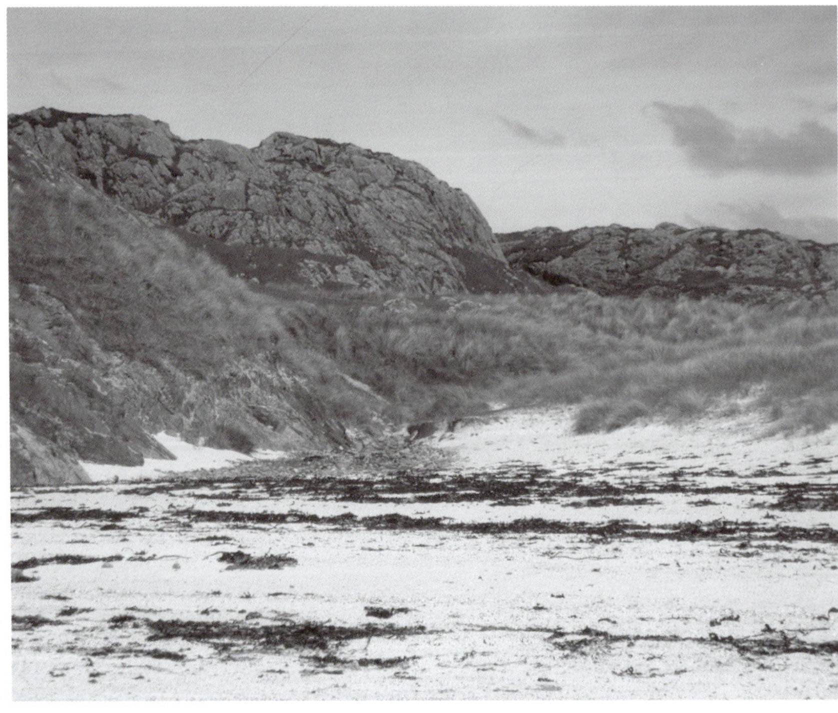

Photograph 2009

This is the view inland from the beach. The pink crag in Plates 188 and 190 is out of the picture to the left.

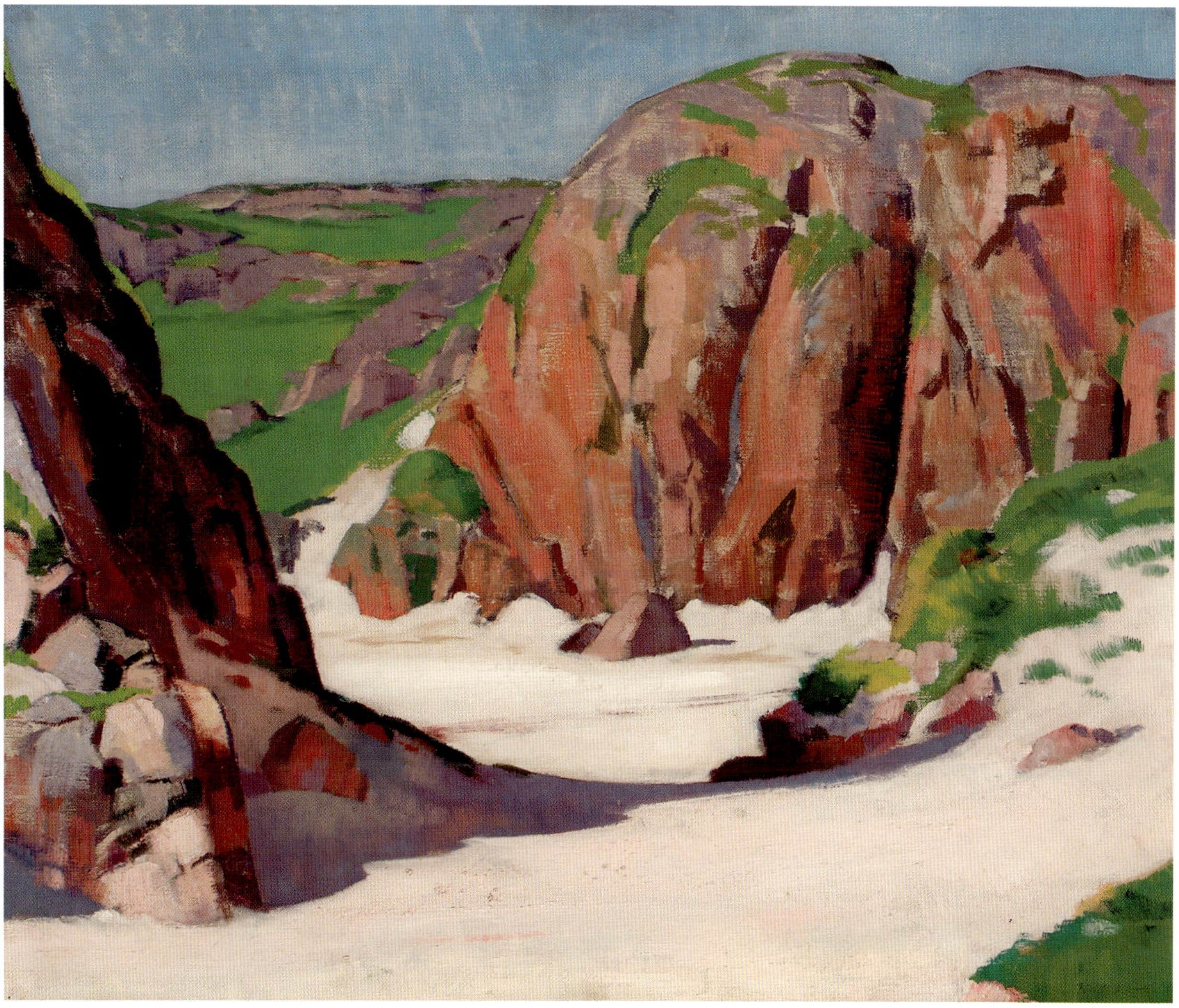

[PLATE 190]
F. C. B. Cadell
Port Bhan
Oil 25 x 30

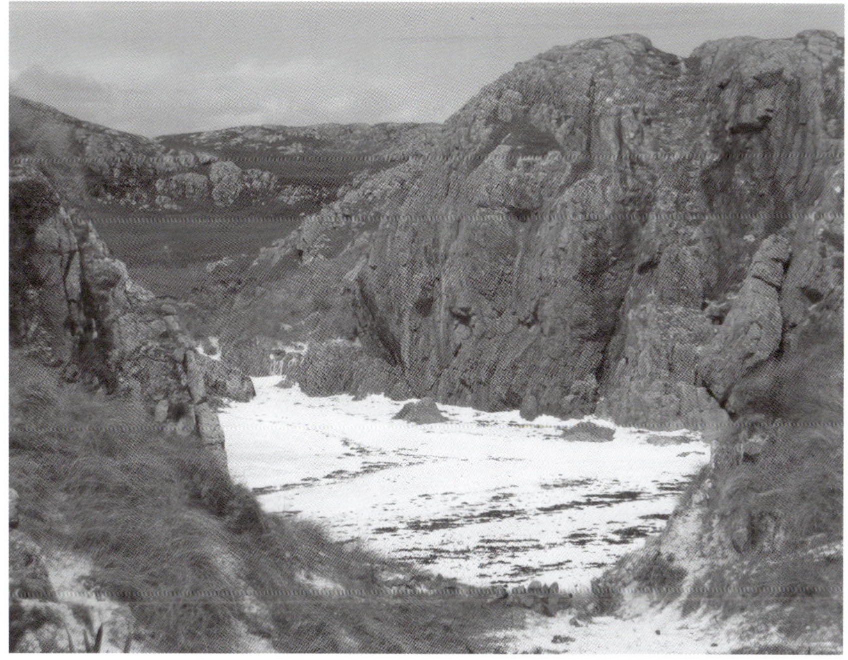

Photograph 2009

Although the sea does not appear in this painting, the highest tides do reach the base of the crag.

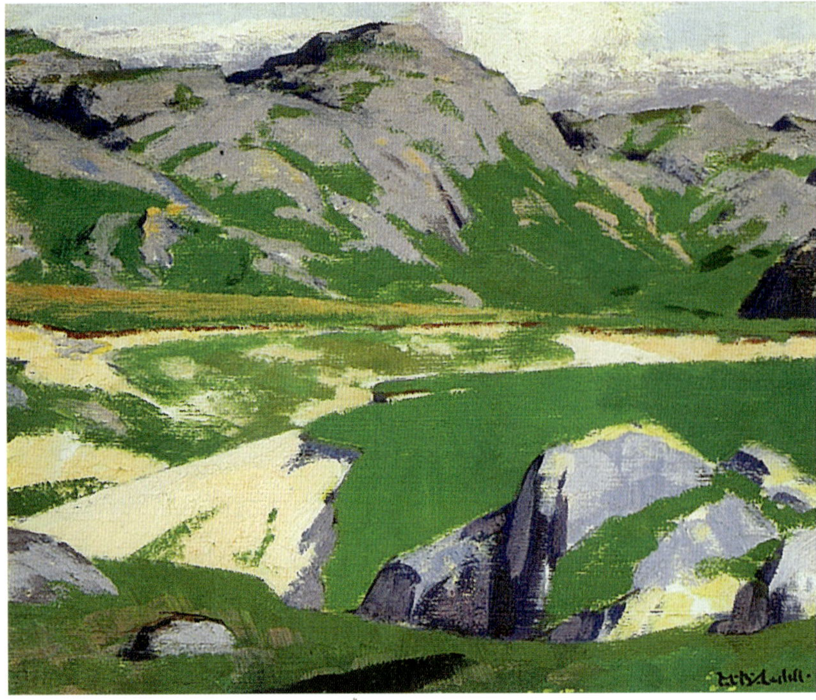

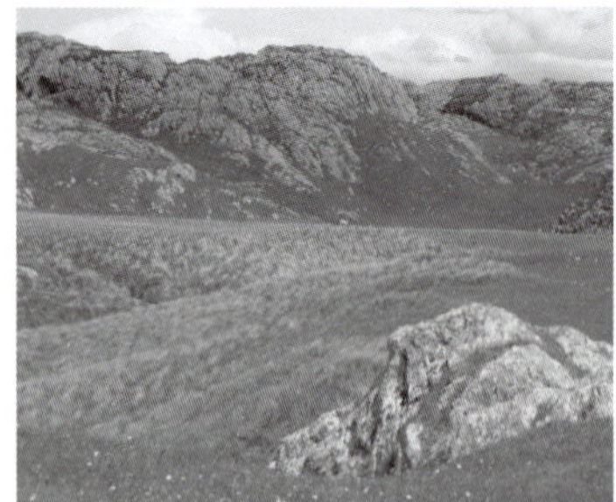

Photograph 2009

[PLATE 191]
F. C. B. Cadell
Port Bhan
Oil 15 x 17

Painted from the top of the crag that separates Port Bhan from Port Pollarain, this is the view to the east away from the sea. The white sand, which provides a bright tonal contrast in Cadell's picture, was covered in marram grass when the corresponding photograph was taken.

THE EAST SHORE FROM THE MARBLE QUARRY TO THE VILLAGE

From Port Bhan to the Marble Quarry, the site of the next painting location, is a walk of three kilometres (nearly two miles). The route is shown on page 17. On the way up to Loch Staonaig from The Machair one passes the place where the photograph of Peploe, his wife Margaret and son Denis was taken, with the Bay at the Back of the Ocean behind them (Figure 19).

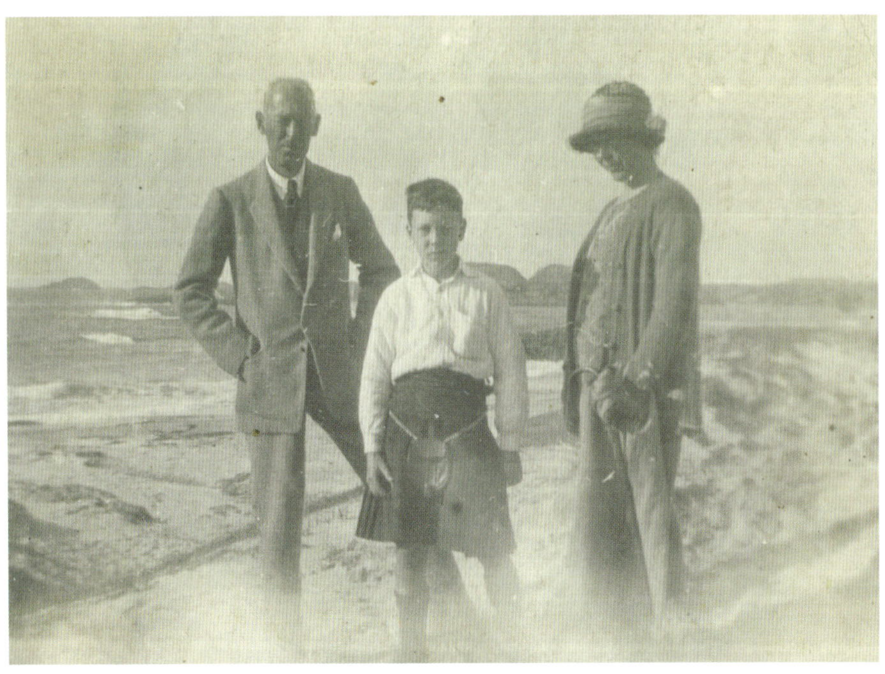

[FIGURE 19]
Peploe, Denis, and Margaret on Iona c. 1925

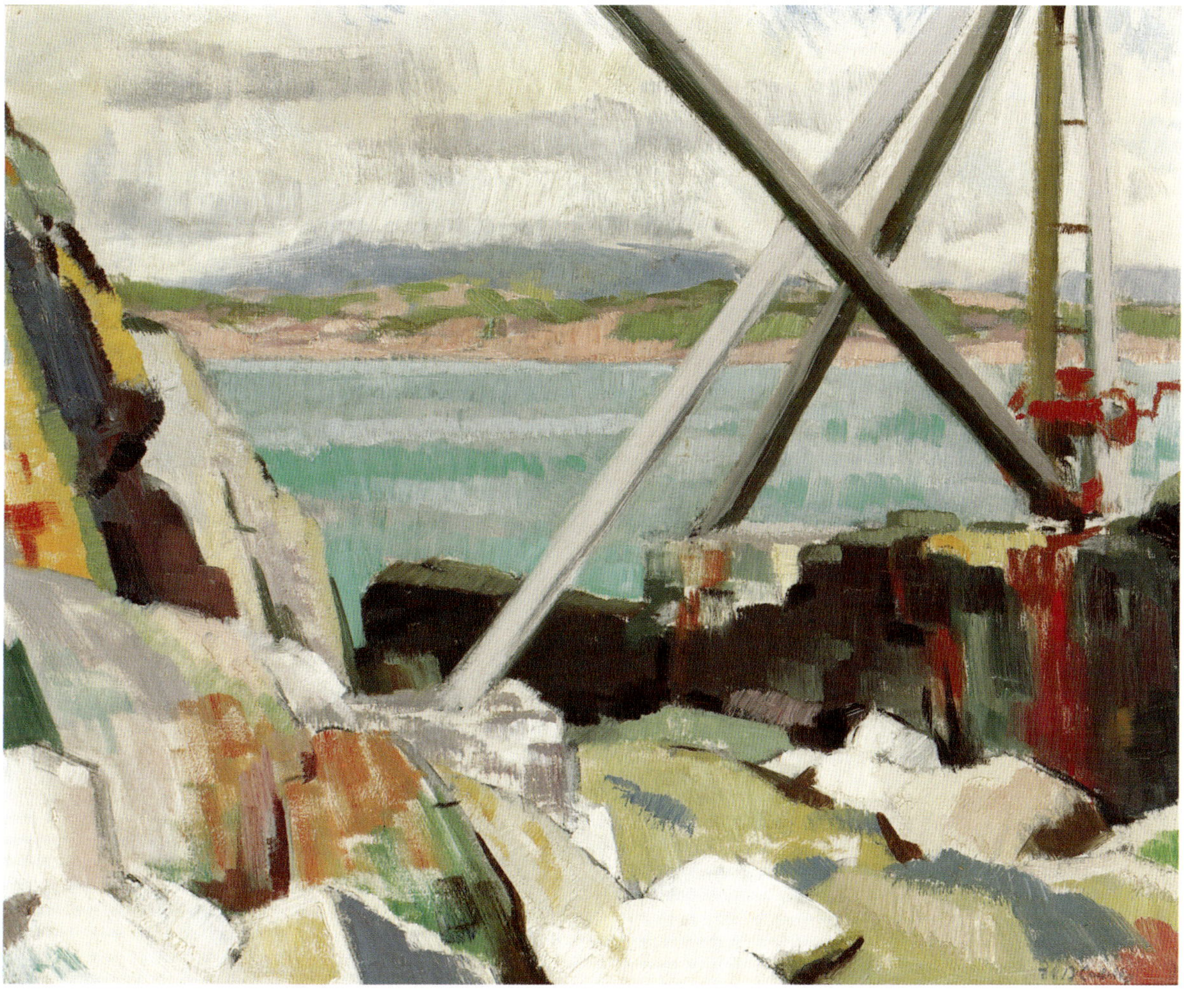

[PLATE 192]

F. C. B. Cadell

The Marble Quarry

Oil 15 x 18

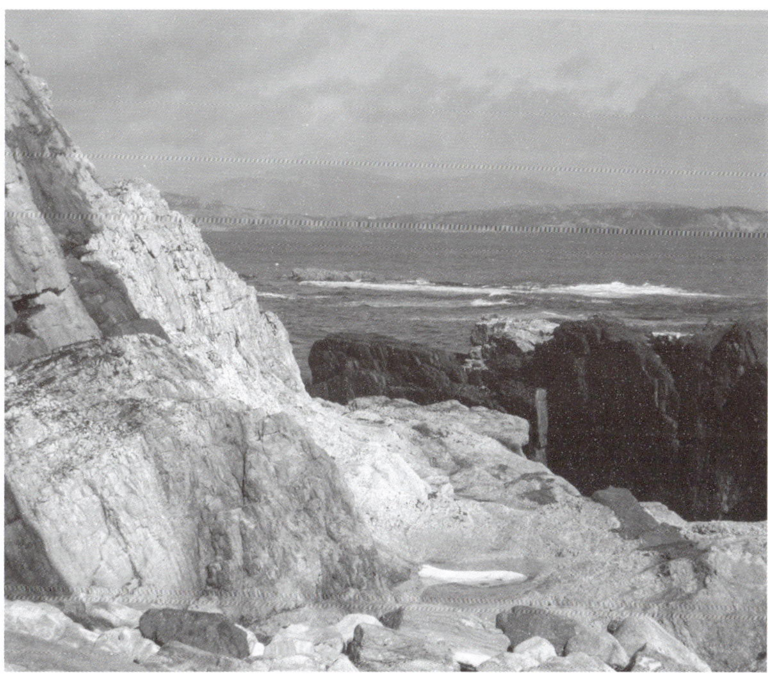

Photograph 2010

The derrick, which was used for loading the marble into boats, is no longer there, but its pivot and the bolts that secured it remain and mark its former position. However some other pieces of machinery do survive. The view is across the Sound of Iona, with the Ross of Mull and the Burg in the background.

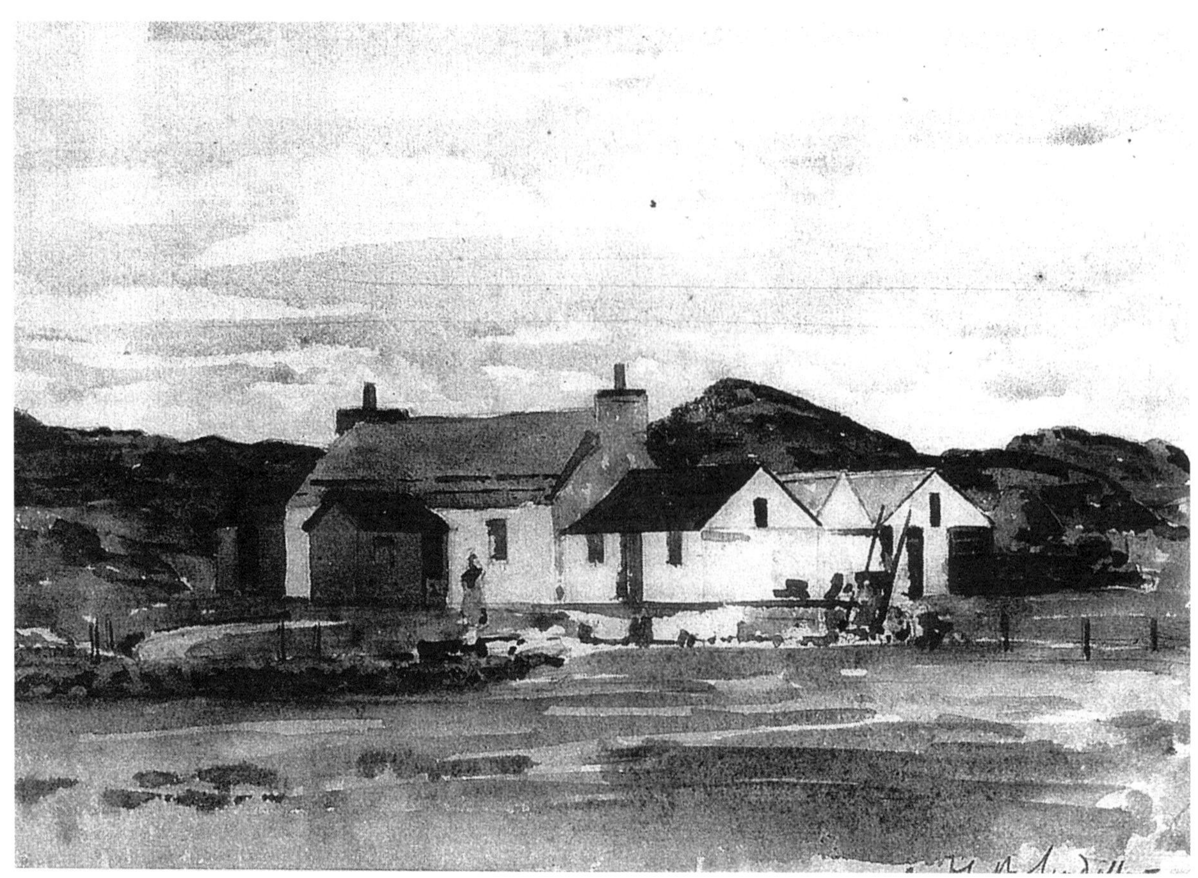

[PLATE 193]
F. C. B. Cadell
Ruanaich Croft
Watercolour 7 x 10

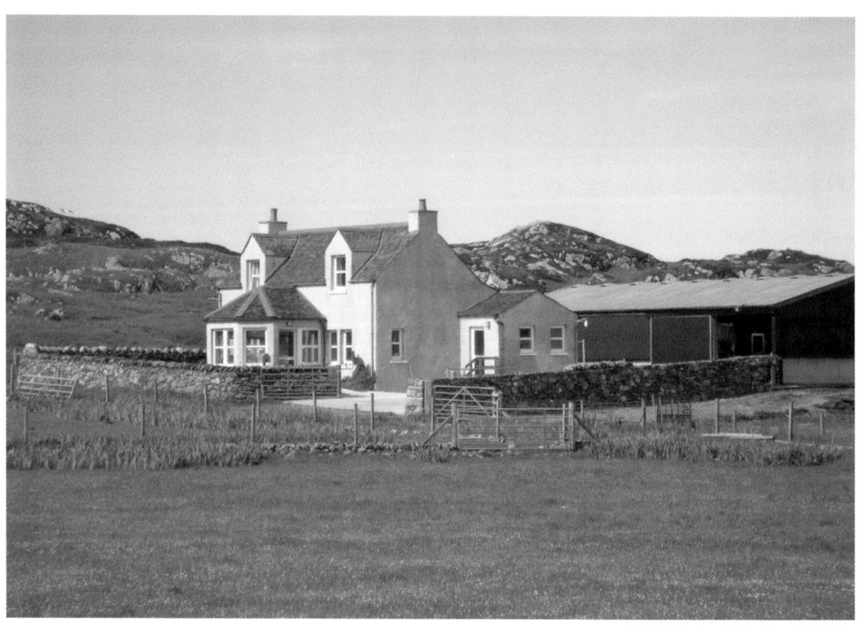

Photograph 2009

The track from the Marble Quarry back over the moorland is somewhat indistinct, but returns to the end of the lane which passes in front of the Ruanaich Croft.

The buildings in Cadell's painting stood behind the present house, which was built in 1966. The old buildings were finally demolished in 2004, and were replaced by the farm store seen on the right in the photograph.

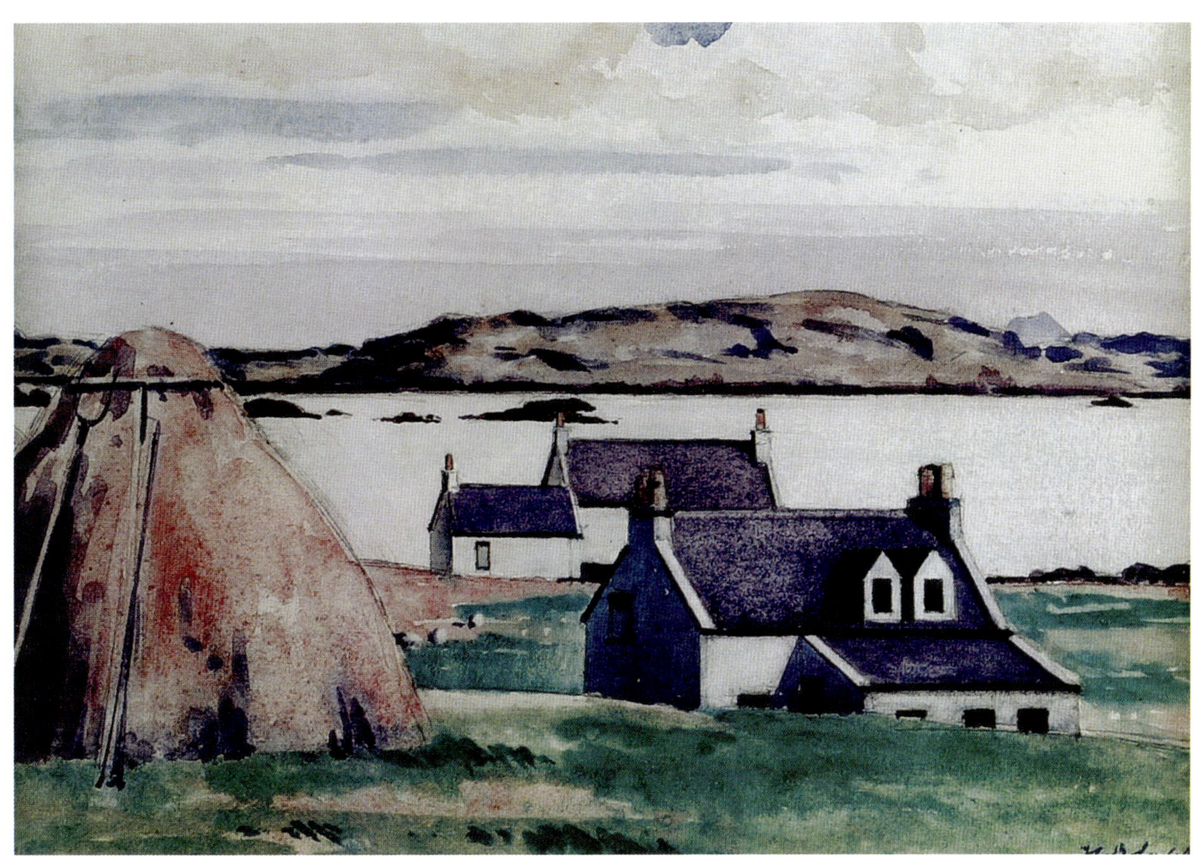

[PLATE 194]
F. C. B. Cadell
Tigh Shee
Watercolour 7 x 10

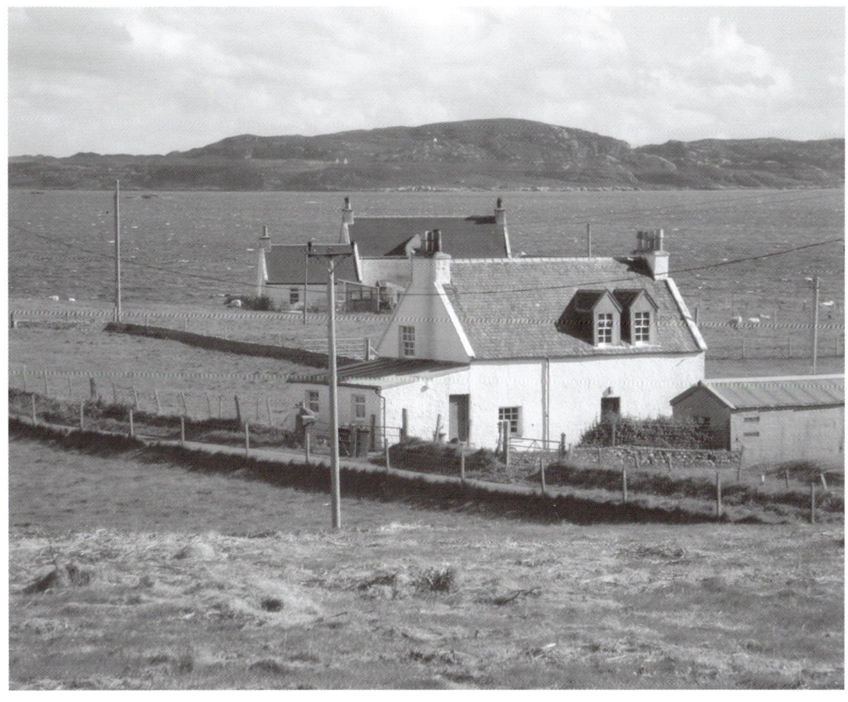

Photograph 2010

Cadell stayed here for some of his visits to Iona; it is probable that the pictures of this part of the island were painted on these occasions. The house in the background is Greenbank (see Plate 197). The Ross of Mull is in the distance.

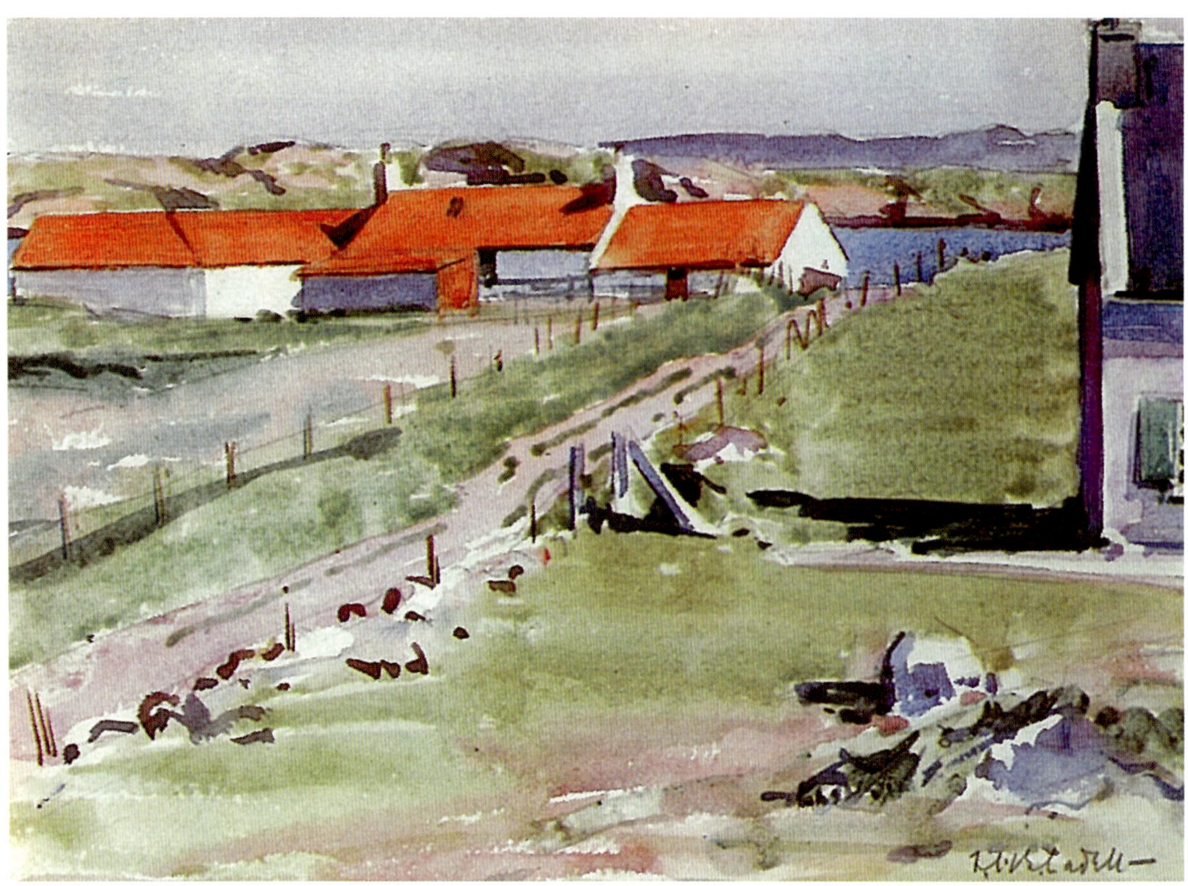

[PLATE 195]
F. C. B. Cadell
Towards the Sound from Tigh Shee (Red Roofs, Iona)
Watercolour 10 x 14

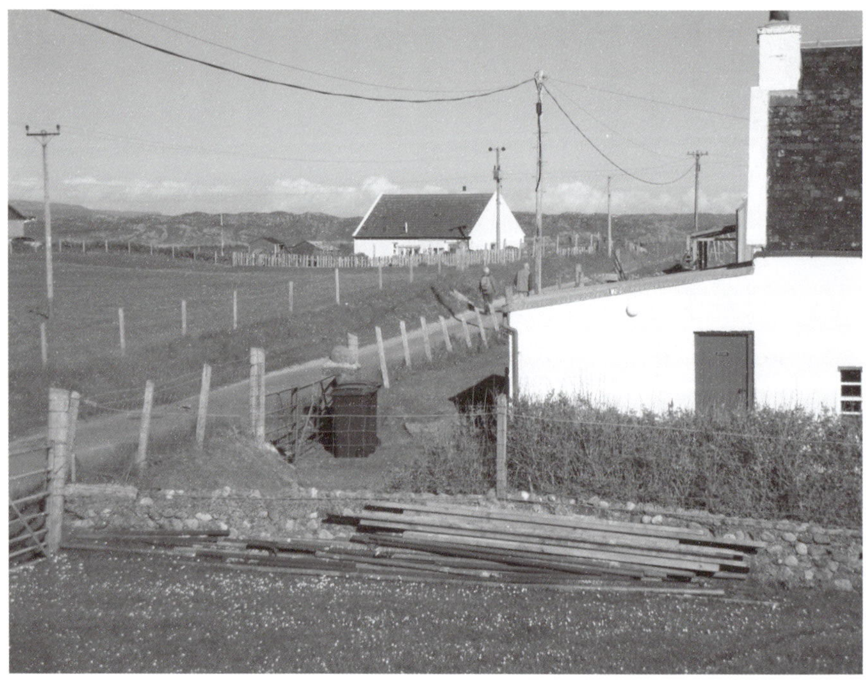

Photograph 2013

The gable wall of Tigh Shee is at the extreme right-hand side of this view down the lane, known as Bruthach na Ceapaich, which leads from Four Roads down to the shore at Port Beag na Sligeanaich.

The red-roofed buildings in the painting were demolished in the 1960s, and the house that replaced them, seen in the photograph, was built in 1983.

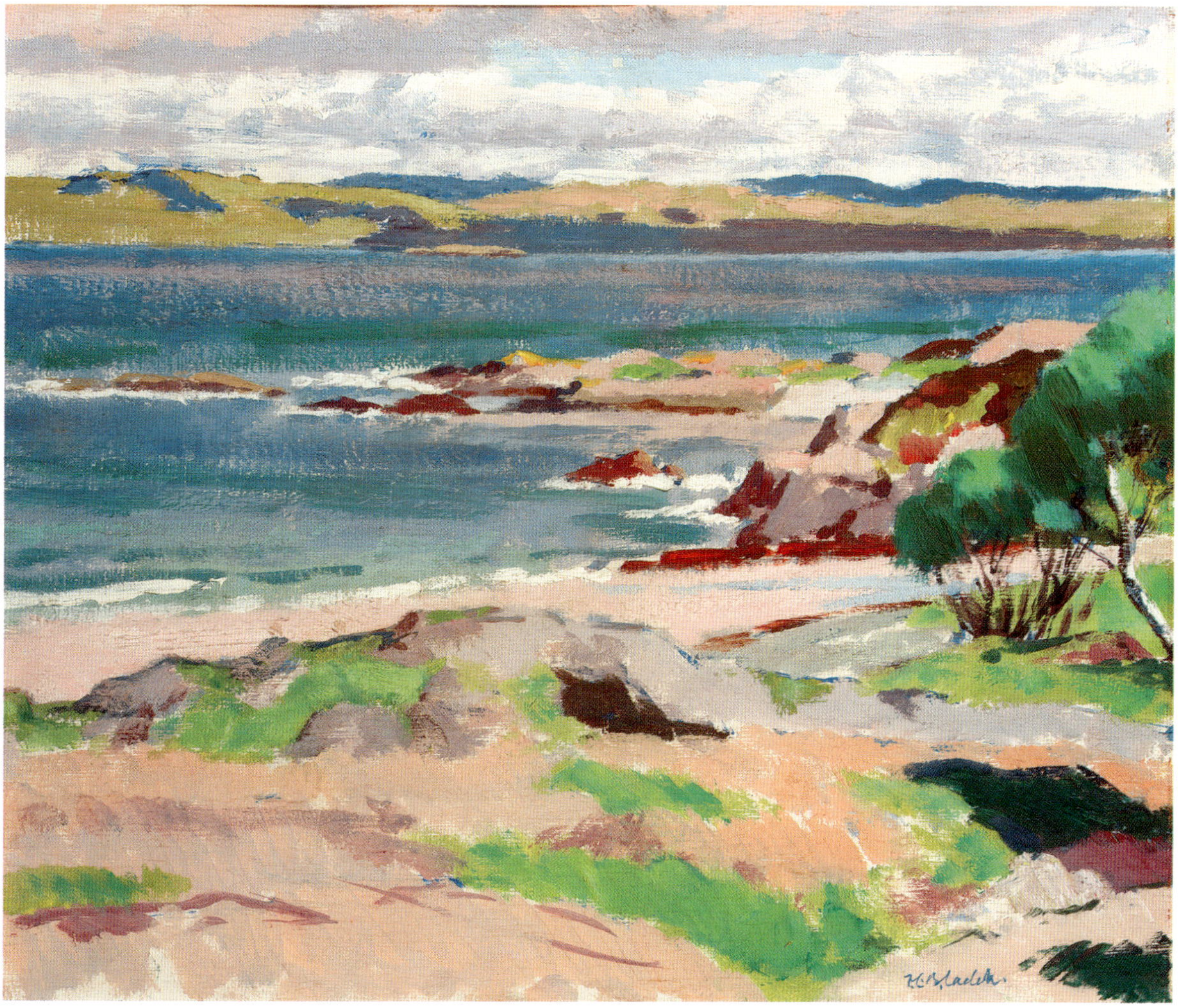

[PLATE 196]
F. C. B. Cadell
Ross of Mull
from Traigh Mhor
Oil 14 x 17

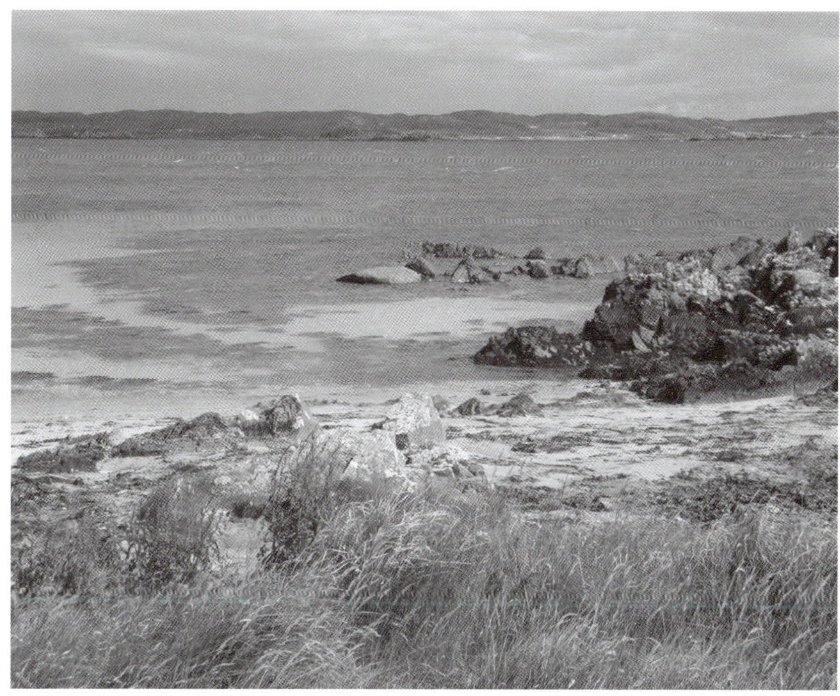

Photograph 2009

From this location it is just a short walk to Sandeels Bay, which may be reached along the sands of Traigh Mhor at very low tide, but otherwise is most easily approached via Bealach na Leacaich (Flagstone Pass). Sandeels Bay has always been a popular picnic spot. Stewart Orr and William C. Crawford both painted there, and there is also a painting by Cadell (not illustrated).

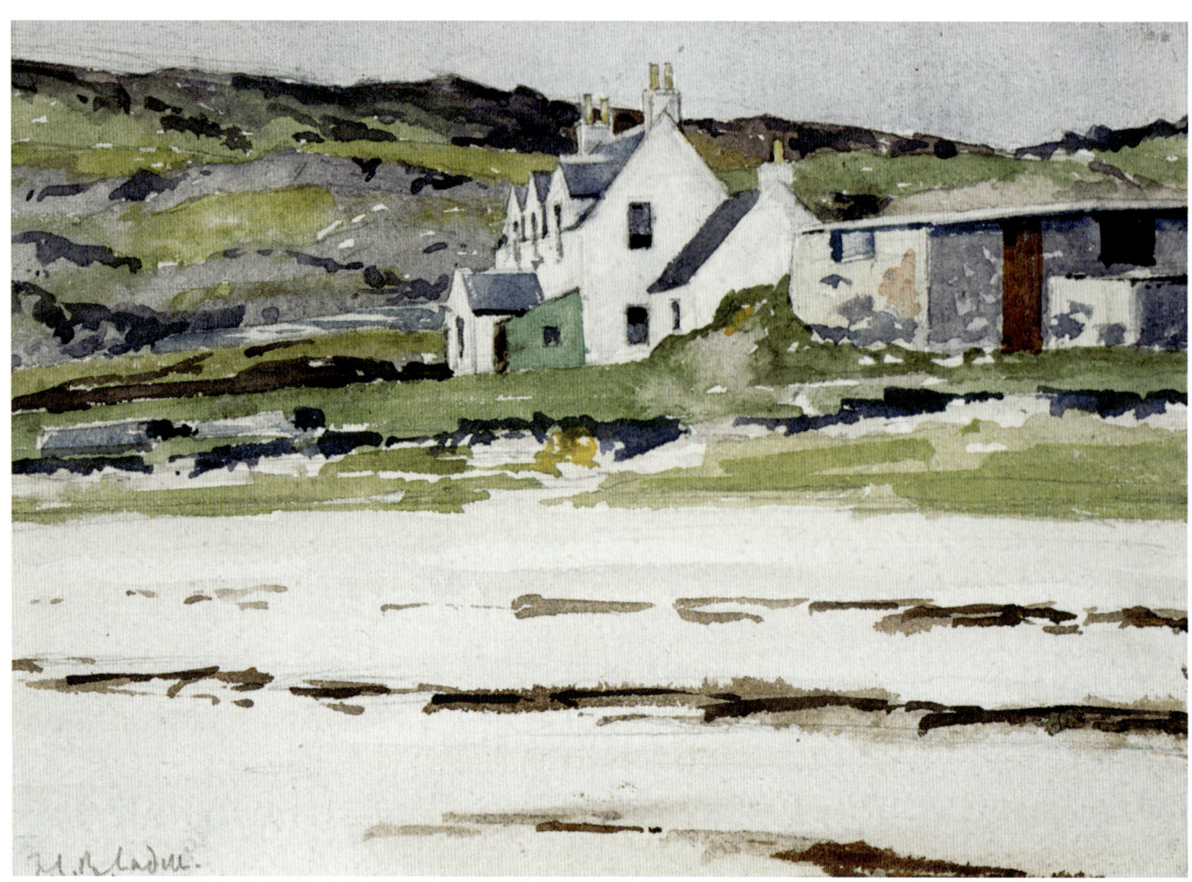

[PLATE 197]
F. C. B. Cadell
Greenbank
Watercolour 5 x 7

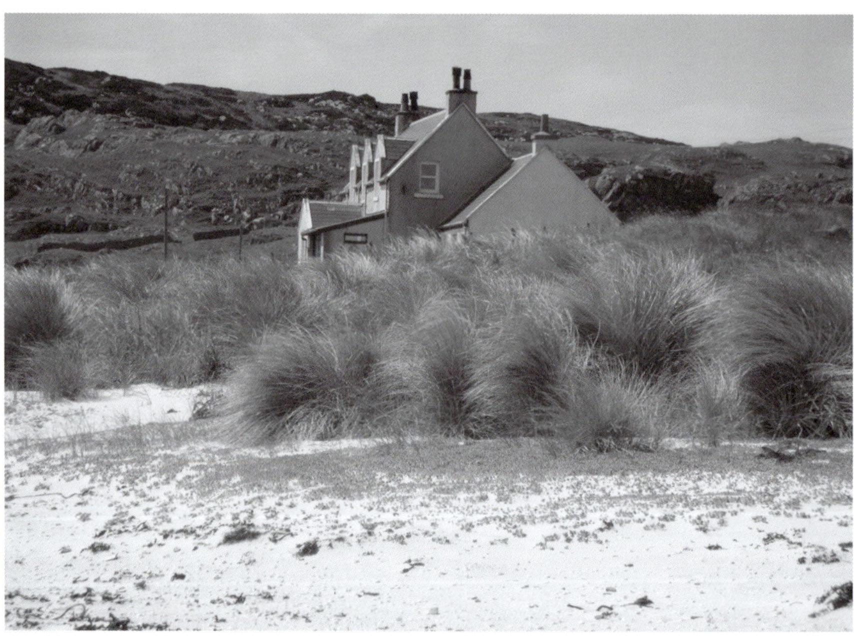

Photograph 2009

This view of Greenbank was painted from the beach opposite the end of the lane which descends from Four Roads.

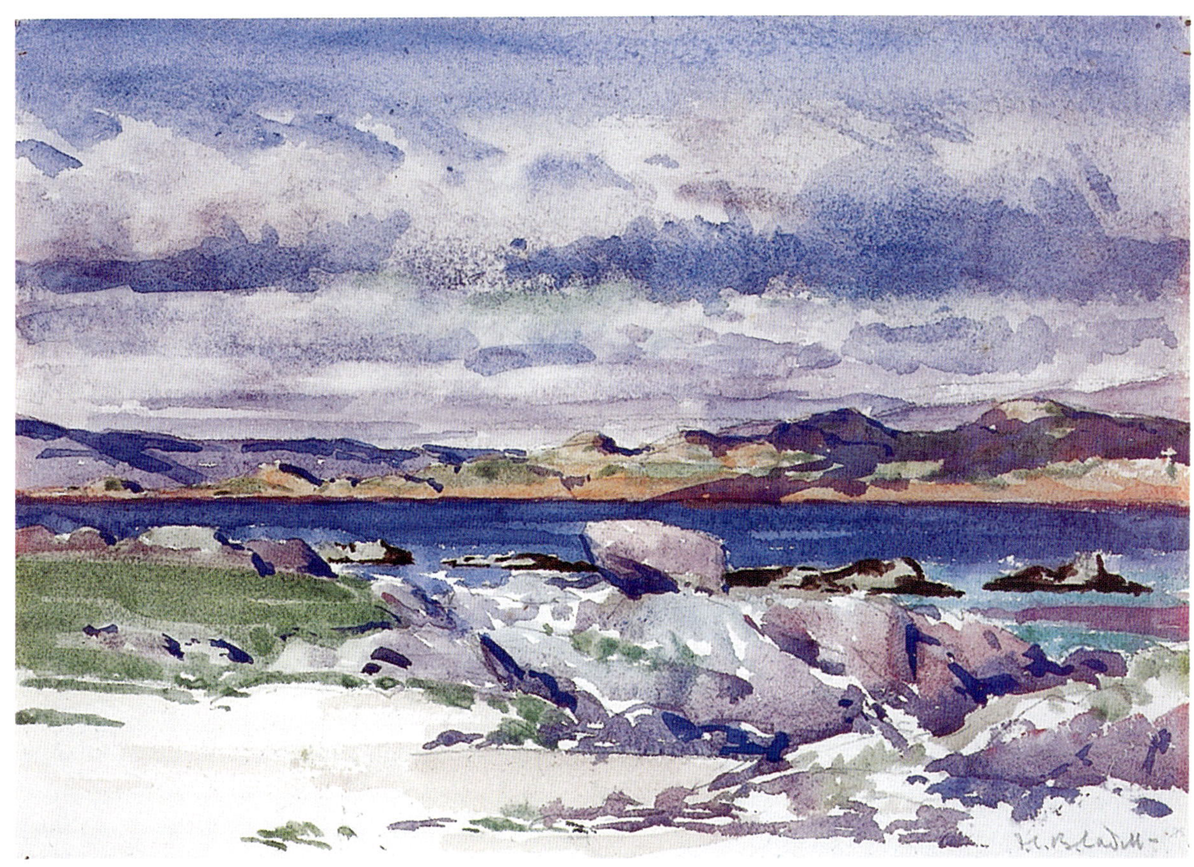

[PLATE 198]
F. C. B. Cadell
Erratic Boulder at Port Beag na Sligeanaich (Ross of Mull from Iona)
Watercolour 7 x 10

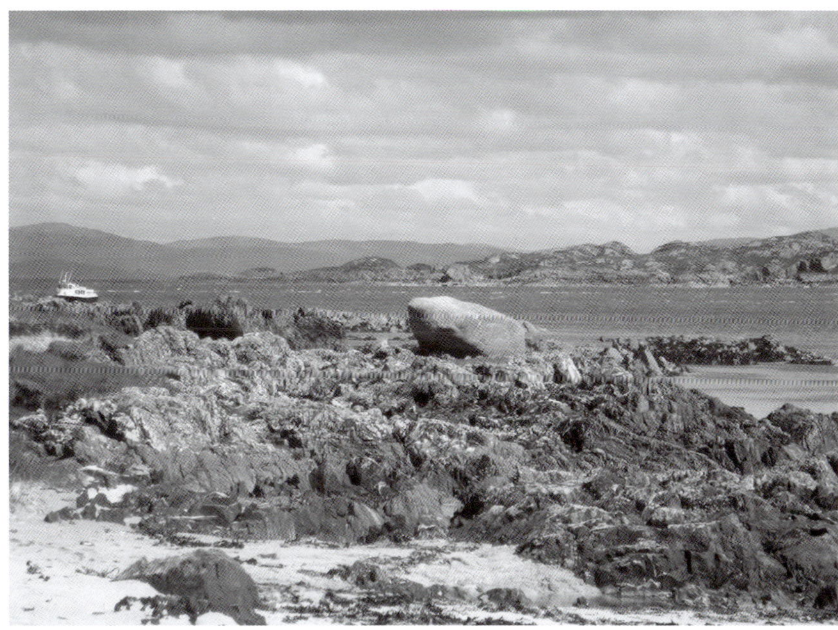

Photograph 2009

This boulder of Caledonian granite was transported to its present position from Mull during the last Ice Age. Resting on the Torridonian rocks, it is an unmistakable feature of this part of the shore.

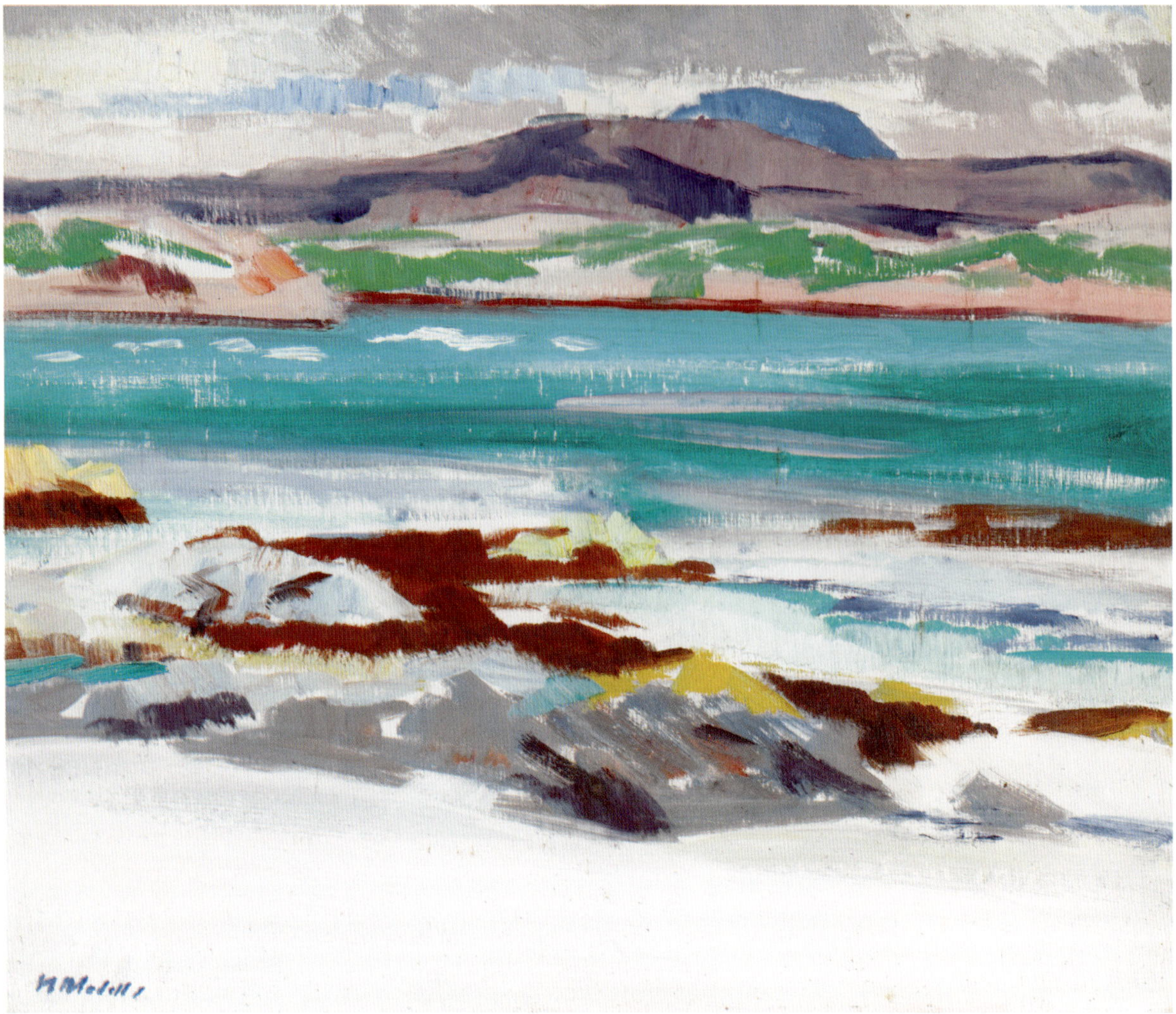

[PLATE 199]

F. C. B. Cadell

Ben More
from the East Shore
Oil 15 x 18

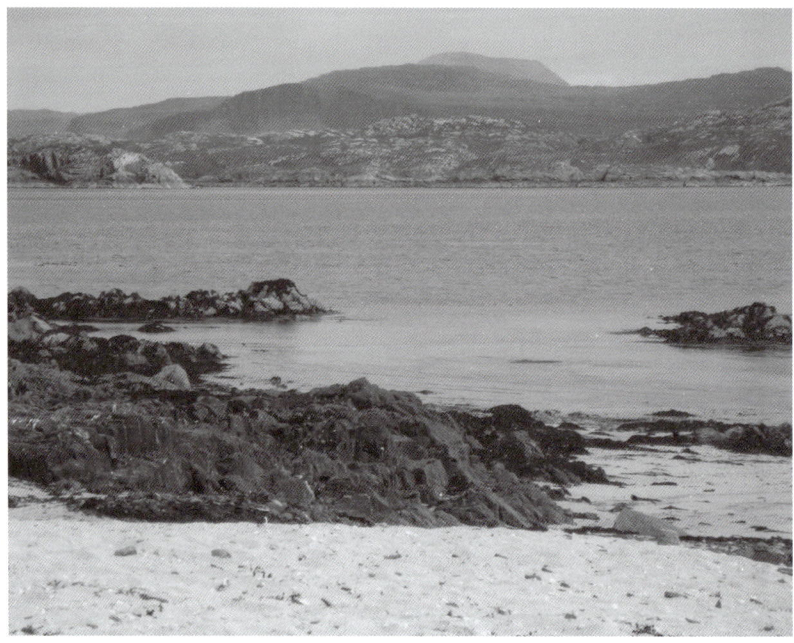

Photograph 2012

Painted from the same position as the previous painting, this is the view towards Ben More, seen here above the Burg. The Ross of Mull is in the middle distance and the south end of Eilean nam Ban is seen at the left-hand side.

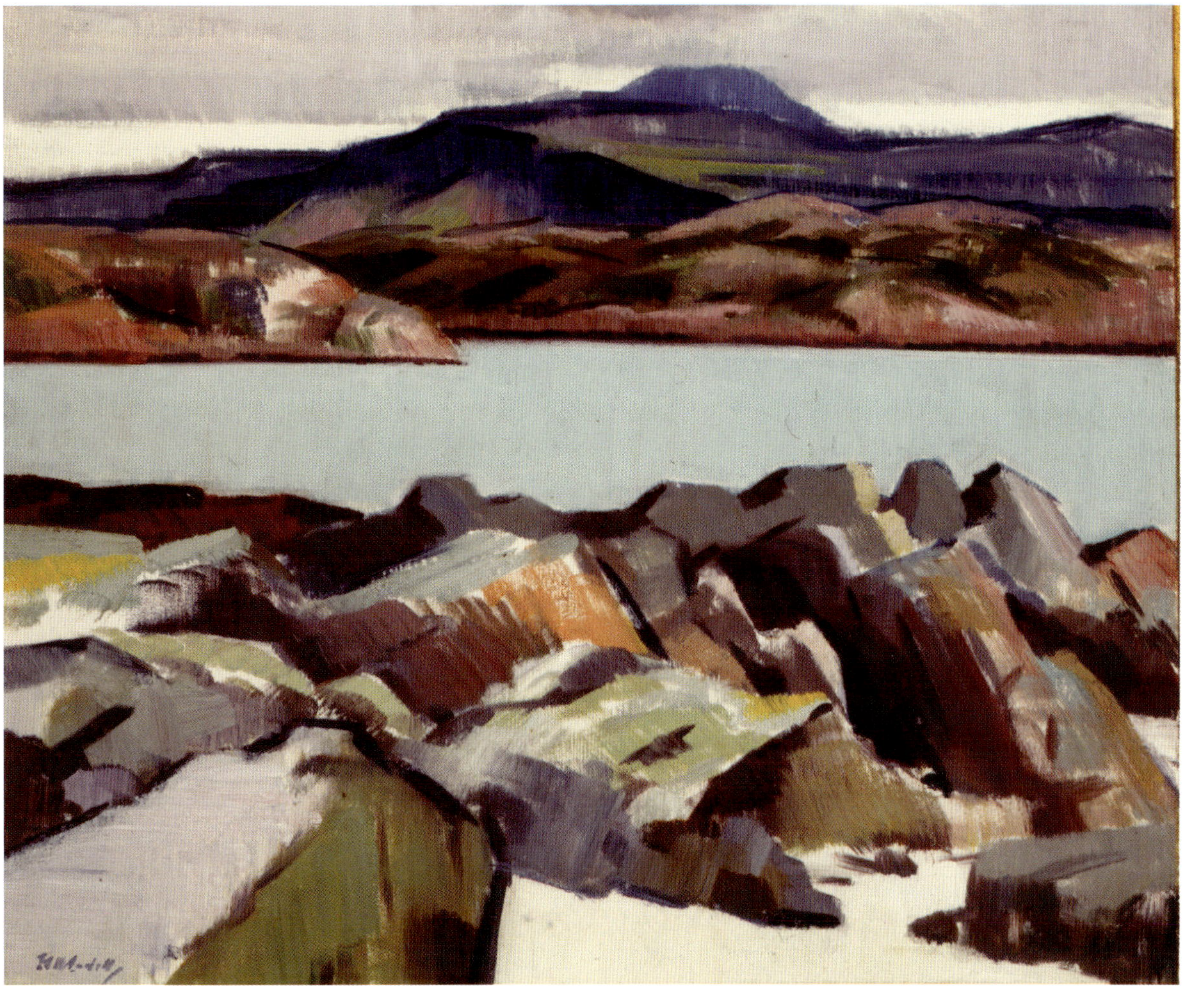

[PLATE 200]

F. C. B. Cadell

Ben More from above
Port Beag na Sligeanaich

Oil 15 x 18

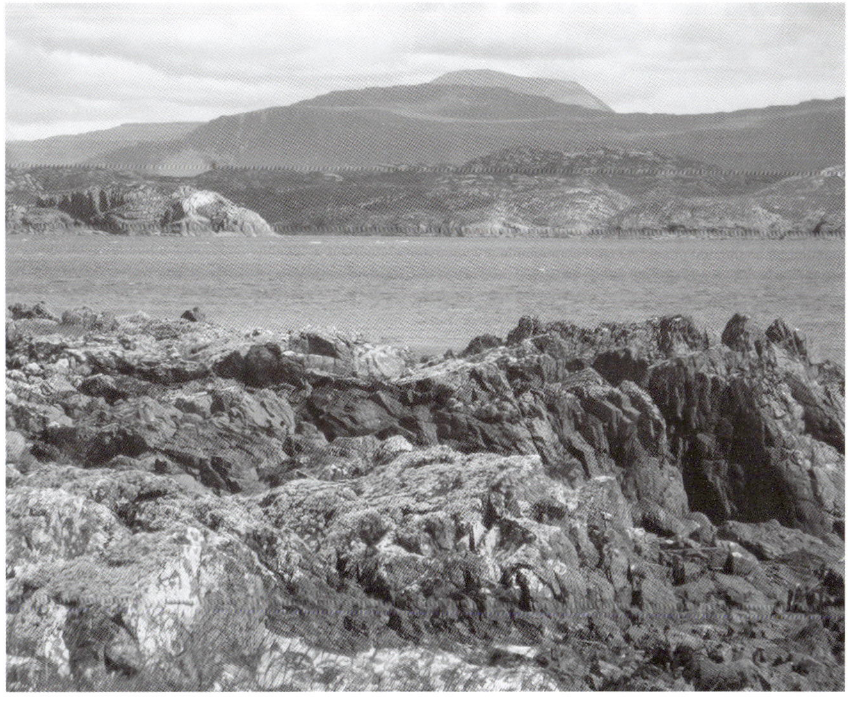

Photograph 2009

The distant elements in this picture are almost identical to those in Plate 199 opposite. However, having been painted from a little further along the shore, the foreground is different, but is easily identified by the group of pointed rocks at the right-hand side.

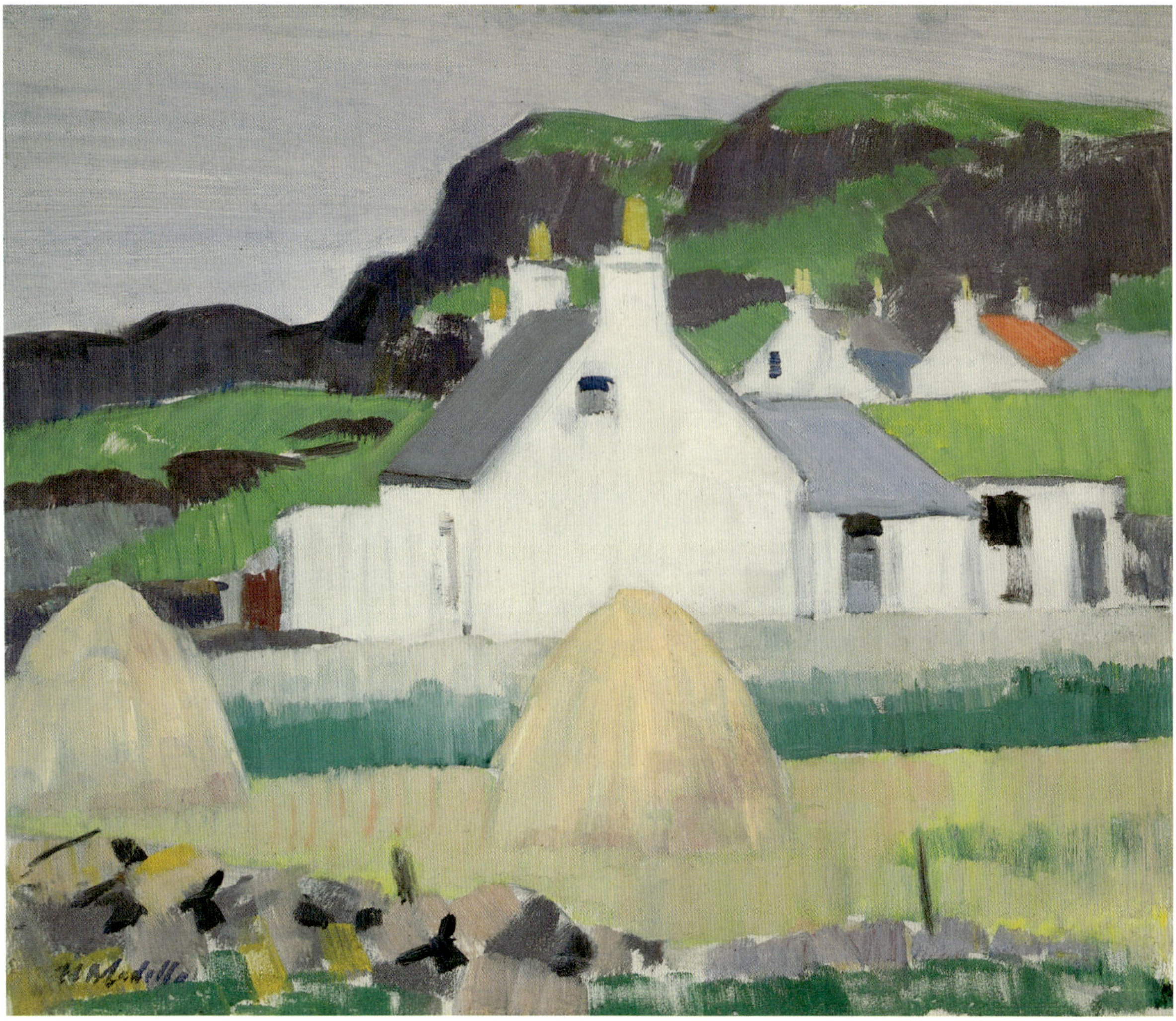

[PLATE 201]

F. C. B. Cadell

Gair na Mara

Oil 15 x 18

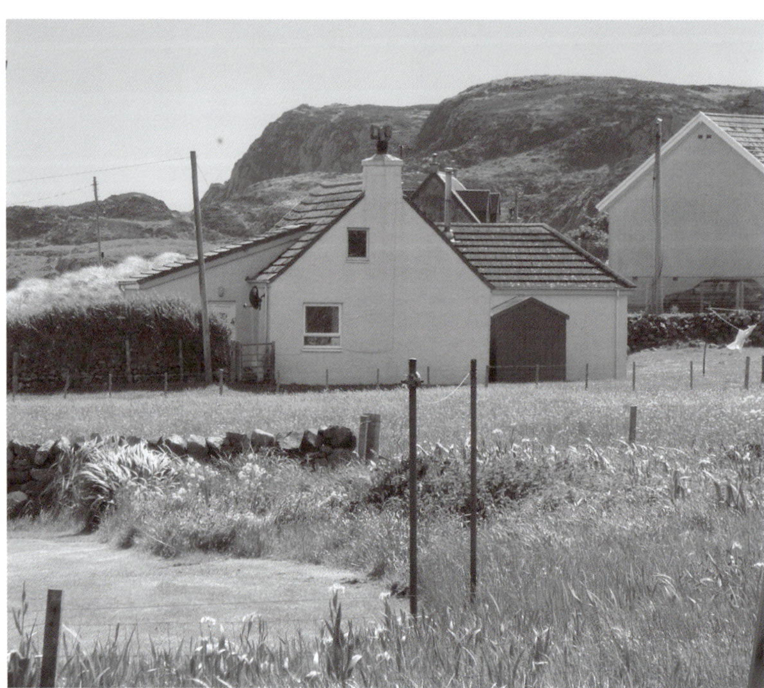

Photograph 2009

The ridges of Druim Dhughaill and Druim an Fhaing are in the background.

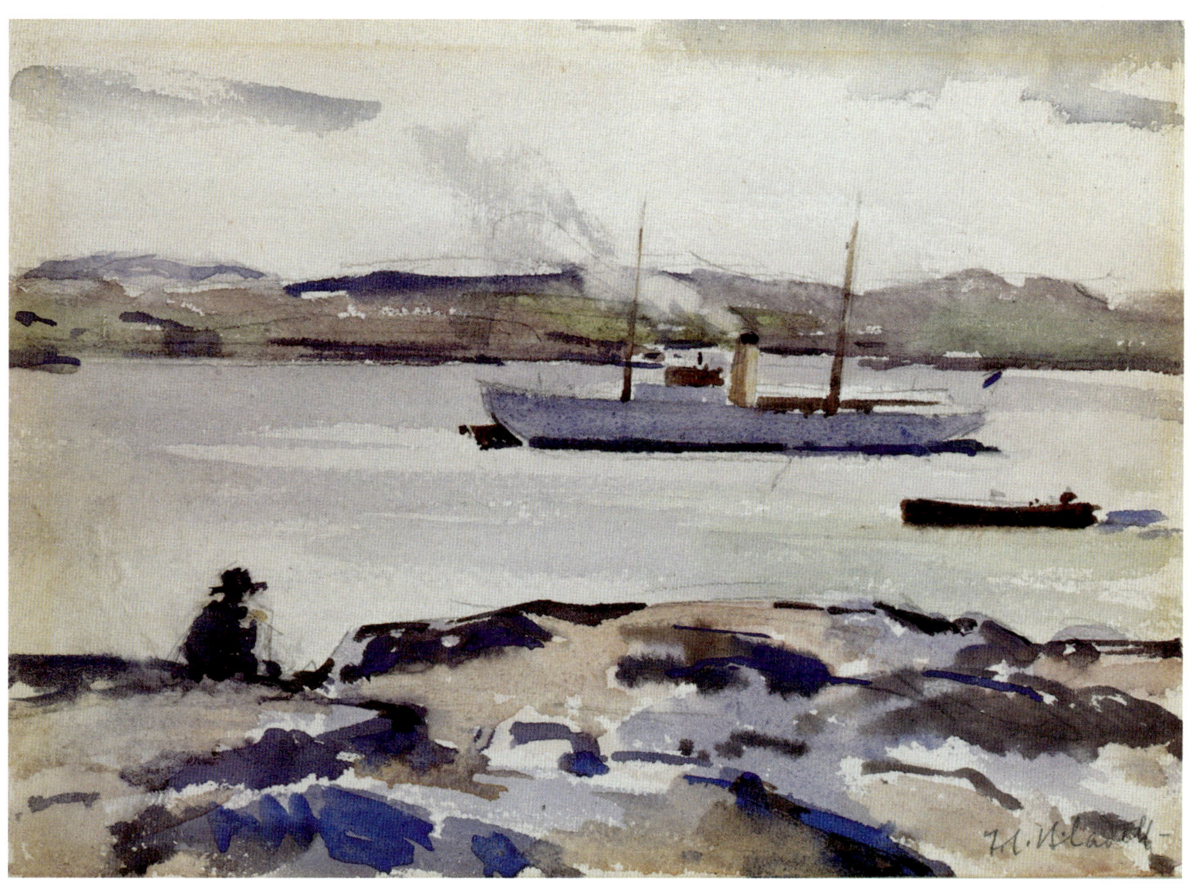

Cadell recorded a great variety of boats, from stylish yachts to workhorses of the seas, such as the coal barge in Plate 15. Many of these were painted in the Martyrs' Bay area, such as this example looking across the Sound of Iona to the Ross of Mull.

[PLATE 202]
F. C. B. Cadell
From the East Shore towards Fionnphort
Watercolour 7 x 10

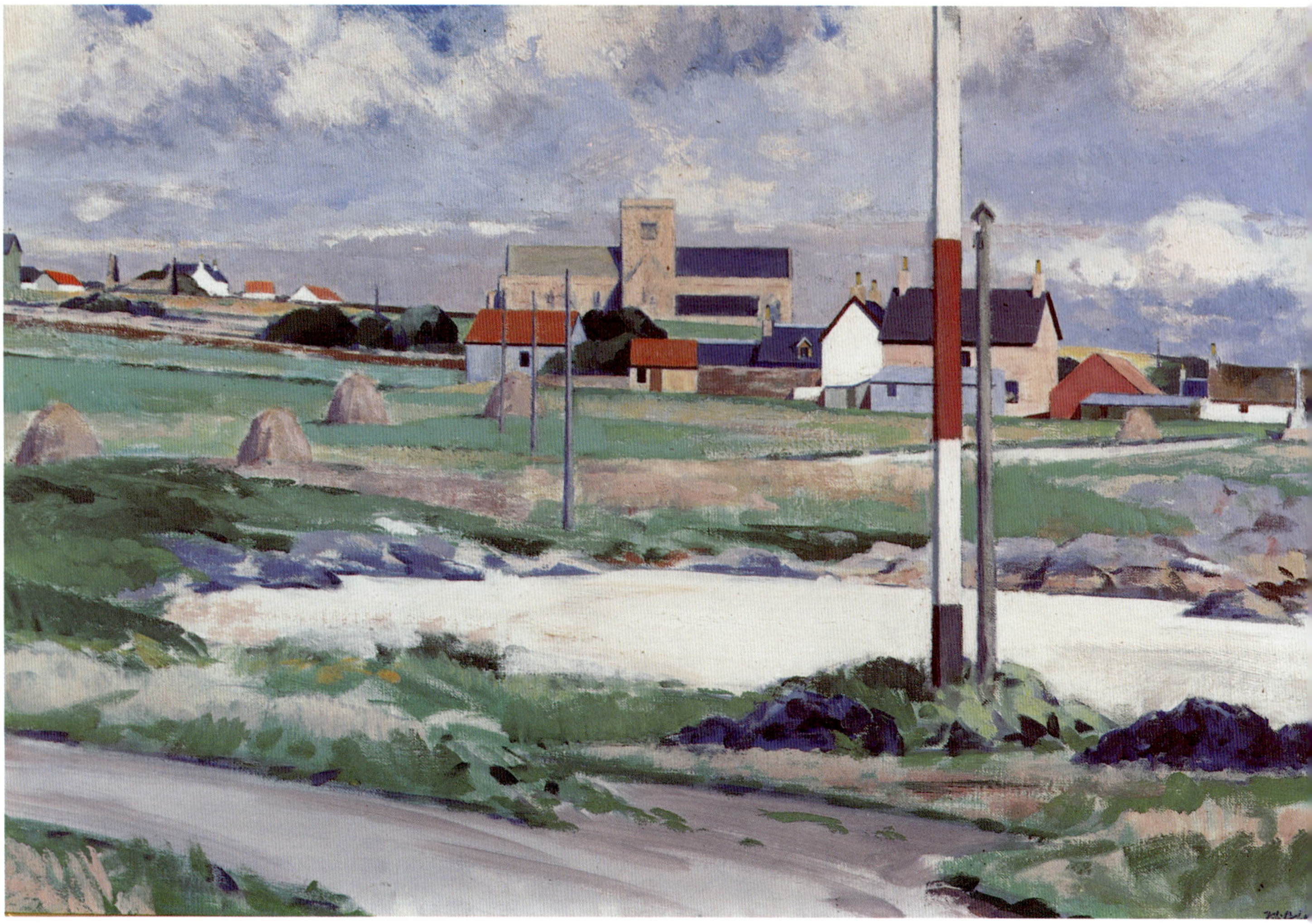

[PLATE 203] **F. C. B. Cadell** *The Village, Iona* Oil 20 x 30

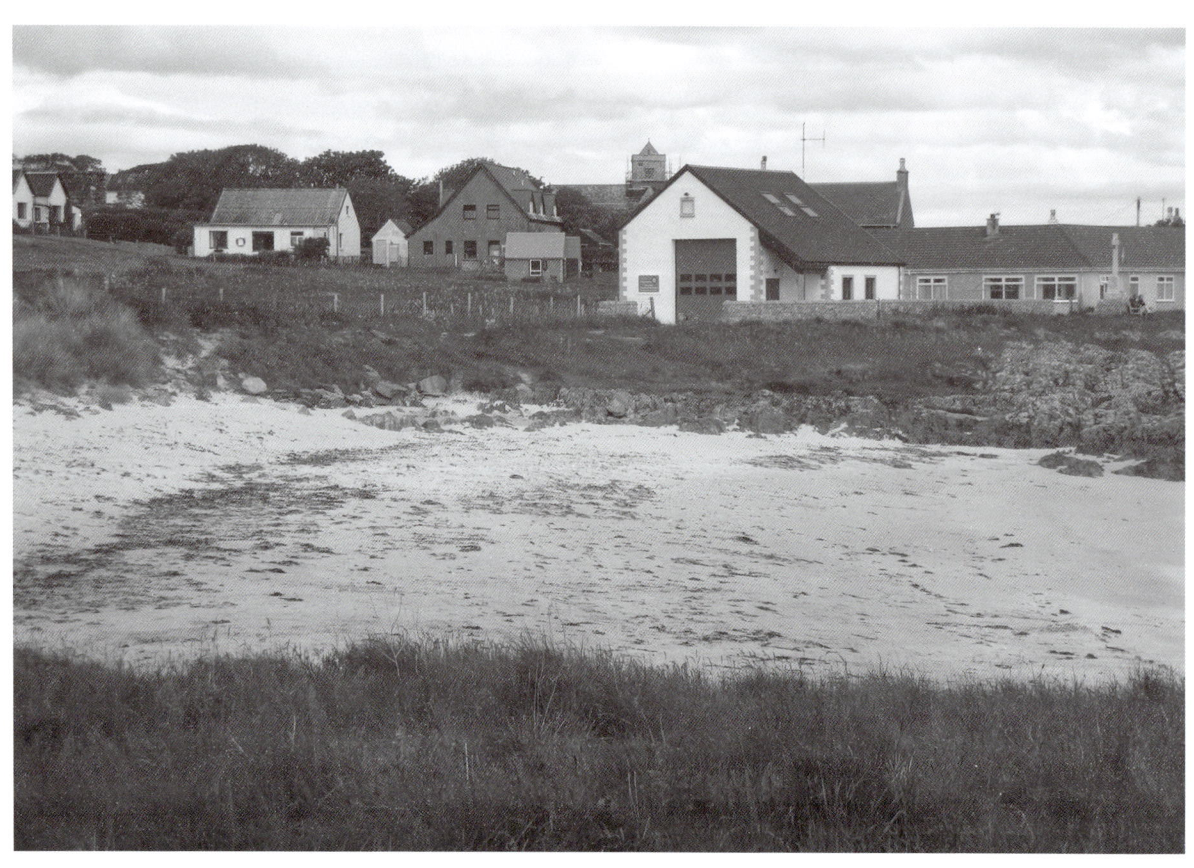

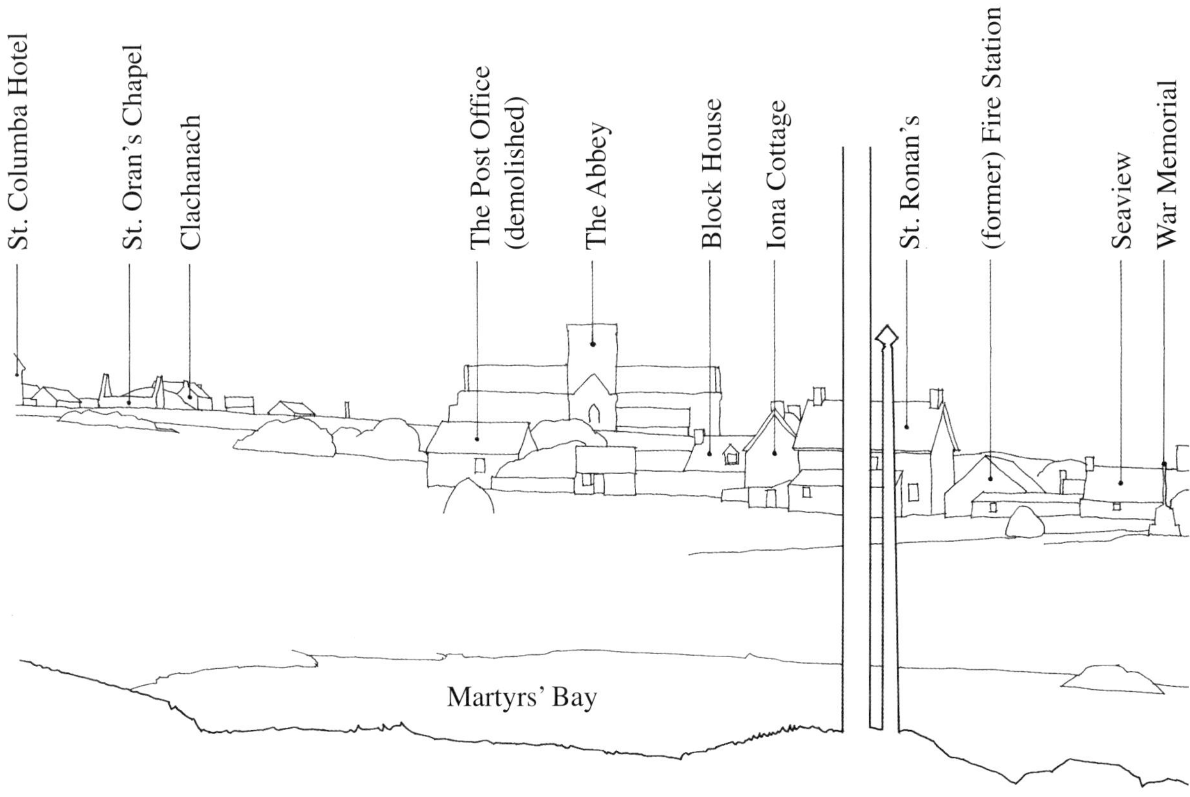

Painted from the south side of Martyrs' Bay, Plate 203 is Cadell's most comprehensive view of the Village.

Many features in the painting still exist and these are identified in the diagram above. However, much is now hidden by trees and subsequent building, as will be seen by comparing the painting with the recent photograph.
The red and white pole in the foreground, which is such an important element in the composition, is no longer there, but at the time of writing the stump could still be found in the grass.

Photograph 2009 (left)

The Abbey is central in the photograph. The large white building right of centre is the new Fire Station, which hides Iona Cottage and most of St. Ronan's. To the left of the Abbey is the Spar Shop which replaced the former Post Office shown in the diagram above. To the left again is the Craft Shop built in 1965, and finally the house on the extreme left is Darrach Bheag. The view through to St. Oran's Chapel and Clachanach seen in the painting is now obscured by trees and the subsequent buildings. St. Oran's Chapel had no roof at the time Cadell was on Iona, and the gable walls of the Chapel, seen edge on in the painting, appear rather like two obelisks.

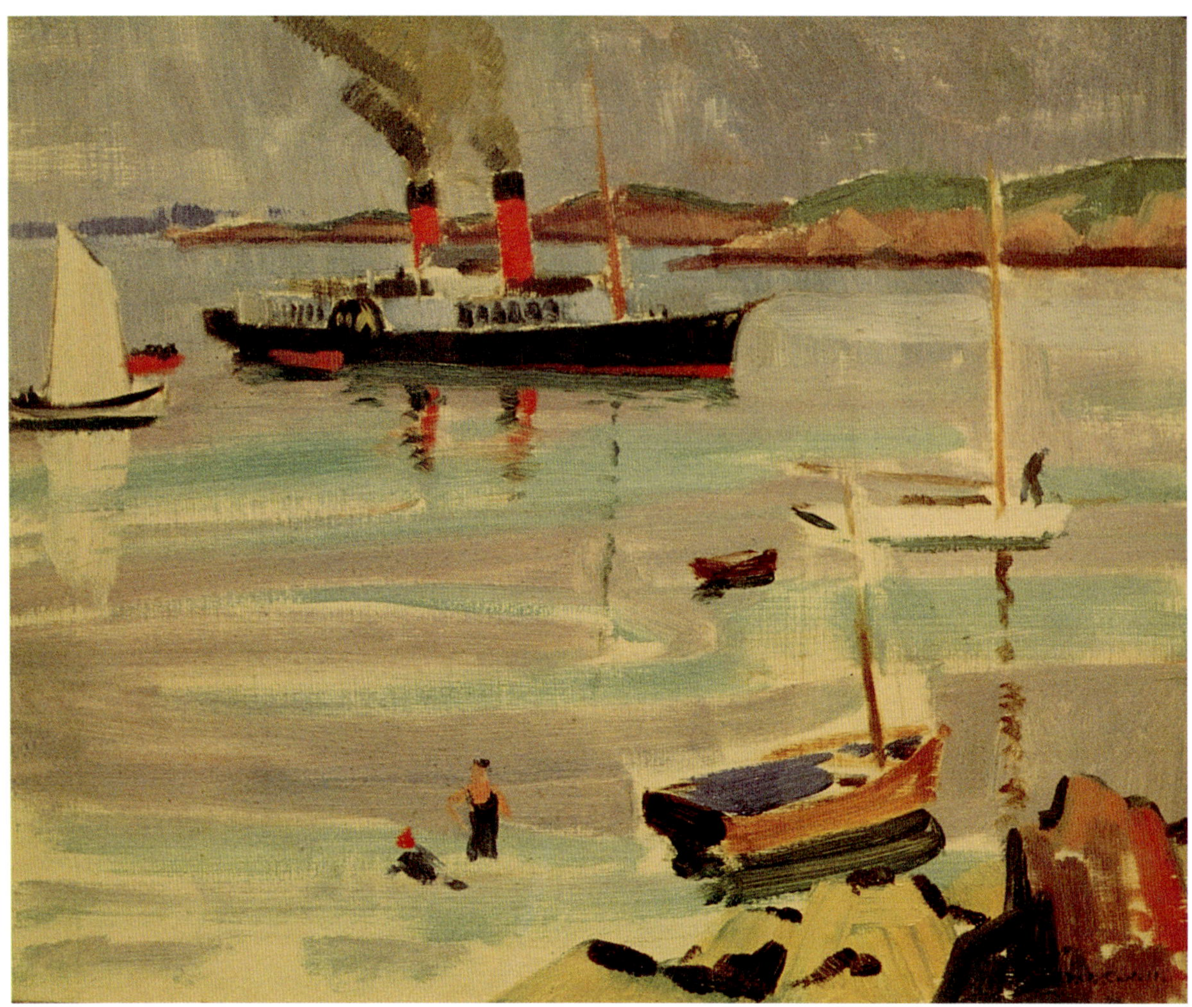

In the tourist season visitors came to Iona in large numbers, sailing from Oban on boats such as the paddlesteamer Grenadier seen here. It was necessary to disembark into smaller boats in order to come ashore, and this was not always possible in a heavy swell. Here, in calm conditions, passengers are being ferried ashore to the jetty which is just out of sight to the left. The picture was painted from the south side of Martyrs' Bay and the Grenadier is moored in about the same position as the Dunara Castle in Plate 1.

The Grenadier was launched in 1885. Always regarded as a very pretty ship, she was the only MacBrayne's paddlesteamer to see active service in the First World War, on mine-sweeping duties in the North Sea. She survived the war, but sadly was destroyed by fire in 1927, whilst alongside the pier at Oban.

[PLATE 204]

F. C. B. Cadell

The Paddlesteamer Grenadier

Oil 15 x 18

[PLATE 205]

F. C. B. Cadell

The Paddlesteamer Grenadier

Oil 25 x 18.5

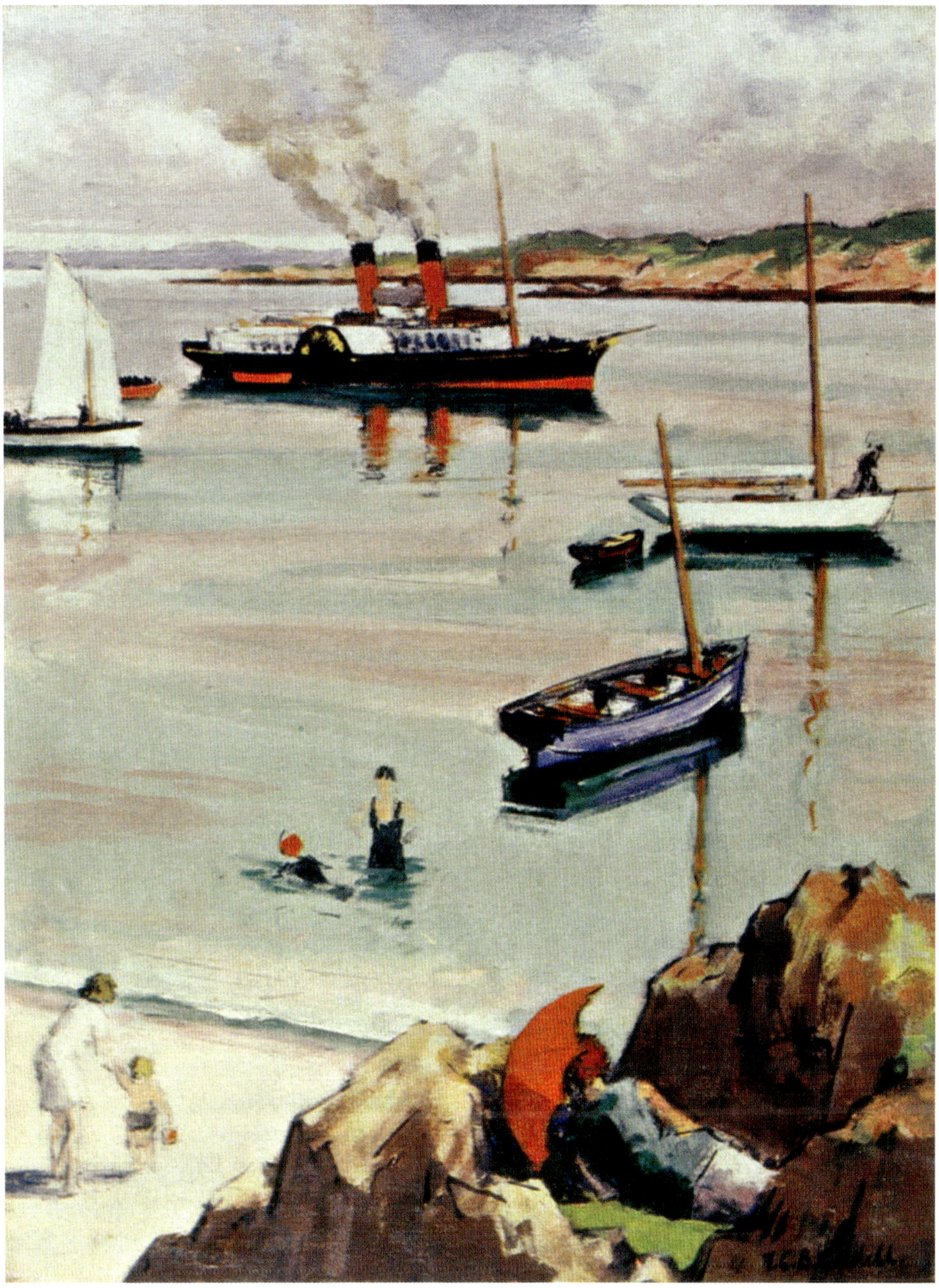

Cadell painted this larger version of *The Paddlesteamer Grenadier* for use in one of the three posters he designed for MacBrayne's Steamers. Working, probably in the studio rather than on location, he has repeated the composition of Plate 204 in the upper part of the painting, and to achieve the vertical format required for the poster has used a larger area of sky and additional rocks and figures in the foreground.

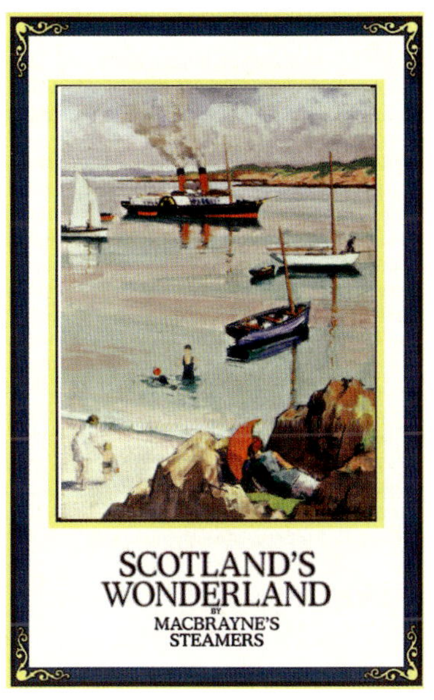

Poster for MacBrayne's Steamers

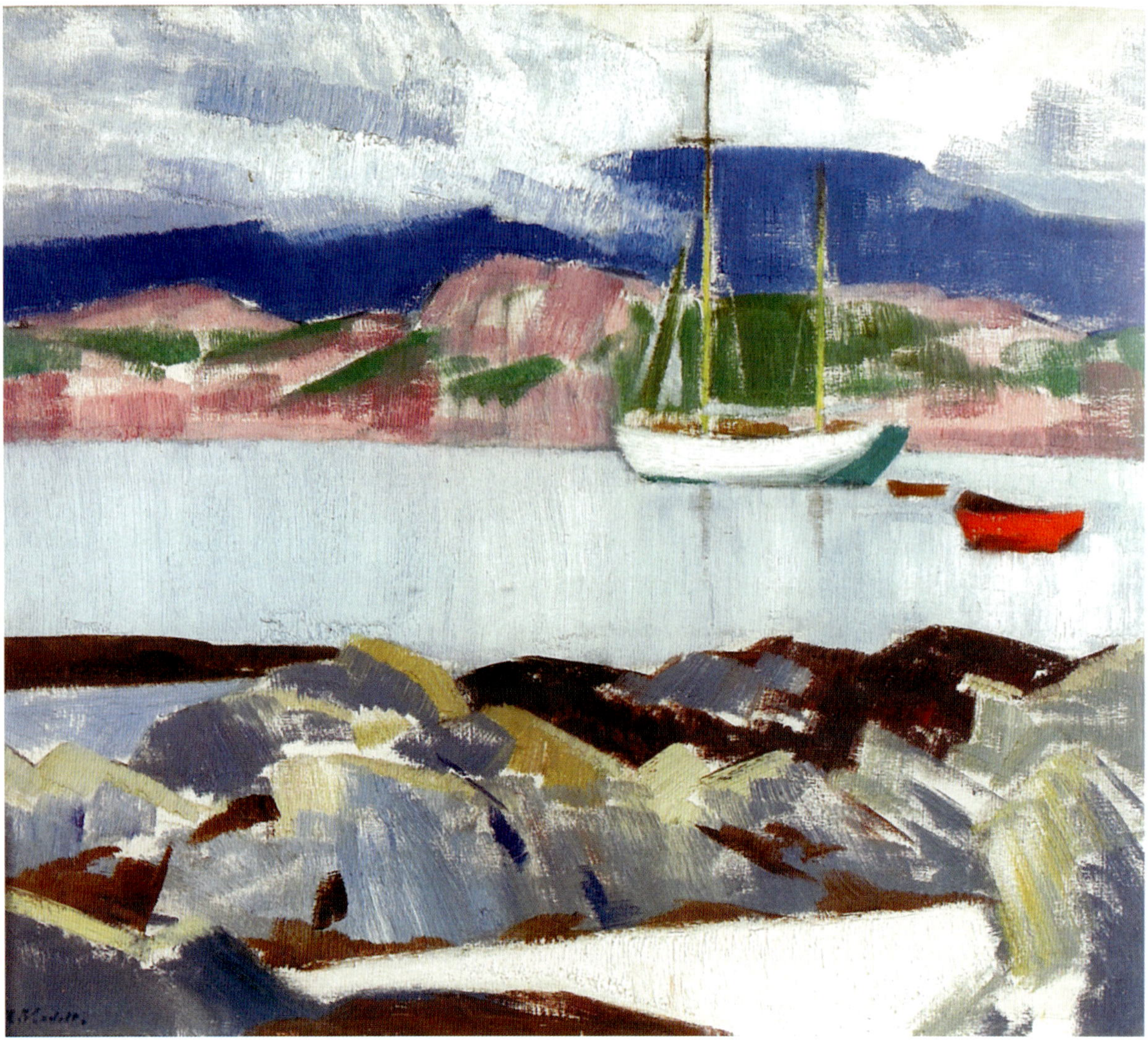

[PLATE 206]
F. C. B. Cadell
Ross of Mull from Martyrs' Bay
Oil 15 x 18

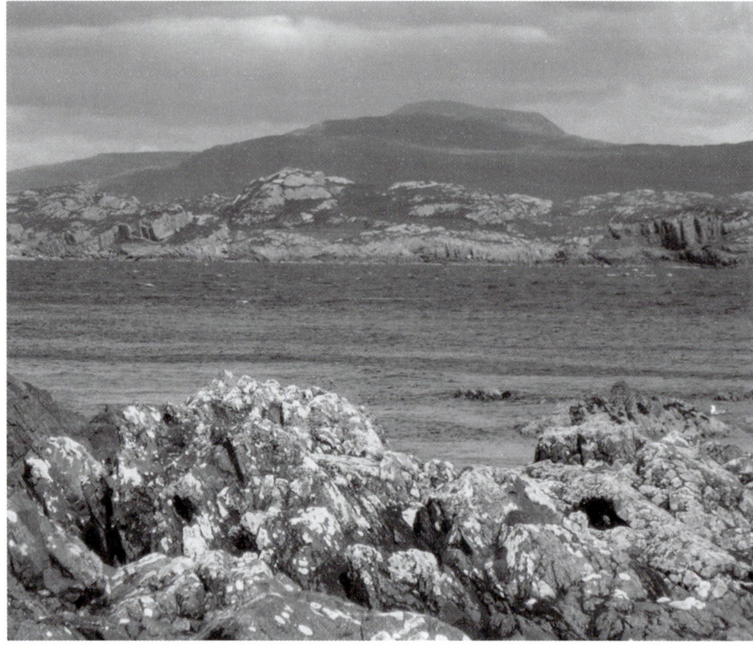

Photograph 2009

Painted from the north side of Martyrs' Bay, this is the view over the Sound to Eilean nam Ban, the pink rock of which contrasts with the dark blue of the Burg beyond, shown in deep shadow and partly obscured by cloud.

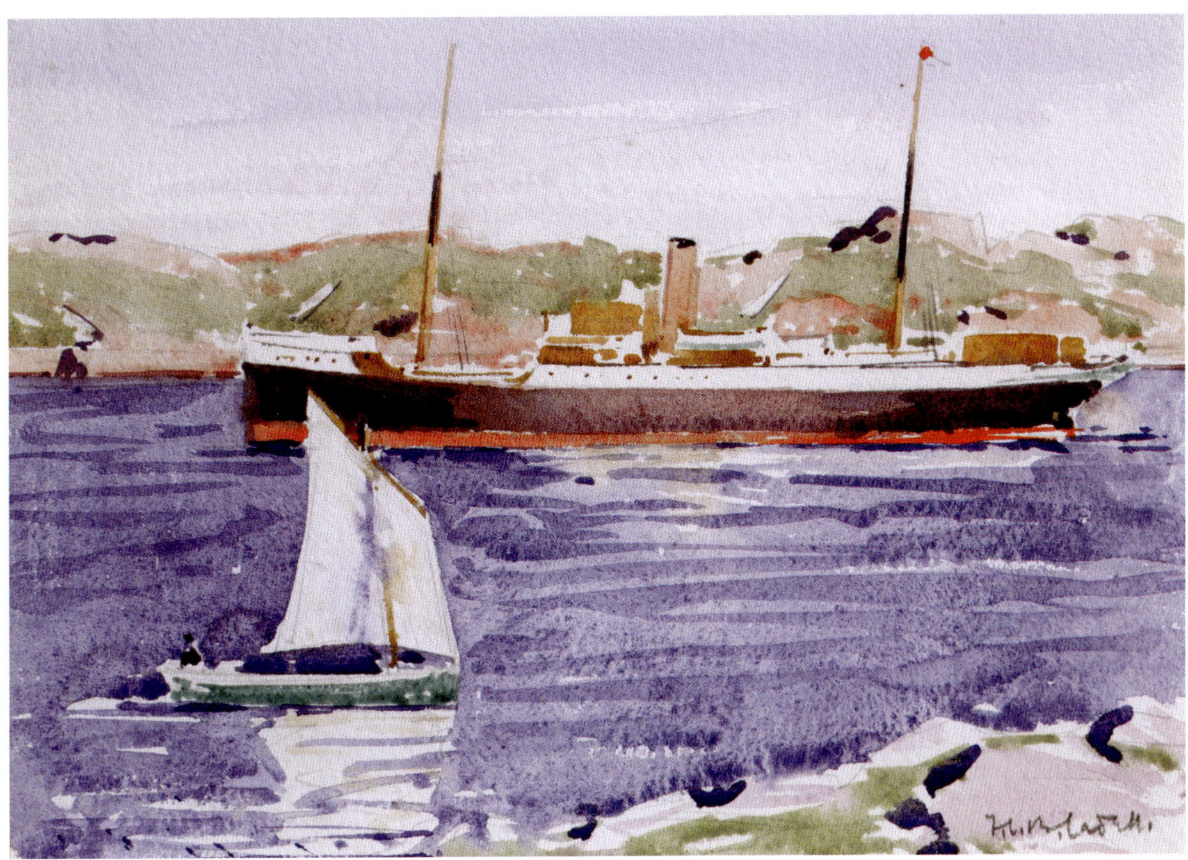

Boats are a vital part of life on Iona, and having started the book with a painting of a boat, we also end with one. The watercolour above is similar in composition to Cadell's oil painting of the Dunara Castle (Plate 1). However, this is a different vessel with a quite different function. The Dunara Castle carried passengers and cargo, whereas the Hesperus serviced the lighthouses on the west coast, from as far south as the Isle of Man to Cape Wrath, the most northerly point on the west coast of Scotland. The normal mooring of the Hesperus was further south in the Sound than that of the Dunara Castle and also closer to the Ross of Mull.

[PLATE 207]
F. C. B. Cadell

STEAMER AND YACHT, IONA

The Steamship Hesperus in the Sound of Iona
Watercolour 7 x 10
The Fleming-Wyfold Art Foundation

BIBLIOGRAPHY

Billcliffe, Roger	*The Scottish Colourists.* Pub: John Murray, London 1989.
Christian, Jessica, and Charles Stiller	*Iona Portrayed.* Pub: The New Iona Press 2000.
Cursiter, Stanley	*Peploe: An Intimate Memoir of an Artist and His Work.* Pub: Thomas Nelson and Sons, Edinburgh 1947.
Dulau, Anne, and Selina Skipwith	*Intimate Friends: Scottish Colourists from the Hunterian Art Gallery and Fleming Collection.* Pub: Fleming-Wyfold Art Foundation in association with the University of Glasgow, London 2003.
Fraser, Fiona F.M.	*The Lewisian and Torridonian Geology of Iona.* Unpublished Ph. D. Thesis, University of St. Andrews, 1977. Copy available for reading at the Heritage Centre, Iona.
Hardie, William, with foreword by T.J. Honeyman	*Three Scottish Colourists Exhibition Catalogue.* Pub: Scottish Arts Council, Edinburgh 1970.
Hewlett, Tom, and Duncan Macmillan	*F.C.B. Cadell: The Life and Works of a Scottish Colourist 1883–1937.* Pub: Lund Humphries 2011.
Honeyman, T.J.	*Three Scottish Colourists.* Pub: Thomas Nelson and Sons 1950.
Long, Philip, with Elizabeth Cumming	*The Scottish Colourists 1900–1930.* Pub: National Galleries of Scotland, Edinburgh 2000.
MacArthur, E. Mairi	*Columba's Island: Iona from Past to Present.* Pub: Edinburgh University Press 1995. Reprinted Polygon, Edinburgh 2001.
SNGMA	*S.J. Peploe 1985 Exhibition Catalogue.* Essay by Guy Peploe: "S.J. Peploe: Painter in Oils." Bibliography by Ailsa Tanner. Pub: Scottish National Gallery of Modern Art.
Peploe, Guy	*S.J. Peploe, 1871–1935* Pub: Lund Humphries 2012.
Strang, Alice	*F.C.B. Cadell.* Pub: National Galleries of Scotland 2011.
Strang, Alice, Elizabeth Cumming and Frances Fowle	*S.J. Peploe.* Pub: National Galleries of Scotland 2012.

Picture Credits

Numbers refer to Plate numbers and not pages

MUSEUMS AND ART GALLERIES

Aberdeen Art Gallery and Museums Collection	83, 122, 129, 154
Art Gallery and Museum, Kelvingrove, Glasgow	170 (Photograph by the author)
City Art Centre, Edinburgh Museums and Galleries	107, 146
Dundee Art Galleries and Museums	77
Fleming-Wyfold Art Foundation	1, 117, 207
The Hunterian, University of Glasgow	49, 55, 80, 105, 109, 126, 153, 155 (Photographs by the author)
Fife Cultural Trust (Kirkcaldy Galleries) on behalf of Fife Council	45, 46, 128, 150
National Galleries of Scotland	4, 18, 37, 147, 177 72, 82 (Photographs by John McKenzie)

PRIVATE GALLERIES

The Roger Billcliffe Gallery, Glasgow	39, 185
Bourne Fine Art, Edinburgh	34, 40, 93, 180
The Fine Art Society, London	89, 151, 173, 191
The Richard Green Gallery, London	166
Iona Gallery	183
The David Messum Gallery, London	102
Duncan R. Miller Fine Arts, London	2, 9, 20, 36, 43, 53, 96, 104, 119, 120, 134, 156, 184, 201, 202
Ewan Mundy Fine Art, Glasgow	54, 57, 114, 138, 142, 148, 152, 168, 182, 186, 203
Portland Gallery, London	5, 7, 10, 11, 12, 17, 24, 27, 33, 62, 67, 74, 75, 78, 79, 91, 97, 162, 164, 175, 188, 195, 205
The Scottish Gallery, Edinburgh	41, 47, 48, 50, 65, 68, 69, 76, 86, 115, 137, 159, 167, 198
Anthony Woodd Gallery, Edinburgh	135

AUCTION HOUSES

Bonhams	8, 73, 90, 101, 144, 145, 160, 163, 206
Christie's (Bridgeman Art Library)	13, 14, 15, 19, 22, 23, 28, 29, 30, 31, 51, 56, 59, 61, 70, 71, 94, 95, 98, 99, 106, 118, 124, 125, 127, 131, 133, 139, 140, 141, 143, 158, 161, 165, 169, 171, 174, 176, 181, 190, 196, 200
Lyon and Turnbull	25, 60
Sotheby's	3, 21, 26, 32, 35, 52, 63, 66, 81, 84, 92, 100, 103, 108, 111, 116, 121, 123, 130, 132, 136, 172, 187, 189, 192, 193, 194, 197, 199

Picture Credits (continued)

OTHER SOURCES

Private collections photographed by:

John McKenzie 42;

Philip MacLeod Coupe 16, 38, 88, 112, 157, 185, 204;

Fiona Menzies 44;

Giclee UK Limited, Edinburgh 58, 64, 85, 151A, 151B;

Plate 87 and the quotation from *Peploe: An Intimate Memoir of an Artist and His Work* by Stanley Cursiter (page 14) reproduced courtesy of the publishers, Nelson Thornes.

PHOTOGRAPHIC CREDITS

Figure 3, courtesy of Mrs Joan Faithfull, daughter of William C. Crawford (Collection of Mairi E. MacArthur)

Figure 4, Tom Hewlett, Portland Gallery;

Figure 9, National Library of Scotland, Edinburgh;

Figure 11, Collection of Mairi E. MacArthur;

Figure 19, Collection of Guy Peploe;

Inside front and back covers R. Martin Tomlinson.